D0227710

CLINICAL
NEGLIGENCE

Books are   ...n or before
                                   ...elow.

Second Edition

MULTIDISCIPLINARY LIBRARY PRINCE PHILIP LIBRARY	
SUP	REC'D.
CLASS W 44	PR

Cavendish
Publishing
Limited

K06643

MULTIDISCIPLINARY LIBRARY
PRINCE PHILIP LIBRARY

SUP. TQYav

REC'D. 19.8.02

CLASS WU49

PR 43.15 (8295)

CLINICAL NEGLIGENCE

Second Edition

Malcolm Khan, LLB (Hons), Barrister at Law
Principal Lecturer in Law
University of Northumbria at Newcastle

Michelle Robson, LLB, Solicitor
Senior Lecturer in Law
University of Northumbria at Newcastle

Kristina Swift, LLB, Solicitor
Lecturer in Law
University of Northumbria at Newcastle

Cavendish
Publishing
Limited

London • Sydney

Second edition first published in Great Britain 2002 by Cavendish Publishing Limited, The Glass House, Wharton Street, London WC1X 9PX, United Kingdom
Telephone: + 44 (0)20 7278 8000   Facsimile: + 44 (0)20 7278 8080

Email: info@cavendishpublishing.com
Website: www.cavendishpublishing.com

© Khan, Malcolm, Robson, Michelle and Swift, Kristina 2002
     First edition   1997
     Second edition   2002

All rights reserved. No part of this publication may be reproduced, stored in a retrieval system, or transmitted, in any form or by any means, electronic, mechanical, photocopying, recording, scanning or otherwise, except under the terms of the Copyright Designs and Patents Act 1988 or under the terms of a licence issued by the Copyright Licensing Agency, 90 Tottenham Court Road, London W1P 9HE, UK, without the permission in writing of the publisher.

British Library Cataloguing in Publication Data

Khan, Malcolm
Clinical negligence – 2nd ed
1 Medical personnel – malpractice – Great Britain
I Title II Robson, Michelle
344.4'1' 0411

ISBN 1 85941 492 3

Printed and bound in Great Britain

PREFACE

For several months the idea that we would be sitting down to write the preface to this book seemed as unlikely a project as one of us winning the lottery. However at long last the labours of Hercules, alias three bleary eyed lecturers, are complete much to the relief and astonishment of the Cavendish team.

Our aim in writing this book remains unchanged from that stated in the first edition: to provide practitioners and students with an insight into the substantive and procedural aspects of this vast subject, a book which is neither wholly substantive nor procedural but a marriage of the two. The format of the second edition is also unchanged; basic principles embodied as a series of rules followed by explanatory notes and references.

So what has changed since the first edition of this text? Firstly there has been an abundance of new case law; however we have singled out here only three decisions for comment. *Bolitho v City & Hackney Health Authority* [1998] AC 232 is the first of our chosen three. The *Bolitho* case is notable for its re-defining of the *Bolam* standard and the encroachment of the *Bolam* rule into the area of causation. It is a decision which has given some power back to the courts and yet has added to the claimant's difficulties in establishing causation. Ultimately what singles *Bolitho* out is that it was a bad decision, the very worst example of the judiciary allowing the medical profession to hide behind their cloak of accepted practice. Our second choice is *McFarlane v Tayside Health Board* [1999] 4 All ER 961 and is, like *Bolitho,* a House of Lords decision and, also like *Bolitho* (in our opinion), a bad decision. Now responsible parents who seek to limit the size of their family, only to find that their efforts have been in vain due to the negligence of their health carers can expect no financial help in caring for their 'unwanted' but loved offspring. The third of our chosen three cases is the much debated Siamese twins case, *Re A* [2000] 4 All ER 961. There are so many questions as yet unresolved arising from this decision; the eroding of parental rights, the potential effect on active voluntary euthanasia and the re-defining of the doctrine of necessity. These and other issues are the focus of Chapter 2.

With the exception of case law there have been two other significant changes affecting the clinical negligence landscape. First, the introduction of the Civil Procedure Rules. The courts are now able to take a pro-active approach to case management, but will their efforts always be thwarted unless the substantive rules are also reformed? The Woolf reforms also produced a change in terminology; the term 'plaintiff' is no more having been substituted with the more meaningful word 'claimant' and we now refer to 'clinical' rather than 'medical' negligence. These terms are used throughout this text. And finally, perhaps the most significant development has been the implementation of the Human Rights Act 1998. Much of our discussion of the Act is still in the realms of speculation; lawyers and claimants are still at the learning stage of how the Act will affect them and how it can be used to their advantage. Does the Act herald the dawn of a new era for clinical negligence claims, or will we come to view it as another version of the Millennium bug? How will the courts reconcile the rights of an individual with the needs of society and the much used defence of health carers, namely lack of resources?

As a final note, there is yet another change the first two named authors wish to pass comment on, and that is that two becomes three! Kristina Swift, much to our relief, agreed in a moment of rashness to assist with this edition. All we can say is that we couldn't have done it without you!

The law is as stated at 31 June 2001. As always, we expect to be corrected, and we apologise in advance for any errors that may be lurking in the following pages.

Malcolm Khan
Michelle Robson
Kristina Swift

ACKNOWLEDGMENTS

The authors gratefully acknowledge the permission granted by the following bodies and persons for reproduction of material in this edition:

Action for Victims of Medical Accidents
44 High Street
Croydon
Surrey CR0 1YB
Tel 020 8688 9555
Fax 020 8667 9065
email pachiefexec@avma.co.uk

Crown copyright material is reproduced with the permission of the Controller of Her Majesty's Stationery Office

Crown copyright legislation is reproduced under the terms of Crown Copyright Policy Guidance issued by HMSO

General Medical Council

Voluntary Euthanasia Society

****

And finally we would all like to thank Cara Annett, Jo Reddy, Ruth Massey and all the team at Cavendish Publishing who throughout the production of this text remained cheerful, friendly and calm in the face of great adversity. Cara is now safe in the knowledge that she will not have to deal with the three musketeers for a while, if ever again!

Malcom Khan dedicates this book to Susan Khan, Tom and Audrey Linsley, Dandelion (the cat!) and Caroline (who tried to fathom his handwriting).

Michelle Robson wishes to personally thank her two co-authors for keeping her sane through the trials and tribulations of balancing parenthood with authorship. Finally she wishes to thank her family, all of whom made her smile in the most stressful of moments. A special thanks goes to Tim Clarke, who cheerfully and patiently read through numerous drafts and never failed with words of encouragement. She dedicates this book to him and to Derek Robson, a much loved father and friend; his guidance and support are sorely missed.

Kristina Swift would like to thank Michelle and Malcolm for asking her to contribute to this book and for their assistance and support throughout. She dedicates this book to her parents.

CONTENTS

TABLE OF CASES

xi

TABLE OF LEGISLATION

European Union law

TABLE OF STATUTORY INSTRUMENTS

TABLE OF ABBREVIATIONS

ABI	Association of British Insurers
AHA	Area Health Authority
AVMA	Action for Victims of Medical Accidents
BMA	British Medical Association
CHC	Community Health Council
CRU	Compensation Recovery Unit
DSS	Department of Social Security
DVLC	Driver and Vehicle Licensing Centre
GMC	General Medical Council
GP	General Practitioner
HA	Health Authority
LREC	Local Research Ethics Committee
NHS	National Health Service

CHAPTER 1

MEDICAL CONFIDENTIALITY

RULE 1(A)

Health carers who are treating patients owe both a legal and an ethical duty of confidentiality to their patients. In practical terms this means that the health carer must not disclose (except in clearly defined circumstances) information regarding his patient to a third party, whether that third party is a relative or a stranger.

Commentary

It is well settled that there is an abiding obligation of confidentiality as between doctor and patient, and in my view when a patient enters a hospital for treatment, whether he be a model citizen or murderer, he is entitled to be confident that details about his condition and treatment remain between himself and those who treat him [*per* Lord Phillips MR in *Ashworth Security Hospital v MGN Ltd* [2000] 1 WLR 515 at p 527].

The justification for this information being kept confidential is that it both sustains and enhances the doctor-patient relationship. Without this rule the patient might not entrust full, possibly intimate, details to the health carer with the result that the treatment given might not be in the patient's best interests. It has to be stressed that the rule is not dependent on any conscious or expressed wish of the patient for confidentiality; it arises from the very existence of the medical relationship. Thus, while a patient may fervently hope that a discussion with the health carer about an embarrassing problem will go no further and may indeed ask that it should be kept confidential, in less embarrassing situations the health carer's obligations to respect confidence will still exist even though the patient may not consciously look for or request confidentiality. This rule is frequently expressed as if it were a self-sustaining proposition. In fact, while there is no denying the ethical origins and consequences of the rule, its legal origins are more difficult to state with the same degree of certainty.

Ethically the duty exists because well known declarations such as the Hippocratic Oath, the Declaration of Geneva, etc, and GMC and BMA guidelines say so. For example, in the GMC's booklet on *Confidentiality: Protecting and Providing Good Information* (September 2000), para 1 states:

Patients have a right to expect that information about them will be held in confidence by their doctors. Confidentiality is central to trust between doctors and patients. Without assurances about confidentiality, patients may be reluctant to give doctors the information they need in order to provide good care. If you are asked to provide information about patients you should:

* seek patients' consent to disclosure of information wherever possible, whether or not you judge that patients can be identified from the disclosure.
* anonymise data where unidentifiable data will serve the purpose.
* keep disclosures to the minimum necessary.

You must always be prepared to justify your decisions in accordance with this guidance.

One can now add to the above list the recent establishment of the National Confidentiality and Security Advisory Body. This body will:

- Set national standards governing the confidentiality and security of information held on patients.
- Promote general awareness of the issues surrounding patient records, including rights of access to records and the security of records.
- Provide support, advice and guidance for the Caldicott Guardians.
- Advise ministers, the NHS Executive, the Department of Health and the NHS Information Authority on an extensive range of issues relating to confidentiality and security.

(Above information taken from *Health Law*, April 2000, p 8.)

This ethical rule applies to all branches of health carers, for example, nurses, doctors, physiotherapists, etc. If a disclosure is made in unauthorised circumstances, then disciplinary action may follow if a complaint is lodged. The 'punishment' will very much depend on the Code of the particular branch of the profession involved. Thus, if a GP was to carelessly divulge confidential information, a complaint to the Health Authority or the GMC would be in order. Again, if the disclosure occurred against the background of hospital treatment, then the hospital complaints procedure could be invoked. While it is more than likely that the patient's first thoughts will turn to the profession's complaints machinery, legal redress will be available for those situations where the patient may be dissatisfied with the internal handling of his complaint, or where the disclosure has resulted in serious consequences for the patient and the patient has decided to bypass the local resolution procedure and proceed immediately to the courts.

But what about the legal basis for the rule? It cannot be the already mentioned ethical codes because these lack legal status. Given that there is as yet no specific statutory provision which deals with unauthorised disclosures, is the remedy available contractual, tortious, equitable, fiduciary or *sui generis*?

As regards a private patient, the answer is clear: a claim lies in contract because there is a contractual relationship between the patient and the hospital and/or the health staff providing the private treatment and the contract will either contain an express term of confidentiality or the courts will properly 'read in' an implied term to that effect in appropriate circumstances (see *Cornelius v de Taranto* [2001] EMLR 12).

But what of the NHS patient who has no contract with the hospital or its staff? At first the authors were of the opinion that the legal underpinning of the rule could lie in the tort of negligence so that non-disclosure might be viewed as part of the health carer's overall duty of care to the patient. But on careful reflection this is probably not a correct analysis since negligence implies a certain degree of non-intentional conduct, whereas in the case of an unauthorised disclosure the actions of the person disclosing are invariably deliberate. To this extent, the New Zealand case of *Furniss v Fitchett* [1958] NZLR 396 may now be regarded as founded on an unsound legal premise. In that case the unauthorised disclosure was followed by a successful negligence claim based on the argument that it was reasonably foreseeable that the disclosure would cause physical harm to the patient. Furthermore, if negligence were to be considered the correct form of action then it should follow that the *Bolam* rule would be applicable (see Chapter 5, Standard of Care, p 155, and *Bolam v Friern Hospital Management Committee* [1957] 1 WLR 582), and that in turn would mean that a health carer would not be liable for any unauthorised disclosure provided a responsible body of peer practitioners would have made the disclosure in similar circumstances.

Could medical confidentiality be regarded as an independent duty (that is, not as part of the doctor's overall duty of care)? It is an interesting thought and one which, if true, could have a profound effect on the general legal liability of the medical profession. It would then be possible to argue that, instead of one indivisible duty owed to the patient with one standard of care (the *Bolam* standard), in reality there were separate duties owed, not all of which need necessarily attract the *Bolam* standard (see, for example, the Australian case of *Rogers v Whittaker* [1993] 4 Med LR 79). But to do so would mean jettisoning the House of Lords approach in *Sidaway v Board of Governors of the Bethlem Royal Hospital and the Maudsley Hospital* [1985] AC 871 where it was said that the doctor's duty to his patient was indeed indivisible. Apart from avoiding the *Bolam* rule this approach has little to recommend it.

Is there a tort of breach of confidence which, if committed, could give rise to such remedies as an injunction or damages? According to some of the standard works on tort the answer is yes. Seemingly, there are three questions which have to be answered:

(1) Was the relevant information of a confidential nature?

(2) Was it entrusted in such circumstances that the other person knew that it was not to be disclosed without prior permission, that is, was there some special relationship between the giver and receiver of the information?

(3) Was it in the public interest that the information should not be divulged?

If the answer to all these questions is in the affirmative, then a claim may be brought for any unauthorised disclosure. According to Mr Justice Scott in *W v Egdell* [1989] 1 All ER 1089 the claim should be framed in equity. At page 1101 he said:

> Counsel for W relies on two sources for the obligations of confidence or of non-disclosure on which W's action against Dr Egdell is based. One source is implied contract, the other is equity. The two sources will in most cases cover the same ground. It is convenient for me first to ask myself what duty of confidence a court of equity ought to regard as imposed on Dr Egdell by the circumstances in which he obtained information from and about W and prepared his report.

Later at p 1105 he continued:

> In my judgment ... the circumstances of this case did not impose on Dr Egdell an obligation of conscience, an equitable obligation to refrain from disclosing his report ...

It is submitted that the whole tenor of Scott J's judgment in the *Egdell* case is to suggest that the legal basis for the claim is the equitable obligation imposed on the receiver of the information with the principal remedy one of injunction but that damages may be awarded in appropriate circumstances (see *Cornelius v De Taranto* [2001] EMLR 12). The success of the claim will rest not so much on the nature of any specific agreement between the parties but rather on the claimant establishing that the information was imparted in confidence and the receiver should not have taken advantage of it in the circumstances.

Now that it has been agreed that a right to privacy can be enforced by claimants/patients using equitable principles, mention must be made of the fact that Art 8 of the European Convention on Human Rights 1950 seems to reinforce the existence and enforceability of such a right, but using the human rights approach (for practical purposes the remedies will be the same).

Article 8 says:

(1) Everyone has the right to respect for his private and family life, his home and his correspondence.

Prior to the introduction of the Human Rights Act 1998, the European Court of Human Rights had established the potential breadth of Art 8 by such cases as *Halford v UK* (1997) 24 EHRR 523 (the right to make private calls at work), and *Z v Finland* (1997) 28 EHRR 371 and *MS v Sweden* (1997) 28 EHRR 371 (both of these cases involved the disclosure of confidential medical information but in both the breach of Art 8 was said to be justified).

Since the introduction of the 1998 Act, the English courts have used Art 8 to uphold the right to privacy of two famous movie stars (*Douglas v Hello! Ltd* [2001] 2 WLR 992 and a patient's medical confidentiality (*A Health Authority v X and Others* (2001) 19 May, see Medical Law Monitor, June 2001, p 7 for the facts of this case). Therefore, if it can now be agreed that a right to privacy also exists for claimants/patients using Art 8, the question remains whether the equitable approach or the human rights approach is the better practical option. Or is there no difference? Given that the equitable approach relies on the special relationship between the giver and the receiver of the information, whereas the human rights approach is not so limited (see *Douglas v Hello! Ltd*), then Art 8 would seem the better alternative. But Art 8 does not confer an absolute right, rather it offers the claimant a qualified right (see Art 8(2), 'there shall be no interference ... with the exercise of this right except such as is in accordance with the law and is necessary in a democratic society in the interests of national security, public safety or the economic well-being of the country, for the protection of health or morals or for the protection of the rights and freedom of others'). But would an equitable claim exist in the sort of circumstances envisaged by Art 8(2)? Doubtful. In which case, all things considered, perhaps the human rights approach is the preferable practical option.

REFERENCES

English case law

(1) Ashworth Security Hospital v MGN Ltd [2000] 1 WLR 515
See above.

(2) Cornelius v de Taranto [2001] EMLR 12

This was an action against a doctor who had sent copies of a medico-legal report, which the claimant had commissioned and paid for, without permission to her GP and to a consultant psychiatrist. The report contained defamatory and confidential material relating to her mental state. Damages were awarded for injury to feelings caused by the breach of confidence.

(3) Bolam v Friern Hospital Management Committee [1957] 1 WLR 582; [1957] 2 All ER 118

See Chapter 5, Standard of Care, p 155.

(4) Sidaway v Board of Governors of the Bethlem Royal Hospital and the Maudsley Hospital [1985] AC 871; [1985] 1 All ER 643

See Chapter 3, Duty, pp 72–74.

(5) W v Edgell [1989] 1 All ER 1089 affirmed at [1990] 1 All ER 835

See Rule 1(D)(v), at p 18. See, also, *AG v Guardian Newspapers (No 2)* [1988] 3 All ER 545

On the question of whether the claimant need show detriment, Lord Keith commented that the erosion of privacy was a sufficient reason for the court to act.

(6) Douglas v Hello! Ltd [2001] 2 WLR 992

The claimants, well known celebrities and newly-wed, obtained interim injunctions restraining the defendants, until trial, from publishing their wedding photographs, on the ground that publication would be a breach of confidence (the claimants had contracted to give exclusive publicity rights to a rival publication).The defendants successfully appealed against a continuation of the injunctions.

Per Sedley LJ at 1025:

> I would conclude, at lowest, that Mr Tugendhat has a powerfully arguable case to advance at trial that his ... clients have a right to privacy which English law will today recognise and, where appropriate, protect. To say this is in my belief to say little ... that our courts have not said already over the years ... It is to say ... that the right grounded as it is in the equitable doctrine of breach of confidence, is not unqualified ... The law no longer needs to construct an artificial relationship of confidentiality between intruder and victim; it can recognise privacy itself as a legal principle drawn from the fundamental value of personal autonomy.

(7) A Health Authority v X and Others (2001) unreported, 19 May

(8) Venables and Thompson v News Group Newspapers Ltd [2001] 2 WLR 1038

The claimants, V and T, had been convicted of the murder of a young boy. Injunctions restricting the information which the media could publish during their detention were coming to an end as V and T approached their 18th birthdays. V and T were now seeking injunctions against specific newspaper publishers and against the whole world which would indefinitely restrain publication of any information about them. Granting the injunctions, Dame Elizabeth Butler-Sloss said at p 1054:

> The onus of proving the case that freedom of expression must be restricted is firmly upon the applicant seeking the relief. The restrictions sought must, in the circumstances of the present case, be shown to be in accordance with the law, justifiable as necessary to satisfy a strong and pressing social need, convincingly demonstrated, to restrain the press in order to protect the rights of the claimants to confidentiality, and proportionate to the legitimate aim pursued. The right to confidence is ... a recognised exception within Article 10(2) ...

Foreign case law

Australia

Rogers v Whittaker [1993] 4 Med LR 79; [1992] 3 Med LR 331; (1992) 109 ALR 625
See Chapter 3, Duty, at pp 72, 76.

New Zealand

Furniss v Fitchett [1958] NZLR 396
The defendant doctor wrote a letter stating that in his opinion the claimant was exhibiting signs of paranoia and should be examined by a psychiatrist. The defendant passed this letter to the claimant's husband (both the claimant and her husband were patients of the defendant), who then used the letter in separation proceedings. The claimant sued the defendant for breach of duty of care.

Held: the defendant ought to have reasonably foreseen that the letter might come to his patient's knowledge and that if it did it might injure her health; he did not have to foresee the precise way in which it would come to the claimant's attention. The defendant was therefore in breach of his duty of care to the claimant and she could recover damages.

United States

Morris v Consolidation Coal Co (1994) 446 SE (2d) 648
The Supreme Court of Appeal of West Virginia considered the relationship between a treating physician and his patient and recognised it as being of a fiduciary (equitable) nature. Further it was held that a third party who induces the health carer to break the confidence of his patient may be liable to that patient. Such a claim will exist when the third party is aware of the physician-patient relationship and the information is wrongfully disclosed.

European Court of Human Rights

(1)   Halford v UK (1997) 24 EHRR 523
The applicant's office telephone calls were intercepted by the police with the intent of using them against her in a sex discrimination case.

Held: interception was unlawful.

(2)   Z v Finland (1997) 25 EHRR 371
Z's husband, who was HIV positive, was charged with manslaughter in that he had raped his victims with full knowledge of his medical condition. The police wanted to ascertain Z's medical condition but she refused to tell them. They therefore seized her medical records from a hospital and the information contained therein was subsequently incorporated into the court's judgment (Z was thus identified as HIV positive).

Held: *prima facie* a breach of Art 8.

(3)   MS v Sweden (1999) 28 EHRR 313
It was held to be a *prima facie* breach of Art 8 for a hospital to pass on confidential medical information to officials investigating a claim for social security benefits.

Statutes/statutory instruments

(1) *Law Commission Report No 110, Breach of Confidence (Cmnd 838, 1981)*

(2) *Human Rights Act 1998, ss 7 and 8. (See Appendix A). See also European Convention on Human Rights, Art 8*

RULE 1(B)

If the claimant's legal claim for an unauthorised disclosure is successful then the court is entitled to grant an injunction and/or award damages.

Commentary

Injunction

Under s 37 Supreme Court Act 1981, an injunction can be granted in all cases where it appears to the court to be just and convenient to do so (see, also, s 38 County Courts Act 1984 which gives a similar jurisdiction to the county court). Breach of the injunction is punishable as contempt of court.

The courts will only act at the instance of the party to whom the duty of confidence is owed. In the case of an injunction, it matters not whether the parties' relationship is in contract or in tort (that is, whether the claimant is a private patient or a NHS patient); what is required is that the person who possesses the confidential information must be under a legal obligation to maintain that confidence.

The injunction will be an interim prohibitory injunction. It may be qualified, for example, to prevent the defendant disclosing information to the press but to permit the disclosure to the appropriate authorities who should receive the information in the public interest (see Rule 1(D)(v)). It may be refused altogether where the court considers damages to be an adequate remedy, whether or not the claimant has applied for damages in his particulars of claim (see s 50 Supreme Court Act 1981).

The precise circumstances in which an injunction may be granted are as follows:

(1) where there is serious harm which is likely to continue; or

(2) where the harm is irreparable or cannot be quantified in financial terms; or

(3) where the defendant does not have the means to pay the damages.

Additionally, before granting an injunction the court will require an undertaking from the claimant to compensate the defendant for any harm caused by the injunction at a later date. This requirement will not apply, however, where the order is in the nature of a final order which, it is suggested, the majority of claims for breach of confidence will be.

If it is intended to proceed to trial, the principles laid down in the case of *American Cyanamid v Ethicon* [1975] AC 396 will need to be followed. This means the claimant will have to show the following:

(1) He has a good arguable claim to the right he seeks to protect, that is, it is not frivolous or vexatious.

(2) There is a serious action to be tried. (This means the court will be looking to see if the claimant has a good arguable case, not that he will necessarily win.)

(3) If the claimant satisfies (1) and (2), then whether or not the court chooses to exercise its discretion depends on the balance of convenience. The court will consider: (i) are damages an adequate remedy and/or is the defendant able to pay them?; (ii) whether the damages are an appropriate remedy; and (iii) whether more harm will be done by granting or refusing an injunction.

If all things are equal, the court will favour maintaining the *status quo*. It will take into account social and economic factors and the relative strength of the respective parties' cases. If it is not self-evident that the injunction should be granted on the criteria stated above then it can be influenced by the fact that one of the parties has a stronger case.

The most obvious reason for applying for an injunction is to prevent a breach of confidence taking place. But will this ever happen? How will the claimant know that the defendant is about to breach confidence? There may be some warning but if not then the action will always be for a past breach. Where the confidence has already been breached then the person to whom the confidence is owed may still be entitled to an injunction, for example, to prevent the defendant from continuing to disclose the information or disclosing further information. However, it will perhaps be thought that damages, in these circumstances, are a more appropriate remedy. Interestingly, in the notes to RSC Ord 29, *The White Book* (29/1/3) (these are still relevant under the new Civil Procedure Rules) points out that, in assessing the balance of convenience test, damages may not be an appropriate remedy if the damage is:

(a) irreparable; or

(b) outside the scope of pecuniary compensation; or

(c) too difficult to assess.

It seems apparent that for the majority of claims for breach of confidence, the damage done will be irreparable.

Alternatively, if the intention is not to proceed to trial then invariably the claimant will want the matter decided once and for all. *The White Book*, at 29/1/2, provides that where neither side is interested in monetary compensation and the decision on the application will be the equivalent of a final judgment, then the court should assess the relative strength of each side's case before deciding whether the injunction should be granted, see *Cambridge Nutrition Ltd v BBC* [1990] 3 All ER 523. Admittedly, this principle is more often to be found where the case concerns a public broadcast (see *Cambridge*) or article but it is suggested that the same could equally apply in a breach of confidence case where the claimant is not looking for financial compensation.

We would argue, however, that although technically the courts may consider the principles stated in *Cambridge*, in a breach of confidence case the court should favour the claimant every time and grant an interim injunction. As for the defendants, they will have ample time to justify their actions at the trial or a later interim hearing by showing that their conduct comes within one of the GMC exclusion criteria (see, further, Rule 1(D) at p 18 *et seq*).

Damages

Damages are appropriate to compensate for a past breach of confidence where there is no likelihood of the breach recurring and where the court deems an injunction to be inappropriate. The award of damages may be made up of any of the following:

(1) mental distress, injury to feelings or annoyance from the breach;

(2) loss of society;

(3) loss of employment;

(4) any adverse effects on promotion prospects.

It is at this point that a distinction begins to emerge depending on the legal relationship of the parties, that is, whether the patient is being treated privately or under the NHS. In a contractual claim, the courts have held that damages will not be awarded for mental distress or injury to feelings (see *W v Egdell* [1990] 1 All ER 835) unless the contract itself was a contract to provide peace of mind or freedom from distress (see *Jarvis v Swan Tours* [1973] 1 QB 233). As regards the other heads of damage, they could be substantial and, under general contract principles, will be for all those losses which flow naturally from the breach, for example, if it is revealed that the claimant is HIV positive his business may suffer and his insurance may be affected, etc.

There is some confusion over what damages are available in a non-contractual relationship, for example, where a NHS patient is involved. Certainly, the English courts have recognised that damages may be an appropriate remedy, as illustrated in the case of *X v Y* [1988] 2 All ER 648. Furthermore, the defendant in a breach of confidence claim will need to account for a loss of profits. However, the courts are also able to award damages not based on any loss of profit (see *Seager v Copydex* [1967] 2 All ER 415); these should be assessed on the basis of reasonable compensation for the use of the confidential information. In reality, however, a claimant's claim for the breach of confidence by a doctor is unlikely to be concerned primarily with loss of profit.

An equity-based claim should not be affected by the ruling in *W v Egdell* [1990] 1 All ER 835 which ruled out damages for mental distress in a contractual claim, although there are comments in this case which seem to imply that the position would be the same in equity. Moreover, there is no tort remedy in damages for mental distress falling short of a recognised psychiatric illness, see *McLoughlin v O'Brian* [1983] AC 410; *Alcock v Chief Constable of South Yorkshire* [1992] AC 310 and Chapter 7, Damages, at p 263 *et seq*.

Apart from damages for mental distress, what other compensation will the claimant receive? As the claim is in equity the position appears to be that he will not recover financial losses flowing from the breach. However, it does seem inequitable that a private patient, suing in contract, could recover such a loss whereas an NHS patient could not. To be 'equitable', the claimant should be able to recover for all foreseeable loss as a result of the breach of confidence whether the claim is in contract, tort or equity.

REFERENCES

English case law

(1) American Cyanamid v Ethicon [1975] AC 396; [1975] 1 All ER 504
See above, at p 7.

(2) Cambridge Nutrition v BBC [1990] 3 All ER 523
The claimant sought an injunction for prevent the BBC broadcasting a programme about the 'Cambridge diet'.

Held: the subject of the programme was in the public interest and the action failed. It was also held that the *American Cyanamid* principle was not of universal application and in this instance Kerr LJ said (at p 536):

> ... I do not think that it makes any difference whether this case is decided in accordance with the *Cyanamid* test or not. On either basis the answer is the same.

Gibson LJ said the case came within the category stated in *American Cyanamid*, namely (at p 543):

> ... many other special factors to be taken into consideration in the particular circumstances of individual cases.

In this case, because the loss was said to be uncompensatable and the action would not proceed to trial, the court was not bound by the *American Cyanamid* principle.

(3) W v Edgell [1990] 1 All ER 835
See Rule 1(D)(v), at p 26 *et seq*.

(4) Jarvis v Swan Tours [1973] 1 QB 233
Here, for the breach of a holiday contract costing £63.45, the court awarded £125 damages. As Stephenson LJ said (at pp 240–41):

> I argue that ... there may be contracts in which the parties contemplate inconvenience or breach which may be described as mental frustration, annoyance, disappointment and as Mr Thompson accedes that this is such a contract, the damages for breach of it should take wider inconvenience or discomfort into account.

(5) X v Y [1988] 2 All ER 648
See Rule 1(D)(v), at p 26 *et seq*.

(6) Seager v Copydex [1967] 2 All ER 415
The claimant had told the defendants about a new type of carpet grip; the defendants then developed the idea which had been given to them in confidence. The claimant was awarded damages for their having used the idea without paying for it.

(7) McLoughlin v O'Brian [1983] AC 410; [1982] 2 All ER 298
See Chapter 7, Damages, at p 265 *et seq*.

(8) Alcock and Others v Chief Constable of South Yorkshire [1992] 1 AC 310; [1991] 4 All ER 907
See Chapter 7, Damages, at p 264.

Statutes/Law Commission material

(1) Law Commission Report No 110, Breach of Confidence (Cmnd 838, 1981)
This recommended that damages for mental distress caused by breach of confidence should be available. However, to date this recommendation has not been acted upon.

(2) Medical (Professional Performance) Act 1995
Discussed below, and see Appendix A.

Professional/ethical guidelines

- If legal redress is not to be sought, a complaint may be lodged with the GMC accusing the doctor of 'serious professional misconduct'.

  The GMC's *Maintaining Good Medical Practice* booklet (July 1998) lists the type of conduct which should be referred to it (pp 14–16); breach of medical confidentiality falls within this category (see p 17 of the booklet). It is clear that the outcome of such disciplinary procedure could be of considerable evidential value in any subsequent civil proceedings and, even though there is no right of appeal against the GMC's findings (judicial review may be available), the unsuccessful patient may still pursue a civil claim for breach of confidence. However, although the courts can depart from the GMC's decision, in practice this is unlikely to happen (see *W v Egdell* [1990] 1 All ER 835 and *X v Y* [1988] 2 All ER 648 discussed at Rule 1(D)(v), at p 26 *et seq*).

  Faced with the criticism that the phrase 'serious professional misconduct' was being given too narrow a meaning, for example, it was alleged to be more focused on the sexual behaviour of health carers than the proper practice of medicine, the GMC published, in May 1992, a Consultative Paper, *Proposals for New Performance Procedures*. Out of that paper came the Medical (Professional Performance) Act 1995, which has widened the GMC's jurisdiction. Now, in addition to 'serious professional misconduct', the GMC can take jurisdiction where the doctor's performance is 'seriously deficient'. Although this phrase has deliberately not been defined, it is doubtful, given the tenor of the debates in Parliament, whether 'seriously deficient' is intended to cover such matters as the breaking of a medical confidence. See, also, the National Health Service (Service Committees and Tribunal) Regulations 1992 (SI 1992/664).

Practice points

- Making the application for an injunction:

  CPR Part 25 and CPR Practice Direction 25A set out the procedural requirements for making an application for an interim injunction. An application must be filed at court. The application must state the order sought together with the date, time and place of the hearing. This must be served (together with the evidence in support) as soon as practicable after it has been issued by the court and in any event not less than three days before the hearing date of the application. An application for an interim injunction has to be supported by evidence. This would generally be contained in a witness statement or a statement of case (that is, the particulars of claim) or the application itself, unless affidavit evidence is required by the court. The evidence will set out the facts the applicant relies on, to include all material facts about which the court should be informed. If the respondent to the application is not to be given notice of the application, the evidence has to set out reasons for this.

- Urgent applications and applications without notice:

  These applications can be made before or after issue of the claim form. No notice of the application is given to the respondent. Where an application is to be made after a claim form has been issued the application notice, together with the evidence in support and a draft order, are to be filed at court two hours before the hearing (if possible). The applicant should attempt to inform the respondent informally of the application, unless secrecy is necessary. If an application is made before the claim form has been issued the applicant generally has to provide an undertaking to the court to issue a claim form immediately unless the court orders otherwise. Where the matter is extremely urgent, the application can be dealt with by telephone.

- Under CPR Practice Direction 25A an order for an injunction has to contain the following (unless the court orders to the contrary):

  (1) the applicant's undertaking to pay any damages the respondent sustains;

  (2) (if the order is made without notice) the applicant's undertaking to serve the respondent as soon as practicable with the application notice together with the supporting evidence and the order made;

  (3) (if the order is made without notice) the return date for a second hearing at which the respondent is able to be present;

  (4) (if the order is made before filing the application notice) an undertaking from the applicant to file the application notice and pay the necessary fee that day or the next working day; and

  (5) (if the order is made before the claim form is issued) an undertaking from the applicant to issue a claim form and pay the necessary fee that day or the next working day. Alternatively the court may make directions regarding the commencement of the claim.

  The order must precisely state what the respondent has to do or must not do.

- Bear in mind an interim injunction is only a temporary remedy. However, if the court grants an interim injunction the defendant may well accept that if the matter proceeded to trial, the trial judge may well order a final injunction. The defendant may not, therefore, proceed to trial on the issue.

Ethical obligation

- In law, it seems that the doctor's duty of confidence does not survive a patient's death (like an action for defamation) unlike the ethical obligation imposed by the GMC. Paragraph 40 of the GMC's *Confidentiality* booklet (September 2000) states:

  > You still have an obligation to keep personal information confidential after a patient dies. The extent to which confidential information may be disclosed after a patient's death will depend on the circumstances ...

  Query – will a defence try and drag out the case as long as possible until the patient has died, and therefore escape legal, if not professional, liability?

- In *X v France* (1992) 14 EHRR 483, it was held that the excessive length of proceedings brought to obtain compensation before the French administrative authorities and the Paris administrative court violated an AIDS sufferer's rights under Art 6 para 1 of the European Convention on Human Rights. The applicant had developed full AIDS and the court held that, because of his reduced life expectancy, exceptional diligence was required. In this case, it was the administrative court that was penalised; however, there is no reason why this principle should not be applied to an unscrupulous defence lawyer or a health authority or trust that was deliberately 'dragging its feet'.

- While it may be possible to prove the doctor has made an error in breaching the patient's confidence, one should always stress to the patient that the damage has been done and an action which may drag the whole matter up again, perhaps even bring it to the attention of the media, should not be undertaken lightly.

- The claimant may have a claim in defamation in addition to a breach of confidence claim. However, such a claim is likely to be a rare occurrence for a number of reasons. First, public funding is not available for defamation actions, an obvious deterrent to many would-be litigants. Secondly, with the exception of those actions that are actionable *per se* in England, the law of slander requires that the claimant should be able to prove special damage, that is, pecuniary losses. This latter point will effectively rule out those cases which are simply a claim for mental distress and anguish. Finally, if the defendant has acted responsibly he is likely to have a defence. If what he stated is true then he will have a complete defence, and even if it is found that part of the statement is not true, provided he had reasonable grounds for holding that belief and he communicated the information to the proper authorities, he will be found not liable. For example, in a suspected child abuse case, informing the police or the social services would be protected by the defence of qualified privilege. However, the defendant who informs an employer that his employee is HIV positive treads an unstable path. The courts will again look at whether the disclosure was justified along the same principles as those used for a breach of confidence claim, see 'disclosure in the public interest' at Rule 1(D)(v), at p 26 *et seq*. We believe that it will only be the reckless defendant or the defendant motivated by malice who will find himself liable.

- See the end of the chapter for checklist, draft pleadings and order regarding breach of confidence.

RULE 1(C)

If a health carer who is treating a patient decides not to disclose information about that patient he will not be liable to a third party who is subsequently harmed by the patient.

Commentary

In deciding whether or not to disclose information a health carer will undoubtedly consider the risk posed by the patient, weigh his duty to the patient against the harm that could be done to society (including the third party) by the patient, and consider whether disclosure is necessary. If this approach is properly adopted, then the health carer should not be held culpable by the courts. Should the health carer act in the public interest, that will excuse a breach of confidence, but the public interest does not impose a new duty on him. Hence, while he can foresee a risk to a third party, for example, the spouse of an AIDS patient, that does not place him under a duty to disclose to the third party. If such a duty were to be imposed then it could place the health carer in the difficult position of being forced to juggle his respective obligations. It is suggested that this should never occur because the duty of confidence is paramount and can only be breached where it is in the public interest to do so: disclosure remains the exception not the rule. In English law, it is still very much the position that one person will not usually be held liable for harm done by another person (see *Smith v Littlewoods Organisation Ltd* [1987] 1 All ER 710; *Goodwill v British Pregnancy Advisory Service* [1996] 2 All ER 161 and *Palmer v Tees HA* [1999] Lloyd's Rep Med 351). Only where the health carer exercises some degree of control over the patient might a duty be imposed (see *Holgate v Lancashire Board* [1937] 4 All ER 19 and *Home Office v Dorset Yacht Club Ltd* [1970] AC 1004).

In certain states of the United States a different approach is evident. In *Tarasoff v Regents of the University of California* (1976) 551 P (2d) 334, a medical centre was found liable to a third party in negligence for failing to disclose information to the third party. There the Supreme Court of California held a psychiatrist liable for the actions of his student patient who murdered his girlfriend in a case of unrequited love. The girl was identifiable and identified and it was clear that the relationship between the psychiatrist and the patient was one in which the patient was under the control of the health professional. In *Bradshaw v Daniel* 854 SW (2d) 865 (1993), the Supreme Court of Tennessee, following *Tarasoff*, imposed a similar duty on a physician where, although there was an identifiable claimant, there was no 'special' control. In that case, a woman died from a non-contagious disease, Rocky Mountain Spotted Fever. The defendant physician had been treating the woman's husband for the same disease from which he had died shortly before the wife began to show symptoms of the disease. The court held that the physician-patient relationship was sufficient to impose upon the physician a positive duty to warn identifiable third parties in the patient's immediate family against foreseeable risks resulting from the patient's illness; here, although it was a non-contagious disease, members of the family were in danger of contracting the disease.

These cases can be contrasted with *Webb v Jarvis* (1991) 575 NE 2d 992 where the claimant had been shot by a patient who was being treated by the defendant physician. The victim brought an action in negligence against the defendant, arguing that the latter:

(1) had a duty to administer medical treatment to the patient in such a way as to take into account possible harm which might be done to unidentifiable third persons;

(2) had breached this duty by prescribing anabolic steroids which had made the patient violent; and

(3) had a duty to warn others of the patient's propensity for violence.

The Supreme Court of Indiana dismissed the claim. In deciding whether the defendant owed a duty it took into account three factors:

(1) *The relationship between the parties.* On this the court ruled that a professional person had no duty to a third party unless the former had actual knowledge that the latter was relying on him to render professional services. Here there was no evidence that the claimant was in fact relying on the defendant in this way. This is somewhat different from the *Tarasoff* case where the defendant must have been aware that the third party was relying on his treatment of the patient. Does this therefore mean that a spouse who wishes to claim against her husband's health carer for failing to warn her that her husband was infected with HIV would have to show not only that the health

carer knew of her existence but also that she was relying on the person who was treating her husband? How would she demonstrate such reliance?

(2) *The extent and nature of the duty of care.* On this issue it was said that the duty should be owed to a foreseeable victim with the particular harm also being foreseeable; whether or not the third party is a foreseeable victim was considered to be a matter for the jury. In *Webb's* case it was said that it was not reasonably foreseeable that prescribing steroids would make the patient violent.

(3) *Public policy.* Strictly this should have led to the conclusion that the physician was liable; here it did not because it would impose too onerous a burden on the physician to predict a patient's reaction to medication and to identify possible claimants who might be at risk. One has to ask whether this would always be the case. If the health carer knew that, by prescribing a certain treatment to his patient, there was a high degree of risk that the patient would harm a third party, should he not be under a legal/moral duty to warn that third party?

What clearly emerges from these cases is that some American courts see no objection in principle in imposing what may be called a third party positive duty on a doctor. What is less clear are the circumstances which must prevail for such a duty to exist. In our view the American cases suggest that:

(1) A reasonably foreseeable identifiable individual must be at risk. In *Tarasoff* there was such an individual, while in *Bradshaw* the members of the family (a distinct and identifiable group) were the people at risk. If the patient in *Tarasoff* had uttered threats of a general nature, for example, to society as a whole, then we would have expected a different decision because it would not have been possible to isolate any specific identifiable third party at risk. While not a perfect analogy, it could be said that one of the reasons why Mrs Hill failed in her claim against the police in *Hill v Chief Constable of West Yorkshire* [1988] 2 All ER 238 was that she was 'at no special or distinctive risk', that is, she was not sufficiently identifiable.

(2) Some control must be exercisable over the patient and was indeed exercised by the defendant health carer over the patient. It is our contention that the nature of this control needs to be of the type which existed in *Tarasoff*, bearing in mind the nature of the patient's illness rather than the 'normal control' which exists between any doctor and his patient. To this extent the nature of the illness will play a significant part in determining whether a duty exists.

(3) The risk to the third party must be real and not illusory.

Demonstrating that a duty exists in some American states is one thing; arguing from that premise that English law is wrong in denying the existence of such a duty is a more difficult proposition. While it is correct to say that at present the American approach is unlikely to be followed in the United Kingdom, we would argue that where a defendant exercising control over an individual can reasonably foresee that the individual's actions will harm identifiable third parties, then a duty should be imposed on the defendant to warn the third party. We would extend this principle to the situation where the defendant, by his own actions over an individual, creates the real risk that an identifiable third party may be harmed. When this approach is applied to health carers we do not give much credence to the argument that the latter would be placed under too onerous a duty to predict a patient's reaction to medication; surely this is part of his job. We would further extend the duty to all identifiable third parties whether or not they are immediate members of the family, because any attempt to limit the duty to family members would, in our opinion, be unfairly restrictive and vague (for example, who are members of the family – only those living in the same household?). The health carer could comply with his obligations by informing the third party or the appropriate authorities, see Rule 1(F), at p 33.

This is how we believe the law should develop. The bottom line still appears to be that the health carer must act in what he perceives to be the public interest, even if this does not accord with the majority's view of how he should have acted. If he does so and harm befalls a third party, it seems that at present he will not be held liable.

See, also, Chapter 3, Duty, at p 82 *et seq*.

REFERENCES

English case law

(1)   Smith v Littlewoods Organisation Ltd [1987] 1 All ER 710
The defendants purchased a cinema intending to demolish it and build a supermarket. The property, however, remained empty for over a month during which time vandals entered the property and attempted to start fires. Neither the defendants nor the police were informed of this. Eventually the vandals were successful in starting a fire, and as a result, the claimant's adjoining property was damaged. The claimant brought an action against the defendants in negligence.

Held: there was no general duty of care to prevent third parties from causing damage. The foreseeability of the damage was not in itself sufficient to create a positive duty on the defendant to act.

(2)   Goodwill v British Pregnancy Advisory Service [1996] 2 All ER 161
The defendants had arranged for M to have a vasectomy. He was subsequently informed that the operation had been a success and that he no longer needed to use contraception. Three years later he began a sexual relationship with the claimant; as the vasectomy operation had been successful the parties did not use any contraception. At some point in the relationship the vasectomy reversed spontaneously and the claimant became pregnant. She sued the defendants in negligence on the ground that they had failed to advise M of the risk of a spontaneous reversal.

Held: no duty was owed to her. At the time of the operation she was not an identifiable or identified third party.

(3)   Palmer v Tees HA and Others [1999] Lloyd's Rep Med 351
The claimant's daughter was abducted, sexually assaulted and murdered by A. A lived in the same street as the claimant and her family and had a history of sexual abuse by his

mother and neglect by the authorities put in charge of his care and protection. The claim, by the victim's mother, was against the health authorities for breach of duty to the victim and her mother.

Held: no duty was owed; there was no proximity between the parties.

(4)   Holgate v Lancashire Mental Hospitals Board [1937] 4 All ER 19
The defendant was held liable for negligently releasing a dangerous patient who had been compulsorily detained following convictions for violent offences. The patient subsequently assaulted the claimant.

(5)   Home Office v Dorset Yacht Club Co Ltd [1970] AC 1004; [1970] 2 All ER 294
Borstal trainees escaped due to the negligence of the Borstal officers who were in charge of them. The trainees caused damage to the claimant's yacht.

Held: the Home Office, as the employer of the officers, were responsible for the damage caused by the trainees. It must be emphasised that in this case there was a high degree of control being exercised by the officers over the trainees.

(6)   Hill v Chief Constable of West Yorkshire [1998] 2 All ER 238
The claimant was the mother of the Yorkshire Ripper's thirteenth victim and she alleged that the West Yorkshire police force had breached their duty of care to her daughter by failing to apprehend the Ripper earlier. The court dismissed the action partly on the ground that the victim 'was one of a vast number of the female general public who might be at risk from his activities but was at no special distinctive risk ...' (*per* Lord Keith, at p 243).

Foreign case law

United States

(1)   Tarasoff v Regents of the University of California (1976) 551 P (2d) 334
Here it was held that a psychiatrist had a duty to inform a third party of the threats made against her by his patient. The patient had repeatedly told his psychiatrist that he intended to kill his former girlfriend. He did in fact carry out his threat and the woman's family brought a successful negligence claim against the employers of the psychiatrist.

(2)   Bradshaw v Daniel [1994] Med L Rev 237; 854 SW (2d) 865 (1993)
See commentary above, at p 14.

(3)   Webb v Jarvis (1991) 575 NE (2d) 992
The claimant's wife had petitioned the court to have the claimant voluntarily hospitalised for psychiatric treatment. The claimant's psychiatrist disclosed communications which had been made to him several months earlier. On appeal, the claimant succeeded in an action for negligence against his psychiatrist. In doing so the court held that the duty of confidentiality may be breached in the following instances:

(1)   if there is a voluntary waiver by the patient; or

(2)   a waiver by operation of law; or

(3)   a disclosure which is justified in the interests of society or a third party or a patient. This was rightly treated as a matter for the jury but it had not been established in this case.

In commenting on the duty of the doctor to act in such instances, the court stated that the 'overriding public or private interests to which we refer merely excuse the psychiatrist's breach of duty to maintain confidentiality, and do not impose a new duty on the psychiatrist or affect any pre-existing duties'. This is very much in line with the English position, that is, a health carer has a discretion to break his duty of confidentiality; he is never under a duty to do so unless statute so orders.

RULE 1(D)

The rule against disclosure is not an absolute rule. There are exceptions to it.

Commentary

The rules about to be discussed are based largely upon GMC and the BMA guidelines. Although the point that we are about to make is, strictly speaking, a practice point it seems appropriate to make it here. In all cases the GMC advise that, should the health carer decide to disclose confidential information, he must be prepared to explain and justify his decision. We suggest that, unless he is sure of his position, he should discuss any intended disclosure of information with a colleague or seek advice from his defence organisation. Moreover, any defence practitioner should advise his client to do just that if the breach has not taken place. If it has, then his first question to the defendant ought to be: did he consult the aforesaid person or bodies? While these guidelines are not legally binding, the courts have tended, as in most cases involving medical matters, to follow the lead given by the medical profession.

Rule 1(D)(i)

A health carer is legally and ethically justified in disclosing confidential information about his patient if the patient willingly consents to the disclosure.

Commentary

Both the legal rules and the ethical guidelines confirm that, in well-defined circumstances, a disclosure can be made by either the health carer or someone in receipt of the confidential information from the health carer. One such circumstance is where the patient willingly consents. Since the confidence is that of the patient, the health carer should be seen as a temporary custodian of that confidence; as such, the patient is free to do whatever he (the patient) wishes with the information. Consequently any adult patient, that is, one who is 16 years of age or over, can give oral or written, express or implied, consent for disclosure and the health carer will be bound to acquiesce to those wishes. No court, it is submitted, will uphold the argument that in the health carer's view the disclosure would not have been in the patient's best interests; that would be taking paternalism too far. Having said that, it is clear that the consenting patient must fully understand both the nature and the consequences of the disclosure, for example, what is to be revealed, why it is being revealed and who is the intended recipient, etc; also the consent has to be freely and willingly given. Finally, there is no reason why the consent may not be conveyed to the health carer by a third party, for example, the patient's relative or legal adviser on behalf of the patient. In such circumstances, however, the health carer would be well advised to ascertain the relationship between the patient and the third party and to note this information on the patient's records.

The patient lying in a hospital bed may not know whether the person having a conversation with him and discussing his case is a consultant or a social worker, etc. Clearly, patients have no problem with their consultants sharing information with fellow health carers. But will they feel equally content if they learn that the person with whom the information has been shared is a medical student or a social worker? Probably not, and that is why it is important for the health carer or consultant not to assume that consent exists or will be given if sought; it is legally and ethically safer to seek the patient's consent. Again, where a health carer asks whether medical students can watch a procedure being undertaken, the patient is unlikely to refuse, but one must query whether there is any consent and whether it is voluntary and freely given. The health carer may genuinely feel that the patient has consented to student observation when in fact that is not the case. See, further, Rule 1(D)(ii), at p 21.

Can a patient under the age of 16 consent to disclosure? It is arguable that, since the *Gillick* case (*Gillick v West Norfolk and Wisbech Health Authority* [1986] AC 112) permits the mature under-16 to consent in law to medical treatment without parental permission, then such a person should rightly be able to consent to his confidential information being disclosed or not as the case may be. Were this not so, the somewhat farcical situation would be reached where a health carer could rely on the patient for consent to be treated but would then have to turn to the parents for permission to disclose information about the said treatment. Guidelines issued by the BMA, the Royal College of General Practitioners, the Family Planning Association and the Brooke Advisory Centres (and supported by the government-funded Health Education Authority) now advise that the under-16s' confidentiality should be respected and that parents should only be informed in 'exceptional circumstances'. Although these guidelines relate specifically to young girls seeking contraceptive advice, it is submitted that, for mature under-16s, capacity to consent to any medical treatment or procedure will carry with it confidentiality. Support for such a conclusion exists, in the authors' opinion, with the passage of the Human Rights Act 1998 and, in particular, Arts 8 and 14 of the European Convention on Human Rights. We would contend that Art 14, which prevents discrimination on age ground linked to Art 8, which advocates a right to respect for one's private life, effectively means that the mature under-16 year old patient has the legal right to consent to disclosure of his/her personal and private health records. In *Re W (A Minor) (Medical Treatment)* [1992] 4 All ER 627, the Appeal Court endorsed the view that a mature under-16 year old (and someone between 16 and 18 years of age) had no legal right to refuse medical treatment; rather, such a refusal lay with the parents or others with parental responsibility ('The fundamental principle is that the authority of any one party with the power to consent trumps the refusal of any other, unless a court otherwise directs': Francis and Johnston, *Medical Treatment: Decisions and the Law*, p 37). It should therefore follow that consent to any disclosure about the refusal should also rest with the parents, etc; any other conclusion would result in yet another farcical situation. But if in the not too distant future *Re W* was to fall foul of Arts 8 and 14 of the European Convention on Human Rights – and it is submitted here that it should – then the mature under-16 year olds and the 16 to 18 year olds would not only have the legal capacity to refuse treatment but also the capacity to consent to its disclosure.

REFERENCES

English case law

(1) *Gillick v West Norfolk and Wisbech Area Health Authority [1986] AC 112; [1985] 3 All ER 402*

See Chapter 2, Consent, at p 46 *et seq.*

(2) *Re W (A Minor) (Medical Treatment) [1992] 4 All ER 627*

The Court of Appeal held that, although a competent minor can give consent to medical treatment, he does not have an absolute right to refuse treatment where his parent/guardian has consented to the treatment (see, further, Chapter 2 at p 48.) This decision would seem to take paternalism to dizzy heights!

See, also, cases discussed in Chapter 2, Consent, at p 47 *et seq.*

Professional/ethical guidelines

GMC's Confidentiality: Protecting and Providing Information booklet (September 2000), paras 1, 2, 13–16

European Convention on Human Rights

Article 8
See above.

Article 14:
> The enjoyment of the rights and freedoms set forth in this convention shall be secured without discrimination on any ground such as sex, race, colour, language, religion, political or other opinion, national or social origin, association with a national minority, property, birth or other status.

Practice points

A court, in the course of legal proceedings, may order a health carer who is either a witness or a defendant to disclose information about his patient. In doing so, the court will have to strike a balance between the need for all relevant information to be disclosed, thereby ensuring justice is done, against the need to keep the patient's confidence secret. The decision to order disclosure will not be taken lightly, but if the court orders then, subject to the rules of legal professional privilege, the health carer has no choice: he must answer or be in contempt of court.

Further, the rules of the court provide for pre-trial disclosure of such things as expert medical reports on which one or other party is seeking to rely. If this is so then again the health carer has no choice: his report will be made public. As Sir John Donaldson said in *Naylor v Preston AHA* [1987] 1 WLR 958 (at p 967):

> ... the general rule is that, whilst a party is entitled to privacy in seeking out the 'cards' for his hand, once he has put his hand together, the litigation is to be conducted with all the cards face up on the table. Furthermore, most of the cards have to be put down well before the hearing.

Furthermore, the courts have held in *Hay v University of Alberta Hospital* [1991] 2 Med LR 204 that, where the nature of the claimant's action is against either his health carer or the health authority for damages, then the claimant will be deemed to have implicitly consented to the defence having access to his medical records and discussing the case with the physicians who treated him. This decision may have to be reviewed in the light of the Human Rights Act 1998, Art 8 of the ECHR and the case of *MS v Sweden* (1999) 28 EHHR 313. In that case, where a compensation claim had been made for a back injury caused by a fall, the Social Insurance Office sought and obtained, without the patient/claimant's consent, all her medical records from the client which had treated her for the injury. Although the European Court of Human Rights ruled that the interference was lawful under Art 8 (economic well being of the state had to be protected from abuse), it nevertheless found that the patient, as a claimant, had not waived her right to privacy generally under Art 8; it therefore meant that all her medical records were not automatically available to the defence; see, further, p 6.

Rule 1(D)(ii)

The health carer may disclose confidential information to other persons responsible for the clinical treatment of the patient; ideally the patient should give his consent to such disclosure.

Commentary

The points already made in Rule 1(D)(i) in relation to whether or not the patient is competent to give consent to disclosure to third parties apply, as do the legal rules on how the consent may be given. Disclosure under this rule is permitted to third parties whether the latter are simply involved in an isolated act of treatment or responsible for the continuing care of the patient. If the patient had to be consulted every time the health carer liaised with a fellow professional the health carer's job, if not already difficult, would become demonstrably difficult; therefore, it is accepted that disclosure can be made to, for example, nurses, radiologists, physiotherapists, etc, whenever the best interests of either the patient or fellow health carers (see below, at p 22 *et seq*) so demand.

The health carer's duty is to ensure that the third party appreciates that the information is being imparted in strict confidence, although it seems unlikely that any claim will succeed against the health carer should the third party decide not to maintain the confidence. Perhaps the only grounds on which a claim against the health carer could succeed are that:

(1) he failed to state unequivocally to the third party that the information was of a confidential nature (unlikely in many circumstances, given the nature of the information being disclosed and the fact that the receiving health care professional would, it is suggested, be bound to assume that the information is confidential); or

(2) where the third party is outside the permitted group to which the health carer can legally disclose.

As regards the latter point it is not certain to what extent people outside the medical profession can receive such information. For example, can a social worker be told the specific details of a patient's illness? In cases involving terminal illnesses they should be told, in the absence of which they may not be able to participate in providing the palliative care the patient requires. But what about other cases? The decision will be the health carer's and, providing he has acted in accordance with good clinical management and in the best interests of the patient, it is unlikely that he will be regarded as having imparted information to the wrong person.

If the patient should steadfastly refuse to give consent then the health carer can disclose the confidential information if he is of the opinion that the health of any of his colleagues in the treatment team is at risk. This disclosure must only take place in exceptional circumstances. In effect, this is little more than a restatement of the public interest defence (see, further, Rule 1(D)(v), at p 26); the health carer must balance the risk to his colleague(s) as against the public interest in maintaining the confidence of his patient. What if he acts too late? Will his colleague, affected by this inactivity, have any recourse against the silent colleague? We would argue not, in line with the position of third parties who allege that the health carer owes them a duty of care to breach the patient's confidence (see Rule 1(C), at p 13). However, the court may feel inclined to treat the patient slightly differently given the identity of the third party, for example, if the third party is a GP then in most cases there is a much higher degree of intimate contact (for example, blood) than there would be between someone diagnosed as HIV positive and his work colleagues.

REFERENCES

Professional/ethical guidelines

GMC's Confidentiality: Protecting and Providing Information booklet (September 2000), paras 7–10

This deals with disclosure to other members of the health team. In particular, it notes that the health carer must explain to the patient why such disclosure is necessary; that in limited circumstances, for example, an emergency, the patient's consent to disclosure need not be obtained; that if the patient refuses permission his decision will be respected, and that all members of the team have a duty to ensure their colleagues understand the obligation of confidentiality. See also the GMC booklet, *Serious Communicable Diseases* (October 1997), paras 18–19.

Rule 1(D)(iii)

When a health carer considers it undesirable for medical reasons to seek the patient's consent or where the patient refuses consent to the disclosure of information, then, if the health carer considers it to be in the patient's best interests, he may disclose that information to a third party.

Commentary

What circumstances will come within this rule? The GMC refers to disclosures which will have personal consequences for patients ('to protect the patient, or someone else, from the risk of death or serious harm' (see paragraph 14 of the *Confidentiality: Protecting and Providing Information* (September 2000) booklet)) and those disclosures which are unlikely to have personal consequences for patients ('for purposes such as epidemiology, public health safety, or the administration of health services, or for use in education or training, clinical or medical audit, or research' (see paragraph 15 of the *Confidentiality* booklet (September 2000))). For our purposes we intend to focus on the first of these two categories. Consequently, we are of the opinion that cases involving neglect or physical/sexual abuse of the patient or occasions where there is evidence that the patient is immature or where the nature of the patient's illness, including mental illness, prevents him from giving consent, are the type of cases which will fall within this exception. Indeed, all of these cases could legitimately come within the public interest exception; the present breakdown is more for the sake of convenience.

But before considering these scenarios in some slight detail, three general points must be borne in mind:

(1) a properly considered clinical decision to disclose cannot be unlawful and therefore would not give rise to a claim;

(2) relatives have no special status regarding receiving information, although it is more likely than not that the disclosure here will be made to such a person;

(3) if the patient were to place a total ban on communication, that would have to be respected in line with patient autonomy; however, in exceptional cases, disclosure may be made even if it is contrary to the patient's wishes.

Sexual/physical abuse

The health carer's dilemma may turn on the identity of the patient. If his patient is an adult woman then she has (in theory) the ability to sort out her own situation by either informing the police or seeking the protection of the law (see the Domestic Violence and Matrimonial Proceedings Act 1976). All a health carer can do here is advise and help the patient; disclosure to the authorities will only be justified if the health carer is of the opinion that the woman's life is at risk and that the risk is real.

In the case of child abuse, the situation is quite different because the patient invariably cannot give and will not have given consent; therefore the health carer will have to act on the basis of the best interests of the child and inform the appropriate authorities. Obviously a misdiagnosis could lead to an action for defamation, but it is likely that the health carer would be able to rely on the defence of public interest, provided he were to disclose the information to the proper authorities. Given that some authorities may undertake not to disclose the name of the informant, this is something which may encourage the health carer to act. The GMC's *Confidentiality* booklet (September 2000) reiterates that disclosure should only be made without the patient's consent if the patient is unable to give consent and such disclosure is in the patient's best interests (see paras 10–12 of *Confidentiality*).

Immaturity

In relation to consent to treatment, confidentiality is owed to a patient who is under the age of 16 but *Gillick* competent in the same way that it is owed to a patient over the age of 16. But what if the patient is under 16 years of age and is not *Gillick* competent? Normally, consent will lie with the parents or others with authority, eg guardians. But, relying on GMC guidelines, disclosure without consent will be justified if, in the health carer's opinion, such a disclosure is deemed to be in that child's best interests. The GMC stress that any disclosure should be based on the child's ability to understand the nature and consequences of the medical treatment and/or procedure involved (see para 23 of the GMC booklet, *Seeking Patients' Consent: The Ethical Considerations* (November 1998)).

One would have expected the patient who is competent (either over 16 or *Gillick* competent) to consent to treatment to be entitled to have that confidence maintained, whereas the non-competent patient would not be so entitled. Not so; even where the patient is non-competent, that is, immature to consent to treatment, confidentiality should still be maintained unless there are convincing arguments to the contrary.

Illness

Disclosure may be permitted where, because of illness, the patient lacks the capacity to consent or to agree to the involvement of the appropriate person. If that were the case, it is submitted that the health carer could legally disclose in the patient's best interests. Ethically he may, before disclosing, discuss the matter with a relative of the patient. Disclosure may also take place where he judges that it would be emotionally damaging to the patient to seek the latter's consent to such disclosure.

REFERENCES

English case law

Gillick v West Norfolk & Wisbech AHA [1986] AC 112; [1985] 3 All ER 402
See Chapter 2, Consent, at p 46 *et seq.*

Statutes/statutory instruments

(1) Domestic Violence and Matrimonial Proceedings Act 1976
Section 1 allows an application for an injunction to restrain the other party to the marriage from molesting the applicant or a child or to exclude him or her from the matrimonial home. Section 2 extends this provision to a man and wife living together as though they were parties to the marriage.

(2) Civil Procedure Rules 1998
Part 21 (Children and Patients)

Practice Direction, Children and Patients (PD/21).
See pp 309–10.

Professional/ethical guidelines

GMC's Confidentiality: Protecting and Providing Information booklet (September 2000), paras 3, 7–11, 14–16

This deals with disclosure without the patient's consent. Generally, it echoes the exceptions discussed in the preceding paragraphs. At para 9 it deals with disclosure to employers and insurance companies; it reminds health carers that in these circumstances they should carry out an assessment of the patient's condition for these bodies with the patient's written consent.

Rule 1(D)(iv)

Information may be disclosed for the purposes of teaching and medical research; in the latter case the research must have been approved by a local clinical ethical committee.

Commentary

This exception recognises that there is a public interest in properly conducted research and learning. To qualify, the research must be sanctioned by an approved ethical committee.

The GMC's booklet on *Confidentiality: Protecting and Providing Information* (September 2000) confirms the basic rule. Paragraph 31 says:

> Where research projects depend on using identifiable information and samples, and it is not practicable to contact patients to seek their consent, this fact should be drawn to the attention of a research ethics committee so that it can consider whether the likely benefits of the research outweigh the loss of confidentiality. Disclosures may otherwise be improper, even if the recipients of the information are registered medical practitioners. The decision of a research ethics committee would be taken into account by a court if a claim for breach of confidentiality were made, but the court's judgment would be based on its own assessment of whether the public interest was served ...

(See also paragraph 32, which says: 'You must obtain express consent from patients before publishing personal information about them as individuals in media to which the public has access, for example in journals or text books ... Express consent must ... be sought prior to the publication of ... case-histories about, or photographs of, patients ...')

Two points need to be made in respect of paragraph 31. First, in cases where the information relates to anonymous patients, the consent of the latter is certainly not needed. Secondly, where it is not possible to anonymise the information then the patient's consent (or someone on the patient's behalf) should be sought. If this consent cannot be obtained then para 16 details what must be done, namely 'that fact should be drawn to the attention of a research ethics committee which should decide whether the public interest in the research outweighs patients' right to confidentiality' (see *R v Department of Health ex p Source Informatics Ltd* [2000] 2 WLR 940).

REFERENCES

English case law

R v Department of Health ex p Source Informatics Ltd [2000] 2 WLR 940; [2000] 1 All ER 786
Here an American company, Source Informatics Ltd (S), wanted information on doctors' prescribing habits; this they intended to sell to pharmaceutical companies who, in turn, might use it to market their products more effectively. S were particularly interested in doctors' names and the products they prescribed; what they were not interested in were

the names and identities of the patients involved. The method used to elicit the information was for the pharmacists to collect the anonymised information by computer. Was this a breach of confidence? The Department of Health argued it was and they issued a policy document to this effect in July 1997. S replied that it was not, using as one of its main arguments the fact that the patients would remain anonymous. At first instance Latham J refused S's application that the 1997 DOH document was erroneous in law but the Appeal Court upheld S's appeal. It rightly concluded that there was no breach of confidence by the pharmacist to the patient if, having dispensed the medicine prescribed, he then used the prescription form as a means of passing on the anonymised information to S. *Per* Simon Brown LJ at 953:

> The patient has no proprietorial claim to the prescription form or to the information it contains. Of course he can bestow or withhold his custom as he pleases ... But that gives the patient no property in the information and no right to control its use provided only and always that his privacy is not put at risk ...

Professional/ethical guidelines

HSG 91(5)

The government has provided additional guidance in the document Local Research Ethics Committee HSG 91(5). Among its recommendations are the following:

(1) no individual should be recognisable from the research without their explicit consent and the information should be destroyed when it is no longer needed;

(2) where a situation arises where it would be impracticable to seek a patient's consent the LREC must be satisfied that the research is in the public interest, albeit that if the patient has indicated that he does not want his records released this should be respected;

(3) information should not be obtained without the consent being obtained from the health care professional and no approach should be made to the patient without the consent of the health care professional responsible for his care.

Rule 1(D)(v)

A health carer will have a defence to an action for breach of confidence if it can be shown that the disclosure of information was in the public interest. In determining whether or not the particular disclosure was in the public interest, the court will balance the harm that would have resulted had the health carer not disclosed the information against the public interest in maintaining the health carer-patient confidence.

Commentary

In establishing the parameters of this exception, the courts have over the years relied heavily on guidance from the GMC's *Confidentiality booklet* (September 2000), paras 18–20. In balancing the various public interests, the courts have demonstrated certain definite approaches.

Public interest

Disclosure of the information must be in the public interest; it is not sufficient that the information is interesting to the public. In *X v Y* [1988] 2 All ER 648, a health authority successfully obtained an injunction prohibiting a tabloid newspaper from publishing the names of two doctors who were being treated for AIDS. While the information would have been of interest to the public, public interest maintained that their identities should not be revealed, as this could have potentially discouraged fellow AIDS sufferers from seeking treatment.

The health carer should also be able to rely on this defence where the confidence is breached to protect an individual from harm; there is a public interest in protecting a member of the public. Hence, the HIV patient who refuses to inform his sexual partner is unlikely to succeed in an action against his health carer if the latter breaches his duty of confidence and informs the partner. But for this defence to be available there must be a specific individual at risk and that risk must be real. If the HIV patient is sexually promiscuous or is unattached, so that there is no identifiable third party at risk, then the doctor should only encourage the patient to seek help.

Risk

How great must the risk to the public be for a health carer to rely on this defence? In *W v Egdell* [1990] 1 All ER 835 Dr Edgell, a psychiatrist, had been asked by W's legal advisers to prepare a report in support of W's application for transfer to a regional secure unit. The report was unfavourable to W and, as a result, W abandoned his application for a transfer. Dr Egdell, however, was concerned that W might make a further application for a transfer at a later date and that his report would not be included in the patient's notes. He considered that W would be a danger to the public if he was ever released; as a result he sent his report to the director of the hospital who then passed it on to the Home Secretary. The Court of Appeal, relying on the GMC guidelines, held that Dr Egdell was justified in disclosing the information. This case was followed in *R v Crozier* [1991] Crim LR 138 where a psychiatrist acting for the accused handed his report to the prosecutor for the Crown. The Court of Appeal held that there was a stronger interest in the public knowing that the appellant was a danger to the public than in the confidence being maintained.

What these cases reveal is that there must be a real as opposed to an illusory risk of harm to the public and that it must be necessary for the information to be disclosed. Even if the exact degree of risk to the public or individual is uncertain, that is irrelevant; all that matters is that there should be some definite risk of danger to the public.

Practical application of the above

Below we consider certain common situations where the health carer will be faced with these two competing public interests.

Crime

The GMC says a breach of confidence is justified if there is a risk of harm to a third party or if there is a risk of serious crime being committed (see Appendix E). It is significant that they use the word 'serious'; a health carer is unlikely to be able to rely on the public interest defence if the crime which has been committed or threatened is of a trivial nature. The fact that the patient has committed a crime, or is about to commit a crime, does not change the nature of the health carer-patient relationship. However, in cases such as rape or child abuse, a health carer would be justified in disclosing such information because of the serious risk to the public and/or a specific individual. Child abuse is particularly difficult because often not only the child but also the rest of the family are patients of the health carer. The paramount duty is to secure the safety of the child, so the health carer must admit the child to hospital and consult with a paediatrician. Given these circumstances, if he should choose not to disclose the information it is submitted that the law will be powerless against his inactivity, except if statute otherwise prescribes; however, he may be censored for professional misconduct.

AIDS

Although in law HIV/AIDS has to be treated in the same way as any other contagious disease, because it is incurable and can be transmitted via venereal or blood contact it raises special dilemmas. Simply being tested positively for such a disease can lead to the assumption that the person in question must be in a high risk category, and consequently is leading a dubious lifestyle. This may have repercussions in relation to such matters as employment, life insurance and mortgages.

The GMC has published a booklet on serious communicable diseases (HIV, hepatitis B and tuberculosis) and the ethical ramifications these illnesses pose for the health carer. The health carer may disclose information:

(1) to other health care professionals responsible for the care of the patient (para 19); or

(2) to the patient's sexual partner/spouse, that is, specific identifiable individuals who are at risk of infection (paras 22–23).

In both instances, the disclosure can only be made after the patient has received counselling from the health carer in charge of his case and has refused to give his consent to the disclosure. In line with the defence of disclosure in the public interest, there must be a serious risk of injury involved and it must be an urgent situation; hence a health carer will only be permitted to inform a specific individual or individuals, for example, if several members of a health care team are at risk. With regard to disclosure to a patient's sexual partner, where the patient is not in a permanent sexual relationship and/or it is unclear whether or not the risk may materialise, then there is not the same degree of urgency about the situation. In addition, it is in the public interest that, as far as possible, the confidences of such patients should be maintained or else patients may feel disinclined to seek treatment. In both the above examples, the advice from the GMC is intended to be binding; in all cases the health carers must make their own judgment. However, it is submitted that should a health carer follow the afore-mentioned advice then he will not be subject to the wrath of the courts or the profession.

Finally, we consider the situation where it could be said that certain individuals consent to run the risk of contracting diseases and infections, namely sportspersons. The two infections that they are most at risk of are HIV and HBV (Hepatitis B Virus); HBV can be cured, to date HIV cannot. Should the sports health carer disclose to team mates the fact that one member of the team has the HBV/HIV virus? Is the situation any different because each player implicitly consents to run the risks associated with the sport? Could it be argued that the sportsperson affected has not given true consent because he does not know of the risk? Unlike other health care professionals he is not subject to the National Health Service Trust (Venereal Diseases) Regulations 1974 (SI 1974/29) or the National Health Service Trust (Venereal Diseases) Directions of 1991. It therefore seems apparent that he will not be placed under any more of an onerous obligation than his NHS counterpart. As a matter of routine, sportsmen/women should be vaccinated against HBV, although there is little that can be done to prevent the spread of HIV except screening, which has obvious drawbacks. As a final point perhaps the obligation for a sportsperson's safety lies solely with the employer – they are the ones who make the profits, so perhaps they should bear the risks (see, further, AA McConnell and MG McKay in *Medicine, Science and the Law* (1995) Vol 35, No 1, at p 45).

REFERENCES

English case law

(1)   X v Y [1988] 2 All ER 648
This case is also referred to at Rule 1(B). A tabloid newspaper had acquired information identifying two GPs as HIV positive. The newspaper argued that the public had a right to know the names of the said individuals because they were continuing to practice and were therefore a risk to the public. The court rejected this argument in favour of the Health Authority, who argued that where a health carer had received proper counselling the risk to the public was negligible. Furthermore, emphasis was placed upon maintaining the confidence of AIDS sufferers, otherwise there was a substantial risk they would not seek treatment.

(2)   W v Edgell [1990] 1 All ER 835
(For the facts of this case, see commentary above, p 27.) W brought an action in contract and equity alleging breach of confidence. The court relied on the advice of the GMC and found that the public interest in disclosure outweighed W's public interest. Dr Edgell was right to disclose his report on W to the appropriate authorities, as W posed a real danger to the public should he ever be released.

(3)   R v Crozier [1991] Crim LR 138
For the facts of this case, see p 27.

Held: the psychiatrist had acted reasonably and in the public interest.

Statutes/statutory instruments

National Health Service Trust (Venereal Diseases) Regulations 1991 (SI 1991/29)

Professional/ethical guidelines

GMC's Confidentiality: Protecting and Providing Information booklet (September 2000), paras 36–37:

Three situations are given as examples which may justify disclosure in the interests of others:

(1) disclosure to the DVLC where the patient continues to drive contrary to medical advice;

(2) where a medical colleague is ill and is placing patients at risk; and

(3) where disclosure is necessary to prevent or detect a serious crime.

RULE 1(E)

A health carer will have to breach the confidentiality of a patient if he is ordered to do so by the courts or if legislation (primary or delegated) so requires.

Commentary

Two separate sets of circumstances are envisaged here.

Court orders

A court, in the course of legal proceedings, may order a health carer who is either a witness or a defendant to disclose information about his patient. In doing so, the court will have to strike a balance between the need for all relevant information to be disclosed, thereby ensuring justice is done, against the need to keep the patient's confidence secret. The decision to order disclosure will not be taken lightly, but if the court orders then, subject to the rules of legal professional privilege, the health carer has no choice: he must answer or be in contempt of court.

Further, the rules of the court provide for pre-trial disclosure of such things as expert medical reports on which one or other party is seeking to rely. If this is so then again the health carer has no choice: his report will be made public. As Sir John Donaldson said in *Naylor v Preston AHA* [1987] 1 WLR 958 (at p 967):

> ... the general rule is that, whilst a party is entitled to privacy in seeking out the 'cards' for his hand, once he has put his hand together, the litigation is to be conducted with all the cards face up on the table. Furthermore, most of the cards have to be put down well before the hearing.

Furthermore, it was held in the Canadian case of *Hay v University of Alberta Hospital* [1991] 2 Med LR 204 that where the nature of the claimant's action is against either his health carer or the health authority for damages then the claimant implicitly consents to the defence having access to his medical records and discussing the case with the physicians who treated him. But this rule may be inapplicable in English law in view of the decisions in *MS v Sweden* (1999) 28 EHRR 313 and *Nicholson v Hatton Green Hospital NHS Trust* [2000] Medical Litigation Cases 0189. In the latter case, the Appeal Court ruled that:

> ... there is the right of confidentiality between a patient and his treating doctor which the law will uphold ... the only restriction which a claimant ... can reasonably seek is that the information which is requested should be confined to that which is relevant to the issues then existing between the parties.

Clearly instituting proceedings will be treated as implicit consent on the part of the claimant to the disclosure of confidential medical information about him, but only as regards such information as the court rules is relevant to the particular issues in dispute.

Legislation

There are Acts of Parliament and delegated legislation which require disclosure to be made. Among the more familiar are the Public Health (Infectious Diseases) Regulations 1988 (SI 1988/1546) and the Abortion Regulations 1991 (SI 1991/499). Among the less familiar are s 18 of the Prevention of Terrorism (Temporary Provisions) Act 1989 and s 8 of the Police and Criminal Evidence Act 1984. It would be futile to look for a common thread running through these various measures; suffice to say that Parliament usually regards such disclosures as being necessary in the interests of society as a whole.

REFERENCES

English case law

(1) Naylor v Preston AHA [1987] 1 WLR 958
See above, at p 30.

(2) Nicholson v Hatton Green Hospital NHS Trust [2000] Medical Litigation Cases 0189
See above.

Foreign case law

Australia

Australian Red Cross Society v BC [1992] 3 Med LR 273
The Court ruled that the identity of a blood donor should be revealed to the claimant in the interests of justice. This outweighed the public interest in maintaining the confidentiality of blood donors.

Canada

Hay v University of Alberta Hospital [1991] 2 Med LR 204
See above, at p 30.

European Court of Human Rights

MS v Sweden (1999) 28 EHRR 313
In this case, a compensation claim had been made for a back injury caused by a fall. The Social Insurance Office obtained, without the applicant's permission, all her medical records from the clinic which had treated her. The European Court of Human Rights ruled that there had been an infringement of the applicant's rights under Art 8 but that

the infringement was, in the circumstances, lawful. But it also found that the applicant in bringing the claim had not waived her right to privacy generally; consequently all her medical records were not automatically available to the defence.

Statutes/statutory instruments

(1) Prevention of Terrorism (Temporary Provisions) Act 1989
18(1) A person is guilty of an offence if he has information which he knows or believes might be of material assistance:
  (a) in preventing the commission by any other person of an act of terrorism connected with the affairs of Northern Ireland; or
  (b) in securing the apprehension, prosecution or conviction of any other person for an offence involving the commission, preparation or instigation of such an act,

and fails without reasonable excuse to disclose the information as soon as reasonably practicable.

(2) Police and Criminal Evidence Act 1984
See, in particular, ss 8, 9, 11 and 12.

Section 8 allows a Justice of the Peace to issue a search warrant where he is satisfied that a serious arrestable offence has been committed and that there is material on the premises which is likely to be of substantial value in the investigations and which is not subject to legal privilege. See, further, ss 9 and 11 for what may be seized. *Note* that an application may be made to seize 'excluded material' such as personal records, human tissue, etc. The government's objective in these sections is to protect the community as a whole. According to s 12, 'personal records' means documentary and other records concerning an individual (whether living or dead) and includes those records relating to his physical or mental health. The provision may apply to medical records and human tissue fluid taken for purposes of diagnostic or medical treatment.

(3) Public Health (Control of Disease) Act 1984 supplemented by Public Health (Infectious Diseases) Regulations 1988 (SI 1988/1546)

(4) Abortion Regulations 1991 (SI 1991/499)

(5) National Health Service (Notification of Births and Deaths) Regulations 1982 (SI 1982/286)

(6) Misuse of Drugs (Notification of and Supply to Addicts) Regulations 1973 (SI 1973/799)

(7) National Health Service (Venereal Diseases) Regulations 1974 (SI 1974/29)

Note that these regulations are said to apply to a sexually transmitted disease; would this apply to someone who was infected with HIV following a blood transfusion?

Practice points

In any legal proceedings medical evidence will remain privileged unless that privilege is waived, eg because the party wishes to adduce the evidence at trial. No party may call an expert or use written evidence from an expert without the court's permission – CPR r 35.4. The court will usually give permission at the directions stage. The party applying for permission must identify the field in which he wishes to rely on expert evidence and, if possible, give details of his chosen expert. Ordinarily this information will usually be provided in the allocation questionnaire, see CPR Part 26 and p 304.

Professional/ethical guidelines

GMC's *Confidentiality: Protecting and Providing Information booklet (September 2000), paras 43-46*

Disclosure should be confined to information which is necessary for the judicial or statutory proceedings and should not be given in the absence of a court order.

RULE 1(F)

If the circumstances permit disclosure, a health carer must ensure that the information is disclosed only to the appropriate person or authority.

Commentary

If a health carer chooses to broadcast the confidential information to all and sundry then his actions will be reprimanded by both the courts and his profession. Consequently, in the case of an epileptic driver disclosure should be made to the DVLA as the appropriate body and, in cases of child abuse, the appropriate social services body or NSPCC should be informed. As such, the health carer not only has the difficult decision of whether or not to disclose but also he must be certain that he is revealing the information in the correct format and to the correct person(s). Again, if he is preparing a report on a patient for the patient's employer or insurance company, he owes a legal and ethical duty to the recipients of the report and should, in such circumstances, only examine the patient on the clear understanding that the patient is aware that the report, with its confidential information, will be forwarded to the employer, etc.

REFERENCES

English case law

(1) *W v Edgell [1990] 1 All ER 835*
Dr Edgell was not in breach of his duty of confidence because he had disclosed the information to the 'proper authorities' (see the judgment of Bingham LJ, at p 853).

(2) *X v Y [1988] 2 All ER 648*
Disclosure could not be authorised to a tabloid newspaper; it was a matter for the health authority who were responsible for GPs and their patients.

Foreign case law

New Zealand

Duncan v Medical Practitioners' Disciplinary Committee [1986] 1 NZLR 513
A GP was found 'guilty of professional misconduct in that he breached professional confidence in informing lay people of his patient's personal medical history'.

The patient, a bus driver, had undergone a triple coronary bypass operation and was certified fit to drive by his surgeon. However, his GP asked that the patient's driving licence be withdrawn and, in addition, warned the patient's passengers of the potential danger. The decision of the Disciplinary Committee was the subject of judicial review and the court duly commented:

I think a doctor who has decided to communicate should discriminate and ensure the recipient is a responsible authority.

Checklist for patient/claimant's solicitor

(1) Is the claimant:
  - (a) a patient?
  - (b) a third party injured by the defendant following a refusal to breach the confidence (claim unlikely to succeed; see Rule 1 (C), at p 13)?
  - (c) a minor (who is acting by his or her litigation friend)?
  - (d) a person under a disability (see (c) above)?
  - (e) dying (is there a need for surgery)?
  - (f) dead, that is, is the claim being brought by dependants (note that only the ethical obligation survives death)?
  - (g) a patient being treated privately (claim will be brought in contract) or under the NHS (claim in equity)?

(2) Is the proposed defendant:
  - (a) a GP?
  - (b) a consultant?
  - (c) other health care professional?
  - (d) a third party, that is, was the information disclosed to a third party who then breached the confidence?
  - (e) a health authority?

(3) What does the client want:
  - (a) an apology/explanation?
  - (b) disciplinary action against the defendant?
  - (c) financial compensation?
  - (d) an injunction to either:
    - (i) prevent the breach occurring; or
    - (ii) prevent further breaches?
  - (e) an action for defamation?

(4) Has the breach already taken place?
  If yes:
  - (a) when did it occur?
  - (b) what was the nature of the breach?
  - (c) to whom was the disclosure made?
  - (d) did the defendant attempt to persuade the patient to consent to the disclosure earlier?
  - (e) did the claimant know the defendant was going to breach his confidence?

  If not:
  - (a) how does the claimant know the defendant is about to breach his confidence?
  - (b) has the defendant tried to persuade the claimant to give his consent to the disclosure?

(c) to whom will the disclosure be made?

(d) is the claimant still under the care of the defendant?

(5) What happened / will happen as a result of the breach? Did the claimant:

(a) write a letter of complaint to the defendant?

(b) use the internal complaints machinery (local resolution)?

(c) lose his job?

(d) suffer distress, inconvenience, illness?

(e) sustain damage to his business, for example, loss of profit?

Furthermore:

(f) was the information disclosed accurate? Was it defamatory?

(6) Does the defendant have any defence?

(a) did the claimant consent to the disclosure?

(b) is the information confidential?

(c) was the information imparted in the context of a doctor-patient relationship?

(d) did the defendant have just cause for disclosing the information:

(i) in the patient's best interests?

(ii) in the public interest?

(iii) to another health carer?

(iv) for research purposes?

(e) was the information disclosed not by the defendant but by a third party?

(7) Do immediate steps need to be taken, for example, an *ex parte* injunction?

Checklist for defendant's solicitor

Refer to the claimant's checklist, with the following amendments.

(1) Points 1 and 2 will be reversed, that is, the client is the defendant and will want to know who is the alleged claimant.

(2) At point 3 the question will be what is the alleged claim?

(3) Refer to points 4, 5 and 6 but in addition:

(a) did the defendant consult with any bodies / organisation before the disclosure, for example, Medical Defence Union, BMA, etc? If yes, what was the nature of their advice?

(b) how often did he try (if he did) to persuade the patient to allow him to disclose the information?

(c) on what basis will he try and justify the disclosure?

(4) What emergency steps (if any) are required?

SUGGESTED PRECEDENTS TO BE USED IN A BREACH OF CONFIDENCE CLAIM

DOCUMENT 1

IN THE HIGH COURT OF JUSTICE   Claim No NE123456
CHANCERY DIVISION
NEWTOWN DISTRICT REGISTRY

BETWEEN

	STANLEY SMITH	CLAIMANT
	and	
(1)	DR FRANCIS FINLAY	
(2)	DR MARY FERGUSON	
(3)	DR HANNAH HYDE	
(4)	DR JAMES BELLAMY	DEFENDANTS

PARTICULARS OF CLAIM

1   At all material times the First Defendant was a medical general practitioner practising at Willow Surgery, Grey Street, Newtown, Blankshire in partnership with the Second to Fourth Defendants.

2   At all material times the Claimant was a patient under the care of the First Defendant and as such a doctor-patient relationship existed between the Claimant and First Defendant ('the relationship').

3   It was an implied term of the relationship that all and any information imparted by the Claimant to the First Defendant was of a private and personal nature ('the information') which would be treated by the First Defendant as confidential and would not be communicated in any form to any other party.

4   In breach of the obligation pleaded at para 3 the First Defendant has communicated certain of the information to other parties without the consent of the Claimant or other good cause.

PARTICULARS

(i) On or about 4th January 2001 the First Defendant divulged in writing information concerning the Claimant's medical condition and treatment to the Claimant's then employer.

(ii) On or about 5th January 2001 the First Defendant divulged in writing the same information to the Claimant's wife.

5   By reason of the aforesaid breach the Claimant has suffered loss and damage.

PARTICULARS

(i) On 7th January 2001 the Claimant's then employer dismissed the Claimant from employment justifying such dismissal on grounds based on information from the First Defendant.

(ii) On or about 6th April 2001 the Claimant's wife left the matrimonial home and has since that date refused to cohabit with the Claimant justifying such action on grounds based on the information from the First Defendant.

(iii) The Claimant has suffered mental distress and anguish.

6　Further, by reason of the First Defendant's breach the Claimant believes that unless restrained by injunction the First Defendant will commit further breaches of the implied term.

AND the Claimant claims:

(1) An injunction to restrain the First Defendant whether by himself or by his servants or agents or otherwise from communicating or disclosing in any form whatsoever to any party or parties whomsoever the information.

(2) Against all Defendants damages and interest thereon pursuant to s 35A of the Supreme Court Act 1981 for such a period and at such a rate as the court considers just.

(3) Further, or other relief.[2]

Dated 13th May 2001

STATEMENT OF TRUTH

*(I believe) (The claimant believes) that the facts stated in these Particulars of Claim are true.

*I am duly authorised by the claimant to sign this statement.

Full name: ....

Name of claimant's solicitors firm: ....

Signed: .... position or office held: ....

*(Claimant) (Litigation friend)　(if signing on behalf of a firm or company)

* delete as appropriate

Address for receiving documents

[name and address of claimant's solicitors]

Notes

The action is being brought against all of the partners in the practice, enabling the claimant to enforce any award of damages against any or all of the partners.

It is usual to include this all-embracing claim in the claim form and particulars of claim. It is possible that the court will order an enquiry as to what damages the claimant has sustained by reason of the defendants' breach.

DOCUMENT 2

THE CLAIM FORM

The claim form will set out the claimant's name and address, the defendant's name and address, brief details of the claim and value of the claim (if appropriate).

Brief details of the claim could be set out as follows: 'the claimant's claim is for an injunction and damages due to the first defendant's breach of the implied duty of confidentiality arising in the course of the relationship between the parties of the claimant as patient and the first defendant as doctor and the second to fourth defendants as partners to the first defendant.'

3   The full details of the claim can be set out in the claim form or set out in separate Particulars of Claim (see document 1 above), which will be served with the claim form.

4   The claim form will contain a statement of truth at the end. (See document 1 above, which sets out the format of a statement of truth).

DOCUMENT 3

IN THE HIGH COURT OF JUSTICE   Claim No NE123456
CHANCERY DIVISION
NEWTOWN DISTRICT REGISTRY

Before Mr Justice Henry

BETWEEN

	STANLEY SMITH	CLAIMANT
	and	
(1)	DR FRANCIS FINLAY	
(2)	DR MARY FERGUSON	
(3)	DR HANNAH HYDE	
(4)	DR JAMES BELLAMY	DEFENDANTS

This claim having come before Mr Justice Henry without a jury at Newtown District Registry on the 3rd day of August 2001 and the said Mr Justice Henry having on the 3rd day of August 2001 ordered that judgment as provided below be entered for the Claimant.

IT IS ORDERED that:

1   The First Defendant be restrained whether by himself or by his servants or agents or otherwise howsoever from communicating or disclosing in any form whatsoever to any part or parties whomsoever the information imparted by the Claimant to the First Defendant of a private or personal nature as described in the Particulars of Claim dated 13th March 2001.

2   An inquiry be taken and made as to what damages the Claimant has sustained by reason of the acts the repetition of which is restrained by the Order.

DOCUMENT 4

THE APPLICATION NOTICE

The application notice is a standard form of application. CPR Part 23 and CPR Practice Direction 23 contain general rules regarding applications for court orders. The application notice must set out the order the applicant is seeking and give brief details why the applicant is seeking the order. It must also include the title of the claim, the reference number of the claim, the full name of the applicant and a request for a hearing, or alternatively a request that the application is dealt with without a hearing.

DOCUMENT 5

On behalf of the Claimant:
Stanley Smith: 1st
First Witness Statement
Exhibits SS 1 & 2
Dated:

IN THE HIGH COURT OF JUSTICE
CHANCERY DIVISION
NEWTOWN DISTRICT REGISTRY

BETWEEN

	STANLEY SMITH	CLAIMANT
	and	
(1)	DR FRANCIS FINLAY	
(2)	DR MARY FERGUSON	
(3)	DR HANNAH HYDE	
(4)	DR JAMES BELLAMY	DEFENDANTS

WITNESS STATEMENT OF STANLEY SMITH

I, Stanley Smith, of 34 Northside, Newtown, Blankshire, Head Chef, will say as follows:

1   I am the Claimant in this action.

2   I first met the First Defendant about 10 years ago and since then I have been a patient under the care of the First Defendant.

3   During the years I was under the care of the First Defendant I disclosed to the First Defendant information of a private and personal nature ('the information') on the implicit understanding that the information would be treated by the First Defendant as confidential and would not be communicated in any form to any other party.

INSERT HERE THE EXACT NATURE OF THE BREACH, for example, WHAT INFORMATION WAS DISCLOSED, EXHIBIT LETTERS, etc.

4   I have been informed by a Mr James Brown, a friend of the First Defendant[1] and verily believe that the First Defendant intends to disclose the information to other parties without my consent or otherwise good cause and I respectfully ask this court that an injunction be granted in the terms specified in the notice of application herein pending trial or further Order.

I believe that the facts stated in this witness statement are true.

Signed .... Dated ....

Notes

1   It may be that the claimant has been informed by the defendant that he intends to disclose the information, or he may have been informed by a third party. Whatever the source of his belief, we think it unlikely that the claimant will be granted an injunction unless he can produce substantial evidence that the defendant is intending to breach his confidence, that is, the claimant will not be granted an injunction if he is merely apprehensive that the defendant will breach his confidence because the information is highly confidential.

DOCUMENT 6

THE DEFENCE

We have not thought it necessary to include a defence or a witness statement in reply to the claimant's witness statement opposing an application for an interim injunction restraining breach of confidence. However, any defence/witness statement would, it is suggested, be along the following lines:

1   That the defendant did not/does not owe the claimant a duty of confidence (unlikely to figure much in a doctor-patient action).

2   That the breach never took place, that is, that the breach occurred without the fault of the defendant. This could be a possible defence where the information was imparted to a third party in confidence, who subsequently disclosed the information. However, it is possible the doctor could still be liable for the third party's breach.

3   That the information was not confidential – that is, it was public property. The defendant here may rely on the public interest defence at Rule 1(D)(v), at p 26.

4   The claimant consented to the disclosure.

5   That the defendant had just cause to disclose the information. In this instance, the defendant will attempt to rely on one of the defences to a breach of confidence claim (see Rules 1(D)(i)–(v), at p 18 *et seq*).

CHAPTER 2

CONSENT

RULE 2(A)

Since most forms of medical treatment will involve some touching of the patient, then any touching without the express or implied consent of the patient will be actionable as trespass to the person. There is no need for the claimant to show hostile intent on the part of the health carer.

Commentary

In England an adult patient is invariably said to have complete autonomy over his body to the extent that he can consent to any form of medical treatment and no one can veto that consent. As Cardozo J put it in *Schloendorf v Society of New York Hospital* (1914) 211 NY 125 at p 126, 'Every human being of adult years and sound mind has a right to determine what shall be done with his own body; and a surgeon who performs an operation without his patient's consent commits an assault ...' More recently, Wall J in *Re JT (Adult: Refusal of Medical Treatment)* [1998] 1 FLR 48 expressed it equally succinctly, 'It is in general terms a criminal and tortious assault to perform physical invasive treatment without a patient's consent' (p 51). In reality, patients have never had complete autonomy, for example, they cannot consent to treatment which would constitute a criminal act. What the rule means is that a patient can choose whether to have the treatment on offer or not, even if, without that treatment, his condition may worsen to the point where he may die. Consequently, before treating a patient the health carer must ensure that he has the patient's express or implied consent. This can be given orally, in writing or a combination of the two; from the point of view of the health carer the 'safest' is undoubtedly written consent (see *Thompson v Sheffield Fertility Clinic* (November 2000) where the claimant contended that she had only agreed to two embryos being implanted whereas the Clinic were equally convinced that she had agreed to three embryos being implanted: a successful breach of contract claim was brought and it is tempting to suggest that the cost and trauma of the litigation could have been avoided had a signed consent form with the relevant details been obtained).

In the Canadian case of *Malette v Shulman* [1991] 2 Med LR 162, the claimant, who was seriously injured in a road accident, was taken to a hospital where she was treated by the defendant. As her condition worsened and she lapsed into unconsciousness, the need to treat her as an emergency arose; in particular, it became necessary to give her a blood transfusion. A Jehovah's Witness card was found among her belongings which, when translated, read as follows:

NO BLOOD TRANSFUSION

As one of the Jehovah's Witnesses with firm religious convictions, I request that no blood products be administered to me under any circumstances. I fully realise the implications of this position but I have absolutely decided to obey the Bible command ...

The defendant was made aware of both the card and its contents but as the patient's condition deteriorated he decided to administer blood. The patient's daughter, on arrival at the hospital, confirmed her mother's wish not to be given a blood transfusion and actually signed a 'consent to treatment and a release of liability form'. Despite this the defendant continued to administer the blood. The Ontario Court of Appeal held that the defendant was liable in trespass. As Robins JA said (at p 166): 'the instructions imposed a valid restriction on the emergency treatment that could be provided ... and precluded blood transfusions.'

In our view, the *Malette v Shulman* case accurately represents the position in English law: any unauthorised touching is technically a battery and a civil claim can be maintained even if there is no evidence of damage to the claimant. It may seem harsh to hold that a defendant is legally liable in damages when the only thing that he is 'guilty' of is trying to help another human being. But a person's choice, however misguided, must be respected if autonomy is to have any meaning. Although English law has not been entirely consistent in its approach when autonomy is taken to its logical conclusion, for example, in the area of euthanasia, it is clear that an adult, conscious, competent patient can choose his treatment. This explains why the court in *Re C (Adult: Refusal of Medical Treatment)* [1994] 1 All ER 819 decided that a paranoid schizophrenic who chose not to have his leg amputated when gangrene was diagnosed, should be left alone and not treated. It also explains why patients who, for religious or other reasons, choose not to undergo a particular form of treatment must have their wishes respected; this is supported, the authors contend, by Art 14 combined with, for example, Arts 2 and/or 3 of the European Convention on Human Rights.

Patients may give consent thereby negativing any trespass. They frequently do so impliedly, for example, when the GP asks to examine their throat and the patient, without hesitation, opens wide his mouth; certainly they do so expressly when, in a hospital, they sign a consent form. Hospitals may be both surprised and disturbed to learn that a signed consent form is not conclusive that there has been no trespass; it is, however, very strong evidence that consent has been given for the invasive treatment. Consequently it would be possible for a claimant to argue that his signature on a consent form had been improperly obtained, for example, by the undue influence of a relative. Furthermore, where a patient consents to treatment A and, during that treatment, treatment B is also effected, *prima facie* a trespass claim could be maintained in respect of B unless the defendant could show that the additional treatment was immediately necessary in the patient's best interests. For example, a hysterectomy performed while a woman is in the operating theatre having a foetus removed following a miscarriage is actionable if the woman has not consented to the hysterectomy and it could not be shown that the treatment was immediately necessary in her interests (*Devi v W Midlands AHA* [1981] CA Transcript 491).

REFERENCES

English case law

(1) Re JT (Adult: Refusal of Medical Treatment) [1998] 1 FLR 48
See above, p 41.

(2)   Thompson v Sheffield Fertility Clinic (November 2000)
See above, p 41.

(3)   Re C (Adult: Refusal of Medical Treatment) [1994] 1 All ER 819
C, a 68 year old patient suffering from paranoid schizophrenia, developed gangrene in his foot; the diagnosis was that he was likely to die immediately if the leg was not amputated below the knee. C refused the amputation.

Held: C was capable of making the decision whether to receive treatment or not; having decided that he did not want to be treated, that decision had to be respected.

(4)   Devi v West Midlands AHA (1981) CA Transcript 491 F5-017
The claimant, aged 29, had four children and hoped for more. Her religious beliefs precluded sterilisation and contraception. She was admitted to hospital for a minor operation on her womb. In the course of the operation her womb was found to be ruptured. Without her consent or knowledge the surgeons decided to sterilise her because they feared that if she became pregnant again her womb could rupture. Although acting in the patient's best interests there was no immediate urgency to perform the operation without permission. The defendants admitted liability and damages of £4,000 were awarded.

(5)   Re T (Adult: Refusal of Medical Treatment) [1992] 4 All ER 649

> An adult patient who ... suffers from no mental incapacity has an absolute right to choose whether to consent to medical treatment, to refuse it or to choose one rather than another of the treatments being offered [pp 652–53].

Foreign case law

Canada

(1)   Malette v Shulman [1991] 2 Med LR 162
See above, at p 41, for facts.

(2)   Murray v McMurchy (1949) 2 DLR 442
During a caesarean operation a doctor tied the patient's fallopian tubes as he was concerned about the consequences of a second pregnancy. No consent had been given. As there was no evidence of immediate danger, the defendant was found liable.

(3)   Marshall v Curry (1933) 3 DLR 260
In the course of a hernia operation, the patient's diseased testicle was removed.

Held: there was no liability because this was an emergency.

(4)   Allen v Mount Sinai Hospital (1980) 109 DLR (3d) 634
Battery was committed when a patient expressly instructed a doctor not to give her an anaesthetic in her left arm and he subsequently did.

United States

Schloendorf v Society of New York Hospital (1914) 211 NY 125
See above, p 41.

European Convention on Human Rights

Articles 2, 3 and 14
See Appendix A.

RULE 2(B)

The consent required to defend a trespass claim is true consent.

Commentary

Commentators have not always been consistent in deciding whether the consent the patient has to give is to be termed 'informed consent', 'valid consent', 'true consent', 'real consent', or, simply, 'consent'. In our view, the only meaningful distinction that can and should be made is the one between 'informed consent' and 'true consent'. It is our intention to use the term 'informed consent' in the way the American and Canadian courts have used that phrase in cases such as *Canterbury v Spence* (1972) 464 F (2d) 772 and *Reibl v Hughes* (1980) 114 DLR (3d) 1. In those jurisdictions the phrase does not simply mean 'being better informed than you were before'; rather it has the particular legal meaning that all material risks should be disclosed to a patient prior to obtaining the patient's consent. Furthermore, a material risk is defined as 'when a reasonable person, in what the physician knows or should know to be the patient's position, would be likely to attach significance to the risk ... in deciding whether or not to forego the proposed therapy'. (See, also, the judgment of Lord Scarman in *Sidaway v Bethlem Royal Hospital* (1985) 1 AC 871 where he said at page 889: 'The critical limitation is that the duty [to warn patients of risks inherent in treatment] is confined to material risk. The test of materiality is whether in the circumstances of the particular case the court is satisfied that a reasonable person in the patient's position would be likely to attach significance to the risk.')

In effect, this means that the patient in the United States, before consenting, will be in receipt of the information which the health carer thinks the patient would want to have. Because American health carers are ever conscious of the financial consequences of getting it wrong, they are more likely to err on the side of caution and to give more information (a beneficial aspect of defensive medicine attitude!). In England, on the other hand, 'informed consent' as explained above was categorically ruled out by the majority of the House of Lords in *Sidaway* where only Lord Scarman was prepared to adopt the transatlantic doctrine. Instead, the English approach is evidenced by the judgment of Bristow J in *Chatterton v Gerson* [1981] QB 432, later approved by the House of Lords in *Sidaway*, and it is this: the patient need only be informed in broad terms as to the nature of the proposed treatment; in turn, that will be determined by what other responsible practitioners, in similar circumstances, would have done (see the *Bolam* test). If the patient has been so informed and thereafter gives his consent he cannot subsequently sue in trespass, although if the procedure is not properly carried out, he will be able to sue in negligence. In short, the patient in England is not as well informed as his American counterpart and the decision as to what he is to be told is definitely that of the health carer. As such our argument is for an acceptance of a distinction between 'true consent' and 'informed consent' and the adoption of the term 'true consent' in so far as English law is concerned.

REFERENCES

English case law

(1) Sidaway v Board of Governors of the Bethlem Royal Hospital and the Maudsley Hospital [1985] AC 871; [1985] 1 All ER 643
See p 74 for facts of this case.

(2) Chatterton v Gerson [1981] 1 All ER 257
The claimant sued in trespass and negligence. She alleged that she had not been warned of the side effects of the treatment, namely, loss of muscle power. In finding for the defendant, Bristow J said (at p 265):

> In my judgment, once the plaintiff is informed in broad terms of the nature of the procedure which is intended, and gives her consent, that consent is real, and the cause of action ... is negligence, not trespass ...

> ... even taking the plaintiff's evidence at its face value, she was under no illusion as to the general nature of what an intrathecal injection of phenol solution nerve block would be, and in the case of each injection her consent was not unreal.

(3) Bolam v Friern Hospital Management Committee [1957] 1 WLR 582; [1957] 2 All ER 118
See Rule 5(A), at p 155.

Foreign case law

Canada

Reibl v Hughes (1980) 114 DLR (3d) 1
See p 178 for facts of this case.

> *Per* Laskin CJC:

> In saying that the test is based on the decision that a reasonable person in the patient's position would have made, I should make it clear that the patient's particular concerns must also be reasonably based; otherwise there would be more subjectivity than would be warranted under an objective test ... In short, although account must be taken of a patient's particular position, a position which will vary with the patient, it must be objectively assessed in terms of reasonableness.

United States

(1) Canterbury v Spence (1972) 464 F (2d) 772
Per Robinson J (at p 787):

> [A] risk is ... material when a reasonable person in that the physician knows or should know to be the patient's position, would be likely to attach significance to the risk or cluster of risks in determining whether or not to forego the proposed therapy.

(2) Rizzo v Schiller [1995] 6 Med L Rev 209; Supreme Court of Virginia (1994) 445 SE (2d) 153
Informed consent required by the law of Virginia.

(3) Arato v Avedon (1994) 6 Med L Rev 230
The Supreme Court of California held that informed consent required the disclosure of all material information the patient needed to make an informed decision, but it did not require any particular species of information to be disclosed. This was because material

information in any given context was to be assessed by the clinical setting, informational needs and the degree of the patient's dependency. The court also made it clear that the informed consent doctrine did not apply to the disclosure of non-medical interests, for example, business and/or investment interests.

RULE 2(C)

A patient who has given true consent to medical treatment cannot have that consent vetoed by another person. The rule applies with equal force whether the patient is an adult or a *Gillick* competent minor.

Commentary

Those who are related to patients, whether by blood or marriage, may view this rule with some disquiet and surprise. Probably the most vivid illustration of the rule's legal consequences centres around the case of a woman seeking a legal abortion. Here the courts have held that neither the woman's spouse nor her partner can legally object to the abortion on the ground that their rights are being ignored, see *Paton v British Pregnancy Advisory Service* [1978] 2 All ER 987. What that decision did was to uphold the right of a woman to determine for herself what should or should not be done to her body. Ethically, the partners or spouses should be involved in the discussions preparatory to procedures such as abortions, sterilisations and vasectomies, but that is the limit of their involvement. Sir George Baker, in *Paton*, said (at p 990):

> No court would ever grant an injunction to stop sterilisation or vasectomy. Personal family relationships in marriage cannot be enforced by the order of the court.

Is the denial of the husband's or partner's rights a breach of Art 8 of the European Convention on Human Rights 1950? That is the Art which says that, 'Everyone has the right to respect for his family life ...'; while noting that the right is a qualified and not an absolute right, could it not be argued that the assertion of the female to do with her body as she wishes will, in the particular circumstance of a case like *Paton*, destroy the male person's right to have a family? What if the male person is middle-aged and sees this as his last chance to start a family? Despite this the authors are of the opinion that the proportionality principle and the desire to keep the *status quo* may well mean that the woman's right prevails and *Paton* remains good law.

In *Gillick v West Norfolk and Wisbech AHA* [1986] AC 112, the House of Lords held that a mature girl under the age of 16 could seek contraceptive advice and treatment from her health carer without her parents' knowledge and involvement (and, therefore, veto) although every effort should be made by the health carer to encourage the girl to involve them. Ultimately, however, the decision is that of the patient, and no one else. The *Gillick* principle applies to both males and females and is not intended to be confined to contraceptive counselling and advice.

REFERENCES

English case law

(1)   Paton v British Pregnancy Advisory Service [1978] 2 All ER 987; [1978] 3 WLR 687
A wife, having discovered she was pregnant, obtained a certificate to a legal abortion. The husband sought an injunction to restrain his wife and the defendants from proceeding with the abortion. The court refused to grant the injunction.

(2)   Gillick v West Norfolk and Wisbech AHA [1986] AC 112; [1985] 3 All ER 402
See below, at p 49 *et seq.*

(3)   Arndt v Smith [1996] 7 Med LR 35
Hutchinson J (at p 40) quoted with approval the following statement from the Canadian Supreme Court's decision in *Tremblay v Daigle* (1989) 62 DLR (4th) 634 (at p 665):

> No court in Quebec or elsewhere has ever accepted the argument that a father's interest in a foetus which he helped create could support a right to veto a woman's decision in respect of the foetus she is carrying.

European Convention on Human Rights

Article 8
See Appendix A.

RULE 2(D)

A patient does not have an unfettered right to refuse medical treatment. In appropriate circumstances the patient's refusal to be treated may be ignored.

Commentary

It might seem self-evident that any legal system which supports the contention that 'every adult has the right and capacity to decide whether or not he will accept medical treatment' (*per* Lord Donaldson MR in *Re T* [1992] 3 Med LR 306, at p 313) must equally uphold the rule that the same person has a right to refuse treatment, whether that decision is founded on a rational or an irrational basis. In the case of *Re C* [1994] 1 All ER 819 that is exactly what the court did. There a 68 year old schizophrenic patient with a gangrenous leg refused to give permission for his leg to be amputated; the prognosis was – and this was never doubted – that, without the operation, he would die (he did later agree to some treatment which meant that the immediate threat to his life had receded). Thorpe J held that the mere fact that the patient was a schizophrenic did not necessarily mean he lacked the capacity to consent and, as there was insufficient evidence to show that he did lack capacity, the patient had a right to refuse treatment.

But the law in the early 1990s seemed to indicate that, where a refusal might bring about the death of an unborn foetus or the decision was made by someone lacking capacity (including being under the age of 16), the courts could and would lawfully ignore the refusal and proceed with the treatment, especially if there was someone else, either a parent or guardian, who was willing to sanction the treatment. In *Re T (Adult: Refusal of Medical Treatment)* (1992) 3 Med LR 306 a pregnant woman's decision not to have a blood transfusion for religious reasons, while given careful consideration by the court, was ultimately ignored on the ground that she lacked the capacity to make that particular decision. While the judge at first instance based his decision on the fact that the treatment was needed in the patient's best interests, the Appeal Court adopted a slightly different stance. They queried whether the woman's refusal was meant to apply in the circumstances which subsequently arose; in other words, a refusal given at a certain point in time when a particular set of circumstances were in existence might not be intended to apply when later the patient's condition worsened. There was also some evidence to suggest that the woman's will was completely overborne by that of her mother, to the extent that the court seriously doubted whether it was her decision.

In *Re W (Minor) (Medical Treatment)* [1992] 4 All ER 627 a 16 year old girl suffering from anorexia nervosa refused to undergo a particular form of treatment. Again, a strong Appeal Court held that she should be treated since, by the time the case came before the court, her condition had deteriorated to the point where there was a real fear that her future capacity to bear children would be seriously in jeopardy and ultimately non-treatment would threaten her life. The case has also been explained on the ground of the patient's lack of capacity, namely that she was not old enough to refuse treatment. The implication of the decision is that, while a person may be mature enough at the age of 16 to consent to treatment without parental involvement (see the *Gillick* case), at that same age a person is not sufficiently mature to decide to refuse to be treated.

In *Re S (Adult: Refusal of Medical Treatment)* [1992] 4 All ER 671, a declaration was granted allowing a hospital to perform a non-consensual emergency caesarean section on a pregnant woman. This was done in the interests of both the woman and her unborn baby since, according to the evidence, without the operation both would have died. While the court in this case was seemingly 'prepared' to accede to the mother's choice were she the only person involved, they were certainly not prepared to do so given that her decision impacted on the life of a third party. This particular decision is unfortunate for three reasons. First, it elevates the rights of the foetus to a superior status over the mother's right of autonomy: a doubtful principle. Secondly, the reliance on the American case of *Re AC* (1990) 573 A (2d) 1235 was regrettable because that case ultimately rejected the notion of compulsory treatment, except in extreme circumstances. Thirdly, the decision is yet another instance of medical paternalism over autonomy.

But in *St George's Healthcare NHS Trust v S* [1998] 3 All ER 673 the Appeal Court ruled that the pregnant woman's right of autonomy prevailed over the rights of an unborn foetus; consequently the woman's treatment decision, which could or would result in the death of the foetus, was not to be ignored, provided she had the requisite capacity, etc to make that decision. As Judge LJ said in that case, '[a foetus's] need for medical assistance does not prevail over her [the mother's] rights' (at p 692). Ethically, this may seem a harsh decision given that the mother was putting her unborn child at risk and that she was indeed 36 weeks pregnant. Legally the decision has merit unless statements such as, 'whatever else it may be, a 36 week foetus is not nothing; if viable, it is not lifeless and it is certainly human' (*per* Judge LJ at p 687) and '... the interests of the foetus cannot be disregarded on the basis that in refusing treatment which would benefit the foetus, a mother is simply refusing treatment for herself' (*per*

Judge LJ at p 688), were going to be given some practical effect. In truth they were not, partly because the mother and child were seen as one and therefore there was only one treatment involved, namely to her and partly because – dare it be said? – of the Appeal Court's visible displeasure at the way the woman in this case was treated and the obscene use which was made of the Mental Health Act 1983 to give her the caesarean section. Again as Judge LJ said, at p 688, '... how can a forced invasion of a competent adult's body against her will even for the most laudable of motives (the preservation of life) be ordered without immediately damaging the principle of self-determination? When human life is at stake the pressure to provide an affirmative answer authorising unwanted medical intervention is very powerful. Nevertheless, the autonomy of each individual requires continuing protection ...'.

The position regarding the mature under-16 who refuses treatment is more difficult to appreciate. The *Gillick* case had clearly allowed such persons to consent to treatment provided, in the eyes of the healthcare, they were mature enough to appreciate the nature and consequences of their action. What seemed to be the logical conclusion from that decision, namely that the same mature under 16 year olds who could consent could refuse consent to treatment, has not proved to be true. For a short time it did seem true; for example, Lord Scarman (*obiter*) in the *Gillick* case did say, '... I would hold that as a matter of law the parental right to determine whether or not their minor child below the age of 16 will have medical treatment terminates if and when the child achieves a sufficient understanding and intelligence to enable him or her to understand fully what is proposed (pp 188–89), and s 44(7) of the Children Act 1989 also says, "where any direction is given under sub-s (6)(b), the child may, if he is of sufficient understanding to make an informed decision, refuse to submit to the examination or other assessment"'.

But in *R and W* [1992] 4 All ER 627 Lord Donaldson poured cold water on this approach arguing, amongst other things, that the *Gillick* case had nothing to do with refusal. Since that ruling other cases have similarly held that a mature under-16 does not have an unfettered right to refuse treatment: that decision rests with the child's parents or guardians (see *Re R (A Minor) (Wardship: Consent to Treatment)* [1992] 3 Med LR 342 and *Re M (Medical Treatment: Consent)* [1999] 2 FLR 1097). The rationale for this different approach, it is submitted, is so that the patient in question can appreciate the consequences of consenting to treatment which probably and hopefully will make them better, whereas such a person really cannot appreciate the consequences of refusing to be treated which, regretfully, may lead to serious problems or even death. Is this not taking paternalism too far? What has happened to the autonomy which gives these patients the right to consent? More importantly, can decisions like *R and W* and *Re M* stand in the light of Art 14 combined with either Arts 2 or 3 of the European Convention on Human Rights? Is not the approach in the above cases discriminatory on the grounds of age (Art 14) and either a denial of a right to life (Art 2) including medical treatment or subjecting the patient to inhuman (or degrading) treatment (Art 3)? We would content that it is, but until there is case law it has to be accepted that at present under 16 year olds can consent but cannot refuse consent.

REFERENCES

English case law

(1)   Re T (Adult: Refusal of Medical Treatment) [1992] 3 Med LR 306; [1992] 4 All ER 649
T, an adult who was 34 weeks pregnant, was injured in a road traffic accident. The case report indicated that she was not a Jehovah's Witness, although she was brought up by her mother who was a fervent member of that faith. T indicated that she did not want a blood transfusion; shortly before so deciding she had been alone with her mother. A decision was taken to deliver the baby by caesarean section. A refusal to consent to a blood transfusion was signed by T, although it was never explained to her that it might be necessary to giver her a transfusion to prevent injury to her health or even to preserve her life. The caesarean section was performed but the baby was stillborn. As T's condition deteriorated a declaration was made by Ward J that it would not be unlawful to administer blood in the circumstances as that would be in her best interests. Two days later he ruled as follows: (a) although T was under the influence of her mother, she did reach the decision of no treatment on her own; (b) T was misinformed as to the availability and effectiveness of alternative procedures; (c) T's refusal of a blood transfusion did not extend to the question of whether she should have a transfusion in the extreme situation which subsequently arose; (d) since T was no longer able to express any view the doctors could lawfully treat her in her best interests.

With this, the Appeal Court agreed. On the issue of patient autonomy versus society's interests in keeping the patient alive, Lord Donaldson MR said (at p 661):

The patient's interest consists of his right to self-determination – his right to live his own life how he wishes ... society's interest is in upholding the concept that all human life is sacred and that it should be preserved if at all possible. It is well established that in the ultimate the right of the individual is paramount. But this merely shifts the problem where the conflict occurs and calls for a very careful examination of whether, and if so the way in which, the individual is exercising that right. In case of doubt, that doubt falls to be resolved in favour of the preservation of life ...

(2)   Re C [1994] 1 All ER 819
See above, p 47.

(3)   Re W [1992] 4 All ER 627
See earlier, at p 48.

(4)   Re C (A Minor: Medical Treatment) [1998] Lloyd's Rep Med 1
A baby was born with spinal muscular atrophy. The consultant paediatric neurologist in charge considered that it was not in the child's best interests for her to be further ventilated and, when the ventilation was withdrawn, it should not be reinstituted in the event of a further respiratory arrest. The parents, orthodox Jews, did not agree with the proposed treatment.

Held: the treatment proposed by the consultant would be sanctioned.

(5)   Re MM (Medical Treatments) [2000] 1 FLR 224
For a variety of reasons, for example, breakdown in communications between the parties, there was a marked difference in the nature of treatments to be administered to a 2 year old Russian boy who was suffering from primary immunodeficiency. His parents wanted him to have immunostimulant therapy; the local authority, supported by the

official solicitor, considered that the child should receive replacement immunoglobin intravenously.

Held: in the child's best interests, the parents' wishes would be overridden.

(6) Re C (HIV Test) [1999] 2 FLR 1004
The local authority wanted a baby born to an HIV mother to be tested for HIV. Both parents were opposed to such testing. The trial judge concluded that the arguments for overriding the parents' wishes were overwhelming; the test was needed in the baby's best interests. Permission to appeal was refused.

Foreign case law

United States

Re AC (1990) 573 A (2d) 1235
In an unusual set of circumstances involving (*inter alia*) the patient being resuscitated and indicating that she did not wish to undergo a caesarean section, the court nevertheless ruled that a pregnant woman suffering from cancer should undergo a caesarean operation. All the available evidence at the time indicated that she would probably not withstand the operation. As it turned out, both the baby and the mother died shortly after surgery.

Associate Judge Nebeker:

> The fundamental right to bodily integrity encompasses an adult's right to refuse medical treatment, even if the refusal will result in death ... The state's interest in protecting third parties from an adult's decision to refuse medical treatment ... may override the interest in bodily integrity.

RULE 2(E)

True consent in English law can be given by a conscious, competent, adult patient voluntarily. Such a person must also be in possession of a certain amount of information relating to his treatment and it must be established that the patient has understood the information received.

Commentary

For true consent to exist, six conditions have to be met. The person giving the consent must:

(1) be an adult, that is, aged 16 or over as laid down in s 8 Family Law Reform Act 1969;

(2) be competent, that is, not subject to any mental/physical disability which would make suspect his decision on his treatment;

(3) be conscious;

(4) be in possession of a certain amount of information on which to base his decision;

(5) have understood the information provided;

(6) have given his consent voluntarily.

RULE 2(F)

True consent can be given by a patient of adult years, that is, someone aged 16 or over. But a person under the age of 16 may consent to treatment without involving their parents or guardians in certain well-defined circumstances.

Commentary

According to s 8 Family Law Reform Act 1969 a patient aged 16 or over is competent to consent to surgical, medical or dental treatment which, 'in the absence of consent, would constitute a trespass ... and the consent given is effective as it would be if he were of full age'.

Taken at face value s 8 would seem to be suggesting that anyone aged 16 or over can consent to any form of medical treatment. That would be misleading since it is generally accepted that an adult cannot legally consent to treatment which would otherwise be a criminal act; that much is clear. What is less clear is whether all non-criminal treatment can be agreed to by an adult as defined above; for example, could a 16 year old consent to organ donation? We would argue that such a question should be answered in the negative for one good reason. Section 8 refers to consenting to 'treatment'; is organ donation 'treatment'? It may be therapeutically beneficial for a person to donate a kidney to his brother or sister but it is our contention that 'treatment' should be taken to mean a procedure which necessarily makes the donor physically or mentally better; procedures such as organ donation are generally undertaken by choice and do not make the donor worse than he/she was before the donation. Consequently our contention is that, legally and ethically, a mature 16 year old should be denied the ability to donate an organ. Although there is no 'magic' in attaining the age of 18, it is submitted that that should represent the minimum age for non-necessary medical treatment. Lord Donaldson in *Re W* [1992] 4 All ER 627 confirmed this and included blood donation in the 'no' list when he held that: '... section 8 ... gives minors who have attained the age of 16 a right to consent ... such a consent cannot be overridden by those with parental responsibility ... This statutory right does not extend to consent to the donation of blood or organs' (p 639).The above analysis should cater for the majority of situations which health carers will encounter.

Additionally, patients under the age of 16 can consent to treatment without their parents' involvement provided they are '*Gillick* mature'. This was the decision of the House of Lords in *Gillick v West Norfolk and Wisbech AHA* [1986] AC 112 where Lord Fraser laid down the following guidelines for determining and assessing maturity in the context of contraceptive counselling and advice. He said (at p 174) that the doctor had to be:

(1) satisfied that the patient understood the advice;

(2) prepared to try and persuade her to tell her parents or let him do so; only if she refused would he then be entitled to proceed with the treatment;

(3) of the opinion that she was very likely to have sexual intercourse with or without the contraceptive advice or treatment;

(4) of the opinion that, unless she had the advice, etc, her physical or mental health or both would suffer;

(5) sure that the girl's best interests required the advice, etc.

The rationale of *Gillick* should not be construed as being restricted to contraceptive counselling and advice; at no stage did the Law Lords try to so limit it. As Lord Scarman said (at pp 188–89):

> ... I would hold that as a matter of law the parental right to determine whether or not [a] minor child below the age of 16 will have medical treatment terminates if and when the child achieves a sufficient understanding and intelligence to enable him or her to understand fully what is proposed.

Consequently, mature under 16s can consent to medical treatment to the same extent as someone aged 16 or over and this should be subject to what was said earlier about the limitations on the latter group.

It follows that the consent for treatment in respect of non-*Gillick* mature under 16 year olds should rest with their parents and guardians. It does especially (but not always, see *Re C (A Minor: Medical Treatment)* [1998] Lloyd's Rep Med 1) if it is a case of consent to treatment having to be given. But the courts do not allow unfettered control over the healthcare of their children, especially if the situation is one where the parents, etc, are refusing to give consent for the treatment; in such circumstances the treatment, if in the opinion of the court is in the child's best interests, will be sanctioned. This explains why parents who, for religious reasons, refuse blood transfusions for their children will often find the child being dealt with, for example, under the Children Act 1989 (see, also, *Re MM (Medical Treatment)* [2000] 1 FLR 224 and *Re C (HIV Test)* [1999] 2 FLR 1004).

Probably the best example in recent years of the courts refusing to follow the parents' wishes is the landmark case of the Siamese twins, Jodie and Mary. In *Re M and J (Medical Treatment: Siamese Twins)* [2001] 1 FLR 1, a hospital sought permission to separate conjoined twins, M and J. The medical facts were not in dispute. Jodie was the stronger twin with strong lungs and a sound heart but the twins shared an aorta which meant that Jodie's heart pumped blood through Mary's body; Mary had no capacity for independent life and consequently the strain on Jodie was such that, without a separation operation, both twins would die, whereas with an operation Jodie could live but Mary would eventually certainly die. The parents, being Roman Catholic, objected to the operation; their view was that this was God's will. At first instance the Judge gave permission for the operation to take place. The Appeal Court agreed with this and dismissed the parents' appeal. A number of interesting points were raised by the Court's decision, not least whether this was not a case of active voluntary euthanasia; also, what about the Human Rights issue? Did Mary have any human rights? Was she a legal persona?

Against the backdrop of such newsworthy ethical issues the question of the legality of the parents' wishes being ignored seems to have been by-passed. In one sense the parents' refusal, having been founded on religious grounds, was rightly refused (see the Jehovah's Witnesses cases); but there was another aspect to their refusal: they (it seemed) did not wish to sanction a procedure which would definitely kill one of their children. Did such a reason have any force? In the light of the Appeal Court's decision, apparently not. From our viewpoint it was always going to be the case that the operation was going to be sanctioned; no English court was ever going to go along with the parents' wishes and effectively condemn two children to die. The only issue was what legal answers would be found to deal with the opposing arguments to the operation. In so far as parental control is concerned, the answer given is that the court was acting in the best interests of the stronger twin. As regards the other issues and how they were dealt with, the controversy will undoubtedly rage on as to whether the right decision, legally and ethically, was made by the Appeal Court and whether the answers offered by the decision are based on sound legal grounds. Given the unique nature of the case and the fact that, unfortunately, the official solicitor (at the parents' request, it must be said) chose not to appeal the decision to the House of Lords, no definite answers or conclusions are possible.

REFERENCES

English case law

(1)   Re W (A Minor) (Medical Treatment) [1992] 4 All ER 627
See above, p 48.

(2)   Gillick v West Norfolk and Wisbech AHA [1986] AC 112; [1985] 3 All ER 402
A circular was issued by the DHSS to area health authorities advising them that, if a girl under 16 consulted a doctor at a family planning clinic seeking contraceptive counselling and advice, in exceptional cases the treatment could be provided without consulting the parents or obtaining their consent. The claimant, a mother of five daughters, sought a declaration that the circular was *ultra vires* and unlawful.

The House of Lords held that it was lawful.

(3)   Re C (A Minor: Medical Treatment) [1998] Lloyd's Rep Med 1
See above, p 50.

(4)   Re MM (Medical Treatment) [2000] 1 FLR 224
See above, p 50.

(5)   Re C (HIV Test) [1999] 2 FLR 1004
See above, p 51.

(6)   Re M and J (Medical Treatment: Siamese Twins) [2001] 1 FLR 1
See above.

Statutes/statutory instruments

(1)   Family Law Reform Act 1969

8   (1)   The consent of a minor who has attained the age of 16 years to any surgical, medical or dental treatment which, in the absence of consent, would constitute a trespass to his person, shall be effective as it would be if he were of full age; and where a minor had by virtue of this section given an effective consent to any treatment it shall not be necessary to obtain any consent for it from his parent or guardian.

(2)   In this section, 'surgical, medical or dental treatment' includes any procedure undertaken for the purposes of diagnosis, and this section applies to any procedure (including, in particular, the administration of an anaesthetic) which is ancillary to any treatment as it applies to that treatment.

(3)   Nothing in this section shall be construed as making ineffective any consent which would have been effective if this section had not been enacted.

RULE 2(G)

The person giving consent to treatment or refusing to give consent to treatment must be mentally competent to do so.

Commentary

A patient will be presumed to have the necessary mental capacity to consent or refuse consent to the medical treatment on offer; the onus will be upon those who seek to argue that the patient is indeed mentally incompetent to show this. In *Re C* [1994] 1 All ER 819, Thorpe J said, 'I am completely satisfied that the presumption that C has the right of self-determination has not been displaced' (p 824).

It was in this very case that the Learned Judge laid down the legal requirements for mental capacity to consent; they were stated to be:

(1)   to take in and retain treatment information;

(2)   to believe it; and

(3)   to weigh that information, balancing risks and needs [p 822].

Thereafter the rules governing consents will depend on whether the patient is to be treated as a voluntary/informal patient suffering from a mental disorder or someone who is compulsorily detained under the Mental Health Act 1983. In the former situation, the common law will apply and the rule there is that the patient can be treated out of necessity and in his/her best interests (see *R v Bournewood Community and Mental Health NHS Trust* [1998] 3 All ER 289 where Lord Goff said, '... The basis upon which a hospital was entitled to treat and to care for persons who were admitted as informal patients ... but lacked the capacity to consent to such treatment ... was the common law doctrine of necessity' (pp 297–98).

What was said in the previous rule about best interests (of unconscious patients) applies with equal force to the mentally incompetent patient.

As regards patients who are detained pursuant to the 1983 Act, the position has become somewhat unsatisfactory over the years. The basic rule is that treatments, other than those covered by ss 57 and 58, may not require the patient's consent. Section 57, which involves such treatments as psychosurgery and hormone implants to reduce the male sex drive, requires the patient's consent as well as the consent of a second opinion appointed doctor (SOAD). Section 58 stipulates that treatments such as ECT (electro-convulsive therapy) and drug treatment after three months or more have elapsed since drugs were first given during the detention period, require the patient's consent or a second opinion, but s 63 defines the circumstances when medical treatment for mental disorder can be given without the patient's consent. The courts have shown that they are prepared to ask this section to confer wide ranging powers on the health carers; for example, the section has been used to permit the force feeding of a patient by a nasogastric tube (*B v Croydon HA* [1995] 1 All ER 683) and the administering of a caesarean section to a pregnant woman (*Tameside and Glossop Acute Services Trust v CH* [1996] FLR 762). These cases and others led Jonathan Montgomery in his book *Health Care Law* (p 327) to conclude that the courts '...

have extended the concept of treatment for mental disorder to such a degree that it would appear that non-psychiatric medical care can be given under s 63 without consent in a wide range of circumstances. Provided that the physical problems are related to the mental disorder, either in their origins or their effects, consent will be strictly unnecessary'. It is expected that the proposed reform of the Mental Health Act 1983 will see the disappearance of s 63; its extensive authority may, in any event, have been a thing of the past given the Appeal Court's decision in *St George's Healthcare NHS Trust v S* [1998] 3 All ER 673 and Art 5 of the ECHR – see Rule 2D at p 48.

REFERENCES

English case law

(1) Re C [1994] 1 All ER 819

A paranoid schizophrenic was allowed to refuse the amputation of a gangrenous foot. See, further, p 47.

(2) R v Bournewood Community and Mental Health NHS Trust [1998] 3 All ER 289

See above, p 55.

(3) B v Croydon HA [1995] 2 WLR 294

B, who suffered from a psychopathic disorder, was compulsorily detained under the Mental Health Act 1983. One of her symptoms was a compulsion to hurt herself; as such she had stopped eating to a point where her weight fell to a dangerous level. The hospital decided to feed her by nasogastric tube without her consent.

Held: tube feeding was medical treatment for the purposes of s 63 and could therefore lawfully be carried out without B's consent.

(4) Tameside & Glossop Acute Services Trust v CH [1996] 1 FLR 762

Here it was held that the pregnant woman was suffering from a mental disorder and consequently treatment for that disorder – in this case a caesarean section using reasonable force – could be carried out under s 63.

(5) St George's Healthcare NHS Trust v S [1998] 3 All ER 673

Section 63 of the [1983] Act may apply to the treatment of any condition which is integral to the mental disorder ... provided the treatment is given by, or under the direction of, the responsible medical officer [*per* Judge LJ at p 693].

(6) SW Hertfordshire HA v Brady [1994] Med L Rev 208

As regards a patient who was suffering from anorexia nervosa, feeding by nasogastric tube was treatment under s 63 of the Mental Health Act 1983 and consequently did not require the patient's consent.

Statutes/statutory instruments

Mental Health Act 1983

    Treatment requiring consent and a second opinion

57 (1)   This section applies to the following forms of medical treatment for mental disorder:

        (a)   any surgical operation for destroying brain tissue or for destroying the functioning of brain tissue; and

    (b)   such other forms of treatment as may be specified for the purposes of this section by regulations made by the Secretary of State.

(2)   Subject to s 62 below, a patient shall not be given any form of treatment to which this section applies unless he has consented to it and:

    (a)   a registered medical practitioner appointed for the purposes of this part of this Act by the Secretary of State (not being the responsible medical officer) and two other persons appointed for the purposes of this paragraph by the Secretary of State (not being registered medical practitioners) have certified in writing that the patient is capable of understanding the nature, purpose and likely effects of the treatment in question and has consented to it; and

    (b)   the registered medical practitioner referred to in paragraph (a) above has certified in writing that, having regard to the likelihood of the treatment alleviating or preventing a deterioration of the patient's condition, the treatment should be given.

(3)   Before giving a certificate under subsection 2(b) above the registered medical practitioner concerned shall consult two other persons who have been professionally concerned with the patient's medical treatment, and of those persons one shall be a nurse and the other shall be neither a nurse nor a registered medical practitioner.

(4)   Before making any regulations for the purpose of this section the Secretary of State shall consult such bodies as appear to him to be concerned.

Treatment requiring consent or a second opinion

58 (1)   This section applies to the following forms of medical treatment for mental disorder:

    (a)   such forms of treatment as may be specified for the purposes of this section by regulations made by the Secretary of State;

    (b)   the administration of medicine to a patient by any means (not being a form of treatment specified under paragraph (a) above or s 57 above) at any time during a period for which he is liable to be detained as a patient to whom this part of this Act applies if three months or more have elapsed since the first occasion in that period when medicine was administered to him by any means for his mental disorder.

(2)   The Secretary of State may by order vary the length of the period mentioned in subsection (1)(b) above.

(3)   Subject to s 62 below, a patient shall not be given any form of treatment to which this section applies unless:

    (a)   he has consented to that treatment and either the responsible medical officer or a registered medical practitioner appointed for the purposes of this part of this Act by the Secretary of State has certified in writing that the patient is capable of understanding its nature, purpose and likely effects and has consented to it; or

    (b)   a registered medical practitioner appointed as aforesaid (not being the responsible medical officer) has certified in writing that the patient is not capable of understanding the nature, purpose and likely effects of that treatment or has not consented to it but that, having regard to the likelihood of its alleviating or preventing a deterioration of his condition, the treatment should be given.

(4) Before giving a certificate under subsection (3)(b) above the registered medical practitioner concerned shall consult two other persons who have been professionally concerned with the patient's medical treatment, and of those persons one shall be a nurse and the other shall be neither a nurse nor a registered medical practitioner.

(5) Before making any regulations for the purposes of this section the Secretary of State shall consult such bodies as appear to him to be concerned.

Urgent treatment

62 (1) Sections 57 and 58 above shall not apply to any treatment:

    (a) which is immediately necessary to save the patient's life; or

    (b) which (not being irreversible) is immediately necessary to prevent a serious deterioration of his condition; or

    (c) which (not being irreversible or hazardous) is immediately necessary to alleviate serious suffering by the patient; or

    (d) which (not being irreversible or hazardous) is immediately necessary and represents the minimum interference necessary to prevent the patient from behaving violently or being a danger to himself or to others.

(2) Sections 60 and 61(3) above shall not preclude the continuation of any treatment or of treatment under any plan pending compliance with s 57 or 58 above if the responsible medical officer considers that the discontinuance of the treatment or of treatment under the plan would cause serious suffering to the patient.

(3) For the purposes of this section treatment is irreversible if it has unfavourable irreversible physical or psychological consequences and hazardous if it entails significant physical hazard.

Treatment not requiring consent

63 The consent of a patient shall not be required for any medical treatment given to him for the mental disorder from which he is suffering, not being treatment falling within s 57 or 58 above, if the treatment is given by or under the direction of the responsible medical officer.

RULE 2(H)

The patient must be conscious to be able to consent. If the patient is unconscious, treatment can only be administered if it is in his best interests.

Commentary

A conscious patient can make a rational or irrational decision regarding his treatment. But the unconscious patient lacks this luxury; he cannot articulate his wishes (however, see below, at p 59 *et seq*) and yet he may require treatment. It would be most unwise for the health carer to work on the premise that, if he were to treat the patient, when the patient recovers consciousness and learns that he has been treated, he will be eternally grateful to the medical profession. The health carer might just find that the patient did not want the particular treatment in question and would have said so had he been conscious (see *Malette v Shulman* [1991] 2 Med LR 162).

As such, the rule to which the health carer must normally adhere is, 'act in the best interests of the patient'. This means that the unconscious patient can be treated (he can even have invasive treatment) provided the treatment is necessary to save his life 'or to ensure improvement or prevent deterioration in [his] physical or mental health' (*per* Lord Brandon in *Re F (Mental Patient: Sterilisation)* [1989] 2 WLR 1025, at p 1067) and is in the best interests of the patient. Or, as Lord Goff put it, at pp 1086–87):

> Where ... a surgeon performs an operation without his consent on a patient temporarily rendered unconscious in an accident, he should do no more than is reasonably required in the best interests of the patient, before he recovers consciousness ... but where the state of affairs is permanent or semi-permanent, as may be so in the case of a mentally disordered person, there is no point waiting to obtain the patient's consent. The need to care for him is obvious; and the doctor must then act in the best interests of his patient just as if he had received the patient's consent to do so.

If the unconsciousness is likely to last for some time but the treatment is immediately necessary then the treatment can be administered; it is in the patient's best interests. If, however, the treatment is not immediately needed then much will depend on when the patient is likely to regain consciousness; it could be that some treatment will have to be given at some time and if the patient is still unconscious then it is most doubtful if an English court would find the health carer's actions unlawful. On the other hand, if the prognosis is that the unconsciousness will only last for a short period of time then it is submitted that only emergency treatment, including treatment to improve the patient's condition, should be given; all other treatment should wait until the patient regains consciousness. What is clear is that in neither situation envisaged does the legal right of consent pass to the relatives; their wishes or views will be listened to and respected but at the end of the day it is what it is in the patient's best interests that matters.

The real difficulty for all concerned is to decide how the patient's best interests are to be determined and who will make that determination. In some cases the health carers themselves will make the decision and decide on the appropriate treatment using their professional expertise and acting in the patient's best interests. In any subsequent litigation they will have to justify their actions accordingly. But with certain forms of treatment the decision has often (not always) been correctly left to the courts which, if the circumstances are right, will grant declarations permitting treatment or non-treatment, as the case may be, in the patient's best interests. In doing so the courts will invariably be guided by experts within the relevant medical specialism; these experts should be other than and additional to the patient's health carers. What the courts will be looking for is unequivocal evidence of the following:

(1) the inability of the patient to make the decision for himself;

(2) whether the patient had earlier expressed any choice as to his proposed treatment;

(3) the need for that particular treatment to alleviate that particular condition;

(4) the consequences should that treatment not be administered; and

(5) the wishes of those closest to him, for example, a spouse or relative.

Consequently, in cases where the compulsory sterilisation of mentally handicapped females is deemed to be in their best interests, prior permission from the courts is rightly sought (see *Re F* [1989] 2 WLR 1025 and *Practice Note (Minors and Mental Health Patients: Sterilisation)* [1993] 3 All ER 222).

An approach similar to the one described in *Re F* has been adopted in the treatment of patients described as being in a persistent vegetative state (PVS). This somewhat indelicate term describes patients who are not clinically dead but who have 'lost the function of the cognitive part of the brain' (BMA Consultation Paper on *Treatment of Patients in Persistent Vegetative State*, September 1992). Put another way, they are patients who are unable to do anything for themselves, are almost totally dependent on life support machines and the prognosis is that they will be in that condition for the foreseeable future. As the patient is unable to give his consent to anything, common law jurisdictions have resorted to the rule of allowing the health carer to do what is in the patient's best interests. To date this has resulted, via applications to the court, in hydration and nutrition being lawfully withdrawn (see *Airedale NHS Trust v Bland* [1993] 2 WLR 316 and *Re G* [1995] Med L Rev 80); gastrostomy tubes not being replaced when they have become dislodged (see *Frenchay Healthcare NHS Trust v S* [1994] 2 All ER 403); and artificial ventilatory support being withdrawn (*Auckland Area Health Board v AG* [1993] NZLR 235).

When the need arises to move quickly, health carers may even treat without obtaining the court's prior approval; here, if the health carer can subsequently justify his actions on the ground not only that it was in the patient's best interests but also that it accorded with accepted medical practice, then it is doubtful if any court will hold the health carer liable in civil law. This is so even when it is hydration, etc, that is to be withdrawn from the PVS patient with its inevitable consequences. As Sir Thomas Bingham MR (*obiter*) said in *Frenchay Healthcare NHS Trust v S* [1994] 2 All ER 403 (at p 409):

> I have in mind the acute emergency when a decision has to be taken within minutes or at most hours as to whether treatment should be given or not, whether one form of treatment should be given or another, or as to whether treatment should be withheld.

Given the serious consequences of this type of 'treatment', it is fervently to be hoped that the *Frenchay* case will not be followed in the future for two reasons. The first is that it is questionable whether PVS cases should be treated as emergencies; after all, the circumstance in which the patient now finds himself is one which was known for some time, so why the rush? Secondly, in an emergency the Official Solicitor – the one person who is likely to argue against the proposed action – will be denied that very opportunity. Should not the PVS patient have his day in court, figuratively speaking? Is that not in his best interests?

What the PVS cases demonstrate is that, in respect of such patients:

(1) The courts will closely scrutinise the medical profession's prognosis and diagnosis that the patient is in a PVS state. To this end the BMA have suggested that:

  (a) every effort should be made to rehabilitate the patient for at least six months from the date of the injury;

(b) a PVS diagnosis should not be confirmed until at least one year has elapsed from the date of injury; and

(c) a PVS diagnosis should be confirmed by two other independent doctors.

Despite this, both the courts and the BMA have justifiably become alarmed at the news that two PVS patients have started to communicate with their families and health carers after periods of seven and two years respectively.

(2) The views of the relatives are important and indeed it is good medical practice to discover those views, but ultimately it is the health carer's duty to decide what is in the patient's best interests (subject to (4) below). So far in almost all the cases the relatives and the doctors have been in complete agreement, but in *Re G* [1995] Med L Rev 10, the patient's wife agreed with the doctors while the mother disagreed.

(3) With PVS patients the courts have decided that what they have to determine is whether the continuation of medical treatment is in the patients best interests, that is, it is medically pointless to continue with the treatment? It is interesting to speculate what the actions of health carers should be once a diagnosis of PVS is made and upheld by the courts: must the treatment be discontinued immediately or can it legally be continued? In the light of the English decisions we would suggest that health carers should discontinue the treatment even if such action were to be taken in the face of opposition from the relatives. This is because the court's decision, made in the patient's interests, must be obeyed; it could hardly be seen to be in his interests to continue a treatment which both the medical and legal professions have decreed is futile.

(4) An application must be made to the High Court for a declaration to discontinue the treatment (see above). Each case will be treated on its own merits.

One thing which would certainly assist the courts in determining the patient's best interests is the discovery of whether the patient had ever voiced his views on what treatment should or should not be administered to him at some time in the future and, more significantly, whether treatment should ever continue or be discontinued in a given situation. But where is this knowledge to come from? It could come from having communicated his views to friends or relatives; it would be much better if the patient had taken the trouble to put his views in written form. The issue then is the legal effect which should be accorded to such written views.

In some American states, advance directives on future medical treatment (or 'living wills') are legally acceptable (see the Patient Self-Determination Act 1991). In Denmark, they have been accorded limited recognition. In England, some degree of level of recognition has already been accorded to advance directives. In *Bland* [1993] 2 WLR 316, two Law Lords (*obiter*) approved the use of living wills as a way of informing the medical profession about future treatments. Lord Keith said (at pp 360–61):

> The first point to make is that it is unlawful ... to administer medical treatment to an adult, who is conscious and of sound mind, without his consent ... This extends to the situation where the person, in anticipation of his ... entering into a

condition such as PVS, gives clear instructions that in such event he is not to be given medical care, including artificial feeding, designed to keep him alive.

In similar vein, Lord Goff said (at p 367):

On this basis, it has been held that a patient of sound mind may, if properly informed, require that life support should be discontinued ... Moreover, the same principle applies where the patient's refusal has been expressed at an earlier date, before he became unconscious or otherwise incapable of communicating it ...

In our view, a strong argument exists for their legal acceptance in English law; can it be seriously questioned that there is any meaningful difference between the directions issued by the claimant in *Malette v Shulman* (see above) and the directions found in 'living wills'? (See the efforts of the Voluntary Euthanasia Society in this field and Appendix G for a sample advance directive.) Their introduction should be by way of legislation, if only because there will need to be clear, unambiguous safeguards, for example, minimum age, provided to counter potential abuse. As such, we would contend that the legislation should lay down a standard form of words to be used (for example, 'I do not want any life sustaining treatment to be administered to me if any disease or illness or cardiac arrest or accident or other similar conditions result in such a severe state of disability that I will thereafter be permanently, physically and mentally, unable to look after myself'). Further, the legislation should demand that the patient makes a clear statement that the nature and effect of making a living will has been explained to him; that there should be two independent witnesses (not members of his family – the word 'family' would need to be defined) to the patient's signature (who sign themselves). Finally, there should be a standard form of words which would have to be used and signed by two medical practitioners that the medical conditions set out in the living will have been reached. When the above factors exist, the legislation should then decree that the patient is not to be given any life extending treatment nor should he be given anything, for example, lethal injection, which would hasten his death. Instead, he is to be left for nature to take its course.

REFERENCES

English case law

(1)   Re F (Mental Patient: Sterilisation) [1989] 2 WLR 1025
A 36 year old mentally handicapped woman, who was a voluntary in-patient in a mental hospital, formed a sexual relationship with a male partner. It was the professional opinion of the hospital staff that she would be unable to cope with the effects of pregnancy and childbirth; that since all other forms of contraception were unsuitable, sterilisation should be resorted to. The House of Lords agreed with the hospital. As Lord Bridge said (at p 1063):

... I agree ... that the court has the jurisdiction to declare the lawfulness of such an operation proposed to be performed on the ground that it is ... in the best interests of the woman.

See above p 59.

(2)   Re A (Male Sterilisation) [2000] 2 FLR 549

A 28 year old Down's syndrome male patient lived with his mother, aged 63. Fearful that as her health declined she might become unable to supervise A and worried that he might make a woman pregnant, the mother sought a declaration that the sterilisation of A was in his best interests. Both the trial judge and the Appeal Court refused the declaration. In declaiming that the treatment was not in his best interests, for example, the risk of A entering a casual sexual relationship was low, the Appeal Court made two interesting points. First, the best interests of a male patient were not the same as the best interests of a female. Secondly, best interests encompassed medical, emotional and all other welfare issues but the question of third party interests was left open (see Dame Butler-Sloss's judgment at pp 555 and 557).

(3)   Re S (Sterilisation: Patient's Best Interests) [2000] 2 FLR 389

A declaration was sought for a hysterectomy to be performed on a 29 year old woman who was incapable of giving her consent to any medical treatment. The official solicitor opposed the application arguing that an intra-uterine device would be more appropriate. The trial judge granted the declaration but an appeal was allowed. On the facts the Appeal Court concluded that the trial judge had failed to give proper weight to the relevant medical evidence which supported the intra-uterine device; as such that treatment had not been properly considered in the context of the patient's best interests. In arriving at their decision the Court made the following interesting observations:

(a) the *Bolam* test – accepted medical practice – should be seen as the starting point of any medical decision (p 400);

(b) where the medical profession is seeking a declaration as to the lawfulness of a proposed treatment, the judge not the doctor has the duty to decide what is in the patient's best interests (p 400); and

(c) referring to the test laid down by the President in *Re GF (Medical Treatment)* [1992] 1 FLR 293 at p 294 for bringing applications for leave to perform a sterilisation operation, the Court said that that test had been expressed in broad terms and therefore if a particular case was anywhere near the boundary line it should be referred to the Court by way of an application for a declaration of lawfulness (p 405).

(4)   Re ZM and OS (Sterilisation: Patient's Best Interest) [2000] 1 FLR 523

Somewhat similar facts to *Re S* (above). Here Bennett J held that the hysterectomy was in the patient's best interests. Commenting on this case in *Re S*, Dame Butler-Sloss noted that there was disagreement on the medical evidence offered to the Judge.

(5)   Airedale NHS Trust v Bland [1993] 2 WLR 316

A patient, aged 17, was seriously injured in the Hillsborough football disaster of 1989. As a result he was left in a PVS condition. The prognosis was that there was no hope of any improvement in his condition. Declarations were sought that the hospital could lawfully discontinue all life-sustaining treatment.

Held: the declarations would be granted. Lord Goff said (at p 371):

... the question is not whether it is in the best interests of the patient that he should die. The question is whether it is in the best interests of the patient that his life should be prolonged by the continuance of this form of medical treatment or care. The correct formulation of the question is of particular importance in a case such as the present, where the patient is totally unconscious or where there is no hope whatsoever of any amelioration of his condition. In circumstances such as these, it may be difficult to say that it is in his best interests that the treatment should be ended. But if the question is asked ... whether it is in his best interests that treatment which has the effect of artificially prolonging his life should be continued, the question can sensibly be answered to the effect that his best interests no longer require that it should be.

(6) Re G [1995] Med L Rev 10
The Hospital Trust sought a declaration that it would be lawful to withdraw artificial hydration and nutrition from a PVS patient. The matter was discussed with the patient's wife and she agreed that it would not be in her husband's best interests to continue the artificial feeding, etc, but the patient's mother disagreed.

Held: the declaration would be granted. The doctors had to act in the patient's best interests, although the views of the relatives would not be ignored.

(7) Frenchay Healthcare NHS Trust v S [1994] 2 All ER 403
The Appeal Court upheld a declaration that it would be lawful not to reconnect a feeding tube, which had become dislodged, to a PVS patient.

(8) Swindon and Marlborough NHS Trust v S [1995] Med L Rev 84
The principles applicable to PVS patients apply whether they are being treated in a hospital or at home. In either case it is to do what was in the patient's best interests. Ward J held that, in treating such a patient, if a doctor were to follow the practice of the Medical Ethics Committee of the BMA, he would be acting in accordance with a responsible and competent body of relevant professional opinion.

Foreign case law

Canada

Malette v Shulman [1991] 2 Med LR 162
See above, p 41.

New Zealand

Auckland Area Health Board v AG [1993] 1 NZLR 235
A declaration was granted by the New Zealand High Court permitting the withdrawal of artificial ventilation from an incompetent adult patient, even though it was inevitable that such action would lead to his death. The court stressed that sanctity of life was not an absolute; fundamental values of human dignity and personal privacy also had to be obeyed.

South Africa

Clarke v Hurst [1994] 5 Med LR 177
The court held that a patient who had made a 'living will' could have artificial feeding discontinued.

Practice directions/notes

Practice Note (Minors and Mental Health Patients) [1993] 3 All ER 222

Foreign statutes

Patients' Self-determination Act 1991 (USA)

Practice points

See Appendix G for sample advance directive.

RULE 2(J)

The patient must be in possession of a certain amount of information prior to giving true consent.

Commentary

See Rules 2(A) and (B).

It should be pointed out that in recent years informed consent has either been introduced or is being discussed as the appropriate mile in certain specific medical areas. If the authors are correct in their conclusion that it is the *Canterbury v Spence* (1972) 464 F (2d) 7721 doctrine of informed consent that is being advocated for these areas, then the question must be asked, why is the doctrine not being applied across the broad spectrum of medical matters? Is it because to do so would be impossible given the current predicament in time and resources of the National Health Service? Would health carers know what further information to impart? Would the patient understand or even appreciate the extra information? The answers to these questions would suggest that, as far as the medical profession is concerned, informed consent is not necessary – there are far more important matters which, in their view, need reforming. But is this a sensible attitude? Might not the broad outlines approach of *Chatterton v Gerson* infringe Art 8 of the European Convention on Human Rights 1950 which refers to the right to respect for private and family life, home and correspondence?

Earlier it was indicated that in certain areas of healthcare law the rule now seemed to be (or soon will be) informed consent. For example, the Senate of Surgery of Great Britain and Ireland in their *Guidance for Surgeons* (October 1997) talked of information being provided in the 'detail required by a reasonable person in the circumstances of the patient to make a relevant and informed judgment' (p 6). Also, in their discussion documents, 'Whose hands on your genes?', the Human Genetics Commission at p 9 say this:

> 5.2 Consent must be informed ... in both English and Scots Law, the test is that of what the reasonable doctor in the circumstances would deem necessary to disclose to the patient, although recent Court decisions now confirm that there will be circumstances in which the Court will depart from this standard in favour of the test of a standard of disclosure of risk determined by the Court itself.

Finally, the recent scandal arising from the removal and retention of organs from babies without parental consent or knowledge looks almost certain to result in, amongst other things, changes to the Human Tissue Act 1961; one such change that has been flagged up is the need for informed consent on the part of parents before the organs can be removed.

So far this discussion has centred on the type of information which should be volunteered by the health carer, that is, without questions being asked by the patient. But what about the 'concerned' patient who, before signing the consent form, asks specific questions relating to his treatment which demand information that would not otherwise be voluntarily disclosed? What is the health carer to do? According to Lord Bridge in *Sidaway*: '... when questioned specifically by a patient of apparently sound mind about risks involved in a particular treatment proposed, the doctor's duty must ... be to answer both truthfully and as fully as the questioner requires.' [1985] 1 AC 871, at p 898. But in *Blyth v Bloomsbury HA* [1993] 4 Med LR 151 the Appeal Court seemingly took the view that the answer need only to adhere to the *Bolam* standard, namely how would other health carers respond in similar circumstances? Clearly they may respond truthfully and fully but then again they may not. In that case the patient, a nurse, was admitted to hospital for antenatal care. It was diagnosed that she had no or insufficient immunity to rubella, but because of the late stage of her pregnancy, a rubella vaccination could not be administered; also the vaccine, if given, could adversely affect a foetus if she became pregnant again within three months. However, as it was essential that she was provided with some form of contraceptive protection, the decision was made to use a progesterone-only contraceptive, Depo-Provera. Unlike many other patients she had specifically and repeatedly questioned the doctor beforehand as to the risks associated with the drug. In his summary of the facts Kerr LJ (at p 154) noted that the particulars of negligence included the following allegation:

(iv) failing to answer the plaintiff's enquiries concerning Depo-Provera accurately and of failing to obtain answers to her questions before attempting to give her the said assurance about the said drug.

In giving judgment for the defendants the point was dealt with by Kerr LJ this way (at p 157):

As regards the judge's repeated reference to the need to give a full picture in answer to a specific enquiry, it must be borne in mind ... that no specific enquiry was found to have been made ... Secondly, I think the judge's conclusions equally cannot properly be based on the remarks of Lord Diplock and Lord Bridge in *Sidaway*. The question of what a plaintiff should be told in answer to a general enquiry cannot be divorced from the *Bolam* test, any more that when no such enquiry is made. In both cases, the answer must depend upon the circumstances, the nature of the enquiry, the nature of the information which is available, its reliability, relevance, the condition of the patient and so forth.

It is submitted that the distinction being drawn by both Lord Bridge and Kerr LJ is the difference between a general enquiry ('Will I get better'? 'Are there likely to be any complications'?) and a specific enquiry ('Will my spinal cord be damaged'?). In the former, the *Bolam* rule will apply and the defendant need only respond in the way a responsible group of his peers would reply; thus, if they would not have answered truthfully and/or fully, the defendant likewise does not. But in the case of a specific enquiry it seems that the question must be answered truthfully, etc, but subject to the further proposition that, if the truth is not therapeutically beneficial to the patient, the specific question need not be answered truthfully. Either way the patient is completely in the hands of the health carer. Is this true consent? Doubtful, in our view.

REFERENCES

English case law

(1)   Chatterton v Gerson [1981] 1 All ER 257
See above, pp 44, 45.

(2)   Sidaway v Board of Governors of the Bethlem Royal Hospital and the Maudsley Hospital [1985] AC 871
See pp 44, 74.

(3)   Blyth v Bloomsbury Health Authority [1993] 4 Med LR 151
See above, p 66.

(4)   Bolam v Friern Hospital Management Committee [1957] 1 WLR 582; [1957] 2 All ER 118
See pp 66, 155.

Foreign case law

United States
Canterbury v Spence (1972) 464 F (2d) 772
See above, p 44.

RULE 2(K)

The patient must have understood the information provided.

Commentary

In a multicultural society it would be most surprising if all patients had the same level of capacity for reading, writing or understanding the English language. So, what does 'true consent' mean for the patient from Vietnam or Bangladesh who cannot speak or write English? What should the health carer do to satisfy himself that the patient has reasonably understood what is being said to him? Furthermore, what if the information is imparted in complex technical jargon so that even an English-speaking person would not understand what has been said?

In our view, the information should be given in non-technical English language accompanied, if necessary, by diagrams or charts. The health carer needs only to be reasonably (not absolutely) assured that the patient has understood; this may be achieved by simply asking if he has any question or if he has understood everything. However, to comply with this standard more needs to be done if, because of the patient's ethnic origins, the health carer is of the opinion that the information has not been understood. In most situations where this is likely to occur relatives may be resorted to as interpreters; in extreme circumstances, professional interpreters may be used. Certainly, some of the more commonplace information which has to be imparted to patients, for example, their rights of complaint, could and should be conveyed in a number of languages.

It is evident from the foregoing that we are arguing for the patient actually to understand the information imparted as opposed to merely possessing an ability to understand the information. In *Re L (Medical Treatment: Gillick Competency)* [1998] 2 FLR 810, a 14 year old Jehovah's Witness girl, described as a person with sincere convictions and mature for her age, refused medical treatment which might involve the possibility of a blood transfusion. The court held that the treatment (including the blood transfusion) could be administered. In the course of doing so Sir Stephen Brown seemed to indicate that she had not actually appreciated certain aspects of the treatment, in particular that without it she would suffer a horrible death.

REFERENCES

English case law

Re L (Medical Treatment: Gillick competency) [1998] 2 FLR 810
See above, p 67.

RULE 2(L)

The patient must give his consent voluntarily.

Commentary

As a general rule a patient's ability to consent to treatment is not determinable by his status at the particular time. Consequently, a detained adult prisoner of sound mind has the same right to consent to or refuse treatment as a 'free' person and that is a right which has to be respected (see *Home Secretary v Robb* [1995] 1 All ER 677). Also there should be no duress, undue influence or misrepresentation used to obtain the consent; if such were shown to exist then it is arguable that no true consent had been obtained. As regards fraud, in *R v Tabassum* [2000] Lloyd's Rep Med 404, the traditional distinction between fraud going to the defendant's identity or fraud going to the nature and quality of the act complained of – both of which would vitiate consent – as opposed to other aspects of fraud was considered.

Which would not legally vitiate consent has been considerably modified. In *Tabassum* the defendant had asked several women to take part in a breast cancer survey as he was preparing, so he said, a software package to be sold to doctors. The three complainants agreed to the defendant showing them how to examine their own breasts, in the course of which he was alleged to have indecently assaulted them. At the trial the defence argued that the complainants had indeed consented to the acts in question. This seemed to be a situation where the fraud went neither to the defendant's identity nor to the nature and quality of his conduct; instead the complainants seemed to be saying that they would not have agreed to the defendant's acts had they known all the facts, namely that he had neither any medical qualifications nor medical training. The defendant was convicted and his appeal against the conviction and sentence was dismissed. The Appeal Court ruled that the complainants had consented to the nature but not to the quality of the acts complained of; they had agreed to be touched but for medical purposes only. Therefore there was no genuine consent. Philip Gainsford, Barrister, in his comment on the decision has this to say in so far as the decision has relevance to health carers and consent to treatments:

> It now behoves those carrying out physical examinations to ensure that no question can subsequently be raised as to their training or qualifications since they are otherwise vulnerable to allegations of assault and, in the case of intimate examinations, to allegations of indecent assault [p 410].

At the same time it should be pointed out that Gainsford, like the authors, has problems with the decision itself. As he expressed it, also at page 410:

> This decision is difficult, if not impossible, to reconcile with those in the above cases and, in particular, with the case of the unregistered dentist ... [here he was referring to the case of *R v Richardson* [1998] 2 Cr App R 200].

REFERENCES

English case law

(1)   Home Secretary v Robb [1995] 1 All ER 677
A prisoner of sound mind had a right to refuse nutrition.

(2)   R v Tabassum [2000] Lloyd's Rep Med 404
See above, p 68.

(3)   R v Richardson [1998] 2 Cr App R 200
See above, p 69.

Professional/ethical guidelines

GMC booklet, Seeking Patients' Consent: The Ethical Considerations (November 1998)

CHAPTER 3

DUTY

RULE 3(A)

A patient is owed a legal duty of care by a health carer. This duty is said to be a single, indivisible duty.

Commentary

Whether or not a duty of care is owed in any given situation will be determined as an issue of law by the English courts (see *Watson v British Boxing Board of Control Ltd* [2001] 2 WLR 1256). Patients using the National Health Service or NHS Trust facilities have no contract with the NHS or the Trust (see *Pfizer Corpn v Ministry of Health* [1965] AC 512); they can only look to the law of tort (in particular the tort of negligence) for redress. For the private patient, that is, the person who is being treated privately, the law of contract exists as an additional alternative to this tort liability. If the claim is brought in contract, then cases such as *Thake v Maurice* [1986] QB 644, *Scuriaga v Powell* (1979) 123 SJ 406 and *Eyre v Measday* [1986] 1 All ER 488 demonstrate that, in the absence of any contrary evidence, the contract will be interpreted as one to treat the patient with reasonable skill and care, not as one guaranteeing a particular outcome. However, should the health carer, orally or in writing or by gestures, go further and guarantee an outcome, for example, permanent sterility, and, should that outcome fail to materialise, then the defendant will be liable in contract. As Kerr LJ said in *Thake* (p 678):

> ... it seems to me that the plaintiffs could not reasonably have concluded anything other than that his agreement to perform the operation meant that ... he had undertaken to render Mr Thake permanently sterile.

Unlike NHS patients, those who are treated privately will not be regarded as coming within the ambit of the European Convention on Human Rights 1950 and the Human Rights Act 1998, since the NHS is a public authority and a private health concern is not. This, in practical terms, will mean that the NHS patient will be able to argue that he/she is owed the new duties said to arise from the incorporation of the Convention into English law, for example, the duty to receive specific treatment under Art 2. But, given that some NHS patients may, henceforth, actually receive their treatment in private facilities because of the resources (etc) problems within the NHS, will such patients continue to get the benefit of the Convention and the 1998 Act? It is submitted that they should, since it is their status as NHS patients which matters and not where and by whom the treatment is actually provided; their rights should remain unaffected by any agreement entered into on their behalf by the Department of Health.

The legal duty of care in the tort of negligence is regarded by the English courts as a single duty, broken down for convenience into individual duties such as a duty to diagnose, a duty to treat, etc. One consequence of this is that there will, again according to the courts, be a uniform standard of care. But what if that standard should prove to be unsatisfactory? Should the standard be redefined? Or might it be argued that, in law, the duty owed is not the single indivisible duty which the House of Lords did, indeed, confirm in *Sidaway v Board of Governors of the Bethlem Royal Hospital and the Maudsley Hospital* [1985] AC 871? In that case, Lord Diplock unhesitatingly said (p 895):

> In English jurisprudence, the doctor's relationship with his patient which gives rise to the normal duty of care to exercise his skill and judgment to improve the patient's health ... has hitherto been treated as a single comprehensive duty ... This general duty is not subject to dissection into a number of component parts to which different criteria ... apply ...

The difficulty with this approach lies with the standard applied to this single duty: the *Bolam* standard (see below, Chapter 5, p 155). It has been argued successfully in the Australian courts, and by many English academics, that the *Bolam* standard places too much control in the hands of the medical profession and results in the English courts declining to impose an objective standard, which could lead to the conclusion that the standard medical practice or procedure is itself negligent. The reluctance of the English courts to adopt such an objective approach could be the result of not wishing to impose their judgment in matters of life and death, or not wishing to see the courts used as a forum for squabbling over which is the correct medical procedure. But, even accepting the merits of such arguments, it is questionable whether the same reasoning could be applied with the same force where negligence results from the doctor's failure to warn the patient about the risks of, for example, invasive surgery. Certainly, the Australian courts in *Rogers v Whittaker* [1993] 4 Med LR 79; [1992] 3 Med LR 331; (1992) 109 ALR 625 have taken the view that disclosing risks associated with the medical procedure could, and should, be treated differently from diagnosis and treatment, and, while they were prepared to apply the *Bolam* rule exclusively to the latter two areas, they were not prepared to do so in the area of risk disclosure.

It could be argued that the English courts have now moved in a similar direction to the Australian courts. In *Bolitho v City and Hackney HA* [1997] 4 All ER 771, Lord Browne-Wilkinson, correctly interpreting McNair J's judgment in the *Bolam* case, handed back to the courts the power to determine whether a medical practice produced by the defence had a logical foundation or basis, but in doing so he seemed to draw a clear distinction between medical practices associated with diagnosis and treatment and those linked to risk disclosure. With the former, he appeared to be saying that the medical standard offered by the medical profession was almost conclusive, but not so with the latter. As he said (p 779):

> These decisions [for example, *Hucks v Cole*] demonstrate that in cases of diagnosis and treatment there are cases where, despite a body of professional opinion sanctioning the defendant's conduct, the defendant can properly be held liable for negligence (I am not here considering questions of disclosure and risk).

Would it be going too far to conclude that there is now no longer a single indivisible duty, but rather two broad duties: diagnosis/treatment and risk disclosure?

However, until such time as the courts unambiguously assert that the duty is not single and indivisible, the reader should proceed on the basis that it is. And there is some merit in such an approach. In addition to the two reasons mentioned earlier, there is the obvious symmetry in having all aspects of the health carer's duty dealt with by the same principle; also, a legal objective standard might only serve to increase the number of instances where the health carer might be held negligent, and that, in turn, could result in the practice of defensive medicine – something which is generally regarded as unwelcome in England. But, as cases such as *Rogers v Whittaker* and *Hucks v Cole* (1968) (reported at [1993] 4 Med LR 393) gain a wider audience, it is possible that more and more claimants' lawyers will argue that a distinction can and should be drawn between diagnosis/treatment and the risks, and that while for both broad areas an objective standard should be adopted, the courts should and would be more willing to find that, on the evidence, an accepted practice was founded on an illogical basis in cases of risk disclosure than in the diagnosis/treatment cases (see the judgments of Morland J in *Smith v Tunbridge Wells HA* [1994] 5 Med LR 334 and Rougier J in *McAllister v Lewisham and North Southwark HA* [1994] 5 Med LR 343).

REFERENCES

English case law

(1)   Watson v British Boxing Board of Control [2001] 2 WLR 1256
Here the BBC was held to owe a duty to the boxer, Michael Watson. *Per* Lord Phillips of Worth Matravers MR at 1261:

> In *Caparo Industries plc v Dickman* [1990] ... and in many subsequent cases, the House of Lords and this court have approved the approach to the development of the law of negligence recommended by Brennan J in the High Court of Australia in *Sutherland Shire Council v Heyman* (1985) ... where he said, 'It is preferable ... that the law should develop novel categories of negligence incrementally ... rather than by a massive extension of a *prima facie* duty of care' ...

(2)   Pfizer Corpn v Ministry of Health [1965] AC 512; [1965] 2 WLR 387
Per Lord Pearce (p 548):

> There is no consensual bargain between the patient and the Minister or his agent. The Minister is by statute bound to provide the drug and the patient is entitled to receive it.

Per Lord Upjohn (p 552):

> When the National Health Service Act 1952 authorised the Minister to make 'a charge' it seems to me that the basic nature of the transaction was not ... turned from a statutory relationship into a contractual relationship of bargain and sale.

(3)   Thake v Maurice [1986] QB 644; [1986] 2 WLR 337; [1986] 1 All ER 479
The claimant had four children and a fifth was on the way. It was agreed that the surgeon, M, would perform a vasectomy on the claimant's husband. The husband had been told that the operation was irreversible but he was not warned that there was a small chance that the vasectomy would not sterilise him. When later recanalisation occurred and the wife found herself pregnant, the claimants sued for breach of contract and negligence.

Held: there was no breach of contract but there was negligence. Nourse LJ said ([1986] QB 644, p 688):

> In my view, a doctor cannot be objectively regarded as guaranteeing the success of any operation or treatment unless he says as much in clear and unequivocal terms.

(4)   Scuriaga v Powell [1979] 123 SJ 406

The defendant doctor agreed to terminate a pregnancy by a legal abortion. He performed the operation but it failed to terminate the pregnancy. The claimant then gave birth to a healthy child by Caesarean section. Subsequently, she claimed damages for breach of contract, arguing that the doctor had negligently performed the operation and had failed to carry out the necessary further investigations, procedures and treatment.

Held: the claimant succeeded. Watkins J considered that the sole and effective cause of the continuation of the pregnancy was the breach of contract.

(5)   Eyre v Measday [1986] 1 All ER 488

The defendant gynaecologist agreed to perform a sterilisation operation on the claimant. The nature of the operation was explained, including the fact that it was irreversible, but the claimant was not told that there was a small risk of pregnancy occurring after the operation. The claimant subsequently became pregnant and an action was brought for damages for (*inter alia*) breach of contract.

Held: judgment for the defendant. The contract was to carry out a particular type of operation and not to render the claimant absolutely sterile.

(6)   Sidaway v Board of Governors of the Bethlem Royal Hospital and the Maudsley Hospital [1985] 1 AC 871; [1985] 2 WLR 840; [1985] 1 All ER 643

During an operation to relieve the claimant of persistent pain in her back and shoulder, her spinal cord was damaged. Her claim in damages was based not on the operation being performed negligently, but rather on the failure by the surgeon to warn her of the risk of damage to the spinal cord, which, at the trial, was agreed to be less than 1%. Her claim was dismissed; the court ruled that, since there was a responsible body of medical opinion who would have warned the claimant in substantially similar terms to those used by the defendant, the latter was not negligent. Lord Diplock said ([1995] 1 AC 871, (pp 895):

> To decide what risks the existence of which a patient should be voluntarily warned and the terms in which such warning, if any should be given ... is as much an exercise of professional skill and judgment as any other part of the doctor's comprehensive duty of care ... the *Bolam* test should be applied.

(7)   Bolam v Friern HMC [1957] 1 WLR 582; [1957] 2 All ER 118

The claimant was treated for depression by ECT (electro-convulsive therapy). No relaxant drugs were administered, nor was any form of manual restraint used; this was in line with the hospital's practice. During the treatment, the patient suffered severe injuries. In directing the jury, McNair J (p 587) uttered the oft-quoted words, 'A doctor is not guilty of negligence if he has acted in accordance with a practice accepted as proper by a responsible body of medical men skilled in that particular art'. See, further, below, Chapter 5, p 155.

(8) Bolitho v City and Hackney HA [1997] 4 All ER 771; [1996] 7 Med LR 1; [1998] AC 232
The defendant's employee omitted to turn up and treat a patient under her care. While accepting that, in doing so, negligence had been committed, the defendants argued that there was no causation. In introducing the *Bolam* principle into the area of hypothetical causation, the House of Lords took the opportunity to explain the *Bolam* rule.

(9) Hucks v Cole (1968) reported at [1993] 4 Med LR 393
During and after her confinement, the claimant was under the control and care of the defendant, a GP. When her finger became swollen, the doctor reassured her that there was nothing to worry about. After the hospital had diagnosed her to be suffering from fulminating septicaemia and prescribed an antibiotic, the GP failed to start her on a course of penicillin treatment. Ultimately, the claimant's voice was permanently damaged.

Holding the doctor negligent, Sachs LJ said (p 397):

When the evidence shows that a lacuna exists by which risks of great danger are knowingly taken, then, however small the risks, the courts must anxiously examine that lacuna – particularly, if the risks can be easily and inexpensively avoided.

If the court finds, on an analysis of the reasons given for not taking precautions that, in the light of current professional knowledge, there is no proper basis for the lacuna, and that it is definitely not reasonable that those risks should be taken, its function is to state that fact and where necessary to state that it constitutes negligence. In such a case the practice will no doubt thereafter be altered to the benefit of the patients.

On such occasions the fact that other practitioners would have done the same thing as the defendant practitioner is a very weighty matter to be put in the scales on his behalf; but it is not ... conclusive.

See, further, below, Chapter 5, p 172.

(10) Smith v Tunbridge Wells HA [1994] 5 Med LR 334
In this case Morland J held a consultant negligent for not giving a patient a warning of a particular risk, even though it was agreed and accepted that, in failing to do so, the defendant was doing what other experienced, competent surgeons would have done. *Per* Morland J (p 388):

I accept the defendant's submission that Mr Cook's [the consultant] personal view as to his duty is not definitive evidence that in law he owed that duty. In my judgment, it is, however, cogent evidence that general surgeons in 1988 ... would have regarded it as the proper and accepted practice to warn such a patient of the risk of impotence.

(Why was *Bolam* not regarded as conclusive? Was it because this case had to do with risks?)

(11) McAllister v Lewisham and North Southwark HA [1994] 5 Med LR 343
Here, Rougier J held a senior consultant neurosurgeon liable in negligence for failing to disclose adequate information regarding the risks associated with a particular operation. *Per* Rougier J (p 352):

I have come to the conclusion that those who say that the warnings given ... were inadequate were right ... It is in this sphere that I am compelled to hold that Mr Strong [consultant neurosurgeon] fell below the standard which could have been expected from him.

(Is it a coincidence that, like the *Smith* case, disclosure of risks was involved here?)

(12) Joyce v Merton and Sutton and Wandsworth HA [1996] 7 Med LR 1; [1995] 6 Med LR 60
Per Roch LJ (pp 13–14):

The second misdirection of which complaint is made, is ...

> In the field of diagnosis and treatment, a defendant is not guilty of negligence if his acts or omissions were in accordance with accepted clinical practice.

Had that been the totality of the judge's direction to himself on the law I would have agreed that it amounted to misdirection. However, the judge added these words:

> Provided that clinical practice stood up to analysis and was not unreasonable in the light of the state of the medical knowledge at the time.

The addition is very important because, without it, it leaves the decision of negligence or no negligence in the hands of the doctors, whereas that question must at the end of the day be one for the courts. In my view, the judge's direction would have been better phrased if, instead of the words:

> ... if his acts or omissions

he had used:

> ... if his acts or decision not to act,

because it is to be hoped that an omission would never be part of accepted clinical practice. In the present case, the question was not whether Dr Stewart had omitted to re-explore the artery but whether his decision not to re-explore because there was a palpable pulse, albeit of small volume, was in accordance with accepted clinical practice and whether that clinical practice stood up to analysis.

(13) Russell v Harley Medical Centre Ltd and Kingdom [2000] Medical Litigation cases 0205
Breach of contract (and negligence) upheld in a case where the patient had plastic surgery.

Foreign case law

Australia

(1) Rogers v Whittaker [1993] 3 Med LR 79; [1992] 3 Med LR 331; (1992) 109 ALR 625
The claimant, who was almost blind in one eye, consulted the defendant, an ophthalmic surgeon, about an operation and the possible risks associated with such an operation. However, she omitted to ask specifically whether sympathetic ophthalmia (damage to the good eye) would result. The Australian High Court held that the surgeon was under a duty to inform the patient of the slight risk to the good eye.

Per Mason CJ (p 82):

> In Australia, it has been accepted that the standard of care to be observed by a person with some special skill or competence is that of the ordinary skilled person exercising and professing to have that special skill. But, that standard is not determined solely or even primarily by reference to the practice followed or supported by a responsible body of opinion in the relevant trade or profession. Even in the sphere of diagnosis and treatment ... the *Bolam* principle has not always been applied. Further, and more importantly, particularly in the field of non-disclosure of risk and the provision of advice and information, the *Bolam* principle has been discarded and, instead, the courts have adopted the principle that, while evidence of acceptable medical practice is a useful guide for the

courts, it is for the courts to adjudicate on what is the appropriate standard of care ...

See, further, below, Chapter 5, p 185–86.

(2)   F v R (1983) 33 SASR 189

After an unsuccessful tubal ligation, a woman became pregnant. She brought a negligence action alleging a failure by the medical practitioner to warn her of the procedure's failure rate. In refusing to apply the *Bolam* rule, King CJ said (p 194):

> The ultimate question, however, is not whether the defendant's conduct accords with the practice of his profession or some part of it, but whether it conforms to the standard of reasonable care demanded by the law. That is a question for the court and the duty of deciding it cannot be delegated to any profession or group in the community.

Canada

(1)   Brushett v Cowan [1991] 2 Med LR 271

Per Marshall JA (p 275):

> Whether a particular relationship gives rise to a duty of care owed by one to another is a question of law. That question was not in issue since the existence of legal obligations of a surgeon towards his or her patient in relation to post-operative care is not really subject to dispute.

(2)   La Fleur v Cornelis (1979) 28 NBR (2d) 569

A cosmetic surgeon entered into a contract to reduce the size of the claimant's nose. He omitted to tell her that there was a risk of scarring. After the operation the claimant was indeed scarred. Barry J held the surgeon liable in breach of contract (and negligence).

RULE 3(B)

The legal duty of care arises as soon as medical treatment is undertaken by the health carer.

Commentary

This means that patients who register with doctors, and patients who enter the accident and emergency ward of a hospital, are all owed a duty of care, because they either have a legal right to be treated or have actually been treated; in short, their treatment has been undertaken. The word 'treatment' includes diagnosis and any suggested courses of action which ought to be followed, whether the patient has been seen or has not been seen by the doctor; for example, the doctor in the casualty department of a busy hospital who instructs a nurse via the telephone of the treatment which the patient is to undergo (see *Morrison v Forsyth* [1995] 6 Med LR 6) or, in the case of what has been referred to as telemedicine, where the patient is treated at a long distance using modern technological methods of communication.

But the legal duty will not arise where the person has been examined by a health carer for some purpose other than to receive medical advice and treatment, for example, someone who is being examined for drunkenness at a police station or who is being assessed for the purposes of insurance cover. In *Baker v Kaye* [1997] IRLR 219, the claimant was seen by the defendant for a pre-employment assessment. Blood samples taken from the claimant showed, in the defendant's opinion, alcohol related abnormalities. In the circumstances the defendant felt unable to recommend the claimant for the 'highly stressful and demanding job'. In a subsequent claim alleging negligence in carrying out the pre-employment assessment, it was held that the defendant did owe a duty of care to the claimant. The judge summed up the position in the following manner:

> I have come to the conclusion that, upon a true analysis of the relationship between the defendant and the company, and between the company and the plaintiff [claimant], there is no conflict inconsistent with the imposition of a duty of care [p 226].

Two years earlier, in non-medical cases involving child abuse and education, the House of Lords had ruled, *obiter*, that only a limited duty of care was owed in the circumstances envisaged. In *X (Minors) v Bedfordshire CC* [1995] 2 AC 633, Lord Browne-Wilkinson said (pp 752–53):

> The social workers and the psychiatrists were retained by the local authority to advise the local authority, not the plaintiffs ... But the fact that the carrying out of the retainer involves contact with and relationship with the child cannot alter the extent of the duty owed by the professionals under the retainer from the local authority. The Court of Appeal drew a correct analogy with the doctor instructed by an insurance company to examine an applicant for life insurance. The doctor does not, by examining the applicant, come under any general duty of medical care to the applicant. He is under a duty not to damage the applicant in the course of the examination; but beyond that his duties are owed to the insurance company and not to the applicant.

In short, the ordinary health carer/patient duty of care which was envisaged in *Baker v Kaye* was at variance with the views of the Law Lords in the *Bedfordshire CC* case.

It was left to the Court of Appeal in the later case of *Kapfunde v Abbey National plc and Another* [1998] 46 BMLR 176 to attempt some clarification. In that case, the claimant was assessed, via a questionnaire filled in and handed to the defendants, by a GP who worked part time for the defendants, as prone to higher than average levels of absence. As a result, the claimant lost the chance of a job with the defendants. The trial judge held that there was insufficient proximity between the claimant and the GP to give rise to a duty of care. The Appeal Court agreed; it concluded that there was no doctor/patient relationship since the parties had never met and the claimant was blissfully ignorant of the existence of the GP. The conclusion could be drawn that, if the parties had met, as in *Baker v Kaye*, then a health carer/patient duty of care would have arisen. But, in view of the fact that the Appeal Court in *Kapfunde* expressly disapproved of *Baker v Kaye*, such a conclusion must be doubted.

Consequently, it would seem that, where a claimant is seen by a health carer not for treatment purposes but for assessment pre-employment or for obtaining insurance, etc, then there is no health carer/patient duty of care. There is, however, a common law duty owed by the assessing health carer but it is no more than the duty expressed in the *Bedfordshire CC* case: it is a duty not to make the claimant's condition worse in the course of the assessment. This means that in assessing the claimant if a broken needle were to be left inside the claimant, the assessing health carer would have 'damaged' or made the claimant's condition worse and as such would be liable in negligence, but it would not be a health carer/patient type of negligence. What is the practical difference between these two 'types of negligence'? Probably the answer lies in the standard of care: in the health carer/patient relationship, the defendant health carer need only act as a responsible peer group would act, whereas in the non-health carer/patient situation the duty is to act as a reasonable person would act in the circumstances.

A similar argument applies to the 'good Samaritan' health carer who, for example, stops at the roadside to treat the victim of a motorway accident. In stopping to treat he is acting ethically (see BMA Guidelines, *Medical Ethics: Its Practice and Philosophy*, 1993), but there is no legal duty to do so (except where Sched 1, para 9(i)(h) of the terms of contract with the health authority apply; this says that, if an emergency were to occur in his practice area, a GP has to render emergency assistance if called upon to do so). If he does stop and treat, it is submitted that the treatment provided is not your health carer/patient treatment; rather, it will be governed by the *Kapfunde* principles.

For the sake of completeness, it should be emphasised that the legal duty of care is owed by all categories of health carers, for example, doctors, nurses, physiotherapists, irrespective of their experience. Thus, the junior health carer owes the same duty of care to his patient as his more experienced senior colleague; this must be correct, since the patient has a right to expect a certain standard of care when he puts himself in the hands of the hospital authority or health carer. From a practical standpoint, this means that the hospital or health authority should avoid placing the health carer in a position where, unassisted, he will have to do things which are beyond his abilities. Furthermore, the employer of such health carers, that is, the health authority or Trust, owes a direct, as opposed to a vicarious, duty of care to the patient. In *Wilsher v Essex AHA* [1986] 3 All ER 801, two of the Appeal Court judges positively asserted that such a duty did exist. The Vice Chancellor's approach was that 'a health authority which so conducts its hospital that it fails to provide doctors of sufficient skill and experience to give the treatment offered ... may be directly liable in negligence to the patient ... I can see no reason why, in principle, the health authority should not be so liable if its *organisation* is at fault' (p 833). Glidewell LJ expressed it this way (p 831): '... there seems to be no reason in principle why, in a suitable case ... a hospital management committee should not be held directly liable ... for failing to provide sufficient qualified and competent staff.'

In truth, this direct duty is not a recent creation of the courts. In *Cassidy v Ministry of Health* [1951] 2 KB 343, Denning LJ had already signalled that such a duty did exist. To paraphrase what he said at p 365, when a patient puts himself in the hands of a hospital he expects there to be sufficiently qualified people and adequate facilities to look after him properly and hopefully make him better; if that fails to materialise, then it is fitting that the health authority should be made liable. In many ways, the word 'organisation' used by the Vice Chancellor in *Wilsher* is most significant; if the hospital 'set-up' is inadequate so that, for example, the patient on the ward becomes vulnerable to attacks by other patients or members of the public, then the duty is owed and broken. It was because of the breakdown in its organisational set-up that the health authority in *Bull and Another v Devon AHA* [1993] 4 Med LR 117 was held to be liable to the patient; their system of cover in the field of obstetrics had produced a real risk of danger to their patients.

The legal duty continues as long as the patient is being treated; it ends when the treatment is completed or the patient or health carer dies. But it can also come to an end when, having been referred by a GP to a hospital or consultant, the GP then writes and informs the hospital or the consultant that the patient does not need to be seen any longer; or, having been told to return for further treatment, the patient fails to reattend. In the latter case, health carers are advised to try and find out, either by contacting the GP or by writing direct to the patient, why the patient was unable to attend. However, it is not suggested that an infinite number of reappointments should be made; there will come a point in time, dictated by hospital practice and common sense, when the patient's non-attendance will release the health carer and the hospital and its staff from their legal duty of care.

REFERENCES

English case law

(1)   Morrison v Forsyth [1995] 6 Med LR 6
The defendant was covering for the claimant's GP. In response to the claimant's account of his symptoms, he telephoned the local pharmacy to make a prescription available. The claimant's symptoms worsened and he eventually died. The widow and children brought an action contending:

- that a reasonably competent GP would not have relied upon taking a history and issuing a prescription over the telephone; and
- that the GP was negligent in not asking further questions, particularly as the patient was reduced to communicating via an intermediary.

Held: the action failed because it had not been shown that, (a) on the facts, it was negligent to have given medical advice; (b) a doctor exercising reasonable care would have questioned the claimant further.

(2)   Baker v Kaye [1997] IRLR 219
See above, p 77.

(3)   X (Minors) v Bedfordshire CC [1995] 2 AC 633
See above, p 78.

(4)   Kapfunde v Abbey National plc and Another [1999] Lloyd's Rep Med 48
See above.

(5)   Powell and Another v Boladz and Others [1998] Lloyd's Rep Med 116
A claim by the parents of a deceased child patient failed on the ground that no duty was owed to them. *Per* Stuart-Smith LJ, p 124:

I do not think that a doctor who has been treating a patient who has died, who tells relatives what has happened, thereby undertakes the doctor-patient relationship towards the relatives.

(6) Re N [1999] 7 Lloyd's Rep Med 257

The Court of Appeal held that no duty of care was owed by a forensic medical examiner, who had examined the claimant following a serious sexual assault, to attend and give evidence at the resulting trial. Per Stuart-Smith LJ, p 260:

> In my judgment ... the defendant, in carrying out an examination at the behest of the police or Crown Prosecution Service, did not assume any responsibility for the plaintiff's psychiatric welfare; the patient/doctor relationship did not arise.

(7) Wilsher v Essex AHA [1986] 3 All ER 801

The claimant was born three months prematurely with breathing problems, as a result of which he needed extra oxygen. To monitor the partial pressure of oxygen in the arterial blood of a baby, the standard practice was to pass a catheter through the umbilical artery into the aorta. Regrettably, a house officer in the special care baby unit inserted the catheter into a vein; the outcome was that false readings of the level of oxygen were shown. The claimant contracted retrolental fibroplasia and was nearly blind. In a negligence claim, the Appeal Court held that the inexperience of the house officer was no defence. In a dissenting judgment, the Vice Chancellor considered that it was more appropriate to sue the health authority directly as opposed to vicariously, on the ground that it had run the hospital in such a way that it had failed to provide health carers of sufficient skill and experience to give the necessary treatment.

See, further, below, Chapter 5, p 158.

(8) Cassidy v Ministry of Health [1951] 2 KB 343; [1951] 1 All ER 574

The claimant was diagnosed as suffering from Dupuytren's Contracture (forward curvature of one or more fingers). After the operation, his hand and arm were bandaged by a nurse. Following complaints that he was suffering excruciating pain, it was found, on removal of the splint, that he had lost the use of four of his fingers. The Appeal Court held that there was a *prima facie* case of negligence.

Per Denning LJ (pp 365–66):

> If the plaintiff had to prove that some particular doctor or nurse was negligent, he would not be able to do it. But he was not put to that impossible task: he says, 'I went into the hospital to be cured of two stiff fingers. I have come out with four stiff fingers, and my hand is useless. That should not have happened if due care had been used'. I am quite clearly of the opinion that that raises a *prima facie* case against the health authorities.

(9) Bull and Another v Devon AHA [1993] 4 Med LR 117

When it took 68 minutes between the spontaneous delivery of one twin and the surgical delivery of the other, resulting in damage to the latter, the Appeal Court held that the liability on the health authority was direct for failing to have a registrar in attendance at a critical period in the second delivery.

Statutes/statutory instruments

(1) Terms of service for doctors in general practice (issued pursuant to the *National Health Service (General Medical Services) Regulations 1992 (SI 1992/635))*.

Professional/ethical guidelines

BMA Guidelines, Medical Ethics: Its Practice and Philosophy, 1993.
See, above, p 79.

RULE 3(C)

**In appropriate circumstances, a legal duty of care may be directly owed by the
health carer to a third party injured by the patient's acts or omissions.**

Commentary

This rule is stated with the utmost caution, since the significant authorities to
support it are almost exclusively foreign. To illustrate the problem, consider the
following two scenarios.

Scenario 1

A is B's patient. In the course of his treatment for depression, A tells B that he is
very much in love with C but that C sees him only as a friend, not a lover. He
further reveals to B that, if he cannot be with C as a lover, then she (C) would be
'better off dead'. Although alarmed, B decides that the confidentiality of his
patient is paramount and therefore he does not inform C or her parents or the
authorities of A's threat. A subsequently kills C. Could C's relatives pursue a
civil claim against B, arguing that C was owed a duty of care by B? Or is B's
duty only to A, his patient?

Scenario 2

X is Y's patient. Tests reveal that X is HIV positive. Y knows that X has a regular
partner, that the union has produced two children and that the parties have a
healthy sex life. Y counsels X as regards his future lifestyle, including advice as
to what and how to tell his partner of his illness. X agrees to think about it.
Some months later, Y discovers that X has not told his partner of his illness. X,
however, is adamant that he, not Y, will tell the partner. If X still does not
inform his partner and she subsequently tests positive for HIV, could she bring
a claim in negligence against Y, alleging that he owed her a duty of care?

In at least two cases in the US courts, it has been held that a legal duty was
(directly) owed by the health carer to the third party; in both cases, the harm
that was sustained by the third party was said to outweigh the confidentiality
owed to the patient. In *Tarasoff v Regents of the University of California* 551 P (2d)
334 (1976), the facts of which are similar to those in Scenario 1, the Supreme
Court of California held that the defendant health carer could not escape
liability by simply arguing that the third party was not his patient; there was a
positive obligation to use reasonable care to protect the undefended victim from
the source of the danger. In *Bradshaw v Daniel* [1994] Med L Rev 237, the facts of
which are reminiscent to those in Scenario 2 except that the case involved Rocky
Mountain spotted fever, the Supreme Court of Tennessee held that a physician
did owe a duty to a non-patient third party in respect of injuries caused by the
physician's negligence, in circumstances where that injury could have been

reasonably foreseen. Writing in the Medical Law Review ([1994], p 239), Ian Kennedy noted that 'English law has yet to decide whether to recognise such a duty of affirmative action', but ventured to suggest:

> [It] may well be, however, that the availability of limits, established by cases such as *Gamill* and reflected in the instant case, would persuade an English court to recognise the duty and hence impose liability for its breach if damage occurred.

In general, English courts have been reluctant to impose a duty in favour of third parties who have suffered harm as a result of the actions of someone who is being 'looked after' by the defendant. This could be explained on the basis either that the reasonable foresight test for a duty situation has not been satisfied or that it was not fair, just or equitable to impose a duty in the particular circumstance. In non-medical cases, a duty to a third party has been upheld. For example, in *Home Office v Dorset Yacht Co Ltd* [1970] AC 1004, liability was imposed for the negligent supervision of borstal trainees by Home Office employees. In that case, it could be argued that there was an element of control which was, in theory, being exercised by the defendants over the perpetrators. The same could also be said of *Tarasoff* given the nature of the student's illness. But if the 'modern' test for establishing a duty is to be proximity/reasonable foresight/just and equitable, then we would suggest that a duty should be owed where harm to *identifiable* and *identified* third parties is foreseen. Will the English courts adopt such a general principle? At present, they give no indication that they will and we can only conclude that, as a matter of policy, they are unwilling to impose additional duties on a profession which, in their view, already carries a heavy responsibility in respect of matters of life and death. This apparent deferential attitude of the judiciary towards the medical profession may soon become a thing of the past. In a speech (17 January 2001) made by the Lord Chief Justice at University College, London, he said that the courts in the past had been 'excessively deferential' to doctors and the traditional view that 'doctor knows best' was and is changing; he seemed to be indicating that a more interventionist era was just around the corner – assuming it had not already arrived. Is it mere coincidence that such a stance should now be flagged up given the present human rights culture?

To revert briefly to the subject of HIV/AIDS, it is to be noted that the GMC's booklet, *Serious Communicable Diseases* (October 1997), permits disclosure of clinical details to a patient's spouse or other sexual partner in the following circumstances:

> You may disclose information about a patient, whether living or dead, in order to protect a person from risk of death or serious harm. For example, you may disclose information to a known sexual contact of a patient with HIV where you have reason to think that the patient has not informed that person, and cannot be persuaded to do so. In such circumstances you should tell the patient before you make the disclosure, and you must be prepared to justify a decision to disclose information [para 22].

See, also, above, Rule 1(D)(v), p 26.

REFERENCES

English case law

(1)   Home Office v Dorset Yacht Co Ltd [1970] AC 1004; [1970] 2 WLR 1140; [1970] 2 All ER 294
The allegation here was that, while officers in charge of some borstal trainees were asleep, the trainees escaped and caused damage to property. The House of Lords held that a duty of care was owed by the appellants (employers of the officers) to the persons whose property was damaged.

Per Lord Reid (p 1026):

The case for the Home Office is that under no circumstances can Borstal Officers owe any duty to any member of the public to take care to prevent trainees under their control or supervision from injuring him or his property.

He continued (p 1032):

It is argued that it would be contrary to public policy to hold the Home Office or its officers liable ... The basic question is who should bear the loss caused by that carelessness – the innocent respondents or the Home Office, who are vicariously liable for the conduct of their careless officers?

(2)   Goodwill v British Pregnancy Advisory Service [1996] 7 Med LR 129; [1996] 2 All ER 161
The Court of Appeal held that a woman who became pregnant by a man who had had a vasectomy some years before he started a relationship with her, could not sue the defendants who had performed the vasectomy and assured him that it had been successful. One reason was that no duty of care was owed to her by the defendants. As Thorpe LJ said (p 133):

In my judgment ... the defendants were not in a sufficient or any special relationship with the plaintiff such as gives rise to a duty of care. I cannot see that it can properly be said of the defendants that they voluntarily assumed responsibility to the plaintiff when giving advice to Mr MacKinlay. At that time, they had no knowledge of her, she was not an existing sexual partner of his, that is to say a member of an indeterminably large class ... I find it impossible to believe that the policy of the law is or should be to treat so tenuous a relationship ... as giving rise to a duty of care...

(3)   Palmer v Tees HA and Hartlepool and East Durham NHS Trust [1999] 9 Lloyd's Rep Med 351
A, who had been sexually abused as a child and had a drink and drugs problem, had been in and out of hospitals on a number of occasions. On one such occasion when he was out, he abducted, sexually assaulted and murdered the claimant's four year old daughter. In a negligence action brought against the defendants, the claimant alleged (*inter alia*) that the defendants had failed to diagnose that there was a 'real, substantial and foreseeable risk of A committing serious sexual offences against children and of causing serious bodily injury to any child victims'. The Court of Appeal held that no duty was owed: proximity between the parties had not been established. Stuart-Smith LJ approved of the trial judge's reliance on the *Home Office v Dorset Yacht Co* case to conclude that 'the potential victim was not identified or identifiable' (p 356). (Contrast this case with the recent decision of *L (A Minor) and Another v Reading BC and Another* (2001) not yet reported, 12 March (CA), where proximity was established.)

(4)   Kent v Griffiths, Roberts and London Ambulance Service [2000] 3 Lloyd's Rep Med 109
The claimant, K, had suffered an asthma attack. At 4.25 pm, the first defendant, the claimant's GP, telephoned the third defendant ambulance service, requesting an ambulance. At 4.38 pm, K's husband made a second call and, at 4.54 pm, the first defendant called for the second time. At 5.05 pm the ambulance arrived. As result of the delay, K suffered respiratory arrest and brain damage.

Held: The ambulance service owed K a duty of care.

Per Lord Woolf MR (p 117):

Here, what was being provided was a health service. In the case of health services under the Act the conventional situation is that there is a duty of care. Why should the position of the ambulance staff be different from that of doctors or nurses? In addition, the arguments based on public policy are much weaker in the case of the ambulance service than they are in the case of the police or the fire service ... It is therefore appropriate to regard the LAS as providing services of the category provided by hospitals and not as providing services equivalent to these rendered by the police or the fire service.

Foreign case law

United States

(1)   Tarasoff v Regents of the University of California 551 P (2d) 334 (1976)
A student psychiatric patient was receiving therapy at the University's hospital. He informed his therapist (an employee of the University) that he was going to kill an unnamed but readily identifiable young lady. At no time was the young lady or her parents informed of the threat. The threat was carried out and the claimants (the parents) sued the therapist and the University in negligence. It was held by the Supreme Court of California that a duty was owed to the young lady; in the circumstances, the confidentiality due to the patient was outweighed by the duty to the third party.

Per Justice Tobriner:

... When the avoidance of foreseeable harm requires a defendant to control the conduct of another person, or to warn of such conduct, the common law has traditionally imposed liability only if the defendant bears some special relationship to the dangerous person or the potential victim. Since the relationship between a therapist and his patient satisfies this requirement, we need not here decide whether foreseeability alone is sufficient to create a duty to exercise reasonable care to protect a potential victim of another's conduct.

Although the California decisions that recognise this duty have involved cases in which the defendant stood in a special relationship ... we do not think that the duty should logically be constricted to such situations. Decisions of other jurisdictions hold that the single relationship of a doctor to his patient is sufficient to support the duty to exercise reasonable care to protect others against dangers emanating from the patient's illness.

(2)   Bradshaw v Daniel [1994] Med L Rev 237; 854 SW 2d 865 (1993)
A woman died from a non-contagious disease, Rocky Mountain spotted fever. It transpired that the defendant physician had been treating the woman's husband for the same disease from which he had died shortly before the wife started to show symptoms of the disease. The plaintiff (the son) argued that the defendant had been negligent in failing to warn the mother of the risks of exposure to the disease. The Supreme Court of Tennessee agreed. It reasoned that the physician/patient relationship was sufficient to

impose on the physician a positive duty to warn identifiable third parties in the patient's immediate family against foreseeable risks resulting from the patient's illness.

Professional/ethical guidelines

GMC Guidelines, Serious Communicable Diseases (October 1997), para 22.
See above.

RULE 3(D)

Employers of health carers will be held vicariously liable for negligence committed by the health carer in the course of the latter's employment.

Commentary

It is a well established rule of common law that a health authority, a Trust, a GP or a medical practice can and will be held legally responsible for the negligence of both the health carers it employs, for example, consultants, nursing staff, paramedical staff, and the support staff, such as receptionists and secretaries, it employs, provided that the wrong done was in the course of the employee's duties (*Cassidy v Ministry of Health* [1951] 2 KB 343; *Roe v Minister of Health* [1954] 2 QB 66). We do not intend to go into the details of what constitutes an employee or what is meant by the phrase 'in the course of employment'; other, fuller works, such as *Street on Torts*, and a recent case like *Lister v Hesley Hall Ltd* [2001] 2 WLR 1311 should be consulted. What does need emphasising is that consultants are regarded as employees, even though the idea of any form of control being exercised over them by the hospital authorities or Trust is illusory. As Denning LJ said in *Cassidy* (p 326):

> I can see no possible reason why they [hospital authorities] should not also be responsible for the house surgeons and the resident medical officers on their permanent staff ... where the doctor or surgeon, be he a consultant or not, is employed and paid not by the patient but by the hospital authorities.

Although this rule is well tested and uncontroversial, some relationships in the field of medicine do require further special attention.

Locum or deputising doctor

From time to time, a GP or medical practice may have to use the services of a qualified doctor to act as a temporary replacement for the GP or one of the doctors in the practice. The responsibility of the GP or the practice is to ensure that a suitably qualified person is appointed to deputise; failure to do so will result in direct (not vicarious) liability. Researchers from the magazine *Health Which?* recently reported (Wednesday 13 December 2000) that they found the vetting of locums poor and recruitment agencies could not be relied upon to make the appropriate checks; for example, only 13% of the 591 locum doctors surveyed said that they had been asked for their references the last time they worked at a new surgery. If the locum is negligent when treating a patient, there will be no vicarious liability on the GP or the practice, since the relationship between the parties is not seen as one of employer/employee; instead, the locum is in the position of an independent contractor and therefore any action should be brought against him in his personal capacity.

Agency nursing staff

Hospitals and medical practices frequently use the services of nursing staff supplied by an agency. In the event of negligence by such staff, it is submitted that whether direct or vicarious liability exists and, if so, against whom it exists may well depend on the cause of the negligence, the terms of the contract between the agency and the nurse and the legal relationship between the agency and the hospital. For example, if the agency chosen is not a reputable/reliable one, or if the hospital fails to instruct the nurse adequately in her duties, then we submit that a direct action should lie against the health authority or Trust. But, if the agency is reputable and the nurse has been properly instructed but is nonetheless negligent, we would argue that, since the agency nurse has become, albeit temporarily, an integral part of the hospital set-up and is acting under the control of and in the interests of the health authority at the point of the delivery of the treatment, then the health authority, not the agency, should be held vicariously liable.

NHS staff treating private patients

It is not unknown for some beds on a ward or even a whole ward in an NHS hospital to be reserved for private patients under an agreement between the health authority and the private provider. In these circumstances, the agreement will be the determining factor as to who will be ultimately responsible for the negligence of the doctors, etc, treating the private patients (see *Ellis v Wallsend District Hospital* [1990] 2 Med LR 103).

REFERENCES

English case law

(1)   Cassidy v Ministry of Health [1951] 2 KB 343; [1951] 1 All ER 574
See above.

(2)   Roe v Minister of Health [1954] 2 QB 66; [1954] 2 WLR 915; [1954] 2 All ER 131
The claimant was given an injection of Nupercaine at the hospital. The Nupercaine was stored in glass ampoules which were, prior to use, immersed in a phenol solution. Unfortunately, some phenol had leaked into the syringe and the outcome was that the patient became paralysed. At that time, it was not known that phenol could leak into syringes through invisible cracks. The Appeal Court held that there was no negligence; the defendant's conduct had to be judged by the standard of a reasonable person with the knowledge available at the time.

See, also, below, Chapter 5, pp 166, 168.

(3)   Lister v Hesley Hall Ltd [2001] 2 WLR 1311
See above, p 86.

Foreign case law

Australia

Ellis v Wallsend District Hospital [1990] 2 Med LR 103
Per Samuels JA (p 126):

... I would reduce my question to more fustian terms by asking whether in treating the appellant was Dr Chambers engaged in his own business or the hospital's ...?

And (p 127):

Considering the totality of the relationship ... I conclude that it points convincingly to the conclusion that, in treating the appellant, Dr Chambers was engaged in his own business and not the hospital's. He was conducting his independent practice as a neurosurgeon and his relationship was not one of employer and employee.

RULE 3(E)

A legal duty of care is owed to an embryo.

Commentary

What a health carer will want to know here is whether he can be sued by a child born with disabilities resulting from the negligence of the health carer towards the mother. It should be clear from the earlier discussion that a duty is owed to the pregnant mother: she is being treated. But can it be said that a duty is also owed to the embryo/foetus while it is in the mother's womb?

According to the Appeal Court decisions in *Burton v Islington HA* [1993] 4 Med LR 8; *De Martell v Merton and Sutton HA* [1993] 4 Med LR 8, a claim can be brought in respect of the child's injuries, but only after the child has been born. In the *Burton* case, the negligence was said to have occurred during a dilation and curettage operation; in *De Martell,* the child was born with brain damage following a failed forceps delivery and subsequent delivery by a Caesarean section. The courts said two things. First, a duty is owed to an embryo, but it is a contingent one which will only be brought to fruition when the child is born alive; secondly, again because of the contingent nature of the duty, the mother is unable to bring a claim for and on behalf of her unborn baby. As Potts J said in the *Burton* case (p 136):

In my view, the actual damage suffered by the plaintiff, that is being born suffering from physical abnormalities, was 'potential damage which was foreseeable' and was the result of the breach of a 'possible duty'. The fact that the plaintiff was undefined in law and without status ... is neither here nor there.

And later:

However, what had been a 'potential' or 'contingent' duty vested on the birth of the plaintiff ...

Would it make any difference if the claim was for pre-conception negligence? In the Australian case of *X and Y v Pal and Others* [1992] 2 Med LR 195, X became pregnant in January 1973. Unknown to her, she was at that time suffering from syphilis. In March 1973, she consulted P, an obstetrician and gynaecologist, who submitted her to a number of tests but not one for syphilis. In October 1973, she gave birth to a child who later died from gross hydrocephaly and other physical deformities. Reassured in mid-1974 that there was no reason why she could not have another child, she became pregnant in September 1974. The child, Y, was born in March 1975, dysmorphic and mentally retarded. Shortly after the birth, it was discovered that both X and Y were suffering from syphilis. Y's action against P and the other doctors was that her abnormalities stemmed from the failure of all the doctors to submit her mother, X, for syphilis testing. One of the issues which the New South Wales court had to determine was whether a duty was owed to a person conceived *subsequent* to the act/omission alleged to be the breach. At first instance, Sully J held that a duty was not owed; this was reversed on appeal. Clarke JA gave the Appeal Court's approach thus (p 205):

> In principle ... it should be accepted that a person may be subjected to a duty of care to a child who was neither born nor conceived at the time of his careless act or omissions such that he may be found liable in damages to that child. Whether or not that duty will arise depends upon whether there is a relevant relationship between the careless person and the class of person to whom the child is one.

Does a similar duty exist in English law? In *Reay v BNF plc; Hope v BNF plc* [1994] 5 Med LR 1, the claimants brought their actions under the Fatal Accidents Act 1976 and the Law Reform (Miscellaneous Provisions) Act 1934 alleging paternal preconception irradiation (PPI) which, they said, caused mutation in their fathers' sperm which in turn caused a predisposition to leukaemia and/or non-Hodgkin's lymphoma in the next generation. Judgment was given for the defendants, principally on the ground that the claimants had failed, on the balance of probabilities, to show causation. Although French J did not specifically consider the duty issue, he did say *obiter* that, if PPI had been found to cause or materially contribute to the resultant illnesses, he would have found for one of the claimants (the other would still have lost, but not because a duty was not owed).

This would suggest that the court did not have a problem in imposing a legal duty on the defendant. But it does not necessarily follow that a similar duty would or should be imposed on the medical profession. English courts are not renowned for willingly extending the liability of the medical profession; public policy has played a conspicuous part in circumscribing that profession's duties. A closer look at the judgment of Clarke JA in *Pal* reveals that what he did say was that there was no reason *in principle* why a duty could not be owed; but that is some way from saying that a duty will be owed in any given situation. In English law, proximity is only one factor in determining duty situations; reasonable foresight and public policy are other very important issues and it is submitted that public policy will prevent a duty being owed by the medical profession in these circumstances.

Under the Congenital Disabilities (Civil Liability) Act 1976, a statutory duty of care is owed to an embryo. This Act applies to births occurring after the passage of the Act, that is, 22 July 1976; for births before that date, the common law rules apply (see above). According to the Act, the child has a claim if he was born disabled as a result of an occurrence before his birth and someone (other than the mother) was answerable to the child for that occurrence; in such circumstances, the child's disabilities are to be regarded as stemming from the wrongful act of that person (s 1(1)). An occurrence is defined as one which:

- affected either parent of the child in his or her ability to have a normal healthy child (this would cover pre-conception negligence, but causation would still be an important issue); or

- affected the mother during her pregnancy, or affected her or the child in the course of its birth, so that the child was born with disabilities which would not otherwise have been present (s 1(2)).

Linking these provisions with the requirements that the defendant must be liable or would be liable in tort to the parent (if sued in time) (s 1(3)) and that the child must have been born alive (s 4(2)(a)), the following emerge as the conditions for a claim under the 1976 Act:

- the health carer must have owed a duty to the parents which is subsequently broken and would have therefore given rise to liability;
- as a result of that breach, a child is born disabled; and
- the child is born alive (that is, no claim can be brought while the child is in the mother's womb, even if damage to the embryo is ascertainable).

The disability envisaged by the Act is prescribed by s 4(1) and it is 'any deformity, disease or abnormality, including predisposition ... to physical or mental defect in the future'. From this it would appear that the resultant injury must be one which is quantifiable in monetary terms, thus ruling out, after 22 July 1976, a claim by a child for 'wrongful life' – that is, that life with all its disabilities is or would be so awful that the child would be better off dead – since such claims are considered to be impossible to quantify in monetary terms.

As regards 'wrongful life' claims before 22 July 1976, the case of *McKay v Essex AHA* [1982] QB 1166 decided that such claims were not possible in English law. In addition to the argument that such claims were impossible to quantify, the court used both the floodgates argument, that is, to allow this type of claim would simply open the way to many other claims, and the public policy argument, that is, to allow the claim would send out the wrong signal – that English courts preferred no life to a wretched life. None of these arguments is totally convincing. The courts could have drawn a distinction between some existence and a very poor existence; why did it have to be a contrast between a poor existence and no existence at all? Furthermore, how many more cases could be envisaged if the claim in *McKay* was upheld? Whatever the figure, it seems scandalous that a meritorious argument should fail simply because there might exist other meritorious claims. Finally, can it really be said that English law is consistent in preferring some life to no life? What about the cases where lifesaving machines are turned off or nutrition is withheld because the patient's quality of life is said to be very poor?

REFERENCES

English case law

(1)   Burton v Islington HA [1993] 4 Med LR 8
This was an appeal against a decision to strike out the claimant's statement of claim as disclosing no cause of action. The appeal was dismissed. *Per* Dillon LJ (p 11):

> ... I think it would be open to the English courts to apply the civil law maxim directly to the situations we have in these two appeals, and treat the two plaintiffs as lives in being at the times of the events which injured them as they

were later born alive, but it is not necessary to do so directly in view of the effect which the *Montreal Tramways* case has already had on the development of the common law in this field in other common law jurisdictions.

(2) *De Martell v Merton and Sutton HA [1993] 4 Med LR 8*

Here, the defendants were appealing against a finding on a preliminary issue. The issue was whether, assuming the allegations set out in the statement of claim, the defendants were liable in tort to the claimant for the acts and omissions committed before the claimant's birth. The appeal was dismissed.

(3) *Reay v BNF plc; Hope v BNF plc [1994] 5 Med LR 1*

Per French J (p 53):

> As to Vivien, she was brought up until the age of six in Drigg, a village rather over two miles to the south of Seascale. When she was six years old her family moved to and remained in Seascale and Vivien's NHL (non-Hodgkin's lymphoma) was diagnosed when she was living there.

> Thus, she did not satisfy the Gardner study criterion of being born as well as diagnosed in Seascale. Nonetheless, had I been satisfied that NHL was properly to be considered as a form of leukaemia and had I been satisfied that PPI did cause or contribute to the Seascale excess including NHL, I would have found that Vivien Hope was part of the excess and her claim ... would have succeeded ...

(4) *McKay v Essex AHA [1982] QB 1166; [1982] 2 WLR 890; [1982] 2 All ER 771*

The claimant argued that, while in her mother's womb, she was infected with rubella (German measles) as a result of negligence by an employee of the health authority. Specifically the claim was that the doctor, who had taken blood samples and sent them for laboratory analysis, had not informed the mother that she and the unborn baby were infected. Consequently, the claimant was born with severe disabilities. Part of the claim was 'for entry into a life in which her injuries are highly debilitating' (that is, 'wrongful life').

Held: to uphold such a claim would be contrary to public policy. Further, such a claim would be incapable of quantification in damages, as it involved comparing existence with non-existence. Ackner LJ said (p 1188):

> I cannot accept that the common law duty of care to a person can involve, without specific legislation to achieve this end, the legal obligation to that person, whether or not in utero, to terminate his existence. Such a proposition runs wholly contrary to the concept of sanctity of human life.

Per Stephenson LJ (p 1180):

> But, because a doctor can lawfully by statute do to a foetus what he cannot lawfully do to a person who has been born, it does not follow that he is under a legal obligation to a foetus to do it and terminate its life, or that the foetus has a legal right to die.

Foreign case law

Australia

(1) *X and Y v Pal and Others [1992] 3 Med LR 195*

The New South Wales Court of Appeal held that a gynaecologist and an obstetrician owed a duty of care to an unborn child or a child not conceived at the time of the negligence.

Per Clarke JA (p 203):

I would express the position in these terms – A may be liable in damages to B notwithstanding that B had not been conceived at the time A acted carelessly if the following conditions be satisfied:

(a) in all the circumstances A owed a duty to take care to a particular class of persons;

(b) A breached that duty;

(c) B was subsequently born suffering from damage which was causally related to those acts/omissions of A which constituted the breach of duty to the particular class of persons; and

(d) B was a member of the relevant class of persons.

(2) *Lynch v Lynch and Government Insurance Office of NSW [1992] 3 Med LR 62*
A pregnant woman was held to owe a duty of care to her unborn child.

Per Grove J (p 66):

... I would hold that an injury to an infant suffered during the stages of the journey through life between conception and parturition is not an injury to a person devoid of personality ... Nicole's personality was identifiable and recognisable ... Secondly, it does not seem to me to be contrary to any principle that in the class of unborn persons to whom a duty to take reasonable care is undoubtedly owed ... there should be included those children who will be born out of the tortfeasor's own body.

Canada

Montreal Tramways v Leveille (1933) 4 DLR 337
The majority of the Canadian Supreme Court held that when a child, not actually born at the time of an accident, was subsequently born alive and viable, it was clothed with all the rights of action it would have had if actually in existence at the date of the accident to the mother.

RULE 3(F)

New positive duties may be owed by the National Health Service, as a public authority, to a patient under the Human Rights Act 1998 and the European Convention on Human Rights 1950.

Commentary

At the time of writing, speculation is rife that, in the area of health care law, enterprising claimants' lawyers are feverishly plotting to launch novel demands on the already stretched resources of the NHS. In the context of duties and clinical negligence, Art 2 of the European Convention of Human Rights would appear to be the source of such a contention. That Art provides for a right to life. It is arguable that it provides for more than just a right not to have one's life taken away (except in certain well defined circumstances): that it provides positively for a certain quality of life. If this is so, then it follows that claims *may* be brought for:

• not receiving medical treatment for a life threatening condition;
• not receiving different but better and (probably more expensive) treatment, for example, a right to receive new and more effective cancer drugs;
• not receiving specific non-life threatening treatments and/or procedures, for example, the right to receive IVF treatment irrespective of age or background, etc.

Whether any or all or none of these claims will succeed in an English court is debatable. Much will depend on the court's view of the following issues:

• the earlier Strasbourg decisions;
• the nature of the Arts in question, that is, is the Art absolute or qualified?;
• the wording of the Art;
• the doctrine of proportionality.

Further, it could be that the defence of lack of resources may be successfully invoked; but even this point cannot be stated with any degree of conviction. To illustrate, compare what Laws J said in *R v Cambridge District HA ex p B* [1995] 1 FLR 1055, 'But where the question is whether the life of a 10 year old child might be saved, by however slim a chance, the responsible authority ... must do more than toll the bell of tight resources' (p 1065), with what the court said in *Osman v UK* [1999] 1 FLR 193 – a non-medical case – 'such an obligation must be interpreted in a way which does not impose an impossible or disproportionate burden on the authorities ... not every claimed risk to life can entail for the authorities a convention requirement to take operational measures to prevent that risk materialising' (p 223).

It is possible that, over the next two years, many claims may be pursued on the basis that new legal duties have been created by the Convention, but few will succeed; this would mirror the experience of the Scottish courts, where 98% of claims brought have failed (specific figures are not available for medical claims). But it could also mean the NHS spending valuable time and money defending speculative claims; that would be unfortunate. The future looks interesting!

REFERENCES

English case law

(1) R v Cambridge District HA ex p B [1995] 1 FLR 1055, overturned at [1995] 2 All ER 129; [1995] 1 FLR 1066
A health authority declined to fund further treatment for a 10 year old girl on the ground that it was not in her best interests. The cost of the further treatment was estimated to be about £75,000 and, according to the relevant medical advice, it had a 10–20% chance of success. It was held that the health authority was not obliged to provide the treatment. *Per* Sir Thomas Bingham MR (p 1073):

> [Health authorities] cannot provide all the treatments they would like ... difficult and agonising judgments have to be made as to the maximum advantage of the maximum number of patients. That is not a judgment which the court can make.

(2)   *R v North and East Devon HA ex p Coughlan [1999] 8 Lloyd's Rep Med 306*
A disabled woman who was resident in an NHS home was assured that it would be her home for life. The Appeal Court held that a decision to close the home was a breach of Art 8 of the European Convention ('Everyone has the right to respect for ... his home'). See the judgment of Sedley LJ at p 330.

Foreign case law

European Court of Human Rights

(1)   *Ireland v UK (1980) 2 EHRR 25*

(2)   *Osman v UK [1999] 1 FLR 193*
Following a history of harassment by a teacher of one of his pupils and investigations, etc, by the police, the teacher then shot and killed the pupil's father and seriously injured the pupil. The family of the victims brought a negligence claim against the police, which was struck out on the grounds of public policy. The family then alleged, before the European Court of Human Rights, a breach of their human rights, including a breach of Art 2, in that the police had failed to protect the right to life of the deceased father against the threat posed by the teacher.

Held: no breach of Art 2 (see p 93).

(3)   *X v UK (1995) 14 DR 81*

Statutes/statutory instruments

(1)   *Human Rights Act 1998, ss 2, 3, 4, 6, 7, 8 and 9 (see below, Appendix A). See also European Convention on Human Rights 1950, Arts 2, 3, 8, 12 and 14 (see below, Appendix A).*

GENERAL PRACTICE POINTS – RULE 3(A)–(E)

Costs

Clinical negligence claims can be both costly and lengthy. Solicitors should try to inform their client (as far as they are able) of the probable cost of them going to court and the length of time it might take for their claim to conclude. Claimants who are not going to be in receipt of public funding (formerly known as legal aid) have the choice of either funding the case privately (in some cases, if they belong to a professional body such as a trade union, funding may be provided for them), entering into a funding arrangement with their solicitor, known as a 'conditional fee agreement', or pursuing the path of non-litigation. In the latter case, this could mean a complaint to the Health Authority, the General Medical Council, the Health Service Ombudsman or making a complaint under the NHS Complaints Procedure. These non-litigious approaches are invariably quicker and less formal but they will not provide the claimant with financial compensation; what they may offer is an explanation of why things went wrong and, in some circumstances, this explanation may shed light on the negligence issue; for example, the hospital report may indicate that a nurse had queried the doctor's recommended treatment. Many claimants may have sought these explanations before consulting their solicitors; therefore, one of the first tasks of a solicitor at the initial interview is to ascertain whether, following a complaint, the claimant has or is aware of a report of the investigation.

Note: NHS Trusts can refuse to investigate complaints if they are of the view that litigation is pending (see, for example, *R v Canterbury and Thanet District HA, South East Thames RHA ex p F and W* [1994] 5 Med LR 132).

Privately funded cases are relatively rare. For those cases which are going to be funded privately, the client should expect to spend at least £1,500 and £2,500 before discovering whether he has a viable clinical negligence claim. The solicitor will need to obtain the necessary medical records and consider these before instructing a medical expert to prepare a report on whether the treatment received was negligent. A letter of claim would then be sent to the defendant setting out the basis of the claim. The defendant would then investigate the claim and send a letter of response, indicating whether liability was to be admitted or denied. How should the client thereafter decide whether to proceed with his action? This will depend on whether his solicitor takes the view that he is likely to succeed if the matter proceeded to trial. Furthermore, a private client should bear in mind that, even if he is successful, he may not recover all the costs of the action from the losing side. Also, if he does not succeed he will be responsible for his own solicitor's costs together with the reasonable costs of the defendant.

Due to the potential costs consequences of funding a case privately, the possibility of entering a 'conditional fee agreement' with a solicitor is generally a more attractive option. A conditional fee agreement (to be distinguished from a contingency fee agreement, under which the solicitor would receive, as his fee, a proportion of the successful claimant's damages) is a method by which, in the event of a claim succeeding, the claimant's solicitor, by prior agreement with the claimant, can be paid a 'success fee' together with his basic charges (commonly known as profit costs) and disbursements (such as fees for medical reports, etc). A 'success fee' becomes payable because the solicitor has taken a risk when agreeing to enter into a conditional fee agreement with a claimant. There is no guarantee the case will be won and, even if it is, the solicitor will only receive payment at the end of the case. (This can be contrasted with a case which is privately funded: in such a case, the solicitor can require the claimant to make 'payments on account' of costs as the case progresses and deliver interim bills to the claimant.) On this basis, the solicitor running a case on a 'conditional fee' basis can charge an uplift on his costs to reflect the risk the solicitor is taking. The success fee is based on a percentage uplift on the solicitor's basic charges for attending on the claimant, preparing documents, etc. The percentage uplift (known as additional liability) cannot be more than 100%. There are two parts to the success fee. The first part is calculated to reflect the risk that the claimant may not succeed (the riskier the case, the higher the percentage uplift). The accepted calculation for setting the percentage is chances of failure divided by chances of success, multiplied by 100; for example, for a case with a 75% chance of success, the percentage increase would be 33%. The second part reflects the fact there would be a delay in payment of the solicitor's charges and the fact that the solicitor may have been paying for the disbursements on behalf of the claimant. Even if those disbursements are eventually recovered from the opponent, there is still a cost to the firm in doing this. The solicitor may even agree with the client that he will ultimately be responsible for the disbursements if they are not recoverable from the opponent and thus increase the percentage accordingly.

The provisions governing conditional fee agreements are set out in the Access to Justice Act 1999 and the Conditional Fee Agreement Regulations 2000 (SI 2000/692). If the claimant wins the case, he should be able to recover from the defendant his solicitor's basic charges, disbursements and (for conditional fee agreements signed after April 2000 only) the part of the success fee which reflects the risk that the claimant's solicitor is taking. The claimant will be responsible for the part of the success fee that reflects the fact his solicitor has had to wait for payment. If the claim is lost, then, under the agreement, the solicitor will not recover any costs; however, the claimant will still be responsible for his disbursements and the defendant's costs and disbursements. A client can take out insurance when he enters into the conditional fee agreement to meet this liability. The insurance premiums payable are high and may be prohibitive to a claimant. In clinical negligence cases insurers tend to assess on a case by case basis because of the complexities involved in clinical negligence litigation, eg much lower chance of success and the likelihood of high costs. Thus the premium has to be high to cover the high costs risks. If the client is successful then, pursuant to s 29 Access to Justice Act 1999, he may recover from the other party the cost of the insurance premium. If he is unsuccessful he will not be able to recover that premium. However, there are now insurance policies which will, in the event that the case is unsuccessful, not only pay the other party's costs and the client's own solicitor's disbursements but will also cover the premium.

To counteract the problem of the client being unable to pay the insurance premium at the outset, the client can take out a loan through an insurer's approved lender to pay the premium. Both the loan and interest are repayable at the conclusion of the case. If the client is unsuccessful, the insurance policy will pay the loan and interest. If the case is successful, then the client will be responsible for the loan and interest (though see s 29 Access to Justice Act 1999 discussed above).

A basic example of how a conditional fee agreement would work in practice is set out below.

Rob succeeds in his clinical negligence claim and obtains damages from the NHS Trust. He had entered into a conditional fee agreement with his solicitor when the case commenced. His solicitor's basic charges for representing him are £5,000. The agreed additional liability (which is set out in the agreement) is 50%. Remember, however, that there are two elements to the success fee:

(a) The agreed additional liability to reflect the risk the solicitor took in handling the matter in this case is 45%. The success fee which reflects this risk is:

$$£5,000 \times 45\% = £2,250.$$

This is recoverable from the defendant NHS Trust.

Note: the success fee relating to risk can only be recovered from the opponent if he has been informed of the date of the agreement and the claim to which it relates – see Costs Practice Directions 1.2 and 19.4 and CPR r 44.3B(1)(c).

(b) The agreed additional liability to reflect the fact that the solicitor has had to wait for payment of his charges in this case is 5%. The success fee which reflects this delay is:

$$£5,000 \times 5\% = £250.$$

Rob will have to pay this to his solicitor.

The total success fee payable to the solicitor is £2,500. This is divided and paid by the parties as set out above.

Note: Remember that the defendant NHS Trust will also have to pay Rob's solicitor's basic charges and disbursements, and possibly any insurance premium (see s 29 Access to Justice Act 1999) together with the 'risk' element of the success fee.

If a client is in receipt of benefits or receives a low income, eligibility for public funding should be considered. If a client is financially eligible a solicitor can give up to two hours of help and advice under the 'Legal Help' scheme, which is administered by the Legal Services Commission (formerly the Legal Aid Board). During this time, the solicitor should be able to give initial advice to a client and submit an application for legal representation to the Legal Services Commission if the solicitor considers that the case has merit. To receive public funding, a client must be financially eligible. The claim must also satisfy the Legal Services Commission's cost-benefit criteria, which are based on the claim's prospects of success, the likely damages the claimant could receive and likely legal costs that would be incurred in pursuing the case. If the application is successful, a certificate of public funding will be granted to cover 'investigative help' initially. This will allow the solicitor to undertake the work that has to be done before court proceedings are commenced. Investigative help may be refused if the claim is less than £10,000 and it is considered more appropriate to use the NHS complaints procedure. The certificate can then be amended to permit 'full representation' to enable the solicitor to represent the claimant once court proceedings commence.

Note: if the limitation period is about to expire, an emergency application can be made to the Legal Services Commission for funding. See generally s 8 Access to Justice Act 1999 and the Funding Code Parts 1, 2 and 3.

Note: Art 6 of the European Convention on Human Rights states:

6(1) In the determination of his civil rights and obligations or of any criminal charge against him, everyone is entitled to a fair and public hearing within a reasonable time by an independent and impartial tribunal established by law.

Consider the situation where the client was unable to obtain funding for his claim. Would his rights under Art 6 have been violated?

How long will a case take?

With a contentious claim, a claimant could expect to be involved in litigation for two to four years. There can be good reasons for delay, for example, it may be necessary to wait and see how a claimant's condition improves. Also, clinical negligence cases are reliant on expert evidence and delays can occur when waiting for an appointment and waiting for the report to be prepared. There had been concern, however, that litigation was too lengthy, which could be frustrating to the claimant. Under the Civil Procedure Rules 1998, which govern claims once court proceedings are issued, judges will take an active approach in handling cases to ensure that unnecessary delay does not occur. The judges have case management powers to help them further the court's overriding objective of enabling it to deal with cases justly, which includes ensuring that the case is dealt with expeditiously and fairly (CPR r 1.1). Judges will set timetables to be complied with.

Access to medical records

There are a number of statutory provisions that allow the patient access to his own health records. First, there is the Access to Personal Files Act 1987 and the Access to Medical Reports Act 1988, which, combined, allow the patient sight of his medical records in certain, well defined circumstances, for example, if the report had been prepared for life insurance or employment purposes. Until March 2000, the main statutory provision was the Access to Health Records Act 1991, which permitted patients access to all their health records post-November 1991; there was, however, no statutory right to see anything that was written prior to that date. Access was denied where there was a genuine risk to the physical or mental health of either the applicant or a third party. This Act has now been partly repealed (except in relation to applications for manual health records by the personal representatives of dead patients and for applications for records made before 1 March 2000) and replaced by the Data Protection Act 1998. This Act now covers paper as well as computerised health records. See, also, the Data Protection (Subject Access Modification) Health Order 2000 (SI 2000/413).

The Act derives from a European Directive which states its objective as being 'to protect the fundamental rights and freedoms of natural persons, and in particular their right to privacy with respect to the processing of personal data'. The Act sets out eight Data Protection principles which, subject to certain specified exceptions (for example, in relation to crime and national security), all information relating to or capable of identifying a living individual (known as personal data) must be processed fairly, lawfully, accurately and securely. The term 'processing' includes disclosure and use lawfully in accordance with the requirements of the common law. Patient records come within the definition of sensitive personal data, and to disclose (process) them fairly, the data controller (GP/Trust/health authority) must fulfil one of the conditions in Sched 2 together with one condition in Sched 3 to the Act, as amended by the Data Protection (Processing of Sensitive Personal Data) Order 2000 (SI 2000/417). One example of where disclosure may be permitted is where the patient gives explicit consent, but others include:

- where processing or disclosure is required by law or in legal proceedings;
- to protect the vital interests of the subject;
- for medical purposes;
- for the detection or prevention of crime in the public interest;
- for insurance or pension purposes;
- for research purposes.

The exception 'for medical purposes' is to be given a wide interpretation and includes preventative medicine, medical research and the management of healthcare services. It follows that almost any activity involving the use and disclosure of medical records falls within the scope of this condition and, further, the information may be put to several uses without the patient's consent, either explicit or implied. Hence, should a patient allege the unlawful use of personal information about himself, the data controller will invariably rely on the defence that the processing was necessary for medical purposes.

The Data Protection Act establishes the right of every individual (subject to stated exceptions) to require the relevant data controller to confirm the nature and extent of the data being held and the recipients to whom they are or may be disclosed. Any person may also be entitled to a copy of the information in an intelligible form. When a request for records is made under the Data Protection Act, the records must be supplied within 40 days of the request. A request should generally only be refused where the data controller is of the opinion that such disclosure is likely to cause serious harm to the mental or physical health of the patient or any other person. The data controller may demand a fee for the access or inspection of the records; see the Data Protection (Subject Access Fees and Miscellaneous Provisions) Regulations 2000 (SI 2000/191). For example, a fee of £10 is charged if the patient simply wishes to inspect their record, and this rises to £50 if a copy is required (note that this will fall to £10 after 24 October 2001). See, also, *Hubble v Peterborough Hospital NHS Trust*, 21 March 2001, MLC 0347, at p 103. Where the processing of the data subject's personal data causes unwarranted and substantial damage or distress, he is entitled to send a notice to the data controller requiring him to cease such processing. The data controller must respond within 21 days and either send the patient a written notice that he has compiled with the request or the reasons why he feels the data's subject request to be unjustified. In more serious cases, the patient can seek an enforcement notice, prosecution and fine for unlawfully obtaining or selling personal data.

As a final point, it is worthwhile mentioning the effect of Art 8 of the European Convention on Human Rights 1950 (see Appendix A). It may be that, at present, given that the Data Protection Act 1998 derives from a European Directive, the Act, together with the common law, acknowledges the duty of confidentiality as a fundamental right and is entirely compatible with the Convention. Note, however, that the Secretary of State for Health plans to give himself powers to override the common law and extend the range of circumstances in which medical records can be disclosed, both within and outside the NHS. We wait to see what these new powers will be and whether they are found to be in violation of Art 8.

The Clinical Negligence Pre-Action Protocol (set out in Appendix D) sets out various steps that the parties should take before court proceedings are issued. It also sets out various 'good practice commitments', covering various areas, including medical records. It is stated that health care providers ought to establish efficient and effective systems of recording and storing patient records, notes, diagnostic reports and X-rays, and also retain these in accordance with Department of Health guidance.

The Protocol sets out a protocol for obtaining hospital medical records at Annex B. A standardised form for obtaining hospital medical records has been produced in order to standardise the disclosure of medical records. The use of this form is voluntary, however; it is intended to save time and costs. The form is used when applying for a patient's hospital records when court proceedings are contemplated (either in a clinical negligence claim or in other court proceedings). The form requests the following general information:

- the name of the patient;
- the current address of the patient and the address at the start of treatment;
- date of birth (and date of death, if appropriate);
- hospital reference number and national insurance number (if available);
- the department where treatment was received;
- the name(s) of the consultant(s) at the hospital in charge of the treatment;
- whether treatment at the hospital was private or NHS, wholly or in part;
- a description of the treatment received with approximate dates.

If the application is made because a claim is considered against the hospital, the following information should be given:

- the likely nature of the claim;
- the grounds for the claim;
- approximate dates of the events involved.

If the patient is pursuing an action against someone else, the patient should give the names of the proposed defendants and give details of the claim and action number (if appropriate).

Copy records should be provided by the healthcare provider within 40 days of the request. If there will be a difficulty in complying with this time limit, this should be explained and details of what is being done to resolve the problem should be given. The patient or their solicitor can apply to the court for an order for pre-action disclosure if the health care provider does not provide the records within 40 days. The court can impose costs sanctions where there has been unreasonable delay in providing records.

There are certain quality standards, which should be met by healthcare providers when copying records:

- all documents should be legible and complete;
- documents larger than A4, for example ITU charts, should be reproduced in A3 or reduced to A4 if they can still be read;
- documents should only be copied on one side of paper, unless the original document is two sided;
- documents should not be shuffled or bound unnecessarily and holes should not be made in the copied papers.

Privilege

The defendant in a clinical negligence action may claim privilege in respect of some or all of the documents sought. According to CPR r 31.19, he may refuse to hand over documents on the ground that they are privileged communications, that is, that the documents represented communication(s) between the defendants (as clients) and their legal representatives. In *Waugh v British Railways Board* [1980] AC 521, the House of Lords, in a non-medical case, ruled that, where the prepared document had two objectives (to communicate with solicitors and to improve matters internally), then the document's main purpose had to be the communication to the solicitor for the privilege to exist. If the main purpose was not that but rather to improve matters within the organisation in question, as in *Lask v Gloucester HA* (1985) *The Times*, 13 December, the privilege will not attach; furthermore, the court showed in that case that it was prepared to go behind the veil of privilege to examine the true purpose of the communications. Consequently, patients could feel quietly confident about the way in which the law on privilege was being interpreted. But in *Lee v SW Thames RHA* [1985] 1 WLR 845, the Appeal Court handed down a ruling which, in some respects, gave the initiative back to the defendants. There, a claimant, who was badly burnt, was taken to a hospital run by Health Authority A. On the same day, he was transferred to the burns unit of a hospital run by Health Authority B. After he developed respiratory problems, he was put on a respirator and sent back to the first hospital in an ambulance whose service was in the control of Health Authority C. Three days later, he was found to have been severely brain damaged, very likely through a lack of oxygen when he was in the ambulance. The claim was brought against Health Authority C, but pre-action discovery was sought from all three health authorities. It soon became evident that one vital piece of evidence was a memorandum which had been prepared by the ambulance crew at the request of Health Authority B in the event of litigation against them; Health Authority C (the defendants) claimed privilege for the memorandum. In effect, what Health Authority C was claiming was the privilege of Health Authority B, since at no time was it ever suggested that the memorandum in question was prepared for impending litigation against Health Authority C. The Court of Appeal held that privilege did exist. It ruled that the action against Health Authority C arose out of the same set of circumstances which made Health Authority B a likely defendant; it went on to argue that, to say evidence was privileged if the action was against Health Authority B but not if the action was against Health Authority C, would be to defeat the whole purpose of privileged communications. For the claimant this was a harsh decision; the real evidence as to what may have caused the brain damage was not available and so the decision about whether to bring an action had to depend on less weighty evidence.

Public interest immunity

Claimants may also find themselves confronting the public interest immunity argument, which says that documents, if revealed, may prove embarrassing for the defendants or damaging to the public interest. The Department of Health unsuccessfully raised this defence in *Re HIV Haemophiliac Litigation* (1990) 140 NLJ 1349 (see, also, below, Chapter 5, p 168). There, the claimants, who had been infected with the AIDS virus as a result of being treated with contaminated blood from the US, sought disclosure of various documents relating to the policy of self-sufficiency in blood products. But they were met with the public interest defence: that to reveal the information would hinder the proper functioning of the National Blood Transfusion Service and the need for effective, candid advice between ministers and their advisers. The Court of Appeal disagreed and ordered disclosure, arguing that the public interest in having a full, fair trial overrode the Department's claim for secrecy.

Who to sue?

Practitioners for claimants should always consider suing an employing health authority in tort, whether on the ground of vicarious liability or on the ground that the authority breached its direct duty to provide reasonable care for the patient. In such circumstances, it is inadvisable to sue the individual health carer additionally, if only because any award of damages may go unsatisfied: one could go further and advise that the health carer's name should not even be added as a second defendant. But, in the situation where there is no employing health authority, then the action must be against the GP or locum personally.

Form of action

Whenever the opportunity presents itself, lawyers for private patients should consider using contract rather than tort as the form of action. Although the limitation period will be the same, namely, three years if the claim is for a breach of contract resulting in personal injuries, yet, if the claim is for damages for loss of earnings following a failed sterilisation, then it may be possible to argue that the limitation period should be six years. However, this has now been put in doubt following the decision in *Walkin v South Manchester HA* [1996] 7 Med LR 211 (see below, Chapter 4, p 106). Also, in a contractual claim, the terms of the agreement dominate and the problems associated with the *Bolam* rule will be largely ignored.

REFERENCES

English case law

(1) R v Canterbury Thanet DHA, SE Thames RHA ex p F and W [1994] 5 Med LR 132
See p 95. NHS Trusts may refuse to investigate complaints if they are of the view that litigation is pending. The court took the view that medical staff could be less likely to co-operate in the investigation of complaints.

(2) R v Mid-Glamorgan FHSA and Another ex p Martin [1995] 1 WLR 110; [1994] 5 Med LR 383
The respondents held the medical records of the appellant, which included reports on his psychiatric behaviour. Numerous requests had been made by the appellant to see his records but, for a variety of reasons, they were not released. The appellant then sought judicial review of the respondent's decision but both Popplewell J and the Appeal Court held that:

- he had no common law right to see his records; and
- there had been no breach of Art 8 of the European Convention for the Protection of Human Rights and Fundamental Freedoms. (Art 8 says, 'Everyone has the right to respect for his private and family life, his home and his correspondence'.)

(3)   Hall v Wandsworth HA (1985) 129 SJ 188

Where the claimant started proceedings for the production of documents in a personal injury case, costs could be awarded against the defendant where the defendant had, without excuse, delayed the production of the documents.

(4)   Hubble v Peterborough Hospital NHS Trust (2001) not yet reported, 21 March, MLC 0347

The claimant's solicitors had requested copies of her medical records from the defendant and had accepted responsibility for the defendant's fees as set out within the meaning of the Data Protection Act 1998. The defendant had demanded a fixed fee of £50 and an additional charge for copying X-rays and CTG traces.

Held: X-rays were part of the health records; they consisted of and/or included information about the individual's physical health or condition at that time and, therefore, the defendant was obliged to provide copies of the claimant's health records, including X-rays, upon payment only of a maximum fee of £50.

(5)   Waugh v British Rlys Board [1979] 3 WLR 150; [1980] AC 521

Following an accident which resulted in the death of the claimant's husband, the Board conducted an internal enquiry and produced a report. The report was headed, 'Further information of the Board's solicitors'. However, the affidavit produced by the Board showed that the report had two objectives: to establish the cause of the accident (and consequently take the necessary safety measures to avoid future accidents) and to enable the solicitors to advise in the likelihood of litigation.

Held: the House of Lords ruled that a document would only be privileged if the purpose of its preparation was that it would be submitted to the legal adviser for advice. Since, on the evidence, that was not the purpose of this report, the claim for privilege failed.

(6)   Lask v Gloucester HA (1985) The Times, 13 December

The Appeal Court held that, where NHS circulars require health authorities to prepare confidential accident reports, both for the use of solicitors in the event of litigation and to prevent a repetition of the accidents, those reports would not attract legal professional privilege.

(7)   Lee v SW Thames RHA [1985] 2 All ER 385

Per Lord Donaldson MR (p 389):

... we consider that the appeal has to be decided by reference to principle rather than authority. The principle is that the defendant shall be free to seek evidence without being obliged to disclose the result of his researches to his opponent. Hillingdon can certainly waive its rights and, were it to do so, the memorandum would clearly be disclosable by SW Thames. However, it has not done so. Furthermore, it would, we think, be impossible to seek in this case to impose a term that disclosure should take place after all proceedings against Hillingdon are terminated or abandoned. If Hillingdon is to be sued as well as SW Thames, the actions must be tried together. SW Thames and their employees have no rights as witnesses, but we can see no way of protecting the rights of Hillingdon as potential defendants if disclosure is ordered against SW Thames.

(8) Re HIV Haemophiliac Litigation (1990) 140 NLJ 1349
The Appeal Court held that, even if the National Health Service Act 1977 did not confer a right to claim damages, a private individual could, on the same facts, sue in negligence.

(9) Walkin v South Manchester HA [1996] 7 Med LR 211
See below, Chapter 4, p 90.

(10) Bolam v Friern HMC [1957] 1 WLR 582; [1957] 2 All ER 118
See below, Chapter 5, p 155.

Foreign case law

Australia

(1) Breen v Williams [1995] 6 Med LR 385
The New South Wales Appeal Court held that a patient had no (common law) right to inspect or obtain access to her medical files; nor did she have any proprietary rights over the contents of her file. Further, the court refused to imply a term into the contract to the effect that she had such a right.

Statutes/statutory instruments/international Conventions

(1) Sections 27 and 29 Access to Justice Act 1999
See below, Appendix A.

(2) Conditional Fee Agreement Regulations 2000 (SI 2000/692)
See below, Appendix B.

(3) Section 8 Access to Justice Act 1999
See Appendix A.

(4) Access to Personal Files Act 1987
See above, p 98.

(5) Access to Medical Reports Act 1988
See below, Appendix A.

(6) Access to Health Records Act 1990
See above, p 98.

(7) Data Protection Act 1998
See below, Appendix A.

(8) Data Protection (Subject Access Modification) Health Order 2000 (SI 2000/413)
See above, p 98.

(9) Data Protection (Processing of Sensitive Personal Data) Order 2000 (SI 2000/417)
See above, p 98.

(10) Data Protection (Subject Access Fees and Miscellaneous Provisions) Regulations 2000 (SI 2000/191)
See above, p 99.

(11) Article 8, European Convention on Human Rights 1950
See below, Appendix A.

CHAPTER 4

LIMITATION

RULE 4(A)

A clinical negligence claim must be commenced within three years of:
- **the date on which the cause of action accrued; or**
- **if later, the date of knowledge of the existence of the cause of action.**

Commentary

Since a clinical negligence claim is a claim normally involving personal injuries or death, it falls within ss 11–14 of the Limitation Act 1980. The court has a discretion to extend this three year period by virtue of s 33 of the Act (this is considered below, at Rule 4(B)). Section 11 covers personal injury actions, while s 12 deals with fatal accidents (see below, p 131 *et seq* for commentary on this section). Only by issuing proceedings will time cease to run; therefore, the issue of proceedings and not the service must be within the limitation period, although the proceedings must be served within four months of issue (see CPR r 7.5(2), PD 7 para 5.1 and p 148 *et seq*).

The three year period applies to personal injury actions resulting from negligence, nuisance, breach of contract (for example, private patients) or breach of the duty of care, but not to those injuries resulting from a deliberate assault. In *Stubbings v Webb* [1993] AC 498, the claimant sued in respect of psychiatric harm which she had suffered as a result of sexual and physical abuse during childhood. The court held that the three year period did not apply because she had been injured deliberately; her case should have been pleaded as a battery and consequently she had six years to commence the action (see, further, s 2 of the Act). This case may have considerable implications for a claim brought against a doctor for battery. If he proceeds to carry out treatment without the consent of the patient, conceivably he comes within the ambit of the decision in *Stubbings*; after all, his conduct can be said to be intentional. Hence, our advice is that, when the solicitor is faced with a potential claim where the allegation is that the patient did not consent to the procedure, the claim should be framed as a claim in trespass and not in negligence. This approach would also extend to those situations where the patient has consented to the treatment but, for some reason, the doctor goes beyond the ambit of the consent, for example, removing an ovary when he suspects cancer rather than simply performing a diagnostic operation. In this example, the doctor's defence may be that it was implied in the patient's consent that he would remove the ovary if he thought it necessary. The patient may counter this by saying that the information about the possibility of removal of her ovaries was not disclosed to her, in which case a claim could be brought in negligence, the doctor having breached his standard of care in relation to disclosure of information. However, a claim may also be brought in trespass because the patient did not consent to the procedure. Solicitors should always take the trespass option where there is a choice, not only to take advantage of the decision in *Stubbings*, but also to avoid the often insurmountable problems posed by the *Bolam* and causation rules; see, further, below, Chapters 5 and 6.

Personal injuries are defined by s 38(1) as being 'any disease and any impairment of a person's physical or mental condition'. It had been thought that, where the claim was limited to financial losses, the three year period would not apply; however, following the decision in *Walkin v S Manchester HA* [1996] 7 Med LR 211, this is not the case. The negligence claim was for a failed sterilisation and was limited to financial losses consequent on the treatment; no compensation was sought for pain, suffering or inconvenience. The court held that this was a claim for personal injuries and was therefore statute barred. Potter J argued that, unlike a failed vasectomy, a failed sterilisation involves the mother suffering an unwanted birth and that brought it within the ambit of s 11; Mrs Walkin had simply abandoned her claim for personal injuries following the birth but was still claiming a loss consequent on that injury. It may seem strange to view pregnancy as an injury. Not all of the judges in the subsequent Court of Appeal hearing took the view that it was; Auld LJ held that the distinction made by Potter J between a vasectomy and a sterilisation was artificial – in each case the personal injury was the unwanted pregnancy. Roch LJ had, he confessed, great difficulty in appreciating a normal conception and pregnancy as a disease or impairment when the only reasons for the pregnancy being unwanted were purely financial ones. All their Lordships agreed, however, that because the pregnancy was unwanted the woman had been injured. This must be right, and it is perhaps worth noting that, as every pregnancy carries recognised risks, then where the woman suffers an unwanted pregnancy, clearly she has been injured. In any event, it is true to say that whilst the claimant may not have specifically claimed damages for personal injuries, the damages she was claiming were as a consequence of the injury. The Appeal Court therefore held that the cause of action arose on the unwanted conception, though time would not begin to run until the woman had knowledge of the pregnancy.

Walkin was recently considered in the case of *Shade v The Compton Partnership* [2000] PNLR 218. In *Shade,* the claimant sued his former solicitors for professional negligence and included a claim for psychological distress and bodily harm. The action was commenced against the defendants more than three years but less than six years after the cause of action arose. The defendants argued that, as the claimant was claiming personal injuries, then the three year limit applied and hence the claim was now statute barred. The Court of Appeal was therefore invited to consider whether a claim for personal injury could be severed from the claimant's other claim for economic loss, thereby leaving the claimant to pursue a claim for economic loss alone. It was held that it could. In reaching this decision, the court considered the following points. First, that litigants should not be allowed to amend existing proceedings to bring claims which they would not now be allowed to bring in fresh proceedings because those claims were now statute barred. In *Shade,* the claimant, if he so desired, could have simply brought new proceedings omitting his claim for personal injuries as he was still within the limitation period of six years. Secondly, the court distinguished the decision in *Walkin* from the present case. The court stressed that in *Walkin* the whole claim arose solely from the effect of the unsuccessful medical treatment. The fact that a second writ was issued claiming only economic loss did not alter the fact that *Walkin* was really a claim for personal injuries. In *Shade*, however, the claimant's claim for psychological injury did not make up a large part of the damages and therefore the court held that this part of the claim could be struck out and the remainder of the claim allowed to continue. In reaching this decision, Walker LJ considered that there might be three different types of cases which might pose a problem similar to that faced in *Shade*. The first is a case where the claimant claims a large amount of damages for economic loss plus an insignificant amount for the cost of a psychiatric consultation and accompanying medication. In that scenario, it would be inconceivable that the limitation period would not be six years. In the second scenario, the *Walkin* type case, where the claimant has suffered physical injury but is also claiming economic loss, since the claim for economic loss was directly attributable to the injury, the three year rule would apply. The *Shade* case, in Walker LJ's opinion, was an example of the third scenario, in that it fell midway between these two extremes. However, it was possible for the personal injury element of the claim to be struck out, leaving the remainder of the claim to proceed in accordance with the given directions for trial. Further, as the claim for economic loss did not flow from any alleged personal injuries caused by the defendant (unlike *Walkin*), this again suggested that this part of the claim was severable and the remainder of the claim for economic loss should be permitted to proceed.

It is suggested that this analysis is correct. In reality, the claim in *Shade* consisted of, in the main, a professional negligence case against the claimant's former solicitors with the claim for psychological distress simply 'tacked on'; each claim was, however, quite distinct from the other. In *Walkin*, all heads of the claim were inexorably bound up with each other and the claim for economic loss would not have been made but for the claim for personal injuries.

Finally, on the theme of what is a personal injury within the context of s 11, see the decision in *Norman v Ali and Another, Norman v Aziz* (1999) unreported, 13 December, CA. In this case, the claimant had sustained personal injuries as a result of the negligent driving of the first defendant. There was an unresolved question as to whether the first defendant had been insured to drive the car, which was owned by Mr Aziz. The claimant notified the Motor Insurance Bureau of her claim, who then requested her to join in Mr Aziz in the proceedings on the grounds that he, as the vehicle owner, permitted uninsured driving. The claimant had subsequently obtained a declaration that the limitation period was six years on the grounds that the vehicle owner did not actually cause the personal injuries but, rather, created a situation in which the injured person could claim damages. Otton LJ, however, held that it was unnecessary that the breach of duty caused the personal injury in order to bring the claim within the three year rule – what was important was that the damages claimed for the breach of duty should consist of, or include, damages for personal injury. Hence the three year rule applied.

(See, also, *Howe v David Brown Tractors (Retail) Ltd (Rustons Engineering Co Ltd; Third Party)* [1991] 4 All ER 30; *Pattison v Hobbs* (1985) *The Times*, 11 November; and *Whiteford v Hunter* [1950] WN 553.)

Accrual of the cause of action

Normally in a clinical negligence claim this will be fairly uncontroversial: it will arise when the damage occurs; but the damage must not fall within the *de minimis* rule, that is, trivial damage will be ignored. However, in some cases the damage might occur some time after the breach, for example, in relation to industrial deafness. In such a case, provided that the breach is a continuing one, the court will generally find that a new cause of action accrues each time the damage reoccurs as a result of a wrongful act. In any event, in most claims this point is irrelevant, as time will inevitably begin when the claimant has knowledge.

Date of knowledge

Under s 11(4), time begins to run from the date of knowledge as defined by s 14(1) and (3). Essentially, the claimant is deemed to have knowledge when he has knowledge of the following facts (s 14(1)):

- that the injury in question was significant; and
- that the injury was attributable in whole or in part to the act or omission which is alleged to constitute negligence, nuisance or breach of duty; and
- the identity of the defendant; and
- if it is alleged that the act or omission was that of a person other than the defendant, the identity of that person and the additional facts supporting the bringing of an action against the defendant; and
- knowledge that any acts or omissions did or did not, as a matter of law, involve negligence, nuisance or breach of duty is irrelevant.

By virtue of s 14(3), knowledge includes constructive knowledge. This means that the claimant is deemed to have knowledge from the facts which he might reasonably be expected to acquire:

- from facts observable or ascertainable by him; or
- from facts ascertainable by him with the help of medical or other appropriate expert advice which it is reasonable for him to seek,

but a person shall not be fixed under this sub-section with knowledge of a fact ascertainable only with the help of expert advice so long as he has taken all reasonable steps to obtain (and, where appropriate, to act on) that advice.

The significance of the injury (s 14(1)(a), (2))

The injury will be thought of as significant if the particular claimant would have thought it so serious as to justify instituting proceedings for damages against a defendant who did not dispute liability and was able to satisfy a judgment. Whether or not the claimant had other personal reasons for not commencing proceedings is irrelevant (although the court may invoke s 33: see Rule 4(B), p 129). The court is only concerned with whether 'the particular claimant', not some hypothetical claimant, thought it reasonable to sue. In *Stephen v Riverside HA* [1990] 1 Med LR 261, the claimant did not sue in respect of her erythema and anxiety. She began the proceedings only when she knew that the overdose of radiation she had been subjected to could cause cancer. The court held that this was reasonable.

As most injuries will be deemed to be significant in monetary terms, the claimant should begin the proceedings as soon as he suspects the injury. Even if a more serious injury should develop later, time begins to run from the date of the lesser injury. Similarly, if the claimant knows there is a risk of deterioration, a claim should be brought in respect of that risk even though it may not yet have materialised. In the case of injuries caused by the side effects of drugs, time will not start to run until the claimant knows that the side effects are dangerous and not just an accepted consequence of using the drug (see *Nash v Eli Lilly* [1992] 3 Med LR 353). In *Dobbie v Medway HA* [1994] 5 Med LR 160 (discussed in detail at p 110), the court reiterated that 'significance' referred to the *quantum* of the claim and not the claimant's belief as to its cause. The Master of the Rolls said (p 165):

> Time does not run against a claimant, even if he is aware of the injury, if he would have reasonably have considered it insufficiently serious to justify proceedings against an acquiescent and credit-worthy defendant if (in other words) he would reasonably have accepted it as a fact of life or not worth bothering about. It is otherwise if the injury is reasonably to be considered as sufficiently serious within the statutory definition: time then runs (subject to the requirement of attributability) even if the claimant believes the injury normal or properly caused.

Finally, in *Brigg v Pitt Payne and Lias* [1999] 1 Lloyd's Rep Med 1, the Court of Appeal dismissed the claimant's argument that, in order for him to know that he had suffered a significant injury, a benefit-deficit equation had to be applied. In *Brigg*, it was argued that the claimant only had to know that the undesirable side effects from which he was suffering were unacceptable, that is, that they were not simply those side effects which a patient would tolerate because of the supposed benefit of the drugs.

That the injury was caused by the defendant's act or omission (s 14(1)(b), (3))

There are two points to consider here:

(a) Does the claimant have the degree of knowledge to satisfy s 14(1)(b) (*actual knowledge*)?

(b) Failing that, will the court deem that the claimant had the requisite constructive knowledge as required by s 14(3) (*constructive knowledge*)?

Actual knowledge

(i) The first point which should be emphasised is, as a matter of law, knowledge that the acts or omissions did or did not constitute negligence, nuisance or breach of duty is irrelevant, as stated in s 14 of the Act. The claimant must merely have knowledge that the defendant's acts might have caused his injuries. Furthermore, according to *Nash v Eli Lilly* [1992] 3 Med LR 353, the court said that knowledge meant more than just 'some vague and generalised conduct', for example, knowing that something had gone wrong as a result of an operation at a hospital would not amount to knowledge under s 14(1). Rather, knowledge referred to some specific factor, as Purchas LJ put it (p 368):

What is required is knowledge of the essence of the act or omission to which the injury is attributable.

On the other hand, it does not mean that the claimant is required to have knowledge of every specific act or omission contained within the statement of claim. In *Nash*, a case which concerned claims against the manufacturers of the drug Opren, the crucial acts/omissions were:

(a) providing for the use of patients a drug which was unsafe, in that it was capable of causing persistent photosensitivity in those patients; and/or

(b) failing to discover that that was the case so as to properly protect those patients (see Hidden J at [1991] 2 Med LR 183).

The appeal court held that (a) and (b) above were all that the claimant was required to know. She was not required to know, for example, that the marketing of an unsafe drug was due to a lack of care in testing or in informing the medical profession about it. *Nash* was applied in the important case of *Broadley v Guy Clapham & Co* [1993] 4 Med LR 328. In *Broadley*, the claimant underwent an operation in 1980 to remove a foreign body from her knee. For seven months after the operation she could only walk with the aid of two sticks, as she was suffering from foot drop. The claimant's claim was against her solicitor for failing to issue proceedings within the limitation period (see, further, below, p 122). The court held that s 14(1) required it to look at the way the claimant put her case and whether she had broad knowledge of the facts on which the complaint was based. As such, the claimant must have realised that something was wrong by virtue of the fact that she realised she could not walk unaided seven months after the operation. A reasonable person in her position should have sought further legal and medical advice, and that would bring her within the ambit of constructive knowledge under s 14(3). The claimant, however, did not have sufficient knowledge to fall within s 14(1). The court, applying *Nash*, stated that she would have had to have *'knowledge of the essence of the act or omission to which the injury is attributable'* ([1993] 4 Med LR 328, p 334, and see *Nash*, p 368). This, of course, begs the question: what is meant by the 'essence of the act' and 'attributable'? In this case, the court held that the essence of the claimant's complaint was that her nerve was damaged during the course of her operation.

In *Dobbie v Medway HA* [1994] 5 Med LR 160, the claimant claimed damages for an operation negligently performed in 1973. The claimant underwent a lumpectomy; however, the surgeon went on to remove her whole breast, a procedure to which she had not consented. The growth was later discovered to be benign and the claimant was told by the surgeon and a nurse that she was fortunate that the growth had not proved to be malignant. She went on to suffer considerable psychiatric stress in reaction to the unnecessary removal of her breast. She did not, however, progress her claim until 1988, when she heard of a similar case where a woman successfully sued. The court ruled, however, that the claim was statute barred. At [1994] 5 Med LR 160, p 166, *per* Beldam LJ:

The personal injury on which the claimant seeks to found her claim is the removal of her breast and the psychological and physical harm which followed. She knew of this injury within hours, days or months of the operation and she at all times considered it to be significant. She knew from the beginning that this personal injury was capable of being attributed to, or more bluntly, was the clear and direct result of an act or omission of the health authority. What she did not appreciate until later was that the health authority's act or omission was (arguably) negligent or blameworthy. But her want of that knowledge did not stop time beginning to run.

Dobbie was then considered in the Lloyd's underwriters case of *Hallam-Eames and Others v Merrett* [1996] 7 Med LR 122. The Court of Appeal said that *Dobbie* had been misinterpreted. Hoffmann LJ said that the claimant must:

> have known the facts which can fairly be described as constituting the negligence of which he complains. It may be that knowledge of such facts will also serve to bring home to him the fact that the defendant has been negligent or at fault. But that is not in itself a reason for saying that he need not have known them [p 125].

In *Hallam-Eames*, the court was at pains to point out that it was not enough for Mrs Dobbie to know that her breast had been removed; rather, it was a healthy breast that had been removed. Hoffmann LJ said:

> If all that was necessary was that a claimant should have known that the damage was attributable to an act or omission of the defendant, the statute would have said so. Instead, it speaks of the damage being attributable to 'the act or omission which is alleged to constitute negligence'. In other words, the act or omission of which the claimant must have knowledge must be that which is casually relevant for the purposes of an allegation of negligence [p 125].

Continuing in his review of *Broadley* and *Dobbie*, he said:

> If one asks what is the principle of common sense on which one would identify Mrs Dobbie's complaint as the removal of a healthy breast rather than simply the removal of a breast, it is that the additional fact is necessary to make the act something of which she would *prima facie* seem entitled to complain [p 126].

Similarly, Mrs Broadley's complaint was that the surgeon had caused damage to her foot when he was supposed to be treating her knee. It is these additional facts – namely the removal of a healthy breast in *Dobbie* and the damage to a knee instead of a foot – which gave the claimant knowledge.

Recently, in *Harrild v MOD, Robert Jones, Agnes Hunt and Orthopaedic and District Hospitals NHS Trust* [2001] 3 Lloyd's Rep Med 117, Toulson J, applying *Hallam-Eames*, held that the claimant did not have knowledge until he was informed of certain medical knowledge which confirmed his suspicions. Although this claimant believed that he should have undergone an ECG following a possible heart attack, it was only when his suspicions were confirmed by his sister, a cardiac nurse, that he could be deemed to have knowledge. Again, as in *Broadley* and *Dobbie*, it is only when the claimant knows that something should or should not have been done that the courts will start the limitation clock ticking.

Sometimes, the question of whether the claimant knew that his injuries were attributable to the defendant's conduct is not too difficult to determine. In *Brigg v Pitt Payne and Lias* [1999] 1 Lloyd's Rep Med 1, the Court of Appeal held that, once this particular claimant knew that the side effects he was suffering were caused by valium, then it was reasonable for him to infer that it was the doctors who had prescribed it who were indeed responsible for his condition.

(ii) Also, the knowledge required will depend on the claimant's state of mind, his ability to understand the information and the strength of his belief. To quote from Purchas LJ, again in the *Nash* case (p 365):

> Whether or not a state of mind for this purpose is properly to be treated by the court as knowledge seems to us to depend, in the first place, upon the nature of the information the claimant received, the extent to which he pays attention to the information as affecting him, and his capacity to understand it ... The court must assess the intelligence of the claimant; consider and assess his assertions as to how he regarded such information as he had; and determine whether he had knowledge of the facts by reason of his understanding of the information.

The court then went on to state that in some cases the claimant would not acquire knowledge until he had received expert advice:

> If it appears that a claimant, while believing that his injury is attributable to the act or omission of the defendant, realises that his belief requires expert confirmation before he acquires such a degree of certainty of belief as amounts to knowledge, then he will not have knowledge until that confirmation is obtained [*per* Purchas LJ, p 366].

See, further, on this point *Khan v Ainslie* [1993] 4 Med LR 319, *Baig v City and Hackney HA* [1994] 5 Med LR 221 and *Forbes v Wandsworth HA* [1996] 7 Med LR 175.

The latter case is of particular importance. Proceedings were issued 10 years after the allegedly negligent treatment. The complaint was that, had the defendant operated sooner, the claimant's leg need not have been amputated. At first instance, it was held that the claimant had neither actual nor constructive knowledge until he received an expert report. The Court of Appeal agreed that the claimant did not have actual knowledge until he received the expert report but held that he had constructive knowledge. This is discussed below, p 115 and see, further, p 124. The case makes some useful points for the claimant so far as actual knowledge is concerned. Discussing knowledge of an omission, Stuart-Smith LJ said that the claimant could not know there has been an omission until he was aware that there had been 'a lost opportunity to prevent the injury which he later suffered'. Stuart-Smith went on to say (p 185):

> The fact that in such cases it may be necessary for the claimant also to know of the negligence before he can identify the omission alleged to have been negligent is nothing to the point.

As far as actual knowledge is concerned, this approach is in line with the decisions in *Hallam-Eames v Merrett* [1996] 7 Med LR 122 and *Smith v Lancashire HA* [1995] PIQR 514 (see p 117) and is in conflict with the *Dobbie* decision. In the latter, the Court of Appeal held that Gatehouse J had erred at first instance in holding that Mrs Dobbie had to know that her breast had been 'unnecessarily removed'; for the purpose of actual knowledge, that was irrelevant.

Since the publication of the first edition of this book, the judiciary has continued to refine the concept of what constitutes 'actual knowledge' and, in particular, to give consideration to whether the claimant's state of mind is a relevant factor. One case which has featured prominently in these discussions is *North Essex DHA v Spargo* [1997] 8 Med LR 125. There, Brooke LJ said at p 129:

1   The knowledge required to satisfy section 14(1)(b) is a broad knowledge of the essence of the causally relevant act or omission to which the injury is attributable.

2   'Attributable' in this context means 'capable of being attributed to' in the sense of being a real possibility.

3   A plaintiff has the requisite knowledge when she knows enough to make it reasonable for her to begin to investigate whether or not she has a case against the defendant. Another way of putting this is to say that she will have such knowledge if she so firmly believes that her condition is capable of being attributed to an act or omission which she can identify (in broad terms) that she goes to see a solicitor to seek advice about making a claim for compensation.

4   On the other hand she will not have the requisite knowledge if she thinks she knows the acts or omissions she should investigate but in fact is barking up the wrong tree: or if her knowledge of what the defendant did or did not do is so vague or general that she cannot fairly be expected to know what she should investigate; or if her state of mind is such that she thinks her condition is capable of being attributable to the act or omission alleged to constitute negligence, but she is not sure about this, and would need to check with an expert before she could be properly said to know what it was.

Spargo, like the *Nash* decision, said that the claimant must have a 'broad knowledge of the essence of the act'. Sometimes this will be when the claimant has enough knowledge that she goes to see a solicitor to investigate her claim but she will not have knowledge if in fact she is 'barking up the wrong tree'. Again, like *Nash* and in contrast to *Forbes* (see p 112), *Spargo* said that the claimant's state of mind will be relevant.

In at least one respect, the principles stated in *Spargo* appear to be flawed. Very few prospective claimants will truly come within *Spargo* principle 3 given the nature of a clinical negligence claim and the intrinsic problems of identifying whether the unexpected injury or outcome was the result of negligence or the already existing illness or disease. For example, see the decision in *Ali v Courtaulds Textiles Ltd* [1999] 8 Lloyd's Rep Med 301, which aptly illustrates this point, and the authors' comments on *Roberts v Winbow* [1999] 2 Lloyd's Rep Med 31, below.

Spargo, however, has continued to find favour in a number of cases. In *Roberts v Winbow* [1999] 2 Lloyd's Rep Med 31, the Court of Appeal held that a claimant will be fixed with knowledge when she has a firm belief that her injuries were caused by the defendant's act or omission, even if that firm belief is unreasonable or ill-founded or unsupported by medical opinion. Again, this is a decision which has been the subject of some criticism. What it is in effect saying is that a claimant who cannot possibly know without expert consideration what caused her injury will have the requisite knowledge that her injury is a result of medical inadvertence. In this particular case, the claimant was held to have a firm belief that her oesophageal stricture was caused by the drugs prescribed by the defendant, despite the fact that the doctors had informed her that her condition was of an unknown aetiology and perhaps due to the ingestion of some caustic substance. The claimant was found to come within *Spargo* principle 3 and not, as her lawyers argued, *Spargo* principle 4. It is suggested that, on these particular facts, harsh as it may seem, perhaps this is the correct approach. The claimant in this particular case knew that her condition was not the result of any of the causes put forward by her doctors (she *knew* that she had not ingested any caustic substance) but, rather, by the misprescription of drugs. Her knowledge was not so 'vague or general that she cannot fairly be expected to know what she should investigate' (*Spargo* principle 4); her knowledge amounted to a firm belief. However, what appears to the writers to be wrong is that, until that belief is confirmed by expert opinion, then in reality the claimant can never truly be said to have knowledge because everything up to that point is simply the claimant acting on her own instincts or, one could say, following a hunch. In *Roberts*, the claimant might have known that one of the possible causes put forward by her doctors was wrong, but could she know for certain that it was not the result of an unknown aetiology?

(iii) Finally, in *Nash*, it was decided that, if the claimant had taken legal advice and instituted proceedings, he will be deemed to have knowledge. However, there is a question mark as to whether time will begin to run from the moment the claimant goes to see his solicitor. This will be particularly harsh given that at this stage the claimant cannot know if he has a viable claim. In accordance with *Spargo* principle 3, it could be argued that where the claimant 'firmly believes' that he knows the act or omissions which constitute knowledge, then time will begin to run the moment he contacts his solicitor. Conversely, note the decision of *Ali v Courtaulds Textiles Ltd* [1999] 8 Lloyd's Rep Med 301. The claimant, a Bangladeshi, had come to England in the 1950s but never became particularly competent in the English language. He worked in the cotton mills from 1969 until 1988. By 1990 he had suffered substantial deafness but it was only in 1991, following the advice of a friend who told him that his deafness could be as a result of working in the cotton mills, that he consulted a doctor and a solicitor. At first instance, the court found that the claimant had knowledge when he visited his solicitor. The Court of Appeal reversed this decision, finding that the claimant knew in 1991 that his deafness could be as a result of either the noise or the ageing process but until he received expert opinion he could not know which. Hence the mere seeking of advice did not of itself fix him with knowledge. The knowledge that the claimant had in *Ali* was said to come within *Spargo* principle 4, that is, it was 'vague or general' or he thought he knew what his condition was but needed to check with a solicitor. It is suggested that the majority of claimants should come within this category; not many non-lawyers are confident enough to say that they have a claim without confirming their belief with their legal adviser. Unfortunately, *Spargo* has created this unique category of claimants: people who have such a 'firm belief' that they need no confirmation of it for the court to find they have knowledge. It is the authors' opinion that perhaps it is better to be a vague and unknowing claimant rather than a determined and convinced litigant.

The Court of Appeal in *Nash* also doubted the proposition put forward in *Davis v Ministry of Defence* (1985) *The Times*, 7 August, that the claimant lost the knowledge he had previously acquired if he subsequently received expert advice which contradicted his belief that he may have had a claim. It is suggested that, in the light of such decisions as *Roberts v Winbow* [1999] 2 Lloyd's Rep Med 31 (see p 113), which held that the claimant has knowledge even if that is unsupported by medical opinion, then the reservations expressed in the *Nash* decision must be correct.

Constructive knowledge

If the claimant does not have actual knowledge, then the court will consider whether he has constructive knowledge. In *Broadley*, the claimant was held to have such knowledge because she could have ascertained with the aid of medical advice that an injury had been caused to her nerve. In considering this particular question, *Nash v Eli Lilly* [1992] 3 Med LR 353 emphasised that the character and intelligence of the claimant had to be taken into the equation. At p 368, Purchas LJ, in discussing constructive knowledge, said:

> The standard of reasonableness in connection with the observations and/or the effort to ascertain are therefore finally objective but must be qualified to take into consideration the position, and circumstances and character of the claimant.

However, an entirely different view was taken in *Forbes v Wandsworth HA* [1996] 7 Med LR 175 (see p 112 for the facts). By the time the case had come to trial, the claimant had died. The Court of Appeal, considering the test for constructive knowledge, held that the test should be solely objective and the characteristics of the particular claimant were irrelevant. By a majority of 2:1, the claimant was held to have had constructive knowledge. Stuart-Smith LJ gave the example of a man who, following an operation on his leg which he expected to be successful, discovers that he now has only one leg instead of two. After the initial shock, the patient then has a choice: either (a) to simply accept it as a cruel blow and not to make any inquiry, or (b) to decide that something is not right and to investigate further. In Stuart-Smith LJ's view, this choice would be made about 12–18 months after the injury. He said:

> ... where, as here, the claimant expected or at least hoped that the operation would be successful and it manifestly was not, with the result that he sustained a major injury, a reasonable man of moderate intelligence, such as the deceased, if he thought about the matter, would say that the lack of success was 'either just one of those things, a risk of the operation or something may have gone wrong and there may have been want of care; I do not know which, but if I am ever to make a claim I must find out' [p 185].

Roch LJ dissented from this view and held that, if such a test applied, then many patients would feel compelled to seek a second opinion following an unsuccessful operation. He said:

> In my view, it would be unfortunate if the question asked in s 14(3)(b) were to be resolved by imputing to a would-be claimant an unconscious decision to do nothing and then requiring him to stand by that 'decision'. Such an approach would encourage those undergoing medical treatment, which did not achieve the desired result, to go automatically to another specialist for an opinion whether the treatment given could have been more effective [p 192].

It certainly seems that there is something to be said for Roch LJ's argument. As we have seen in *Dobbie*, many patients do not even recognise that they have been injured rather than treated, let alone make a decision that their predicament is simply a cruel twist of fate as opposed to their carer's negligence. Additionally, to place a time limit on this decision and to ignore the characteristics of the particular claimant appears to be totally unrealistic.

The debate received yet another airing in *Smith v Leicester HA* [1998] 3 Lloyd's Rep Med 77, where the Court of Appeal held that *Forbes* has been misinterpreted and misapplied. Roch LJ (the dissenting judge in *Forbes*) said the following:

> Whether it was reasonable for the [claimant] to seek such advice depends upon the facts and circumstances of each case, but excluding the character traits of the individual [claimant] [p 87].

However, how does one draw the line between circumstances and intelligence when the claimant is mentally disabled and has learning difficulties? What if the claimant was entirely dependent on a third party? Would that have any bearing on his ability to have knowledge? In *Ali v Courtaulds Textiles* [1999] 8 Lloyd's Rep Med 301, the Court of Appeal endorsed the subjective approach of *Nash* (see above, p 115) and notably failed to mention *Forbes*. Finally, in *Fenech v East London and City HA* [2000] 1 Lloyd's Rep Med 35, the Court of Appeal once again sought to resolve the *Nash* versus *Forbes* debate. Unfortunately, little progress was made, as Simon Brown LJ chose not to reconcile the decisions in *Nash*, *Forbes* and *Ali* but simply stated that a degree of objectivity was required in determining when someone should seek advice. In *Fenech*, the claimant's pain had begun immediately following the birth of her first child in 1960. The pain had continued throughout the subsequent births of her five other children and had been so great as to almost destroy her marriage, in that it had not only affected her enjoyment of sexual intercourse but also affected her day to day enjoyment of life. Simon Brown LJ held that, given these circumstances, it was reasonable to infer that the claimant should have sought advice in the 1960s and thus considered her to have constructive knowledge. Despite the fact that she was shy in discussing intimate matters with her male GP, the claimant must have had the opportunity of discussing her problems with other health care workers and therefore her personal characteristics, that is, her embarrassment, would be disregarded.

It would be a foolish man (or woman!) who would assert that this is the last word on the *Forbes* versus *Nash* debate and one would be even more foolhardy to try and predict just how things will progress. Even the judiciary have avoided reconciling the decisions in those two cases and failed to give a definitive ruling. However, there is a vague pattern emerging from cases such as *Smith v Leicester HA* [1998] (see p 126) and that seems to be that the test is now both objective – was it reasonable for the claimant to seek further advice, and subjective – the reasonable man in the claimant's shoes. For example, in a *Fenech*-like situation, it would be reasonable for someone faced with persistent pain to seek help. Hence, looked at objectively, that is what one would expect the reasonable claimant to do; but also looked at from a subjective stance, that is what you and I 'in the claimant's shoes' would have done. Whatever the position, it is to be hoped that the courts will never lose sight of the claimant's own particular circumstances when considering whether the claimant has acted reasonably and that the approach of Stuart-Smith LJ in *Forbes* continues to diminish in importance. Perhaps the court should also look at the nature of the injury when considering the claimant's state of mind. For example, consider the position of Mrs Dobbie (*Dobbie v Medway HA* (1994)): she was someone who was completely traumatised after her mastectomy. Even if she had been aware that she had been injured rather than treated, would she have been rational enough to act?

The authors are in agreement with the courts' view that they cannot be expected to take account of all the individual idiosyncrasies of the claimant. However, it may be too simplistic to say that character traits should be excluded completely. Consider the claimant who, after being ill-treated by her husband for a number of years, is now completely subservient and would not think to question or make enquiries. This is her character, yet it has been created by her circumstances and, as such, surely the court must consider these facts in determining when she has knowledge? Hence the objective/subjective test again; viewed objectively, the reasonable man would have made enquiry, but subjectively the reasonable person in the claimant's shoes living the claimant's life would not. Perhaps, therefore, it would be better to say that the court will generally consider only the facts and circumstances of the case unless the character traits of the claimant are so important that they must be considered to make sense of the claimant's conduct. The authors will end this discussion with a plea; could the judiciary take a pragmatic and robust approach on this one instead of being caught up with questions of semantics?

Finally, what if the claimant does seek medical advice? Can he always rely on it or must he seek further advice in given circumstances? In *Smith v West Lancashire HA* [1995] PIQR 514, the court held that, as the claimant had been reassured by his GP that his treatment was appropriate for his condition, he was not caught by s 14(3), which states that a claimant will be deemed to have constructive knowledge if he failed to seek medical advice. This must be right, otherwise it would seem that the claimant can never rely on the reassurances of the medical profession and that he must obtain several opinions before he can be satisfied that he has taken all steps in accordance with s 14(3). However, in *Gregory v Ferro (GB) Ltd* [1995] 6 Med LR 321, the claimant relied on assurances from her GP that the pain in her leg was caused by her recurrent arthritis. The Court of Appeal held that she had constructive knowledge and they took into account that the claimant was 'an intelligent woman' who doubted whether the continuing pain was solely attributable to her arthritis. In both these cases, the claimant relied on the reassurances of their GP. Could the defendant argue that in all cases the claimant should obtain the advice of a specialist to totally fulfil the requirements of s 14(3)?

Further, given the decision in *Roberts v Winbow* [1999] 2 Lloyd's Rep Med 31 (see p 113), where the claimant was held to have knowledge despite medical assurances that her condition was of unknown aetiology, it is arguable that the courts have moved away from the decision in *Smith* and now expect claimants to take a more proactive approach and challenge their expert's views. In the case of *Sniezek v Bundy (Letchworth) Ltd* [2000] PIQR 213, the Court of Appeal held that a distinction had to be made between a claimant who had a firm belief that he had a significant injury which he retained whatever contrary advice he was given, and a claimant who believed that he might have or probably had an injury which was attributable to the defendant's conduct but he was not sure which and felt that he needed expert advice. Only the first of these claimants had knowledge within the meaning of s 14. Further, the court ruled that it was not sufficient to postpone knowledge that the claimant recognised the need to get both legal and medical advice and that advice was adverse. In *Sniezek*, the claimant had always been convinced that his throat symptoms had been caused by his working conditions; so firm was his belief that he sought legal advice despite receiving a medical opinion that failed to support his belief. The claimant's conduct was in no way at fault; he had knowledge within the meaning of s 14(3) and, as in *Roberts v Winbow*, the court exercised their s 33 discretion (see, further, Rule 4B and below, p 129 *et seq*). Providing the courts continue to take this approach of exercising their discretion under s 33 where the claimant has acted reasonably and yet received false assurances, then there are no problems caused by finding that the claimant has knowledge within the context of s 14(3). However, the authors still find it slightly incredulous that a claimant is supposed to have knowledge even when his belief is contradicted by the full weight of the legal and/or medical profession. The humble claimant, all knowledgeable in the face of such opposition? Surely not! This is simply an expedient way for the court to look at this problem but the logical way – we think not.

Is the position any different where the claimant seeks legal advice? As a general principle, the claimant will be fixed with the knowledge ascertained by his solicitor. What, however, if the solicitor fails to find out the facts of the case; will the claimant still have constructive knowledge? This is different from the point discussed above, that the claimant receives negative advice.

From recent case law it appears that the claimant may still have knowledge within the meaning of s 14 but the court will not penalise him for his solicitor's inertia and will exercise their s 33 discretion. There are two views as to whether this is the correct approach. First, that as the claimant has sought legal advice then he should not be penalised for his solicitor's failings. In *Das v Ganju* [1999] 6 Lloyd's Rep Med 198, Buxton LJ (p 205) stated that the failings of the claimant's lawyers were 'not to be visited upon her'. Previously, however, in *Whitfield v North Durham HA* [1995] 6 Med LR 32, it was held that a litigant's action or inaction cannot be divorced from his lawyer's. *Whitfield* was referred to in *Das* where the court held that *Whitfield* was not laying down any binding principle but, rather, making a concession in the given circumstances. Which is the correct view? The answer is far from certain but, in line with s 14(3), we would argue that the claimant's knowledge includes only that which 'he might reasonably be expected to acquire' and that he shall not be fixed with knowledge only ascertainable with expert help 'if he has taken all reasonable steps to obtain ... that advice'. Clearly, by taking legal advice the claimant will have taken all reasonable steps and cannot be found wanting for his solicitor's inactivity.

However, a different viewpoint is that, although we do have some sympathy with a claimant who, through no fault of his own, finds his case statute barred because of his lawyer's failings, the law does provide a remedy, in that he may, instead of suing his medical advisors, now sue his legal advisors. Before the decision in *Das*, it had been thought that the claimant's lawyers acted as his agents. Now it seems that it does not matter how long the claimant's lawyers take because their conduct is not considered together with the claimant's actions. This is very unfair on the defendant, for he has no right of action against the claimant's lawyers and is also deprived of defending the case at a much earlier stage. Finally, in *Das*, the court seem to have overlooked the fact that much of the delay was caused by the claimant's lack of funding. The present position, in our opinion, is on balance unjust to the defendant. See, also, *Corbin v Penfold Metallising Co Ltd* [2000] 6 Lloyd's Rep Med 247, which affirms the decision in *Das*.

From the above, the following principles emerge:

- If the patient knows that he has been injured by an operation/treatment which is unexpected and knows in general terms how the injury occurred, then the limitation period may begin to run or, at the very least, the patient will be under an obligation to make further enquiries.
- A patient should always seek further advice if he has any reason to suspect that he has suffered an injury which would not normally have occurred. It appears that the mere seeking of advice may not necessarily give him knowledge. If the claimant, in the court's opinion, has failed to act reasonably in an attempt to obtain information, the court may fix him with constructive knowledge (s 14(3)). It is as yet unresolved whether the character or personal circumstances of the claimant will be taken into consideration. What is apparent, however, is that, at some point, the courts will display a degree of objectivity and the claimant may be deemed to have knowledge if he has a 'firm belief' (*Spargo*) and despite medical assurances to the contrary (*Roberts v Winbow*).
- If the patient fails to obtain further advice, then whether or not the patient is deemed to have knowledge will be determined by reference to s 14(1)(b).

The identity of the defendant (s 14(1)(c))

In a clinical negligence case, this should not pose too many problems given that the health authority will be vicariously liable for its nursing and medical staff. In the case of a private patient, the individual surgeon or physician may be sued in addition to the hospital or clinic. The only potential difficulty with identifying the defendant is where a claim is one for product liability. For example, more than one company may produce the drugs which caused the injury and it may be difficult to ascertain exactly who is responsible for its manufacture. If a claim is brought under the Consumer Protection Act 1987 (see Rule 4(C), p 144), the defendant could be:

- the producer of the product;
- anyone who holds himself out as a producer;
- an importer; or
- a supplier.

The claimant may bring a claim against any of the above; if the claim is brought against the supplier, then it is highly likely that he will seek an indemnity from the importer, and so on.

Summary

In the first edition of this book, the authors stated that this area of law was unclear. Despite an abundance of new case law, the authors remain of the same view. We simply urge the reader to consider the cases listed below at Rule 4B in conjunction with the principles that have emerged from the decisions in *Nash, Broadley, Dobbie* and the like. However until the courts come to some agreement on what is the meaning of 'attributable' when looking at actual knowledge and finally decide on whether to take a subjective or an objective approach, or even a mix of the two in cases of constructive knowledge, then many of the judgments will continue to lack consistency. What lawyers will find is that, in reality, judgments will depend on individual facts alone rather than on any definitive legal approach to what is still a difficult area of law.

REFERENCES

English case law

(1) Stubbings v Webb [1993] AC 498
See p 105.

(2) Bolam v Friern HMC [1957] 1 WLR 582; [1957] 2 All ER 118
See below, Chapter 5, p 155.

(3) Walkin v S Manchester HA [1996] 7 Med LR 211
Here, there was a failed sterilisation. The claimant's claim was for the upkeep of her child.

Held: damages for loss of earnings fell within the meaning of s 11(1) of the Act and the limitation period ran from the moment of conception.

(4) Shade v The Compton Partnership [2000] PNLR 218
See above, at p 106. The claimant sued his former solicitors for professional negligence for failing to commence proceedings within the limitation period. The claim included a claim for psychological distress and bodily harm. The defendant applied to strike out the entire claim on the basis that it was statute barred.

Held: the claims for personal injury could be severed from the remainder of the claim, leaving the claim for economic loss only. The decision in *Oates v Harte Reade* [1999] PNLR 763 was doubted.

(5) Norman v Ali and Another, Norman v Aziz (1999) unreported, 13 December, CA
For the facts of this case see above, at p 107.

Held: to bring a claim within the scope of s 11, it was not necessary that the breach of duty should have physically caused the personal injury; what was important was that the damages claimed for the breach of duty should consist of or include damages for personal injury.

(6) Howe v David Brown Tractors (Retail) Ltd (Rustons Engineering Co Ltd; Third Party) [1991] 4 All ER 30
The claimant was injured by some defective agricultural machinery. He claimed damages for negligence as part of a partnership.

Held: a claim for financial loss resulting from physical injuries is a claim for damages in respect of personal injuries. The claimant could not circumvent the three year rule by seeking damages only for his loss of earnings.

(7)   Pattison v Hobbs (1985) The Times, 11 November
A claim arising out of a failed vasectomy was not a personal injury claim.

(8)   Whiteford v Hunter [1950] WN 553; 94 SJ 758
See p 105 and below, Chapter 5, p 168.

(9)   Stephen v Riverside HA [1990] 1 Med LR 261
The claimant underwent a mammography in which the radiographer took 10 films instead of the usual four or six. She was told that there was a danger from the effects of radiation. She began proceedings nearly 11 years later in respect of her increased risk of developing cancer.

Held: although she had a suspicion or belief that she did have cancer, contrary to what the experts had told her this did not amount to knowledge and therefore her claim was not statute barred.

(10) Nash v Eli Lilly [1992] 3 Med LR 353
The claimants claimed that, as a result of being prescribed the drug Opren, they had suffered side effects. The drug had been prescribed to relieve arthritic pain and was withdrawn in August 1982 amid intense publicity. The side effects included skin sensitivity to sunlight and in some cases any sort of bright light, acute red rashes, injury to eyes, abnormal hair growth and liver and kidney failure.

See, also, *Hepworth v Kerr* [1995] 6 Med LR 135: the limitation issue here was tried as a preliminary issue. The claimant alleged that his paraplegia was caused by the negligence of the defendant anaesthetist in 1979. In the operation notes a diagnosis was made that there may have been an anterior spinal artery thrombosis (the hospital rejected this claim). Soon after this operation, the claimant was examined by Dr Cook, a neurologist, who formed the opinion that the claimant's condition was not the result of the operation. The claimant subsequently showed this report to a solicitor in 1980, who said that there was nothing more to be done.

In 1987, the claimant changed his GP and saw solicitors who obtained his medical records. They commissioned a new medical report which attributed the claimant's injuries to the operation. The claimant's action was commenced within three years of this date.

The defence argued that the claimant's claim was statute barred, because the solicitor in 1979 should have requested the hospital notes and realised that Dr Cook was the wrong expert. Consequently, the claimant had the requisite knowledge at that time.

Held: dismissing the defendant's argument, the court ruled that Dr Cook was not simply acting as an expert, he was acting as a clinician attempting to identify the cause of the claimant's condition. Furthermore, it was unreasonable to require the claimant or his solicitor to question whether Dr Cook had obtained the notes. Accordingly, the claimant would not be fixed with knowledge pursuant to s 14(3) of the Act which he might reasonably be expected to acquire with the help of his solicitor, because it was not the sort of knowledge that would have reasonably been ascertained with the help of a solicitor.

(11) Dobbie v Medway HA [1994] 4 All ER 450; [1994] 5 Med LR 160
See above, p 110 and Rule 4(B), p 132.

(12) Brigg v Pitt-Payne & Lias [1999] 1 Lloyd's Rep Med 1
The claimant sued his GPs for continuing to prescribe Valium and not warning him of the dangers of continuing to take it. He complained that, as a result of not being withdrawn from Valium earlier, he had suffered a number of symptoms, including drowsiness, personality changes, incontinence at night and bowel problems. In 1992, the claimant was joined in a group action against the manufacturer of Valium, Roche Products. This action was subsequently discontinued. The claimant issued proceedings in 1994 and the defendants raised a limitation defence which was tried as a preliminary issue in 1997. At first instance, the court found that the claim was time barred. The claimant appealed.

Held: the action was time barred. The benefit-deficit equation was not relevant in determining whether the claimant was aware that the injury from which he was suffering was significant. The claimant knew, by February 1991 at the latest, that the harmful effects from which he was suffering might be attributable to the doctors who had prescribed Valium for him. The judge had been correct in deciding not to exercise the s 33 discretion to take account of the fact that the claimant had been advised that, at the time of his participation in the group litigation, he only had a negligible chance of success and that much of the evidence in this action depended on the oral recollection of witnesses from several years earlier.

(13) Broadley v Guy Clapham & Co [1993] 4 Med LR 328
The claimant underwent an operation on her knee in 1980 and afterwards suffered from foot drop. In June 1983, the claimant saw a solicitor who consulted an expert who told the claimant that the operation might have been performed negligently (no report was obtained). The claimant consulted new solicitors in August 1990, and these new solicitors began proceedings.

Held: time started to run immediately after the operation (the claimant must have known that something was wrong when she was compelled to walk with sticks for seven months). Therefore, the claim was statute barred.

(14) Hallam-Eames v Merrett [1996] 7 Med LR 122
At first instance, the claims against the underwriters were held to be statute barred. However, in the Court of Appeal, it was held that *Dobbie* had been misinterpreted at first instance: for time to start running, the claimant must realise not only that something had gone wrong but also that the defendant's act or omission had caused that wrong. See p 111.

(15) Harrild v MOD, Robert Jones, Agnes Hunt and Orthopaedic and District Hospitals NHS Trust [2001] 3 Lloyd's Rep Med 117
The claimant was admitted to hospital on 11 February 1995 with a history of chest pains, shortness of breath and nausea. During his admission, on 13 February he suffered a heart attack and was transferred to a cardiac care unit. On 22 February 1995 the claimant suffered a cerebral embolism. On 24 February 1995 he was informed by his doctors that he had suffered a heart attack. On consultant review in February 1996 the claimant was given an optimistic view of his condition and was led to believe that he would recover sufficiently to play rugby again. However, in April 1996 the claimant was informed that

his prognosis was not as good as he had believed. He was also informed for the first time that he had suffered a stroke during his admission in February 1995.

After April 1996 his condition deteriorated and he came to consider the treatment he had received in 1995. He also noticed in television hospital dramas that patients with chest complaints appeared to routinely undergo ECGs. His concerns led him to consult with his sister, a cardiac nurse, about the treatment he received in 1995. His discussions with his sister led him to believe that the defendants had failed to carry out diagnostic tests such as an ECG, and that his heart attack should have been avoided. He consulted solicitors in 1997 and proceedings were issued in 1999. The defendants contended that the claim was time barred as the claimant knew in 1995, amongst other facts, that he had not undergone an ECG on admission.

Held: the claimant only had actual knowledge when his sister confirmed his suspicions that his condition may have been avoidable. Until then he did not explore in his own mind whether his condition was avoidable. He also did not have constructive knowledge until August 1996, as before then he was concentrating on getting better and did not act unreasonably in taking time to consider matters and then approach his sister for medical advice.

(16) Khan v Ainslie [1993] 4 Med LR 319
The claimant had been suffering from acute angle glaucoma which the defendant optician had been treating with the administration of mydriatic fluid. For some time, the claimant had believed that it was negligent to administer the fluid notwithstanding expert evidence to the contrary. His real complaint, however, was only revealed when he received a further expert report which indicated that the defendant had failed to recognise the glaucoma and should have referred the claimant to hospital immediately. The claimant was held to have acquired knowledge on receipt of the later report.

(17) Baig v City and Hackney HA [1994] 5 Med LR 221
The claimant had suffered from chronic partial deafness. In 1973, an ear, nose and throat surgeon performed a stapedectomy on the claimant's ear. The claimant alleged that within a matter of weeks all his hearing had been lost. He returned to Pakistan in 1976 and did not return to the UK until 1984. In 1985, he wrote to the defendant alleging negligence. In 1986, he consulted solicitors but it was not until 1989 that he received an optimistic report confirming that the operation was the cause of his handicap. The writ was issued in 1991.

Limitation was tried as a preliminary issue. The court first considered whether the claimant had knowledge sufficient to satisfy s 14(1). Rougier J held that knowledge equated with a 'sufficiently firm conviction' and that conviction must be right in accordance with specialist opinion. In any event, the claimant must know in general terms what it was that the defendant had done or failed to do which had caused the damage. The court held that the claimant's position was analogous to *Broadley v Guy Clapham & Co* [1993] 4 Med LR 328 and, consequently, the claimant did not have knowledge pursuant to s 14(1). However, the claimant was held to have constructive knowledge pursuant to s 14(3). The claimant was an educated man capable of reading his own case notes; thus, when an operation which he had been assured was virtually certain of success was a disaster, this should have put him on inquiry. Shortly after the operation he should have sought professional help but he did nothing until 1985.

In refusing to exercise its discretion under s 33, the court gave the following reasons:

- There was considerable and inordinate delay.
- The defendant was responsible for six months' delay in providing the medical records but that appears to have been a genuine mistake.
- One of the claimant's arguments was that the defendant had failed to warn him of the dangers of the operation. The evidence depended on personal recollection and, as such, the defendant would be unduly prejudiced given the length of time that had elapsed, much more so than the claimant for whom this was a 'one-off' event.
- The defendant's insurance arrangements had changed. (See *Antcliffe v Gloucester HA* [1992] 1 WLR 1044.)
- There was considerable delay in issuing the writ when the claimant did find out the position.
- The claimant's chances of success were doubtful: he had one report which was favourable to him, as opposed to three unfavourable reports.

See, further, Rule 4(B), p 134.

(18) Forbes v Wandsworth HA [1996] 7 Med LR 175
The claimant had a history of circulatory problems and underwent a bypass operation in October 1982. This was unsuccessful and so another operation was carried out the next day. The claimant was informed that his leg would have to be amputated to prevent gangrene.

In 1991, the claimant consulted his solicitor to obtain financial advice. His medical notes and an expert report was obtained, and a writ was issued the following year.

Held: the claimant had constructive knowledge in 1982 and declined to exercise its discretion under s 33. For further commentary, see pp 133, 140.

(19) Smith v West Lancashire HA [1995] PIQR 514
In 1981, the claimant attended an accident and emergency department, complaining of an injury to his right hand. The claimant was X-rayed and reviewed over the next few weeks but no change was made in his treatment until eight weeks after the injury, when he was advised that the treatment had not worked and he required an urgent operation. The claimant continued to see his GP after the operation but was never told that the operation should have been performed shortly after the injury and not some eight weeks later. As a result of the failure to operate promptly, the claimant sustained pain and degenerative changes.

Held: the claimant had been reassured by his GP that he had been given the appropriate treatment; therefore, he would not be deemed to have constructive knowledge.

(20) North Essex DHA v Spargo [1997] 8 Med LR 125
The claimant had been mistakenly diagnosed as suffering from irreversible selective brain damage and was the subject of a compulsory admission order to a mental hospital. She was confined to the hospital between 1975–81. In January 1986, an expert report indicated that she was not suffering from brain damage and, in October 1986, she consulted a firm of solicitors who were acting for her in connection with divorce proceedings. In 1993, proceedings were issued against the defendant health authority claiming damages for personal injuries. She alleged that, as a result of the wrong diagnosis, she was not given the correct treatment which would have at the very least secured her release at an earlier time and would not have have left her with the stigma of

suffering from organic brain damage. The defendant health authority pleaded a limitation defence. At first instance, the court held that the claimant did not have knowledge until she received the confirmation from the expert of the link between the misdiagnosis and her mental condition which constituted the personal injury. The defendant appealed.

Held: the appeal would be allowed because, for the purposes of s 14(1)(a), the actual injury was the alleged negligence surrounding the diagnosis of organic brain syndrome which constituted the omission or omissions relied upon and, therefore, the claimant knew in October 1986 of her 'injury' and of the causally relevant 'omission'.

(21) Ali v Courtaulds Textiles Ltd [1999] 8 Lloyd's Rep Med 301

The claimant had worked for 20 years in a cotton mill run by the defendant. In 1990, he told his GP that he had been unable to hear for six months. In November 1991, the claimant was told by a Mr Ali, a community worker, that his deafness could have been caused by working in the cotton mill and that he should consult a doctor and a solicitor. The claimant consulted a solicitor the next day and a consultant ENT surgeon reported on 20 August 1992 that the claimant's hearing loss had probably been caused by exposure to industrial noise. The claimant issued proceedings on 5 May 1995. The defendant relied on limitation as a defence. At first instance, the court found that the claimant had constructive knowledge when he was told in 1991 that deafness could be attributed to industrial noise, and this was not a case where it would be equitable to allow it to proceed under s 33. The claimant appealed.

Held: the appeal would be allowed. The claimant knew in 1991 that his deafness could have been caused by exposure to noise, but he also knew that the ageing process could cause deafness. The claimant could only discover whether his deafness was noise induced or age induced with the aid of expert medical help and he had taken all reasonable steps to obtain such help from the moment the community worker informed that his disability could be noise induced.

(22) Roberts v Winbow [1999] 2 Lloyd's Rep Med 31

In January 1988, the claimant was admitted to hospital under the care of the defendant, a consultant psychiatrist, suffering from severe depression. She was prescribed a number of drugs, including carbamazepine. Shortly after discharge, she developed flu-like symptoms and then an erythematous rash. In February, she saw the defendant who diagnosed drug-induced urticara; he advised the claimant to stop taking some of the drugs but to continue taking the carbamazepine. The claimant's condition deteriorated and she was admitted to hospital. She was dangerously ill for two weeks and the doctors attributed her illness to carbamazepine sensitivity. After discharge from hospital, the claimant complained of difficulty in swallowing and weight loss. She was diagnosed as having a low oesophageal stricture. The claimant was admitted to hospital on several occasions between May 1988 and May 1990 for treatment of the stricture which her doctors said was caused by an unknown aetiology or due to caustic irritation of the oesophagus. In April 1989, the claimant instructed solicitors; she felt that the defendant had failed to diagnose an adverse drug reaction quickly enough and because of the delay she had suffered permanent damage to her gullet. It was not until June 1992 that a clinical pharmacologist report was received which indicated carbamezepine as the cause of the stricture; proceedings were issued in 1995. The claimant contended that she did not have knowledge until she received the pharmacologist report and, therefore, proceedings were commenced within the limitation period. The trial judge agreed. The defendant appealed.

Held: the claimant had actual knowledge in April 1989, as she had a firm belief that her oesophageal stricture was attributable to a failure on the part of the defendant to withdraw her drug regime; this belief was sufficiently strong and it prompted her to consult a solicitor. The case, therefore, fell within principle 3 of the principles laid down in *North Essex DHA v Spargo* [1997] 8 Med LR 125. The court, however, exercised its s 33 discretion, as the claimant would suffer extreme prejudice if the discretion was not exercised, whereas the only prejudice to the defendant would be the loss of the limitation defence.

(23) Davis v Ministry of Defence (1985) The Times, 7 August

The claimant firmly believed that his dermatitis was the result of his employment, but he accepted medical and legal advice that it was not. He subsequently experienced another, far more severe attack and received further expert advice which confirmed his original belief that the dermatitis was caused by his work conditions.

Held: he did not acquire knowledge within the meaning of s 14(1)(b) until he received this second expert advice.

(24) Smith v Leicester HA [1998] 3 Lloyd's Rep Med 77

In 1950, the claimant, then aged seven, developed a weakness in her right leg and occasional incontinence. She was diagnosed as having spina bifida in 1952. She then underwent a series of operations to alleviate her incontinence which were unsuccessful. Unfortunately, the radiologist failed to report an enlargement of her spinal canal, clearly visible on the claimant's X-rays, which was causing her problems and which could have been removed with little or no risk. It was not until 1957 that, following an exploratory laminectomy, an operation was carried out. The claimant experienced breathing difficulties following the operation and a tracheotomy was performed. The claimant became tetraplegic as a result of the operation.

In December 1983, the claimant heard a doctor use words to the effect that someone had 'made a mistake' in her case. She was advised by the Spinal Injuries Association that the limitation period for bringing her claim had expired. She then did nothing since she could not afford to seek legal advice.

The claimant met her solicitor in 1988 who suggested that she might have a claim. Legal aid was obtained and proceedings were eventually issued in 1992. At the trial in 1996, the court found for the defendants. Although the defendants' negligence had clearly caused the claimant's injuries, the claim was statute barred as the claimant had constructive knowledge that she had a claim more than three years before the issue of proceedings. It was reasonable for someone in the claimant's position who had suffered a devastating injury in 1957 as a result of the unsuccessful operation to make a prompt enquiry. The court would not exercise its s 33 discretion, as the prejudice caused to the claimant if the action did not proceed was equal to that caused to the defendants if it did proceed, and the length of the delay was enormous. Additionally, changes in funding and insurance arrangements meant that the defendants would now have to bear some £100,000 more than if the action had been brought in 1990. The claimant appealed.

Held: the appeal was allowed. The claimant did not know in 1957 that her operation had been unsuccessful; rather, she believed that it had saved her life. It was also not reasonable to expect someone in the claimant's position (in a wheelchair with no means of her own) to have sought medical advice prior to 1989. She had been told by her consultant that it would not be possible to establish the physical cause of her paralysis after the lapse of time and this had been confirmed by the Spinal Injuries Association who had informed her that it was not worthwhile pursuing this line of enquiry.

(25) Fenech v East London and City HA [2000] 1 Lloyd's Rep Med 35

In July 1960, the claimant gave birth to her first child at the defendant's hospital. Afterwards, the doctor suturing the claimant's episiotomy informed her that the needle that he had been using had broken. In fact, a two inch piece of needle had been left inside the claimant. The claimant experienced pain in the area of her episiotomy for two weeks, with persistent pain on sexual intercourse and discomfort on walking and performing her household chores. Despite giving birth to five more children, she remained too embarrassed to discuss her problem with her male GP. In 1983, she came under the care of a female GP and underwent a number of negative gynaecological investigations and operations over a period of 11 years. The fragment of a needle was identified on a hip X-ray in April 1991 but it was not until a repeat X-ray in 1994 that the claimant was told of its presence. The claimant issued proceedings in 1997 and the issue of limitation was tried as a preliminary point. At first instance, the claimant was held to have constructive knowledge long before 1994. The claimant appealed, contending that the trial judge had failed to take into consideration the embarrassment she had felt in relation to her symptoms.

Held: the appeal would be dismissed. There was no evidence that the claimant's failure to seek advice could be attributed to her being misled or deceived. As she had appreciated the pain shortly after the birth of her first child, it was only reasonable for her to connect the pain with the defendant's care. Her failure to give her doctors a full history of her symptoms had prevented them focusing their enquiries.

(26) Das v Ganju [1999] 6 Lloyd's Rep Med 198

The claimant consulted the defendant (who was then her GP) in 1978 with a facial rash. She was seven weeks pregnant and it was her case that that was made known to the defendant, although the medical notes made no reference to this. She subsequently gave birth to a severely handicapped child who was diagnosed as suffering from congenital rubella in 1985. The claimant first consulted solicitors in 1987 and was offered legal aid subject to a large financial contribution. She and her husband also obtained counsel's opinion (which they paid for privately) in May 1988. That opinion referred to the claim as not being one for personal injuries and that it was now statute barred. There then followed a series of delays. The claimant, acting on the advice of her solicitors, chose to delay bringing proceedings until her daughter reached the age of 16 as she was informed that her daughter would then be eligible for legal aid in her own right. Proceedings were eventually issued in 1996. On the trial of a preliminary issue as to limitation, Garland J held that the claimant's claim was statute barred but exercised his discretion under s 33 in the claimant's favour. The defendant appealed. It was agreed that the action was one for personal injuries within the meaning of s 11 and that the date of knowledge was between 1987 and 1988. The only issue in dispute was whether the judge was correct to exercise his s 33 discretion when the delay was caused by the legal advice received.

Held: the defendant's appeal was dismissed. The failings of the claimant's lawyers were not to be visited upon her. The claimant would suffer considerable prejudice if she were not allowed to bring her claim, in that she would then have to bring a speculative claim against her former solicitors. In considering the cogency of the evidence, the court had to consider the time after the date of knowledge had arisen.

(27) Gregory v Ferro (GB) Ltd [1995] 6 Med LR 321
See above, p 117. See, also, *Burton v Islington HA* [1993] 4 Med LR 8; *De Martell v Merton and Sutton HA* [1993] 4 Med LR 8; [1995] 6 Med LR 234

The claimant's mother became pregnant in 1966 as a result of a secret liaison with her uncle. Due to the alleged negligence of the defendant in the claimant's delivery, he was born with athetoid cerebral palsy. The claimant was 18 years old on 5 February 1985 but proceedings were not issued until 15 November 1988. The defendant contended that the claimant must have known that something must have happened at his birth at an earlier age when he realised his disability. The claimant contended that he did not learn the truth until 1987, when he requested a medical report before undertaking a pioneering trip to Hungary for further treatment. The court accepted this argument. The claimant had adduced evidence that his birth was never discussed in the household because of the secret surrounding his conception. It was only when he had the chance of further treatment that he felt bound to investigate the circumstances of his birth.

In this case, if it was necessary, the court would have applied s 33. The court did not feel that the defendants would have been unduly prejudiced, as they had confessed that they had no recollection of the claimant's birth; therefore, any further delay was irrelevant.

See also *Driscoll-Varley v Parkside HA* [1991] 2 Med LR 346, where the court accepted that the claimant did not seek further advice as to the merit of her treatment because she was terrified of having her leg amputated and wished to retain her present surgeon. She had absolute faith and trust in him and therefore did not question his acts.

Query: could this not be applied to the vast majority of patients, that is, they hold the belief that their doctor can do no wrong? Or will it only apply to the less intelligent patient?

(28) Sniezek v Bundy (Letchworth) Ltd [2000] PIQR 213
The claimant visited his GP in 1989 with throat problems which he associated with his working conditions. Despite receiving negative medical advice, he contacted solicitors a year later. There were then a number of long delays in issuing proceedings due to the inability to obtain any positive medical advice. At first instance, the claimant was found to have knowledge within the meaning of s 14 but the court exercised its discretion under s 33. The defendant appealed.

Held: the appeal was dismissed. There was a distinction to be made between a claimant who had a firm belief that he had an injury attributable to his working conditions, a belief that he retained whatever contrary advice he received and a claimant who thought that he might have a significant injury but he was not sure and felt it necessary to have expert advice on those questions. The former had knowledge for the purposes of s 14, the latter did not. This claimant fell into the former category. The claimant, however, could not be faulted for failing to do more than he did to identify his injury and its cause; it was therefore equitable that the court should exercise its discretion under s 33.

(29) Corbin v Penfold Metallising Co Ltd [2000] 6 Lloyd's Rep Med 247
See p 135.

Statutes/statutory instruments

Limitation Act 1980
See Appendix A.

Consumer Protection Act 1987
For persons who may be liable, see s 2 of the Act and Rule 4(C), p 144.

RULE 4(B)

The three year rule for commencing a clinical negligence/personal injury claim will not apply in the following instances:

- In the case of person under a disability, time will not start to run until the claimant dies or ceases to be under the disability, whichever occurs first (s 28(1), (6)).

- Where an action is brought under the Fatal Accidents Act 1976 or the Law Reform (Miscellaneous Provisions) Act 1934, time will start to run from the date of the deceased's death, or the date of the dependants' or personal representatives' knowledge, whichever is the later (ss 11(5), 12).

- By virtue of s 33, the court may disapply the limitation period if it is equitable to do so.

- Where the defendant has deliberately concealed any fact from the claimant which would have notified him that he has a right of action, time does not start to run until the claimant discovers or could, with reasonable diligence, have discovered the nature of the concealment (s 32(1)).

Commentary

Claimants under a disability

A person is under a disability if he is an infant (that is, under the age of 18; see s 1(1) of the Family Law Reform Act 1969) or is of unsound mind (that is, someone who, under the Mental Health Act 1983, is incapable of managing or administering his property affairs – s 1(2)); see, also, r 21.1(2)(a), (b) of the Civil Procedure Rules 1998. As stated above, time will not start to run until the claimant ceases to be under the disability or dies; thus, a child can commence an action any time before he attains the age of 21 (18 plus three years' limitation period); while a person who comes within s 1(2) Mental Health Act 1983 can bring an action within three years of becoming sane. Although the claimant may be suffering from a mental illness, he may still be capable of managing his own affairs and, if this is indeed the case, s 28 will not apply and he will be subject to the usual three year rule. If the person will never recover from his mental disability, the limitation period may never run. It is interesting to note that, in *Headford v Bristol and District HA* [1995] 6 Med LR 1, the court held that it did not matter how long those caring for a claimant under a disability took to issue proceedings. In that case, the delay was 28 years, but it might well have been 40, 50 or greater (see p 138 for the facts of this case). This will undoubtedly place the defendant under an awesome burden; imagine how difficult it will be to locate medical records and witnesses from several decades previously.

A claimant may still commence an action while under a disability (see CPR r 21.2, PD 21, paras 1.3, 1.5)). If the action itself caused the mental disability, time will not run provided that the disability was immediate. However, where the disability occurs after the cause of action accrued, time will still run, although in such a case it is highly probable that the court will exercise the s 33 discretion.

An interesting point in this area was raised by the case of *Colegrove v Smyth* [1994] 5 Med LR 111. The claimant, born in 1959, claimed for negligent delay in the diagnosis of a congenital displacement of the hip. She alleged that the defendant should have diagnosed the condition when she was 12 months old instead of at three years of age; consequently, the claimant had suffered ever since from a debilitating condition. The claimant succeeded on the limitation issue, since the court held that she was under the impression that she had simply been born with a disability until, applying for a job in 1984, an examining doctor suggested to her that that might not be have been the case. In fact, even this was said not to have given the claimant knowledge until she had the condition confirmed by an expert report. What is significant is the treatment by the court of the knowledge that the claimant acquired while she was a minor. The claimant admitted that, at the age of eight, a doctor had basically said the very same thing which was said to her in 1984 and, furthermore, that she understood what he was saying. However, the court held that this neither constituted knowledge nor put the claimant under an obligation to enquire further when she came of age. The court ruled that the doctor's statement merely indicated that there had been a delay in diagnosis and nothing further. This is contrary to the decision in *Nash v Eli Lilly* [1992] 3 Med LR 353, which states that knowledge once acquired cannot be lost. As a matter of policy, however, it appears that the court will not attribute knowledge to a child which is recalled on the age of majority. In any event, it appears that the court in *Colegrove* would have resorted to their s 33 discretion, if necessary.

How does this decision fit with the decision in *Gillick v West Norfolk and Wisbech AHA* [1986] AC 112? *Gillick* is widely thought of as being the seminal case in the area of children consenting to medical treatment. Is it the case that a child, although *Gillick* competent, will never be regarded as having acquired knowledge for the purposes of the Limitation Act 1980? In *Colegrove*, it appears that the child may have been '*Gillick* competent'; however, that in itself did not put her under any obligation to make further enquiries when something went wrong. It is a curious situation but we suggest that, both legally and ethically, it must be correct; we would never advocate that merely because a child can take an active part in deciding the nature of his treatment that he should be placed under an obligation to make further enquiries when something goes wrong.

Recently, the courts have again looked at the question of when a minor is deemed to have knowledge. In *Appleby v Walsall HA* [1999] 5 Lloyd's Rep Med 154, the claimant, born in 1971 suffering from cerebral palsy, was deemed not to have knowledge until 1996. The claimant was aware in 1984 (from the age of 13) that he was suffering from cerebral palsy. His mother had been aware since 1977 that the claimant's condition was the result of lack of oxygen to the brain during his birth but did not tell the claimant until 1996 when, because of concerns for his own son's health, the claimant pressed his mother for more information about his birth. The defendant argued that, as the claimant was not someone whose mental state was impaired, then, on reaching the age of majority, he should have questioned his mother more closely as to what happened to him during his birth. Given that the claimant would have been aware by reading newspapers that claims could be made, this should have prompted him to make further enquiries. Popplewell J rejected this argument, stating that the general possibility of making a claim was not sufficient to require the claimant to question his mother about it. The defendant had also argued that, when the claimant reached majority, since his mother had knowledge, that was to be directly imputed to him. Popplewell J quite rightly rejected this argument and held that this approach was contrary to the Act.

Fatal accidents, etc

For limitation purposes, these claims are dealt with under ss 11, 12 and 13 of the Limitation Act 1980. Claims brought on behalf of the estate under the Law Reform (Miscellaneous Provisions) Act 1934 are governed by s 11(5) and those claims brought on behalf of the dependants under the 1976 Act fall under s 12. Effectively, both ss 11 and 12 state that the three year limitation period begins at the date of death or, if later, the date of knowledge of either the dependants or personal representatives, depending on which Act the claim is being made under. If there is more than one dependant and each has a different date of knowledge, then different limitation periods apply (s 13(1)), whereas if the personal representatives have different dates of knowledge then time runs from the earliest date (s 11(7)). If the claim is not brought within this period, it is *prima facie* statute barred, although the court may invoke s 33. If the three year period had expired before the deceased's death, any action brought by the personal representatives/dependants will be statute barred. No account is taken of the possibility that the deceased could have invoked s 33. However, the court may, of its own accord, invoke s 33 in favour of the deceased's dependants or personal representatives.

The s 33 discretion

By virtue of s 33, the court may allow an action to continue notwithstanding that it is outside the limitation period, if it would be equitable to do so having regard to the prejudice caused to both the claimant and the defendant if the action were not allowed to proceed. The question is not whether the claim itself is equitable, but whether it would be equitable to allow it to proceed (see *Ward v Foss and Heathcote* (1993) *The Times*, 29 November). Section 33(3) (set out in full at Appendix A) states that, in deciding whether or not to exercise its discretion, the court must consider a number of factors including the length and the reasons for the claimant's delay, the effect the delay has had on the evidence, the defendant's conduct (for example, did he respond to any requests the claimant made for information?), whether or not the claimant was suffering from any disability after the cause of action accrued, and, once the claimant realised that he had a claim, the speed of his actions and in particular the steps he took to obtain advice. The court will not consider any of these points in isolation; it will have regard to the circumstances of the claim as a whole and may take into account any factors not specifically listed in s 33(3).

The length of delay (s 33(3)(a))

This refers to the time that elapses between the expiry of the limitation period and the issue of a claim form. However, in *Donovan v Gwentoys Ltd* [1990] 1 All ER 1018, the court said the whole period, that is, the delay from the commencement of the limitation period must be taken into account in assessing prejudice to the defendant, see, further, at p 140. This was recently reaffirmed in *Margolis v Imperial Tobacco Ltd, Gallaher Ltd Hergall (1981) (In Liq)* [2000] MLC 0204. The Court of Appeal dismissed the claimant's appeal against the first instance decision of Sachs J and said that, although the delay referred to in s 33(3)(a) meant the delay subsequent to the expiry of the limitation period, the court was entitled when considering the degree of prejudice to both parties to take into account all the circumstances of the case, including the staleness of the claim when it was first notified. However, see *Das v Ganju* [1999] 6 Lloyd's Rep Med 198, discussed at p 118.

The claimant's reasons for the delay (s 33(3)(a))

A short delay will not usually prejudice the claim, as illustrated in *Hartley v Birmingham City DC* [1992] 2 All ER 213 (where proceedings were issued only one day late), and *Hendy v Milton Keynes HA* [1992] 3 Med LR 114 (a delay of nine days). What is more important are the reasons for the delay and in assessing these the court will look at why the claimant acted as he did.

In *Dale v British Coal Corpn* (1992) *The Times*, 2 July, the claimant was advised by Arthur Scargill in 1975 that he had a good case, but he did not act on that advice, and did not see a solicitor until 1987. The court ruled in favour of the defendant, holding that the claim was now so stale that it would be unfairly prejudicial for the defendant to defend it, given that 15 years had elapsed and the claimant had known that he had a cause of action since 1975.

In *Dobbie v Medway HA* [1994] 5 Med LR 160, the court held that Mrs Dobbie knew she had a cause of action in 1973 and it refused to exercise its discretion under s 33; after all, the claimant knew that her breast had been wrongly removed in 1973 and, consequently, a delay of 16 years was inexcusable. Perhaps the court should have taken into account the fact that the claimant was under great emotional strain immediately after the lumpectomy and had been told in effect that she should not complain – after all, she might be minus a breast but at least she did not have cancer! In fact, the evidence indicates that she repeatedly overdosed and was admitted to psychiatric hospitals after the loss of her breast. In our opinion, this case is harsh in the extreme.

We contend that Mrs Dobbie did not appreciate that something had gone wrong and was therefore unaware that she had suffered an injury as opposed to having been treated. In 1973, it would have been unheard of to question the actions of the medical profession. Unfortunately, the Court of Appeal in *Dobbie* did not share this view (see, also, *Baig v City and Hackney HA* [1994] 5 Med LR 221, p 123). Generally, where the delay is the result of a discouraging expert opinion or incompetent legal advice, the court will favour the claimant, though a delay because of fear of what the legal action will cost is unlikely to find favour; however, see *Das v Ganju* [1999] 6 Lloyd's Rep Med 198. Nevertheless, the court must be satisfied that the claimant took steps to obtain expert advice or, if he did not, that he had a cogent reason for not doing so.

The evidence (s 33(3)(b))

In *Hartley v Birmingham City District Council* [1992] 2 All ER 213, the court held that problems associated with the evidence were the most significant issues for consideration in the exercise of its discretion. (See, also, *Dale v British Coal Corpn* (1992) *The Times*, 2 July, where Stuart-Smith LJ said that the court should take into account the claimant's prospect of success in considering whether the limitation period should be disapplied, but it should not attempt to determine the merits solely on the affidavit evidence. All that the court must do is determine the overall prospects. Further, in *Forbes v Wandsworth HA* [1996] 7 Med LR 175, the court noted that the factual evidence of the case was highly questionable, and this, together with the fact that the claimant was legally aided, placed a heavy burden on the defendant which ultimately persuaded the court not to exercise its discretion. In *Dobbie,* the fact that the documentary evidence was still available was not enough to persuade the court to exercise its discretion. Furthermore, in *Whitfield v N Durham HA* [1995] 6 Med LR 32, the court still felt that there would be difficulties in reconstructing the events despite the fact that the relevant documents and the original slide on which the diagnosis was made were still available,

More recently, in *Davis v Jacobs and Camden and Islington HA and Novartis Pharamaceuticals (UK) Ltd* [1999] 3 Lloyd's Rep Med 72, the Court of Appeal held that, in exercising its discretion, great care should be taken when considering the prospects of success. At first instance, Turner J doubted the credibility of the claimant's evidence, which contributed to him ultimately refusing to exercise his discretion. However, the Court of Appeal stressed that, given the interlocutory nature of the proceedings, it was important that all matters were taken into consideration. Where there is a real possibility that the claimant may succeed, issues as to credibility were not of such importance. With the advent of the new Civil Procedure Rules 1998, either party who contends that the prospects of success or defence are significant can, of course, bring an application for summary judgment under CPR r 24.

In *Brigg v Pitt-Payne and Lias* [1999] 1 Lloyd's Rep Med 1, the Court of Appeal upheld the decision at first instance not to exercise its s 33 discretion because of the clear evidential difficulties; the alleged injury had occurred several years previously and the only evidence available was witness recollection. Additionally, this claimant had the opportunity to pursue his claim at a much earlier stage and had been advised that he had only a negligible chance of success.

Generally, where there has been a long delay, the courts will favour the defendant, with one notable exception; in the case of minors, where there has already been a considerable delay before beginning proceedings (see pp 129, 130 *et seq*), the courts sensibly have decided that any extra delay which was avoidable is unlikely to have any effect on the cogency of the defendant's evidence (see *Doughty v North Staffordshire HA* [1992] 3 Med LR 81 and *Colegrove v Smyth* [1994] 5 Med LR 111).

Another factor which the solicitor must bear in mind is the nature of the claim being pursued. Where, for example, the claim is for a failure to treat, the action is more likely to be allowed to proceed, since the evidence is usually contained in available medical notes, etc. However, where the claim is based on a failure to disclose a risk, then the evidence is often based on the recollections of witnesses and the court will take into account the number of patients who will inevitably have passed through the doctor's door since the relevant incident, plus the fact that most people are normally forgetful.

How did the defendant respond (s 33(3)(c))?

The defendant can expect to be penalised where the delay is of his own making. Instances where this may occur are failing to supply the claimant with his medical records promptly or failing in any way to respond to reasonable requests from the claimant. In *Atkinson v Oxfordshire HA* [1993] 4 Med LR 18, the court held that it would have exercised its discretion because a large part of the delay had been caused by the defendant's failure to inform the claimant's mother what had happened during a second operation. The defendant cannot lie to the claimant, but at the same time does not have to volunteer information, as aptly illustrated by *Dobbie* above, p 110 and *Fenech v East London and City HA* [2000] 1 Lloyd's Rep Med 35. See p 116.

Was the claimant under a disability (s 33(3)(d))?

This was considered above, at p 129.

Note that the court is only concerned with a disability that arises after the date of the accrual of the cause of action. In *Davis v Jacobs and Camden and Islington HA and Novartis Pharamaceuticals (UK) Ltd* [1999] 3 Lloyd's Rep Med 72, the Court of Appeal held that it was entitled to consider as part of 'all the circumstances of the case' the fact that, although the claimant was not suffering from a disability within the meaning of s 38(1) of the Act, he was suffering from a condition which was very relevant to the delay, namely drug induced hypomania, and he had undergone brain surgery and radiotherapy.

What steps did the claimant take to investigate the claim (s 33(3)(e), (f))?

In particular, what steps did he take to obtain legal/medical advice, and if he did take such steps, what was the nature of the advice? This section should be read in conjunction with the section on constructive knowledge, at p 115. The court will consider how quickly the claimant progressed his case once he was aware he had a cause of action. In particular, the court will be interested to see whether the claimant obtained medical and/or legal advice and whether that advice was negative. In *Nash*, Purchas LJ had indicated that the claimant may not acquire knowledge until he received a positive expert report (see pp 117, 118 and *Baig v City and Hackney HA* [1994] 5 Med LR 221, *Bentley v Bristol and Western HA* [1991] 2 Med LR 359 and *Khan v Ainslie* [1993] 4 Med LR 319, at p 123).

When taking s 33(e) into account, the court should only consider the claimant's conduct and not that of his advisors; see *Davis v Jacobs and Camden and Islington HA and Novartis Pharamaceuticals (UK) Ltd* [1999] 3 Lloyd's Rep Med 72, above.

In *Das v Ganju* [1999] 6 Lloyd's Rep Med 198, the court exercised its s 33 discretion, ruling that the delay was the result of mainly misleading advice by the claimant's lawyers and that their failings were not to be visited upon her.

This is an interesting development, because it clearly divorces the claimant's actions from that of her lawyers, and also because part of the delay here seems to have been caused by the claimant's lack of funding (see p 118 for more discussion of this case). The *Das* decision has recently been affirmed in *Corbin v Penfold Metallising Co Ltd* [2000] 6 Lloyd's Rep Med 247. There, the claimant's solicitors had issued proceedings five and a half months outside the limitation period; no explanation had been given for the delay, but at first instance the judge found the delay attributable to the claimant's lawyers and refused to exercise his s 33 discretion. At p 251, Buxton LJ, commenting on the *Das* case, said, 'there was certainly no rule of law to visit the faults of the lawyer upon the claimant'. This decision runs contrary to previous decisions: see, for example, *Htec Information Systems Ltd v Coventry* [1997] 1 WLR 1666. If one examines the facts of *Corbin*, it is difficult to find fault with the claimant's actions; therefore, the court's decision appears entirely reasonable. Unlike *Das*, the delay in *Corbin* was attributable solely to the lawyers. But to adopt the approach taken in *Corbin* would seem to imply that the claimant's lawyers could be as incompetent as they like; the claimant would never be penalised, as the court would not consider delay by the lawyers in exercising its s 33 discretion. It would also follow that, if the defendant wished to resist the s 33 application, he must now produce evidence to demonstrate that the delay was the claimant's doing and not that of his lawyer. On balance, this outcome, in the authors' opinion, is neither desirable nor meaningful. Clearly, if the claimant has the intelligence to seek help, then is it too harsh to expect that perhaps he should question his solicitor's inactivity after a certain length of time? In *Corbin*, it was some three years before proceedings were issued after the initial consultation; Corbin had received an expert report some 18 months earlier confirming that his injuries were a result of his working conditions. Would the reasonable man not have queried why his claim was taking so long to come to fruition and, therefore, should he not bear a little of the responsibility for the delay? If this is too onerous a burden to place upon the shoulders of the claimant, an alternative approach could be that the claimant should not be deemed to have knowledge until he receives the necessary confirmation or expert report to confirm his suspicions. However, when he does receive the said report, then, for the purposes of the proceedings, he and his lawyers should be viewed as one and, if his lawyers fail, then he must look to them for compensation. Whatever the approach, the current situation is, in our opinion, entirely unsatisfactory and requires the judiciary's urgent attention.

Generally, if the claimant can show that he was attempting to progress the case, the court will rule in his favour.

Other matters that the court may consider are set out below.

The alternative remedy

Can the claimant substitute his solicitor as the defendant for failing to bring proceedings within the limitation period? This alternative remedy is something which the courts will consider. The two factors which are significant in deciding whether the claimant should pursue this alternative remedy are:

(a) would the claimant suffer any unfair prejudice in suing his solicitors as opposed to the defendant?

(b) whether the defendant, if deprived of the limitation defence, was nonetheless insured and hence would be able to claim on his insurance.

Two cases on this point have favoured the claimants continuing their action against the defendants notwithstanding that there was a viable claim against the claimant's solicitors. In *Ramsden v Lee* [1992] 2 All ER 204, the accident occurred in September 1985 and proceedings were issued in April 1989, but the defendants had been notified of the claimant's claim within two months of the accident and had themselves done a substantial amount of work investigating the accident and had, additionally, made a voluntary interim payment. In refuting recourse to the alternative remedy, the court held that to find for the defendant would be to provide them with 'an undeserved windfall'. The court also took into account the fact that the claimant's solicitors might have known of some weaknesses in the claimant's case and, as such, could exploit these facts in defending any action that might be brought against them. Finally, note the decision in *Das v Ganju* [1999] 6 Lloyd's Rep Med 198, where the court held that the claimant's lawyers' failings were not to be 'visited upon her'. Therefore, despite having an obvious claim against her lawyers for their repeated delays, the court exercised its s 33 discretion and allowed the claimant's case to proceed. See, further, pp 118, 135 for a discussion of the rights and wrongs of this case.

In *Hartley v Birmingham City DC* [1992] 2 All ER 213, the court noted that the defendants were insured and hence the claimant was allowed to proceed with the claim notwithstanding that he had a good claim against his solicitors. The courts obviously felt that there was no good reason why the burden should be shifted to the solicitor's insurers instead of being met by the defendant's insurers.

The 'sword of Damocles'

Effectively, what this means is that the courts will at some stage rule that the defendant has been threatened with the issue of proceedings for too long and that threat must be removed (see *Biss v Lambeth HA* [1978] 1 WLR 382, p 142). In *Dobbie*, the court said that the defendant could not use this argument when the doctor had absolutely no idea that there was any threat of litigation hanging over him. Surely, this argument must hold good for the majority of cases, the exception being when the defendant is fearful that there may have been negligence but does not reveal this to the claimant in the hope that it will remain undiscovered. Perhaps this is another reason for placing defendants under a duty to disclose their mistakes!

The 'Crown indemnity prejudice'

Clearly, this argument will diminish in importance with each passing year. This is where the defendant argues that its resources are in effect prejudiced by the operation of the Crown indemnity rule, in that any judgment which it is ordered to meet must now come out of its budget whereas, had the claimant prosecuted his claim earlier, any damages award would have been met by the Medical Defence Union. See, on this point, *Antcliffe v Gloucester HA* [1993] 4 Med LR 14, *Whitfield v North Durham HA* [1994] 6 Med LR 32 and, more recently, *Forbes v Wandsworth HA* [1996] 7 Med LR 175.

Beginning and discontinuing

Finally under this section, for the sake of completeness, we consider the effect of beginning an action, discontinuing it and then issuing for a second time, where those second proceedings are outside the limitation period. This is what happened in *Walkley v Precision Forgings Ltd* [1979] 1 WLR 606, where the court refused to exercise its discretion under s 2D of the Limitation Act 1939 (the forerunner to the 1980 Act). Therefore, if the solicitor fails to start an action and the limitation period expires, the court retains a discretion to invoke s 33. If, however, the proceedings were issued but not served, or if the writ was served only for the action to be discontinued or struck out at a later date, the court has no discretion to reinstate the action. In *Walkley*, the court indicated that even in the last mentioned scenario it can exercise its discretion if there are exceptional circumstances, such as where the claimant has been encouraged to discontinue the action because of the misrepresentations of the defendant. But beware the moral of this tale – the claimant does not get two bites at the cherry!

Concealment

There are two points to make under this heading:

(a) Concealment does not necessarily mean fraud. It could simply be an assurance from the defendant 'not to concern yourself' when the claimant asks if something has gone wrong.

(b) In personal injury claims, the claimant will not normally have to invoke s 32 because he will be deemed not have acquired the knowledge as required by s 14. Nonetheless, s 32 may be relevant for non-personal injury claims, since in those cases time will start to run from the date on which the action accrued. In the case of *Sheldon and Others v RHM Outhwaite (Underwriting Agencies) Ltd and Others* [1995] 2 WLR 570, the court held that the deliberate concealment of a cause of action which occurred after the accrual of the cause of action postponed the running of the limitation period.

In the case of *Brocklesby v Armitage and Guest* [2000] PNLR 33, the Court of Appeal considered what amounted to a deliberate concealment within the meaning of s 32(2). The claimant brought a claim against his former solicitors in 1997, alleging that they had been negligent in 1989 and had failed to inform Mr Brocklesby of their negligence. It appeared that the claim was statute barred and the defendants applied to have the claim struck out. Mr Brocklesby, however, relied on s 32(1)(b), which applies in cases of 'deliberate concealment' of facts relevant to the claimant's right of action; this provision allows a claimant six years from the date on which he discovers or could have discovered, with reasonable diligence, the concealment to commence his action. It was undisputed that Mr Brocklesby discovered the defendant solicitors' negligence in 1992. The Court of Appeal, allowing the claimant's appeal, held that, in order to rely on s 32(1)(b), the claimant only had to show that the act giving rise to the concealment was intentional. The court stated that the claimant did not have to establish that the defendant also committed the concealment knowing that he would benefit from a certain legal consequence. Morritt LJ said (p 42):

Accordingly, the conclusion I reach is that it is not necessary, for the purpose of extending the limitation period pursuant to section 32(1)(b), to demonstrate that the fact relevant to the claimant's right of action has been deliberately concealed in any sense greater than that the commission of the act was deliberate in the sense of being intentional and that that act or omission, as the case may be, did involve a breach of duty whether or not the actor appreciated the legal consequence.

Brocklesby is important because there was no suggestion of dishonest conduct on the part of the defendant solicitors and yet the court still found that the claim was within the ambit of s 32. Seemingly now all that is required under s 32 is that the act giving rise to the concealment must have been intentional; it is irrelevant as to whether or not the defendant knows he is negligent. This is a significant decision and one which favours the claimant enormously, though there are grave doubts as to whether it is the correct decision. Clearly, there would be no argument that a defendant who knows that he is doing poor work but conceals this fact from the claimant, should not be allowed to escape litigation. However, what about the defendant who is unaware that he has made a mistake? Should he be tarred with the same brush?

As indicated above, s 32 will only apply to non-personal injury claims and therefore is not as important a decision in this area of law as it is for other professional negligence cases. However, it may be of some importance in cases where the claim brought against the defendant is in battery, either where the conduct was deliberate or where the health carer exceeds the ambit of the patient's consent. If a health carer, albeit acting in what he perceives to be the patient's best interests, performs an operation which is an extension of the procedures that the patient has consented to and fails to tell the patient of this, then he will be held to have deliberately concealed facts from the patient. This will be the case whether or not the health carer is of the opinion that the patient would agree to the procedure. There is no unconscionable conduct here, yet it is still within s 32. Harsh though that may be for the defendant, all health carers must now surely be aware of the patient's right to refuse treatment and therefore perhaps should not complain too vociferously.

REFERENCES

English case law

(1) Headford v Bristol and District HA [1995] 6 Med LR 1
The claimant underwent an operation in 1964 as a baby, during which he suffered a cardiac arrest and brain damage. Proceedings were not issued until 1992, the claimant relying on s 28 of the Act. The defendant succeeded before the deputy judge in their claim to strike out the action as an abuse of process. The judge held that the defendant was prejudiced because of the 28 year delay, because several witnesses had died, medical records had been lost and medical practice had changed since the incident, as had the defendant's insurance arrangements. The claimant appealed to the Court of Appeal.

Commenting on the application of s 28, the court made the following points:

- Section 28 of the Act was not to be compared to s 33. The court was not interested in the degree of prejudice that would be suffered by either party should the action be allowed to proceed or struck out.

- As Parliament had already legislated to allow an action to proceed within six years of the disability, that is, 28 years after the incident, then there was no objection to a delay of 28 years or longer.
- Section 28(1) contained no long stop provision as per s 28(4).
- Generally, s 28 was permissive; however, it conferred a right in general to bring proceedings during the period of continuing disability.
- Any prejudice arising to the defendant from a change in their insurance arrangements (that is, the introduction of Crown indemnity) was immaterial.
- The case was distinguishable from *Hogg v Hamilton and Northumberland HA* [1993] 4 Med LR 370. The claimant had suffered brain damage in 1976; a writ was issued in 1978. In January 1982, the claim was struck out for want of prosecution. The claimant later instructed a second firm of solicitors who, whilst investigating the alleged negligence of the claimant's former solicitors, asked the health authority responsible for the claimant's treatment for disclosure of his medical records. The claimant's solicitors gave an assurance that he would not sue the health authority in return for disclosure of the said records. The action was struck out as an abuse of process. Merely issuing fresh proceedings itself within a current limitation period would not necessarily amount to an abuse, but it could do depending on the circumstances of the case and where the previous action had been struck out for want of prosecution.

(2) Colegrove v Smyth [1994] 5 Med LR 111
See above, p 130.

(3) Nash v Eli Lilly [1992] 3 Med LR 353
See above, p 130.

(4) Gillick v West Norfolk and Wisbech AHA [1986] AC 112; [1985] 3 All ER 402
See above, p 54 for the facts of this case.

(5) Appleby v Walsall HA [1999] 5 Lloyd's Rep Med 154
The claimant was born in 1971 suffering from cerebral palsy. He issued proceedings against the defendants in May 1997, claiming damages for personal injury caused by a negligent birth. The defendants argued that his claim was statute barred and that the court should not exercise its discretionary power under s 33. See above, p **130** for the additional facts.

Held: the mere possibility of a claim was not sufficient to require the claimant to press his mother about his birth; further, to impute the knowledge of the parent to the child on the latter reaching the age of majority would be contrary to the Act. Also, although the defendants may be caused some difficulties by the unavailability of records and witnesses, the claimant would be equally affected by the absence of live witnesses and hence the prejudice to the defendants was such as to prevent the court from exercising its s 33 discretion.

(6) Ward v Foss and Heathcote (1993) The Times, 29 November
See above, p 131. After the death of their parents in 1982, actions were commenced on behalf of the dependent children seven years later under the Law Reform (Miscellaneous Provisions) Act 1934 for the benefit of the estate and under the Fatal Accidents Act 1976 for the benefit of the children. The claim under the Fatal Accidents Act was within time; however, the estates claim was statute barred and an application was made under s 33.

Section 4(2) of the Administration of Justice Act 1982, which applies to all actions after 1 January 1983, prevents an award of damages for loss of income in respect of any period after the death of the injured person. The court had to decide whether the injustice caused by this provision should dictate whether or not it was 'equitable', pursuant to s 33, to disapply the limitation period. The court ruled that the question was not whether the claim was equitable or not but whether it was equitable to allow the claim to proceed. Here, it held that there was little prejudice to the defendant despite the delay and, further, that the claims had been promptly notified in 1982; consequently, the claim was allowed to proceed.

(7) Donovan v Gwentoys Ltd [1990] 1 All ER 1018
See above, p 132. The claimant, then aged 16, suffered an accident in 1979. The limitation period therefore began in 1981 and, in 1984, a writ was issued, five months after the limitation period had expired. Due to the various ineptitudes of the claimant's solicitors, the defendant only learned of the nature and date of the accident in June 1987. Therefore, the defendants were faced with a claim which was now eight years old. The court held that it would be unfairly prejudicial for the defendants to have to defend the claim.

Note that the claimant's solicitors were criticised in this case for not obtaining emergency legal aid and issuing proceedings. Waiting for legal aid should not prevent issuing within the limitation period.

(8) Margolis v Imperial Tobacco Ltd, Gallaher Limited Hergall (1981) (In Liq) [2000] MLC 0204
See above, p 132.

(9) Das v Ganju [1999] 6 Lloyd's Rep Med 198
See above, p 132.

(10) Hartley v Birmingham City DC [1992] 2 All ER 213
See above, p 133. The writ was issued one day late. This insignificant delay did not really have any prejudicial affect on the defendant.

(11) Hendy v Milton Keynes HA [1992] 3 Med LR 114
See above, p 132.

(12) Dale v British Coal Corpn (1992) The Times, 2 July
See above, p 133. *Held*: that the test as to whether the claimant had acted reasonably was an objective one.

(13) Dobbie v Medway HA [1994] 4 All ER 450; [1994] 5 Med LR 160
See above, p 133. See, also, *Whitfield v North Durham HA* [1995] 6 Med LR 32 below and at p 133.

(14) Baig v City and Hackney HA [1994] 5 Med LR 221
See Rule 4(A) above, p 123.

(15) Forbes v Wandsworth HA [1996] 7 Med LR 175
See above, p 124. In considering whether to exercise its discretion under s 33, the court took into account the fact that the claimant had now died. It also took into account the prejudice caused to the defendant by changed insurance arrangements, missing medical records and changing medical standards.

(16) Whitfield v North Durham HA [1995] 6 Med LR 32

The claimant's solicitors had negligently omitted to issue proceedings against one of the defendants, the cytologist. As to the court's discretion under s 33, the following points were made:

- The court held that it would be inequitable to allow the claimant to gain an advantage from the negligence of his solicitors. Although this was not conclusive, the court had to take this into account in assessing whether to exercise its discretion.
- As to Crown indemnity prejudice, the trial judge had erred in assuming altruism on the part of patients whose expectations of prompt medical treatment would be lessened because of the use of part of the health authority resources to pay damages to the claimant.
- The claimant's conduct could not be considered in isolation. The court had to look at her conduct in conjunction with the conduct of her legal advisers.
- The paramount question was whether it would be equitable to allow the action to proceed having regard to all the circumstances together with the claimant's and her advisers' conduct.
- The medical evidence on which the defendant relied was still available but the court should take into account the fact that the delay must have had some prejudicial effect.

The court considered the prejudice to both parties, and refused to exercise its discretion.

Note that the court is not concerned with any hardship caused to either party but with what is fair in the circumstances. Therefore, the claimant cannot rely on the default of his solicitors, notwithstanding that there is still prejudice to the defendant.

Note that this case also is relevant in considering the application of s 14, the court ruling that it is sufficient for the claimant to have 'a generalised sense of grievance'.

(17) Davis v Jacobs and Camden and Islington HA & Novaritis Pharamaceuticals (UK) Ltd [1999] 3 Lloyd's Rep Med 72

See above, p 134.

(18) Brigg v Pitt Payne & Lias [1999] 1 Lloyd's Rep Med 1

See above, p 133.

(19) Doughty v North Staffordshire HA [1992] 3 Med LR 81

The court was faced with a 28 year old claim brought on behalf of a minor which could have been commenced 17 years earlier. The court held that, where minors were involved, there would always be considerable delay, and any extra delay will be largely insignificant. The court refused to penalise the claimant's mother for not progressing the case as quickly as she could, since much of her time was taken up with looking after her child.

(20) Atkinson v Oxfordshire HA [1993] 4 Med LR 18

See above, p 134.

(21) Fenech v East London and City HA [2000] 1 Lloyd's Rep Med 35

See above, pp 110, 116.

(22) Bentley v Bristol and Western HA [1991] 2 Med LR 359

See above, p 134. The claimant had received negative medical and legal advice.

Held: it was only when she received a positive report that she acquired knowledge.

(23) Khan v Ainslie [1993] 4 Med LR 319
See Rule 4(A) at p 123.

(24) Corbin v Penfold Metallising Co Ltd [2000] 6 Lloyd's Rep Med 247
The claimant was employed by the defendant as a metal air blasting and spraying worker between 1979 and 1992. In 1993, his consultant wrote a letter to his GP which stated, 'I am sure that he has got an "industrial" disease'. In September 1993, the claimant consulted solicitors. An expert report in 1995 confirmed that his lung disease could be attributed to his working conditions in the factory. Proceedings were issued in 1996 and a statement of claim served in 1998. The defendant successfully applied to have the action struck out as being statute barred. The court found that the claimant had knowledge in March 1993 and proceedings were issued five and a half months out of time. The court refused to exercise its s 33 discretion. The claimant appealed.

Held: the appeal was allowed. The claimant did have knowledge in March 1993. The court found that the delay was attributable to the solicitors but the claimant would not be held responsible for his solicitors' failings, which occurred due to no fault of his own. The delay was not great and did not affect the cogency of the evidence and the claimant had instructed the solicitors promptly. The court therefore exercised its discretion under s 33.

(25) Ramsden v Lee [1992] 2 All ER 204
See above, p 136.

(26) Biss v Lambeth, Southwark and Lewisham HA [1978] 1 WLR 382
In considering an application to strike out for want of prosecution, the court said that there would be prejudice to the defendants where they lived in fear of an action hanging over them.

(27) Antcliffe v Gloucester HA [1992] 4 Med LR 14
Held: by Scott LJ that if, as a consequence of the delay in bringing proceedings, the defendant suffered prejudice because of his business or insurance arrangements, the court should consider that prejudice.

(28) Walkley v Precision Forgings Ltd [1979] 1 WLR 606
See above, p 137. The claimant issued and served a writ in 1971 and later discontinued that action. He sought to commence proceedings again in 1977.

Held: the court refused to exercise its discretion. The result is that, if proceedings are issued and not served, or the action is discontinued, then any future action outside the limitation period will not be allowed.

See, also, *Whitfield v North Durham HA* [1995] 6 Med LR 32, p 141. The claimant underwent surgery to remove what was thought to be a malignant lump from her neck. During the operation, damage was caused to the claimant's nerve, causing neurological damage. It later transpired that the lump was benign. The claimant had taken medical and legal advice early on and knew that the original diagnosis was wrong but proceedings were not instituted until six years and nine months after the operation. During these six years, the claimant had consulted a first set of solicitors, who had issued proceedings for personal injuries but had failed to serve it, as counsel had advised that the claimant did not have a claim. The claimant subsequently instructed a second set of solicitors. By this time, the writ had expired. The claimant argued that the principle in *Walkley* was not applicable; however, the court decided differently – although the proceedings had not been discontinued but remained alive (the court could still renew the writ), the *Walkley* principle was relevant. Furthermore, the court held that, where an action against a second defendant in respect of the same cause of action was not begun at the time of the first action because of the default of the claimant's first solicitors, the claimant should not be entitled to take advantage of s 33 to exclude the limitation period as against that second defendant.

(29) Sheldon and Others v RHM Outhwaite (Underwriting Agencies) Ltd and Others [1995] 2 WLR 570
The claimants issued proceedings against the defendant in April 1992 for breaches of contract and duty by the defendants in or before 1982. The defendants asserted that the claim was statute barred. The claimants contended that, pursuant to s 32(1)(b) of the Act, the limitation period had been postponed because the defendants had deliberately concealed facts relevant to their cause of action, and consequently time did not start to run until such concealment was discovered, which occurred less than six years before the proceedings were issued.

At first instance, the claimants were successful. However, the Court of Appeal allowed the defendants' appeal, holding that s 32(1)(b) could not be relied upon when the limitation period had already begun to run. The House of Lords overturned the Court of Appeal decision by a majority of 3:2.

Held: s 32(1)(b) of the Act provides that time shall not run when 'any fact relevant to the claimant's right of action has been deliberately concealed from him by the defendant'. The House of Lords ruled that this provision covered both where the concealment was contemporaneous with the accrual of the cause of action and where the concealment occurred some time later. The court relied on s 1(2) of the Act, namely, that if the case fell within the ambit of s 32, then the ordinary time limits would be excluded until the discovery or imputed discovery of the facts by the claimants. Browne-Wilkinson LJ's opinion was that it would be absurd that a claimant, who had been prevented by the dishonourable conduct of the defendant from learning the facts, should not be entitled to the full six year period from the date of the discovery of such concealment. However, it would be equally absurd if the claimant's right of action became time barred before he became aware of the full facts of the case because of the deliberate concealment of the defendant, an argument endorsed by the Court of Appeal.

(30) Brocklesby v Armitage and Guest [2000] 1 All ER 172; [2000] PNLR 33
See above, p 137.

Note: the *Brocklesby* decision has recently been applied by the Court of Appeal in *Cave v Robinson, Jarvis and Rolfe* (2001) unreported, 20 February. The judges, however, expressed some reservations about the merit of the *Brocklesby* decision but refused leave to appeal to the House of Lords.

Statutes/statutory instruments

Family Law Reform Act 1969, s 1(1)
See above, p 129.

Fatal Accidents Act 1976
See below, Appendix A.

Law Reform (Miscellaneous Provisions) Act 1934
See below, Appendix A.

Limitation Act 1980, ss 11(5), 12, 33
See below, Appendix A.

Mental Health Act 1983, s 1(2)
See above, p 129.

Civil Procedure Rules 1998, Part 21
See below, Chapter 7, p 309.

RULE 4(C)

A claim brought under the Consumer Protection Act 1987 for personal injuries must be brought within three years of the date when the damage occurred or the date of knowledge of the claim, whichever is the later, subject to a maximum time limit of 10 years.

Commentary

For the purposes of the 1987 Act, the date of knowledge is interpreted in much the same way as under the 1980 Act: see s 14(1)(A). However, the main difference is with regard to personal injury claims, which must be brought within 10 years of the product being put into circulation. The court has no discretion to overrule this time limit, irrespective of the substance of the mitigating factors (s 33(1A)), or if the claimant is under a disability (s 28(7)) or has been the victim of fraud or concealment (s 32(4A)). Therefore, in order to rely on the courts' s 33 discretion, many claimants will be forced to sue in negligence or ensure that the application under s 33 is made before the limitation period expires.

REFERENCES

Statutes/statutory instruments

(1) Limitation Act 1980
See below, Appendix A.

(2) Consumer Protection Act 1987

Persons who may be liable under s 2 of the Consumer Protection Act 1987
... (a) the producer of the product;

   (b) any person who, by putting his name on the product or using a trade mark or other distinguishing mark in relation to the product, has held himself out to be the producer of the product;

   (c) any person who has imported the product into a member State from a place outside the member States in order, in the course of any business of his, to supply it to another.

(3) ... any person who supplied the product (whether to the person who suffered the damage, to the producer of any product in which the product in question is comprised or to any other person) shall be liable for the damage if ...

Note that this section then continues to state that a supplier shall be held liable if he fails, within a reasonable time of a request by the person who suffered the damage, to identify the person to whom sub-s (2) applies, that is, the producer of the product.

RULE 4(D)

A claim for latent damage must be brought within six years from the date when the cause of action accrued, or three years from the date on which the claimant discovered or ought to have discovered the damage, subject to an absolute time limit of 15 years from the date of the defendant's negligence (s 1 of the Latent Damage Act 1986; ss 14A, 14B of the Limitation Act 1980).

Commentary

Rules 4(A)–(C) have essentially dealt with the limitation periods applicable to claims for personal injuries, which will make up the vast majority of all clinical negligence claims. As we have seen (above, p 105 *et seq*), where a claim is for pure financial loss only, a six year limitation period will apply, whether the claim is in contract or in tort (s 2).

The six year period runs from the date on which the damage occurs or, in the case of a number of negligent acts, the last instance on which damage occurs or three years from the starting date (see s 14A (3), (4) below), whichever expires later. The 'starting date' is defined in s 14A(5), (6) and (8) as the time that the claimant must have had knowledge of the material facts about the damage and that it was caused by the defendant's negligence. The degree of knowledge is defined in s 14A(7), but is similar to that specified in s 14(2).

The 15 year time bar on latent damage claims is laid down in s 14B and is an absolute bar, notwithstanding that the cause of action or the damage may not have occurred yet or the damage is still latent. The two exceptions to this rule are where the action has been concealed or the claimant is under a disability (see Rule 4(B), p 129 *et seq* and ss 28A, 32(5) of the Act).

We have not dealt with latent damage in great detail, as this rule will only be applicable in limited circumstances, for example, where the claimant, relying on the negligent diagnosis of a doctor, gave up work and subsequently suffered loss of earnings for more than six years, only then to find out that the diagnosis was negligent.

Strangely, a similar scenario has, however, recently been the subject of judicial debate in *Oakes v Hopcroft* [2000] 9 Lloyd's Rep Med 394. The facts of this case are slightly unusual. The claimant had suffered an accident at work in 1980 and brought proceedings against her employer. She eventually settled her claim on the advice of her solicitors in 1983 for £2,000. Mr Hopcroft was the orthopaedic surgeon who had prepared two medical reports on behalf of the claimant for the proceedings against her employer. After the settlement, the claimant continued to suffer as a result of her injury and, in 1991, commenced proceedings against the defendant alleging misdiagnosis and reporting of her injury causing her action to be settled for less than it was worth, thereby causing her economic loss.

The defendant argued that the claim was statute barred; the claimant had the requisite knowledge long before 1988 and, since her claim was not one for personal injuries, the court had no discretion to disapply the limitation period. The claimant argued that she did not have knowledge until 1990, which is when she first received an expert report stating that her accident had caused injuries significantly more serious than those reported by the defendant and that her claim should not have been compromised at £2,000.

At first instance, the judge found that the claimant had the necessary knowledge at the time of her settlement against her employer and thus her claim was statute barred. The claimant, however, was successful on appeal. Interestingly, the Court of Appeal decided that it was appropriate to go beyond the findings of fact of the judge, using the argument that he had failed to consider the effect on the claimant's state of mind of the advice from her solicitor and counsel regarding the settlement of her claim. Although there was ample evidence that she should have questioned the medical evidence, there was no justification for saying that she should have questioned her legal advice regarding the settlement of her claim. The Court of Appeal found that she was entitled to assume that her legal advice was correct until there was some incident to challenge it, and the knowledge that she was required to have was the knowledge of the low settlement and its cause, and not simply knowledge of her physical symptoms and their cause. Lord Justice Walker stated (p 399, para 35): 'There is an important distinction between knowing that something has been missed and knowing that the missing of that something is negligent.' So, despite the fact that the claimant knew that she was unfit for work in the years immediately following the settlement of her claim and knew that she remained incapacitated, which should have led her to doubt the validity of the defendant's reports and counsel's advice, there was no finding of constructive knowledge under s 14(A)(10). She was entitled to rely on the legal advice given some seven years previously. This is a surprising outcome because, in a personal injury claim, the equivalent s 14(3) requires an objective approach; would it therefore not have been reasonable for a claimant who knew that she was not fit to return to work to question any advice given or any settlement reached on the basis of a report which said that she was fit to return to work? The Court of Appeal stated that it would be an excessive burden to expect the claimant to challenge counsel's advice; but was it, given that the claimant knew that the medical report was in direct contradiction to her ongoing symptoms and, more importantly, her inability to work? In February 1988, she *knew* that her condition was not a ganglion as stated in the report but an aneurysm, she *knew* her inability to work was because of the accident, and she *knew* her loss of earnings was £30 per week, which when totalled would exceed her low settlement of £2,000. Yet it was not until 1990, when she received a second medical report making it blatantly clear that the first medical report was negligent, that the court found her to have knowledge. The Court of Appeal has indeed been kind to this claimant. Even on a generous interpretation of the facts, Mrs Oakes knew that something was fundamentally wrong with her settlement and yet did nothing. There is little by way of objectivity with this judgment and it is clearly not in line with those decisions discussed at p 115 and which, in the authors, opinion, are more likely to be followed in subsequent cases.

REFERENCES

English cases

Oakes v Hopcroft [2000] 9 Lloyd's Rep Med 394
See above, p 145.

Statutes/statutory instruments

(1) Limitation Act 1980, s 14A
See below, Appendix A.

RULE 4(E)

A claim brought under the Human Rights Act 1998 must be begun within a period of one year of the date on which the act complained of took place unless there is a prescribed shorter time limit for the proceedings, s 7(5) HRA 1998.

Commentary

See Rule 5J and the accompanying commentary for a discussion of a possible claim under the HRA at p 194. Claims for judicial review should be brought within three months from when the grounds of the application first arose.

Note that only if the act or the decision complained of has affected an individual personally can he/she bring a claim. Further, any claim can only be brought against a public authority and not against another individual (private patients cannot bring a claim against their health carer).

REFERENCES

Statutes/statutory instruments

Human Rights Act, s 7(5) – see Appendix A.

GENERAL PRACTICE POINTS – RULES 4(A)–(E)

We strongly advise any solicitor to bear in mind the following points in relation to limitation:

- Ascertain from the facts when the cause of action accrued and when the claimant had knowledge. When these dates have been decided, diarise the earlier of the two as the date from which the limitation period will run, and consequently when the limitation period will expire or has expired.

  Note that this date may have to be revised on receipt of further evidence, for example, medical records. The claimant's medical records will often confirm whether or not the claimant had knowledge, for example, did the claimant make any complaint after the procedure or visit his GP on several occasions?

- Late instructions from the client can cause obvious problems. The solicitor should adopt the following measures:

  (a) Obtain emergency community legal service funding (if appropriate).

  (b) Obtain medical records and contact a medical expert.

  (c) Inform the intended defendant immediately of the claim. If there is any doubt as to the contractual relationship between the managers or owners of the hospital and their staff, then seek clarification from the managers. Normally, in accordance with the Clinical Negligence Pre-Action Protocol (see below, Appendix D), proceedings should not be issued until three months after the letter of claim; however, para 3.21 of the Protocol recognises that, if there is a limitation problem, then it may not be possible to wait that long.

(d) Issue the claim form within limitation period if at all possible. Time will stop running on issue of the proceedings. Generally, proceedings are commenced when the court issues a claim form at the claimant's request, but for the purposes of the Limitation Act the claim is 'brought' when the claim form is received in the court office (see CPR PD 7, para 5.1). The date on which the claim form was received by the court will be recorded by a date stamp either on the claim form held on the court file or on the letter that accompanied the claim form when it was received by the court (see CPR PD 7, para 5.2). However, PD 7, para 5.4, goes on to state that parties who are proposing to begin a claim which is approaching the expiry of the limitation period should take appropriate measures to ascertain the date on which the court received the claim form and ensure that the date is recorded. Even if a medical report confirming the merit of the claimant's claim is not yet available, always issue (even though the client may have to fund this particular step himself). The claim form should be served within four months of the date of issue (CPR r 7.5(2)). Where, however, the solicitor has issued proceedings solely to protect his client's position, he may require longer than four months in which to investigate his client's claim and to satisfy himself as to the merits of the claim before serving on the defendant. An application for an extension of time for serving the claim form is permitted under CPR r 7.6 but should be made within the period for serving the claim form, that is, four months from the date of issue. Such an application must be supported by evidence (a witness statement) and may be made without notice to the other side (see CPR r 7.6(4)). There is no limit on the length or number of extensions that the court may grant. The CPR 1998 are silent on the test that the court will apply in deciding whether to grant an extension, but it is suggested that such a scenario as described above (that is, where the solicitor has issued proceedings hurriedly as the limitation period is about end) will constitute a good reason. It is also highly likely that the claimant's solicitor will require the extra time to comply with the Pre-Action Protocol (see Appendix D and para 3.21 of the Protocol). As an alternative, the solicitor may choose to serve the claim form and then simply agree with the defendant's solicitors to extend the period of time for serving the particulars of claim (see commentary at CPR r 7.6.3).

If acting for the defendant, time will stop on the issue of the Part 20 claim.

- If the limitation period has expired, notify the intended defendant of the claim and issue proceedings.

Note that the court will not refuse to issue a claim form which is to be served out of time. Neither CPR r 16 nor the corresponding Practice Direction make any reference to the claimant including a point of limitation in his particulars of claim. However, r 16.4 states that the particulars of claim should include 'a concise statement of the facts on which the claimant relies' and the corresponding commentary refers to the claimant stating all the facts necessary for the purpose of formulating a complete cause of action. Thus, it is suggested that, in order to fulfil that requirement, the claimant must state in the particulars of claim, as precisely as he can, the date when he first knew of the facts and matters specified in s 14 and the facts which led to such knowledge.

The defendant, however, in accordance with PD 16 para 14.1, must give details of the expiry of the limitation period relied on.

Thus, the defendant should state positively the date on which the defendant alleges that the claimant had knowledge; if the defendant intends to assert that the claimant had constructive knowledge pursuant to s 14(3), he must give supporting details.

Finally, if the claimant intends to resort to s 33, all facts on which he intends to rely in asserting that ss 11 and 12 of the Act do not apply must be stated and, conversely, the defendant should state all facts in support of the argument that the court should not exercise its discretion.

- Before serving the proceedings, the claimant's solicitors must consider the likelihood of the s 33 application succeeding (see p 149 *et seq*) and the costs implications should the claimant fail. The solicitor should explain this to the client in writing. However, while the solicitor must consider the merits of a s 33 application, he must endeavour to serve the proceedings as soon as possible after they are issued.

The court may have reference to the criteria for extending the limitation period as laid down under s 33. More generally, the court will examine the potential hardship to the parties (for example, where the claimant is receiving Community Legal Service funding, the court will have regard to the fact that the defendant is unlikely to recover his costs (see *Lye v Marks and Spencer plc* (1988) *The Times*, 15 February)) and, where the limitation period has now expired, the reason why the claimant's solicitors failed to apply for an extension of the time for service of the claim form within the time as prescribed by the Rules.

The s 33 procedure

See generally, on this area, *Blackstone's Civil Practice 2000*, 2000, London: Blackstone, para 10.30–10.31.

The application

The burden is on the claimant to satisfy the court that it should exercise the s 33 discretion and disapply the limitation period. The application is generally made to a judge, though in the county court, following the decision in *Hughes v Jones* [1996] PIQR P380, the application can be made to a district judge provided that the value of the claim does not exceed £15,000 (the trial jurisdiction of district judges). The application may well be made at the same time but as an alternative to the main argument that the limitation period has not expired.

The application to disapply the limitation period may be dealt with at an interim stage by a master, district judge or judge, usually as a preliminary issue before the trial (see CPR r 2.4). This may seem rather late in the proceedings to deal with the application, but it is often not until disclosure of documents and other interim procedures are completed that the degree of prejudice to both parties becomes apparent; in particular, the exchange of witness statements often clarifies any remaining ambiguities. A case on this point is *Fletcher v Sheffield HA* [1994] 5 Med LR 156, p 151. Further, if much of the evidence to be given will be duplicated at the full hearing, then it may be prudent not to deal with it as an interim hearing. One important drawback of leaving the matter until trial is that no costs will be saved. The application should be supported by a witness statement setting out the facts relied on.

The witness statement

- The witness statement should cover the material as required by s 33.
- If the limitation period has been missed due to the error of the solicitors, the witness statement should specify these facts (after the solicitors have agreed the matter with the other partners and insurers).
- Always check that the witness statement explains why the action was not brought within the limitation period; if it was the fault of the solicitors, they should appear suitably apologetic. Whatever the facts, a full chronology should be set out, detailing the claimant's character, in particular, his ability to understand legal or medical advice and the reason for any delays. The witness statement should also cover events prior to the expiry of the limitation period. It is vital that the claimant gives a full and frank disclosure of all matters affecting his medical condition if he wishes to rely on s 33 (see *Long v Tolchard and Sons Ltd* (2000) *The Times*, 5 January).

The claimant should also detail the defendant's conduct, for example, was there prompt disclosure of medical records, replies to letters, etc? The defendant often argues that, because of the delay, there are problems in collecting the evidence. The claimant can, however, counter that as soon as the defendant was notified of the claim the latter should have been on notice to begin this procedure.

Once the claimant has acquired knowledge, the witness statement should detail all the steps he took regarding medical and legal advice, etc. If the claimant is under a disability (and that began after the limitation period started to run), then the litigation friend should show that they acted with diligence and sought to prosecute the case.

Miscellaneous points

- The judge must, if he chooses to exercise his s 33 discretion, explain his reasons for doing so (see *Mold v Hayton Newson* [2000] MLC 0207).
- In the county court, the appeal will be by way of a re-hearing to the circuit judge, whereas in the High Court the appeal is to a judge sitting in private. Appeals from either a county court or High Court judge to the Court of Appeal require permission (see CPR r 52.3). Whilst it is preferable that any appeal against the court's exercise of the s 33 discretion should be made

within time, the court may still entertain an appeal if it is out of time (see *Briody v St Helen's and Knowsley AHA* [1999] 6 Lloyd's Rep Med 185).

- When acting as the defendant's solicitor, always consider an application for summary judgment on the grounds that the claimant has no real prospects of succeeding on the claim or issue (see CPR r 24.2). To defeat the application, the claimant must show some prospect of success and that success must be real. In practice, however, the claimant may simply reply to the application by making a s 33 application.

- The claimant must prove that all relevant parties are joined in the action. The court will not add another party to the action after the limitation period has expired unless the case falls within one of the exceptions in s 35(3), see, also, CPR r 19.5. In addition, r 19.5(4) of the CPR empowers the court to make an order adding a new party after the expiry of the limitation period where it has exercised its s 33 discretion and directed that either s 11 or 12 shall not apply, or where it directs that this issue shall be decided at trial. See, also, r 17.4, which deals with the application to amend a statement of case after the limitation period has expired. The court may allow an amendment whose effect will be to add or substitute a new claim, but only if the new claim arises out of the same or substantially the same facts as a claim in respect of which the party applying for permission has already claimed a remedy in the proceedings (r 17.4(2)). The court will also allow the correction of a name of a party, but only when it appears that the mistake is genuine and the identity of the party was never really in doubt (see r 17.4(3)). The rule also allows an amendment to be made in respect of the capacity in which a claimant sues, for example, perhaps allowing a claimant to sue as an executor or executrix after a grant of probate (see r 17.4(4)).

REFERENCES

English case law

(1) Lye v Marks and Spencer plc (1988) The Times, 15 February
See above, p 149.

(2) Hughes v Jones (1996) The Times, 18 July
See above, p 149.

(3) Fletcher v Sheffield HA [1994] 5 Med LR 156
The claimant was born jaundiced with rhesus incompatibility. She alleged negligence by the defendant at her birth and also during a series of leg operations carried out when she was aged 16–17 (in 1975). The question that the court had to resolve was whether the claimant should have knowledge of the alleged negligence during 1975 and whether that should have led her to discover the alleged negligence at birth and, therefore, whether she had constructive knowledge.

The court was asked to determine whether the limitation issue should be tried as a preliminary issue or whether it was so closely bound up with the evidence that it should be dealt with at the trial.

Held: the limitation issue and the substantive issues overlapped: the same experts would be required to cover both the alleged negligence at birth and in 1975–76, and therefore all matters should be dealt with at the trial.

This will usually be the case where causation is at issue.

(4) Long v Tolchard & Sons Ltd (2000) The Times, January 5
The claimant commenced a personal injury action in 1990 in connection with a back injury sustained in 1983 whilst working for the defendant. The judge concluded that the claimant's injuries only came to light in 1987 and, therefore, the claim was in time and did not give detailed consideration as to whether he should exercise his s 33 discretion. Liability was established and a separate trial ordered to consider quantum. At this trial, it came to light that the claimant had experienced previous back problems prior to 1983. The defendant appealed.

Held: the discretion to apply the limitation period would only be exercised if it was equitable to do so, having regard to all the circumstances, including the length of the delay and any prejudice which had been caused to the defendant. The Court of Appeal held that the judge had erred in exercising his s 33 discretion by failing to take account of all the relevant circumstances, notably the fact that the claimant had taken four years to commence his action, during which time he never notified the defendant of his pending claim. This, coupled with the undisclosed evidence concerning the claimant's back injury, meant that it would be inequitable to exercise the s 33 discretion.

(5) Mold v Hayton Newson [2000] MLC 0207
The claimant sued two GPs in partnership for failing to discover in 1979 or early 1980 that she was in the early stages of cervical cancer, which could have been treated with light doses of radiation. As it was, she was not diagnosed until late 1980 and was subsequently treated with much larger doses of radiation. She issued proceedings in 1998.

Held: by 1982, as the claimant had been in and out of hospital a number of times, she might reasonably have been expected to acquire knowledge from the facts ascertainable by her with the help of expert advice which it was reasonable for her to seek. The judge was under a duty to explain his reasons for exercising the s 33 discretion where he gave such an extension of time. Where no reasons were given, it was impossible to tell where he had gone wrong and, therefore, the losing party would be deprived of his right of appeal unless the lack of reasons of itself afforded such a right. Thus, the Court of Appeal was entitled to exercise its discretion afresh and would refuse to exercise its discretion, as the length of the delay was enormous and the defendant had done nothing to add to it.

(6) Briody v St Helen's and Knowsley AHA [1999] 6 Lloyd's Rep Med 185
Whilst it is preferable that any appeal against the court's exercise of the s 33 discretion should be made within the specified time for making such an appeal, the court may still entertain such an appeal if it is out of time. Here, the defendants appealed out of time against the decision of Kennedy J in 1995, when he refused to strike out the claim as being time barred. The defendant was also appealing against the judgment of Garland J. The defendant argued that the outcome of the trial depended on the findings of fact of Kennedy J.

Held: there was no authority on whether leave to appeal the exercise of the s 33 discretion should be given so as to invalidate the conclusions of the trial judge. However, the court has a discretion to admit fresh evidence of events that occur after the trial from both sides. Assuming that the fundamental assumption on which Kennedy J's order had been made had been falsified, the court must then consider other matters, such as justice, that the defendant had consented to limitation being tried as a preliminary issue and that the application had been made three years out of time. The court could make no criticism of the way in which the trial had been conducted and hence the application would be dismissed.

Law Commission

Limitation of Actions, Law Com 270

As a final word in this chapter solicitors should be aware of the recent Law Commission Report: *Limitation of Actions*. In brief it recommends that for all claims there should be a primary limitation period of three years starting on the date which the claimant knows, or ought reasonably to know (a) the facts which give rise to the cause of action; (b) the identity of the defendant; (c) if the claimant has suffered injury, loss or damage or the defendant has received a benefit, that the injury, loss or damage or benefit was significant. The Commission recommends that the court continues to retain its discretion to disapply the primary limitation period.

For further details see www.lawcom.gov.uk.

CHAPTER 5

STANDARD OF CARE

RULE 5(A)

To establish negligence, the claimant must show that the defendant's acts fell below the required standard of care. The standard of care applicable to the medical profession is that stated by McNair J in *Bolam v Friern HMC* [1957] 1 WLR 582, pp 587–88, now commonly known as the *Bolam* test:

> A doctor is not guilty of negligence if he has acted in accordance with a practice accepted as proper by a responsible body of medical men skilled in that particular art.

Commentary

To establish negligence on the part of the defendant, the claimant must show:

- what is the standard of care; and
- on the facts of the case, that the defendant's conduct fell below that standard.

In the field of medical negligence, the *Bolam* test is now recognised as almost determinative of both the above points; moreover, as a test it is not restricted to doctors but is of general application to any branch of the medical profession (see *Gold v Haringey HA* [1987] 2 All ER 888).

In *Bolam*, the claimant was given electro convulsive therapy and, as a result of this treatment, sustained fractures. He argued that the doctor was negligent, first, in not giving him relaxant drugs (which admittedly would have excluded the risk of fracture); secondly, if drugs were not used, in failing to restrain him manually; finally, in not warning him of the risks involved in the treatment. There were different opinions in the medical field as to whether the claimant should have been given relaxant drugs and whether he should have been so warned. The defendant doctor was found not negligent because he was able to show that he had acted in accordance with the accepted medical practice of his peers.

The defendant health carer will be tested against the standard of other health carers in his particular field of medicine, for example, the GP must meet the standard of the reasonably competent GP; likewise, the consultant must meet the standard of his reasonably competent fellow consultant. A patient suffering from a rare skin disorder cannot expect his GP to be an expert dermatologist unless the GP held himself out as having that type of skill. This principle is not new – in all professional negligence cases, like is compared with like.

The defendant is not to be judged by the standards of the most experienced, or the most skillful, nor by the standards of the least qualified and experienced. In accordance with *Bolam*, the standard is that of the ordinary competent practitioner in the defendant's field of medicine: 'the norm'. The standard of care is to be judged by reference to the status of the defendant, and not to his personality or experience. No allowance is made for the personal idiosyncrasies or, for that matter, the physical or mental illness of the defendant (see *Nickolls v Ministry of Health* (1955) *The Times*, 4 February and *Barnett v Chelsea and Kensington HMC* [1969] 1 QB 428).

Further, the standard of care does not differ because of the unique circumstances the defendant is placed in, for example, an emergency situation. The standard is that dictated by *Bolam*. Sensibly, the court will not expect a health carer working in extremely adverse conditions to achieve the same results as his colleague operating within the confines of a hospital and will not judge the defendant's conduct too harshly simply because, with hindsight, a different course would have been adopted had the situation not been an emergency. However, the defendant may be held negligent if, knowing that an emergency situation might develop, he did not cater for that emergency (see *Bull and Another v Devon AHA* [1993] 4 Med LR 117 and above, pp 80, 81).

Nor does the standard change depending on the nature of the medical treatment. It is still the *Bolam* test irrespective of whether the defendant is dealing with a diagnosis or a disclosure of information or post-operative care. Attempts have been made to introduce a different standard of care in the realms of risk disclosure, and in some jurisdictions such attempts have been successful; see *Rogers v Whittaker* [1993] 4 Med LR 79 and the doctrine of informed consent (Chapter 2, p 44); however, until the recent case of *Bolitho*, the English judiciary had only sparingly deviated from the *Bolam* standard (see, for example, *Hucks v Cole* (1968), reported at [1993] 4 Med LR 393 (discussed at pp 72, 74 and 172), *Clarke v Adams* (1950) 94 SJ 599, *DeFreitas v O'Brien and Connolly* [1995] 6 Med LR 108 (see p 165) and r 5(D) at p 172).

Do the personal idiosyncrasies of the claimant have any bearing on the standard of care? In English law, the answer given is that it does not. In *Blyth v Bloomsbury AHA* [1993] 4 Med LR 151, Mrs Blyth alleged that her doctor was negligent in not informing her of the potential side effects of the contraceptive drug Depo-Provera. Unlike many patients, she had specifically and repeatedly questioned the doctor beforehand as to the risks associated with the drug. The court ruled that the defendant had complied with accepted practice; there was no obligation to pass on to the patient all the information available to the hospital. Kerr LJ held (p 157):

> The question of what a claimant should be told in answer to a general enquiry cannot be divorced from the *Bolam* test, any more than when no such enquiry is made.

In the same case, Balcombe LJ said (p 160) that there was no rule of law that, if the patient asks questions or has doubts, a doctor must disclose all the information he possesses on the subject to the patient:

> Furthermore, I do not understand that the decision of the House of Lords in *Sidaway v Governors of Bethlem Royal Hospital* [1985] AC 871 ... either Lord Diplock or Lord Bridge were laying down any rule of law to the effect that where questions are asked of a patient, or doubts are expressed, a doctor is under an obligation to put the patient in possession of all the information on the subject ... The amount of information to be given must depend on the circumstances, and as a general proposition it is governed by what is called the *Bolam* test.

Readers are invited to agree that, by relying exclusively on accepted medical practice, the courts in medical negligence are really doing little more than paying lip service to the usual approach in negligence, gauging whether or not the defendant fell below the required standard of care. Normally, the court will have regard to the following:

(a) The magnitude of the risk (see, for example, *Paris v Stepney BC* [1951] AC 367). The more serious the damage to be prevented, the greater the precautions that must be taken. When determining this equation, the court must also consider the likelihood of the damage occurring and the foreseeability of that risk. *Vernon v Bloomsbury HA* [1995] 6 Med LR 297 is an interesting and pertinent example of the courts applying the risk/benefit analysis. In this case, the court found the defendant not negligent notwithstanding that the administration of the drug in question was in excess of the manufacturer's guidelines. The court applied a risk/benefit approach – the claimant was suffering from a serious illness, and medical experts confirmed that higher dosages of the drug than recommended by the manufacturer had been prescribed on other occasions. The lesson being, therefore, that it is dangerous to rely solely on guidelines and the like – whether the defendant is in breach will be a question of fact.

(b) The availability and practicability of precautions which can be taken in order to prevent the potential damage occurring (see, for example, *Latimer v AEC Ltd* [1953] AC 643 where the only alternative which was available to the employer was to close down his factory, which the court held was not commercially viable).

(c) Usual and accepted practice. This will invariably be considered after (a) and (b) above. However, following an accepted practice will not always exculpate the defendant; the court will consider whether it is a reasonable practice or whether it is *Wednesbury* unreasonable (see *Associated Provincial Picture Houses v Wednesbury Corpn* [1948] 1 KB 223). Unfortunately in clinical negligence cases, somewhere along the line factors (a) and (b) tend to become blurred and consequently the courts frequently consider not the degree of risk or the precautions that should have been followed, but simply whether the defendant had acted in accordance with accepted practice in the particular circumstances. The courts shy away from their self-appointed role of assessors and instead simply ask the defendant's peers if this particular defendant had acted in accordance with an accepted practice. In a clinical negligence case, the courts argue that they are advised by medical experts on the degree of risk and the measures which could have been taken to avoid the damage. This in itself may not be too damaging a consequence, except that, in matters of medical judgment, the judiciary seem to place too much emphasis on who is giving the opinion rather than considering whether the opinion given is a reasonable one. Although the courts have substituted their opinion for the views of experts in non-medical fields, they have shown a marked reluctance to use the same initiative in the world of the medical expert. But, obviously buoyed by Lord Browne-Wilkinson's judgment in *Bolitho*, it is noticeable that the medical expert no longer appears to be a 'protected species' (see *Walsh v Gwynned HA* [1998] Current Law Yearbook 3977 and *Marriott v W Midlands RHA* [1999] Lloyd's Rep Med 23).

Finally, an error of judgment does not of itself amount to negligence; it may be indicative of such, but the *Bolam* test should be applied. In *Whitehouse v Jordan* [1981] 1 WLR 246, Lord Denning argued in the Court of Appeal that an error of clinical judgment by a medical practitioner did not amount to negligence. He indicated that the law allowed for errors of judgment which did not of themselves amount to negligence. The House of Lords rejected Lord Denning's interpretation and stated that some errors of judgment may be negligent and some may not. Whether or not a defendant has committed an error of judgment may be indicative of negligence, but the proper test to be applied was the *Bolam* test.

Below, we consider the standard of care expected of health carers with differing levels of experience.

Specialists

A specialist must exercise the standard of care of a reasonably competent specialist in his field. If a GP embarked on a specialist task, he would be judged by the standards of that speciality. To date, the courts have shied away from demanding a higher standard of care from a specialist (that is, higher than the standard of a reasonably competent specialist): see *Ashcroft v Mersey RHA* [1983] 2 All ER 245. We submit that, in certain circumstances, the defendant's specialism should warrant a higher degree of care because the claimant indeed expects more of the defendant due to his apparent expertise. However, there is a potential problem with imposing this higher standard of care and it revolves around the distinction between the private patient and the NHS patient. Clearly, any contractual term could be implied (subject to the reasonableness requirement) into a contract; consequently, it could be argued that a higher degree of care could be demanded from the private specialist than his NHS counterpart, thus placing the private patient in a better position. For this reason, the courts are unlikely to change their current approach.

The novice

With regard to the junior doctor, inexperience is no defence; he must meet the standard of care expected of his rank/status. This is nothing new in the law of tort (see *Nettleship v Weston* [1971] 2 QB 691, where the same standard of care was expected of a learner driver as of an experienced driver).

The leading authority on this point in clinical negligence is *Wilsher v Essex AHA* [1986] 3 All ER 801. Martin Wilsher was born prematurely, suffering from various illnesses including oxygen deficiency. He was placed in a special care baby unit at the hospital. While he was in the unit, a catheter was twice inserted into a vein rather than an artery and on both occasions he was given excess oxygen. The doctors administering the oxygen were a junior and an inexperienced doctor. The position of the catheter was not in itself negligent, as it was a mistake that a reasonably competent doctor could have made. The catheter could have been checked by means of an X-ray, which was in fact done in this case; however, the senior registrar failed to spot the mistake. The baby was subsequently found to be suffering from retrolental fibroplasia, which causes blindness.

In the Court of Appeal it was argued that the standard of care expected of the junior doctor was not the same as that of his experienced counterpart. It was suggested that a junior doctor had to learn on the job, otherwise it would be impossible for medicine to develop and function; it was therefore unavoidable that mistakes would be made. Sir Nicholas Browne-Wilkinson VC agreed with this argument, stating (p 833):

> ... a doctor ... should only be held liable for acts and omissions which a careful doctor with his qualifications and experience would have done or omitted.

But the majority of the Court of Appeal dismissed this argument. Glidewell LJ applied the *Bolam* test, commenting (p 831) that, if there was not a uniform standard of care, then:

> ... inexperience would frequently be urged as a defence to an action for professional negligence.

The legal practitioner should bear in mind that:

• The judgment of Glidewell LJ represents the current legal position. What is reasonable conduct on behalf of the defendant will not change with the post he holds, nor with his level of inexperience. It may be that the hospital was at fault in placing the junior doctor in such a situation (see above, p 79 for direct liability on health authorities); however, the wrong inflicted on the junior doctor should not be remedied at the expense of the patient.

• Once a health carer performs a task, the patient can assume that he has the competence to perform the task with care and skill. If the health carer either unwittingly or knowingly attempts something beyond his experience, then that will constitute a breach of the standard of care (refer to p 79, above).

• The junior doctor will not be liable if he was to seek the advice of a senior/more experienced colleague (as was the case in *Wilsher*). The liability will then fall upon the shoulders of the more experienced doctor for lack of supervision. A common illustration of this inexperience is that, often, the doctor does not realise that the task at hand is beyond his capabilities and therefore he does not seek help. In the Canadian case of *Fraser v Vancouver General Hospital* (1951) 3 WWR 337, the court held that an intern had to exercise the 'ordinary skill of a junior doctor' and must have an appreciation of his own limitations. Quite what this means is uncertain: it is all very well saying that a doctor must appreciate his own capabilities, but in most situations the junior doctor is already acting under the firm belief that this is in fact what he is already doing.

• The more experienced doctor could be held liable for failing to reasonably supervise the junior doctor, or the hospital could be made directly liable for placing the junior doctor in a position with which he was not qualified to cope (see *Bull and Another v Devon AHA* [1993] 4 Med LR 117, above, p 156 and pp 80, 81). We urge that the latter of these options be resorted to: we have no qualms about placing the health authorities under this onerous obligation, it may even make them consider the working environment of junior doctors more closely. However, we are wary of increasing the demands on their colleagues, as it seems to us that the only way in which they could escape liability would be to place their inexperienced staff under constant supervision; not only would this increase the pressure on the supervisors but also it might make the inexperienced staff insecure.

- What about the converse situation where the doctor again either knowingly or unwittingly holds himself out as being more experienced than he actually is? The position seems to be that, once the doctor has held himself out as possessing that degree of skill and knowledge and has accepted the responsibility and undertaken the treatment, then he must reach that standard (see *R v Bateman* (1925) LJKB 791).

- What if the patient accepts the treatment knowing that the doctor does not have that skill? Will this prevent the patient from bringing an action in negligence against the doctor should something go wrong? It is suggested that the particular factual circumstances will be all important. If it is an emergency situation, then the patient may have had no alternative. However, if the patient has a range of available options, could it be said that he must have consented to run the risk, that is, that he was *volenti*? Perhaps the situation can be likened to one where a person accepts a lift from a drunken driver (see *Owens v Brimmell* [1977] 1 QB 859). We would contend that the two situations cannot be held to be truly analogous: the patient does not really have a choice: he requires treatment and he does not really have knowledge of what the doctor can and cannot do; the passenger clearly has a choice and a great deal more knowledge about his situation. We therefore say that *volenti* is inappropriate, although contributory negligence may be considered.

Recently, the courts have again looked at this question of inexperience in relation to the standard of care to be expected. In *Bouchta v Swindon HA* [1996] 7 Med LR 62, the junior operating surgeon was under the supervision of a more senior surgeon. The court held that, at a certain time during the operation, despite the supervision of the senior surgeon, the junior surgeon failed to exercise reasonable care. In *Wilsher*, it was accepted that, had the junior doctor sought supervision, then he might have escaped liability. The junior surgeon was under constant supervision in *Bouchta* but despite this he was still liable. In *Wilsher*, the court went on to say that the senior doctor could be held liable for failing to supervise adequately – this point was either not discussed in *Bouchta* or the court was satisfied with the level of supervision that took place; indeed, the report states that the senior surgeon 'supervised as far as he could'. The court went on to say that had the senior doctor carried out the operation it would have been difficult to reach the same conclusion – why? If the more senior surgeon had acted as his junior counterpart, why would the decision have been any different? (See, also, *Djemal v Bexley HA* [1995] 6 Med LR 269.)

The medical student

To our knowledge, there is no case law concerning the medical student; but it is our contention that *Wilsher* should apply and that the student's inexperience should not be a defence. Furthermore, there is the guidance given by the DHSS to health authorities in September 1971 (DS 256/71). Essentially, this states that the consultant in charge has overall supervisory responsibility, that a student should not initiate treatment for the patient on his own diagnosis but should have that diagnosis confirmed by a registered medical practitioner, that he is not to be regarded as a locum and that he should not prescribe or request X-rays.

The nurse

Finally, what about the legal position of the nurse? She should show the standard expected of a reasonably competent nurse. If she finds herself in a difficult position, she should always seek the advice of her superiors; this could be a line manager or a doctor depending on the nature of the difficulty. The nurse should act on the doctor's instructions but should not follow those instructions if they are clearly erroneous or criminal.

REFERENCES

English case law

(1) Bolam v Friern HMC [1957] 1 WLR 582; [1957] 2 All ER 118
See Commentary above, p 155.

(2) Gold v Haringey HA [1987] 2 All ER 888
There is no difference in the standard of care between advice given in a therapeutic context and advice given in a contraceptive context. The judge at first instance in this case preferred one body of medical opinion to the other. The Court of Appeal dismissed this approach and held that the test to be applied was *Bolam*. For further details, see above and Chapter 2.

(3) Nickolls v Ministry of Health (1955) The Times, 4 February
The surgeon, who was suffering from cancer, operated on the claimant. The court held that he was in a fit condition to operate and consequently was not negligent.

(4) Barnett v Chelsea and Kensington HMC [1969] 1 QB 420
A casualty officer who was unwell refused to see three nightwatchmen in casualty.

Held: he was negligent in telling them to go home and contact their own doctors.

Note that the case eventually failed on causation, as the court found that even if the men had been treated they would have still died from arsenic poisoning.

(5) Bull and Another v Devon AHA [1993] 4 Med LR 117
Refer to pp 80, 81 and 156 above – failure of hospital administration/organisation.

(6) Hucks v Cole [1993] 4 Med LR 393; (1968) 112 SJ 483
For a detailed commentary, see p 172

(7) Clarke v Adams (1950) 94 SJ 599
See p 175

(8) DeFreitas v O'Brien and Connolly [1995] 6 Med LR 108
See r 5(B), p 165.

(9) Blyth v Bloomsbury AHA [1993] 4 Med LR 151; (1989) 5 PN 169
See above, p 156.

(10) Paris v Stepney BC [1951] AC 367
The claimant was already blind in one eye when a scrap of metal fell into his good eye during the course of his employment. His employer had not provided him with safety goggles, although that was in accordance with accepted practice.

Held: the defendant employer was negligent in failing to provide goggles: he owed a duty of care to each individual employee. Consequently, the employer must take account of the degree of risk posed to each employee, that is, the employer must take greater care over the precautions for a partially sighted man.

(11) Vernon v Bloomsbury HA [1995] Med LR 297
See above, p 157.

(12) Latimer v AEC Ltd [1953] AC 643
A factory floor became very slippery after heavy rainfall, which resulted in the water mixing with oil. Despite the fact that the defendant had covered the floor with sawdust, the claimant slipped. It was argued that the factory should have been closed down. However, the court held that this was not commercially practicable.

(13) Associated Provincial Picture Houses v Wednesbury Corpn [1948] 1 KB 223
See above, p 157.

(14) Walsh v Gwynedd HA [1998] Current Law Yearbook 3977
See p 175 for the facts.

(15) Marriott v W Midlands HA [1999] Lloyd's Rep Med 23
See p 176 for the facts.

(16) Joyce v Merton, Sutton and Wandsworth HA [1996] 7 Med LR 1; [1995] 6 Med LR 60
See r 5(D) and p 236.

(17) Whitehouse v Jordan [1981] 1 WLR 246; [1981] 1 All ER 267
See above, p 157.

(18) Ashcroft v Mersey RHA [1983] 2 All ER 245
Per Kilner-Brown J (p 247):
> The more skilled a person is, the more care that is expected of him.

The claimant's case failed in this instance because expert evidence was divided between a body which stated that the damage could occur without negligence and a body which stated that the injury occurred because of the fault of the defendant. The claimant had sustained severe damage to his ear, despite the fact that it was a relatively simple operation. However, Kilner-Brown J indicated, as stated above, that the court would expect a higher degree of care from someone professing to be a specialist.

(19) Nettleship v Weston [1971] 2 QB 691
Held: a learner driver must meet the standard of care of a qualified driver even vis à vis his instructor. The Court of Appeal was heavily influenced by the presence of compulsory insurance.

Note that the High Court of Australia has refused to follow this decision (see *Cook v Cook* (1986) 68 ALR 353), holding that it was 'contrary to what is common sense'.

Note, also, *Phillips v William Whiteley Ltd* [1938] 1 All ER 566, where the court held that a jeweller piercing ears is not bound to take the same precautions as a surgeon but must meet such standards as may reasonably be expected of a jeweller. In this day of AIDS and other highly infectious diseases, we submit that the standard of care of a jeweller would be rather high.

(20) Wilsher v Essex AHA [1988] 2 WLR 557; [1988] 1 All ER 871; [1986] 3 All ER 801
See above, p 158. See, also, on this point, the following five cases:

- *Burgess v Newcastle HA [1992] 3 Med LR 224*

  Whether the doctor is sufficiently competent and experienced to carry out an operation unsupervised is a question of fact and degree on the evidence.

- *Jones v Manchester Corpn [1952] 2 All ER 125*

  A doctor was found negligent and it was held that his inexperience was no defence. The hospital board was also found negligent for not supervising the defendant.

- *Payne v St Helier Group HMC (1952) The Times, 12 November*

  A casualty officer was held to be negligent for failing to detain a patient for examination by a doctor of consultant rank.

- *Sa'ad v Robinson [1989] 1 Med LR 41*

  In the case of a junior doctor, a failure to summon a senior colleague might constitute negligence even though the problem was not unusual or did not appear complicated, or a senior colleague might not have been able to do anything in the circumstances (see, further, p 182).

- *Scott v Bloomsbury HA [1989] 1 Med LR 214*

  Failure to summon a senior colleague might not constitute negligence; it will depend on all the circumstances of the case.

(21) Bouchta v Swindon HA [1996] 7 Med LR 62
The claimant sustained damage to her ureter. The court held that, as damage to the ureter was a well known risk of hysterectomies, the degree of care must reflect that risk. See above, and below, p 227.

(22) Djemal v Bexley HA [1995] 6 Med LR 269
The defendant contended that the standard of care and skill to be applied was that of a reasonably competent senior officer of about four months' experience on the job. The court, applying *Wilsher*, said that the test was that of a reasonably competent houseman acting as a casualty officer, without any reference to the length of experience.

(23) R v Bateman (1925) LJKB 791
See above, p 160.

Foreign case law

Readers will note that other jurisdictions do not adhere as stringently to the *Bolam* test as their English counterparts (see p 72).

Australia

Rogers v Whittaker [1993] 4 Med LR 79; [1992] 3 Med LR 331; (1992) 109 ALR 625 discussed above, pp 72 and 176.

Canada

(1) Crits v Sylvester (1956) 1 DLR (2d) 502
Held: an anaesthetist handling dangerous substances which he knew to be highly inflammable was subject to a proportionately higher degree of care and consequently he was bound to take special precautions to prevent injury. It was stated (p 508):

> Every medical practitioner ... is bound to exercise that degree of care and skill which could reasonably be expected of a normal, prudent practitioner of the

same experience and standing, and if he holds himself out as a specialist, a higher degree of skill is required of him than of one who does not profess to be so qualified by special training and ability.

(2)   Fraser v Vancouver General Hospital (1951) 3 WWR 337; affirmed (1952) 3 DLR 785
A patient was admitted to casualty after being involved in a road accident. He was examined by junior doctors, X-rays were taken and examined, and the claimant was then sent home. The patient subsequently died.

Held: the junior doctors were negligent in attempting to read the X-rays themselves and in failing to consult a specialist. They should have sought the advice of the radiologist and not relied on their own knowledge.

Statutes/statutory instruments

(1)   Unfair Contract Terms Act 1977
Section 2(1) deals with excluding liability for death or personal injuries. A private patient has a contractual relationship with his doctor and as such is technically free to negotiate the terms, but this is subject to the Unfair Contract Terms Act 1977 which states that a doctor will not be able to exclude any liability for his negligence which results in death or personal injuries. In reality the court will imply a term into the contract that the doctor must reach the same standard of care as his NHS contemporary.

(2)   Emergency treatment and GPs
Although it is stated that there is no legal duty on a GP to be a good Samaritan, the GP must give treatment to anyone in an emergency in his practice area, providing he is available and the patient's own doctor is not available to give immediate treatment. See, also, the National Health Service (General Medical Services) Regulations 1992 as amended. See, also, the GMC booklet, *Good Medical Practice* (May 2001), para 9.

(3)   Medical (Professional Performance) Act 1995
This Act came into force on 1 May 1995 and amends the Medical Act 1983. Section 1 of the Act gives the GMC power to act where the doctor's conduct is found to be 'seriously deficient' in the performance of his professional duties. Guidelines as to what will constitute a seriously deficient performance are yet to be finalised.

Professional/ethical guidelines

The GMC has published a series of pamphlets under the general title 'Protecting Patients, Guiding Doctors'. One of the booklets is entitled *Good Medical Practice* (May 2001) and deals with what it considers to be a good standard of practice and care. In particular, it itemises what it regards as good clinical care, which includes an adequate assessment of the patient's condition, providing or arranging necessary investigations or referring the patient to another practitioner. Further, it states that practitioners must appreciate their own limitations and be willing to consult others. The booklet stresses the need to keep accurate records and, interestingly, to consider the appropriate use of resources (see paras 2–8).

Practice points

- The effect of *Your Guide to the NHS* (which replaces the Patient's Charter) on the patient's right to sue in negligence is unknown. We suggest that a breach will only add evidential weight to the claimant's allegations.

- Know your specialisms. If you are claiming against a specialist then it is vitally important to use an expert in the specialist's field (see below, Appendix G).
- Although the degree of the defendant's experience and rank is relevant when evaluating whether the defendant has been negligent, that is, specialists will be compared with specialists, etc, in practice it does not matter whether the breach of duty was that of the novice or the specialist; the standard of care will be determined by the *Bolam* test.

RULE 5(B)

Accepted practice means a practice accepted as proper by the defendant's peers. If the defendant has complied with such a practice, then that is strong evidence that he is not negligent; if he does not, then it is likely that he will be regarded as negligent.

Commentary

In ascertaining whether or not the defendant has met the appropriate standard of care, the court is governed by the *Bolam* test (as modified by the *Bolitho* decision). This test demands that the defendant acts in accordance with accepted practice, which means the practice followed by a responsible body of medical opinion. It does not matter that there is a body of medical opinion which takes the contrary view or that there is more than one accepted practice. The rationale for the *Bolam* rule was that the courts were not the appropriate forum for the medical profession to squabble over what was the 'right practice'. This much is evident from cases such as *DeFreitas v O'Brien and Connolly* [1995] 6 Med LR 108 and *Sidaway v Board of Governors of the Bethlem Royal Hospital and the Maudsley Hospital* [1985] AC 871, where Lord Scarman stated (p 881):

> In short, the law imposes the duty of care but the standard is a matter for medical judgment.

In the *DeFreitas* case, the Court of Appeal ruled that a small number of medical practitioners could constitute a 'responsible body of medical opinion against which the practices of a doctor could be measured'. The claimant had sought to argue that although a small number of surgeons could be considered responsible, nevertheless they had to be a substantial body. In support of this contention he had relied on the judgment of Hirst J in *Hills v Potter* [1984] 1 WLR 641 (p 653):

> I do not accept that ... by adopting the *Bolam* principle, the court in effect abdicates its power of decision to the doctors. In every case the court must be satisfied that the standard contended for on their behalf accords with that upheld by a substantial body of medical opinion, and that this body of medical opinion is both respectable and responsible, and experienced in this particular field of medicine.

This approach had also been evidenced in the Irish case of *Dunne v National Maternity Hospital and Jackson* [1989] IRLM 735 where Findlay CJ had said (p 746):

> General and approved practice need not be universal but must be approved of and adhered to by a substantial number of reputable practitioners holding the relevant specialist or general qualifications.

But the court in *DeFreitas* rejected this approach, ruling that 'substantial' did not simply refer to numbers. The issue could not be determined by counting heads – it was a question of fact. However, we submit that numbers must play a part in determining whether or not the practice is accepted and responsible. Referring back to the *dicta* of Hirst J in *Hills v Potter* [1984] 1 WLR 641, we find it difficult not to construe the word 'substantial' as meaning 'of a great number'. Just how many this number is, however, is irrelevant to the argument. However, we submit that the greater the number the higher the degree of respectability it is likely to attract. In the light of *DeFreitas*, conceivably there is now a situation where a 'body' of two medical practitioners could outweigh the views of a group of 50. This cannot be what McNair J intended in *Bolam*. In determining whether or not a practice is responsible, the first thing that the court should do is to see who has adopted the practice and count heads. It follows that the greater the number adopting a practice, the more likely it is that the practice is both accepted and responsible. What is not being advocated is that the matter can be determined *solely* by counting heads: before anything else the court should examine the risk in relation to the precautions adopted, if any. *DeFreitas* sets a worrying precedent in that perhaps now a small fringe group practising experimental techniques can legitimately constitute a responsible body despite being contrary to the norm.

Complying with an accepted practice is strong evidence that the defendant is not negligent, but it is not conclusive, otherwise adopting a practice and calling it 'accepted' would exculpate the defendant every time. However, pre-*Bolitho*, in all but a few cases, accepted practice did get the seal of approval from the courts. As has been mentioned before, courts in other jurisdictions have not accepted this approach without reservation, and in some cases have actually held it not to be appropriate to the case in question (see p 172 *et seq*). The concept of accepted practice is not new in the law of tort; what is different is the apparent reluctance of the courts to challenge 'accepted practice' in the medical law field.

The accepted practice must be a current practice. This means that the health carer has to keep up to date with new developments in his field of medicine (see *Hepworth v Kerr* [1995] 6 Med LR 139, p 139). The medical practitioner cannot stick steadfastly to the principles learnt in his training; he must endeavour to keep up with new developments. But this does not mean he must read everything published within a few weeks of its publication; all he is required to do is to act responsibly and reasonably. Like any other practice, medical practice will be judged by the standard of care prevailing at the time of the incident, not at the time of the trial. In *Roe v Minister of Health* [1954] 2 QB 66, anaesthetic was kept in glass ampoules stored in disinfectant; the disinfectant seeped through cracks into the anaesthetic. This was impossible to detect at the time, and so the defendant was found not negligent. (See, also, *Re HIV Haemophiliac Litigation* (1990) 140 NLJ 1349 and *ter Neuzen v Korn* (1993) 103 DLR (4th) 473.) This principle has found its way into the Consumer Protection Act 1987. This Act is important in the medical field as it covers pharmaceutical products, in particular contraceptive drugs, appliances and even blood. While purporting to be a strict liability Act, under s 4(1)(e), a producer can escape liability if it can be shown that the state of scientific knowledge was not such that the defendant could have been expected to have knowledge of the defect (the development risks defence). Thus, a defendant can escape liability if, for example, it can be shown that the defect constituting a breach in 1993 was not generally known until 1995. This seems to go against the very spirit of the Act and perhaps will not prevent a 'thalidomide' tragedy occurring again. As the law now stands, it would be right to conclude that Britain is little more than a testing ground for new drugs.

The problem for any solicitor who alleges that the defendant has been negligent in failing to adopt a new practice is to determine when the defendant should have adopted the new practice, that is, how long does a health carer have before he is found negligent in not adopting a new technique? Each case will have to be judged on its own facts but we submit that the court will look at:

- how widespread the knowledge is;
- the length of time it has been available; and
- if the new practice is a precaution, the expense of adopting that precaution, the practicality of doing so and the benefit to the patient.

Finally, whose practice is being referred to when the phrase 'accepted practice' is being used? Is it an English practice only, or can the practices in other jurisdictions be looked at? In the Canadian case of *ter Neuzen v Korn* (1993) 103 DLR (4th) 473 (see p 169), the court said that, although Canadian doctors were not expected to be aware of the practices of their Australian counterparts, they should be aware of the US guidelines. However, it is submitted that, to be judged negligent in not following an accepted practice, the court must have regard to an English accepted practice; otherwise, we could be faced with a situation where an English doctor could be held negligent for failing to operate because it was an accepted practice in, say, the US. Conversely, could a health carer 'save himself' by saying, for example, that his practice was an accepted practice in another country? Would it matter which country had adopted his practice? If we accept that a health carer will not be held negligent for not following a foreign accepted practice, then surely he should not be permitted to rely on a foreign medical practice as a last ditch attempt to escape liability.

REFERENCES

English case law

(1)   *Bolam v Friern HMC [1957] 1 WLR 582; [1957] 2 All ER 118*
See p 155.

(2)   *Sidaway v Board of Governors of the Bethlem Royal Hospital and the Maudsley Hospital [1985] AC 871; [1985] 1 All ER 643*
See p 185.

(3)   *Bolitho v City and Hackney HA [1997] 4 All ER 771*
This case involved the failure of two paediatricians to attend and treat a patient. The defendants admitted that there was negligence but argued that that negligence had not caused the patient's death.

Held: causation had not been established (House of Lords).

(4)   DeFreitas v O'Brien and Connolly [1995] 6 Med LR 108
The claimant had suffered from intense back pain since 1981. She had exploratory surgery which later became infected. Her condition deteriorated and eventually she was discharged from hospital suffering from chronic arachnoiditis. She alleged that her exploratory operation should not have been carried out because there was insufficient clinical or radiological evidence to warrant such an operation.

Held:

- The *Bolam* test did not impose any burden of proof upon the defendant to show that the diagnosis/treatment would be acceptable to a responsible body of medical opinion. The burden of proof was on the claimant.
- The body of spinal surgeons did not have to be substantial. It was sufficient that the court was satisfied that it was a responsible body.

(5)   Hills v Potter [1984] 1 WLR 641; [1983] 3 All ER 716
See p 184.

(6)   Hepworth v Kerr [1995] 6 Med LR 139
See p 171.

(7)   Roe v Minister of Health [1954] 2 QB 66; [1954] 2 All ER 131
The events giving rise to the action occurred in 1947. The claimant had a spinal anaesthetic administered to him in preparation for a minor operation. The anaesthetia was contained in a glass ampoule which had been stored in a solution of phenol. Some of the phenol had penetrated the ampoule which contaminated the anaesthetia. As a result the claimant was paralysed from the waist down. The ampoule had been inspected prior to the operation. However, the possibility of invisible cracks was not something which was generally recognised as capable of occurring.

Held: the defendant was not negligent as the risk of invisible cracks was not apparent to the profession until 1951. Current practice is not retrospective. The standard of care is to be judged at the date of the incident, not the date of the trial. See the following additional cases:

- *Crawford v Charing Cross Hospital* (1953) *The Times*, 8 December, concerned the liability of an anaesthetist. He failed to read an article in *The Lancet* which had been published six months earlier concerning the best position of the arm when using a drip. The Court of Appeal found him not negligent.
- *Whiteford v Hunter* [1950] WN 553; 94 SJ 758 concerned a mistaken diagnosis of cancer. If the defendant had used the instrument commonly found in the US and had been aware of the American way of diagnosing such a condition, the mistake would not have been made. However, both the instrument and method were rarely used in England and the defendant was held not negligent. This illustrates that doctors are not negligent if they fail to keep up to date with foreign practices.
- *Gold v Haringey HA* [1987] 2 All ER 888 concerned the appropriate standard regarding disclosure of information; such was to be judged by 1979 standards, not the standards applicable at the time of the trial.

(8)   Re HIV Haemophiliac Litigation (1990) 140 NLJ 1349
Claimants sued the government in negligence and for breach of statutory duty under the National Health Service Act 1977 for infecting them with the HIV virus (which leads to AIDS) after receiving Factor 8 (the clotting agent) which had been imported from the US.

The case was settled; hence it still remains uncertain whether the government were negligent in failing to implement screening processes for blood in the early 1980s.

Foreign case law

Australia

(1) Dwan v Farquhar [1988] Qd R 234

An article had been published in March 1983 about the risk of contracting AIDS from blood transfusions. The patient contracted AIDS from a blood transfusion performed in May 1983. The defendant was held not to be negligent.

(2) H v Royal Alexandra Hospital for Children [1990] 1 Med LR 297

An infant haemophiliac was infected with the HIV virus from blood products during Factor 8 replacement therapy.

Held: the claimant was owed a duty of care by the treating hospital, the manufacturer and the distributor of the product. However, the evidence did not establish that, in March 1982 when the incident took place, the defendant had been negligent in excluding certain groups (notably homosexuals) from the blood donor pool. It was not until June 1983 that the Australian Red Cross Society had recommended that, as an interim measure, blood or blood components should not be collected from certain groups of people until tests for AIDS became available. The court also held that even where the risk of transmitting AIDS through blood products was known it was not practicable to recall the products.

(3) E v Australian Red Cross Society [1991] 2 Med LR 303

The applicant, E, received a transfusion of frozen human plasma which was HIV infected. E commenced proceedings against three respondents (the Australian Red Cross Society, the New South Wales Division of the Society and the Central Sydney Service, which was created by statute in 1986 to take over responsibilities for the liabilities of hospitals). It was alleged that the Society had been negligent in the collection and distribution of blood.

The court did not apply the *Bolam* rule; instead it applied the test as enunciated in *F v R* (1983) 33 SASR 189 (p 194):

> The ultimate question, however, is not whether the defendant's conduct accords with the practices of his profession or some part of it, but whether it conforms to the standard of reasonable care demanded by the law. That is a question for the court and the duty of deciding it cannot be delegated to any profession or group in the community.

Canada

ter Neuzen v Korn (1993) 103 DLR (4th) 473

The claimant contracted HIV from an artificial insemination procedure carried out in 1985. The risk of transmission of HIV by this procedure was known in Australia since late 1984, but this information did not filter through to British Columbia until mid-1985. At first instance, the defendant was found liable in negligence. On appeal the court said the test should be whether the defendant had conducted himself as a reasonable doctor would have done in similar circumstances and as such the jury had to look at the prevailing standards of practice at that time.

Held: Canadian practitioners had acted in accordance with accepted practice at that time. Therefore the only question was whether the doctor had failed to protect his patients against sexually transmitted diseases; if he had failed to do so then he would be negligent, even if he did not foresee the risk of HIV.

Ireland

(1)   Dunne v National Maternity Hospital and Jackson [1989] IRLM 735
See p 165.

(2)   Best v Wellcome Foundation [1993] IR 421; [1994] 5 Med LR 81
See p 212.

Note that, in determining the appropriate standard of care, the court held that simply complying with the requirements imposed by health authorities would not necessarily amount to a sufficient degree of care. This would be the minimum requirement only.

Statutes/statutory instruments

(1)   Consumer Protection Act 1987

   The state of the art defence
   4(1)(e)   that the state of scientific and technical knowledge at the relevant time was not such that a producer of products of the same description as the product in question might be expected to have discovered the defect if it had existed in his products while they were under his control.

(2)   Medicines (Labelling) Amendment Regulations 1992 (SI 1992/3273); Medicines (Leaflets) Amendment Regulations 1992 (SI 1992/3274)
From 1 January 1994, drug manufacturers must supply an information leaflet with any new product. All existing drugs will have to comply with this when the product license is renewed; such renewal takes place on a five year interval.

Professional/ethical guidelines

Solicitors should refer to the pamphlet *Good Medical Practice* published in May 2001 by the GMC. With regard to keeping up to date, the GMC stress the need for practitioners to participate in educational activities, to work with colleagues, to take part in regular audits and to keep up to date with any laws affecting their practice (see paras 10–12).

Practice points

In any case where the allegation is that the defendant has failed to keep up to date with current practice, it is vitally important to obtain the latest medical publications, for example, *The Lancet*, government guidelines, GMC guidelines, etc, and to ascertain how long these publications have been in circulation.

RULE 5(C)

A health carer may be held liable in negligence when he departs from accepted practice. This will be determined as a question of fact.

Commentary

Departing from an approved, accepted practice is in itself not negligent. As the reader will have observed, if the defendant conforms with accepted practice, legally he may escape liability. If he departs from the approved practice, he will not be negligent if he can justify his actions, but if he cannot justify his departure from the accepted practice the claimant should have little difficulty in establishing negligence. The negligent performance of an approved practice will also constitute a departure. Generally, the more serious the resulting damage, the more difficult it will be for the defendant to justify his actions. The rationale behind these comments is that the medical profession should not be discouraged from trying new innovative techniques and that the development of medical science should be encouraged.

However, neither should patients be subjected to reckless experimentation. This point was explored in the case of *Hepworth v Kerr* [1995] 6 Med LR 139, where an anaesthetist was found negligent for reducing a patient's blood pressure to a level lower than the accepted norm. The fact that the defendant argued that he had performed the technique on 1,500 patients was not enough to show that he had proper scientific validation of his technique; this begs the question what will be and when will a technique be deemed accepted practice (see, further, p 166). In *Hepworth*, the court did give some guidance: the defendant had failed to follow up any of his previous 1,500 patients; there was no expert support or endorsement of his work; it was not known how many of his previous 1,500 patients had the characteristics of the claimant; the defendant had no safety margin for error and there had been no proper validation of the technique.

REFERENCES

English case law

(1)   Hepworth v Kerr [1995] 6 Med LR 139
See Commentary above.

(2)   *Clark v McLennan [1983] 1 All ER 416*
The claimant suffered from stress incontinence after the birth of her first child. The defendant operated one month and 11 days after the birth to repair the weakness in her bladder and muscles. The operation and a subsequent operation were unsuccessful. Accepted practice was that the operation should not have been performed until at least three months after the birth.

Held: where the defendant has failed to take a precaution and the very damage occurs which the precaution was designed to prevent then the burden of proof is on the defendant to show he is not in breach of his duty and did not cause the damage. Pain J said (p 425):

... in a situation in which a general duty of care arises and there is a failure to take a precaution, and that very damage occurs against which the precaution is designed to be a protection, then the burden lies on the defendant to show that he was not in breach of duty as well as to show that the damage did not result from his breach of duty.

This decision has been severely criticised, most notably in *Wilsher v Essex AHA* [1986] 3 All ER 801. Mustill LJ (pp 814–15) denied that in such a situation the burden of proof was reversed.

(3) Robinson v Post Office [1974] 2 All ER 737; [1974] 1 WLR 1176
A doctor waited only a minute instead of the usual half hour before administering a tetanus injection after the usual test. He was found negligent in not conforming with accepted practice. (The case failed on causation: see p 212.)

RULE 5(D)

The courts can now condemn an accepted practice on the ground that it does not have a logical basis.

Commentary

An accepted practice has to meet certain basic criteria. There were a number of cases, albeit outside the area of medical law, where the courts had readily intervened and held a practice to be negligent (see *Re Herald of Free Enterprise Appeal* (1987) *The Independent*, 18 December and *Edward Wong Finance Co Ltd v Johnson, Stokes and Master* [1984] AC 296). In the area of medical law, however, the cases were few and far between, but there were the decisions in *Clarke v Adams* (1950) 94 SJ 599 and *Anderson v Chasney* (1949) 4 DLR 71. As these cases pre-date *Bolam*, they had to be viewed with caution, although McNair J in *Bolam* did state that the *Bolam* principle was nothing new and was simply restating the law as of old. Post-*Bolam*, there was the 1968 case of *Hucks v Cole* reported at [1993] 4 Med LR 393. There, a GP was found negligent for failing to treat Mrs Hucks with penicillin and, as a result, septicaemia developed. Mrs Hucks had recently given birth and developed puerperal fever, a condition which had been extremely common before the Second World War but was very rare in the 1960s. The defendant said he acted in accordance with the reasonable practice of other doctors with obstetric experience. It was contended that this was no defence; the doctor should have taken the requisite steps when he could see that the absence of treatment posed a serious risk to the woman's health. Sachs LJ said (p 397):

> When the evidence shows that a lacuna in professional practice exists by which risks of grave danger are knowingly taken, then, however small the risks, the courts must anxiously examine that lacuna – particularly if the risks can be easily and inexpensively avoided. If the court finds on analysis of the reasons given for not taking those precautions that, in the light of current professional knowledge, there is no proper basis for the lacuna, and that it is definitely not reasonable that those risks should have been taken, its function is to state that it constitutes negligence. In such a case the practice will no doubt thereafter be altered to the benefit of the patients.

In *Hucks v Cole,* the correct approach was adopted by the court; it focused on the magnitude of the risk involved and the ease of avoiding it. The pathologist's report had signalled that a form of septicaemia infection was present while the expert evidence was that it should have been treated. Dr Cole had received the test results indicating the infection but had done nothing. The court considered the likelihood of death resulting and the extent of the foreseeability of the risk; although the possibility of fulminating septicaemia was extremely rare, where the infection occurred in a maternity ward the consensus of the experts was that it should be treated. Also, the court considered the practicality of the precautions: penicillin was readily available and posed no danger to the patient's health. Bearing all this in mind the court decided that the necessary precautions should have been taken; as they were not, Dr Cole was held to be negligent. It is worthwhile noting that at no time in their judgment did the court refer to the *Bolam* principle.

Despite decisions like *Hucks v Cole (supra)*, *Djemal v Bexley HA* (1995) 6 Med LR 269 and *Lybert v Warrington HA* (1996) 7 Med LR 71, these cases were very much in the minority; the majority clung tenaciously to the words of Lord Scarman in the *Sidaway* case: '... the standard is a matter for medical judgment.' (See *Maynard v W Midlands RHA* [1984] 1 WLR 634.) And so, the courts seemed to have little or no role to play on the issue of breach, except in the most blatant of circumstances. Commentators like Margaret Brazier rightly questioned the wisdom of this. Not only did such an approach smack of a deferential attitude on the part of the courts towards medical practitioners, it was also not the way they treated other professions.

And then came the *Bolitho* decision (*Bolitho v City and Hackney HA* [1997] 4 All ER 771). In this case, the House of Lords introduced the *Bolam* test into the area of causation and omissions to treat; fortunately for all concerned, they took the opportunity to spell out the *Bolam* test as they saw it. Lord Browne-Wilkinson said (p 778):

> The use of these adjectives – responsible, reasonable and respectable – all show that the court has to be satisfied that the exponents of the body of opinion relied on can demonstrate that such opinion has a logical basis. In particular, in cases involving, as they often do, the weighing of risks against benefits, the judge before accepting a body of opinion as being responsible, reasonable or respectable, will need to be satisfied that, in forming their views, the experts have directed their minds to the question of comparative risk and benefits and have reached a defensible conclusion on the matter.

It is submitted that what Lord Browne-Wilkinson has done is to correctly hand back to the courts the jurisdiction to objectively declare an accepted medical practice as not being able to provide a defence if the practice is found to be lacking a logical basis. It is further submitted that this 'modern' restatement of the *Bolam* test was exactly what McNair J really intended back in 1957; the gloss which the courts, post-*Bolam*, sought to put on the words of the learned judge was evidence of a public policy hands-off approach towards the medical profession. Rightly, that approach has been jettisoned.

But has it? At p 779 of the report, this is what Lord Browne-Wilkinson went on to say:

These decisions (*Hucks v Cole* ...) demonstrate that in cases of diagnosis and treatment there are cases where, despite a body of professional opinion sanctioning the defendant's conduct, the defendant can properly be held liable in negligence (I am not here considering questions of disclosure of risk). In my judgment that is because, in some cases, it cannot be demonstrated to the judge's satisfaction that the body of opinion relied on is reasonable or responsible. In the vast majority of cases the fact that distinguished experts ... are of a particular opinion will demonstrate the reasonableness of that opinion ... But if in a rare case, it can be demonstrated that the professional opinion is not capable of withstanding logical analysis, the judge is entitled to hold that the body of opinion is not reasonable or responsible. I emphasise that ... it will very seldom be right for a judge to reach the conclusion that views genuinely held by a competent medical expert are unreasonable.

It is suggested that the House of Lords having given the power back to the courts then, in a demonstration of what they would probably call realism but is nothing more than a throwback to the 'bad old days', sought to suggest that in diagnosis and treatment cases the chances of being able to argue a non-logical basis were not very high; but were probably higher in cases of risk disclosure.

In fact, subsequent case law has not borne out this distinction; could this be a case of lower court judges, having been given the 'green light' by the House of Lords, flexing their muscles? In five cases post-*Bolitho*, a non-logical basis was found to exist and they were all cases which had more do do with diagnosis and treatment than with risk disclosure (*Penney, Palmer and Cannon v E Kent HA* [2000] 1 Lloyd's Rep Med 41; *Walsh v Gwynned HA* (see Medical Litigation, May 1998 p 9; [1998] Current Law Yearbook 3977); *Marriott v W Midlands RHA* [1999] Lloyd's Rep Med 23; *Zinzuwadia v Home Secretary* (2000), reported in [2001] Medical Law Monitor, January, p 6; and *Calvert v Westwood Veterinary Group* [2001] 1 Lloyd's Rep Med 20).

REFERENCES

English case law

(1)   Re Herald of Free Enterprise Appeal (1987) The Independent, 18 December
This case was heard on appeal following the ferry disaster at Zeebrugge. Although the court agreed that it was common practice for masters not to check the bow doors to confirm that they were closed, there had been a failure to adopt the necessary precautions which were required for the safety of the ship.

(2)   Edward Wong Finance Co Ltd v Johnson, Stokes and Master [1984] AC 296
Conveyancing practice in Hong Kong was held to be negligent despite the fact that it was followed by other solicitors.

(3)   Clarke v Adams (1950) 94 SJ 597
A physiotherapist was found negligent despite the fact that he had acted in accordance with the practice approved by the Chartered Society of Physiotherapists.

(4)   Bolam v Friern HMC [1957] 1 WLR 582; [1957] 2 All ER 118
See p 155.

(5)   Hucks v Cole [1993] 4 Med LR 393
See p 172 above.

(6) Djemal v Bexley HA [1995] 6 Med LR 269

(7) Lybert v Warrington HA [1996] 7 Med LR 71
The court held that a warning given by the defendant was inadequate.

(8) Sidaway v Board of Governors of the Bethlem Royal Hospital and the Maudsley Hospital [1985] AC 871; [1985] 1 All ER 643
In a case about disclosure of information, Lord Bridge stated that the courts might depart from the standards set by the profession, where (p 663):

> ... disclosure of a risk was so obviously necessary to an informed choice on the part of the patient that no reasonably prudent medical man would fail to make it.

Lord Templeman stated that it is (p 665):

> ... for the courts to decide, after hearing the doctor's explanation, whether the doctor has in fact been guilty of a breach of duty with regard to information.

(9) Maynard v West Midlands RHA [1984] 1 WLR 634; [1985] 1 All ER 635
The claimant was provisionally diagnosed as having TB, although this was far from certain; she could have been suffering from Hodgkins disease. It was agreed that further tests should be carried out and in the course of a biopsy the recurrent laryngeal nerve was damaged and the patient rendered hoarse. The claimant based her case on the grounds that the diagnosis was so obvious that the operation should never have been performed.

The case eventually went to the House of Lords. There were two schools of thought, one which supported the claimant, the other the defendant. Lord Scarman said ([1984] 1 WLR 634, p 639):

> ... a judge's 'preference' for one body of distinguished professional opinion to another also professionally distinguished is not sufficient to establish negligence in a practitioner whose actions have received the seal of approval of those whose opinions, truthfully expressed, honestly held, were not preferred ... For in the realms of diagnosis and treatment, negligence is not established by preferring one respectable body of professional opinion to another. Failing to exercise the ordinary skill of a doctor (in the appropriate speciality, if he be a specialist) is necessary.

Consequently, as the defendant's conduct was approved by a body of medical opinion, the claimant's action failed.

(10) Bolitho v City and Hackney HA [1997] 4 All ER 771
See p 235 *et seq.*

(11) Penney, Palmer and Cannon v East Kent HA [2000] 1 Lloyd's Rep Med 41
The case involved cervical smears obtained from each of the claimants which were screened at the defendant's hospital. In each case the smears had been reported as normal or negative, yet all the claimants had gone on to develop adenocarcinoma of the cervix. The claim was that the cytoscreeners had been in breach of their duty in reporting the smears as negative. The trial judge held there was negligence. The appeal was dismissed.

(12) Walsh v Gwynned HA [1998] Current Law Yearbook 3977; [1988] Medical Litigation, May
W's father had committed suicide whilst a voluntary psychiatric patient under the care of the defendants. W contended that the defendants had negligently failed to provide proper care and treatment to her father and this had led to his suicide. The defendants denied negligence and causation.

In holding the defendants liable the trial judge indicated that their expert opinion could not withstand logical analysis.

(13) Marriott v W Midlands RHA and Others [1999] Lloyd's Rep Med 23
The claimant fell down some stairs and was unconscious for 20–30 minutes, having sustained a head injury. He was admitted to the first defendant hospital. Following X-rays and neurological observations, he was discharged the next day. Finding that his condition was not improving, the claimant asked his GP – the third defendant – to attend him at his home. The GP examined the claimant but neurological tests showed no abnormality; he therefore told the claimant's wife to contact him again if the claimant's condition deteriorated. Four days later, the claimant's condition suddenly deteriorated, he became unconscious and was returned to hospital. He had sustained a massive extradural haematoma. During the operation which followed, a linear fracture of the skull was discovered and he was found to be bleeding from the middle meningeal artery. The outcome was that the claimant was left with hemiplegia, dysanthria and severe disability.

The claim against the GP was that he had been negligent in failing to realise the seriousness of the claimant's injury and to refer him back to hospital. The trial judge and the Appeal Court agreed there was negligence. Two of the Appeal Court judges (Beldam and Swinton-Thomas LJJ) applied the *Bolitho* decision.

(14) Zinzuwadia v Home Secretary (2000) – see [2001] Medical Law Monitor, January, p 6
This was a claim by the widow of a man who, while a prisoner, had committed suicide. The claim alleged that a psychiatrist had been negligent in failing to diagnose that the man was a potential suicide risk.

Held: no negligence.

(15) Calvert v Westwood Veterinary Group [2001] 1 Lloyd's Rep Med 20
The claim here was that a veterinary surgeon had been negligent in not administering prophylactic antibiotics to a thoroughbred mare owned by the claimant.

Held: no negligence.

See, also, the following foreign case law:

Foreign case law

Australia

(1) Rogers v Whittaker [1993] 4 Med LR 79; [1992] 3 Med LR 331; (1992) 109 ALR 625
In this case, the claimant, who was nearly blind in her right eye, developed an extremely rare condition in her left eye. After a routine checkup she was referred to the defendant for possible surgery. He advised that she should have surgery on the right eye to remove scar tissue which would improve its appearance and restore significant sight to the eye as well as hopefully prevent the onset of glaucoma. She agreed to an operation on this eye. She did not ask whether the operation could cause damage to her 'good' eye. However, the evidence at the trial showed that she had questioned the defendant repeatedly as to any possible complications and was very concerned that her good eye could be injured. In fact, an entry had been made in the hospital notes indicating that she was concerned that her 'good eye' would be operated on by mistake. Following the operation, she developed an inflammation in her treated eye which caused a condition, sympathetic ophthalmia, in her left (good) eye which resulted in almost total loss of sight

in this eye, consequently rendering her nearly blind. There was a one in 14,000 chance of this sympathetic ophthalmia developing, but this had not been mentioned by the defendant. Had the defendant disclosed the risk, the claimant contended she would not have undergone the operation. She claimed the defendant had been negligent for failing to disclose the risk. The High Court of Australia ruled in her favour. It rejected the *Bolam* test and instead applied the test already entrenched in a number of Australian cases and endorsed the dissenting judgment of Lord Scarman in *Sidaway* (see p 42). Mason CJ, commenting on the standard of care, said (p 83):

> ... that standard is not determined solely or even primarily by reference to the practice followed or supported by a responsible body of opinion in the relevant profession or sphere ... Further ... in the field of non-disclosure of risk and the provision of advice and information, the *Bolam* principle has been discarded and instead, the courts have adopted the principle that, while evidence of acceptable medical practice is a useful guide for the courts, it is for the courts to adjudicate on what is the appropriate standard of care after giving weight to the paramount consideration that a person is entitled to make his own decisions about his life.

(2) Ellis v Wallsend District Hospital [1990] 2 Med LR 103; (1989) 70 NSWLR 553

The claimant had a background of intractable and severe neck pain, was dependent on drugs and had overdosed. All other treatment had failed. She was advised to have nerve separation microsurgery. The evidence was that the operation carried a remote risk of paralysis but a more substantial risk was that it would fail to cure the pain. She contended that had she known of the risk then she would not have undergone the operation. Although the case failed on causation the court made some interesting comments re disclosure of risk. The judge at first instance, relying on Lord Scarman's dissent in *Sidaway v Board of Governors of the Bethlem Royal Hospital and the Maudsley Hospital* [1985] AC 871 and the judgment of King CJ in *F v R* (1983) 33 SASR 189, pp 192–94, held that the doctor was in breach of duty in failing to warn of the risk of paralysis and of failure to obtain relief from pain. This decision was not challenged on appeal. As a result the defendant was found to be in breach of his duty to warn of the risks involved in the operation, despite medical evidence to the contrary in support of non-disclosure.

(3) F v R (1983) 33 SASR 189

The case concerned a failed tubal ligation. The claimant's husband had queried whether he should have a vasectomy instead. The claimant alleged that the defendant had been negligent in failing to warn of a less than 1% failure rate.

No alternatives were discussed with the patient and the operation was carried out at the same time as a Caesarian section. Although the defendant was found not negligent the court made the following comments on standard of care:

Per King CJ:

> The ultimate question, however, is not whether the defendant's conduct accords with the practice of his profession or some part of it, but whether it conforms to the standard of reasonable care demanded by law. That is a question for the court and the duty of deciding it cannot be delegated to any profession or group in the community.

Per Bollen J:

> ... nothing in *Bolam* ... which justifies any suggestion that evidence of the practice obtaining in the medical profession is automatically decisive of any issue in an action ... for damages in negligence.

Canada

(1)   Anderson v Chasney (1949) 4 DLR 71

A surgeon was found negligent after leaving a sponge in the base of a child's nostrils following a tonsillectomy. His defence was that it was not his practice nor the hospital's practice to use sponges with ties on nor to keep a count of the number of sponges used.

Held: complying with general practice does not constitute a complete defence. The court reasoned that if common/accepted practice was always a defence then a group of operators by adopting an accepted practice could avoid liability, even if that practice was clearly negligent.

(2)   Reibl v Hughes (1980) 114 DLR (3d) 1

The defendant did not disclose the risk of a stroke resulting from surgery. The risk was rare and might not have affected the claimant's decision but for the fact that he was nearing retirement and would have been eligible for a full pension. The risk of the stroke was therefore very significant to him as he could not risk the loss of his pension; consequently the court ruled that it should have been disclosed if a reasonable patient in the position of the claimant would not have undergone the operation.

STANDARD OF CARE IN PARTICULAR INSTANCES

As discussed in the preceding paragraphs the same standard of care is applicable no matter what the stage, nature or context of medical treatment, namely, the *Bolam* standard as modified by the *Bolitho* case. However, for ease of reference, the cases below are split into the following categories: diagnosis, treatment, disclosure of information and prescriptions.

RULE 5(E)

A health carer may be held liable for a faulty diagnosis, etc.

Commentary

First, a health carer may fail to consider the patient's medical history. He is under an obligation to give this full consideration for obvious reasons, for example, the patient may be allergic to a particular drug, be suffering from a pre-existing illness or may have had treatment for the condition previously. In any event, common sense says that it is inherently dangerous to attempt to make a diagnosis without first considering the patient's medical records, and then asking him relevant questions (see *Cassidy v Ministry of Health* [1951] 2 KB 343). The doctor must listen to the patient's account of the illness, while being careful not to attach too much significance to the patient's self-diagnosis, for example, the patient who says he has pains in his chest and that it is probably due to indigestion. The health carer must examine the patient and come to his own diagnosis.

An error in diagnosis will not necessarily amount to negligence (see *Whitehouse v Jordan* [1981] 1 WLR 246). The court will take into consideration the nature of the symptoms present (if any), the difficulty in making the diagnosis (see *Hulse v Wilson* (1953) 2 BMJ 890), what further tests may be appropriate and the actual steps required to make an accurate diagnosis, for example, the use of diagnostic aids (see *Whiteford v Hunter* [1950] WN 553). A common area for mistaken diagnosis involves fractures (see *Fraser v Vancouver General Hospital* (1951) 3 WWR 337 and *Hotson v East Berkshire HA* [1987] AC 750). It could be said that, in all cases where there is a suspected fracture, the defendant should avail himself of X-rays, bearing in mind that such a precaution is readily available. In *Hucks v Cole* [1993] 4 Med LR 393, Sachs LJ said (p 140) that, where the precaution was readily available and relatively inexpensive, it would seem sensible that the defendant doctor should avail himself of it.

Another area which causes problems is the diagnosis of cancer. Breast cancer has been subject to a great deal of publicity and yet cases still arise of incorrect or missed diagnosis (see *Judge v Huntingdon HA* [1995] 6 Med LR 223). The problem here is that, notwithstanding the cancer, the breast itself often contains lumps and therefore an accurate diagnosis can often be difficult without an operation which the patient and the doctor may be loathe to undertake. In *Judge*, an experienced surgeon was convinced of the innocence of the lump even after the second referral. Delay in the diagnosis of cancer often leads to another problem, namely how to estimate the damage to the patient's chance of survival, which is considered at p 217 *et seq*. Lack of physical signs of injury or illness is not of itself determinative of liability (see *Bova v Spring* [1994] 5 Med LR 120); what is important is the whole picture as presented by the facts.

Apart from the medical factors, the court will have regard to the practicality and the expense of the precautions (see *Latimer v AEC Ltd* [1953] AC 643 and the discussion above, p 157). However, the solicitor must always remember that the test is what a reasonable health carer would have done by reference to the *Bolam* test, as modified, ignoring the fact that the precaution may seem sensible to him (the solicitor) and was readily available.

In some cases, the allegation of negligence is not that the diagnosis was incorrect but that the claimant's condition appeared so serious that the defendant should have referred the claimant to a specialist or, at the very least, carried out further tests (see *Dale v Munthali* (1976) 78 DLR (3d) 588 and *Gordon v Wilson* [1992] 3 Med LR 401). The health carer is advised that, where he suspects that the condition is more serious, he must carry out further tests, even though there is a viewpoint which suggests that he could be sued for over testing. We suggest that such cases would be few and far between and that, in view of the consequences if he failed to test, he should always err on the side of caution.

In determining whether the health carer has failed to reach the requisite standard of care, he would do well to bear in mind that diagnosis is an ongoing factor. A health carer who refuses to budge from his initial assessment of the claimant's condition, notwithstanding the patient's apparent deterioration, is at risk of being negligent (see *Stacey v Chiddy* [1993] 4 Med LR 345). At all stages, the treating health carer should be alert to the patient's response to the treatment prescribed and whether he has the expertise to continue to treat the patient, that is, should the patient be referred to a specialist? In *Judge v Huntingdon HA* [1995] 6 Med LR 223, the court found the specialist at fault for failing to arrange with the claimant to see her again, taking into consideration that she was adamant that the lump in her breast was painful and the letter of referral from her GP. GPs, however, usually see their patients over a long period of time; they should therefore continually be monitoring the patient's condition (see *Langley v Campbell* (1975) *The Times*, 6 November). Although the patient may have difficulty in establishing negligence after one visit to his GP, the greater the number of visits and the longer the time before the correct diagnosis is made, the more likely a negligence claim becomes. The moral for the defendant is: if the patient's symptoms persist, think twice. At the very least, the health carer should make an accurate contemporaneous note of why he did not refer to a specialist.

Having made the diagnosis that the patient has to be, for example, referred to hospital, what if the hospital then fails to give the patient an appointment? Although the GP who made the referral would not be responsible for the hospital's failure, he would be liable for failing to make the hospital aware that the patient's condition was serious or had become so while waiting for the appointment (see *Coles v Reading and District HMC* (1963) 107 SJ 115).

Finally, another area which continues to attract media headlines is the number of incidences where patients have caught infections while in hospital, notably from blood transfusions (see *Re HIV Haemophiliac Litigation* (1990) 140 NLJ 1349 and *H v Royal Alexandra Hospital for Children* [1990] 1 Med LR 297). Whether the defendant is negligent will often turn on what he could have reasonably been expected to do at the time of the alleged incident, for example, in *ter Neuzen v Korn* (1993) 103 DLR (4th) 473, the question was whether the defendant should have known in 1985 that there was a risk of HIV infection from artificial insemination.

REFERENCES

English case law

(1)   Cassidy v Ministry of Health [1951] 2 KB 343; [1951] 1 All ER 574
Hospital staff failed to listen to the claimant's complaints of excessive pain. See, also:

- *Payne v St Helier Group HMC* (1952) *The Times*, 12 November, where the claimant was admitted to casualty after being kicked by a horse. He was sent home and subsequently died. The casualty officer was found negligent in failing to examine the claimant.

- *Barnett v Chelsea and Kensington HMC* [1969] 1 QB 420; [1968] 2 WLR 427 on the obligation of casualty officers.

(2)   Whitehouse v Jordan [1981] 1 WLR 246; [1981] 1 All ER 267
A child suffered brain damage at birth as a result of the obstetrician's negligence in his use of forceps. In the Court of Appeal, Lord Denning expressed the opinion that a mere error of judgment did not amount to negligence. The House of Lords forcibly stated that whether or not the practitioner was negligent depended on if he had exercised reasonable care. It was held that here he had, because the error was one that could have been made by any of his contemporaries.

(3) Hulse v Wilson (1953) 2 BMJ 890
Held: it was not unreasonable on the part of the defendant not to diagnose cancer of the penis because it was so unusual in a man of the claimant's age.

See, also, *Thornton v Nicol* [1992] 3 Med LR 41, where the doctor diagnosed conjunctivitis but failed to diagnose meningitis. He failed to refer the patient (a baby) to hospital. Meningitis was diagnosed by a subsequent doctor; however, earlier diagnosis would have avoided the worst consequences. The earlier doctor was found not negligent – the patient did not appear so ill that the doctor should have immediately referred him to hospital.

(4) Whiteford v Hunter [1950] WN 553; (1950) 94 SJ 758
Availability of diagnostic aids: see p 168.

(5) Hotson v East Berkshire HA [1987] AC 750; [1987] 2 All ER 909
A young boy fell from a tree and hurt his leg. The accident and emergency department failed to X-ray him and he was sent home. After five days, he went back and a fracture of the femur was diagnosed. The claimant succeeded in showing that the failure to X-ray him on his first visit was negligent. The case failed on causation (see p 217 *et seq*).

See, also, *Wood v Thurston* (1951) *The Times*, 5 May, where the patient entered hospital in an intoxicated condition. He was allowed to go home and died the next day. It was revealed that he had several injuries. The defendant argued that the deceased's intoxicated condition had dulled his sensitivity to pain. The defendant was held liable for not examining the deceased thoroughly, notwithstanding that he might have been misled by the deceased's intoxicated condition.

(6) Hucks v Cole [1993] 4 Med LR 393
See p 172.

(7) Judge v Huntingdon HA [1995] 6 Med LR 223
See above p 179 and Chapter 6 Causation, p 223.

(8) Bova v Spring [1994] 5 Med LR 120
The claimant had been moving concrete and had developed pains in his chest. A week later, his GP was called. The claimant complained of diarrhoea, breathlessness and of feeling shivery, and also of increased pain on movement. The GP diagnosed a muscular strain and attributed the other symptoms to a virus infection. He did not arrange a further appointment. The claimant collapsed and died two days later. The cause of death was suppurative lobar pneumonia.

The defendant GP was held liable in negligence in that he did not arrange a follow-up appointment. Expert evidence indicated that, had the claimant been examined the following day, his condition would have indicated that urgent treatment was required.

See, also, *Sutton v Population Services Family Planning Programme Ltd* (1981) *The Times*, 7 November, which involved a failure to follow up a diagnosis of cancer. For a detailed commentary, see p 223.

Other cases involving the diagnosis of cancer include: *Phillips v Grampian Hospital Board* [1991] 3 Med LR 16; *Gascoine v Ian Sheridan & Co and Latham* [1994] 5 Med LR 437; *Judge v Huntingdon HA* [1995] 6 Med LR 223; and *Stacey v Chiddy* [1993] 4 Med LR 216.

In *Sa'ad v Robinson* [1989] 1 Med LR 41, a GP was held negligent for failing to refer to hospital a child who had sucked hot tea from a teapot. The GP had merely prescribed some medication to soothe the child. The child's mother telephoned the surgery some hours later and reiterated her child's symptoms. The duty doctor instructed that the child should be propped up with pillows, but he did not visit the child. Eventually the duty doctor was called to the house and the child was admitted to hospital and later referred to casualty, where she had an anoxic fit and suffered irreversible brain damage.

The court ruled that the GP was negligent in failing to realise that, in sucking tea from a hot spout, the child might have inhaled steam which could reach her throat directly without burning her mouth. The duty doctor was also found negligent in failing to visit the child immediately and for not admitting the child to casualty, or emphasising the seriousness of her condition.

(9)   Latimer v AEC Ltd [1953] AC 643
See r 5(A), p 157.

(10) Bolam v Friern HMC [1957] 1 WLR 582
See r 5(A), p 155.

(11) Gordon v Wilson [1992] 3 Med LR 401
The claimant had visited her GP on several occasions complaining of deafness and difficulties with balance, impaired vision and difficulty in eating and drinking. She was eventually referred to a specialist who removed a benign melanoma from her brain. She sued the GP, alleging that her symptoms were such that she should have been referred at an earlier stage. The court accepted that her combination of symptoms should have prompted her GP to refer her to a specialist at an early stage.

See, also, *Chin Keow v Government of Malaysia* [1967] 1 WLR 813 (failure to inquire into family history – inquiry would have revealed that the claimant was allergic to penicillin – patient died from an allergic reaction to the drug); *Gardiner v Mountford* [1989] 1 Med LR 205 (doctor failed to listen to the patient's suggestion that she could be pregnant).

(12) Langley v Campbell (1975) The The Times, 6 November
This case concerned a failure to diagnose malaria. The GP diagnosed the patient as having influenza.

Held: although the GP did not routinely come across malaria, the fact that the claimant's symptoms persisted and that the claimant had recently returned from Uganda, coupled with the fact that his family had told the GP that he had suffered from malaria previously and had himself suggested blood tests, should have alerted the GP that he might be dealing with a tropical disease.

See, also, *Meyer v Gordon* (1981) 17 CCLT 1 (failure to consider the patient's previous obstetric history which would have revealed that the patient's previous labour was rapid).

(13) Coles v Reading and District HMC (1963) 107 SJ 115
The deceased suffered a finger injury and went to the local cottage hospital for treatment. He was advised to go to the main hospital for a tetanus injection but failed to do so and instead visited his GP. His GP failed to inquire what treatment he had undergone at the cottage hospital. The patient died of toxaemia; neither the treating hospital nor the GP gave the patient a tetanus injection. The cottage hospital was found negligent in failing to communicate the claimant's symptoms, and the GP for not inquiring what treatment the claimant had received and for not contacting the cottage hospital.

(14) Re HIV Haemophiliac Litigation (1990) 140 NLJ 1349
See p 168.

Foreign case law

Australia

(1)   Stacey v Chiddy [1993] 4 Med LR 216, affirmed [1993] 4 Med LR 345
The claimant visited her GP after finding two lumps in her breast. The GP arranged a mammogram and an ultrasound scan, which gave normal results but did not confirm that the lumps were cystic. She re-attended her GP on several occasions. However, he failed to re-examine her breasts for lumps and relied on the inconclusive ultrasound scan. Eventually she was referred to a specialist, where it was established that the cancer had spread to her spine. In the New South Wales Supreme Court, the GP was held negligent for placing too much reliance on inconclusive results and for failing to re-examine the claimant. The court held that, although the defendant had not acted irresponsibly with his advice, he should have taken into consideration the magnitude of the risk to which the appellant was exposed if the diagnosis was incorrect. The action failed on causation.

(2)   Giurelli v Girgus (1980) 24 SASR 261
A doctor failed to listen to the patient's complaints about persistent pain, claiming that the patient was difficult.

(3)   H v Royal Alexandra Hospital for Children [1990] 1 Med LR 29
See p 169.

Canada

(1)   Dale v Munthali (1976) 78 DLR (3d) 588
The claimant complained of aching all over and later developed diarrhoea and began vomiting. He also had difficulty in hearing. He was diagnosed as suffering from influenza. His condition deteriorated over the next two days and he was admitted to hospital where meningitis was diagnosed.

Held: the defendant GP was not negligent for failing to diagnose meningitis, but the claimant's symptoms were so severe that he should have carried out further tests.

(2)   Layden v Cope (1984) 28 CCLT 140
The claimant had a history of gout. He complained of a sore foot and the GP diagnosed gout. His condition deteriorated but the doctor continued the treatment for gout. He was eventually diagnosed as having blood poisoning which resulted in his leg being amputated below the knee.

Held: the defendant was negligent in failing to revise his initial diagnosis in the light of the claimant's deterioration.

(3)   ter Neuzen v Korn (1993) 103 DLR (4th) 473
See p 169.

Statutes/statutory instruments

National Health Service (General Medical Services) Regulations 1992 (SI 1992/635)
These Regulations apply to NHS patients and provide for GPs' terms of service to include a condition that they must give to their patients all necessary and appropriate personal medical services of the type usually provided by general medical practitioners

including arranging for the referral of patients as necessary to any other services provided under the Health Services Acts.

RULE 5(F)

A health carer may be held liable for failing to disclose to the patient the risks associated with the treatment.

Commentary

All medical treatment will involve some side effects and/or risks, ranging from the trivial to the not so trivial. Consequently, in treating a patient, two things need to be borne in mind:

(a) what are chances of the side effects/risks occurring and are they reasonably foreseeable?; and

(b) what are the consequences of those side effects?

Those issues will have a direct bearing on the nature of information to be imparted to the patient prior to the treatment being undertaken. At the same time, this information itself could depend on such things as the treatment involved and the characteristics of the particular claimant (see *Blyth v Bloomsbury HA* [1993] 4 Med LR 151 and *Chatterton v Gerson* [1981] QB 432). The general rule is that disclosure of risks is governed by the *Bolam* modified rule.

Where the claimant claims that he was not given sufficient information about the procedure, then, technically, he may be able to claim in either battery or negligence. In *Hills v Potter* [1984] 1 WLR 641, the court held that, where there was a lack of information as to the nature of the procedure, the claim should be brought in battery, but where the claim was based on the failure of the health carer to disclose the risks inherent in the procedure the claim should be brought in negligence. While this distinction appears to be clear and firmly entrenched (see, for example, *Sidaway*), it is not without its problems. For example, it has been said that some inherent risks are so significant that they go to the very nature of the procedure. Our advice to the doctor is that, where the risk is common, even if it is trivial, then it should be disclosed. However, where it is not certain how serious the risk could be, the issue is more problematical. One approach would be to instruct the patient to return if certain symptoms appear; in that case, if the patient fails to return, he could be regarded as contributorily negligent (see, further, p 241).

If the consent is induced by fraud or misrepresentation, it could be invalid. However, for a claim in negligence, it does not really matter why the risks have not been disclosed; what matters is that they have not been disclosed and that, if they had been, the patient would not have consented to the procedure. This latter point is crucial; many claims fail because the claimant is unable to show that, even if disclosure had taken place, he would not have consented to the procedure (see *Goorkani v Tayside Health Board* [1991] 3 Med LR 33 at p 189 and p 210). Where the health carer lies to the patient in response to a question, he may be able to escape liability if he can rely on the defence of therapeutic privilege or show that other doctors would have done the same; but much will depend on the nature of the question asked.

The leading authority on disclosure of information is *Sidaway v Board of Governors of Bethlem Royal Hospital and the Maudsley Hospital* [1985] AC 871. The claimant underwent an operation on her spine to relieve pressure on one of the nerve roots. Unfortunately, during the operation her spinal cord was damaged, leaving her disabled. The neurosurgeon had told her about the risk of damage to the nerve root (a risk of about 2%) but had not told her about damage to the spinal cord (a risk of 1%). There was no evidence that the operation had been carried out negligently. The claimant, however, argued that the defendant had been negligent in not telling her of the risk of damage to the spinal cord. The claim failed. The court said that it was a matter for the doctor's clinical judgment which risks should be disclosed to enable the patient to make a rational decision. This case demonstrates how much English courts did indeed favour the medical profession as the body to determine the level of information to be disclosed, as opposed to the 'what would the patient need to know' approach canvassed in, for example, *Rogers v Whittaker* [1993] 4 Med LR 79.

Real innovations with regard to the standard of disclosure have been in other jurisdictions. In *Rogers v Whittaker* [1993] 4 Med LR 79, the court held that the *Bolam* test was inappropriate to cases concerning disclosure of information. What was important was whether the risk was material and, if the answer to that question was yes, then that risk should be disclosed. A risk was material if a person in the position of the claimant, when warned, would deem it significant or if the medical practitioner would know that if the claimant was warned of this particular risk he would attach significance to it. With such an approach the court is not really applying the doctrine of informed consent; it is simply saying that the risk of sympathetic ophthalmia was a risk that the claimant should have been informed about in order to make a reasoned decision about the procedure. The fact that the claimant had repeatedly questioned the defendant regarding the procedure and whether there was any incidental risk to her good left eye was significant. In making its decision, the court departed from the previously established view that asking questions made no difference in determining the standard of care. In *Blyth v Bloomsbury HA* [1993] 4 Med LR 151, Kerr LJ had said (p 157):

> The question of what a claimant should be told in answer to a general enquiry cannot be divorced from the *Bolam* test, any more than when no such enquiry is made ... Indeed, I am not convinced that the *Bolam* test is irrelevant even in relation to what answers are properly to be given to specific enquiries ...

The court in *Rogers* rightly held that the question was not whether the defendant's conduct was in accordance with accepted practice, but whether the defendant had met the standard of care required by law which was a question to be determined by the court. It then went on to distinguish between cases concerning diagnosis and treatment and the present one. In the former, the professional standards of the time would have a large part to play in determining whether the defendant was in breach; however, in cases concerning the apparent failure to disclose information, they were not really about what was accepted practice except for those instances where therapeutic privilege was involved. What was important was whether the defendant communicated the relevant information to enable the claimant to make an informed decision. In *Rogers*, the patient expressed concern about the possible danger to her one good eye and therefore that risk was material; however, there was a body of medical opinion which held that the defendant should only have revealed information about damage to the patient's good eye if the latter had specifically asked about damage to her good eye. This was held to be untenable as this would in effect require the patient to have specific knowledge of medical matters (see *Hollis v Dow Corning Corpn* (1993) 103 DLR 520, p 189).

In addition to warning about risks before treatment, the health carer also has a duty to inform the patient if something goes wrong. It would seem to be the rule that whether or not he decides to tell the patient what has been done to him will still be a matter of clinical discretion and as such determined by the *Bolam* test. However, given the current trend that a patient does have a right to know and the general importance attached to patients' rights, it would seem likely that a court would hold that a health carer who failed to disclose a medical error had not met the required standard of care. In some instances, the health carer may be able to rely on the defence of therapeutic privilege; however, although this concept has been widely accepted by US courts, it has been soundly rejected by other jurisdictions, notably Canada, where it was held that it could not be used as an excuse for non-disclosure (see *Meyer Estate v Rogers* (1991) 78 DLR (4th) 307). An important point to bear in mind is that many clinical negligence cases will fail on the issue of causation; therefore, if the damage has already occurred, then the claimant's ignorance through non-disclosure will be immaterial. In Canada, the test is that of materiality (see *Reibl v Hughes* (1980) 114 DLR (3d) 1), namely, that if an error would be material to a patient, then disclosure must be made.

One notable decision on non-disclosure of an error is the Canadian case of *Stamos v Davies* (1985) 21 DLR 4th 507. In that case, the patient was to have a biopsy of the lung. Unfortunately, in error, the biopsy tissue that was obtained was not of the lung but of the spleen, which resulted in the spleen being removed. The claimant was not informed of the mistake and the court found that the physician had breached his duty to disclose. However, the case failed because the claimant was unable to show a causal connection between the loss of the spleen and the fact that the physician did not tell him that his spleen had been injured. In *Kueper v McMullin* (1986) 37 CCLT 318, a dentist performing a root canal left a piece of the drill bit in the patient's mouth. Although aware of the error he left the bit in place and simply filled the tooth. Eventually, X-rays taken by another dentist revealed the drill bit. The court was faced with the issue as to whether the dentist should have disclosed the error. The question they asked was: what would a reasonable patient choose to do, knowing that the drill bit was there and that there was only a minimal risk if it was left alone? The court held that the reasonable patient would have left it there; consequently, the defendant was not liable for non-disclosure.

The claimant may take a risk or follow a certain type of lifestyle that he would not otherwise have done had the risk been disclosed. In *Gregory v Pembrokeshire HA* [1989] 1 Med LR 81, the patient was never informed that an amniocentesis test had failed to elicit a result. After giving birth to a Down's Syndrome child, she alleged that, if she had been informed, then she would have undergone a second test, and if that proved positive, have had an abortion.

The case failed because, on the evidence, it appeared that she would not have had a second test so late on in the pregnancy in accordance with the doctor's advice.

Whether or not a person would have asked the health carers to do something different or refused further treatment or asked for further tests should be regarded as immaterial in determining whether a medical error ought to have been disclosed. By his inadvertence, the health carer has created the dilemma/risk/injury; therefore he should be accountable for his actions. Is this too harsh an approach? Not if there is no other way of ensuring that an unrestricted flow of information is maintained. In the US, this principle has been adopted in some cases where the court's reasoning is that the health carer, rather than 'the individual consumer who is entirely without fault', should legally bear the consequences. In our opinion, if disclosure is not made, it should be assumed that the health carer will assume responsibility for anything that does go wrong.

A health carer has a duty to liaise with other health professionals; indeed, it is one of the exceptions to the strict confidentiality rule (see p 21). The most obvious case of communication is between the hospital and the GP who has referred the patient to the hospital's outpatient department. The duty demands that the referral letter should be sufficiently detailed for the specialist to be fully familiar with the facts. Initially, the GP may choose to telephone the hospital, but this should be followed up by a letter. If the letter is found to be inadequate, the question becomes one of whether the hospital's treatment would have been different if the correct information had been communicated.

The patient who has attended a hospital will be given a letter indicating the treatment received, which he is then required to take to his GP or another hospital if he is to receive further treatment. What if he does not do this? If the treatment is not yet complete, it should be stressed to him that he must seek further treatment; if there is a danger that he may suffer further injury after discharge, a method by which the patient can contact the treating doctor should be put in place. Is it enough to tell the patient in very strong terms in an attempt to transfer the onus to the patient? What if the patient lives on his own? Is there an obligation to check up on the patient? What if the patient cannot contact the relevant health carer and, in his ignorance, decides not to pursue his enquiry? The extent of this obligation is still, in our opinion, to be clarified. In *Coles v Reading and District HMC* (1963) 107 SJ 115, the patient was not given any document to place before either another hospital or his GP; neither did the GP make any enquiry as to what treatment he had received at the hospital. As a result, the patient was not given a tetanus injection and subsequently died. Both the hospital and the GP were found liable for lack of communication.

If it is alleged that the health carer failed to discharge his responsibility with regard to a follow-up the claimant will have to establish that a further appointment would have made a difference. Causation is considered in greater detail in below, Chapter 6, but for the present it is sufficient to say that the claimant will have to show that:

- if there had been a follow-up, the treatment he received would have been different; and

- if he had been contacted for a follow-up, his prognosis would have been significantly more optimistic.

Within the hospital itself there must be an adequate system of communication between the various professional groups; likewise, there must be a good system of communication between the GP and his employees. There has been an obvious welcome trend to place more emphasis on the role of the nurse/employee; they are not blindly to follow orders but should question matters where they fear for the patient's safety. One area where a GP has to be extremely careful is in the writing of his prescriptions. In *Prendergast v Sam and Dee Ltd* [1989] 1 Med LR 36, a GP was found liable in part when a pharmacist misread his prescription with fatal results for the patient.

The health carer has a duty to give appropriate instructions to his patient. In some cases, this may simply amount to a warning that, should symptoms persist, he should return to the surgery for instructions as to the dosage and frequency of the medication. Whatever the instructions, the health carer must be reasonably convinced that the patient understands these instructions.

REFERENCES

English case law

(1)   Blyth v Bloomsbury HA (1987) reported at [1993] 4 Med LR 151; (1989) 5 PN 169
See p 66.

(2)   Chatterton v Gerson [1981] QB 432; [1981] 1 All ER 257
The claimant was suffering from severe pain. She was injected once near the spinal cord to destroy nerve fibres, but the pain returned. She consented to a further injection which resulted in numbness to her leg. The defendant had indicated that the procedure might involve temporary numbness and the court held that it was sufficient 'that a patient need only be informed in broad terms of the nature of the procedure'.

(3)   Bolam v Friern HMC [1957] 1 WLR 582; [1957] 2 All ER 118
See r 5(A), p 155.

(4)   Sidaway v Board of Governors of the Bethlem Royal Hospital and the Maudsley Hospital [1985] AC 871; [1985] 1 All ER 643
See p 185.

See, also, *McAllister v Lewisham and North Southwark HA* [1994] 5 Med LR 343, which involved a patient suffering from a serious neurological condition. The defendant advised an operation which carried a 20% chance that the condition of her leg would deteriorate, but failed to inform her that the risk also applied to her arm. The said risk materialised.

Held: although the decision to operate was not negligent, applying *Sidaway*, the defendant was in breach for failing to disclose adequate information.

(5)   Hills v Potter [1984] 1 WLR 641; [1983] 3 All ER 716
The claimant was left paralysed after an operation on her neck. This was an inherent risk which the defendant had not disclosed; however, he was deemed to have acted in accordance with the *Bolam* standard.

(6)   Goorkani v Tayside Health Board [1991] 3 Med LR 33

The patient was diagnosed as suffering from Behcet disease. By 1981, he had lost the sight in one eye. After other treatment had failed, he was eventually given Chlorambucil, which was successful in the treatment of the eye but had the side effect of rendering the patient infertile.

The defendant was found negligent for failing to warn of the risks of infertility which was a known side effect from the long term use of the drug Chlorambucil. The court ruled that the defendant had failed to exercise what skill he had with reasonable care and diligence. Interestingly, the court held that it was not concerned with what was accepted practice. (The case failed on causation because the pursuer had not proved that had the discussion taken place the outcome would be any different (see, generally, below, p 210 *et seq*).)

(7)   Gregory v Pembrokeshire HA [1989] 1 Med LR 81
See above p 186.

(8)   Coles v Reading and District HMC (1963) 107 SJ 115
See p 187 above.

(9)   Prendergast v Sam and Dee Ltd [1989] 1 Med LR 36
The claimant was prescribed amoxil tablets for asthma. The pharmacist misinterpreted the prescription and prescribed daonil. The claimant suffered brain damage.

   Held:

* the GP was negligent for failing to write clearly;
* the pharmacist was negligent for blindly following the prescription (he prescribed 21 tablets of 250 mg strength instead of the usual 100 tablets of 5 mg strength).

Foreign case law

Australia

Rogers v Whittaker [1993] 4 Med LR 79; [1992] 3 Med LR 331; (1992) 109 ALR 625
See p 185 above.

Canada

(1)   Hollis v Dow Corning Corpn (1993) 103 DLR (4th) 520
The claimant had implants manufactured by the defendant company inserted surgically into her breasts. The implants later ruptured. She sued the surgeon for failing to warn her of the risk of rupture.

   Held: as the risk of rupture was well known at the time of the surgery, albeit that the risk was comparatively rare, the doctor had a duty to disclose. The company, too, had a duty to disclose the risks of rupture which were well known to it and could not rely on the medical profession to disclose the risks for them. Consequently, both the doctor and manufacturing company were liable.

(2)   Meyer Estates v Rogers (1991) 78 DLR (4th) 307; [1991] 2 Med LR 370
The claimant was suffering from an urinary tract problem and consented to an operation, an IVP (intravenous pyelogram), which was a diagnostic procedure. During the course of the operation a dye, hypaque, was administered to the patient which caused an allergic reaction resulting in death. (The case ultimately failed on causation.)

The Canadian Association of Radiologists divided procedures into high and low risk. For a high risk procedure full informed consent was required, for a low risk procedure, such as IVP, the Association felt that the risks associated with fully informing the patient outweighed the risk of not informing the patient.

Held: this position contravened the standard as required by *Reibl v Hughes* (1980) 114 DLR (3d) 1, which held that, for a patient's consent to be informed, all material risks should be disclosed and here the risk of death was a material risk.

The court went on to reject the defence of therapeutic privilege, quoting the judgment of Lord Scarman in *Sidaway*, holding that the defence only relates to psychological harm to the patient.

(3) Reibl v Hughes (1980) 114 DLR (3d) 1
See pp 186 and 211.

(4) Stamos v Davies (1985) 21 DLR (4th) 507
See p 186 above.

(5) Kueper v McMullin (1986) 37 CCLT 318
See p 186 above.

Professional/ethical guidelines

The GMC publication *Good Medical Practice* (May 2001, paras 36 and 42–47) gives advice for referring patients between GPs and specialists. Generally, the GP has an obligation to give the specialist all relevant information about the patient's history and current condition; the specialist in turn has a duty to provide the GP with details of the care he provided. Normally, the specialist should not accept the patient without a referral from the GP. However, if he does, then he should inform the patient's GP before embarking on treatment unless the patient requests him not to or the patient has no GP. In such cases, the specialist will be responsible for the patient's aftercare.

RULE 5(G)

The health carer may be held liable for errors in treatment, etc.

Commentary

An error in treatment, for example, prescribing the wrong drug, is not of itself negligence (see *Whitehouse v Jordan* [1981] 1 WLR 246). Again, it is not necessarily negligent to depart from accepted treatment; the defendant may have had very good reasons for not following what is commonly regarded as the norm (see r 5(C), p 171).

Many health carers from different branches of the profession may be involved in the treatment. All that the NHS patient has to show is that someone involved in his treatment did something wrong; the hospital will then be vicariously liable. However, where the patient is being treated privately, it will be important to ascertain what went wrong and exactly who was at fault: it could be the surgeon or it could be a lack of facilities in the private hospital, etc.

If a member of the treatment team is at fault, he cannot hide behind his superior's instructions; if in doubt, the instructions should be queried (see *Collins v Hertfordshire CC* [1947] 1 KB 598 and see r 5(A) and the discussion of the relationship between junior doctors and their more senior colleagues, p 158).

A number of cases have arisen where the claim is that, during the course of the treatment, something was left in the patient, for example, a needle or swabs. Generally, if the defendant did not avail himself of the usual precautions that could be taken, such as using swabs with tapes, holding a count and checking the patient before closing, it is likely that the court will find him negligent. The two most well known swab cases are *Anderson v Chasney* (1949) 4 DLR 71 and *Mahon v Osborne* [1939] 2 KB 14. In *Anderson,* a child died after a sponge was left in the base of his nostrils following an operation on his tonsils. The defendant was found negligent for failing to adopt the simple precaution of attaching tapes to the sponge even though he had followed the hospital's accepted practice. However, in *Mahon,* the surgeon was found not negligent for leaving a swab inside a patient. The judge directed the jury that they should consider that this had been an emergency operation and that the surgeon had been anxious to conclude the operation. However, it is suggested that this case would be unlikely to be followed at the present time.

REFERENCES

English case law

(1)   Whitehouse v Jordan [1981] 1 WLR 246; [1981] 1 All ER 267
See r 5(A) and p 178.

(2)   Bolam v Friern HMC [1957] 1 WLR 582; [1957] 2 All ER 118
See r 5(A), p 155.

(3)   Collins v Hertfordshire CC [1947] 1 KB 598
A junior medical officer misheard an instruction to supply procaine as cocaine. The pharmacist at the hospital did not question the unusual dosage and the surgeon did not check.

Held: the surgeon, medical officer and hospital were all liable.

(4)   Mahon v Osborne [1939] 2 KB 14
See above, and p 226.

Foreign case law

Canada

Anderson v Chasney (1949) 4 DLR 71
See p 178 .

RULE 5(H)

A health carer may be liable for faulty prescribing.

Commentary

Here, a defendant could be negligent in a number of ways:

- failing to appreciate the possible side effects of the prescribed drug;
- prescribing the wrong drug or recommending the wrong dosage;
- writing a prescription illegibly.

The defendant can escape liability if he has acted in accordance with the *Bolam* modified test. In prescribing drugs a doctor has a duty to pay heed to any instructions given by the manufacturer; the latter will not normally be liable if the drugs have been provided with a written warning: that will discharge his liability.

There have been a number of recent cases where the claimant has alleged that they 'woke up' in the middle of an operation primarily due to failure of the anaesthetist to administer the correct dosage of anaesthetic (see *Ludlow v Swindon HA* [1989] 1 Med LR 104 and *Taylor v Worcester and District HA* [1991] 2 Med LR 215). If the evidence shows that there was consciousness at the relevant time, then the issue again turns on the *Bolam* rule, as explained in *Bolitho*.

REFERENCES

English case law

(1) Ludlow v Swindon HA [1989] 1 Med LR 104
See p 228.

(2) Taylor v Worcester and District HA [1991] 2 Med LR 215
The claimant alleged that she was awake during a Caesarian operation and she experienced intense pain and terror. The action failed because the court could not find that the anaesthetic technique used had departed from accepted practice. Even if it had been proved that the claimant had been awake during the operation, the defendant would not have been negligent.

(3) Bolam v Friern HMC [1957] 1 WLR 582; [1957] 2 All ER 118
See r 5(A), p 155.

RULE 5(I)

The defendant health authority or Trust may be directly liable to the patient on the ground that it failed to provide reasonable care and treatment.

Commentary

The final area to be considered is where the negligence claim is targeted at the organisation and/or administration of the hospital. Such claims are canvassed as direct liability claims against the hospital, as opposed to vicarious liability. In practice, it does not matter whether the hospital is vicariously or directly liable: the damages will be the same in both cases. The main hurdle in bringing a direct liability claim is that it often brings into focus the level of resources, both personal and physical, and in these matters the court is exceedingly reluctant to intervene, seeing them as administrative matters. In *Wilsher*, the court suggested that where a hospital failed to provide doctors with sufficient skill and care, the hospital may be directly liable to the patient. This statement was taken one step further in the case of *Bull and Another v Devon AHA* [1993] 4 Med LR 117, where the health authority was held liable for not having an adequate system to cater for an obstetric emergency. Devon HA had argued that their levels of staffing were no different to any other hospital in the vicinity; the court was unimpressed with this argument, although it did acknowledge that these matters raised important issues of social policy which the court had to address. This happened in the cases *R v Central Birmingham HA ex p Walker* (1987) and *R v Cambridge HA ex p B (A Minor)* [1995] Med LR 250. The first involved hole in the heart babies and delays in their treatment, and the second concerned the question of expensive treatment for leukaemia for a child, and in both the claimants lost. These social policy cases can be distinguished from *Bull*, in that in those cases the negligence was in failing to provide the service, whereas in *Bull* it was failing to carry out an already existing service properly. Only in the latter cases are the courts tempted to intervene. See, further, Chapter 3, p 80.

REFERENCES

English case law

(1) Wilsher v Essex AHA [1988] 1 All ER 871; [1988] 2 WLR 557; [1986] 3 All ER 801
See p 158.

(2) Bull and Another v Devon AHA [1993] 4 Med LR 117
See commentary above. During the delivery of twins, it was alleged that there was a delay and inadequate supervision. The Court of Appeal held that the health authority were in breach of their duty to the claimant. Such breach had to be decided according to the standards prevailing in 1970. The health authority had failed to discharge the evidential burden of justifying why the registrar or consultant did not attend.

(3) R v Secretary of State for Social Services ex p Hincks (1979) 123 SJ 436

(4) R v Central Birmingham HA ex p Walker (1987) 3 BMLR 32; (1987) The Times, 26 November
In both of these cases, the parents of the children concerned failed in their applications for judicial review. The parents had contended that the hospitals concerned should have provided the necessary facilities to enable heart surgery to be carried out on their respective children. The court held that it would not intervene in questions of the allocation of resources.

(5) R v Cambridge HA ex p B (A Minor) [1995] 6 Med LR 250
B, aged 10 and a half, was originally suffering from non-Hodgkins lymphoma with common acute lymphoblastic leukemia in 1990. At first, the treatment seemed successful but in 1993 she developed myeloid leukemia. She underwent chemotherapy, total body irradiation and a bone marrow transplant and the disease went into remission, but she

suffered a further relapse in January 1995. She was given six to eight weeks to live, no further treatment was deemed appropriate by the doctors who were treating her. B's father, however, found two medical experts who were prepared to treat B, the treatment costing £75,000. B's health authority refused to fund the further treatment. The chances of the treatment being successful were estimated at 10–20% for the chemotherapy and then, if a successful remission was achieved, a 10–20% chance of a successful bone marrow transplant.

The Court of Appeal held that it was not for them to decide how the defendant's health authority limited budget should be allocated. The court found that the defendant's health authority had acted reasonably, taking into consideration the chances of the proposed treatment being successful, and the suffering it would cause to B.

Question: To what extent would the 'resources defence' be available to the new claims brought under the Human Rights Act 1998 and the European Convention on Human Rights 1950?

RULE 5(J)

A claimant may argue breach of a duty using the Human Rights Act 1998 and the European Convention on Human Rights in circumstances where the *Bolam* modified defence may be otherwise effective.

Commentary

In the present circumstances, where there is as yet no case law on the point, this Rule has to be stated most tentatively. The rationale behind it is that the Act and the Convention have conferred rights on individuals which, in the area of health care, effectively mean that the patient ought to be receiving more than the reasonable care offered by any prevailing accepted medical practice. For example, if Art 2's right to life includes a right to a specific and better treatment such as the more expensive cancer drugs and this is not given to a patient, in consequence of which the patient's condition worsens and/or takes longer to get better, then a 'traditional' negligence claim could be met by the argument that there was no breach, since the defendant was only doing what his peer colleagues would have done, and that such an approach was founded on a logical basis; and such a defence might very well succeed. But if, using the same circumstances, the patient was to argue that the defendant health carer had breached his (the patient's) right to life, would a *Bolam* defence or a defence based on lack of resources succeed? Ethically, no; after all, if the Act and Convention are to mean anything in practical terms, then it has to be acknowledged that the patient's right to a certain quality of life has been adversely affected. Legally, the Act and the Convention must mean more than just providing reasonable care, since that is already catered for at common law. We would therefore contend that serious consideration should be given by claimants' lawyers to using the Act and Convention in appropriate circumstances rather than a traditional negligence claim which may be met by a *Bolam* modified defence.

REFERENCES

English case law

(1) R v Cambridge District HA ex p B [1995] 1 FLR 1055; [1995] 6 Med LR 250
Per Laws J (p 1065):

> But where the question is whether the life of a 10 year old child might be saved, by however slim a chance, the responsible authority must in my judgment do more than toll the bell of tight resources. They must explain the priorities that have led them to decline to fund the treatment.

Foreign case law

European Court of Human Rights

(1) Osman v UK (2000) 29 EHRR 245

> While effective investigation procedures and enforcement of criminal law prohibitions ... provide an indispensable safeguard and the protective effect of deterrence, the Commission is of the opinion that for Art 2 to be given practical force it must be interpreted also as requiring preventive steps to be taken to protect life from known and avoidable dangers. However, the extent of this obligation will vary inevitably having regard to the source and degree of danger and the means available to combat it. Whether risk to life derives from disease, environmental factors or from the international activities of those acting outside the law, there will be a range of policy decisions relating ... to the use of State resources, which it will be for the Contracting State to assess on the basis of their aims and priorities ... [p 278].

GENERAL PRACTICE POINTS – RULES 5(A)–(I)

It is assumed at this stage that the solicitor will have identified the parties likely to be at fault, obtained the medical records, etc, and is therefore ready to choose his medical expert to evaluate whether or not the defendant fell below the required standard of care.

Choosing your expert

The right expert can make or break your case.

Do not use anyone:

- who is involved in the case;
- who works at the same defendant hospital/health authority/Trust;
- who works in the same area;
- simply because you have used him before (attitudes change);
- who is already treating the client – they may have an unduly optimistic opinion of how the treatment is progressing, and could be unduly critical of the patient, thus ruining the doctor-patient relationship.

Use:

The right expert and an independent expert.

Select from:

- your own list of experts (choose people who are known to have advised claimants properly);
- an expert who has successfully appeared against you;
- an expert you know (because you are qualified to judge);
- AVMA (Action for Victims of Medical Accidents). This is an organisation set up to help victims of medical accidents. They have an extensive pool of experts on their files. Members have access to these files and AVMA will be pleased to assist with selecting the appropriate expert;
- APIL (the Association of Personal Injury Lawyers) now has a database of medical experts. *Note* that these experts may or may not be appropriate to deal with clinical negligence cases;
- the Law Society Helpline/Law Society's Directory of Expert Witnesses;
- professional journals, for example, *The Lancet, BMJ,* etc;
- experts you have seen in other case reports which have dealt with the same issues that are facing you now;
- UK Register of Expert Witnesses (see *Law Society Gazette,* the *Solicitors Journal*).

The letter of instruction to the expert

Before instructing your expert, it is vital to consider what type of expert you require:

- What medical expert(s) are you concerned with?
- Do you require more than one expert?
- Are separate reports needed on causation and prognosis?
- Did the claimant undergo any supervening treatment or suffer a later illness which could have affected the claimant's present condition?

Instruct an expert conversant with the claimant's treatment.

Check that the expert will accept the case either by telephoning him or, preferably, by a short letter of inquiry. The purpose of such a letter is to deal with the following matters:

- Ascertaining whether the expert will accept this type of case.
- Obtaining the expert's full CV or appropriate evidence of the expert's qualifications. Once received, these should be checked against the appropriate entries in the Medical Directory.

  When these details are received, consider:

  o what is the degree of experience of the expert? Is he still practising? If he is not, only instruct an expert who retired recently as he will still be up to date with common practices;
  o if instructing more than one expert, whether they are from different generations and whether they will work well together;
  o whether the expert is up to date in the relevant field;
  o try to match experts with the intended defendant.

- Determining his likely fee. Medical experts can be expensive and reports prepared for a clinical negligence case are likely to be even more expensive. Ask the expert to give an estimate of his likely fee and his hourly rate. Tell the expert whether the client is paying privately or whether the client has the benefit of a certificate of public funding (in the latter case, the prior authority of the Legal Services Commission (formerly the Legal Aid Board) should be obtained before instructing the expert).
- Obtaining a time estimate: while medical experts will take their time, you do not want to be waiting indefinitely. Tell the expert when the limitation period expires and the date when you want the report.
- Determining how long it will be before he can see the client.
- Informing the expert of the nature of the problem, and the parties involved, that is, which hospital, etc. It may be that he feels that he cannot act against the potential defendant.
- Ascertaining whether the expert has any special requirements regarding instructions.

Once a favourable response has been received to the letter of inquiry, think about drafting the letter of instruction, which should contain the following matters:

- The name, address, date of birth and telephone number of the client.
- What are the issues/facts? Outline the allegations of negligence, for example, disclosure of information, inexperience, etc, and a brief description of how it is alleged that the injury was caused and what the injury is.
- Reiterate the test for negligence, that is, *Bolam*. (Stress to the expert that the defendant will not be negligent if he can show that an accepted body of medical opinion would have acted as the defendant did. Although the expert is probably familiar with *Bolam*, remind him of it.)
- Liability/causation. Ask the expert whether it is clear from the evidence that the alleged negligence caused the damage or whether it is impossible to establish liability.
- Condition/prognosis. Ask the expert to estimate what the client's chances are for a complete recovery, or whether his disability will be permanent. This is obviously required to establish the quantum of damages.
- Whether there are any factors peculiar to the client's case which the expert is required to deal with such as medical history, contributory negligence, and any allegations or reports the defendant has made.
- Progress of the litigation (this should be read in conjunction with the comments on limitation).
- Whether an examination is required and if so what issues are to be addressed.
- Experts should be aware of the requirements set out in the Civil Procedure Rules 1998, which deal with the format of medical reports. It may be prudent for the solicitor to remind the expert of these requirements.

In addition, any of the issues that were not mentioned in the initial enquiry to the expert should be included. With regard to the medical records, although it is possible to simply provide the expert with an authority to obtain the records, in our opinion, the better option is for the solicitor to provide the records with the letter of instruction. This is because:

- it allows the solicitor to read the records before the expert;
- the solicitor can take a copy of the records, so he is able to identify easily any problem the expert has with the records; and
- the solicitor is able to sort the records before they are sent to the expert.

What should be sent to the expert accompanying the letter of instruction? A file should be sent containing, in paginated and chronological order, the documents listed below.

- Hospital records, for example, X-rays and medical notes, nursing kardex, any specialist results of histology, myelograms, blood analyses, etc. Check with your expert that copies will suffice. A copy of the notes should be sent to the expert, annotated with the claimant's comments and any admissions or comments made by the defendant.
- Case notes and GP's records, for example, record cards, correspondence, reports.
- Proof of evidence by the claimant and any other relative, if appropriate, plus any recent photographs or videos taken of the client's injuries which may indicate to the expert whether or not the surgery has healed as it should.
- A copy of any current statements of case.
- Any previous expert reports and statements. Tell the expert whether or not they have been disclosed.
- The client's authority to obtain the medical records (if appropriate).

The expert's report

At the outset, it must be remembered that the overriding duty of the expert is to the court. This overrides any obligation to the person from whom he has received instructions or by whom he is paid (CPR r 35.3). The expert's report must comply with the requirements of CPR Pt 35 and the accompanying Practice Direction. PD 35 para 1.2 states that the report must:

(1) give details of the expert's qualifications

(2) give details of the literature or other material the expert has relied on when making the report

(3) say who carried out any test or experiment which the expert has used for the report and whether this was carried out under the expert's supervision

(4) where there is a range of opinion on matters dealt with in the report the expert should summarise the range of opinion and give reasons for his own opinion

(5) contain a summary of the conclusions reached

(6) contain a statement that the expert understands his duty to the court and he has complied with that duty

(7) contain a statement which sets out the substance of all material instructions (written or oral). This should summarise the facts and instructions given to the expert which are material to the opinions expressed in the report or upon which those opinions are based. (The instructions are not protected by legal privilege, however, cross-examination of the expert on the contents of the instructions would not be allowed unless the court permits it.)

The expert's report must also be verified by a statement of truth in the following form: 'I believe that the facts I have stated in this report are true and that the opinions I have expressed are correct.' If the report contains a false statement (and there was no honest belief in its truth) and the report was verified by a statement of truth, proceedings for contempt of court can be brought against the person who made the statement.

Once the report is received

Once the solicitor has obtained the report, he will be expected to take the following steps:

- Read it carefully with the assistance of a medical dictionary, for example, *Pears' Medical Encyclopaedia*.
- Check whether the report has dealt with all the issues raised in the letter of instruction; if not be prepared to send a follow-up letter to the expert.
- Ascertain whether any part of the report requires clarification, for example, if the claim is for a delay in diagnosis, how much earlier would the diagnosis have had to be made to avoid the injury?
- Does the report indicate that the alleged negligence has merely exacerbated a pre-existing condition? Is the client's present condition solely attributable to the alleged negligence, or would his condition have deteriorated in any event? It is important to be aware of the difficulties of establishing causation at an early stage and to be alive to the fact that it could ultimately reduce the level of damages.
- Ask yourself if you need another report. Does the present report throw up issues that would be best dealt with by an expert in a different field of medicine? Do you need a psychiatrist's report, for example, has the client suffered from depression since the incident? If yes, then the psychiatrist will require access to all records that you have sent to your first expert. Ensure that, if you are acting for a private client, he agrees to this further expenditure. If the client has the benefit of a public funding certificate, then you will require the authority of the Legal Services Commission (formerly the Legal Aid Board).
- Do you need a second opinion because you are not happy with the report for some reason, for example, is it entirely objective? Obviously, if there is anything in the report that you cannot understand, go back to the expert, but if you conclude that you need a second opinion then apply the same criteria to the second expert. If you are acting for a private client then obtain his authority for this extra expenditure. If the client has the benefit of a public funding certificate, you will have to seek the authority of the Legal Services Commission; if you are refused, you will have to advise the client that he

will have to pay for a second report privately (or possibly consider a conditional fee arrangement, see p 94 *et seq*) and arrange for his certificate to be discharged.

- If the expert has indicated that the evidence is incomplete, for example, further proofs of evidence are required, there are missing medical records, etc, or, for that matter, a different expert is required, ensure that all of these matters are attended to before the conference with counsel.

All of these matters should be attended to before the conference with counsel.

Finally, make one last check that there is nothing in the report which would lower your client's level of damages; if there is, go back to the expert for further comment.

If appropriate, send a copy to your client for his comments. You should advise the expert that the report will be shown to the client, and therefore the report should not contain anything which the expert would feel uneasy about the client seeing.

The next step is to arrange a conference with counsel. By this time, it should be clear to you whether the client has a good case; you may therefore consider that there is little point in going to counsel if the report is unfavourable. However, it is advantageous to have a conference at this stage with counsel, the expert and the client, even if the report is unfavourable, for the following reasons:

- It provides a chance to clear up any ambiguities within the report.
- It allows counsel the chance of taking the client through his version of events while at the same time inviting comment from the expert. Counsel will be able from this to estimate how the client and the expert perform as witnesses, and this may ultimately affect what advice he gives, that is, if the client is a poor witness, counsel may advise settlement at an early stage.
- A conference at an early stage provides an opportunity for the 'team' to meet; it gives you an opportunity to iron out any problems with your 'team' and the client can see that his case is being well run.

Selecting counsel

Many of the criteria used for selecting an expert apply equally to your choice of counsel. Unfortunately, we do not as yet have a scheme in place similar to the Law Society's specialist clinical negligence panel, although all firms who are franchised and are members of the Personal Injury Panel or Clinical Negligence Panel will have a list of approved counsel. However, as a brief guide, the solicitor should consider the points listed below:

- Choose from your own list, counsel who specialise in this field. Be wary of relying on the advice of counsel's clerks, especially if you know nothing about the particular barrister. If relying on the advice of counsel's clerks, it is worthwhile asking questions like how many clinical negligence cases that particular counsel has dealt with and what proportion of them were settled or went to trial.
- Consult lawyers' directories, etc.

- Consult law reports and journals for the names of counsel. You should be looking for a recent case similar to the one you are dealing with.
- AVMA; APIL; Law Society Helpline.
- Consult other solicitors who may be more experienced than you in the field of clinical negligence.

The conference

Preparation

To a large extent, many of the problems that will arise, for example, the expert being suddenly called away, are unavoidable. However, to try to minimise these problems, the conference should be timetabled well in advance at the most convenient venue for all the parties – for example, if the client is severely disabled, it may be difficult for him to travel very far. In selecting the venue, the paramount concerns are time and costs. With regard to time, this is to a large extent dictated by train/air times; as to costs, bear in mind that the Legal Services Commission are questioning more and more the level of costs incurred, for example, would it have been cheaper to travel by train rather than to drive? As a final consideration, think about using video facilities.

What to tell counsel

How much information do you include in your instructions? The most important item is a chronology of events, especially when several matters occurred close together. By doing this, the solicitor ensures that counsel has a clear picture of the events. The instructions should basically reiterate the history and identify the issues. Obviously, every solicitor has his own way of identifying these issues but, as a minimum, the instructions should state:

- the facts of the case;
- how far the litigation has progressed;
- if the case is funded by a public funding certificate, what limitations there are on the certificate;
- what counsel is being instructed to do and if there is any urgency;
- what documents are enclosed.

With regard to the last point, ensure that the following are included:

- all proofs of evidence from the client and witnesses;
- all medical reports, together with copies of any supplemental documentation referred to in the report, for example, medical texts;
- all correspondence between the parties, if relevant;
- a brief schedule on the estimated damages claim;
- a copy of the public funding certificate.

Make sure that the records used by the solicitor, expert and counsel are identical, sorted and paginated. Finally, it must be clear what counsel is being asked to do; it is to see whether there is a claim to answer.

The conference meeting

It is not our intention to discuss in detail what should be the main priorities of the conference, as we are sure that all solicitors have their own way of conducting a conference. However, by way of a brief reminder, we will make the following point: before the conference, all papers should be read in advance, along with the relevant medical texts and, if appropriate, think about drafting the allegations of negligence.

If the client is in attendance, the solicitor's first priority will be to explain how the conference will proceed and to put the client at ease. It is important that the client feels involved at an early stage; at all times, the solicitor should remind himself that the client has already been let down by one group of professionals and may find it difficult to place his trust in another. The client should be encouraged to correct what he perceives to be mistakes and to ask questions. It may be that he feels rather intimidated by the other professionals present, so again be alert to this and work to put the client at ease.

During the conference, the solicitor should ensure that a contemporaneous note is taken, from which future action will be decided and the issues of negligence will be formulated. It is a good idea to have the latter in mind during the progress of the discussion. After the conference, it is important that the solicitor's note is circulated to all those who were present, to avoid any misunderstanding and to facilitate further discussion.

After the expert advice has been dealt with, there must be a discussion on how the case should progress; for example, is further advice necessary, does the solicitor need to go back to the Legal Services Commission and have the limitation on the certificate removed, etc?

CHAPTER 6

CAUSATION

RULE 6(A)

The claimant must prove, on a balance of probabilities, that the defendant's breach caused the damage. The claimant will succeed if he can show that:
- **the damage would not have occurred but for the defendant's negligence; or**
- **the defendant's negligence materially contributed to, or materially increased the risk of injury; or**
- **if the claim is for negligent non-disclosure, had he been adequately informed he would not have accepted the treatment.**

Commentary

This is the third step in a negligence claim and perhaps the most problematic of all. Once the claimant has overcome the difficulties posed by *Bolam* (see above, Rule 5A, p 155 *et seq*) then he must face the hurdle of causation. The claimant must show that the damage he suffered was caused by the defendant's negligence. It is not for the defendant to prove that his negligence did not cause the damage (although in some instances a case could be made out for asserting that that should be the rule, see p 235 *et seq*).

The problem with a clinical negligence claim is that there are often several possible factors involved and/or the actual cause of the damage may be unknown. For example, the claimant may have been suffering from an ongoing disease; however, he must still show that the clinical negligence caused the damage complained of. In some cases where the medical evidence is conflicting the court will probably find that the claimant has failed to prove that the defendant's breach was responsible for the ensuing damage (see the whooping cough litigation, and the case of *Loveday v Renton* [1990] 1 Med LR 117).

Below, we examine the various ways in which the claimant can establish causation.

(1) The 'but for' test

The claimant is here saying that 'but for' the defendant's negligence, he would not be in the predicament he is in now in which case it is for him to show that the damage which occurred would not have occurred 'but for' that negligence. The defendant's conduct need not be the sole cause of the damage, there may be other factors which also contributed to the damage (see (2) below). However, the existence of those contributory factors will more often than not make it impossible for the claimant to overcome the evidential burden posed by this test. One such example is *Barnett v Chelsea and Kensington HMC* [1969] 1 QB 428 where the claimant attended the casualty department of his local hospital complaining of vomiting. The casualty officer failed to examine him, and the nurse in attendance sent him home with the instruction to see his own doctor. Shortly afterwards the claimant died of arsenic poisoning. There was no dispute that the casualty officer was negligent in failing to see and examine the patient; however, his lack of care did not cause the claimant's death because the arsenic poisoning was too far advanced for any treatment to have prevented his death (see, also, *Robinson v Post Office* [1974] 1 WLR 1176, p 212).

(2) The material contribution – materially increasing the risk test

The 'but for' test will only work in a minority of cases. Where there are two or more contributing factors, only one of which is the defendant's negligence, it is enough for the claimant to establish that the negligent act materially contributed to the damage. This test was first canvassed in *Bonnington Castings Ltd v Wardlaw* [1956] AC 613. In that case, the claimant contracted pneumoconiosis from inhaling silica dust at his workplace. The dust he inhaled came from two sources: the first as a result of the production process for which the defendant could not be held responsible, the second as a result of the defendant's breach of statutory duty in failing to have adequate extraction fans. Medical evidence indicated that both sources contributed to the claimant's disease even though the greater amount of dust came from the innocent source. The court held that the claimant need only prove on a balance of probabilities that the defendant's negligence materially contributed to the damage to recover the whole of his loss. In this instance the court were prepared to draw an inference that the defendant's breach had materially contributed to the damage even though in reality it was impossible to say. (See, however, *Bolitho v City and Hackney HA* [1998] AC 232, p 235 *et seq* where the court shied away from developing this approach.)

The question which follows from this test is: just what is a material contribution? In *Bonnington,* Lord Reid indicated that it was anything that did not come within the *de minimis* rule. Exactly what this means in terms of percentages is somewhat uncertain. It may seem somewhat harsh that a defendant who was only 10% liable could be held responsible for all the ensuing damage; however, if the defendant creates the risk it seems unjust that he should escape liability merely because there happens to be another concurrent cause (but see, further, *Holtby v Brigham and Cowan Hull Limited* [2000] 6 Lloyd's Rep Med 254, discussed at p 207).

The meaning of 'material contribution' was recently considered in *Brown v Lewisham and North Southwark HA* [1999] 4 Lloyd's Rep Med 110. The claimant underwent a quadruple coronary artery bypass surgery at Guy's Hospital in London on 20 September 1990 and was discharged post operatively on 28 September 1990 by train and taxi to the RVI in Blackpool. On arrival there a deep vein thrombosis in his leg was diagnosed. This condition eventually led to the amputation of his left leg. The claimant argued that the journey he was forced to take by train and taxi had extended or exacerbated the thrombosis so that it made a material contribution to the pathology that led to the loss of his leg. This argument was dismissed by the trial judge and the Court of Appeal. The trial judge found that Guy's Hospital had been negligent in discharging the claimant prematurely with a chest infection and that he should not have been allowed to travel by himself to Blackpool, but this did not cause the loss of his leg because: (1) even if he had remained at Guy's Hospital he would not have been diagnosed any earlier nor would his treatment have been any different; and (2) the journey did not materially affect the development of deep vein thrombosis. This judgment was upheld on appeal. Beldam LJ then went on to say (*obiter*) that it may not be enough to show that the journey played a material part in the injury as it must be shown that the injury suffered by the patient was 'within the risk from which it was the doctor's duty to protect him. If it is not, the breach is not a relevant breach of duty' (p 118). Had the injury been caused by something for which the claimant had been receiving treatment at Guy's Hospital then that may have been foreseeable, but the defendants could not be under a duty to protect the claimant from an undetectable thrombosis; the court reasoned that a health carer is not (a) expected to be a clairvoyant and (b) able to foresee all eventualities. This statement is of interest as it appears that the Court of Appeal is placing limits on the events for which the defendant may be liable (see, further, Rule 6D, p 230).

Bonnington was applied in the other influential case in this area, *McGhee v National Coal Board* [1973] 1 WLR 1. Here the pursuer alleged that as a result of the defender's failure to provide washing facilities he had contracted dermatitis. The defender admitted negligence; however, the evidence was inconclusive as to whether the pursuer would still have contracted the disease. This case differed from *Bonnington* in that it was not being argued that the defender's breach materially contributed to the damage since no one could say that had washing facilities been available the end result would have been different; all that was certain was that there was an increased risk of contracting dermatitis although the exact percentage of increase was unknown. The House of Lords said that this did not matter; a failure to take steps to reduce the risk was the same as a material contribution to the injury. Lord Reid said (p 5):

> From a broad and practical viewpoint I can see no substantial difference between saying that what the defender did materially increased the risk of injury to the pursuer and saying that what the defender did made a material contribution to the injury.

We submit that this reasoning does not hold up. Materially increasing the risk is distinguishable from materially contributing to the damage. A risk may or may not materialise in damage; merely to increase the likelihood that something might happen is very different from positively contributing to the actual damage. The defender in *McGhee* merely increased the chance of the claimant's contracting dermatitis.

McGhee is also renowned for this policy statement of Lord Wilberforce who said (p 6):

> And if one asks which of the parties, the workman or the employers, should suffer from this inherent evidential difficulty, the answer as a matter of policy or justice should be that it is the creator of the risk who, *ex hypothesi*, must be taken to have foreseen the possibility of damage, who should bear its consequences.

This statement would seem to indicate the burden of proof is reversed, that is, the claimant need only show that the defendant's breach had increased the risk; that done, it was for the defendant to rebut the inference. This approach was not new; in *McWilliams v Sir William Arrol & Co Ltd* [1962] 1 WLR 295, a case concerning an employer's breach of duty, Lord Hodson said that the onus was on the defendant to show the claimant would not have used the safety equipment had it been available. Again, in *Clark v McLennan* [1983] 1 All ER 416 (a case concerning breach of duty), Pain J said (p 427):

> It seems that it follows from *McGhee* that where there is a situation in which a general duty of care arises and there is a failure to take a particular precaution, and that very damage occurs against which the precaution is designed to be a protection, then the burden lies on the defendant to show that he was not in breach of duty as well as to show that the damage did not result from his breach of duty.

This approach was severely criticised in *Wilsher v Essex AHA* [1988] 2 WLR 557 (for the facts of this case, see p 158). The House of Lords firmly quashed any belief that the burden of proof can be reversed at all times. They ruled it remains with the claimant, who must establish that the defendant's breach was at least a contributory cause of the harm. Lord Bridge expressed the following sentiments (p 569):

> ... *McGhee v National Coal Board* [1973] 1 WLR 1 laid down no new principle of law whatever. On the contrary, it affirmed the principle that the onus of proving causation lies on the pursuer or claimant. Adopting a robust and pragmatic approach to the undisputed primary facts of the case, the majority concluded that it was the legitimate inference of fact that the defenders' negligence had materially contributed to the pursuer's injury.

McGhee is therefore still good law, subject to the cautionary note in *Wilsher*.

Wilsher also demonstrated the difference between consecutive and discrete contributory factors. In distinguishing *Wilsher* from *McGhee*, the court ruled that where the claimant's injury could have resulted from a number of causes, that did not give rise to a presumption that the injury was caused by the defendant's breach of duty. As Browne-Wilkinson VC had said in the Court of Appeal ([1986] 3 All ER 801, p 835):

> ... A failure to take preventive measures against one out of five possible causes is no evidence as to which of those five caused the injury.

In *Wilsher*, there was a 20% chance that the defendant's breach had caused the damage; the court interpreted this to mean that what the defendant had done was to add to the factors which could have caused the damage. To succeed, the claimant would have to establish that the defendant's breach did cause or materially contribute to the damage; here the defendant had not increased an existing risk but had simply created a further risk. It was a pity that the words of Wilberforce LJ in *McGhee* were not adopted and that the creator of the risk was not held to account for his actions.

How then does *Wilsher* compare with *McGhee*? In *McGhee*, the defendant increased an already existing risk: in *Wilsher* he increased the number of risks. In *McGhee*, the exposure to the risk was consecutive: in *Wilsher*, there were five possible discrete causes of the retrolental fibroplasia. *McGhee* succeeded: *Wilsher* failed. Why? On a question of semantics only? For some reason the Court of Appeal wanted to distinguish between the enhancement of an existing risk and merely adding to other risks. In both *McGhee* and *Wilsher* the defendant had increased the risk, whether by increasing the likelihood of an existing risk occurring or by adding to a list of possible factors which might have caused the damage; whatever the interpretation both increased the risk to the claimant. In neither case could the claimant show that the defendant's breach materially caused the damage, but in *McGhee* the court was prepared to infer that it did. Is this because they were only faced with two factors as opposed to five in *Wilsher*? Why should it make any difference how many factors there are as long as it can be said that the particular breach by the defendant does not fall within the *de minimis* rule?

In reality, in neither case could it be said that the defendant's breach materially contributed to the damage, yet it is apparent that both materially increased the risk. Consequently, it is illogical and plainly wrong that the courts were prepared to adopt a robust approach in *McGhee* but not in *Wilsher*. Our advice to the claimant's solicitor is never be caught out by *Wilsher* – always assert that the defendant's breach materially increased the risk and therefore materially contributed to the damage, thus adopting a robust and pragmatic approach so much favoured by the courts.

Other jurisdictions adopt a much more innovative approach to the issue of causation. In *Snell v Farrell* (1990) 72 DLR (4th) 289, the Supreme Court of Canada ruled that causation need not be determined with scientific precision; it was not essential that the claimant's case should be supported by a firm expert opinion.

Whilst the authors knew that much of the first edition of this book would require up-dating we did not envisage that the '*Bonnington* rule' would be the subject of attack – this was one rule that we thought would and should remain intact. However in clinical negligence one should never be complacent as the decision of the Court of Appeal in *Holtby v Brigham and Cowan Hull Limited* [2000] 6 Lloyd's Rep Med 254 illustrates. We have not, however, altered Rule 4A and the preceding discussion in the hope that this decision will be clarified in subsequent rulings and that the approach taken by the courts in *Bonnington* is universally and unequivocally adopted by all members of the judiciary.

In *Holtby* the claimant had developed asbestosis and was suing the defendant employer. The claimant had been exposed to asbestos dust for over forty years, half of which was in the defendant's employment and the other half working for other employers doing the same kind of work for periods of time varying from a few months to several years. He alleged that the defendant was negligent and in breach of its statutory duty. At first instance the judge held that the defendant was liable only to the extent of the damage it had caused and consequently reduced the damages by approximately 25%. The evidence indicated that, had the claimant only been exposed to asbestos whilst working for the defendant, his condition would not have been as severe. The decision was upheld on appeal.

Holtby therefore ran contrary to *Bonnington*, which held that if the claimant could demonstrate that the defendant's breach of duty materially contributed to the injury then the claimant could recover in full subject to the *de minimis* rule (see above, at p 204). Only where the defendant's contribution is known is the defendant liable to that extent and no more (see *Thompson v Smith Shiprepairers (North Shields) Ltd* [1984] 1 All ER 881).

Whilst the Court of Appeal were in agreement about the outcome of the appeal there was a divergence of reasoning. Stuart-Smith LJ attached great emphasis to the fact that in both *Bonnington* and *McGhee* it was never argued that the defendant was only liable to the extent of the material contribution. He stated that, if the defendant fails to argue that its liability should be only to the extent of their material contribution, then the claimant would succeed in full. The burden of proof therefore shifts to the defendant. With respect this new slant on *Bonnington* and *McGhee* is entirely implausible. We are asked to accept that simply because the defendant's lawyers in *Bonnington* failed to argue the 'split contribution' point the court ruled that they should be liable for all ensuing damage even though their material contribution could be as little as 10% or anything which satisfies the *de minimis* rule (see p 204). This does not show the defendant's lawyers in *Bonnington* in a good light! Stuart-Smith LJ went on to say, relying on the decision in *Thompson v Smith Shiprepairers* [1984] 1 QB 405 p 443, that quantification would be difficult but the court must simply do the best it can.

Clarke LJ took a more pragmatic approach and at p 261 he said:

> If the position were that the claimant cannot, as a matter of law, recover anything more than the contribution which the defendant has tortiously made to his disease, it does seem to me to be surprising that none of their Lordships mentioned that point in either *Bonnington* or *Nicholson*.

He too relied on *Thompson* and said that although the job of assessing damages was 'shot through with imprecision' (*per* Mustill J in *Thompson* p 443E) the courts should not shy away from it. The defendant bears a burden to prove contributory negligence and similarly he bears a burden to show that others have contributed to the claimant's disease. It does not matter whether this is classified as a legal or evidential burden of proof; what matters is that the defendant must plead the point if it wishes to rely upon it. However the assessment of damages is more often than not a jury issue and it will rarely be the case that recourse to the burden of proof is required. Furthermore Clarke LJ contended that this was not such a case as, similar to *Thompson*, the injury was not truly indivisible.

What does this case mean for the causation rules as we know them?

1   It could be argued that *Bonnington* and *Holtby* are distinguishable in that in *Bonnington* it was accepted that the injuries were caused partly as a result of the innocent dust and partly as a result of the defendant's breach, whereas in *Holtby* the asbestosis was caused purely as a result of negligence albeit not entirely by the defendant's own hand. Apportionment of damages is only possible in the *Holtby* type case. This reasoning, however, is dealt a blow when we look at *Thompson* which was extensively relied on in *Holtby*. In *Thompson* the apportionment was between a negligent and a non-negligent cause. On the other hand it might be said that the various employers of Mr Holtby who were not joined in the proceedings could be thought of as being blameless, similar to the innocent dust in *Bonnington*. There is, however, an obvious flaw in this argument – this view fails to appreciate that parties are not joined to litigation for a variety of reasons, one of the most compelling being the lack of belief as to a party's ability to satisfy any judgment.

2   In the opinion of Clarke LJ the defendant should shoulder the responsibility of showing the extent of his contribution. Stuart-Smith LJ stated that if the defendant fails to raise this argument then the claimant would succeed in full. Consequently any solicitor must ensure that if his client alleges that someone else is partly responsible then this should be pleaded in full in the defence. However, in *Holtby* the defendant failed to plead material contribution yet the court said that, since the matter had been raised at trial, they were still able to deal with the issue. To sum up; the defendant must plead a positive case (in line with the Woolf reforms); a bare denial will not suffice (even though in *Holtby* this is what the defendant did).

3   The claimant must ensure as a first step that he joins in all of the possible contributors to the action and further adduces evidence to show to what extent he has been damaged by each of the defendants if he is to recover in full. This seems rather a heavy burden for the claimant to bear and one which the claimant will find difficult to satisfy; for example, what evidence will he have to adduce? In the authors' opinion the preferred option should be that if the defendant alleges that he is not entirely to blame then he should commence Part 20 proceedings. If, however, a claimant has misgivings about the financial status of any of the defendants he would be wise to join all possible tortfeasors in the action.

The authors have grave misgivings about the decision in *Holtby* and some of our reservations have been expressed in the paragraphs above. However to sum up we are of the opinion that the following rules should be applied:

(a) The claimant should not be denied damages simply because he does not join all possible tortfeasors in the action because he has either evidential difficulties or because he does not know their identity. The job of apportionment should be left to Part 20 claims and it is the defendant's responsibility to bring such a claim if he alleges that any other party/parties is/are wholly or partly at fault.

(b) Should the court decide to apportion damages then any apportionment should not take place without a hearing from all the contributors unless the apportionment is blatantly obvious. *Holtby* gives little guidance as to how the court arrived at their decision to reduce damages by 25%.

(c) *Bonnington* should be restored to its rightful position and the claimant should recover all or nothing unless there are exceptional circumstances, for example, both parties accept that the defendant cannot be more than x% responsible. In *Holtby* the claimant's condition gradually worsened as he inhaled more dust, therefore logically it could be contended that, as he spent only half his time employed by the defendant, then the defendant should only be liable for 50% of his loss. However not all diseases or injuries progress in this way: it is often the case that the claimant's condition remains static for some time and then suddenly an event causes his condition to deteriorate rapidly. In this situation how does the claimant prove his case? *Bonnington* and *McGhee* held that the claimant should not have to bear this burden and it is a sentiment with which we agree.

(d) If, however, the *Holtby* approach is accepted then there is an argument that the claimant should have succeeded in *Wilsher* to the extent of 20% of the damages, that is, the defendant's breach was one of the five factors that may have caused the injury. As we have already argued, in *Wilsher* the defendant, by adding to the possible causes of the RLF, was also increasing the risk of damage occurring. The courts have stressed that this is the same as a material contribution, hence there is no need to distinguish between those cases of consecutive causes and the *Wilsher*-like discrete causes.

Causation and non-disclosure

This section should be read in conjunction with Chapter 2, Consent, and Chapter 5, Standard of Care, p 44 *et seq* and p 184 *et seq*. Readers will already have noted that in Chapter 4, p 105, we advised the solicitor wherever possible to frame a claim for non-disclosure of risks as a trespass claim rather than as a negligence claim, in order to avoid the problems of causation. Where the claim is brought in negligence, once the claimant has overcome the *Bolam* test, he must then prove that if he had been warned about the inherent risk in the procedure he would not have accepted the treatment. In the majority of cases the claimant's claim will fail at this juncture because the court will hold that, on balance the claimant would still have undergone the operation. In the English courts a subjective test is applied: would *this claimant* have accepted this treatment?

Although at first glance this test would seem unduly favourable to the claimant, case law demonstrates that the courts apply the test stringently (see *Chatterton v Gerson* [1981] QB 432; [1981] 1 All ER 257, *Hills v Potter* [1984] 1 WLR 641 and *Smith v Barking, Havering and Brentwood HA* [1994] 5 Med LR 285). In *Chatterton v Gerson* [1981] QB 432 (an action brought in battery), the defendant had explained to the claimant that the treatment would involve some numbness and possibly a temporary loss of muscle power to her leg. However, the claimant suffered total numbness in her leg which affected her mobility. She argued that she had not given her consent to the operation because the doctor had not informed her of the inherent risks associated with the procedure. The court ruled that since the claimant had been informed in broad terms of the nature of the procedure her consent was real, and any claim should have been brought in negligence. The court remained unconvinced that the claimant would not have proceeded with the procedure had she received more information about it.

However, there have been some successes. In *Thake v Maurice* [1986] QB 644, the claimant did succeed, although the case can perhaps be distinguished on the grounds that here the claim was not that the male claimant would not have had a vasectomy had he been informed of a risk of reversal, but that if his wife had been given this advice, she would have realised that she had subsequently fallen pregnant earlier than she did, and consequently she could have sought an abortion.

In other jurisdictions, notably Canada, an objective test is applied, see, for example, *Reibl v Hughes* (1980) 114 DLR (3d) 1, where the court asked whether a reasonable person in the claimant's situation, knowing of the risks, would have declined the treatment. In *Reibl's* case, the claimant succeeded largely because of the high risk of a stroke resulting (10%) and the fact that the claimant was only about a year-and-a-half away from being eligible for a full pension, consequently this information was very important to him. Conversely in *Stamos v Davies* (1985) 21 DLR (4th) 507 (see, also, Chapter 5, Standard of Care, p 186) as the claimant was suffering from a life threatening condition and had also turned down other forms of treatment the court held that he would not have had the treatment even if the risk had been disclosed.

A different approach, however, was adopted by the Australian courts in *Chappel v Hart* [1998] HCA 55. There the claimant suffered injury to her vocal chords and voice loss. The defendant argued that she had suffered injury randomly, the risk she was exposed to would have eventually occurred at some time. Gaudron J however rejected this argument and made the point that the degree of risk varies with whoever is carrying out the treatment. Hence the claimant successfully argued that she would have deferred treatment until someone more experienced was available. Additionally the claimant's case was based not upon the exposure to the risk but rather the exposure to the physical injury; it may be true that she would eventually have been exposed to the risk of injury but it was not the case that she would have eventually suffered this harm.

However, in most cases where an objective test is applied, causation becomes even more burdensome to the claimant, and tends to obscure what the real issue is, namely: what would the claimant have done had he possessed all the relevant information?

Although there is a difference between the subjective and objective tests, in practical terms whether one or the other is applied will make little difference – the claimant must still convince the court that he would not have had the treatment had the risks been disclosed. The court will therefore look at the claimant's evidence and weigh up its credibility by reference to the reasonable man and by looking at the risks attached to the particular procedure. Indeed, if cases such as *Smith v Barking, Havering and Brentwood HA* [1994] 5 Med LR 285 are to be followed, it would seem that in reality the English courts are applying an objective test and will be persuaded to adopt a subjective approach only on very rare occasions, see the cases immediately below. Accordingly, the court will assess whether or not the claimant's decision was reasonable by reference to what the reasonable man would have done. In practice, this is no different from cases such as *McWilliams v Sir William Arrol & Co Ltd* [1962] 1 WLR 295, although there the burden was on the defendant to show that the claimant would not have used the safety equipment, whereas in an action for non-disclosure the burden falls squarely on the claimant to show that he would not have consented to the treatment. In practice, many cases will fail because the court will rule that the risk is so small it would not have affected the claimant's decision (see *Chatterton v Gerson* [1981] QB 432, *Meyer Estates v Rogers* (1991) 78 DLR (4th) 307 and *Ciarlariello v Schacter* [1991] 2 Med LR 391).

On the issue of burden of proof and non-disclosure, perhaps the better recommendation is that at the very least the burden should be equally shared. Thus the defendant should have to produce substantial evidence to indicate that the claimant would still have undergone the treatment by reference to the claimant's previous decisions regarding treatment (if any) or the claimant's character or, perhaps, the decisions of others in a similar position to the claimant. At the same time, the claimant would have to adduce evidence in support of his decision to refuse medical treatment, referring to his past decisions, etc.

REFERENCES

English case law

(1)   Bolam v Friern HMC [1957] 1 WLR 582; [1957] 2 All ER 118
See Chapter 5, Standard of Care, p 155.

(2)   Loveday v Renton [1990] 1 Med LR 117
The claimant failed to establish that pertussis (the whooping cough vaccine) caused meningitis.

For a more optimistic decision from the claimant's viewpoint, see *Best v Wellcome Foundation Ltd* [1993] IR 421; [1994] 5 Med LR 81.

Note that the court at no time referred to the decision in *Loveday*. In finding the defendant negligent, the court held that it was not their role to resolve scientific disputes, rather it was to apply common sense and logic.

(3)   Barnett v Chelsea and Kensington HMC [1969] 1 QB 428; [1968] 1 All ER 1068

See above, p 203 and Chapter 5, Standard of Care, p 161.

(4)   Robinson v Post Office [1974] 1 WLR 1176; [1974] 2 All ER 737
While at work, the claimant slipped from an oily ladder injuring his shin. He was given an anti-tetanus injection by his GP. In giving the injection the GP did not administer a test dose nor did he wait the customary half hour to see whether the claimant had any adverse reaction.

Held: he had been negligent for failing to adhere to accepted practice; however, the case failed on causation. The claimant's reaction was so severe that it would not have shown itself in the half hour.

(5)   Bonnington Castings Ltd v Wardlaw [1956] AC 613; [1956] 1 All ER 615
See above, p 204.

(6)   Bolitho v City and Hackney HA [1998] AC 232
See Chapter 5, Standard of Care, p 173 and below, p 235 *et seq.*

(7)   Brown v Lewisham & North Southwark HA [1999] 4 Lloyd's Rep Med 110
See above, page 204.

(8)   Holtby v Brigham & Cowan Hull Limited [2000] 6 Lloyd's Rep Med 254
The claimant who had developed asbestosis was suing the defendant employer. The claimant had been exposed to asbestos dust over some forty years, half of which he had been in the defendant's employment and half of which he had been working for other employers doing the same kind of work for periods of time varying from a few months to several years. He alleged that the defendants were negligent and in breach of their statutory duty. At first instance the court found that the defendant had materially contributed to the claimant's injuries, however damages were discounted by 25% as the

judge held that the defendant was liable only for the damage it had caused. The claimant appealed.

Held: the appeal was dismissed. Although the claimant had successfully proved that the defendant's breach materially contributed to his injuries the defendant was only liable to the extent of that contribution. The burden of proof was upon the claimant to show what portion of his disability was caused by the defendant's breach, however if that point was not raised in evidence or argued by the defendant the claimant would succeed in full. It was preferable for the defendant to plead that others were responsible for the injury but here it was sufficient that the matter was properly dealt with at trial.

(9)   McGhee v National Coal Board [1973] 1 WLR 1; [1972] 3 All ER 1008
See above, p 205 *et seq.*

(10) McWilliams v Sir William Arrol & Co Ltd [1962] 1 WLR 295; [1962] 1 All ER 623
The claimant sued his employer in negligence and for breach of statutory duty for failing to provide safety helmets. It was accepted that if the safety helmet had been worn the claimant would not have sustained the head injuries he did. However, the case failed on causation because the defendant successfully proved that, even if helmets had been provided, the claimant would not have worn one.

(11) Clark v McLennan [1983] 1 All ER 416
After giving birth, the claimant was found to be suffering from stress incontinence. The defendant performed an anterior colporrhapy four weeks after the birth. This operation and further operations were unsuccessful and the claimant's incontinence became permanent. It was accepted practice that the claimant should not have been operated on until three months after the birth. The claimant succeeded on causation.

Note, however, that the defendant was able to prove that even with the operation at the correct time, there was a 33% chance that the claimant's incontinence would still have persisted. Accordingly, the court reduced the damages by one-third. See, further, Chapter 7, Damages, p 257.

(12) Wilsher v Essex AHA [1988] 2 WLR 557; [1988] 1 All ER 871; [1986] 3 All ER 801
See Chapter 5, Standard of Care, p 158 and above, p 206 *et seq.*

(13) Thompson v Smith's Shiprepairers (North Shields) Ltd [1984] QB 405
The claimant suffered noise-induced industrial deafness. He had worked in the shipbuilding yard since 1944 but it was generally thought that noise-induced deafness was an inescapable feature of the work. It was not until 1960 that effective protection was available and in 1963 the Ministry of Labour published a pamphlet on the dangers of it. The claimant was not given ear protection until 1970.

Held: the exposure to noise was not negligent until it became a breach of duty. The defendant was only liable for that part of the claimant's deafness that occurred after the exposure to noise became negligent. The defendant would not be liable for any injury caused prior to that time as they had followed an accepted practice adopted by their industry and the consequences of noise exposure was viewed as a risk associated with that industry.

(14) Chatterton v Gerson [1981] QB 432; [1981] 1 All ER 257
See p 44. Bristow J was not satisfied that the defendant was in breach of duty for failing to inform the claimant, but even so, as he explained (at [1981] QB 432, p 445):

... the claimant had not proved that, even if she had been further informed, she would have chosen not to have the operation. The whole picture is on the evidence of a lady desperate for pain relief.

(15) Hills v Potter [1984] 1 WLR 641; [1983] 3 All ER 716

See Chapter 5, Standard of Care, p 184. The claimant underwent an operation to cure a neck deformity; she was rendered paralysed. The defendant had told the claimant there was a small risk of her dying and a risk of paralysis which might be temporary or transient.

Held: the defendant had acted in accordance with accepted practice and, furthermore, the claimant had failed to show that if the risks had been disclosed she would not have consented to the operation.

(16) Smith v Barking, Havering and Brentwood HA [1994] 5 Med LR 285

The claimant had undergone an operation as a child to drain a cyst on her spinal cord. At the age of 18, she began to experience problems again and she was advised to have a further operation in the hope of alleviating her condition, without which she would have been in a wheelchair within three months and a tetraplegic within six months. It was accepted there was a 50% chance that the second operation could immediately worsen the condition; this in fact happened and the claimant was rendered a tetraplegic immediately. It was admitted that the defendant was negligent in failing adequately to disclose to the claimant the risks involved in the procedure. However, the claimant's case failed on causation.

The court applied a subjective test and held that the claimant would have consented to the operation because if nothing was done she faced disability within three months anyway. She would have trusted the defendant as representing the only chance she had to postpone her inevitable disability.

Note that Hutchinson J urged caution in considering the claimant's evidence in 'a wholly artificial situation', that is, in the witness box. The court should consider the evidence objectively, asking what would a reasonable claimant had done. Only if there were other unique factors such as religious beliefs or other social considerations and these assertions were stated immediately following the operation, should the court be persuaded by such evidence.

(17) Thake v Maurice [1986] QB 644; [1986] 1 All ER 479

The claimant underwent a vasectomy operation. The operation failed and the claimant's wife gave birth to a fifth child. The claimant sued the defendant in contract and negligence for failing to warn him of the possibility that the vasectomy might not render him irreversibly sterile.

Held: The claim in contract failed, the court ruling that a reasonable man would not have understood the defendant as giving an absolute guarantee that the operation would be successful. The claim in negligence succeeded; the court ruled the defendant had fallen below the standard of care and had the claimant appreciated that the operation was not foolproof, then Mrs Thake would have suspected she was pregnant at an earlier stage and consequently sought an abortion.

See also *Goorkani v Tayside Health Board* [1991] 3 Med LR 33 in Chapter 5, Standard of Care, p 189.

Foreign case law

Australia

(1)   Chappel v Hart [1998] HCA 55
See above, p 211.

(2) Ellis v Wallsend District Hospital [1990] 2 Med LR 103; (1989) 70 NSW LR 553
For the facts of this case, see Chapter 5, Standard of Care, p 177. On appeal the court held that the judge at first instance was correct in applying a subjective rather than an objective test to the question whether the claimant would have undergone the operation had she been fully informed of the risk of paralysis and the failure to relieve pain. However, at first instance, the judge had held that the claimant had failed to establish a causal link between the negligence and the damage. This was reversed on appeal. The court held that, although there was no rule of law which said the judge was bound to accept the claimant's evidence because it was not challenged on cross-examination, since the claimant's evidence was not 'inherently incredible' or 'inherently improbable' the judge could not dismiss the evidence without an explanation and hence the decision at first instance would be reversed.

Canada

(1)   Snell v Farrell (1990) 72 DLR (4th) 289
The respondent had problems with her right eye and was advised to have surgery to remove a cataract. The appellant explained the operation and the risks involved. The claimant lost the sight in the eye following the operation. The trial judge found that the defendant had acted negligently in continuing the operation after noticing a haemorrhage in the claimant's eye. The medical evidence was that the operation was a possible but not definite cause of the loss of sight. The trial judge held that the burden had shifted to the defendant to disprove causation, that this burden had not been discharged, and therefore the defendant was liable. The defendant's appeal to the New Brunswick Court of Appeal was dismissed, as was a further appeal to the Supreme Court.

   Held: the burden throughout was on the claimant to show that the defendant's negligence had caused her loss, but the evidence adduced by the claimant was sufficient to support an inference of causation based on common sense despite the absence of positive medical opinion. It was stated (p 300):

> Causation need not be determined by scientific precision. It is as stated by Lord Salmon in *Alphacell Ltd v Woodward* [1972] 2 All ER 475, p 490 'essentially a practical question of fact which can best be answered by ordinary common sense rather than abstract metaphysical theory' ... the allocation of the burden of proof is not immutable. Both the burden and standard of proof are flexible concepts.

And (p 301):

> The legal or ultimate burden remains with the claimant but, in the absence of evidence to the contrary adduced by the defendant, an inference of causation may be drawn, although positive or scientific evidence of causation has not been ... This is, I believe, what Lord Bridge had in mind in *Wilsher* when he referred to a 'robust and pragmatic approach to the facts'.

(2)   Patterson v Dutton (1991) 79 DLR (4th) 705
During an operation a congenital displacement of the claimant's spine was aggravated and she suffered immediate paralysis. The claimant alleged that the defendant had been

negligent in failing to make a prompt diagnosis of the spinal displacement and the court found the surgeon had been negligent in the claimant's post-operative care. However, medical evidence was divided as to whether the claimant's paralysis could have been avoided. The court adopted a 'robust and pragmatic' approach, applying *Snell* (see above), stating (p 717):

> Here, we know what caused the paralysis – it was the compression of the spinal cord. What we do not know with certainty was whether the breach of duty, that is, the failure of timely diagnosis made even partial recovery impossible ... What we do not know with certainty is whether if there had been no breach of duty she would have had some recovery.

It was impossible to determine exactly how much traction should have been applied to the claimant to prevent the paralysis and consequently it would be unfair to require the claimant to prove something which scientifically is incapable of proof. As it was very difficult to determine what would have happened had the correct treatment been given, much more so than determining the effect of something which ought not to have been done, the court was prepared to draw an inference and find for the claimant.

Query – is this a loss of chance case? See Rule 6(B), below.

(3) Reibl v Hughes (1980) 114 DLR (3d) 1
See Chapter 5, Standard of Care, p 186.

(4) Stamos v Davies (1985) 21 DLR (4th) 507
The defendant internist accidentally punctured the claimant's spleen whilst performing a lung biopsy with the result that the spleen had to be removed. The defendant failed to inform the claimant that his spleen had been biopsied and not his lung.

Held: the defendant's breach of duty to inform the claimant of the injury to his spleen did not cause the claimant's damage, that is, the loss of his spleen.

(5) Ciarlariello v Schacter [1991] 2 Med LR 391; [1994] 5 Med LR 213
It was held that the risk of a reaction to angiography was less than risk of death caused by subarachnoid haemorrhage, consequently, the claimant would still have consented to treatment even if the risk had been disclosed.

(6) Meyer Estates v Rogers [1991] 2 Med LR 370
See Chapter 5, Standard of Care, p 189. The risk of reaction from an intravenous pyelogram was one in 2,000 and the risk of death between one in 40,000 and one in 1,100,000.

Practice points

The claimant's solicitor should point out to any prospective claimant, the problems associated with a claim for non-disclosure. If the claim proceeds, the solicitor should ensure the claimant has a plausible argument as to why he would not have accepted the treatment. If the claimant's decision is contrary to the view taken by the reasonable man, the evidence will have to be extremely cogent to convince a sceptical judiciary.

RULE 6(B)

Where the nature of the claimant's claim is that the defendant's breach deprived him of the opportunity of making a full recovery from his original illness or injury, the claimant must establish on a balance of probabilities that, but for the defendant's negligence, his chances of making a full recovery exceeded 50%.

Commentary

These 'loss of chance' cases are perhaps most closely associated with the area of diagnosis, with the claimant alleging that, had the diagnosis been made earlier, then the condition would have been treated in time and he might have made a complete recovery. For example, a man visits his GP's surgery on several occasions complaining of severe headaches; the GP negligently fails to examine him or to ask him whether he has any other symptoms or to refer him to a specialist; he attributes the cause of the headaches to stress. Eventually the patient collapses and a brain tumour is diagnosed. The tumour is now so far advanced that the patient's condition is terminal. The GP is not negligent for failing to make the diagnosis, but he is in breach for failing to revise his initial diagnosis. The question is what difference would an earlier diagnosis have made? Would it have given the patient a chance of a full recovery and, if so, how great a chance?

The leading case in this area is *Hotson v East Berkshire HA* [1987] AC 750. After sustaining a fall the claimant was taken to hospital where he was examined and sent home without being X-rayed. Five days later he went back to the hospital complaining of persistent pain; he was again X-rayed and a fracture of the neck of the femur was now diagnosed. Although treatment was undertaken the claimant later developed avascular necrosis, a medical condition causing deformity of the hip joint and permanent disability. The defendant admitted negligence; however, the question to be resolved was, what was the claimant's loss? Since expert evidence established that even with treatment there was a 75% chance of avascular necrosis developing, the claimant's argument was that the defendant's negligence had deprived him of a 25% chance of a cure. Consequently, the trial judge and the Court of Appeal worked on the principle that the claimant was entitled to 25% of the damages in proportion to the 25% chance of the recovery he had lost.

The House of Lords reversed this decision, holding that the proportionate approach was incorrect; the claimant should recover all or nothing. What the claimant had to establish, on the proper application of *Bonnington*, was that the delay in treating him had at least materially contributed to the damage; in this instance, it had been established there was a 75% chance the claimant would have contracted avascular necrosis in any event. The claimant had to establish at least a 51/49 likelihood that had the defendant not been negligent he would have made a full recovery. Once it had been established that the avascular necrosis was the result of the defendant's negligence, then the court could go on to assess damages.

The following points emerge from this decision:

(1) The House of Lords refused to answer the question whether a claim formulated as a loss of chance claim was recognised by the law of tort. However, *Hotson* has been regarded as tolling the death knell in tort for loss of chance cases (this is endorsed by other jurisdictions: see *Lawson v Lafferiere* (1991) 78 DLR (4th) 609 discussed below, p 219. In fact, although the court said that it would not rule that the claimant could never bring such a claim and succeed (p 786) Lord Mackay said, 'I consider that it would be unwise in the present case to lay down as a rule that a claimant could never succeed by proving loss of a chance in a clinical negligence case'), the likelihood of success seems increasingly remote.

(2) The claimant's claim was whether through the defendant's negligence he had lost the chance of a recovery. Once this was established the court should have gone on to see whether the defendant's negligence caused the damage. The House of Lords approached the problem on the basis that either the claimant's original injury (the fall) or the misdiagnosis caused the injury. Having effectively found that, on a balance of probabilities, it was the fall that caused the injury, it then became immaterial to consider how negligent the defendant had been: the claimant had to fail unless he could establish that without the negligence he would have had a 51% chance of making a full recovery. However, in the majority of cases the claimant will never be able to prove this because the defendant's negligence will usually be such that it is impossible to say whether the claimant would have made a full recovery. What seems certain is that a claim for less than a 50% chance is doomed to failure. Can this be right? – see our recommendations, at practice points, p 241.

(3) Perhaps the claimant in this case would have succeeded had he relied on *McGhee* and argued that the defendant's conduct had materially increased the risk. On the facts of *Hotson*, it is possible to argue that the defendant's negligence increased the risk from 75%–100%, but it is impossible to say that the defendant's negligence materially contributed to the damage. However, in *McGhee*, it could not be said that the provision of washing facilities would have made any difference. So why the different outcomes? Is it because in *McGhee* the degree of risk was unknown, whereas in *Hotson* the percentages were clearly known? Why does this make any difference? Although we have stated that 'loss of chance' claims in clinical negligence form the basis of a separate rule in the causation section, we suggest that the claim should not be formulated as a loss of chance claim, but rather along the lines of *McGhee*.

It is worth noting that the courts have not always rejected the loss of chance approach; however, the majority of claims have been brought in contract (see *Chaplin v Hicks* [1911] 2 KB 786). This point was expressly recognised in the Court of Appeal in *Hotson* [1987] AC 750. Dillon LJ said (p 764):

... what is the damage the claimant has suffered? Is it the onset of the avascular necrosis or is it the loss of chance of avoiding that condition? In my judgment, it is the latter.

I see no reason why the loss of chance which is capable of being valued should not be capable of being damage in a tort case just as much as in a contract case such as *Chaplin v Hicks* [1911] 2 KB 786. If that is right, there is no difficulty over causation. Causation – that the damage was caused by the wrongful act of the defendant – has to be proved on the balance of probabilities, but by that standard of proof it was amply proved in the present case that the choice which the claimant on the judge's findings had had was lost by the admitted negligence of the doctor.

It is also relevant to note that in solicitors' negligence cases the claimant in effect is bringing a loss of chance claim, for example, where a solicitor has been negligent in failing to issue proceedings within the limitation period, the claimant's claim is for the loss of opportunity in bringing a claim for which he can only estimate the chance of success; he is not required to prove that he would have won his case (see *Kitchen v Royal Air Force Association* [1958] 1 WLR 563). Can an analogy be drawn between the solicitor–client and doctor–patient relationships? If it can, then the claimant in *Hotson* should have succeeded. In the House of Lords in *Hotson* [1987] 3 WLR 232, Lord Bridge referred to both *Chaplin* and *Kitchen*, but was of the opinion that any analogy with *Hotson* was only 'superficially attractive' and that there were 'formidable difficulties' in accepting an analogy between these cases and *Hotson*. Why the Court of Appeal could draw the analogy but the House of Lords could not is difficult to see.

We must also ask why, ultimately, the House of Lords rejected the approach of apportioning damages. In the Court of Appeal, the Master of the Rolls indicated that the claimant had lost the benefit of timely treatment and that it would be unjust to deprive the claimant of a claim simply because the chance of the treatment being successful was less than 50%. Equally, a claimant should not succeed on 100% liability where the chances of success or cure only marginally exceeded 50%. It was indicated in *Hotson* that the proportionality approach posed too many problems in assessing damages. This argument is untenable. In *Bagley v North Herts HA* (1986) 136 NLJ 1014, the court reduced the claimant's damages by 5% to reflect the medical evidence which indicated that she would still have had a stillbirth had the defendant provided adequate treatment; in *Clark v McLennan* [1983] 1 All ER 416, the claimant's damages were reduced by 33%. Ackner LJ in *Hotson* [1987] 3 WLR 232, p 248) was of the opinion that *Bagley* had been wrongly decided, holding that causation had been fully established by the claimant and therefore there should be no discount. These cases, however, appear not to have been categorised as loss of chance cases and, consequently, the courts did not feel that they were playing a game of chance – yet another reason for suggesting that the solicitor should think twice before labelling a claim as the loss of chance.

The loss of chance approach has also fallen on stony ground in other jurisdictions. In *Lawson v Lafferiere* (1991) 78 DLR (4th) 609 (the facts of which are set out below), the court rejected it, especially since the damage had already occurred, that is, the claimant had died. The claimant, however, was allowed to recover for the psychological damage she had suffered and the better quality of life she would have enjoyed (lost years) if the defendant had not been negligent. This claim for lost years was also successful in the English case of *Sutton v Population Services Family Planning Programme Ltd* (1981) *The Times*, 7 November (see p 223).

Finally, it seems somewhat unjust that a patient who has a good chance of recovery, say as great as 49%, and is deprived of this chance by the defendant's negligence will not be able to recover any compensation because it is not possible to say with certainty that the negligence caused the damage. In our view, that negligence did cause the damage and therefore there should be liability. Also, if death is the natural result of the negligence, then any lay person would say that the defendant has caused the death of the patient. There have, however, been cases in the non-medical field where the court has recognised such a claim in tort. In *Allied Maples Group Ltd v Simmons & Simmons* [1995] 1 WLR 1602, in the Court of Appeal, Stuart-Smith LJ held that the classification of the causation issue into all or nothing on the balance of probabilities or the quantification of a loss of chance depends on whether the negligence is a positive act or an omission.

1   If the negligence is a positive act the question of negligence is determined retrospectively and once proven on the balance of probabilities is taken as true, and the claimant will therefore recover damages in full. It will often be the case however that the claimant's losses may be difficult to predict, for example, how will his physical condition deteriorate? In that situation the court must perform a risk assessment.

2   Where the negligence consists of an omission then the courts are asked to determine a hypothetical question – what would the claimant have done had there been no omission? The claimant must prove, on a balance of probabilities, that he would have acted had there been no omission. If the claimant is successful in proving his case then he will recover his damages in full. It is clear, however, that in this situation the claimant's evidence will undoubtedly be self-serving and may be disbelieved if there is compelling evidence to the contrary.

3   In the *Allied Maples* case, however, the claimant's loss depended on the acts of an independent third party and in this situation the claimant need only show that he had a real or substantial chance as opposed to a speculative one of avoiding the liability – a substantial chance may be less than 50%.

Allied Maples was applied in *Stovold v Barlows* [1996] 1 PNLR 91 and *First Interstate Bank of California v Cohen Arnold and Co* [1996] 1 PNLR 17. In *Stovold*, which concerned the loss of the sale of the claimant's property because of his solicitor's negligence, the Court of Appeal held that it must evaluate the claimant's chance that but for the defendant's negligence the sale would have gone ahead. If the claimant proved that he had lost a real chance as opposed to a speculative one then the court would go on to evaluate that chance.

In the latter case, the Court of Appeal asserted that a loss of chance claim was recognisable in tort. The chance lost had to be 'real or substantial' and in this particular case was valued at 66%. The chance lost, however, does not necessarily have to be 50% or greater. This argument was put forward in *Allied Maples* and failed.

In *Harrison and Another v Bloom Camillin* (1999) *The Times*, 12 November, the claimants had an unhappy relationship with their accountants and had instructed solicitors to sue them for damages. Unfortunately the solicitors failed to issue proceedings within the limitation period. The claimants then sued their solicitors for the loss they claimed to have suffered, that is, a loss of the chance to bring proceedings against their accountants. The court held that assuming the action had not been settled then it was necessary to assess the likely outcome and then apply a certain fraction to that sum to reflect uncertainties. In some circumstances where the claimant's prospects of success appeared so strong then it would be inappropriate to apply any such fraction; on the other hand if it appeared that the prospects of success were slim it would be inappropriate to award the claimant anything. In general the court would more readily infer that the claimant would have failed or succeeded on a point of law rather than go on to determine that the claimant would have failed or succeeded on a point of fact.

Finally, in *Smith v National Health Litigation Authority* [2001] 2 Lloyd's Rep Med 90, a loss of a chance claim was once again considered in a clinical negligence action. The claimant was born at home in 1973 with a congenitally displaced hip (CDH) which was not diagnosed until she was a year old. By the time the displacement was diagnosed, it was not easy to remedy and she underwent several operations and suffered continuing pain. She brought a claim against the defendant (who was responsible for the community health service which provided the claimant's care), alleging that her displaced hip should have been detected either within a few days of her birth or at six weeks of age. The claimant argued that in CDH cases an Otolani-Barlow test should have been performed. The expert evidence indicated that if CDII was detected before or at about eight weeks of age, the chances of successful treatment were in the region of 70%.

Andrew Smith J found that there was no breach of duty by the defendant but then, and this is interesting for our purposes, went on to consider that if there had been a breach of duty for which the defendant was responsible, whether the claimant would be entitled to recover damages for the lost chance of successful treatment. In his review of relevant case law, unsurprisingly, the learned judge began with *Hotson*. He contended that although the House of Lords in *Hotson* had some reservations about the merit of a loss of chance claim, they had not arrived at any definitive conclusion (p 100). It is clear from *Hotson* that their Lordships refused to answer the question as to whether a loss of chance claim could be sustainable in a clinical negligence action; however, the whole tenor of their judgment seems to indicate that it is not – see also *Lawson v Lafferiere* above at p 219. Andrew Smith J then chose to apply the analysis in *Allied Maples*, stating that he believed the judgment was of general application and that there is 'no reason to adopt a different approach because this case concerns a different category of professional negligence' (p 101). *Allied Maples* was, however, clearly different to *Smith* in at least one respect, namely that, unlike *Smith*, in *Allied Maples* the claimant's loss depended on the independent acts of a third party. Andrew Smith J stated that the speculation surrounding what action the third party may have taken in *Allied Maples* was analogous to considering what actions the defendant performing 'a properly competent, but not an unusually thorough or able, examination' (p 102) would have taken following that examination. This is not a true analogy. When speculating on what action a third party would have taken, one is truly asking the question 'would' or 'is it possible that' or 'do you think' this would have happened or occurred. However, in *Smith* there were clues as to what the defendant would have done had he performed the Otolani-Barlow test – those clues could be found in the expert evidence. The defendant's expert, for example, was of the opinion that the claimant's condition was unlikely to be detected in the early weeks of life, whereas the claimant's expert took the contrary view (p 102). Further, there was expert evidence as to the prospects of successful treatment. Either way, the court was not being asked to work in the realms of speculation as they were in *Allied Maples*. The court then came to the novel conclusion in *Smith* that the claimant had been properly treated, and yet had still suffered damage. However, had the claimant not been properly treated, then she would have been able to claim damages for the loss of a chance.

Despite the judgment in *Smith*, the upshot of all these cases seems to be that if causation depends on what the claimant or defendant would have done in a past hypothetical situation the claimant must establish this on the balance of probabilities but if it depends on what a third party would have done then he need only establish a chance. The reasons behind this distinction are not clear. What is apparent however, is that the situation remains unresolved as to whether a loss of chance claim is sustainable in clinical negligence. We think, however, that this is an area which will soon be revisited by the courts and perhaps they will eventually see the injustice of this situation and the loss of chance claim will become more than virtual reality.

REFERENCES

English case law

(1) Hotson v East Berkshire HA [1987] AC 750; [1987] 3 WLR 232
See above, p 217 *et seq.*

(2) Bonnington Castings Ltd v Wardlaw [1956] AC 613; [1956] 1 All ER 615
See above, p 204.

(3) McGhee v National Coal Board [1973] 1 WLR 1; [1972] 3 All ER 1008
See above, p 205 *et seq.*

(4) Chaplin v Hicks [1911] 2 KB 786
The claimant entered into a contract with the defendant as a result of which she might have won a prize. The defendant subsequently broke the contract and the claimant sought damages for the loss of a chance of winning the prize. The court assessed her chances of winning and then assessed her damages to reflect the lost chance. It was stated (p 797):

> The contract gave the claimant a right of considerable value, one for which many people would give money; therefore to hold that the claimant was entitled to no damages for being deprived of such a right because the final result depended on a contingency or chance would have been a misdirection.

(5) Kitchen v Royal Air Force Association [1958] 1 WLR 563
A claim succeeded against a firm of solicitors for the loss of a chance of bringing litigation.

See, also, *Kenyon v Bell* (1953) SC 125 where the claimant sustained an eye injury because of the defendant's negligence. However, the defendant established that even without the negligence there was a more than 50% chance that the claimant would have lost her sight. The court held it was an all or nothing approach and consequently found for the defendant.

(6) Bagley v North Herts HA (1986) 136 NLJ 1014
See above, p 219. The claimant successfully sued the defendant for failure to carry out blood tests during her pregnancy when they knew the claimant had a blood disorder. Liability was admitted by the hospital for failing to carry out the tests and to perform a Caesarian section. If the hospital had not been negligent the claimant would have had a 95% chance of a successful pregnancy. The claimant's award of damages was made up of the following:

(a) the loss of satisfaction in bringing her pregnancy to a successful conclusion;
(b) compensation for the loss of bringing up an ordinary healthy child (the claimant had decided not to attempt a further pregnancy);
(c) physical illness and suffering caused by the loss of the child (relying on *Kralj v McGrath and St Theresa's Hospital* [1986] 1 All ER 54. See Chapter 7, p 292).

(7) Clark v McLennan [1983] 1 All ER 416
See above, p 219 and Chapter 5, Standard of Care, p 171.

(8) Sutton v Population Services Family Planning Programme Ltd (1981) The Times, 7 November
The claimant was suffering from cancer. Due to the negligence of a nurse, the cancer was detected too late. However, as the cancer was highly malignant, an earlier diagnosis would not have prevented it but only meant that the onset of the cancer would have been delayed for four years. Additionally, the claimant's menopause was brought forward. The claimant was compensated for the loss of the four years during which she could have led a normal life. See, further, Chapter 7, Damages, p 257.

See, also, *Judge v Huntingdon HA* [1995] 6 Med LR 223 where the claimant attended her GP's surgery with a lump in her left breast. Her GP referred her to a surgeon who examined her and indicated that he found no discrete lump. The claimant attended her GP's surgery again some months later, complaining that a lump in her breast was painful. She was again referred to a surgeon who this time removed a grade two cancer lump which also had a lymphatic permeation. She later underwent a mastectomy and extensive treatment and her life expectancy was substantially reduced. On causation the court held there was an 80% chance of a cure had the cancer been diagnosed on first referral.

Note that there was a conflict of lay evidence and medical evidence as to whether there was a lump present at the first examination by the surgeon and whether the lymph nodes were present at that time. The court did not take into account the possibility of the cancer recurring and affecting the claimant's life in assessing damages.

See, also, *Phillips v Grampian Hospital Board* [1991] 3 Med LR 16; *Gascoine v Ian Sheridan & Co and Latham* [1994] 5 Med LR 437.

(9) Allied Maples Group Ltd v Simmons and Simmons [1995] 1 WLR 1602
The claimant (a retailing company) had wanted to acquire certain businesses and properties belonging to its rival company, G. Four of the properties, however, could not be conveyed directly to the claimant because of restrictive covenants that were personal to K, a subsidiary of G, in which the properties were vested. The defendant solicitors

advised the claimant to acquire all the shares in K and then pass on the unwanted properties and liabilities to another company, thereby retaining the properties they wanted. However, after completion of the sale the claimant found that K had liabilities for which it was responsible and could not reclaim from G. The trial judge found that the defendant had negligently failed to warn the claimant of this potentially open-ended liability and if they had warned the claimant then it would have tried to protect itself by obtaining some form of warranty from G. The judge also held that on the balance of probability, if asked G would have given that warranty or some other form of protection and that if K's properties had not been included in the sale the deal would not have proceeded. Commenting on a loss of chance claim, the Court of Appeal held that the claimant must prove that he had lost a real or substantial chance as opposed to a speculative one. Should the claimant fulfil this requirement then the court will assess the value of that chance as part of the assessment of quantum.

(10) Stovold v Barlows [1995] NPC 154; (1995) The Times, 30 October
The claimant claimed the defendant's negligence resulted in the sale of his house falling through. The court found that there was a 50% chance of the sale going through but for the negligence of the defendant. The Court of Appeal therefore awarded the claimant damages assessed at 50% of the loss.

(11) First Interstate Bank of California v Cohen Arnold & Co (1995) The Times, 11 December
The claimant bank lent money to the defendant accountant's client. As a large proportion of the loan remained outstanding, the claimant enquired of the defendant what its client's net worth amounted to. The defendant misrepresented its client's net worth and as a result the claimant, relying on this representation, did not begin marketing the property on which the loan was secured until September. The claimant obtained a price of £1.4 million for the property and contended that had it not relied on the defendant's representation that it would have called in the loan in June and sold the property for £3 million. The Court of Appeal held that this was a loss of a 'real or substantial' chance which the law would recognise.

(12) Harrison and Another v Bloom Camillin (No 2) (1999) The Times, 12 November
The claimant instructed solicitors to issue proceedings against his accountants for their alleged negligence in connection with the acquisition of shares. Proceedings were not issued within the relevant limitation period. The claimant therefore pursued a claim for negligence against his solicitors.

Held: the claim succeeded. Where the claim was for lost opportunity the onus was upon the claimant to prove that he would have pursued the matter until he was compensated. When assessing quantum the court did not have to assume that the action would have proceeded to trial as the majority of professional negligence actions did not. If the court was of the opinion that the case would not have settled then damages should be reduced by an appropriate fraction to reflect uncertainties. Where the case was strong then no deduction may be appropriate; however if a case was weak then it might be appropriate to award no damages. The court however would be more ready to accept success or failure on a point of law rather than a point of fact.

(13) Smith v National Health Litigation Authority [2001] 2 Lloyd's Rep Med 90
The claimant was born at home in 1973 with a congenitally displaced hip (CDH) which was not diagnosed until she was more than a year old. By that time, the displacement was not easy to remedy and she had several operations and suffered continuing pain.

In 1996 she began proceedings claiming that the defendant (which was responsible for the liabilities of the community health service that provided the claimant's care) was negligent in failing to diagnose the displaced hip by the performance of the Otolani-Barlow test, either within a few days of the claimant's birth or when she was about six weeks old. Expert evidence indicated that if CDH was detected before or about eight weeks of age the chances of successful treatment were 70%.

Held: there was no breach of duty as the Otolani-Barlow test for CDH had been performed at the appropriate times. If there had been a breach of duty by the defendant, namely a failure to perform the Otolani-Barlow test at six weeks, then, although the CDH would not have been detected at examination, the claimant would have been entitled to claim damages for the loss of a chance of successful treatment.

Foreign case law

Australia

Stacey v Chiddy [1993] 4 Med LR 345 in Chapter 5, Standard of Care, p 183
Note that on appeal the court refused to consider a claim for loss of chance (the doctor had failed to diagnose a malignant tumour) as it had not been explored at trial. As the claimant was found to be suffering from an aggressive tumour it was doubtful whether an earlier diagnosis would have made much difference anyway.

Canada

Lawson v Lafferiere (1991) 78 DLR (4th) 609, also noted at [1994] 5 Med LR 185
The defendant failed to inform the claimant of a biopsy result which confirmed the claimant had cancer. The claimant did not learn of the result until four years later, by which time the cancer had spread throughout her body. She died three years later.

In the Quebec Court of Appeal she was compensated for loss of a chance, but the defendant successfully appealed to the Supreme Court of Canada. The majority of that court held the loss of chance claim should not be introduced into Quebec law, at least where the damage in question had already occurred.

Note that the claimant was awarded compensation for the psychological damage that she suffered as a result of the defendant's failure to inform her of the result. She was also awarded damages for the better quality of life she would have enjoyed had the defendant not been negligent.

In discussing the 'loss of chance' claim, the court held in this instance the damage had already occurred and therefore the court was simply concerned as to whether or not the defendant's negligence had affected the claimant's condition and thus the question was one of probability and not loss of chance. In doing so, the court was not persuaded simply by statistical evidence; it would have found for the claimant even if the statistical evidence was poor.

See, also, *Snell v Farrell* (1990) 72 DLR (4th) 289 and *Patterson v Dutton* (1991) 79 DLR (4th) 705, pp 180, 181.

United States

Herskovits v Group Health Cooperative of Puget Sound (1993) 664 P (2d) 474

The claimant (the widow of the deceased) brought a claim alleging the defendant had been negligent in failing to diagnose her husband's cancer at an earlier stage. It was accepted that had the cancer been diagnosed at an earlier stage then Mr Herskovits' chances for survival would have been 39%, but the delay reduced his chances to 25%. The claimant recovered damages only for her husband's early death, for example, loss of earnings, etc. Dole J said (p 477):

> To decide otherwise would be a blanket release from liability for doctors and hospitals any time there was less than a 50% chance of survival, regardless of how flagrant the negligence.

RULE 6(C)

Where the claimant cannot explain how the accident occurred he may rely on the principle of *res ipsa loquitur*. The defendant must then rebut the inference of negligence.

Commentary

In all tort cases the burden of proof is on the claimant who must show, on a balance of probabilities, that the defendant's negligence caused the damage. As has already been seen, this may be supremely difficult; the patient might be unconscious at the time of the alleged negligence and therefore oblivious as to what actually happened and who gave the treatment, or the procedure being complained of might have been routine, as a result of which there may be very little in the way of written evidence as to how it was carried out. In such circumstances the claimant may rely on the evidential principle of *res ipsa loquitur*. It should be noted that the principle *does not* shift the burden of proof, it merely raises the inference of negligence which the defendant must rebut (see *Ng Chun Pui v Lee Chuen Tat* [1988] RTR 298). Although reliance on the principle will in effect give the claimant a more than equal chance of succeeding the burden still remains with him to establish that the defendant was negligent.

In order to rely on *res ipsa* the claimant must essentially prove two things:

(1) that the defendant had control of the situation; and

(2) that the damage would normally not have occurred in the ordinary course of events.

The most apt illustration of the principle at work is the case of *Cassidy v Ministry of Health* [1951] 2 KB 343. The claimant was suffering from Dupuytren's contracture and two of his fingers were operated on. After the operation he found that four of his fingers were stiff. In the Court of Appeal, Denning LJ held that *res ipsa* was appropriate because the result of the operation was highly indicative of negligence; the defendant was in control of the situation as it was responsible in law for all of the people involved in the procedure.

In *Mahon v Osborne* [1939] 2 KB 14, where a swab was left inside the patient's body, Scott LJ (in a strong dissenting judgment) said that it was wrong to apply the doctrine as a matter of course; the claimant had to prove that the accident was caused by the defendant's want of care. This statement should be borne in mind by a solicitor seeking to rely on *res ipsa*. If the operation is not routine but has associated risks, it may be difficult for the reasonable person to draw the necessary inference. Similarly, the principle should not be used as a stop gap in lieu of a closer investigation of the evidence. In practice, where an object is found in the claimant's body which clearly should not be there, it is most unlikely that any defendant is going to spend a vast amount of time and money in defending a negligence claim.

In *Delaney v Southmead HA* [1995] 6 Med LR 355, the court held that *res ipsa loquitur* would rarely be of assistance after all the evidence had been adduced. Furthermore, the defendant could rebut the inference by either giving a reasonable explanation (the usual 'defence' to *res ipsa*), or by showing that he had exercised reasonable care (which is what happened in this case). As regards the second limb of the test, all the defendant did in this case (which satisfied the court) was to demonstrate that it had followed accepted practice despite the fact that this did not accord with the scientific evidence. This is in line with the decision of *Ng v Lee* (see above); the defendant merely has to show that it has taken care, that is, provided an explanation, not that it has taken all reasonable care. See, also, the recent case of *Bouchta v Swindon HA* [1996] 7 Med LR 62 which, like *Delaney*, again demonstrates the reluctance of the court to apply *res ipsa* to clinical negligence actions. Commenting on the *res ipsa*, Judge Sumner said (p 65):

> I am reluctant to apply such a test to issues of medical judgment unless I am compelled to do so.

Likewise in *Fallows v Randle* [1997] 8 Med LR 160 the court, quoting from *Delaney*, held that the maxim of *res ipsa loquitur* was not helpful; the court simply had to decide what was the most probable explanation of what was an unusual and comparatively rare event. In doing so the *Bolam* principle has no application; the court simply had to determine what happened on a balance of probabilities.

Note, the court also rejected the application of *Bolitho*, see below, p 235.

More recently, in *Ratcliffe v Plymouth and Torbay HA* [1998] 4 Med 162 Hobhouse LJ, doubting the applicability of *res ipsa* in clinical negligence cases, said:

> ... the expression *res ipsa loquitur* should be dropped from the litigator's vocabulary and replaced with the phrase 'a *prima facie* case'. *Res ipsa loquitur* is not a principle of law: it does not relate to or raise any presumption. It is merely a guide to help to identify when a *prima facie* case is being made out. Where expert and factual evidence has been called on both sides at a trial, its usefulness will normally have long since been exhausted [p 177].

The other judges, whilst not as pessimistic about the relevance of *res ipsa*, both emphasised that in clinical negligence actions the weight of expert evidence supports the maxim which, in essence, means that the claimant is not simply relying on the *res ipsa* doctrine. It is apparent that *res ipsa* is now of little importance in the era of the expert witness. See also the more recent decision of *Fryer v Pearson* (2000) *The Times*, 4 April where Lord Justice May observed that lawyers should stop using 'unhelpful Latin phrases'.

The courts will only entertain *res ipsa* in the most clear cut cases. In *Ludlow v Swindon HA* [1989] 1 Med LR 104, the claimant alleged that the defendant had failed to administer halothane during a caesarian operation. Although she was able to describe the symptoms of a caesarian operation and she had experienced the pain, because she had been under the influence of drugs the court doubted the reliability of her version of events. Had the claimant been able to establish conclusively that she had been conscious and had suffered pain the court held, *obiter*, that *res ipsa* would have applied.

Once *res ipsa* has been held to apply, the defendant must seek to rebut the inference by offering a reasonable explanation. In *Saunders v Leeds Western HA* (1984) 129 SJ 225, a child suffered cardiac arrest during an operation. The defendant sought to explain it by suggesting that the child's heart had suddenly stopped. This was rejected as implausible by the court.

If the defendant succeeds in rebutting the inference of negligence (see *Roe v Ministry of Health* [1954] 2 QB 66 and *Brazier v Minister of Defence* [1965] 1 Lloyd's Rep 26), the claimant must then, as for a 'normal' negligence case, prove that the defendant acted without reasonable care. It is submitted that it will be very difficult for him to do this since, if he had evidence of the defendant's want of care, it is unlikely that he would have relied on *res ipsa* in the first instance.

REFERENCES

English case law

(1)   Ng Chun Pui v Lee Chuen Tat [1988] RTR 298; (1988) 132 SJ 1244
The first defendant was driving a coach owned by the second defendant when it crossed the central reservation, colliding with a public bus. The action was brought by the personal representatives of passengers who were killed or injured for damages for negligence. At first instance, judgment was given for the claimants. The claimants had relied on *res ipsa* and the judge had held that the burden of disproving negligence was on the defendants who had failed to discharge it. The Court of Appeal reversed the decision, holding that the defendant had exercised reasonable care in the circumstances. The Judicial Committee upheld this decision. Commenting on *res ipsa*, Lord Griffiths held that the burden of proving negligence rested throughout on the claimant. If the defendant adduced evidence, this had to be evaluated to see if it was still reasonable to draw the inference of negligence from the mere fact of the accident.

(2)   Cassidy v Ministry of Health [1951] 2 KB 343; [1951] 1 All ER 574
Commenting on the claimant's claim Lord Denning said (p 365):

> I went into hospital to be cured of 'two stiff fingers'; I have come out with 'four stiff fingers'. That should not have happened if due care had been used. Explain it, if you can.

(3)   Mahon v Osborne [1939] 2 KB 14
See above, p 226 and Chapter 5, Standard of Care, p 191.

Note that there was a strong dissenting judgment of Goddard LJ who thought that *res ipsa* might apply.

(4) Delaney v Southmead HA [1995] 6 Med LR 355

The claimant underwent a cholocystectomy under general anaesthetic which was in itself successful; however, it was later discovered that the claimant had sustained a lesion of the brachial plexus. The claimant contended that as she had suffered a fracture of her clavicle in 1975, which had been plated resulting in substantial callous formation and reduction of the thoracic outlet, that the defendant should have refrained from using her left arm or hand for the administration of the general anaesthetic. As an alternative, the claimant argued that her left arm had been hyper abducted resulting in excessive strain and stretch on the nerve. The claimant argued that once it was accepted that an injury to the brachial plexus had occurred during the operation and there was no narrowing of the thoracic outlet then the principle of *res ipsa loquitur* was appropriate. The Court of Appeal doubted whether *res ipsa* was appropriate to a clinical negligence case (see above, p 227) and also the recent case of *Hay v Grampian Health Board* [1995] 6 Med LR 128. Here, a voluntary patient who was known to be at a high risk of suicide hanged herself resulting in irreversible brain damage. At the time of the incident, the patient was left unattended, the two ward nurses were occupied with other patients. An action for damages was brought and the claimant established liability but it was held that the doctrine of *res ipsa loquitur* was inappropriate. Here, the facts were known, the patient had been left unsupervised which had resulted in her attempted suicide.

(5) Bouchta v Swindon HA [1996] 7 Med LR 62

See Chapter 5, Standard of Care, pp 160 and 163. The claimant suffered damage to her ureter during a routine hysterectomy. Negligence was established though the doctrine of *res ipsa* was held inappropriate.

(6) Fallows v Randle [1997] 8 Med LR 160

See above, p 227.

(7) Bolam v Friern HMC [1957] 1 WLR 582

See p 155 *et seq.*

(8) Bolitho v City and Hackney HA [1998] AC 232

See p 227 *et seq.*

(9) Ratcliffe v Plymouth and Torbay HA [1998] 4 Med 162

The claimant, in 1989, underwent a triple arthrodesis of his right ankle and was given a general anaesthetic and a spinal anaesthetic. The operation was successful, but the claimant suffered a serious neurological defect on the right side from the waist downwards. On appeal, the claimant argued that, as the claimant's condition raised an inference of negligence, *res ipsa loquitur* applied and the onus was on the defendant to rebut that inference.

Held: the maxim could only be applied in simple situations in the clinical negligence field. In contested clinical negligence claims, the defendant might adduce a plausible explanation of what might have happened that did not connote any negligence on his part. The defendant did not have to prove that his explanation was more likely to be correct than any other. Alternatively, the defendant's evidence might satisfy the judge, on the balance of probabilities, that he did exercise proper care.

(10) Fryer v Pearson (2000) The Times, 4 April
The claimant appealed against a decision that the defendant was not negligent. He had suffered an injury as a result of kneeling on a needle whilst working in the defendant's house. The claimant sought to rely on the maxim of *res ipsa loquitur*.

Held: the appeal was dismissed. It could not be inferred from the defendant's evidence that the defendant had permitted the needle to remain on the floor, knowing that it was there. The use of Latin tags not easily understood by non-lawyers should be discouraged.

(11) Ludlow v Swindon HA [1989] 1 Med LR 104
See Chapter 5, Standard of Care, p 192.

See, also, *Taylor v Worcester and District HA* [1991] 2 Med LR 215, Chapter 5, Standard of Care, p 192.

(12) Saunders v Leeds Western HA (1985) 129 SJ 225
See above, p 228.

(13) Roe v Minister of Health [1954] 2 QB 66; [1954] 2 All ER 131
See Chapter 5, Standard of Care, p 168.

(14) Brazier v Ministry of Defence [1965] 1 Lloyd's Rep 26
The claimant was injected with penicillin. During the injection the needle broke off and lodged in his right buttock. He suffered severe pain and was compelled to give up work. He sued the Ministry of Defence, relying on *res ipsa*. The defendant, however, successfully rebutted the inference by showing that the accident was the result of a latent defect in the needle.

(15) Glass v Cambridge HA [1995] 6 Med LR 91
The claimant suffered a cardiac arrest whilst under a general anaesthetic resulting in severe brain damage. *Res ipsa* was held to apply. The defendant's explanation that a gas embolism had occurred when hydrogen peroxide was used to clean the patient's wound was rejected as the medical evidence did not support this explanation. If the defendant had proffered a reasonable explanation the inference of negligence would have been rebutted.

RULE 6(D)

The defendant will only be held to have caused that damage which was reasonably foreseeable. The defendant, however, must take his victim as he finds him.

Commentary

As with other areas of tort the defendant will not be held responsible for all ensuing damage which befalls the claimant but only for that which is reasonably foreseeable as per *The Wagon Mound* [1961] AC 388. Furthermore, neither the extent of the damage nor the manner of its occurrence need be foreseen (see *Hughes v Lord Advocate* [1963] AC 837 and *Crossley v Rawlinson* [1982] 1 WLR 369). However, the foreseeable damage must be of the same kind as that which occurred. See, also, *Brown v Lewisham and North Southwark HA* [1999] 4 Lloyd's Rep Med 110, where the Court of Appeal made some interesting observations on what a health carer may be expected to foresee (p 205).

The defendant must take his victim as he finds him. This is endorsed by the operation of the 'eggshell skull' rule, the two most important cases in this area being *Bourhill v Young* [1943] AC 92 and *Smith v Leech Brain & Co Ltd* [1962] 2 QB 405. In the latter, an employee who was burnt on the lip by a piece of molten metal contracted cancer as a result of the burn which led eventually to his death. The court held that 'the amount of damage which he suffers as a result of that burn, depends upon the characteristics and constitution of the victim' (p 415). What is important is that some damage was foreseeable as a result of the defendant's negligence; provided that requirement is satisfied, the defendant is responsible for all the ensuing damage.

How this test fits in with the remoteness test based on foreseeability is speculative to say the least; however, it is apparent that the courts have held that the principle remains unaffected by *The Wagon Mound* decision. In *Page v Smith* [1995] 2 WLR 644, the claimant was involved in a road traffic accident with the defendant. Before the accident the claimant had been suffering from ME (chronic fatigue syndrome or post viral fatigue syndrome), which he claimed had become chronic and permanent as a result of the sudden shock caused by the accident. The Court of Appeal held that the claimant's psychiatric illness, which had not resulted from physical injury but from the nervous shock he sustained, was not reasonably foreseeable and the claimant could therefore only recover damages for the harm he suffered if the incident giving rise to the claim would have caused a person of ordinary fortitude to be similarly affected. However, in the House of Lords, the claimant was ultimately successful on a 3:2 majority. The two dissenting Lords applied an objective test and held that a reasonable person in the position of the defendant would not have foreseen that such an accident might inflict on a person of normal susceptibility such mental trauma and nervous shock as to result in illness. The majority, however, took the view that any driver should be able to foresee that driving carelessly might cause physical or psychiatric injury or both, and accordingly restored the award of damages.

It would seem from this decision that the courts have quashed any idea that the eggshell skull rule might not apply where the damage is psychiatric in nature. With this we agree. It is possible that the defendant could not have reasonably foreseen that the claimant was suffering from ME; however, we imagine that the defendant in *Smith v Leech Brain & Co Ltd* [1962] 2 QB 405 did not for one moment foresee that the claimant could contract cancer as a result of a minor burn. In our opinion, the two scenarios are indistinguishable, and there is no justification for applying different rules dependent on whether the damage is physical or psychiatric. It is to be hoped that the majority view of the House of Lords in *Page v Smith* continues to prevail.

See, also, nervous shock, p 263 *et seq*.

REFERENCES

English case law

(1)   Overseas Tankship (UK) v Morts Dock & Engineering Co (The Wagon Mound) [1961] AC 388; [1961] 1 All ER 404; [1961] 2 WLR 126

OT Ltd were demise charterers of *The Wagon Mound* which was moored at the C Oil Co's wharf to take on fuel oil. OT's employees negligently spilt oil onto the water and this spread to MD's wharf where another ship was moored undergoing repair. MD's manager asked C Oil Co whether he should stop the repairs and their answer, together with his own opinion, led him to order that the repairs should continue, taking extensive precautions. However, two days later the oil caught fire causing extensive damage to MD's wharf.

Held:

(a) it was unforeseeable that the fuel oil spread on the water would catch fire; and

(b) the damage which was caused to MD's wharf was foreseeable.

On appeal the Privy Council found for the defendant. The applicable test was the foresight of the reasonable man. It was also said that the damage that occurs must be of the same kind as that which was foreseeable.

(2)   Hughes v Lord Advocate [1963] AC 837

A manhole was left open, covered only by a canvas shelter and surrounded by warning paraffin lamps. It was left unattended in the evening. The claimant, a child of eight, took one of the lamps and entered the shelter. He fell into the manhole causing an explosion and sustained severe burns.

Held: It was unforeseeable that the lamp would explode but it was foreseeable that by leaving the shelter unattended someone might take a lamp and enter. So although the exact sequence of events was unforeseeable, the resulting damage clearly was and thus the defendant was liable.

(3)   Crossley v Rawlinson [1982] 1 WLR 369

The claimant fell when running to put out a fire caused by the defendant's negligence.

Held: For the claimant to recover it had to be foreseeable that his injuries were caused by falling, it was not enough that it was foreseeable that he might be injured.

(4)   Brown v Lewisham and North Southwark HA [1999] 4 Lloyd's Rep Med 110
See p 204.

(5)   Bourhill v Young [1943] AC 92

The claimant, a pregnant fishwife, was standing about 45 ft from a motorcycle accident. She heard a noise, although she did not see the accident and suffered a fright which resulted in severe nervous shock. She gave birth to a stillborn child.

Held: the driver of the motorcycle owed no duty to her as she was not within an area of potential danger resulting from the negligence.

(6)   Smith v Leech Brain & Co Ltd [1962] 2 QB 405
See above, p 231.

(7)   Page v Smith [1995] 2 WLR 644; [1995] 2 All ER 736

Note that the majority judgment distinguished between primary and secondary victims, an example of the latter being the spectators in *Alcock v Chief Constable of South Yorkshire*

[1992] 1 AC 310, whereas someone directly involved in the accident would be regarded as a primary victim. Where the claimant is a secondary victim and is bringing a claim for nervous shock, the damage must be foreseeable – something which does not arise in the case of the primary victim. The court affirmed the decision in *Brice v Brown* [1984] 1 All ER 997 where a mother and daughter were involved in a car accident. The mother was awarded damages for her own shock and also the shock she suffered as a result of being aware of her daughter's predicament. As a result of *Page* the mother can be seen as both the primary and secondary victim.

RULE 6(E)

The claimant's claim will fail on causation if:

(1) there was a break in the chain of causation; or

(2) the defendant's breach of duty amounts to an omission and the claimant cannot show that the defendant's actions were contrary to accepted medical practice.

Commentary

The break in the chain

This is where an act by a third party supersedes the original negligent act of the defendant. The court must decide whether the original act of the defendant was responsible for the damage or if the intervening act constitutes a *novus actus interveniens*, that is, the second act caused the damage. The second act could be an intervening act by a third party or an intervening act by the claimant himself.

By a third party

A good illustration of this principle is the case of *Prendergast v Sam and Dee* [1989] 1 Med LR 36. There a GP's writing was so bad that a prescription was misread by a pharmacist with the result that the patient suffered brain damage. The doctor alleged that the pharmacist's failure to query his illegible handwriting constituted a break in the chain of causation. This argument failed because the court ruled that it was foreseeable that the pharmacist would prescribe the wrong drug because of the GP's illegible handwriting.

The damage must in some way be caused by the initial negligence. So where a GP failed to diagnose appendicitis but the claimant's resulting damage was caused by the negligence of the operating surgeon, the GP could not be said to have caused that damage (see *Yepremian v Scarborough General Hospital* (1980) 110 DLR (3d) 513). This is different from the situation where a doctor negligently fails to diagnose a fracture and then the claimant is negligently treated by a second doctor for that fracture. In that situation, as in *Prendergast*, it is clearly foreseeable that the second doctor will rely on the negligent diagnosis of the first doctor.

Where the claimant's original injuries are exacerbated by negligent medical treatment, is the chain of causation broken? In *Hogan v Bentinck West Hartley Collieries Ltd* [1949] 1 All ER 588, the court ruled that the chain would only be broken where the treatment was unreasonable or lacking in care. Just what will constitute an unreasonable intervention is not defined but we submit that it must mean any treatment contrary to accepted practice.

An interesting point is whether the same principles apply where the supervening act constitutes an omission. Generally, no liability attaches where the negligence constitutes an omission unless the doctor has a duty to treat. Usually the defendant can only rely on the omission where it is totally independent of the original act. It seems apparent, however, that any failure by the doctor to treat should be seen as a failure to minimise the damage rather than a failure to act, and that both the original tortfeasor and the negligent health carer should be held responsible. This results from the application of the 'but for' test, that is, but for the original negligence the claimant would not have been placed in this predicament, but the health carer by his omission has exacerbated the damage and consequently must be held to account for his lack of action.

By the claimant

In some cases the defendant will try to argue that the claimant's conduct amounts to a *novus actus*. For example, the claimant may refuse to follow the prescribed treatment or fail to return to his GP when the very symptoms he has been told to watch out for reappear. Whether such conduct amounts to a *novus actus* must depend to a large extent on whether the patient's conduct is regarded as reasonable. In *Emeh v Kensington and Chelsea AHA* [1985] QB 1012, a woman sued in respect of the birth of her severely handicapped child following a negligently performed sterilisation operation. She had discovered that she was pregnant at about 20 weeks but decided not to undergo an abortion; this, the defendant argued, amounted to a *novus actus*. At first instance, this argument was accepted by the court but was rightly rejected on appeal. Slade LJ stated that the defendant had by his own negligence caused the claimant to be 'faced with the very dilemma she had sought to avoid by having herself sterilised' (p 1053). The court doubted that such a decision could amount to a *novus actus* 'save in the most exceptional circumstances'. Quite what these exceptional circumstances are is unknown but we submit that a woman's decision not to have an abortion should never amount to a *novus actus*; there should never be a duty on a woman to abort. In contrast to the decision in *Emeh,* see the case of *Sabri-Tabrizi v Lothian Health Board* 1998 SC 373. There, the claimant was aware that she was not sterile following a failed sterilisation operation, but she continued to have sexual intercourse without using any contraceptive measures. This was held to constitute a break in the chain of causation between the negligent surgery and the birth of her resulting child.

An area which may cause problems is where the patient refuses treatment on religious grounds. In the criminal case of *R v Blaue* [1975] 1 WLR 1411, it was held that refusal to undergo a blood transfusion did not constitute a *novus actus*. This decision was clearly made on policy grounds, but it can be said to illustrate that the court will be reluctant to regard a decision based on religious grounds as unreasonable.

It is worth noting that the claimant need only take reasonable steps to mitigate his damage, consequently, it should never be unreasonable to make a decision according to one's religion. Also in cases of clinical negligence (excepting in emergency situations) it is more than likely that the defendant will have discussed the variety of treatments available with, for example, a Jehovah's Witness patient and therefore should be able to foresee how the patient would react in any given situation. In this regard, it could not be said to be a totally independent act and consequently a *novus actus*.

We think it unlikely in the majority of cases that the defendant will be able to rely on the principle of *novus actus*, because the court will be reluctant to hold that either the claimant or, for that matter, a third party should be penalised for not taking some step to minimise the damage caused by the defendant. At best the defendant should concentrate on those cases where a blatant lack of care by the claimant or a third party has resulted in damage which could have been avoided; as a defendant he should be relying on the principle of contributory negligence (see Rule 6(F), p 241).

The Bolitho defence

In the first edition of this book we speculated as to whether what we termed the 'Bolitho defence' (*Bolitho v City and Hackney HA* [1993] 4 Med LR 381) would become entrenched in English law. It was not long before our question was answered in the affirmative by the House of Lords ([1998] AC 232). The importance of the decision cannot be underestimated; *Bolitho* was the first clinical negligence case to reach the House of Lords in over ten years. The facts of *Bolitho* are as follows. The claimant (a minor) was admitted to hospital with breathing difficulties. The paediatric registrar failed to attend the child after being summoned by the sister and it was admitted that this was negligent. However, the court could not say that that negligence caused the claimant's injuries because it was not apparent what the registrar would have done had she responded. The claimant's solicitors contended that had she attended she would have intubated the patient which would have prevented the ensuing injury; the defendant argued that she would not have intubated. Both arguments were endorsed by experts. The court held that where the breach of duty consisted of an omission, it had to be decided what course of events would have followed had the duty been discharged. To do so the court was bound to rely on the evidence of experts. As there was a conflict of medical opinion on the appropriate treatment then, since the claimant could not prove that failure to intubate was contrary to medical practice (that is, the *Bolam* test), the claim failed. The Court of Appeal therefore abandoned the probability game canvassed in cases such as *Bonnington* and *McGhee*. There was however at this stage still some hope for the claimant in the strong dissenting judgment of Simon Brown LJ. He chose to adopt the robust and pragmatic approach of *McGhee* and said that it was a matter of common sense to infer that a reasonable doctor would have intubated had he attended. It is possible that he reached this decision out of sympathy, but it can be justified using the risk versus precautions approach:

(1) The sister caring for the claimant would not have summoned assistance unless treatment was required; from the evidence she was of the opinion that there was something wrong and was sufficiently worried to order a nurse to stay with the claimant.

(2) It was an accepted fact that intubation would have benefited the claimant. Furthermore, intubating would have resulted in less risk to the claimant than not intubating.

(3) The claimant had a known history of respiratory problems. One month previously he had undergone a serious operation and had recently recovered from an attack of the croup.

(4) The claimant had been admitted to hospital after collapsing and making wheezing sounds. His medical notes indicated reduced air supply.

If point (2) is acceptable, is it wrong to infer the very thing which would have most benefited the claimant? As Simon Brown LJ pointed out, this approach had been taken in other cases. The House of Lords however held that causation had not been proven. Central to the debate was the role of *Bolam*. Lord Browne-Wilkinson said that where a breach of duty consisted of an omission then the court's role was to determine what would have happened had the breach not occurred. In Bolitho whether the claimant would still have sustained the resulting damage depended upon what the doctor would have done had she attended. Lord Browne-Wilkinson relied on the case of *Joyce v Merton, Sutton and Wandsworth HA* [1996] 7 Med LR 1.

There, the claimant established negligence but failed on causation because even if the occlusion had been discovered earlier, a surgeon would not have operated in time to remove the blockage and, furthermore, it would not have been negligent not to have done so. The fact the court found that the defendant would not have operated is a simple application of the 'but for' test but the court then went on to approve the Court of Appeal judgment in *Bolitho*. Hobhouse LJ said at p 20:

> Thus, a claimant can discharge the burden of proof on causation by satisfying the court either that the relevant person would in fact have taken the requisite action (although she would not have been at fault if she had not) or that the proper discharge of the relevant person's duty towards the claimant required that she take that action ... Properly viewed, therefore, this rule is favourable to the claimant because it gives him two routes by which he may prove his case – either proof that the exercise of proper care would have necessitated the relevant result, or proof that if proper care had been exercised, it would in fact have led to the relevant result.

The claimant therefore had the burden of showing that, (1) the defendant would have acted in a certain way but did not (had she attended), or (2) that she would not have acted and that behaviour was contrary to accepted medical practice. *Bolam* has no part to play in (1) yet in Lord Browne-Wilkinson's words 'it is central to the second'. He then went on to dismiss Simon Brown LJ's approach in the Court of Appeal criticising him for dismissing the evidence of Dr Horn that she would not have intubated, stating that it was for the judge to assess the truth of her evidence.

There is however an intrinsic problem in assessing the truth of Dr Horn's evidence. In reality no-one could say for certain what would have happened had Dr Horn attended. The claimant argued that had Dr Horn attended then she would have intubated so preventing the resulting damage ('but for your breach the damage would not have happened'.) The defendant argued that she would not have intubated; the claimant can no longer assert that had the defendant attended, the injury would have been prevented (the 'but for' test fails). It is at this stage that Simon Brown LJ in the Court of Appeal ([1993] 4 Med LR 381) argued that if it is uncertain as to what course of events would have followed had Dr Horn attended then the question is not, 'Would it have been unreasonable and thus negligent for an attending doctor not to intubate Patrick? ... It is rather: Should and therefore would an attending doctor probably have intubated Patrick?' (p 390).

In reaching this conclusion Simon Brown LJ, having regard to the evidence and in particular the *Maynard* test which he reasoned was not appropriate to causation, stated that:

> No doctor in this case ever took a decision whether or not to intubate. The plain fact here is that no doctor ever arrived at Patrick's bedside. It is that want of attention that constitutes the undoubted negligence in this case [p 388].

The House of Lords ruled that this was the wrong approach; the court could not dismiss out of hand the evidence of the defendant. The burden is upon the claimant to demonstrate that, by not acting, the defendant fell below the standard of accepted medical practice. In turn the defendant must show that his actions or omissions would not have been contrary to accepted medical practice and if he succeeds in doing this the case fails. This was also the approach in the *Joyce* case. Hobhouse LJ said at p 20:

> In assessing what the exercise of proper care necessitates, no different test is to be applied to that to be applied in any case where professional negligence is alleged, essentially the so called *Bolam* test. This is because it is the same question as is involved in the initial allegation of fault; the causation question merely extends the ambit of fault. The claimant's case is still based upon saying what the exercise of proper care required and saying that if proper care had been exercised in all respects and had continued to be exercised, the claimant would not have suffered the injury. Nor do any different principles of burden of proof apply; the claimant has the same general burden but can rely on evidential inferences to discharge that burden. In my judgment, it does not assist to introduce concepts from administrative law such as the *Wednesbury* test ...

Hobhouse LJ contends that the '*Bolitho* rule' is favourable to the claimant because he now has two alternatives to prove his case. Favourable? Surely not. It is difficult, in the authors' view, to see what advantage the claimant gains by the introduction of the '*Bolitho* rule'. The claimant has always had the opportunity to demonstrate that but for the defendant's omission he would not have suffered injury because the defendant would have taken action. That is nothing new, so the first alternative is merely restating the law as we know it to be. But the second? The claimant is being asked to prove not one but two negligent acts: (1) the original breach of duty (in this case the fact that the claimant was not given adequate post-operative care and was discharged) and (2) that had the original breach of duty not taken place that it was negligent not to intervene. A double edged sword? Hobhouse LJ says the causation question 'merely extends the ambit of the allegation of fault'. Surely, however, the 'fault' has already been established – in *Bolitho*, it was the non-attendance, in *Joyce* it was the discharge of the claimant without adequate care. Once this fault had been established to then go on and say that the claimant must now further establish a second fault, namely that the defendant would have fallen below the *Bolam* standard had he not acted, if given the chance, seems to us to be particularly absurd.

However the judiciary's attempt to justify the *Bolitho* decision seems to us fundamentally flawed in that it confuses the question 'what should have been done' (the claimant has then to go on and demonstrate that the defendant's account is plainly illogical) with 'what would have probably been done' (is this the normal way doctors respond?). The true test should be on the balance of probabilities and in a case such as this it would mean asking whether the defendant's conduct materially contributed or materially increased the risk. Like *McGhee* there was a failure to do something; in *McGhee* the failure to provide washing facilities certainly increased the likelihood of the claimant contracting dermatitis; in *Bolitho* the non-attendance of Dr Horn certainly increased the risk of something going wrong with Patrick's treatment. Simon Brown LJ recognised that, as truthful as Dr Horn may be, her evidence could never be relied on because any evidence of a defendant in a similar situation will undoubtedly be self-serving. Would any defendant in a similar situation stand up and say that had she attended she would have taken the very measures needed to avert the injury? Too much weight was attached to what the defendant would or would not have done with the benefit of hindsight. In *Bolitho* there is too little evaluation of the evidence and too much of the judiciary substituting its own opinion on what they think would have happened. Indeed it is arguable that, by finding for the defendant, the court has implicitly rejected the claimant's expert evidence. Notwithstanding that this case should never have been decided on whether the claimant could prove two breaches of duty it appears regrettable that the court believed that *Bolam* and causation do mix. The House of Lords have placed yet another burden on the already *Bolam*-weary claimant, one which will be very difficult to throw off. We have very little by way of words of comfort for the claimant's solicitor except to suggest that he/she try and argue along the lines of material contribution (although even that has its problems, see 204 *et seq*), and to hope that more of the judiciary are like Simon Brown LJ and some of his more pragmatic colleagues (see *Wisniewski* below). After all where there is a case and a more radical judge there is always hope!

Most of the cases post-*Bolitho* have applied the decision with regard to the standard of care. In *Wisniewski v Central Manchester HA* [1998] Lloyd's Rep Med 223 the issue was what steps the doctor would have taken had he attended the claimant's mother whilst she was in labour. This case was unusual in that the doctor (a Dr Rennisson) failed to attend at the actual trial and that played a part in the Court of Appeal affirming the decision at first instance and finding for the claimant. The decision is of interest for its application of *Bolitho*. Brooke LJ emphasised that the first limb of the *Bolitho* test did not require the court to make a finding of what a doctor actually did but rather what a doctor would have done in a hypothetical situation. In such a situation the claimant's case would be strengthened if for no good reason the doctor is unwilling to submit himself to questioning before the judge as to what he would probably have done. The defendant may no longer rely on the fact that the doctor in question is abroad to avoid calling him, given the technological aids such as video link now widely available. So despite the fact that the Court of Appeal held that the views of the defendant's experts did have a logical basis they were prepared to rule in the claimant's favour. Why? The court found that the claimant had established a *prima facie* but weak case that if Dr Rennisson had attended then he would have taken the necessary measures to prevent injury to the claimant. As Dr Rennisson failed to appear at the trial the court was entitled to treat the claimant's case as being strengthened by his absence and so find for the claimant. So although the court could find no fault with the defendant's experts this case illustrates how much importance is placed on the defendant doctor's evidence (although we have already commented that we believe that such evidence will always be self-serving and for that reason should not carry much weight, see above). Presumably, if Dr Rennisson had attended and given evidence that he would not have taken the necessary measures to avoid injury, then the end result would have been entirely different. The moral for defendant solicitors is that although the cards are stacked in your favour, do not be too complacent as there is no substitute for the oral evidence of the parties actually involved.

REFERENCES

English case law

(1)   *Prendergast v Sam and Dee [1989] 1 Med LR 36*
See above, p 233.

(2)   *Hogan v Bentinck West Hartley Collieries Ltd [1949] 1 All ER 588*
Held: an operation that had been unreasonably recommended by a doctor broke the chain of causation. If the treatment had been properly carried out, however, the original tortfeasor would still have been liable for any damage that resulted from the treatment.

(3)   *Emeh v Kensington and Chelsea and Westminster AHA [1985] QB 1012; [1984] 3 All ER 844*
See above, p 234.

(4)   *R v Blaue [1975] 1 WLR 1411*
The claimant was stabbed by the defendant. She refused to undergo a blood transfusion because she was a Jehovah's Witness, and this resulted in her death.

   Held: this did not break the chain of causation. The stab wound caused her death and the defendant could not contend that the claimant's religious beliefs were unreasonable.

(5)   *Bolitho v City and Hackney HA [1998] AC 232*
See above, p 235 *et seq* and Chapter 5, Standard of Care, p 173 *et seq*.

(6)   *Bolam v Friern HMC [1957] 1 WLR 582; [1957] 2 All ER 118*
See above, and r 5(A), p 155.

(7)   Bonnington Castings Ltd v Wardlaw [1956] AC 613; [1956] 1 All ER 615
See p 204 *et seq.*

(8)   McGhee v National Coal Board [1973] 1 WLR 1; [1972] 3 All ER 1008
See p 205 *et seq.*

(9)   Holtby v Brigham & Cowan Hull Limited [2000] 6 Lloyd's Rep Med 254
See above, p 207 et seq.

(10) DeFreitas v O'Brien and Connolly [1995] 6 Med LR 108
See Chapter 5, Standard of Care, p 165 for a more detailed analysis of the case. Briefly, the claimant's claim was that a group of 11 spinal surgeons could not constitute a group for the purposes of the *Bolam* rule; the group had to be substantial as in the *dicta* of Hirst J in *Hills v Potter* [1984] 1 WLR 641. This argument was rejected by the court, which held that whether or not the group was responsible could not be determined by 'counting heads'.

(11) Joyce v Merton, Sutton and Wandsworth HA [1996] 7 Med LR 1; [1995] 2 Med LR 60.
See above, p 236.

(12) Wisniewski v Central Manchester HA [1998] Lloyd's Rep Med 223
The claimant's mother and litigation friend sued on his behalf for injuries suffered at birth as a result of the defendant's negligence. The court was asked to consider whether the midwife was negligent in deciding not to call the doctor during the mother's labour and whether the doctor was negligent in not attending. Further the court was asked to consider, if the doctor had attended, would he have gone on to take the necessary steps to prevent the claimant's injuries, that is, rupture the membrane and perform a caesarean operation? At first instance the court found for the claimant because there was no responsible body of medical opinion which would not have attended and as Dr Rennisson failed to attend the trial it could be inferred that he had no answer to the allegations made against him. The defendant appealed.

Held: the appeal was dismissed. The court found that the views of the defendant's experts could be held by responsible doctors. The judge, however, could draw an adverse inference from the failure of Dr Rennisson to appear at trial because he was a witness who would be expected to give material evidence. As the claimant had established a *prima facie* albeit weak case that Dr Rennisson would have followed the course suggested by his (the claimant's) experts then Dr Rennisson's absence strengthened the claimant's case. If the reason for the witness's absence had satisfied the court then no adverse inference would have been made.

Scotland

Sabri-Tabrizi v Lothian Health Board 1998 SC 373
See above, p 234.

Foreign case law

Australia

(1)   Rogers v Whittaker [1993] 4 Med LR 79; [1992] 3 Med LR 331; (1992) 109 ALR 625
See pp 176 and 185.

Canada

(1)   Yepremian v Scarborough General Hospital (1980) 110 DLR (3d) 513
The first doctor (G) was negligent in his treatment of the claimant's diabetes. The claimant subsequently suffered a cardiac arrest as a result of the negligence of a second doctor (R) after the diabetes had been diagnosed. Consequently, G was not responsible for R's negligence; however, the court indicated that had the cardiac arrest been the result of untreated diabetes then G would have been held liable notwithstanding R's subsequent negligence.

Practice points

The only recommendation we can make to help the hapless claimant's solicitor avoid the operation of the *Bolitho* exception is to use existing case law and try and argue material contribution and also take into consideration the view expressed in *Holtby* (see p 207 *et seq*). In reality, a defendant in breach by non-attendance has materially contributed to the damage in exactly the same way as the employer who failed to provide an extractor fan did in *Bonnington*. To quote Lord Simon in *McGhee* ([1973] 1 WLR 1, p 8) 'a failure to take steps which would bring about a material reduction of the risk involves ... a substantial contribution to the injury'. However, this approach may only work when there is a choice of two alternatives. What about the situation as demonstrated by *Wilsher*? What if the defendant could have chosen any one of, say, five options had he attended? Argue that the defendant's actions materially increased the risk of damage occurring (which the court have held is the same as a material contribution – see p 204, *et seq*). Anything that does not fall within the *de minimis* rule is a material contribution. If the defendant then raises the argument of accepted practice, that is, even if he had attended he would have done nothing and that his action (or lack of) is endorsed by a responsible group of medical opinion, the claimant's solicitor, in reply, should argue the risk versus precautions theory. The greater the likely risk if the defendant fails to act and the simpler the precautions available to avoid the ensuing damage, the stronger the argument that the court should be able to infer that the defendant would have chosen the option which would have prevented the resulting damage. This approach is not foolproof, but at the moment this is the only viable option we can see.

RULE 6(F)

If the claimant's injuries were caused partly by his own fault and partly by the fault of the defendant, the claimant's damages may be reduced by such an amount as the court thinks just to reflect the claimant's responsibility for the damage.

Commentary

Although contributory negligence may have a only a limited part to play in a clinical negligence claim, it should still be borne in mind by any solicitor, especially when it is clear that the claimant himself is not totally blameless.

The Law Reform (Contributory Negligence) Act 1945 defines fault as: 'negligence, breach of statutory duty or other act or omission which gives rise to a liability in tort.' After some debate it now appears that the Act also applies in cases of trespass to the person (see *Murphy v Culhane* [1977] QB 94 and *Barnes v*

Nayer (1986) *The Times*, 19 December) and in contractual claims where, although the defendant's liability is in contract, the same liability would have arisen in tort independently of any contractual liability. In clinical negligence, this means that the Act will apply equally to claims arising out of negligent treatment under the NHS and in private treatment. This accords with the court's intention that private patients should be not be given preferential treatment.

When the defence is raised in a clinical negligence claim, the defendant will have to establish that the claimant's conduct contributed to the damage (see *Jones v Livox Quarries Ltd* [1952] QB 608) and that he has failed to take reasonable care for his own safety. The claimant need not owe any duty to the defendant. The standard of care expected of the claimant is measured objectively and is the same as for negligence itself, although there is of course some discretion in relation to children and those claimants under a disability.

If a solicitor wishes to rely on this defence, then he should look to the Canadian courts for guidance on how the principle may be applied. In *Crossman v Stewart* (1977) 82 DLR (3d) 677, a patient was rendered almost blind from chloroquine retinopathy, the drug having been prescribed for a skin disorder. However, the claimant's damages were reduced by two-thirds because she had obtained some of her supplies of the drug from an unknown source and failed to obtain prescription renewals or to consult her treating physician.

Whether the defence would be appropriate in, for example, a situation where the claimant fails to return to his GP's surgery for follow-up visits is debatable, and we think it could only be invoked where the claimant has been specifically and repeatedly warned to return if certain symptoms persist and these symptoms are of a serious nature. Other than that, it would be unwise to place too much emphasis on this defence, primarily because the court will always view the doctor's duty to his patient as paramount and will be reluctant to hold the patient culpable because of his lack of knowledge and lack of control over any given situation. Also, any defendant who pleads contributory negligence may find that the burden of proof is back on him. For example, if the defendant alleges that the claimant failed to read the prescription properly or return to the surgery if his condition deteriorated, the court may question what advice the defendant gave to the patient regarding the medication condition and whether this advice was adequate.

As to how damages are apportioned if this defence is successfully pleaded see Chapter 7, Damages, p 245.

REFERENCES

English case law

(1) Murphy v Culhane [1977] QB 94
The claimant (widow of the deceased) brought an action against the defendant. The deceased was killed during an assault by the defendant. The defence argued that the assault occurred during and as part of a criminal affray begun by the claimant.

Held: the defendant could rely on the defence of *volenti non fit injuria* and that even if the claimant had been entitled to damages they would have been reduced in consequence of his own fault pursuant to the Law Reform (Contributory Negligence) Act 1945.

(2)   Barnes v Nayer (1986) The Times, 19 December
See above, p 242.

(3)   Jones v Livox Quarries Ltd [1952] QB 608
The claimant was riding on the towbar of a 'traxcavator' vehicle when the driver of another vehicle drove into the back of him.

Held: the claimant had exposed himself not only to the risk of being thrown off but also to the risk of being run into from behind.

(4)   Oxley v Penwarden [2000] 7 Lloyd's Rep Med 347
See Practice points below.

(5)   Huxley v Elctiva Wood Engineering Ltd v James Neal Services Ltd (No 2) [2000] MLC 0201
See Practice points below.

Foreign case law

Canada

(1)   Crossman v Stewart (1977) 82 DLR (3d) 677
See above, p 242.

(2)   Fredette v Wiebe (1986) 29 DLR (4th) 534
The claimant underwent an abortion. She was advised by her GP to return two weeks after the operation to check that the procedure had been successful, and the GP was supposed to check the laboratory report relating to the tissue removed at the operation. The claimant did not return and the GP failed to check the report. In fact, the claimant was still pregnant.

Held: the claimant was contributorily negligent in failing to return to her GP.

Note that this case is similar to *Emeh v Kensington and Chelsea and Westminster AHA* [1985] QB 1012; [1984] 3 All ER 844 where the court held that the claimant was not liable for failing to mitigate her damage by not having an abortion on discovering that she was still pregnant. The court ruled that it is one thing to seek an abortion in the early stages of pregnancy but the claimant might feel quite different as the pregnancy advanced.

Practice points

There are however two points we wish to make here as they are particularly relevant to causation. The first concerns the number of experts parties may call in accordance with the Civil Procedure Rules. In *Oxley v Penwarden* [2000] 7 Lloyd's Rep Med 347 the district judge had agreed that each party should be allowed to call one general practitioner and one vascular surgery expert. However, at a later case management conference the court directed that the parties should agree on a single vascular surgeon and, should they fail to reach agreement, then the court would appoint a single expert. The claimant successfully appealed this decision; the Court of Appeal ruled that this was a case where each side should be allowed to investigate causation through an expert of their own choosing and further they should be permitted to call that evidence. Mantell LJ said that if the court was forced to select a single expert and there was more than one school of thought on the issue that would inevitably mean that the court would have to choose between those competing schools of thought thereby deciding an important issue without the opportunity for challenge. Reference was also made to the note to CPR r 35.7, which states, 'There is no presumption in favour of the appointment of a single joint expert. The object is to do away with the calling of multiple experts where, given the nature of the issue over which the parties are at odds, that is not justified'.

The second point concerns the credibility and professional reputation of the chosen expert. In *Huxley v Elctiva Wood Engineering Ltd v James Neal Services Ltd (No 2)* [2000] MLC 0201 the Court of Appeal held that the trial judge was correct to consider not only what the principal experts on causation said but also what he regarded as their relevant expertise and the impression they created when giving evidence. Two issues emerge from this statement. First, that any solicitor should choose his expert with care having regard to the expert's standing in his own particular field, and second, he should take some time in going over the presentation of the expert's oral evidence. Is the expert completely familiar with his report? Does the expert appear convincing? What is the expert's demeanour? Perhaps a third additional point is that this case illustrates that the courts will not simply accept an expert's view unquestioningly. They will, in line with *Bolam/Bolitho*, be concerned to establish that it is accordance with an accepted school of thought, though to what extent they will challenge accepted practice is debatable.

CHAPTER 7

DAMAGES

RULE 7(A)

Once the claimant has established that the defendant's lack of care caused his injuries, he is entitled to be compensated for all of his losses which are attributable to those injuries. In a case for personal injuries, damages are divided into two categories: special damages and general damages. The claimant may also be awarded interest on these damages.

Commentary

The basic principle in awarding compensation is to put the claimant in the position he would have been had the tort not occurred. Obviously, although the purpose is to compensate the claimant for his injuries, in reality no amount of money can compensate for the pain and suffering sustained. But once liability is established or admitted, the principle *restitutio in integrum* applies and the court must award damages – there is no discretion.

There are various categories of damages and these are discussed under separate headings below with the last three being distinct claims in their own right, that is, the loss of a chance claim (see *Hotson v East Berkshire HA* [1987] AC 750, above, p 217 *et seq*); the claim for wrongful life/birth (refer to Chapter 3, Duty, at p 90) and the claim for nervous shock.

Pain and suffering

Damages for pain and suffering will form part of the general damages award. Damages are assessed at the date of the trial and not the date of injury (see *Jobling v Associated Dairies Ltd* [1982] AC 794). Generally, the court will not draw a distinction between damages awarded for pain and suffering and damages for loss of amenity – they tend to be awarded as a global sum. It is unlikely that any injury will not result in some degree of pain and suffering; therefore as a rule the courts do not recognise the injury itself as a separate head of damage, except where it is specific, for example, loss of an arm or leg where there are recommended awards for such injuries. Solicitors will be familiar with texts such as *Kemp and Kemp, Current Law, Halsbury's Monthly Review* and the *Judicial Studies Board Guidelines for the Assessment of Damages*, which detail the awards.

Pain is suffered as a consequence of the injury; that suffering includes anxiety, embarrassment, etc, caused by the injury, and the court will also take into account any shock suffered by the claimant. The award will be tailored to meet the characteristics of the particular claimant; consequently, if a claimant suffers no pain or is incapable of experiencing pain (for example, someone who is unconscious or paralysed) there will be no award. As with most claims the claimant must present evidence that he suffered pain; in *Hicks and Others v Chief Constable of the South Yorkshire Police* [1992] 2 All ER 65, the personal representatives of relatives who were crushed to death at the Hillsborough Stadium claimed damages under the Law Reform (Miscellaneous Provisions)

Act 1934 for the pain and suffering alleged to have been sustained immediately prior to their relatives' deaths. That claim was rejected by the House of Lords who ruled that prior to the deaths the victims suffered fear which in their view was a normal human reaction and as such damages could not be awarded. This decision was clearly a matter of policy since the court was concerned that if they had taken the opposite stance this would in effect have meant that the people who had escaped the Hillsborough disaster would have had a claim for the distress they had suffered, which was an earlier view expressed by the Court of Appeal. It seems rather harsh that a claimant can suffer appalling treatment but, because of his extraordinary fortitude, not suffer any shock or psychiatric illness and is therefore not compensated. Generally, only where the claimant suffers from a recognisable psychiatric illness as a result of his injuries will the court award compensation (see the commentary on nervous shock claims below, p 263). However, the claimant may be able to recover in a situation where mental distress and grief caused by the death of someone close to him prevents a normal recovery (see *Rourke v Barton* (1982) *The Times*, 23 June).

Other factors which the courts will consider are the degree of pain already suffered and the claimant's future prospects. As regards the latter obviously the claimant's age and life expectancy are determinative but, additionally, the court will consider the way in which the claimant reacted to his predicament.

Clinical negligence cases where damages seem to be awarded purely for pain and suffering include:

(1) where a claimant was awake during an operation due to the negligence of the anaesthetist, for example, conscious during a caesarean section;

(2) where a claimant has suffered an appalling time during the delivery of her child. See *Kralj v McGrath and St Theresa's Hospital* [1986] 1 All ER 54; *Ackers v Wigan HA* [1991] 2 Med LR 232; *Phelan v East Cumbria HA* [1991] 2 Med LR 295 and *Cooper v Nottingham HA* (1989) *The Times*, 17 March; or

(3) where a child suffers injuries in the womb and is born disabled as a result he has a claim for pain and suffering in respect of those injuries under the Congenital Disabilities (Civil Liability) Act 1976. This rule is also now enshrined in the common law. See *Burton v Islington HA* and *De Martell v Merton and Sutton HA* [1993] 4 Med LR 8.

Loss of amenity

Damages under this head will compensate the claimant for his loss of enjoyment as a result of the accident, that is, when can he no longer do the things he was accustomed to doing. Damage within this category will include loss of any of the five senses, loss of sex drive, damage to the claimant's marriage prospects, loss of enjoyment of hobbies, employment and, indeed, loss of any facet of life. The court may also make an award for loss of congenial appointment when a claimant can no longer carry out work which he particularly enjoyed, or for loss of leisure time caused by having to work longer. The court will take into account how long the claimant will be deprived of these amenities; if it is for the rest of his life the amount of damages will be awarded in proportion to the claimant's age and life expectancy. However, age is not necessarily the determinative factor – loss of amenity in an elderly patient can have drastic effects and give rise to high awards of damages.

The claimant need not be aware of the loss of amenity; what matters is that the amenity is lost, for example, someone who is rendered permanently unconscious is still entitled to an award under this head. See *Wise v Kaye* [1962] 1 QB 368 where the claimant remained unconscious from the moment of the accident, was deprived of all the attributes of life and was awarded £15,000. In *H West & Son Ltd v Shepherd* [1964] AC 174, the claimant sustained severe head injuries, cerebral atrophy and paralysis of all four limbs. There was no chance that her condition would improve; her life expectancy was reduced to five years. She was unable to speak although the evidence indicated that she might appreciate her condition. The House of Lords upheld an award of £17,500 for loss of amenity.

Whether damages should be awarded in such situations is debatable. Clearly, such a claimant is in reality in no different a position than a dead claimant. It seems illogical that a claimant who feels nothing should be awarded the same as a claimant who will have to suffer the loss for the remainder of his life. The Pearson Commission (see para 15.1.3) recommended that such damages should only be awarded where they served some useful purpose; however the Law Commission Report on *Damages for Personal Injuries: Non-Pecuniary Loss*, Law Com No 257, 1999 recommended no change. Furthermore, in *Lim Poh Choo v Camden and Islington AHA* [1980] AC 174, the House of Lords refused to endorse any change, ruling that it was a matter for the legislature although they did reduce the award.

Recently the Court of Appeal in *Heil v Rankin* [2000] 5 Lloyd's Rep Med 203 heard eight appeals which were selected as test cases to allow the court to issue guidelines following the Law Commission Report 257 (see above) which recommended an increase in the level of damages for non-pecuniary loss for personal injuries. The Court of Appeal accepted that compensation should not be frozen at inadequate levels and agreed that an increase in general damages was required. However it held that not all awards were deserving of an increase and there should be no increase for those awards of less than £10,000 notwithstanding that the Law Commission had recommended an increase for awards over £3,000 by a factor of 1.5–2. The most serious injuries, those where damages were in the region of £150,000–£200,000, attracted the highest increase of about a third. The court stated that the awards would increase with the Retail Price Index although it was accepted that other changes in society could result in a previously acceptable level of damages no longer being reasonable. Hence the courts would, from time to time, review the awards though only if they appeared out of line with the standards set. In doing so, the court reasoned that, whilst it must not be influenced by the means of a particular defendant it did not mean that economic consequences such as higher insurance premiums for the defendant and less resources available for the NHS were irrelevant and would not be taken into account; the needs of the defendant and society must be considered as a whole. This is perhaps another example of the courts applying the concept of distributive justice (see p 259). The decision to increase general damages would be retrospective and this did not contravene the European Convention Human Rights. The Court of Appeal urged the Judicial Studies Board to produce a new edition of their Guidelines as quickly as possible.

Finally, pursuant to s 1(1)(b) Administration of Justice Act 1982, for all actions arising after 1 January 1983 the court will make an award to a claimant whose expectation of life has been reduced because of his injuries. Before 1983 this was a separate award; now the courts simply take this factor into account in awarding general damages. Any claim for loss of expectation of life will inevitably be coupled with a claim for bereavement which will now be brought under the Fatal Accidents Act 1976.

Loss of future earnings

This head is an exception to the general rule that pecuniary losses fall into the special damages category. The reason is that it is often impossible to say what the claimant's future loss would have been but for his injuries. For example, it may be unclear how long he will require medical attention or when or if he will ever return to work. Furthermore, if he does return to work it is most unlikely that his wage will remain constant. In general, the court will apply the same rules for the assessment of past and future loss of earnings, although obviously there is more guess work involved in the latter. The court's main problem is how to take into account the receipt of a lump sum in advance of future losses. The policy operated by the court is that each future payment will be subject to a reduction or a discount to reflect the fact that the claimant is actually receiving his compensation before the loss or expense has occurred.

As personal injury solicitors will be aware, future loss of earnings and expenses are assessed at the date of trial by reference to a multiplicand and a multiplier. The multiplicand will be the claimant's net annual loss which in practice will already have been calculated in determining the special damages schedule (see below, p 255). The courts will then apply a multiplier – the figure is an arbitrary one calculated as from the date of trial, not the date of injury, see *Cookson v Knowles* [1979] AC 556. The multiplier will be arrived at by reference to the Pearson Commission data, possibly government actuary tables (which are now specifically admissible, see p 249) and previously decided cases. The multiplier is supposed to cover the period from the date of trial up to the time when the loss of earning or expenditure would cease. What is certain is that the court will not fix the multiplier as the number of years from the trial until retirement or death as that would result in over-compensation. The general principle is that the interest and capital should be exhausted at the same time as the claimant's need is extinguished. Additionally, the court will have to assess what is the real return after tax, national insurance and inflation, and on investment of the money. In fixing the multiplier, account will be taken of the general vicissitudes of life (for example, the contingency that the claimant might have died at an earlier date in any event; the possibility that the claimant may have taken time off work due to child-rearing/marriage), and the fact that the lump sum can immediately be invested.

For an illustration of how the court select an appropriate multiplier see *Worral v Powergen plc* [1999] 5 Lloyd's Rep Med 177. There the court said that it should look for 'the most realistic basis to the assumptions made in relation to the likely mortality of the injured party had he not sustained injury'. This could only be done by looking at the mortality rates of the population as a whole and in doing so the starting point was to examine the Ogden Tables (the Actuarial Tables produced by the Government's Actuary Department). The Ogden Tables are based on English Life Tables which contain information on contingencies other than mortality, for example, illness, employment and a list of justifiable deductions in respect of those contingencies. The courts had previously shunned the Ogden Tables but, following the decision in *Wells v Wells, Thomas v Brighton HA* and *Page v Sheerness Steel Co Ltd* [1998] 3 All ER 481 (see below), they are now readily accepted and are specifically admissible in civil proceedings pursuant to s 10 Civil Evidence Act 1995.

The use of The Ogden Tables had been previously recommended by the Law Commission Reports, *Structured Settlements and Interim and Provisional Damages* (Law Com No 224) (see para 6.1) and *Personal Injury Compensation: How Much is Enough?* (Law Com No 225). These reports had also been critical of the rule that stated that the claimant would receive a 4.5% real return on his damages. In estimating the real return of money, until fairly recently a discount rate of 4.5% had been adopted (see, for example, *Cookson v Knowles* [1979] AC 566). In other words the court had assumed that the claimant who received compensation would subsequently invest it and receive a net return of 4.5% per annum after tax and inflation were taken into account. On this assumption the maximum multiplier was usually 18. The Law Commission reasoned however, that what the real return of money will be will depend on how the claimant chooses to invest his money.

The Law Commission Report No 225 analysed what some claimants did with their money. The most common method of saving was to use a building society account, followed by a bank account. Advice was most commonly sought from a bank or building society, though there was still a high percentage of respondents who received no advice. For example, of those who were awarded over £100,000, 16% took no investment advice. In their summary of recommendations, the Law Commission in Report No 224, para 6.2 recommended that legislation should be implemented requiring the court to consider the net return on an index-linked government security ('gilts' – these are published in the *Financial Times*) subject to evidence demonstrating that a different rate is more appropriate in any given case.

The views of the Law Commission and general criticism of the low level of awards eventually came to a head in three consolidated appeals in *Wells v Wells, Thomas v Brighton HA* and *Page v Sheerness Steel Co Ltd* [1998] 3 All ER 481. There the House of Lords held that the discount rate should be based on investment in Index Linked Government Securities (ILGS) which would currently yield a return on income and capital of 3%. The advantage of ILGS from the claimant's perspective is that it is virtually a risk-free investment. The same sum invested in equities might produce a much higher rate of return but equally it might produce a much lower rate of return. The defendant's argument in Wells was that if the claimant acted as a prudent investor then any investment advisor would advise investing in a spread of equities and more secure bonds and gilts. But, as the House of Lords recognised, the claimant needed to be sure that the investment would secure him an income without the risks of the equity market; he could not be expected to take the risk for the benefit of the defendant. The claimant was not in the same position as the ordinary investor who could simply wait for the stock market to recover if it fell; he had to secure his long-term needs and hence choose a safe investment. As the current rate of return on ILGS was 3% that would be a more appropriate discount rate. See *Warren v Northern General Hospital Trust* [2000] 1 WLR 1404.

However, note that on 25 June 2001 the Lord Chancellor made the Damages (Personal Injury) Order 2001 pursuant to s 1 of the Damages Act 1996 in which he lowered the discount rate to 2.5%. He stressed, however, that under s 1(2) of the Act the courts may adopt a different rate in any case if there are exceptional circumstances. Finally, note that the claimant will also be able to recover damages for either the loss of a pension or any reduction in his pension (see further *Auty v National Coal Board* [1985] 1 WLR 784).

Damages for handicap in the labour market – the Smith v Manchester award

Damages under this head are often referred to as damages for loss of a person's earning capacity. A true award under this head is made to a claimant who is able to return to his employment but his injuries mean that he is more likely to lose his job in the event of redundancies and/or he is plainly at a disadvantage in the labour market, for example, predisposition to similar injury or has been unemployed through his disabilities since the injury (see *Smith v Manchester Corporation* [1974] 17 KIR 1; *Moeliker v A Reyrolle Co Ltd* [1976] ICR 253; *Foster v Tyne & Wear County Council* [1986] 1 All ER 567). Under the new Civil Procedure Rules the Practice Direction accompanying Part 16 states at para 4.2, 'The claimant must attach to his particulars of claim a schedule of details of any past and future expenses and losses which he claims', and since a *Smith v Manchester* claim is one for future loss it is arguable that it should be pleaded to allow the defendant to assess the claim thereby acting in the spirit of the overriding objective. Such a claim should also be referred to in the medical report and, perhaps, should be distinguished from the general loss of earnings claim.

The lost years

These damages are incapable of any precise calculation and form part of the general damages award. The claim is made by a living claimant for the 'lost years', that is, the period by which his life has been shortened because of his injuries and during which he would have received remuneration. In *Pickett v British Rail Engineering Ltd* [1980] AC 136, the court allowed such a claim overruling previous decisions to the contrary. Damages will be dependent on the claimant's date of birth and his expectation of life at the date of trial.

The claim is not restricted to lost earnings, although that is the basis of the usual claim. No deduction is to be made in respect of expenditure that the claimant would have incurred on behalf of his dependants during the lost years, but a deduction will be made to reflect the actual living expenses of the claimant (see *Harris v Empress Motors Ltd* [1984] 1 WLR 212). It is important to note that the courts are concerned to ensure that the only sums to be deducted are those that were necessary to maintain the claimant in the standard of life to which he was accustomed and, furthermore, any joint expenditure between the claimant and others should only be deducted to the extent of the claimant's share. It therefore follows that a much larger deduction may be made in respect of a single person, and that in the majority of cases where children are involved there will be no deduction.

Loss of a pension will fall under this head of damages in most cases, except where the claimant has reached pensionable age; in that case, his past losses will come under the sphere of special damages, while his future loss will form part of his general damages. The court must consider what the claimant's pension would have been had he not been injured. Generally, quotations are sought from life insurance companies to calculate this loss, and a comparison is made between the pension the claimant could have expected had he not been injured with the pension he can now expect. In *Phipps v Brooks Dry Cleaning Services* [1996] PIQR Q100, the claimant's life expectancy had been curtailed as a result of coming into contact with asbestos dust during his employment with the defendant. The court applied the judgment of *Harris v Empress Motors* [1984] which concerned the assessment of damages under the Law Reform (Miscellaneous Provisions) Act 1934. In this case, O'Connor J, discussing what amounted to living expenses, said at p 229:

> ... in relation to a man's net earnings that any proportion thereof that he saves or spends exclusively for the maintenance or benefit of others does not form part of his living expenses. Any proportion that he spends exclusively on himself does. In cases where there is a proportion of the earnings expended on what may conveniently be called shared living expenses, a *pro rata* part of that proportion should be allocated for deduction.

The Court of Appeal held that the rationale expressed in *Harris* also applied where the claimant was still living. Hence, a living claimant who lives with one dependant, for example, his wife, will not only have his multiplicand reduced by one-third to reflect his share of the household expenses, but also by half of one-third to represent his share of the joint expenditure: the total deduction being approximately half. This is in contrast to the position of a wife claiming under the Fatal Accidents Act 1976 (see Rule 7(E), p 293 *et seq*) where her dependency would normally be two-thirds of his net annual earnings.

Past and future expenses

The rule for calculating pecuniary loss is as stated in *McGregor on Damages* (15th edition, para 1450):

> The claimant will recover, subject to the rules on remoteness and mitigation, full compensation for the pecuniary loss he has suffered.

In assessing these losses it must be noted that there is no difference between past and future losses; the damages are dealt with under the same categories and the same deductions and/or contingencies are taken into account. The main item under this head will be medical expenses, both past and future. Future medical expenses and any other future expenses will be assessed as part of the claimant's *general damages*; those which have already been incurred will form part of the *special damages*.

The most important aspect of future expense is how long should the expense last and what discount is appropriate? As for loss of earnings, the expenses will be assessed using the multiplicand/multiplier approach. Generally, a greater multiplier will be applied here than for loss of earnings since it is assumed that most expenses will be permanent future expenses, except where the claimant's expectation of life is short, in which case his loss of earnings will be greater.

One of the matters which falls to be determined in estimating the claimant's future medical expenses and loss of earnings is his life expectancy. This is often difficult to determine and it will be the area which will cause most disagreement between the respective parties. For example, in the case of a claimant who has suicidal tendencies, the defendant may argue that the claimant's life expectancy is limited; the claimant's argument, however, would be that with round the clock nursing the risk could be minimised.

Below some of the more usual expenses are discussed in greater detail.

Accommodation

One of the major expenses the claimant may incur is buying new accommodation or adapting his present accommodation. At present, society encourages the care of the disabled at home wherever possible, but the problem the court faces in assessing damages under this head is how to provide for the claimant's reasonable needs without providing a windfall to his estate. This problem was considered in *Roberts v Johnstone* [1988] 3 WLR 1247 where the extra cost of special accommodation was converted into an annual loss, the general multiplier being used to arrive at the sum awarded, and the claimant was allowed to recover the cost of moving and any new furniture. The dominant principle in *Roberts* was to avoid over-compensation and to ensure that any award was exhausted at the death of the claimant. It could be argued that housing costs are special damages in that they are pre-trial costs, thereby removing their speculative nature. The court should also recognise that often a house which has been adapted to cater for the claimant's disabilities may be worth less when sold because of those alterations. Thus, not only will the claimant fail to recoup his expenditure but he will also lose the opportunity to invest a proportion of the award because it is tied up in the house. Perhaps the time has come for the courts to reassess the principles by which they make these awards.

Where the claimant intends to purchase new accommodation, the court must take into consideration the cost of the property as against the benefit of having a new asset. In *Roberts v Johnstone* [1988] 3 WLR 1247, the court ruled that the purchase of residential property should be regarded as the equivalent of buying an investment secured against the risk of inflation. Damages were assessed by taking 2% of the cost of the property and multiplying it by the multiplier. However, this approach may not always be appropriate because the value of property has fluctuated considerably since 1989 when the case was decided.

Nursing care

Where the claimant is being cared for in a private institution, damages awarded under this category must be set off against any domestic savings. However, where the claimant is being cared for at home, the cost may be recovered notwithstanding that it would be cheaper if he was in an institution, but the burden is on the claimant to prove that it is reasonable. This is also the case where the help is provided gratuitously, for example, by family or friend (see *Donnelly v Joyce* [1974] QB 454 and *Housecroft v Burnett* [1986] 1 All ER 332). In *Donnelly*, the claimant's mother gave up work to nurse him and the court ruled that the claimant was entitled to recover damages in respect of the reasonable cost of the special attention required. The one exception to this rule is where the services are provided by the tortfeasor, see *Hunt v Severs* [1994] 2 All ER 385 in which the court ruled that any damages paid to the claimant under this head were paid under the assumption that the claimant would hold them in trust for his carer. It follows that the bizarre situation could be reached where the defendant could be required to pay the claimant damages under this head only for the claimant to repay him at some future date. This decision has serious implications for victims of road traffic accidents where the driver and the injured passenger are often related, but it has limited application in clinical negligence claims where the tortfeasor is usually the NHS, a Trust, etc. However, conceivably there could be a situation where a GP is sued by a relative and the GP goes on to provide care for his relative. In such a situation the solicitor should advise that the care be provided by a relative other than the defendant or, alternatively, that the services be provided pursuant to a contract between the defendant and the victim, as it appears that this would remain unaffected by the decision in *Hunt*.

In their report *Personal Injury: Medical, Nursing and Other Expenses: Collateral Benefits*, Law Com No 262, 1999 the Law Commission proposed that the outcome in *Hunt v Severs* should be reversed by legislation and that the claimant should be under only a personal obligation to his carer in respect of past care. Further a claimant should be under no legal duty to account for any award made for gratuitously provided future care.

The carer may recover for any loss of earnings suffered as a result of caring for the claimant; however, he will not be able to recover for both loss of earnings and the cost of caring for the claimant, because this would amount to double recovery. One exception to this rule is where:

(1) the value of the carer's loss of earnings is more than the cost of care (providing that the carer's decision in giving up his job was reasonable in all the circumstances); and

(2) only the carer can provide that care, for example, a father looking after his children after the death of their mother (see *Mehmet v Perry* [1977] 2 All ER 529).

In *Hardwick v Hudson and Another* [1999] 3 All ER 426 the Court of Appeal held that damages could not be awarded to compensate the victim's wife for giving her unpaid services to her husband's business. The court drew a distinction between voluntary services provided in a commercial setting as distinct from a domestic environment. The victim's wife had provided her services voluntarily for the business; had she not, those services would have had to be provided by someone else, for whom the business would have had to pay. Therefore, as the victim's business had been saved this extra wage bill, it had suffered no loss in this area.

The other main award under this head is in respect of any special facilities the claimant has required in respect of the alterations to existing accommodation, for example, a lift.

Medical expenses

These are recoverable provided they are reasonable and were incurred as a result of the injuries. They can take any form, for example, treatment, medicine, appliances, etc. Often in a clinical negligence claim as a result of the defendant's negligence the claimant will require further surgery, for example, a repeat abortion or sterilisation. The claimant will be awarded the cost of the extra surgery (see *Emeh v Kensington and Chelsea and Westminster AHA* [1985] QB 1012; [1984] 3 All ER 844) where the claimant was awarded the cost of a second sterilisation operation. If the claimant requires further medical treatment then, pursuant to s 2(4) Law Reform (Personal Injuries) Act 1948, he may claim the cost of private medical treatment notwithstanding that the same treatment is available on the NHS. The court, however, will take into account that if the claimant has spent time in a NHS hospital or its equivalent then he must give credit for the savings in his living expenses (see s 5 of the Administration of Justice Act 1982 at p 279).

In *Briody v St Helen's & Knowsley HA* [2000] 3 Lloyd's Rep Med 127, the claimant, who had been left infertile as a result of the defendants' negligence, argued that the defendant was liable to pay for the costs of a commercial surrogacy agreement she had entered into in California; the surrogacy costs claimed totalled nearly £100,000. The claim failed on three grounds:

(a) that it was contrary to public policy to award damages for a commercial surrogacy contract which in English law is unenforceable;

(b) that the chances of conception were so low, that it was unreasonable for the defendant to fund the treatment; and

(c) that to award damages for the costs was neither reasonable nor 'fair, just and reasonable' because the treatment was almost certainly doomed to failure and the unlawfulness of the method to be used.

Note that interestingly the court refused to rule out a claim of this type ever succeeding; their decision was confined to the particular facts of this case.

Other expenses

There are many other pecuniary items which the solicitor should consider; they are not dealt with here but readers are advised to consult *Kemp and Kemp*, Vol 1, Chapter 5, and in particular paras 5-011–5-0112. By way of quick reference, damages may be awarded for any of the following items:

- Clothes.
- Costs of extra home help.
- Costs of special equipment.
- Postal charges.
- Telephone charges.
- Costs of alterations to car or a new car or car hire.

- Any other pecuniary losses, for example, the value of free accommodation, any concessionary fares, a trip abroad, the loss of a job, etc.
- Court of Protection fees where the claimant becomes unable to look after his own affairs; the cost here is dependent on the estate to be administered, *Roberts v Johnstone* [1988] 3 WLR 1247 (also applicable where the claimant is a minor).
- The extra costs of running a household.
- The cost of buying a second home as a consequence of the breakdown of a marriage. This may occur where, as a result of his injuries, the claimant undergoes a complete personality change and the spouse has to move out of the marital home. Although in *Jones v Jones* [1984] 3 WLR 862 the court awarded damages to the claimant's spouse for this very loss, that decision was rejected in *Pritchard v Parrot* (1985) *The Times*, 27 September where the court held that the loss was too remote. For any solicitor looking to prove such a claim it is important that the loss is capable of proof.

See *Pritchard v JH Cobden Ltd* [1987] 1 All ER 300 where the Court of Appeal held that where the claimant's injuries led to the break up of his marriage the financial consequences of the divorce are not recoverable from the defendant but in *(No 2)* [1987] FLR 56 the legal costs of the divorce action were held to be recoverable.

Loss of earnings (past)

In calculating lost earnings they will be net of tax and national insurance contributions and the claimant's contributions to a compulsory pension scheme, with any loss of pension rights calculated separately. For the position as regards social security benefits, see p 281 *et seq*. The claimant's loss is calculated tax year by tax year. In addition, the claimant must give credit for any sums that he would have incurred in earning the income, for example, travelling expenses (see *Lim Poh Choo v Camden and Islington AHA* [1980] AC 174).

Normally, special damages are agreed and there is little dispute about what the claimant would have earned until trial. The claimant should be asked to estimate his loss of earnings over the period and then the employer should be asked to do the same. If there is a difficulty in calculating the amount the claimant would have earned as overtime, a comparison can usually be made with a fellow employee. In comparing the claimant's loss of earnings with a fellow employee, it is important that the figures are gross not net because special factors, for example, individual tax circumstances distorting the true picture. Other considerations the court will take into account in assessing both actual and future loss of earnings are whether the claimant's earnings would have been less as a result of factors other than his injuries, whether he receives any commission, whether it was likely that the claimant would have been promoted, etc.

Solicitors should study the contract of employment; it may be that the claimant was entitled to be paid while he was off work, but this is often subject to a clause in the contract of employment that the claimant will seek to recover these sums (see, further, p 281 *et seq*).

As regards statutory sick pay the employee will be entitled to this payment for the first 28 weeks of absence in any three years. At the end of this period he is no longer eligible for statutory sick pay and so will have to claim DSS benefits (see p 281). Until April 1994, any statutory sick pay paid by the employer was refunded by the state and in these cases the employer must repay to the Compensation Recovery Unit all payments made to the client.

In the case of a self-employed claimant, the services of an accountant will be required and the court will effectively be required to evaluate the loss of a chance of those earnings.

Interest

Pursuant to s 35A Supreme Court Act 1981 and s 69 County Courts Act 1984, if the award is £200 or greater then the claimant is entitled to interest on the damages awarded from the date of issue until trial, unless the court in its discretion decides there are reasons not to make such an award. The guidelines for the award of interest are found in cases such as *Wright v British Railways Board* [1983] 2 AC 773 and *Pickett v British Rail Engineering Ltd* [1980] AC 136, and more recently in *Lawrence v Chief Constable of Staffordshire* (2000) *The Times*, 25 July. In essence, the rules are as follows:

(1) on damages for pain and suffering and loss of amenity, interest is awarded at 2%;

(2) for future pecuniary loss inclusive of possible future handicap on the labour market there is no award; and

(3) for special damages interest is awarded at half the court's special account rates applicable during the period. This rate was reduced to 7% on 1 August 1997. Solicitors should refer to Rodney Nelson-Jones' annual ready reckoner tables in the *Law Society Gazette* (latest edition 27 September 2001). Since June 1987, interest has been paid daily on 1/365 basis, even in a leap year. In *Roberts v Johnstone* [1988] 3 WLR 1247, the court held that damages awarded for unpaid past care and attendance should be treated as special damages for this purpose and that interest should be awarded accordingly. The dates on which interest begins to run will differ depending on the category of damages. For general damages, interest runs from the date of service of the proceedings; for special damages it runs from the date of the accident.

In calculating interest no deduction is made to allow for the receipt of social security benefits by the claimant, see *Wiseley v John Fulton (Plumbers) Ltd; Wadey v Surrey County Council* [2000] 2 All ER 545. Furthermore, in *Davies v Inman* [1999] PIQR 26, the court held that the claimant was still entitled to interest on his loss of earnings even though his employer continued to pay him. The claimant had, however, undertaken to repay his employer from any damages he received.

Loss of chance

This claim is dealt with in detail above, p 217 *et seq*. It has to be said that it remains uncertain whether damages for loss of chance can ever be awarded in a clinical negligence case, even though they have been awarded in contract cases.

To have any chance of success the claimant must be able to prove that, but for the defendant's negligence, he would have had at least a 51% chance of making a full recovery (see *Hotson v East Berkshire HA* [1987] AC 750). *Hotson* did not rule out the possibility of a loss of chance case, but neither did it endorse it. It also appears that the proportionality approach used by the courts in cases such as *Bagley v North Herts HA* (1986) 136 NLJ 1014 and *Clark v McLennan* [1983] 1 All ER 416 will not, in the light of *Hotson*, find any favour with the courts. The courts in those cases assessed damages on a percentage basis to reflect the chance the claimant had lost because of the defendant's negligence. Where the claim is that, had it not been for the defendant's negligence, the claimant would have enjoyed a better quality of life for a longer period the courts are prepared to compensate the claimant for this loss (see *Sutton v Population Services Family Planning Programme Ltd* (1981) *The Times*, 7 November).

There are more recent cases in which the courts have considered the loss of chance claim in a non-medical context. In *Allied Maples Group v Simmons and Simmons* [1995] 1 WLR 262, the court held that if the claimant could establish that he had lost a real or substantial chance then the court must evaluate that chance in the assessment of damages. In *Stovold v Barlows* [1996] 1 PNLR 91, the defendant's alleged negligence caused the sale of the claimant's house to fall through; the Court of Appeal held that had the defendant not been negligent, there was a 50% chance that the sale would have occurred and therefore the claimant was entitled to half the award. See, further, Chapter 6, Causation.

Until this matter is once and for all resolved, the solicitor should think twice before labelling a claim as a loss of chance claim and would be better advised to bring the claim within the ambit of *McGhee v National Coal Board* [1973] 1 WLR 1.

Wrongful life/birth/conception

Before an examination is made of the damages that are awarded under this head, it is necessary first to distinguish between a wrongful life claim and a claim for wrongful birth. The former action is disallowed by the courts since the claimant (the handicapped child) is in effect saying that I was better off dead than being born the way I am – because of your negligence I was not aborted. This was the nature of the claim in *McKay v Essex AHA* [1982] QB 1166 where tests on a pregnant woman failed to disclose rubella resulting in the child being born disabled. The court held that a doctor did not have a duty of care to the child to advise the mother to have an abortion. However, the claim should have been framed differently, namely that the mother was deprived of the loss of an opportunity to have an abortion which is implicitly recognised by the Abortion Act 1967. The court refused to award damages on the following policy grounds:

(1) it would have meant assessing the life of a handicapped child as less worthy than that of a normal child;

(2) the child might have sued the mother for failing to abort;

(3) it was impossible to assess damages as it would mean comparing non-existence with existence.

The Congenital Disabilities (Civil Liability) Act 1976 is said to replace any law in force before 1976; consequently it is thought that it prevents any common law action. In *McKay*, the court said that a wrongful life claim could not be brought under the Act, but it is unclear whether that also includes those claims under s 1A. This section, introduced by s 44 Human Fertilisation and Embryology Act 1992, extends the provisions of the Act to children born disabled as a result of negligent fertility treatment, for example, placing a damaged embryo in the womb.

With a wrongful birth claim, the allegation is that a sterilisation operation, vasectomy or abortion was negligently performed and consequently the claimant became pregnant and gave birth to a handicapped child. The claim is for pain, suffering, physical injury and financial loss. In *McKay* this part of the claim was successful. Damages for wrongful conception have, until fairly recently, been commonly awarded. The claim is for damages for the upkeep of a healthy child that has been born as a result of a failed vasectomy/sterilisation operation. The mother may also claim for the pain and suffering associated with pregnancy and childbirth. In *Allen v Bloomsbury HA* [1993] 1 All ER 651 the court awarded damages for the following:

(1) Pain and suffering associated with the continuance of the pregnancy and birth (although the benefit of not having to undergo an abortion should be offset against this award).

(2) Damages for the cost of bringing the child up to adulthood according to their station in life. Damages under this head include the cost of private education if appropriate and damages may be awarded for additional anxiety and distress at having to bring up a handicapped child.

The claimant may also be able to recover for the cost of a second abortion/sterilisation.

If the mother has to give up work she will be able to recover for her loss of earnings or the cost of maintaining the child but not for both, as this would amount to double recovery (see *Fish v Wilcox* [1994] 5 Med LR 230).

The Australian courts also adopted the approach taken in *Allen* following the birth of a healthy but unwanted child in *CES v Superclinics (Australia) Pty Ltd* [1996] Med L Rev. By a majority of 2–1, the court held that awarding damages under this head was not contrary to public policy though the quantification would depend on the facts of the case. Kirby P said that the court was not required by social policy to view the birth of a healthy child as a blessing. Further, in addition to awarding damages for any financial losses sustained by the parents, the court said that damages should be recoverable for the distress and burden of raising the child without any off-set for the joy and blessing of bringing up the child. The argument that such an award might cause the child to feel unwanted was rejected, the court reasoning that many children were unplanned and if damages were not awarded then it may cause more family difficulties. Meagher JA, in his dissent, said that the sanctity of human life rendered any such award 'improper to the point of obscenity'. Priestley JA said that, whilst he agreed with Kirby J, the damages should not be assessed on the grounds that the claimant had failed to mitigate her loss, she had chosen to keep the child. Damages could be awarded, however, for any anguish and distress caused by giving the child up for adoption. It is unlikely that the English courts would follow such an abhorrent approach; they have already rejected the argument that a claimant may be under an obligation to terminate the unwanted pregnancy (see *Emeh*, p 234) and presumably this reasoning would be given equally short shrift.

The views of the Australian judiciary and indeed the previously held opinions of the English judiciary on the merits of awarding damages for wrongful conception cases now stand in stark contrast to the House of Lords ruling in *McFarlane v Tayside Health Board* [1999] 4 All ER 961, a Scottish case that will undoubtedly be followed in the English courts. The facts were unremarkable. The McFarlanes, after the birth of their fourth child, decided their family was complete and so Mr McFarlane underwent a vasectomy. Relying on the advice that Mr McFarlane's sperm count was negative the couple resumed sexual intercourse resulting in Mrs McFarlane becoming pregnant. She subsequently gave birth to her fifth child. The McFarlanes' claim for damages was initially successful in the Court of Session. However their joy was shortlived as the Health Board successfully appealed against the ruling.

The path taken by each of the five Law Lords in reaching their decision was very different. Lord Slynn based his decision on the grounds that the claim was one for economic loss and asked whether it was 'fair, just and reasonable for the court to impose such a duty' on the defendant to which he answered in the negative. A doctor's duty, he reasoned, was only to avoid a pregnancy and that did not extend to the costs of bringing up a child if that child was born and accepted into the family. Lord Steyn however saw the decision as being one of corrective justice versus distributive justice (that is, the just distribution of burdens and losses among the members of society). According to him a decision had to be made between the two but the decision was not one of public policy (which he likened to quicksand). The authors find this contention difficult to accept. Lord Steyn reasoned that, in this case, distributive justice decreed that parents of a healthy, unwanted child should not be permitted to recover the cost of bringing up that child from the Health Board or doctor. Further, if necessary he said that he would rely on the old stalwart of the claim not being just, fair or reasonable.

Interestingly neither of these Law Lords chose to use the set-off argument, namely that the joys of parenthood outweighed the financial hardship. Lord Hope, although referring to the benefits of parenthood and the set-off principle being relevant, chose to argue that it was impossible to value them against damages for upkeep and hence no recovery was permissible. Lord Clyde concurred with this view although he based his decision on the legal rule of reasonable restitution and stated that 'the cost of maintaining the child goes far beyond any liability in the present case which in the circumstances of the present case the defenders could reasonably have thought they were undertaking'. Finally Lord Millett gave perhaps the most controversial and harsh judgment in that he stuck with the view that 'the law must take the birth of a healthy child to be a blessing, not a detriment'. He went further than his fellow Law Lords in that he rejected Mrs McFarlane's claim in respect of pain and distress associated with the pregnancy as these 'were the price of parenthood'.

What is one to make of this judgment? Previously in the Court of Appeal Lord Cullen had expressed, in the authors' opinion, the following sensible sentiments:

> In the result ... the benefits of the child do not provide an answer to the claim for the costs of her upbringing. Respect for human life should not be allowed to obscure the fact that couples who have decided that they cannot afford to raise another child have been left a way to do so.

To their credit the McFarlanes have accepted and loved an unwanted child and yet by their judgment the House of Lords have effectively penalised them for showing compassion. Undoubtedly the child (Catherine) will give her parents much pleasure in subsequent years but she will also bring an added expense to the household which her parents rightly claim should be reimbursed by those whose negligence resulted in her conception. It is baffling that the expenses of raising Catherine should not be borne by those whose negligence resulted in her birth but rather by the persons who, by responsibly seeking to limit the size of their family, have sought to avoid them. There are occasions for limiting the liability of health carers in tort but this is not one of them. Surely the answer in cases such as this should be that, if a child is born because of the negligence of those health carers who were entrusted to prevent his/her conception, it is precisely those persons who should be accountable for the financial burden of bringing up that child and not the unfortunate parents.

The *McFarlane* case has obviously changed the goalposts for those claims for damages for the birth of an unwanted but healthy child but will it have any impact on those wrongful birth claims where the resulting child is born disabled?

The first wrongful birth case to come before the courts after the *McFarlane* decision was *Rand v East Dorset HA* [2000] 4 Lloyd's Rep Med 181. The parents claimed damages for the defendant's negligent omission to advise Mrs Rand that she may give birth to a disabled child and consequently her loss of opportunity to terminate the pregnancy. The child (Katy) was subsequently born with Down's Syndrome. The court distinguished *Rand* from *McFarlane* on the basis that in the former the defendant was under a clear duty to save the parents from the birth of a disabled child. By its negligence the defendant had deprived the claimants of their chance of seeking a termination under the Abortion Act. The very existence of this Act means that the views of health carers must be made available to parents so that they are aware of the financial consequences of the mother carrying a disabled child. In *Rand* the parents were allowed to recover for those losses relating to their child's disability and not the full cost of bringing up the child, however such losses were not restricted to the child's 18th birthday. The court held that the defendant was not liable for the disability itself but was liable for having failed to protect the claimants from the consequences of the disability. The award was for the additional wear and tear of a disabled child over and above a healthy child. Damages were assessed by reference to the parents' means and not the child's needs. The authors are still left with the injustice that the level of damages recovered will depend to a great extent on how wealthy the parents are, the court reasoning that a child born to wealthy parents would have more spent on his needs and ignoring the fact that whoever the child is born to will still need to look after him/her. There seems something fundamentally wrong to us in a health authority only being liable to pay a lesser amount of damages because the court conclude that the parents' financial status will prevent them from catering for their child's needs.

Interestingly the court applied part of the reasoning of Lord Millett in *McFarlane* who stated that the parents had been denied an important aspect of their personal autonomy and that 'Their decision to have no more children is one the law should respect and protect' (p 201). It is a pity that Lord Millett did not abide by his noble words in *McFarlane*. Finally the Rands were also allowed to recover damages for the birth of their third child as there was evidence to suggest that Mrs Rand only embarked on a further pregnancy to prove to herself that she could have a normal child after the birth of Katy.

In *McLelland and Another v Greater Glasgow Health Board* 7 March 2001, MLC 0364 the Scottish courts adopted the same approach taken by their English contemporaries in *Rand*. Mrs McLelland gave birth to a child suffering from Down's Syndrome. The defenders admitted negligence in failing to diagnose the condition and inform Mrs McLelland of it, thereby depriving her of the opportunity to undergo a termination which, she contended, she would have had. The Appeal Court of the Court of Session (Inner House) held that, although it was 'fair, just and reasonable' that the defenders should be liable for the 'extra economic burdens' attributable to a child suffering from Down's Syndrome, there were no grounds for saying that they were assuming responsibility for the ordinary costs of maintenance. Lord Prosser came up with the unusual and, in our opinion, ludicrous argument that, although the McLellands were relying on their doctors to detect the Down's Syndrome and were entitled to recover damages for the economic loss related to the Down's Syndrome, their reliance did not extend beyond matters not directly related to the Down's Syndrome, namely the ordinary maintenance of the child. Lord Prosser incredulously argued that, although it would be in the hospital's contemplation that if they breached their duty of care (in failing to diagnose the Down's Syndrome) that may lead to loss of the opportunity to terminate the pregnancy, remarkably the possibility of an unwanted birth would not be in the defender's contemplation, even less so than a case such as *McFarlane*. Lord Marnoch, whilst arriving at the same conclusion as Lord Prosser, clearly has some doubts about some of his colleague's reasoning. Relying on *Rand*, he argued that it was evident that Gary was a wanted child and that the McLellands were in the same invidious position as the McFarlanes, as far as the ordinary costs of maintenance. However, unlike Lord Prosser he refused to rule out the possibility that ordinary maintenance costs may never be recoverable, stating: 'But I do not go so far as to say that the birth of a damaged or disadvantaged child can never give rise to a claim for such costs (p 17, para 3).' The most sensible judgment, unfortunately for the claimants, was the minority dissenting judgment of Lord Morrison. He seemingly poured scorn on Lord Prosser's judgment, saying of it: 'I am not able to understand this view (p 19, para 7).' Neither was he of the opinion that the costs of ordinary maintenance should be excluded on the grounds that the child was a benefit as, he argued, the benefit should be set against the whole costs of maintaining the child, not just part of them.

Both *Rand* and *McLelland* are distinguishable from *McFarlane* not just on the basis that the resulting child was born disabled as opposed to healthy, but also on the nature of the respective claims. *Rand* and *McLelland* were both cases concerning a failure to diagnose rather than a failed sterilisation/vasectomy claim. However, recently, in *Parkinson v St James and Seacroft University Hospital NHS Trust* [2001] 6 Lloyd's Rep Med 309, the Court of Appeal has considered what costs are recoverable for the birth of an unplanned disabled child. The claimant, who already had four existing children, had become pregnant with her fifth child following a negligently performed sterilisation operation. She was warned that the child may be born disabled, but chose not to have a termination. The child was subsequently born handicapped. Brooke LJ held that the parents' award should be limited to those extra expenses associated with the child's disabilities. Hale LJ, too, came to the conclusion that to compensate for the financial costs for a healthy child would be going too far. However, she dismissed the argument that the birth of a child was to be thought of as a benefit - she was of the opinion that either the courts should ignore the benefit of a child altogether or assume that the benefit cancelled out any claim for the costs of rearing the child. Referring to Lord McCluskey's comments in *McFarlane,* she noted that many 'would argue that the true costs to the primary carer of bringing up a child are so enormous that they easily outstrip any benefits' and 'The notion of a child bringing benefit to the parents is itself deeply suspect, smacking of commodification of the child, regarding the child as an asset to the parents (p 24, paras 38, 39)'. She argued that the better approach would be to deduct a conventional sum. The authors' argument would, of course, be to deduct no sum at all.

From the tenor of her judgment it is clear that Hale LJ has some reservations about the *McFarlane* judgment. She notes that their Lordships' reasoning was 'variously and elegantly expressed' but 'in truth they all gave different reasons for arriving at ... the same result (p 21, para 29)'. Her judgment is also noteworthy for her eloquent account of the life-changing affect of pregnancy; she refers to the loss of personal autonomy, to the 'hard work' of labour, and to the fact that 'bringing up children is hard work'. One feels that here is one member of the judiciary who is in tune with reality and, unlike her male contemporaries, recognises that pregnancy is more than being 'with child' for nine months.

Finally, Hale LJ also clarifies two other areas of confusion. First, how disabled must a child have to be for the parents to make a claim? Hale LJ simply adopts the test of disability found in s 17(11) of the Children Act 1989. Secondly, although not an issue in the present case, she states that a father who satisfies the proximity test, and who has child caring responsibilities and meets them, should also have a claim.

To conclude this sorry tale let us briefly summarise the position for claims for wrongful conception and wrongful birth. Following the *McFarlane* decision the unplanned birth of a healthy child will attract no award to compensate for the ordinary maintenance of that child. This, in the authors' opinion, is wrong because it quite simply fails to apply the principle that a tortfeasor should be liable for all foreseeable losses. When an unwanted child arrives as a result of a tortfeasor's negligence surely it is unarguable that a foreseeable loss is the cost of care of that child, whether that child is healthy or disabled. Children, healthy or disabled, are a blessing, but even a blessing has its price and the Law Lords' puritanical and moralistic view in *McFarlane* is totally divorced from reality.

Responsible parents are left just hoping that the measures they have taken to curtail their family are successful because if they are not then they will get no help from the courts in paying for that extra mouth to feed. Where the child is born disabled following an unplanned pregnancy or failure to diagnose, damages will be restricted to those additional costs associated with the disability; the courts only compensate for the disability and not for the child him/herself. Perhaps this is mildly acceptable where the negligence is the same for the disabled child as it is for the healthy child. To do otherwise would mean drawing a distinction on the basis that one child was born healthy and the other was born with a disability; that is morally abhorrent. Where, however, the negligence is failing to diagnose the disability, then the authors would suggest the approach should be more straightforward: the defendant has breached their duty of care in diagnosis and the parents should be compensated for all losses resulting from that breach, as was the case in *Nunnerley v Waring HA* [2000] 4 Lloyd's Rep 170, a claim decided in those happier days of pre-*McFarlane*. Whatever the position, it is to be hoped that the *McFarlane* decision is re-visited and all claimants of healthy or disabled children will eventually recover compensation for the entire upkeep of their unwanted but now loved offspring.

Finally, in *Rand v East Dorset HA (No 2)* [2000] 8 Lloyd's Rep Med 377 is a case which concerns the recovery of benefits under the Social Security (Recoupment of Benefits) Act 1997. Following the birth of Katy the claimants had been in receipt of various benefits on their own account and benefits were also received or receivable for the child. The court ruled that the 1997 Act did not apply in cases of economic loss. Any deduction made at common law extended only to unemployment benefit, income support and job seekers allowance but no benefits received/able by the child were deductible at common law. Also invalidity care allowance was not deductible as the claimants had not recovered any sum from the defendant in respect of that care and to require the claimants to give credit would prevent them from recovering the economic loss they had incurred.

For additional case law regarding 'wrongful birth', see references 52–56 at p 274.

Nervous shock

Because of the imprecise nature of the damages awarded and the abundance of case law in this area we think it appropriate to look at damages for nervous shock separately.

The first point to note is that there must be some recognisable psychiatric illness; damages will not be awarded for emotional distress or grief unless this leads to a recognisable psychiatric illness. In *Hicks v Chief Constable of South Yorkshire* [1992] 2 All ER 65 (see p 245), the victims of the Hillsborough disaster were trapped for several hours before dying from asphyxia. It was held that they had suffered from grief and distress and as such this was not recoverable (see, also, *Reilly and Reilly v Merseyside Regional HA* [1995] 6 Med LR 246). However, it has to be said that in cases where the victim suffers some other injury the court will take into account any mental distress in assessing general damages for pain and suffering. For example, in *Kralj v McGrath and St Theresa's*

Hospital [1986] 1 All ER 54 (see r 7(D), p 292), the court ruled that if the claimant's injuries were exacerbated because of the grief she was suffering at that time the court could take that into account. The court ruled that aggravated damages were inappropriate and instead increased the award for pain and suffering. A case which seems to go further is *Salih v Enfield HA* [1991] 2 Med LR 235 where, as a result of a negligent diagnosis, the claimant gave birth to a child suffering from congenital rubella syndrome. She was awarded £5,000 for pain and suffering, although it is to be noted that there was no evidence of any psychological effects or physical defects as a result of the injury. Finally, in *Grieve v Salford HA* [1991] 2 Med LR 295, the claimant, who it was admitted had a vulnerable personality, was awarded £12,500 general damages. This award was for having to undergo a caesarean section after an aborted attempt at forceps delivery of a stillborn child and the court took into account the psychological damage the claimant had suffered.

Vernon v Bosley (No 1) [1997] 1 All ER 577 was a case where the court held that the claimant was entitled to damages for mental illness and no discount was applied despite the mental illness being in part caused by grief and bereavement.

For primary victims, damages will be recoverable if they are foreseeable. In *Page v Smith* [1995] 2 WLR 644 (for the facts, see Chapter 6, Causation, at p 231), the claimant, a primary victim, alleged that a road traffic accident had exacerbated a pre-existing condition of ME. The House of Lords found for the claimant by a majority of 3–2; Lord Lloyd held that where the claimant was a primary victim what must be foreseeable was personal injury of some type. This argument was endorsed by Lord Browne-Wilkinson who said that no distinction should be drawn between physical and psychiatric injury. What is interesting are the propositions put forward by Lord Lloyd for dealing with nervous shock claims. He said that it was important to distinguish between primary and secondary victims. As regards the latter, the law imposes certain control mechanisms to limit the number of claimants. However, the defendant will not be liable unless psychiatric injury is foreseeable in a person of ordinary fortitude, although in the case of a secondary victim it may be appropriate to use hindsight. Subject to these qualifications, a defendant will be liable to the claimant if it can be established that he can reasonably foresee that his conduct will expose the claimant to a risk of physical or psychiatric injury. Once the duty of care is established, the claimant must prove that the nervous shock resulted in a psychiatric illness; it does not matter that this illness is unusually severe; the defendant must take his victim as he finds him.

If the claimant is a secondary victim, that is, someone who witnesses the suffering of others, *Alcock and Others v Chief Constable of South Yorkshire* [1992] 1 AC 310 is the seminal case. There, the claimants had all suffered psychiatric trauma as a result of the Hillsborough disaster in 1989, none had sustained any physical injury and most of them were not even present at the ground. The court ruled that claims for nervous shock should be limited and to that end three criteria had to be satisfied.

The first criterion relates to the class of persons who could claim. It was held that what mattered was the degree of love and affection; such would be presumed in the case of close relatives and would be scrutinised in the case of more distant relatives. The court seemed to leave open the question whether a bystander could sue. Lord Keith said (at p 397):

The case of a bystander ... is difficult. Psychiatric injury to him would not ordinarily ... be within the range of reasonable foreseeability, but could not perhaps entirely be excluded from it if the circumstances of a catastrophe occurring very close to him were particularly horrific.

However, in *McFarlane v E Caledonia Ltd* [1994] 2 All ER 1 (a case concerning the Piper Alpha disaster), the court rejected a claim by a bystander. The claimant, who had previously suffered from depression, witnessed a massive explosion on a North Sea oil rig at least 100 metres away. At the time he was on a support vessel. The court held that, since there was no evidence that the claimant had close ties to any of the crew on the rig, he was simply a bystander and therefore his claim failed. This was so despite the fact that the claimant must have witnessed the horrific events knowing that there would be many deaths. However, he was held not to be involved with the disaster nor to be a rescuer and, as no one else on the support ship had suffered injury or was close enough to be in danger, the claim failed.

The second criterion is that there must be proximity of time and space. This has been held to cover the aftermath of the accident (see *McLoughlin v O'Brian* [1983] AC 410). In *Alcock,* the claim failed because it was nearly nine hours before the claimants saw the victims and then only for formal identification. The same reasoning was applied in *Taylor v Somerset HA* [1993] 4 Med LR 34 where the claimant alleged that she had suffered nervous shock after identifying her husband's body in the mortuary. Additionally, in *Alcock,* the court ruled that the medium by which the claimants were informed of the ensuing events, that is, television, did not come within the aftermath principle as the claimants could only see a general picture of chaos and not the suffering of their own relatives. This principle, however, is not set in stone; it may be that parents who witness their children's injuries on television can succeed.

In *Palmer v Tees HA* [1999] 9 Lloyd's Rep Med 351 the claimant claimed for post traumatic stress disorder and pathological grief following the abduction and murder of her four year old daughter. She alleged that the defendant had negligently failed to identify that the patient posed a serious risk to children and that her condition was the result of being present at the scene of the discovery of her daughter's body (although she was not allowed to see her at that time), being present at the immediate aftermath of her daughter's abduction and the identification of her daughter's body. She was held to be in the same category as the relatives in the *Alcock* case; she had undergone a period of grave worry and anxiety before learning her daughter was dead. She did not come within the immediate aftermath. See, also, *W v Essex CC* (2000) 53 BMLR 1 where at p 8 Lord Slynn stated that 'the concept of the "immediate aftermath" of the incident has to be assessed in the particular situation'.

Just how far the aftermath principle stretches is not certain. In *McLoughlin,* the claimant was allowed to recover because she saw her family before they had been treated by the medical staff, something which is unlikely to happen in a clinical negligence case. Certainly, in *Alcock,* the court refused to give 'aftermath' a precise definition. The conclusion appears to be that unless the claimant sees his relative in an injured state, preferably covered in blood, then the claim will probably fail.

The third criterion is that the nervous shock must arise from the negligence of the defendant which causes injury to the claimant or a third party. However, it is far from clear whether the court was ruling out claims in other types of cases, for example, where the defendant suffers injury through his own fault which in turn causes the claimant to suffer psychiatric illness. What is clear is that the psychiatric illness must be induced by shock (see *Alcock and Others v Chief Constable of South Yorkshire* [1992] 1 AC 310, p 264). In *Jaensch v Coffey* (1984) 54 ALR 417, Brennan J gave two examples which would not qualify for compensation, namely an overworked spouse who had been caring for a husband who was injured by the defendant's negligence and as a result suffers from psychiatric illness, and a parent who suffers as a result of the behaviour of a brain-damaged child. There must be some shock which must be immediate or fall within the aftermath principle, and not simply a period of time spent caring for the claimant. With respect, subject to certain limits, we do not see any reason why the compensation should not be extended to cover the aforementioned situations. It is clearly foreseeable, so why the need for the shock element? The sufferer has still been placed in a position which he would not have been in but for the negligence of the tortfeasor.

The case of *Tredget and Tredget v Bexley HA* [1994] 5 Med LR 178 may be taken as giving support to our proposition. There, the claimants were allowed to recover damages for nervous shock caused by their child's death shortly after his birth. Although the birth itself was a horrifying event – at one point the child's shoulder had to be broken to allow the birth to take place – the shock arose from the parents spending two-and-a-half days knowing that something was gravely wrong until eventually the child's life support machine was switched off. Conversely, in *Sion v Hampstead HA* [1994] 5 Med LR 170, a father was denied a claim for nervous shock which was allegedly caused by watching his son die as a result of clinical negligence. The claimants in *Tredget* and *Sion* clearly satisfied the aftermath test, but were their injuries reasonably foreseeable? Mrs Tredget was a diabetic and had already experienced one difficult delivery; therefore, it could be said that a difficult delivery and the events that followed were foreseeable. Additionally, it could be argued that the events that followed would cause shock in a person of reasonable fortitude. On the other hand it could be that this was just intense grief.

In the case of *Tan v East London and City HA* [1999] 9 Lloyd's Rep Med 39, a father claimed damages for psychiatric injury from the defendant health authority. The defendant had informed him of the death of his child *in utero* and he then spent several hours comforting his wife, watching the caesarian delivery of his dead child and then keeping an overnight vigil. The health authority admitted the stillbirth was the result of their negligence, however the claim failed. The court held that the claimant did not come within the immediate aftermath, (that is, the death of the child *in utero*); secondly, the death, stillbirth and vigil were not all one event and therefore did not satisfy the aftermath test; and, finally, there was no shock element, for example, the caesarian operation was planned.

The reasoning behind *Tan* is tenuous, to say the least. Should it matter that Mr Tan did not attend immediately following his child's death when the hospital knew he would be coming? Does this decision yet again not illustrate the unjustness of the aftermath principle, a view shared by the Law Commission in their Report No 249, *Liability for Psychiatric Illness* (see below). That report had recommended that the only limitation in cases of secondary victims should be that the claimant should be able to demonstrate a close tie of love and affection with the victim. Finally, should it matter whether the claimant can satisfy the shock requirement?

There have been other cases that have tried to widen the categories of claims for which damages may be awarded for psychiatric harm. In the following two cases the claimants argued that the health authority were under a duty to disclose information in a sensitive/appropriate manner. In *AB v Tameside and Glossop HA* [1997] 8 Med LR 91 a large number of patients received treatment at two NHS hospitals from a person who was later found to be HIV positive. As there was a small risk that some of them may have been infected the defendant health authority wrote to the patients informing them of this fact and recommending that they undergo tests to clarify the issue. A telephone counselling line was also set up but this was not operational until the letters were sent out. Although there was no evidence that any of the patients had been infected a number of patients alleged that the letter was not drafted in a suitably sensitive manner and further it ought not to have been sent out until the help-line was operational. They contended that they had suffered psychiatric harm as a result of the defendant's negligence. The Court of Appeal held that the defendant could not be held to be negligent merely because, with hindsight, it did not choose the best method of informing the claimant. Unfortunately the court failed to answer the question of whether the defendant owed a legal duty to take care in releasing the information in the first place.

In *Allin v City and Hackney HA* [1996] 7 Med LR 167 the claimant had undergone a very difficult labour and was then misinformed that her baby was dead. It was some six hours later that she discovered her baby was still alive when a paediatrician came to speak to her about the baby and he kept using the present tense. The claimant's claim for psychiatric harm caused as a result of the defendant's careless dissemination of information succeeded; the defendant's counsel conceded that the *'defendants were under a duty of care in respect of statements of this sort made to the mother'*. Could the same not be said of the previous case? That receiving information of a potentially devastating effect should be dealt with sensitively and, if not, then those disseminating the information should be held accountable? It should be noted that following *Allin*, a woman given correct news that her baby was dead as a result of clinical negligence would not be allowed to recover but a woman given incorrect news would.

The argument against extending the *'Tredget*-like' claims would be that the courts could be confronted with a situation where the death of a neonate, or for that matter anyone, will lead to claims for nervous shock. We are of the opinion that it is justifiable that where there is a particularly serious lack of care by the hospital, and the claimant has to endure a traumatic period watching a loved one die knowing that the death could have been avoided; then, in such cases, the hospital should be held accountable for any lasting psychiatric damage caused to the claimant. There is an inbuilt safeguard in these claims – the claimant must show that he has suffered from a psychiatric illness and not mere grief. This is the way the law should progress. At present, however, a claim resulting from the negligence of the doctor or hospital will only have a good chance of success if:

(1) the claim is made by the victim of the alleged negligence (either as a result of receiving some horrific treatment while still conscious or, if he was unconscious, perhaps waking up to find that the wrong limb has been amputated); or

(2) a third party witnesses the horrific treatment; or

(3) the third party sees the victim in a distressed state as a result of the clinical negligence.

It seems however that it is not only academics who are of the opinion that the 'aftermath' test and the 'shock' requirement are cumbersome and unnecessary in determining whether the claimant has suffered psychiatric damage. In their report, *Liability for Psychiatric Illness*, Law Com No 249, 1998 the Law Commission recommended the creation of a new statutory duty of care for secondary victims that would allow a claimant who has suffered a reasonably foreseeable psychiatric illness as a result of the death, injury or imperilment of a person with whom he had a close tie of love and affection to recover damages regardless of the claimant's closeness in time and space to the accident and its aftermath or the means by which the claimant learned of it. The new statutory duty would retain the requirement for the claimant to show a close tie of love and affection to the victim and there is a list of relationships where that would be presumed but it would still be possible for someone outside that list to prove that he had a sufficiently close relationship with the victim. The reforms would also remove the shock element. Hopefully in the not too distant future these reforms will be implemented and that would probably mean a very different result for cases such as *Sion, Alcock* and *Tan*.

REFERENCES

English case law

(1)   Hotson v East Berkshire HA [1987] AC 750; [1987] 2 All ER 909
See above, p 217 *et seq*.

(2)   Jobling v Associated Dairies Ltd [1982] AC 794
The defendant's negligence resulted in the claimant sustaining a back injury. Three years later he found he was suffering from myelopathy. The defendant argued that its liability was extinguished by the onset of the myelopathy, an argument which ultimately found favour with the House of Lords.

(3)   Hicks and Others v Chief Constable of the South Yorkshire Police [1992] 2 All ER 65
See above, p 245.

(4) Rourke v Barton (1982) The Times, 23 June
The claimant's husband was suffering from terminal cancer. She sustained an injury to her hip which prevented her from caring for her husband when he was at home. The distress caused to her was taken into account in the assessment of damages.

(5) Kralj v McGrath and St Theresa's Hospital [1986] 1 All ER 54
Considered at pp 291 and 292.

(6) Ackers v Wigan HA [1991] 2 Med LR 232
The claimant was not totally anaesthetised during a caesarian section. She was awarded £12,000 for pain and suffering and consequent psychological upset.

(7) Phelan v East Cumbria HA [1991] 2 Med LR 419
The claimant was paralysed but fully conscious while his leg was opened, drilled and four screws inserted. He was awarded £5,000 for his experience on the operating table and £10,000 for the resulting psychological damage.

(8) Cooper v Nottingham HA (1989) The Times, 17 March
The claimant was conscious during a caesarian section – she was awarded £15,000 for pain and suffering.

See, also, *Taylor v Worcester and District HA* [1991] 2 Med LR 215, above, p 192.

(9) Burton v Islington HA; De Martell v Merton and Sutton HA [1993] 4 Med LR 8
Both cases effectively restate the position under the Congenital Disabilities (Civil Liability) Act 1976 and are only relevant to those cases which predate the Act. See, further, above, p 88 *et seq*.

(10) Wise v Kaye [1962] 1 QB 368
See above, p 247. The claimant was aged 20 at the date of the accident. At the time of trial (three years later) she had not recovered consciousness and was unlikely to do so. The court awarded £15,000 general damages (other than future loss of earnings and loss of expectation of life).

(11) H West & Son Ltd v Shepherd [1964] AC 174
See above, p 247.

(12) Lim Poh Choo v Camden and Islington AHA [1980] AC 174

The claimant sustained extensive and irremediable brain damage and was totally dependent on others.

Held: the domestic elements of the claimant's care should be deducted from the cost of care claim and that the expenses she would have incurred in earning her living should be deducted from the loss of earnings claim.

(13) Heil v Rankin [2000] 2 WLR 1173
The claimant was a police dog handler who was involved in a serious accident in 1987. In 1993 he suffered a minor injury caused by the defendant which triggered off a condition of post traumatic stress disorder which had initially manifested itself after the 1987 incident. The claimant gave up working in the police force.

The claimant's appeal was heard jointly with seven other appeals as test cases by the Court of Appeal raising the issue of the level of general damages to be awarded for pain, suffering and loss of amenity.

The Court of Appeal accepted in the main the Law Commission's proposals that there should be an increase in awards for non-pecuniary loss though there was no increase in awards of £10,000 or under. See, further, p 247.

(14) Cookson v Knowles [1979] AC 566
This case involved a fatal accident in which the claimant's husband was killed.

(15) Worral v Powergen plc [1999] 5 Lloyd's Rep Med 177
See, further, p 248.

(16) Wells v Wells, Thomas v Brighton HA and Page v Sheerness Steel Co Ltd [1998] 3 All ER 481
See above, p 249.

(17) Warren v Northern General Hospital Trust [2000] 1 WLR 1404
The claimant had been one of the claimants in *Heil v Rankin* (see ref 13) and had been awarded damages of £2.5 million for future loss on the basis of a discount rate of 3%. On appeal, he argued that the rate of 3% was too high because the Lord Chancellor had failed to set a rate under the Damages Act 1996, and that the court should do so. He also argued that the rate should be reduced because the incidence of taxation on higher awards distorted the rate of return and, consequently, he would in fact be under-compensated.

Held: dismissing the appeal that it was for the Lord Chancellor, using his power under s 1 of the Damages Act 1996, to alter the rate of return from the current 3%.

(18) Auty v National Coal Board [1985] 1 All ER 930; [1985] 1 WLR 784
See above, p 250.

(19) Smith v Manchester Corporation [1974] 17 KIR 1

See above, p 250.

(20) Moeliker v A Reyrolle & Co Ltd [1976] ICR 253
In assessing damages for loss of earning capacity the court had to assess whether the risk was substantial (real) or whether it was fanciful or speculative. Where there is a real risk, the assessment of damages depends on the degree of the risk at the time when the loss of employment might occur and the factors affecting the claimant's prospects of obtaining another job. Each case would be decided on its individual facts.

(21) Foster v Tyne & Wear County Council [1986] 1 All ER 567
An adult claimant was awarded £35,000 for loss of earning capacity. Lloyd LJ said that, in determining the level of the award, it was necessary to weigh up all the chances in all the circumstances of a particular case.

(22) Pickett v British Rail Engineering [1980] AC 136
See above, p 250.

(23) Harris v Empress Motors Ltd [1984] 1 WLR 212; [1983] 3 All ER 561
See above, p 251.

(24) Phipps v Brooks Dry Cleaning Services (1996) The Times, 16 July
See above, p 251.

(25) Roberts v Johnstone [1988] 3 WLR 1247
See above, p 252.

(26) Donnelly v Joyce [1974] QB 454
See above, p 253.

(27) Housecroft v Burnett [1986] 1 All ER 332
See above, p 253.

(28) Hunt v Severs [1994] 2 All ER 385
See above, p 253.

Medical experts agreed that the claimant had a life expectancy of 25 years. The Court of Appeal therefore assessed damages for this fixed period. The House of Lords, however, ruled that this was inappropriate.

(29) Mehmet v Perry [1977] 2 All ER 529
The court may use the earnings of one parent who stays at home to look after the children as the multiplicand.

Held: the claimant had acted reasonably in giving up work on the death of his wife and that it was reasonable that he should not take up employment until his youngest child reached the age of 15. (The claimant's two youngest children, H and S suffered from a rare blood disorder and required frequent blood transfusions.) In these circumstances, the damage for loss of the deceased's housekeeping services should be assessed by reference to the claimant's loss of wages, not by reference to the reasonable cost of employing a housekeeper, because the claimant's loss of wages represented the loss of providing the services of a full time housekeeper in substitution for his wife.

(30) Hardwick v Hudson and Another [1999] 3 All ER 426
The claimant was awarded damages against the defendant for personal injuries suffered as a result of a road traffic accident. He was unlikely to recover fully from his injuries and therefore was unable to carry on his work as a motor mechanic. Before the accident the claimant had been running a garage business in equal partnership with a Mr Hannington. The claimant sought to recover compensation in respect of extra work done by his wife for the business from the time of his accident until she replaced Mr Hannington as full time partner. Before the accident Mrs Hardwick had worked for the business 1–2 days a week but after the accident she had worked an extra 20 hours a week.

Held: the claimant could only recover if there was evidence of an express or implied contract by the business to remunerate Mrs Hardwick for the work done. There was no evidence of that; if there had been the business profits would have had to be reduced to the extent of her remuneration. Therefore the Court of Appeal held that the claimant was not entitled to recover damages in respect of services provided gratuitously by his wife.

(31) Emeh v Kensington and Chelsea and Westminster HA [1985] QB 1012; [1984] 3 All ER 844
See above, p 254.

(32) Briody v St Helen's and Knowsley HA [2000] 3 Lloyd's Rep Med 127
See above, p 254.

(33) Jones v Jones [1984] 3 WLR 862
The claimant suffered a severe personality change after his injuries which caused the breakdown of his marriage. The court awarded damages of £15,000 to compensate the claimant for the money he had paid to his wife and children to enable them to set up a

new home. In fact, the claimant actually paid his wife £25,000 but the court only awarded him £15,000 to reflect the fact that the claimant would inevitably have paid his wife money in respect of the care that she had provided.

(34) Pritchard v Parrot (1985) The Times, 27 September
Initially, the court awarded £42,500 to a claimant whose marriage had broken down as a result of his injuries. The award was made to enable the claimant to purchase a new home, separate from his wife and family and for the cost of maintaining it. This ruling was reversed in the Court of Appeal, which held that the financial detriment suffered by the claimant was too remote, even though it was admitted that the divorce was a result of the claimant's personality change.

(35) Pritchard v JH Cobden Ltd [1987] 1 All ER 300
See above, p 255.

(36) Wright v British Railways Board [1983] 2 AC 773
In this case the court applied the guidelines for the award of interest as discussed at p 256.

(37) Lawrence v Chief Constable of Staffordshire (2000) The Times, 25 July
See above, p 256.

(38) Wiseley v John Fulton (Plumbers) Ltd; Wadey v Surrey County Council [2000] 2 All ER 545
See above, p 256.

(39) Davies v Inman [1999] PIQR 26
See above, p 256.

(40) Bagley v North Herts HA [1986] 136 New LJ 1014
See above, p 257.

(41) Clark v McLennan [1983] 1 All ER 416
See above, p 257.

(42) Sutton v Population Services Family Planning Programme Ltd (1981) The Times, 7 November
See above, p 257.

(43) Allied Maples Group v Simmons and Simmons [1995] 1 WLR 1602
See Chapter 6, p 223.

(44) Stovold v Barlows (1995) The Times, 30 October
See Chapter 6, p 224.

(45) McGhee v National Coal Board [1973] 1 WLR 1; [1972] 3 All ER 1008
See Chapter 6, p 205.

(46) McKay v Essex AHA [1982] QB 1166; [1982] 2 All ER 771
See above, p 257.

(47) Allen v Bloomsbury HA [1993] 1 All ER 651
See above, p 258. The case involved the birth of a healthy child following a failed abortion.

(48) Fish v Wilcox [1994] 5 Med LR 230

The claimant gave birth to a handicapped child and brought a claim for loss and damage as a result of the birth and having to look after a seriously handicapped child. The claimant was later diagnosed as having MS and was unable to look after the child. The judge at first instance awarded the claimant £234,387 by way of damages for negligence, £34,167 was awarded for the nursing care the claimant had provided up until the date of trial. No award was made for loss of earnings, because the judge ruled that this would amount to double recovery. The claimant appealed against this. The appeal was dismissed, the court ruling that:

(1) The claimant could not do two jobs at once and she was not entitled to be paid for doing two jobs at once.

(2) That the judge had awarded on additional burden of looking after her child as opposed to the work the claimant had previously done.

In any event, the judge had awarded a substantial sum over and above the compensation for loss of earnings to reflect the additional burden of caring for a child.

In essence, it appears that these type of awards are subject to the ultimate discretion of the court as to whether to recompense the parent for loss of earnings or the value of services rendered.

Note that this case simply reiterates the decision in *Housecroft v Burnett* [1986] 1 All ER 332 but is the first clinical negligence case on this point.

(49) Rand v East Dorset HA [2000] 4 Lloyd's Rep Med 181

The defendant health authority negligently failed to inform the claimants that Mrs Rand was carrying a Down's Syndrome child thereby depriving them of the opportunity of terminating the pregnancy. It was accepted that had the claimants known of this then the pregnancy would have been terminated. The claimants sought compensation for, amongst other things, the cost of the care of their disabled child for life.

Held: the existence of the Abortion Act 1967 was sufficient to impose liability on the defendant for the consequences of their omission which was the birth of a disabled child. The full costs of care were not recoverable as that would mean comparing existence with non-existence of the child. Hence only the costs relating to the disability were recoverable. Damages were not limited to the child's eighteenth birthday. Mrs Rand could also recover damages for discovering the child was Down's Syndrome and for the additional third pregnancy.

(50) Parkinson v St James and Seacroft University Hospital NHS Trust [2001] 6 Lloyd's Rep 309

See, also, at pp 257, 258.

(51) Nunnerley v Waring HA [2000] Lloyd's Rep Med 170

The claimants' third child was born with a genetic disorder that left him mentally retarded and prone to epileptic fits. The defendant accepted that its staff had been negligent in failing to warn the claimants that their son might be born with the disorder and that if such a warning had been given, the pregnancy would have been terminated. The claimants claimed damages for the cost of their child's care and the additional costs related to his disorder.

Held: the claimants succeeded because the normal rules of compensation applied in this case. The wrong committed was the birth of the claimants' son and hence the claimants were entitled to recover for all costs resulting from this and those included the cost of their son's care. Furthermore there was no rule of law that stipulated that such damages were limited to the child's 18th birthday.

(52) Rand v East Dorset HA (No 2) [2000] 8 Lloyd's Rep Med 377
See above, p 263.

(53) Taylor v Shropshire HA [2000] 2 Lloyd's Rep Med 96
Mrs Taylor gave birth to an unwanted fifth child following a failed sterilisation operation. The child was born seriously disabled.

Held: general damages were awarded for the physical and psychological effects of pregnancy and for the additional burden and anxieties of bringing up a disabled child less a discount for the joy and comfort of the child's existence.

(54) Hardman v Amin [2000] 10 Lloyd's Rep Med 498
The claimant's GP failed to diagnose that she was suffering from rubella and consequently she gave birth to a son who was seriously disabled.

Held: the claimant could recover damages for the suffering and inconvenience of the pregnancy and the shock of the realisation that she had given birth to a disabled child. The continuation of the pregnancy did amount to a personal injury and the claimant could recover loss and expense consequent upon the pregnancy. The defendant could not limit liability by reference to what the claimant would in any event, but for the award, have spent on caring for her child.

(55) Groom v Selby [2001] 2 Lloyd's Rep Med 39
The facts of this case are of interest. The defendant GP had failed to diagnose the claimant's pregnancy and therefore deprived her of the opportunity to have a lawful termination. The claimant gave birth to a daughter three weeks prematurely in May 1995. In June, the baby became unwell and was admitted to hospital. She developed salmonella meningitis and was left permanently brain damaged.

Held: it was foreseeable that if the defendant failed to discover the claimant's pregnancy, the child would be born prematurely. The child had never been born healthy; the infecting bacterium was on the surface of the child's skin and/or gut and remained asymptomatic for about three and a half weeks. The bacterium then entered her bloodstream and, within 12–48 hours, septicaemia followed by meningitis developed. The child would need additional care and supervision because of her disabilities.

Note: The judge was at pains to distinguish this case from *McFarlane v Tayside Health Board* [1999] 4 All ER 961, stating that the child in *Groom* was born 'unhealthy'. Is this right? *McFarlane* seemed to distinguish between a child born seriously disabled (which was not the case in *Groom*) as opposed to a healthy child. Is there not an argument to say that the child in *Groom* was born healthy but then, because of an infection contracted from the mother's vagina, went on to suffer serious illness which led to her disabilities? Hence, is this case distinguishable from *McFarlane*?

(56) Greenfield v Irwin (2001) 6 February , MLC 0341
Following *McFarlane*, the Court of Appeal held that there could be no claim for the mother's loss of earnings when she had to give up employment to look after her healthy unplanned child.

(57) Reilly & Reilly v Merseyside HA [1995] 6 Med LR 246
The claimants were trapped in the defendant's lift for over one hour. On appeal, it was held that there was no compensatable damage – claustrophobia and fear were normal human emotions.

(58) Salih v Enfield HA [1991] 2 Med LR 235
A baby was born with congenital rubella syndrome because of the negligence of the defendant. The mother was awarded £5,000 for her pain and suffering although there was no evidence of any psychological effects or physical defects.

(59) Grieve v Salford HA [1991] 2 Med LR 295
The claimant was delivered of a stillborn child. Liability was admitted by the HA. The court took into account the effect on the claimant's personality of the stillbirth. The claimant had repeatedly been given inconsistent explanations as to the cause of her child's death.

(60) Vernon v Bosley (No 1) [1997] 1 All ER 577
The claimant's two young children were passengers in a car driven by their nanny, the defendant, when it veered off the road and crashed into a river. The claimant did not witness the original accident but was at the scene shortly afterwards and witnessed unsuccessful attempts to salvage the car and rescue his children. The claimant became mentally ill and his marriage and business failed. The defendant accepted that the claimant's illness was a result of the death of his children but contended that it was not caused by seeing them drown but rather by pathological grief at the loss of his family resulting in an illness called pathological grief disorder.

Held: a secondary victim was entitled to recover damages for psychiatric illness where he could establish that he had a close tie of love and affection with the primary victim, proximity to the accident, and that the negligence of the defendant caused or contributed to his mental illness. The claimant could recover compensation regardless of whether his illness consisted of in part an abnormal grief reaction and in part post traumatic stress disorder.

(61) Page v Smith [1995] 2 WLR 644; [1995] 2 All ER 736
See above, p 264.

(62) Alcock and Others v Chief Constable of South Yorkshire [1992] 1 AC 310; [1991] 4 All ER 907
Actions were brought against the police for nervous shock arising out of the disaster at the Hillsborough football ground in April 1989 when 95 were killed and 400 injured by crushing. Too many people had been allowed to crowd into a confined area. The events were shown on live television and broadcast on the news. The actions were brought by those who were present at the ground, those who had witnessed the events on television and those who had identified the bodies at the mortuary. The claims were divided into two categories, those where the claimant was involved as a participant and those who had witnessed the accident. In the case of the latter, the court held that they must satisfy the three criteria discussed above, p 268 *et seq*.

(63) McFarlane v E Caledonia Ltd [1994] 2 All ER 1
See above, p 265.

(64) McLoughlin v O'Brian [1983] AC 410; [1982] 2 All ER 298
The claimant's family was involved in a road traffic accident – one child was killed and her husband and other two children were badly injured. The claimant was told about the accident some two hours later and taken to the hospital where she was told about the death of her child and saw the injuries to her family before they had been attended to. The claimant succeeded in her claim for psychiatric damage. Clearly, most emphasis was placed on the fact that the claimant had seen her family in a distressed state before they had been cleaned up. We advocate that the views of Lord Bridge have some merit – is there really any difference between a mother who imagines the horrors of her family who have been subjected to a hotel fire and Mrs McLoughlin who has the misfortune of seeing them?

See, also, the potential liability of breaking bad news in *Furniss v Fitchett* [1958] NZLR 396 in Chapter 1, Medical Confidentiality, at p 6, and p 267 above.

(65) Taylor v Somerset HA [1993] 4 Med LR 34
The claimant's husband had a heart attack and was taken to hospital, where he later died. The claimant arrived 20 minutes later and identified her husband's body in the mortuary. She alleged that this caused her shock and she suffered from a psychiatric illness. The health authority admitted negligence in failing to treat the deceased's heart condition. However, the claimant's claim failed because she did not witness the accident within the defined aftermath principle. She had simply gone to the mortuary to dispel her disbelief that her husband was dead.

(66) Palmer v Tees HA [1999] 9 Lloyd's Rep Med 351
See above, p 265.

(67) Tredget and Tredget v Bexley HA [1994] 5 Med LR 178
The claimants claimed damages for psychiatric illness which contributed to the breakdown of their marriage. The illness had been caused by the death of their son two days after his birth. It was admitted by the defendant that they were liable for the child's death; however, they alleged that the breakdown of the claimant's marriage was the result of their grief rather than nervous shock. The claimants were allowed to recover damages for nervous shock.

(68) Sion v Hampstead HA [1994] 5 Med LR 170
The claimant's son was injured in a motor cycle accident. The claimant stayed at his son's bedside for some 14 days until his son died. He contended that the hospital were negligent in failing to diagnose bleeding from his son's kidney which led to his son lapsing into a coma. He alleged that as a result of the hospital's negligence in caring for his son he had suffered psychiatric illness and had had to give up work.

Held: there was no shock. The claimant had merely been subjected to a continuing process, and his giving up work resulted from an abnormal grief reaction to his son's death. There was no 'sudden appreciation by sight or sound of a horrifying event which visibly agitates the mind' (*per* Lord Ackner in *Alcock and others v Chief Constable of South Yorkshire* [1992] 1 AC 310; [1991] 4 All ER 907, at p 401).

(69) W v Essex CC (2000) 53 BMLR 1
The claimant parents were approved as specialist adolescent foster carers by the local authority. The claimants had specifically said to the local authority that they were not willing to accept any child that was a known or suspected sexual abuser. In April 1993 the local authority placed with the parents an adolescent who had received a police

caution in respect of indecent assault on his own sister and had been under investigations for alleged rape. These details, although known to the local authority, were not provided to the parents. Their children were all physically and sexually abused by the adolescent whilst he was living in their household. The Court of Appeal struck out the parents' claims for psychiatric injury stating that they were secondary victims and as such did not come within the criteria laid down by *Alcock v Chief Constable of South Yorkshire* [1992] 1 AC 310. The local authority's appeal to the House of Lords to have the children's claims struck out was withdrawn and the House of Lords was then asked to consider whether the parents could recover damages for their own psychiatric injury.

Held: The claimants' psychiatric injury was more than just 'acute grief'. The classification of who are primary or secondary victims is not yet closed and is still a concept to be developed in different factual situations. The concept of the 'immediate aftermath' of the incident has to be assessed in each case. Hence the parents' claims would not be barred.

(70) Tan v East London & City HA [1999] 9 Lloyd's Rep Med 39
See above, p 266.

See, also, *Taylorson v Shieldness* [1994] PIQR 329

The claimants were the parents of a child who was involved in a road traffic accident. They were told of the accident and went to the hospital where although they did not see their son they glimpsed his face with blood on it on the way to intensive care. They did not see him for several hours and then saw him in intensive care over the next two days until his eventual death. Their claim for nervous shock failed because they failed to come within the immediate aftermath principle.

Query – is this case really distinguishable from *Tredget*?

(71) AB v Tameside & Glossop HA [1997] 8 Med LR 91
See above, p 267.

(72) Allin v City & Hackney HA [1996] 7 Med LR 167
See above, p 267.

Foreign case law

Australia

(1) Jaensch v Coffey (1984) 54 ALR 517
The facts were similar to *McLoughlin v O'Brien* – a mother was informed of the death of her husband and children but did not witness the aftermath of the accident.

(2) CES Superclinics (Australia) Pty Ltd [1996] Med L Rev 102
See above, p 258.

Scotland

(1) McFarlane v Tayside Health Board [1999] 4 All ER 961
See above, p 259.

(2) McLelland and Another v Greater Glasgow Health Board (2001) 7 March, MLC 0364
The pursuers claimed damages against the defenders in respect of the loss, injury and damage they had suffered due to their son being born with Down's Syndrome. Mrs McLelland had been worried when she became pregnant that there was a risk that she was carrying a Down's Syndrome child as she had a brother affected by the syndrome

and had been tested herself and found to carry the abnormality. Her GP made reference to it in his referral letter to the ante-natal clinic. Mrs McLelland was subjected to an alphafetaprotein test, a screening test with a 30–35% detection rate, which was not diagnostic of Down's syndrome in the foetus. The test was negative but the mother was not advised that it did not exclude the possibility of Down's and that she should have an amniocentesis. The defenders admitted negligence and liability to pay damages and the court accepted the pursuers' evidence that if they had been advised that the unborn child suffered from Down's Syndrome they would have had the pregnancy terminated.

Held: on appeal, damages were awarded for the following:

1   Physical consequences to the mother's health of continuing with the pregnancy beyond the date when if the defenders had not been negligent, the pregnancy would have been terminated. Damages included an award for the mother's shock and distress at discovering her son was handicapped and the added stress of bringing up a handicapped child.

2   An award to the father in respect of emotional distress at the discovery that his child was affected by Down's Syndrome.

3   An award for the extra expenses associated with the care of a Down's Syndrome child. No award for the ordinary costs of maintenance of that child.

4   An award in respect of the care and maintenance after the age of 40.

5   An award to Mrs McLelland for loss of wages after her son's fifth birthday.

United States

Lovelace Medical Center v Mendez (1991) 803 P (2d) 603
This case concerned a negligent tubal ligation.

Held: damages could be recovered for the care of the child until he reached the age of majority. However, the court overruled the first instance decision that the interest of financial security and limiting the size of a family were not worthy of protection.

Note that in the United States there have been some successful claims in which the claimant has been allowed to recover for the fear of future disease without present physical injury. Generally most of these claims have failed as the claimant has failed to demonstrate a physical injury, but there have been some successes. In *Wisner v Illinois Central Gulf* (1988) RR 537 So (2d) 740, the court allowed recovery for fear of cancer following toxic fume exposure. However, the majority of cases reflect the decision in *Payton v Abbot Labs* (1982) 386 Mass 540; 437 NE (2d) 171. This was a class action brought by women who were exposed to diethylstilbestrol (DES) *in utero*. They claimed that they were more likely to suffer from abnormalities of the reproductive organs, but they presented no physical symptoms at the time of trial. It was held that to recover for negligently inflicted emotional distress, one of the factors that must be present is some element of physical harm.

Practice directions

CPR PD 16 para 4.2.

Statutes/statutory instruments

(1)   Congenital Disabilities (Civil Liability) Act 1976
Sections 1, 1A – see below, Appendix A. See, also, s 44 of the Human Fertilisation and Embryology Act 1990.

(2)   Administration of Justice Act 1982

Reduction of life expectancy
    1(1)(b) if the injured person's expectation of life has been reduced by the injuries, the court, in assessing damages in respect of pain and suffering caused by the injuries, shall take account of any suffering caused or likely to be caused to him by awareness that his expectation of life has been so reduced.

Maintenance at public expense
    5   In an action under the law of England and Wales or the law of Northern Ireland for damages for personal injuries (including any such action arising out of a contract) any saving to the injured person which is attributable to his maintenance wholly or partly at public expense in a hospital, nursing home or other institution shall be set off against any income lost by him as a result of his injuries.

(3)   Fatal Accidents Act 1976
See r 7(E), and below, Appendix A.

(4)   Law Reform (Personal Injuries) Act 1948

Private medical costs
    2(4)   In an action for damages for personal injuries (including any such action arising out of a contract), there shall be disregarded, in determining the reasonableness of any expenses, the possibility of avoiding those expenses or part of them by taking advantage of facilities available under the National Health Service Act 1977 or the National Health Service (Scotland) Act 1978 or any corresponding facilities in Northern Ireland.

(5)   Supreme Court Act 1981
For interest on damages, see s 35A below, Appendix A.

(6)   County Courts Act 1984
For interest on damages, see s 69 below, Appendix A.

(7)   Civil Evidence Act 1995

The admissibility of actuarial tables
    10(1)   The actuarial tables (together with explanatory notes) for use in personal injury and fatal accident cases issued from time to time by the Government Actuary's Department are admissible in evidence for the purpose of assessing, in an action for personal injury, the sum to be awarded as general damages for future pecuniary loss.

      (2) They may be proved by the production of a copy published by Her Majesty's Stationery Office.

      (3) For the purposes of this section:

          (a) 'personal injury' includes any disease and any impairment of a person's physical or mental condition; and

          (b) 'action for personal injury' includes an action brought by virtue of the Law Reform (Miscellaneous Provisions) Act 1934 or the Fatal Accidents Act 1976.

Practice points

Interest

- In fatal accident cases, interest on the bereavement award is awarded at the full special account rate from the date of death. Interest is also awarded on damages from date of death to trial and half the special account rates in place during that time.
- *Note* that interest awarded on personal injury damages is not taxable as income pursuant to s 329 Income and Corporation Taxes Act 1988.
- Interest must be claimed in the particulars of claim (CPR r 16.4).
- For interim payments, the fact that interest will be awarded with the final award must be taken into account in making the final award.
- Finally, note that in *Wright v British Rlys Board* [1983] 2 AC 773 (see p 256), the court indicated that in exceptional cases, where one party is guilty of gross delay, the court could increase or decrease the amount of interest or alter the period for which it is allowed.

Nervous shock

- The claimant will have to adduce cogent psychiatric evidence that he has indeed been affected by nervous shock. As vulgar as this may seem, the claimant will have to adduce evidence that he loved the victim whose distress he witnessed. Be prepared for the fact that defence counsel could allege that there was in fact no love and affection and adduce evidence to the contrary.
- Finally, it appears that the success of the claim will often rest upon whether the claimant witnessed the actual injuries. Thus, in the case of a claimant who is merely told what has happened to her nearest and dearest, it is unlikely that the claim will succeed unless there is some unique factor. For clinical negligence cases this may be the death knell for such claims.

RULE 7(B)

The claimant has a duty to mitigate his damages. The claimant must also give credit for any benefits he has received as a result of his injuries and these will be deducted from the final award.

Commentary

Mitigation

It is for the defendant to prove that the claimant has failed to mitigate his damages (see *McGregor on Damages* (15th edn), para 289):

> The onus of proof on the issue of mitigation is on the defendant. If he fails to show that the claimant ought reasonably to have taken certain mitigating steps, then the normal measure will apply.

Although the rule is expressed in terms of a 'duty to mitigate', the claimant will commit no wrong should he fail in this duty; however, his damages may be reduced. Consequently, if the claimant has lost his job or is unable to return to his employment because of his injuries, he should seek alternative employment if he is still capable of working; if he secures a lower paid job then it follows that he will only be able to recover his net loss, that is, the difference between what he was earning prior to his injuries and what he is now earning.

An interesting point is whether the claimant has an obligation to seek further medical treatment to alleviate or improve his condition. Whatever the treatment it must be reasonable, this is why no claimant will be required to undergo an abortion, *Emeh v Kensington and Chelsea AHA* [1985] QB 1012. As for most questions concerning the claimant's conduct, the test is whether or not it was reasonable for him to refuse further treatment and, in assessing this, the court will look at the degree of risk and whether or not there is a predicted outcome. As the defendant has placed the claimant in the adverse position, it will be rare for the court to find that the claimant has acted unreasonably. If there is conflicting medical advice, or if the risk is such that the doctors leave the final decision to the claimant as in *Selvanayagam v University of the West Indies* [1983] 1 WLR 585, a refusal of treatment will invariably be considered reasonable.

If the court were to find that the claimant had acted unreasonably, then they have the problem of assessing damages, especially where the prospect of success of the treatment was uncertain. In line with the loss of chance cases (see p 217 *et seq*) it may be that, where the operation has a less than 50% chance of succeeding, the court could refuse to take that into account in assessing damages. However, as the courts are accustomed to taking the slightest contingencies into account, it is submitted that they will simply have regard to the chances of the treatment succeeding as against the possibility of it failing. This was the approach used in the Canadian case of *Ippolito v Janiak* (1981) 6 DLR (4th) 1. However, a cautionary note should be introduced here – there have been cases where the courts have simply assessed damages on the principle that the operation would have been successful (see *McAuley v London Transport Executive* [1957] 2 Lloyd's Rep 500).

We wish to make two final points. Where the claimant cannot mitigate his damages because of impecuniosity, the defendant will be liable for the full loss. This could perhaps apply where the claimant requires some expensive treatment not ordinarily available on the NHS. Secondly, the reasonable claimant can recover the increased damages which result from his attempt to mitigate (see *Hoffberger v Ascot International Bloodstock Bureau Ltd* (1976) 120 SJ 130).

Benefits

The rule is that the claimant will not be allowed to recover twice for his injuries. The scheme for the deduction of benefits is contained in the Social Security (Recovery Recovery of Benefits) Act 1997. The defendant ('the compensator') has to refund certain benefits which the claimant has received due to his injuries, to the state. The claimant will receive a sum from the defendant reflecting the gross amount of compensation agreed or awarded by the court, less the amount that has to be refunded to the Compensation Recovery Unit. No deductions can be made from damages awarded for pain and suffering. Deductions can be made where a claim is made for past loss of earnings, the costs of care incurred and loss of mobility. The benefits that can be deducted are set out in Sched 2 to the 1997 Act. There is to be no deduction in respect of any claim for future losses. In any event, deductions can only be made for a period of five years starting from the date of the accident, injury or the first claim for benefit.

Where a claimant makes a claim for past loss of earnings the amount received in respect of the following benefits will be deducted from the award of damages and recouped by the Compensation Recovery Unit:

- Disability working allowance.
- Disablement pension payable under s 103 of the Social Security Contributions and Benefits Act 1992.
- Incapacity benefit.
- Income support.
- Invalidity pension and allowance.
- Jobseeker's allowance.
- Reduced earnings allowance.
- Severe disablement allowance.
- Sickness benefit.
- Statutory sick pay (includes only 80% of payments made between 6 April 1991 and 5 April 1994 and does not include payments on or after 6 April 1994).
- Unemployability supplement.
- Unemployment benefit.

If a claimant makes a claim for the cost of care that has been incurred, the following would be deducted from the award of damages:

- Attendance allowance.
- Care component of disability living allowance.
- Disablement pension increase payable under s 104 or 105 of the Social Security Contributions and Benefits Act 1992.

Where a claim is made for compensation for loss of mobility the following would be deducted from the award of damages:

- Mobility allowance.
- Mobility component of disability living allowance.

Listed below is a series of points concerning the recoupment of benefits, which should be taken into account by both the claimant's solicitor and the compensator.

(1) The compensator must complete form CRU1 and forward this to the Compensation Recovery Unit of the DSS within 14 days of being notified of the claim. The following information must be provided: the full name, address, date of birth and national insurance number of the injured person, together with the date of the accident or injury and the nature of the accident, injury or disease.

(2) The Compensation Recovery Unit will provide a certificate which states the amount of the benefits paid to date.

(3) Before settling the case or before trial the compensator will obtain an updated certificate. A gross sum of compensation will be calculated. The claimant will receive the net sum after the deduction for benefits has been made. The defendant/compensator will pay to the Compensation Recovery Unit the amount stated on the certificate in respect of benefits paid.

(4) A claimant is able to claim interest on his special damages claim (including, for example, loss of earnings). This interest will be calculated on the claimant's full claim before any benefits deductions are made (see *Wadey v Surrey County Council* [1999] 2 All ER 334).

Other benefits

Sometimes, as a result of his injuries, the claimant will benefit in monetary terms in other ways. Whether such sums are deductible is discussed below.

(1) Benevolence.

Any gifts received either from public benevolence (for example, a disaster fund) or private benevolence (for example, a gift from a friend) are to be disregarded.

(2) Insurance moneys.

These are also to be disregarded since the defendant cannot rely on the claimant's foresight and planning to reduce his liability. In *McCamley v Cammell Laird Shipbuilders Ltd* [1990] 1 WLR 963, the House of Lords ruled that, for this rule to apply, the claimant himself must have paid the premiums. In this case, the premiums had been paid by the defendant's employer. Notwithstanding this, the court held that the insurance moneys were still to be disregarded as the payment was an act of benevolence by the employer.

(3) Redundancy payments.

These are not deductible unless the claimant is made redundant because of his injuries.

(4) Pensions.

Whether the pension is contributory or non-contributory it is not deductible (see *Smoker v London Fire and Civil Defence Authority* [1991] 2 All ER 449). Additionally, neither state pensions nor an *ex gratia* pension payable by the employer will be deductible. The claimant, however, must give credit if he is receiving a disablement benefit.

(5) Gratuitous payments by the defendant.

It is still uncertain as to what extent payments made by the defendant which are not legally required are deductible. In *Hunt v Severs* [1994] 2 All ER 385, the court ruled that where the tortfeasor provided the defendant with a wheelchair he could not be charged with the cost of the wheelchair. However, where the defendant makes a payment into a disaster fund there is no deduction. There will be no deduction for sick pay where there is a clause in the claimant's contract of employment that the claimant will repay the money to the employer if his claim is successful.

(6) Maintenance at public expense.

According to the Administration of Justice Act 1982, the claimant must give credit for any saving caused by his maintenance at public expense, for example, because he is in a nursing institution. However, under the Law Reform (Personal Injuries) Act 1948, the claimant can claim the cost of private treatment notwithstanding that the same is available on the NHS. The claimant must give credit for any savings to his living expenses; thus, in *Lim Poh Choo v Camden and Islington AHA* [1980] AC 174, where the claimant, who was totally dependent on others, brought a claim for loss of earnings and the cost of care, the House of Lords held that the domestic elements of the claimant's care should be deducted from the cost of care claim; also, the expenses the claimant would have incurred in earning a living, for example, commuting, should be deducted from her loss of earnings claim.

(7) Compensation order made in the criminal courts.

Any award of compensation made to or in respect of the victim by the Criminal Injuries Compensation Authority is not deductible.

REFERENCES

English case law

(1)   Emeh v Kensington and Chelsea and Westminster AHA [1985] QB 1012; [1984] 3 All ER 844
See above, p 281.

(2)   Selvanayagam v University of the West Indies [1983] 1 WLR 585
The claimant refused to undergo an operation which, if successful, would have allowed him to recover 80% of his mobility and allowed him to resume his career as a professional engineer.

Held: the question as to whether the claimant had failed to mitigate his damages was one of fact and the burden was on the claimant. (In this case, the court held that he had discharged this burden.)

See note 13-009 in *Kemp & Kemp* where the opinion is that this decision was made *per incuriam.*

(3)   McAuley v London Transport Executive [1957] 2 Lloyd's Rep 500
Jenkins LJ said that damages should be assessed on the assumption that had the claimant undergone the operation and it had been successful.

(4)   Hoffberger v Ascot Intended Bloodstock Bureau Ltd (1976) 120 SJ 130
See above, p 281.

(5)   Wadey v Surrey County Council [1999] 2 All ER 334
See above, p 283.

(6)   McCamley v Cammell Laird Shipbuilders Ltd [1990] 1 WLR 963
An employer had taken out a personal accident policy for the benefit of his employees although the employees were unaware of this and in fact made no contributions to the premiums. The sum was payable as a lump sum.

Held: the moneys payable under the policy should not be deducted from an award of damages made by the employer.

(7)   Smoker v London Fire and Civil Defence Authority [1991] 2 All ER 449
The House of Lords held that pension benefits were deferred remuneration in respect of the claimant's past work and the defendant cannot appropriate the benefit of this.

(8)   Hunt v Severs [1994] 2 All ER 385
See above, p 283.

(9)   Lim Poh Choo v Camden and Islington AHA [1980] AC 174
See above, p 284.

Foreign case law

Canada

Ippolito v Janiak (1985) 6 DLR (4th) 1
In this case, the mitigating operation which the claimant had refused to undergo had a 70% chance of success.

Held: the 30% chance of it failing should be taken into account in assessing damages.

Statutes/statutory instruments

Social Security (Recovery of Benefits) Act 1997
See below, Appendix A.

Practice points

For assistance/queries on the recoupment of benefits, contact the Compensation Recovery Unit, DSS, Reyrolle Building, Hebburn, Tyne and Wear NE31 1XB.

RULE 7(C)

Damages are usually awarded as a lump sum. However, in certain instances, damages may be awarded on more than one occasion, in advance of the final resolution of the matter or in a form other than a lump sum.

Commentary

As already noted the claimant can only bring one action in respect of the alleged tort and any compensation is usually awarded in a lump sum. Such a method of payment can create problems where, for example, the claimant's prognosis is uncertain or where the award is large. In such situations, the solicitor may wish to consider alternatives to the lump sum payment. These are considered below. However, before doing so there is another possibility which he may wish to consider, and that is a split trial where the issues of liability and *quantum* are tried separately. This may be appropriate in the case of a brain-damaged baby where it will be sensible to deal with liability at an early stage but resolve *quantum* when the child is older and his future needs will have become apparent (see CPR r 3.1(2)(i)).

Structured settlements

Structured settlements were introduced in England and Wales in 1987 following an agreement between the Association of British Insurers (ABI) and the Inland Revenue. Essentially, the settlement allows compensation to be paid in instalments for the life of the claimant who will also receive part of his damages as a lump sum payment.

What happens when a structured settlement is agreed? The defendant's insurer will agree to pay a lump sum to the claimant but additionally will agree that the majority of this lump sum will be paid by instalments tied to the Retail Price Index with a life office for an annuity on the claimant's life. The annuity is in fact paid to the defendant or the defendant's insurers, who then pay these sums to the claimant. In clinical negligence cases payments may come direct from the paying body, an annuity may not be used. The main advantage of such a scheme is that the claimant receives this sum tax-free as it is regarded as a capital payment and consequently represents a considerable saving to him. Investment income from the lump sum is treated as income and therefore is subject to tax. It is possible that the defendant's insurers will attempt to negotiate a discount on the award, bearing in mind that the claimant will make a tax saving.

The second advantage of a structured settlement is one of security, since there is an increasing worry that the damages may not cater for the claimant's life expectancy. Where the claimant has dependants, any structured settlement will usually provide for a minimum number of payments in case the claimant dies early, and will also provide a capital sum to cater for any contingencies. The claimant is also relieved of the financial pressures of managing a large sum of money.

The defendant insurer is, however, under a disadvantage as he is required to pay the gross amount to the claimant, reclaiming the tax withheld at the end of the financial year. Therefore, although the claimant receives a tax-free annuity, the defendant will suffer an administrative burden and the loss of cash flow in having to pay the gross amount before reclaiming the tax.

In considering whether to elect for a structured settlement, it would be an unwise solicitor who does not consider its potential disadvantages. Not necessarily a disadvantage but a point worth noting is that before making the structured settlement the parties usually estimate what the court would have awarded at trial; thus there is still a guessing element that goes with the lump sum award. Once set up, a structured settlement is there for the life of the claimant and cannot be changed. This can cause problems, for example, where the claimant's condition deteriorates unexpectedly so that he now needs expensive treatment or where he can no longer be cared for at home and requires a place in a residential home. The contingency fund may cope with these problems, but the greater the amount placed in such a fund the less the tax benefit to the claimant; any income generated by the fund is subject to income tax. Finally, there will be no legacy left to the claimant's dependants on his death – this may be considered both an advantage or disadvantage depending on how you view the situation.

Provisional damages

The introduction of provisional damages remedied another deficiency in the lump sum award. Usually, the claimant received his compensation in one sum. The problem arises when, for example, five years after that payment, the claimant finds his condition deteriorating. He cannot go back to court and try to claim more compensation. An award of provisional damages allows the claimant to obtain some compensation and still return to court at a later date should his condition deteriorate. The court can make an award of provisional damages under Supreme Court Act 1981 s 32A or County Courts Act 1984 s 51.

What situations will qualify for an award of provisional damages? In the case of *Willson v Ministry of Defence* [1991] 1 All ER 638 the court refused to make an order for provisional damages because the claimant had not established that there was a serious deterioration in his condition as opposed to a chance of continuing deterioration of his condition. The court held that for an award of provisional damages to be successful:

(1) there had to be a chance of the injury or disease deteriorating and that possibility had to be measurable rather than fanciful; and

(2) the deterioration must be serious in that it was something beyond ordinary deterioration; that was a question of fact, depending on the circumstances of the case.

Thus, for example, a claimant who contracts HIV through contaminated blood could apply for provisional damages on the basis that at some time in the future he may develop AIDS; similarly, a claimant who has a disease which is now in remission may claim for the chance that the disease may reoccur. However, even if those two conditions were satisfied, the court still had a discretion as to whether to award provisional damages. In *Willson,* the court regarded the development of osteo-arthritis as a progressive condition.

Note that the burden of proof is on the claimant to show there is a chance of deterioration.

Dependants can start proceedings under the Fatal Accidents Act 1976 where deterioration occurs and the claimant dies before further damages were agreed or ordered.

For procedural points, see pp 288 and 299.

Interim payment

An interim payment is, as the name suggests, an interim award, an advance on the claimant's damages. In clinical negligence litigation the need for immediate compensation can be great, for example where the claimant requires nursing care or incurs other medical expenses; consequently interim awards are very important.

CPR r 25.6 to r 25.9 deal with interim payments.

The court can make an order for an interim payment only if:

(a) the defendant against whom the order is sought has admitted liability to pay damages or some other money to the claimant;

(b) the claimant has obtained judgment against that defendant for damages to be assessed;

(c) it is satisfied that, if the claimant went to trial, the claimant would obtain judgment for a substantial amount of money (CPR r 25.7).

Clearly, the last ground in effect asks the court to do little more than guess what will be the eventual outcome of the action and, therefore, the claimant must show that his case is as strong as possible. The court can only make an order for interim payment if the defendant is insured (or liability will otherwise be met by an insurer) or the defendant is a public body. It will therefore be possible to obtain an order for interim payment of damages against a NHS Trust or Health Authority.

As the majority of points we wish to make with regard to interim payments are of a procedural nature they are all dealt with in the practice points at p 290.

REFERENCES

English case law

Willson v Ministry of Defence [1991] 1 All ER 638
See p 287.

Practice points

Structured settlements
CPR PD 40C sets out the requirements for making a structured settlement. A structured settlement can be made either on settlement of the case or after the claimant has won at trial. If a structured settlement is to be made after trial the claimant's representative should ask the judge to state the amount to which the claimant is entitled and request an adjournment so that advice can be obtained as to how a structured settlement should be formulated for that sum. If the claimant settles before trial an application for a consent order setting out the structured settlement should be made. A hearing is not required if the claimant is not a child or patient.

If the claimant is a child or patient, the court's approval is required and a hearing must take place. The following documentation/information must be filed in court before the hearing: Counsel's or the legal representative's opinion on the value of the claim, a draft structure agreement, information to enable the court to be satisfied (a) there is enough money retained as a contingency fund and (b) the structured settlement is secure and established insurers are paying the annuities. Details of other assets available to the claimant should be disclosed. If a claimant is a 'patient' for the purposes of the CPR (that is, a person who by reason of mental disorder cannot manage his own affairs) the approval or consent of the Court of Protection is also required. The Court of Protection will require sight of the above documentation together with a copy of the claim form and statements of case. The Practice Direction sets out examples of structured settlements.

Provisional damages
Provisional damages are dealt with by Part 41 of the CPR. Under Part 41 the court can make an order for provisional damages provided that the particulars of claim filed by the claimant include a claim for provisional damages and the court is satisfied that Supreme Court Act 1981, s 32A or County Courts Act 1984, s 51 applies. PD 16 sets out what the claimant must state in his particulars of claim. He must:

(1) state that he is seeking provisional damages under either Act; and

(2) state there is a chance he will develop some serious disease or serious deterioration in his physical/mental condition in the future; and

(3) specify the disease /type of deterioration which may lead to an application.

The particulars of claim may be prepared before the claimant's condition has settled. Where there is doubt as to how the condition will stabilise, it may be good practice to include a provisional damages claim, otherwise permission of the court would be required to amend these if it became apparent such a claim should be made. If the condition does indeed stabilise, the provisional damages element of the claim would not be pursued.

If a defendant fails to file an acknowledgment of service or a defence within the relevant time limits after the claimant has served the claim on him, a claimant can ordinarily apply for 'default judgment'. However, where provisional damages are being claimed, a claimant cannot apply for default judgment unless the claim for provisional damages is dropped. The claimant should instead make an application to the court for directions. The court will then order that the following issues should be decided (PD 41, para 5.1):

(1) whether the claim is an appropriate one for an award of provisional damages and if so, on what terms, and

(2) the amount of immediate damages.

A defendant can make a 'payment into court' for a sum of money to try to settle the case under Part 36 CPR. When offering to settle a claim where provisional damages are claimed a defendant has to specify whether he offers to agree to the making of an award of provisional damages. (See CPR r 36.7 for rules relating to defendants' offers to settle claims for provisional damages).

Where the court makes an order for provisional damages that order:

(1) must specify the disease or type of deterioration in respect of which an application may be made at a future date;

(2) must specify the period within which such an application may be made; and

(3) may be made in respect of more than one disease or type of deterioration and may, in respect of each disease or type of deterioration, specify a different period within which a subsequent application may be made (CPR r 41.2(2)).

A claimant can make more than one application to extend the time for applying for a further award. The court can specify the period for making a subsequent application as being for the duration of the life of the claimant (CPR PD 41 para 2.3).

If the parties agree that an order for provisional damages should be made, an application can be forwarded to court for a consent order to be made. Approval of the court is needed if the claimant is a child or 'patient' and the application for approval would ordinarily be dealt with at a hearing (CPR PD 41 para 4.1).

The practice direction states that the 'case file' documents which would include the judgment, statements of case, medical reports, etc, are to be preserved until the expiry of the period specified by the court.

Interim payments

CPR r 25.6 and CPR PD 25 sets out the general procedure for applying to court for an interim payment. The claimant's solicitor should first try to correspond with the defendant setting out the fact they seek an interim payment and requesting a voluntary payment. If a defendant refuses a court application can be made. *Note* a voluntary interim payment for a child or patient will require the court's permission.

A claimant can make an application to court for an interim payment after court proceedings have been served on the defendant and the time limit for filing an acknowledgment of service has passed. The claimant's application must be supported by evidence which deals with the following:

(1) the sum of money sought by way of an interim payment,

(2) the items or matters in respect of which the interim payment is sought ,

(3) the sum of money for which final judgment is likely to be given,

(4) the reasons for believing that if the claimant went to trial, the claimant would obtain a substantial sum of money,

(5) any other relevant matters,

(6) details of special damages and past and future loss.

Note the applicant does not have to demonstrate a need for the interim payment. Any relevant documents which support the application should be exhibited including any medical reports. If the respondent to the application wants to rely on written evidence at the hearing he must file the written evidence and serve copies on every other party to the application at least seven days before the hearing of the application. If the applicant wants to rely on written evidence in reply he has to file it and serve a copy on the respondent at least three days before the hearing of the application.

The claimant can make more than one application for an interim payment. Sometimes an application for an interim payment will be coupled with an application for summary judgment. If there are more than two defendants and each of the defendants is insured or is a public body, the court can make an order for an interim payment against any or all defendants even if the court at that stage cannot identify which defendant the applicant will succeed against at trial.

RULE 7(D)

Damages are essentially compensatory in nature. In certain circumstances damages may not be compensatory.

Commentary

Damages may be contemptuous, nominal, exemplary or (aggravated) punitive. For the purposes of clinical negligence, only the latter two are relevant.

Exemplary damages

These damages are awarded to teach the defendant a lesson (see *Rookes v Barnard* [1964] AC 1129). In practice, they are only awarded where:

(1) there has been oppressive, arbitrary or unconstitutional action by servants of the government; or

(2) the defendant's conduct has been calculated by him to make a profit for himself which may well exceed the compensation payable to the claimant; or

(3) they are specifically authorised by statute.

Furthermore, in *AB and Others v South West Water Services Ltd* [1993] QB 507, the courts decided that exemplary damages can only be awarded for those torts which were recognised as being appropriate for that particular claim before the decision in *Rookes v Barnard* [1964] AC 1129.

Exemplary damages have little or no part to play in clinical negligence claims in England, but they do feature in other jurisdictions, in particular, the United States. The main thrust of the argument against their introduction is that it would cause confusion between civil and criminal law but, given that the number of cases where they may be applicable are few and far between, this argument seems untenable. For the method of calculating the award, see *Rookes v Barnard* [1964] AC 1129 and *Broome v Cassell & Co Ltd* [1972] AC 1027.

The Law Commission in their report No 247, *Aggravated, Exemplary and Restitutionary Damages* (1997) recommended that exemplary damages should be renamed punitive damages and should be awarded in addition to any other remedy but only as a last resort where other remedies are inappropriate. The Commission stated that the situations they envisaged where such an award would be appropriate were where 'the defendant deliberately and outrageously disregarded the claimant's rights'. Exemplary damages should not, however, be awarded for breach of contract or for any civil wrong arising under statute and, further, the narrow tests laid down in *Rookes v Barnard and South West Water Services* should be abolished. Finally, the report recommended that judges and not juries should determine the level of damages, contrary to the views of APIL (Association of Personal Injury Lawyers).

Aggravated (punitive) damages

Essentially aggravated damages are compensatory in nature, but when the court awards such damages it usually takes into account the way in which the claimant was injured, for example, was the conduct of the defendant wilful and intentional and, consequently, was the claimant's injury and/or pride injured? In such circumstances, the court may award a higher level of damages. It seems that at present, the court is unlikely to award such damages in a clinical negligence field. In *Kralj v McGrath and St Theresa's Hospital* [1986] 1 All ER 54 where the claimant suffered appalling treatment during childbirth, the court ruled that aggravated damages were inappropriate in a clinical negligence case.

In *Appleton v Garrett* [1996] PIQR 1 the defendant dentist's conduct was labelled contumelious as he had deliberately inflicted pain and damage to his patients and had taken advantage of their young age. The defendant had performed unnecessary treatment on his patients' teeth in order to increase his income and had deliberately and in bad faith withheld from the claimants the information that the treatment was unnecessary. In making their ruling the court was clearly influenced by the fact that the defendant had committed this deceit on a large scale and had abused a position of trust.

The Law Commission in their Report No 247 (see above) recommended that aggravated damages should be awarded for mental distress or injury to feelings but should not be used as a means to punish the wrongdoer and neither should there be any restriction in the circumstances in which damages for mental distress may be recoverable. To date these recommendations have not been implemented but we would welcome any increase in damages for the *Kralj*-like case though we are still of the opinion that the courts will simply continue to increase the general damages award for pain and suffering in such situations whether or not these reforms ever become law.

REFERENCES

English case law

(1)   Rookes v Barnard [1964] AC 1129
See above, p 290.

(2)   AB and Others v South West Water Services Ltd [1993] QB 507
This was an action for public nuisance. The defendant had allegedly caused injury to the claimants by supplying contaminated water. As there was no similar claim for exemplary damages prior to 1964, the claimants' claim for exemplary damages was struck out.

(3)   Broome v Cassell & Co Ltd [1972] AC 1027; [1971] 2 QB 354
The commission of a tort in a malicious, insulting or oppressive manner may aggravate the claimant's injury.

(4)   Kralj v McGrath and St Theresa's Hospital [1986] 1 All ER 54
The claimant was pregnant with twins. Because of the defendant's negligence, one of the twins was born severely disabled and died eight weeks later. The claimant suffered a truly horrific time during the delivery and suffered shock at seeing the child's injuries and watching the child die over the eight week period following. The court ruled that aggravated damages were inappropriate in an action for negligence against a doctor and in addition no award was made in respect of the woman's grief, but the court took into account that the claimant's treatment might have increased her pain and suffering in relation to the death of her child.

See above, p 291.

See, also, *Devi v West Midlands Regional HA* (1981) *Kemp & Kemp*, Vol 2, F5-018 and F5-107, where compensatory damages of £4,000 were awarded in a case of non-consensual sterilisation without any reference to aggravated damages.

(5)   Appleton v Garrett [1996] PIQR P1
See above, p 291.

Practice points

Under CPR r 16.4, if a claimant is making a claim for aggravated damages or exemplary damages, the particulars of claim must contain a statement to that effect, together with the grounds for claiming them.

RULE 7(E)

Where a person has a cause of action against the defendant but dies before it has been resolved the defendant may still be liable to the estate of the deceased under the Law Reform (Miscellaneous Provisions) Act 1934, or to the dependants of the deceased under the Fatal Accidents Act 1976.

Commentary

Although these statutory claims have been grouped within one rule, for the sake of convenience they will be dealt with separately. However, the procedural aspects of both claims are dealt with together in the practice points section.

An action under the Law Reform (Miscellaneous Provisions) Act 1934

Section 1 of the 1934 Act does not create a cause of action, rather it allows the deceased's claim (with the exception of defamation) to survive after his death. In addition, s 1(4) of the Act allows an action to continue against a tortfeasor after the latter has died. For example where a GP negligently prescribes the wrong drug and dies before his patient has suffered damage from taking the drug over a long period, the patient will still have an action against the GP's estate.

Generally, the damages recoverable will be the same as if the claimant was still alive (for example, loss of earnings and other pecuniary losses from the date of injury until death), except that neither exemplary damages nor any amounts in respect of loss of income after the deceased's death is recoverable, see s 1(2)(a) of the Act. Claims prior to 1 January 1983 are outside the scope of this provision, see *Kemp and Kemp* 26–001 *et seq* for further guidance and *Gammell v Wilson and Swift & Co Ltd* [1982] AC 27 where the court allowed the estate to recover an amount in respect of the deceased's loss of earnings after his death. However, a bereavement claim is available under s 3 Administration of Justice Act 1982. In assessing a sum to reflect pain and suffering, damages cannot be recovered for pain which is suffered as a result of dying, see *Hicks v Chief Constable of West Yorkshire* [1992] 2 All ER 65. Where the death has been caused by the act or omission which gives rise to the cause of action, no account is to be taken of any loss or gain to the estate in the calculation of damages except that an additional claim may be made for funeral expenses if paid for by the estate.

Where it is the tortfeasor who dies, damages will be assessed in the normal way against his estate. In a clinical negligence claim, this provision is effectively redundant, since the claim will usually be against the health authority, Trust, private hospital, or against the GP's practice, although in the latter case the claim can be brought against the deceased GP's estate as well as against his fellow partners, see s 1(2)(c) of the Act.

An action under the Fatal Accidents Act 1976

Where the wrongful act of the defendant causes the death of the deceased, then a claim under this Act is possible. The claim is brought by the deceased's dependants and it is for the loss which has been suffered or is likely to be suffered. The claim may be brought by any dependant (for the definition of 'dependant', see p 300) and is a new action in its own right. It will only subsist if the deceased whilst alive could have sued the tortfeasor for his injuries, s 1(1). Additionally, if the deceased had already accepted compensation for his injuries before his death or if his claim was statute barred (see above, p 131) then the dependant(s) will have no claim.

The Act provides for three types of compensation: bereavement allowance, a claim for loss of dependency, and a claim for funeral expenses if paid by the dependants. The bereavement payment is fixed at £7,500 for deaths occurring after 1 April 1991, and £3,500 for deaths before that date. Interest will be payable on such a sum at the full rate. This will only be awarded to the spouse of the deceased or the parents of an unmarried minor child (but only the mother of an illegitimate child).

The loss of dependency claim can be brought by a wide class of dependants and, generally, will cover any amounts which they could have reasonably expected from the deceased had he not died. Thus, the court must take into account the characteristics of the dependants, for example, if the dependant has a short life expectancy. The benefit alleged to be lost must arise because of the relationship between the deceased and the dependant but, where the dependency occurs after the injury which causes the deceased's death, the spouse may still bring a claim under the Act (see *Phillips v Grampian Hospital Board* [1991] 3 Med LR 16 (a Scottish case)). Notice should be taken of the fact that there can be no claim under the Act in respect of the claimant's emotional dependency; the court is merely concerned with the financial dependency of the claimant on the deceased. See *Thomas v Kwik Save Stores Ltd* (2000) *The Times*, 27 June, and see, also, Law Commission Report No 263 1999: *Claims for Wrongful Death*.

The usual approach in assessing the damages is to take the deceased's net income and from that deduct a figure which represents an amount which the deceased will have spent on himself. Any other benefits such as a company car or cheap mortgage should be added in calculating the net income. This figure is the multiplicand. The figure can only be an approximate one as it will often be very difficult to apportion expenditure between family members. Alternatively, the multiplicand may be calculated by building up a profile of the deceased's income and expenditure. In the case where a mother has died, there may be other factors to take into account in assessing the multiplicand and the proper award to the child dependants. Where the deceased did not provide any earnings but provided services such as caring for children, the usual figure will be either the cost of employing someone to look after the children (*Regan v Williamson* [1976] 1 WLR 305) or the earnings lost by the other parent in having to stay at home and look after the children (*Mehmet v Perry* [1977] 2 All ER 529) providing that the decision to stay home was reasonable. Where the children would be looked after by a relative, the wage should be net of tax and national insurance contributions. Where children had lost their mother, the court ruled in *Spittle v Bunney* [1988] 1 WLR 847 that the mother's services could not be valued at a constant figure for the whole of the child's dependency; it therefore raised the award by some 10%.

Note that the multiplicand is assessed at the date of trial, that is, the income the deceased would have been earning had he been alive. In practice, the court assesses the deceased's income at the date of his death and the degree of dependency of each claimant and then revises it in the light of his expected income at the date of trial.

Future loss of earnings is calculated in exactly the same way as for a living claimant (see p 248); however, the multiplier is a figure decided at the date of death and not the date of the trial as for a living claimant (see *Graham v Dodds* [1983] 1 WLR 808). Exactly what the multiplier will be depends on the characteristics of the dependants, for example, age, health, expectation of working life, and was it foreseeable that the deceased's income would rise in the immediate future; if so, the multiplier is likely to be increased. In addition, the court must take into account any period which has elapsed between the death and the date of the trial. On this point, see *Corbett v Barking, Havering and Brentwood HA* [1991] 2 QB 408 where on appeal the multiplier was increased to reflect that the claimant was aged eleven-and-a-half at the time of trial (her mother died at her birth). In assessing the multiplier, no account is taken of inflation. Interest is awarded pre-trial at half the short-term investment rates current between the date of death and trial and there is no interest on future losses. Generally, the court assumes that the award will be invested to provide an annuity and will also take into account whether the award is likely to be subject to heavy taxation. As regards the dependant's future prospects, s 3 states that no account shall be taken of the widow's prospect of remarriage; however, the same does not apply for the widower's chances of remarriage, or for that matter a widow when assessing a child's dependency, however, it seems by the application of s 4 as substituted by s 3(1) Administration of Justice Act 1982, the same result is achieved by a widower, see below. With regard to a cohabitee, the court will take into account that there is no legal duty on the deceased to maintain the cohabitee and consequently reduce the damages accordingly. The court can take into consideration the likelihood that the parties might have divorced and in doing so the court will have regard to the fact that one-third of marriages end in divorce (see *Owen v Martin and Another* [1992] PIQR 151).

The court will disregard any benefits the dependants receive in calculating the compensation payable under the 1976 Act (s 4); this includes benefits which have accrued and those which will accrue. But exactly what constitutes a benefit has proved somewhat elusive. In *Stanley v Saddique* [1992] QB 1, the court ruled that the word 'benefit' should be given a wide meaning and in that case it was held to include care provided by a stepmother to a child who had lost his natural mother in an accident, notwithstanding that the care provided was better than that which could have been provided by the child's natural mother. The award, however, was still reduced to reflect the prospects of the services continuing.

The benefit lost must be as a result of the deceased's death and directly related to the relationship between the deceased and the dependant. In *Hayden v Hayden* [1992] 1 WLR 986, the defendant was the father of the infant claimant whose claim was in respect of the loss of her mother's care. The defendant had given up work to look after the child and it was held that this was not a benefit pursuant to s 4 but, rather, it was a factor to be taken into account in calculating the claimant's loss under s 3(1). This decision appears, at first, to be at odds with the cases of *Stanley* and *Hay v Hughes* [1975] QB 790 where the court, in considering the application of s 3(1), held that care provided by the deceased's grandmother could be disregarded as it was provided out of the generosity of the grandmother and not because of the deceased's death. *Stanley* was distinguished from *Hayden* on the ground that in the former an unstable relationship had been replaced by something rather better, whereas in the latter the father was simply carrying out his parental duties. However, it seems clear that the services were provided as a direct result of the mother's death and the court erroneously took into account the continuing benefit of her father's services. Whatever the artificial distinction, it now appears that the courts have resolved the dilemma by adopting the approach taken in *Donnelly v Joyce* [1974] QB 454 and *Hunt v Severs* [1994] 2 All ER 385. In *Donnelly*, the claimant was allowed to claim for his mother's loss of wages as a result of her giving up her employment to care for him, although the court held that such damages should be held in trust for the third party. In *Hunt*, it was held that there can be no claim for services rendered by the tortfeasor, despite the fact that he is insured. This seems a more sensible approach as it is illogical for a claimant to hold damages on trust for the defendant!

See, also, *R v Criminal Injuries Compensation Board ex p K (Minors)* [2000] PIQR Q32 where the court said *Hayden* did not establish any general principle of law applicable to the valuation of children's claims. In this case the mother of three young children was murdered by her husband. The children were then cared for by the husband's brother and his wife. The court had originally found themselves bound by *Hayden* and held that, as the general parental services provided by an uncle and aunt were at least as good as those provided by their mother before her death, the children had suffered no loss and those services should be disregarded by virtue of s 4. The Divisional Court, however, followed the decision in *Stanley v Saddique* and held that *Hayden* was distinguishable because in that case the services taken on by the father (who was also the tortfeasor) after the mother's death were not new but simply an extension of his existing parental duties. In this case, however, the services were provided by an independent third party and provided that those services were at least equivalent to those provided by the deceased s 4 stipulates that the benefit has resulted from the death and is therefore disregarded.

In assessing damages, the court will deduct any amount which they consider just to reflect contributory negligence by the deceased (s 5). Additionally, where the deceased's death was the fault of the deceased and one of the dependants, it seems likely that the dependant will have his compensation reduced to a degree proportionate to his responsibility. If the death was caused by the negligence of the dependant, this would debar him from claiming but it has no effect on the other dependants.

According to s 3(1), damages will be awarded to the dependants in proportion to the injury suffered, but the courts have said they will assess the loss as a whole and then apportion it between the dependants (see *Davies v Powell Duffryn Associated Collieries Ltd* [1942] AC 601). The case of *Harris v Empress Motors Ltd* [1984] 1 WLR 212 acts a as a useful guide (where there are no unusual features): if the husband is killed and the wife does not work, dependency will be approximately 66% of the husband's total income; if both spouses worked, dependency will be 66% of the joint income; if there are children, the figure rises to around 75%. However, this will only apply in a 'usual' case; so where the wife was earning a substantial sum before the deceased's death or perhaps has substantial private income, this rule may be inappropriate (see *Coward v Comex Houlder Diving Ltd* [1984] 1 WLR 212).

Recently, the Court of Appeal looked at the question of dependency in relation to state benefits and fraudulent earnings. In *Hunter v Butler* [1996] RTR 396, the claimant's husband was killed in a road traffic accident. Before his death, he was in receipt of supplementary benefit and was also working part-time; however, he did not disclose these earnings to the DSS. The court held that since, after his death, the claimant had claimed a widow's allowance and a widowed mother's allowance, and continued to receive housing benefit as before, the death of her husband did not cause her any loss, she remained dependent on the State. Moreover, the court held that it would be contrary to public policy to allow dependency on the assumption that the deceased would have continued to claim benefits without disclosing his earnings. The claimant was privy to the deceased's conduct and had also committed an offence, hence she was precluded from recovering damages – see, further, *Kemp & Kemp* para 26-006.

The loss of social security benefits has been held to amount to loss of financial dependency though it will depend on the type of benefit lost see *Cox v Hockenhull* [1999] 3 All ER 577.

Note that the recovery of social security benefits is not applicable to awards made under the Fatal Accidents Act (see further Rule 7(B) at p 281.

Finally, a claim may be made for funeral expenses where those expenses have been paid by the dependants (s 3(3)). Regrettably, there is no definition of funeral expenses in either the 1976 Act or the 1934 Law Reform (Miscellaneous Provisions) Act; however, it will only be reasonable funeral expenses (see *Gammell v Wilson and Swift & Co Ltd* [1982] AC 27, *Quainoo v Brent and Harrow AHA* (1982) 132 NLJ 1100 and *Smith v Marchioness/Bowbelle* (1993) *The Times*, 27 January).

REFERENCES

English case law

(1) Gammell v Wilson and Swift & Co Ltd [1982] AC 27
This case is set out in full at para 20-051 in *Kemp and Kemp*.

(2) Hicks and Others v Chief Constable of the West Yorkshire Police [1992] 2 All ER 65
See above, p 245.

(3) Thomas v Kwik Save Stores Ltd (2000) The Times, 27 June
See above, p 294.

(4) Regan v Williamson [1976] 1 WLR 305
This case involved the death of a non-wage-earning wife and mother. It was held that the court should value the husband's loss by taking the cost of employing a housekeeper plus the value of those services which were not replaceable.

(5) Mehmet v Perry [1977] 2 All ER 529
See above, p 294.

(6) Spittle v Bunney [1988] 1 WLR 847
See above, at p 294. The award was increased from £25,000 to £47,500. The court ruled that it could not value the mother's services at a constant figure for the whole of the dependency.

(7) Graham v Dodds [1983] 1 WLR 808
See above, p 295.

(8) Corbett v Barking, Havering and Brentwood HA [1991] 2 QB 408; [1990] 3 WLR 1037
A claim was brought for the benefit of a boy who was aged 11 and a half at the date of the trial. The court applied a multiplier of 15 (normally a multiplier of 12 would have been used); the court, however, applied a multiplier of 3.5 for the post-trial loss.

(9) Owen v Martin (1992) The Times, 21 May; [1992] PIQR Q151
See above, p 295.

(10) Stanley v Saddique [1992] QB 1
Sec above, p 295.

(11) Hayden v Hayden [1992] 1 WLR 986
See above, p 295.

(12) Hay v Hughes [1975] QB 790
See above, p 296.

(13) Donnelly v Joyce [1974] QB 454
See above, p 296.

(14) Hunt v Severs [1994] 2 All ER 385
See above, p 296.

(15) R v Criminal Injuries Compensation Board ex p K (Minors) [2000] PIQR Q32
See above, p 296.

(16) Davies v Powell Duffryn Associated Collieries Ltd [1942] AC 601
See above, p 296.

(17) Harris v Empress Motors Ltd [1984] 1 WLR 212; [1983] 3 All ER 561
See p above, 296.

(18) Coward v Comex Houlder Diving Ltd [1984] 1 WLR 212
It was held that the judge at first instance had adopted the wrong approach in that it was not for the court to ask whether the evidence displaced the conventional or usual figure of two-thirds/one-third. The judge should have asked whether the evidence required or permitted him to take a larger figure into account. As he did not do so, it was up to the court to examine the findings of fact and the evidence to see whether any larger figure was justified. In this case, the amount of dependency should be calculated by reference to 60% of the net earnings instead of two-thirds.

(19) Hunter v Butler [1996] RTR 396
See above, p 297.

(20) Quainoo v Brent and Harrow AHA (1982) 132 NLJ 1100
This case involved the funeral of a member of the Ghanaian royal family. The cost of transporting the body back to Ghana and the cost of the relatives' air fares and cars for the funeral procession were allowed, but not the costs of funeral cards, wreaths, photographer and the hire of a hall and funeral attire.

(21) Smith v Marchioness / Bowbelle (1993) The Times, 27 January
The claimant was allowed £400 for a reception of wine and canapés for 300 people after the funeral.

(22) Avery v LNER [1938] AC 606
See Practice points below, p 301.

(23) Shepherd v Post Office (1995) The Times, 14 June
See Practice points below, p 301.

Foreign case law

Scotland

Phillips v Grampian Hospital Board [1991] 3 Med LR 16
Although this is a Scottish case, it is more than likely that the same principles would apply in English law. The deceased had begun an action against the defenders for failure to diagnose a testicular tumour. The defenders argued that as the pursuer had married the deceased knowing that he was suffering from a fatal illness she could not sue in respect of his death. Moreover, as her husband was already dying, the pursuer could not claim for loss of society or support because she never had any expectation of obtaining this in her marriage. The court rejected this argument, ruling that s 1(3) Fatal Accidents Act 1976 provided that damages were not simply awarded for an unexpected death but the pursuer had a right to be compensated for loss of support suffered or likely to be suffered as a result of the defender's omission. The date of the marriage was irrelevant because the assumption was that the deceased would not have died but for the negligence of the defenders.

Statutes/statutory instruments

(1) Law Reform (Miscellaneous Provisions) Act 1934
See below, Appendix A.

(2) Fatal Accidents Act 1976
See below, Appendix A.

(3) Administration of Justice Act 1982, s 3(1)

Practice points

- The 1934 and the 1976 Acts are distinct: damages claimed under the former go to the estate, whereas any compensation recovered under the 1976 Act goes to the dependants. Usually, claims under both Acts will be brought together, see the Practice Direction to CPR Part 16 at para 5.3. If the death does not occur until sometime after the accident, it is likely that proceedings will have commenced prior to death.

Note that a missing dependant cannot bring a second action under the 1976 Act (see *Avery v LNER* [1938] AC 606). Conversely, the defendant cannot rely on missing dependants to justify a lowering of the award to other dependants, since each dependant has a separate judgment debt.

- The definition of a dependant under the 1976 Act is set out at Appendix A and includes the following (s 1(3)):
  - (a) the spouse or former spouse of the deceased;
  - (b) a person who has been living with the deceased as 'husband or wife' in the same household two years prior to his or her death;
  - (c) any parent, or other ascendant of the deceased including a person who was treated as a parent;
  - (d) any child or other descendant of the deceased including a child treated as a child of the family by the deceased;
  - (e) any person who is, or is the issue of, a sibling, uncle or aunt of the deceased;
  - (f) an adopted/stepchild/illegitimate child of the deceased;
  - (g) a common law spouse providing he or she has been living with the deceased two years prior to the accident. See the recent case of *Shepherd v Post Office* (1995) *The Times*, 14 June which held that a divorced woman who remarried but later returned to her first husband was capable of being a dependant under the Fatal Accidents Act 1976 as a former wife and did not have to show that she had been living with the deceased in the same household prior to his death. The courts now appear to be more concerned with the facts of the situation rather than being simply bound by the two year rule.

- A claim under the 1976 Act should be brought by the personal representatives of the deceased; however, if they fail to sue within six months of the deceased's death, then any dependant may bring the action in his own name or on behalf of himself and others (s 2). There is a time limit of three years which runs from the date of the deceased's death.

- Where death was instantaneous, damages under the Law Reform (Miscellaneous Provisions) Act will be limited to funeral expenses which in any event are recoverable under the Fatal Accidents Act; thus only a claim under the Act should be brought.

- In a fatal accident claim the particulars of claim must state the following: that the claim is being brought under the Fatal Accidents Act 1976, the dependants on whose behalf it is made, the date of birth of the dependants and details of the nature of the dependency claim. A claim for damages for bereavement can be included. The claimant can, on behalf of the deceased, bring a claim under the Law Reform (Miscellaneous Provisions) Act 1934 (CPR PD, paras 16.5.1–16.5.3).

  Additionally, the particulars of claim must include those matters required by CPR PD 16, para 5.1. These are:
  (i) that the claim is being brought under the Fatal Accidents Act 1976;
  (ii) the names of all dependants on whose behalf the claim is made;
  (iii) the date of birth of each dependant;
  (iv) details of the nature of the dependency claim.

  Additionally, it is usual to state the date of death of the deceased and details of the grant of probate or administration. *Note* that para 5.2 of the Practice Direction states that any fatal accident claim may include a claim for damages for bereavement.

- The schedule of special damages should cover all pre-death losses and losses suffered by the dependants.
- If there is to be an inquest, the client should be advised that public funding will not be available and therefore any attendance will have to be paid for privately. *Note* that inquest evidence cannot be admitted as evidence at the trial unless both parties agree.
- Under CPR r 37.4, where a claim involves a claim arising under the Fatal Accidents Act 1976 and the Law Reform (Miscellaneous Provisions) Act 1934 and the claimant accepts money paid into court in satisfaction of the claims, the court will apportion the money between the claims.
- Where a claim was made under the Fatal Accidents Act 1976 by more than one person or on behalf of more than one person, the court will apportion the sum of money accepted between the persons who are entitled to it, unless the court has already apportioned this or the parties have reached agreement on how this should be apportioned (CPR r 37.4).
- Where a child or patient is to receive part of the sum that is to be apportioned the approval of the court is required (CPR PD 21, para 1.6). For rules relating to children and patients generally, see p 309).

GENERAL PRACTICE POINTS – RULES 7(A)–(E)

Many of the points listed below are dealt with in the paragraphs above in more detail. We do not propose to discuss in detail how a special damages schedule should be calculated; there are numerous texts which deal more than adequately with that subject. What follows is a ready reckoner on the subject; a checklist designed to act more as a reminder than anything else. As a final note it is suggested that the starting point should always be to send the claimant a questionnaire to encourage him to keep a record of his past and continuing loss.

DAMAGES SCHEDULE

Pain and suffering	[What was the nature of the injury? Was the claimant suffering from a previous injury or illness (see above, p 245)?]
Amenity	[What effect has the injury had on the client's lifestyle (see above, p 246)? Consider what additional expenses have been generated by this claim.]
Psychiatric damage	[Is there a recognisable illness? Do you need an expert report? Is it ongoing? (see above, p 263).]
Loss of chance	[Unlikely to succeed; instead formulate as a *McGhee* claim if possible (see above, p 256).]
Wrongful birth:	[Limited damages may be awarded for the birth of either a healthy or disabled child. It is important to find out what is the family's lifestyle (see above, p 257).]

The client's loss of earnings

- Has the client returned to work?
- Is the client a minor? You will have to speculate on what the client could have earned.

Generally, the following matters should be considered for loss of earnings to date:

(1) You need a six month comparison. Remember to check that the figures are truly comparable, for example, overtime, promotion and fluctuating wage rates. Figures are usually obtained from the employer. Obtain an expert's report, if appropriate. Did the client have different employers? Do you need to contact the tax office (you will need client approval)? See also the Court of Appeal decisions of *Langford v Hebron and Another* [2001] All ER 169; [2001] ECWA CIV 36 and *Doyle v Wallace* [1998] PIQR 416 – both cases give guidance for claims for loss of earnings (and other losses) where the claimant's future prospects are uncertain.

If the client is returning to work, what will his salary be and what will be the date of his return? If he has already returned, what is his present salary? Has he returned to work less well paid?

(2) Obtain a copy of the client's contract of employment; check the position as regards statutory sick pay.

(3) Remember that income must be calculated net of tax; what is the client's personal allowance? What was the client's personal allowance for each of the tax years? Do not forget national insurance contributions.

(4) Remember that the client must give credit for all benefits received. Which benefits would he have continued to receive notwithstanding the accident?

Note the client must give credit for all earnings he receives as a result of the accident.

Special cases
If the client is self-employed you may need an accountant's or actuary's report (which will have to be disclosed).

Note that the accountant or actuary will need all the client's personal details. Do not forget that actuarial tables can now be admitted pursuant to the Civil Evidence Act 1995.

Expenses because of the accident
It is very important that the client keeps an up-to-date record of all his expenses whether by diary or otherwise, for example, bank or credit card statements. Such expenses might include:

(1) Transport (for example, to and from hospital: how many visits, did other members of the family incur travelling expenses?).

(2) Special equipment such as handrails, ramps, etc.

(3) Private medical care (see s 2(4) Law Reform Personal Injuries Act 1948).

(4) Any special dietary requirements.

(5) Holidays.

(6) Heating/lighting/telephone.

(7) Damage to clothing; any special clothing required.

(8) Any accommodation losses (likely to be future losses).

(9) Cost of carer, for example, member of the family (likely to be future losses).

(10) Wages lost by any other member of the family as a result of the accident.

Future losses
As above, but in particular consider:

(1) Accommodation – *Roberts v Johnstone* [1988] 3 WLR 1247 (see above, p 252).

(2) Cost of future care – not only for the client but also for the client's children, for example, will someone be required to collect the children from school? Also consider who is to provide the care: if it is a member of the client's family the value of the service may be difficult to calculate – try using home help rates.

(3) Future medical treatment costs.

(4) Counselling – did the client suffer psychiatric damage?

(5) Therapy – this generic term covers all sorts of therapy, for example, occupational, speech, physiotherapy, etc.

(6) Education – if the client is a minor or disabled will he now require any special educational needs, for example, the purchase of a new computer, home tuition?

(7) Fees – will any fees be payable now or in the future, for example, Court of Protection fees, fees payable for financial advice, etc?

(8) Child's earnings.

Loss of future earnings
There is not much to say here which has not already been said (p 248), except to reiterate that account should also be taken of the loss of earnings of anyone affected by the client's injuries.

Finally do not forget

(1) Interest – at applicable rates.

(2) Costs – agree if possible but remember they are always in the discretion of the court.

HOW THE CASE WILL PROCEED

As the discussion of the substantive law of negligence comes to an end it seems appropriate to conclude with some comments on the procedural aspects of a clinical negligence claim. Solicitors will have access to the Civil Procedure Rules. The following therefore is not an exhaustive commentary; rather it is a guide to some of the more important points that should be borne in mind.

Before proceedings are commenced

The Clinical Negligence Pre-Action Protocol governs what steps ought to be taken before court proceedings are issued. The Protocol is designed to encourage the parties to settle the case without starting litigation, encourage early exchange of information and ensure that if proceedings are issued they will be managed efficiently. Under the Protocol the claimant will send a detailed letter of claim to the defendant. The letter must be sufficiently detailed to enable the defendant to investigate the claim properly. The Protocol contains a template of a letter of claim. The defendant should acknowledge the letter within 21 days. The defendant then has three months to investigate the claim and respond to it. If the defendant denies liability, reasons must be given. The claimant should not issue proceedings during the period allowed for investigation, unless proceedings need to be issued because the limitation period is due to expire (see Chapter 4 for discussion regarding limitation periods). The defendant will forward copies of the claimant's medical records to the claimant during this protocol period.

Issue of court proceedings

Court proceedings are issued when the claim form together with supporting documentation are delivered to the court. The court will issue the claim and allocate a claim number. The claim form will be accompanied by the Particulars of Claim. The Particulars of Claim must contain a concise statement of facts on which the claimant relies. For claims brought under the Human Rights Act 1998, the normal rules apply for beginning a claim; however the statement of case must set out the provision of or right arising under the HRA or the remedy available under the HRA and must include all matters as specified by PD 7, para 2.10(2). These include giving precise details of the Convention right allegedly infringed and details of the relief sought.

The claimant then has four months to serve proceedings on the defendant, see CPR r 7.5(2). When the Particulars of Claim is served it must be accompanied by a medical report and schedule of special damages. The defendant must then acknowledge service or file a defence within 14 days of service.

Allocation

Once the court becomes aware a claim is to be defended 'allocation questionnaires' will be sent out to be completed by the claimant and defendant. The judge will use these allocation questionnaires to assist him in allocating the claim to a 'track' (see CPR r 26 and its Practice Direction for the procedure for this and the criteria for allocation to the tracks). Civil litigation cases are split into three tracks: small claims track, fast track and multi-track. As a general principle cases worth less than £5,000 (where damages for pain and suffering are less than £1,000) are allocated to the small claims track and straightforward cases worth £5,000–£15,000 are allocated to the fast track. Cases worth more than £15,000 with a trial estimate of more than one day are generally allocated to the multi-track. If more than one expert per party in more than two expert fields would be needed to give oral evidence this is a factor that should result in a claim being allocated to the multi-track. Clinical negligence claims would ordinarily be allocated to the multi-track (CPR r 29). This is the most flexible track, which accommodates the needs of complex cases.

Case management

The court is obliged to manage cases to further the court's overriding objective of dealing with cases justly. The overriding objective states that dealing with a case justly would include: ensuring the parties are on an equal footing; saving expense; dealing with cases in ways which are proportionate to the amount involved, to the importance of the case, to the complexity of the issues, to the parties' financial position; ensuring that cases are dealt with expeditiously; and allocating an appropriate share of the court's resources to a case (see CPR r 1.1(2)). The judge can manage a case at various stages once proceedings are issued, for example, at allocation. The judge can also order that a case management conference be held. Both parties' solicitors would have to attend such a hearing. Judges' case management powers are wide. They can, for example, bring forward hearing dates, join different proceedings together, decide the order in which issues are to be tried or exclude an issue from consideration. Either on allocation or at a case management conference directions will be ordered. These directions constitute a timetable for the future conduct of the case. Directions, for example, can be made providing for disclosure of documents, exchange of lay witness evidence and expert reports (discussed, further, below).

Disclosure

Both parties are under an obligation to disclose documentation relevant to the case even if it is potentially detrimental to them. The court should make an order providing for each party to serve a 'list of documents' on the other party, together with an order providing for inspection of the documents contained in the list. The court can order each party to provide 'standard disclosure', in which case each party must disclose the following: the documents on which he relies, the documents which adversely affect his own case or support another party's case together with any further documents which must be disclosed under any relevant practice direction (see CPR rr 31.6, 31.10). A party is required to undertake a 'reasonable search' for these documents. Some disclosure and exchange of information should have occurred before proceedings were issued. The defendant ought to have disclosed the claimant's medical records to the claimant during the three month protocol period. Once proceedings have been issued there may be further updated medical records to disclose.

If a party considers that the other party has not made proper disclosure, they may make a court application requesting specific disclosure, describing the document or class of documents that should be disclosed in the application (see CPR r 31.12). A party does not have to disclose a document that is legally privileged. If a document is created for the purpose of giving or receiving legal advice it will be privileged. If documents were created before the possibility of litigation became apparent, they will not be privileged. A party's duty of disclosure is continuing; if relevant documentation comes to light further on in proceedings this must also be disclosed. If a party fails to disclose a document, then they cannot rely upon it at trial without the court's permission, CPR r 31.21.

Witness statements

The witness statement will be an amalgamation of all the client's proofs of evidence adapted to meet the requirements of the Civil Procedure Rules (see CPR r 32.4(1)), which set out various requirements regarding the content and format of witness statements. The initial statement taken from the claimant (proof of evidence) will contain all the evidence the claimant can remember, including opinion evidence. Opinion evidence must be edited out of the witness statement, which will be exchanged with the other side.

Hearsay evidence can be included in a witness statement. It is admissible under s 1 of the Civil Evidence Act 1995. It is defined under s 1(2)(b) as 'a statement made otherwise than by a person while giving oral evidence in the proceedings which is tendered as evidence of the matters stated'. If you were to rely on hearsay evidence, a hearsay notice would have to be served on the other party under s 2 of the 1995 Act. A failure to comply with the notice procedure will not render the evidence inadmissible but the court may take this into account in assessing the weight to be attached to the hearsay evidence and, further, may penalise a party in costs (s 2(4)). Under s 4(1) of the 1995 Act the court will assess what weight should be given to the evidence. The court will consider whether it would have been reasonable and practical to call the witness instead; whether the statement was made contemporaneously; if the statement is multiple hearsay; if the maker has any motive to conceal or misrepresent facts; if the statement has been edited or is the product of collaboration with another; and, finally, if the statement is being adduced as hearsay evidence to try and circumvent a proper evaluation of its weight.

Part 32 of the Civil Procedure Rules and the accompanying practice direction contain various provisions regarding the formal requirements for the content of witness statements. The heading of the statement must be in a certain format. The heading of the action should be at the top of the statement. In the top right hand corner of the statement the following information should be set out: the party on whose behalf the statement is made, the initials and surname of the witness, the number of the statement in relation to that witness, whether there are any exhibits and the date the statement was made. The statement should contain details in chronological order. The name, address, capacity, occupation and relation to the proceedings of those making the statement should be included. If the statement contains information that is not from the witness's own knowledge this must be indicated together with the source of the information. A witness statement must contain a statement of truth at the end in the following form, 'I believe that the facts stated in this witness statement are true'.

It is important that all the witnesses who may be needed are contacted and witness statements prepared. On occasions the solicitor may be unable to trace a witness. In such situations, he may ask for permission to serve a witness summary, which will contain the evidence the witness would probably give. A witness summary would be of use if there is a possibility of being able to trace the witness and calling the witness to give oral evidence.

The witness statement must contain all the evidence which the witness intends to adduce; therefore it must be reviewed in the light of the statements of case (the particulars of the claim and the defence), the medical reports and medical records. Any discrepancies must be considered.

Note: the witness will be unable to adduce any evidence not contained in his statement without the court's permission (see CPR r 32.5).

Tactically what should or should not go into the witness statement is a personal matter; but remember the court must not be misled. What should always be considered is that evidence detrimental to the claimant's case is likely to come out in cross-examination and therefore to lessen its effect it should be adduced as evidence-in-chief.

Once exchange has taken place any inconsistencies between the claimant's evidence and the defendant's statements should be attended to; in addition check that all the defendant's witnesses have given the same version of events.

Expert reports

Clearly, the claimant will have already disclosed at least one medical report with his particulars of claim. In many cases a further report will be required to provide an update on the claimant's condition and prognosis. The court on allocation or at a case management conference will provide a date for exchange of expert reports within the order for directions. Exchange of reports should take place simultaneously.

Written questions can be put to an expert instructed by the opponent under CPR r 35.6. These questions must be served within 28 days of service of the expert's report. Questions must be put for clarification purposes only. The solicitor may well send the expert's report to his own medical expert and instruct him to prepare relevant questions arising from the report. An expert can decline to answer the questions received if the questions go beyond seeking clarification.

Meetings can be held between experts. Where the claimant and defendant have both instructed experts (which is the norm in clinical negligence cases) the court can make an order that the parties' experts discuss the case in order to narrow down the issues in dispute between the parties (CPR r 35.12). The parties should seek to agree an agenda for the meeting. The court will also usually order that the experts prepare a joint report setting out the issues on which they are able to agree and the issues on which they disagree (together with their reasons for disagreement). If they largely disagree it would be appropriate for the experts to attend the hearing in order to give oral evidence. See further Practice points, p 243 and 'Guidelines on experts' discussions in the context of clinical disputes' (2000) 6 Clinical Risk 149–52.

Preparation for trial

When the court makes directions on allocation/at a case management conference, one of the directions would provide for the parties to file 'listing questionnaires' (CPR r 29.6). The questionnaires are completed so that a date can be fixed for trial and a timetable for the trial can be set. At this time the judge can make any further necessary directions. Directions can be made as to whether oral expert evidence is necessary. The court can hold a pre-trial review if the case is complex and involves many parties, or if the case is likely to be lengthy.

Under CPR PD 39A, para 3.1, a claimant must file a 'trial bundle' in court not more than seven days and not less than three days before the start of trial. Generally the trial bundle should comprise copies of the following:

(1) the claim form and all statements of case;

(2) a case summary and/or chronology where appropriate;

(3) requests for further information and responses to the requests;

(4) all witness statements to be relied on as evidence;

(5) any witness summaries;

(6) any notices of intention to rely on hearsay evidence under CPR r 33.2 or other evidence under CPR r 33.6;

(7) any medical reports and responses to them;

(8) any experts' reports and responses to them;

(9) any order giving directions as to the conduct of the trial; and

(10) any other necessary documents.

The originals of the above documents should be available at trial. The bundle should be paginated, indexed and should normally be in a ring binder or lever arch file. The contents of the trial bundle should be agreed between the parties if possible. The party who files the trial bundle should provide identical bundles to all the parties and for the use of the witnesses.

A case summary should also be prepared in accordance with CPR PD 34A. This will help to identify the points that are agreed and the points that are disputed between the parties.

Where witnesses (lay or expert) are to be called to give oral evidence, it is good practice to consider issuing witness summonses (CPR r 34.3) to help ensure attendance at court. Even if a witness is willing to give evidence, a witness summons will assist, for example the witness will be able to obtain leave from work with greater ease.

As a final point, we think it appropriate to say something about the introduction of Part 36 offers and payments, although this is by no means a comprehensive account of the procedure – for further details see CPR Part 36 and its Practice Direction. Part 36 offers and payments have provided both claimants and defendants with a significant weapon with which they can persuade their opponent to settle. In brief, they provide that, if the opponent refuses the offer and goes on to do worse at trial than the offer made, they run the risk of incurring further costs and, in some cases, further interest charges on damages. Claimants can make Part 36 offers to settle the case at any time before or after the commencement of proceedings. Such an offer will invariably be to accept a sum of money in settlement of the claim. The defendant has 21 days in which to accept the offer. If the defendant decides to accept, then the claimant will be entitled to the sum of money he has offered plus his costs up to the notice of acceptance. If, however, the defendant decides to reject the offer and the claimant then goes on to win his case and recovers more than the offer made, then the defendant may be ordered to:

- pay interest on any sum of money awarded to the claimant at a rate not exceeding 10% above base rate for some or all of the period starting with the latest date on which the defendant could have accepted the offer;

- pay the claimant's costs on an indemnity basis from the latest date on which the defendant could have accepted the offer;

- pay interest on the claimant's costs from the latest date on which the defendant could have accepted the offer at a rate not exceeding 10% above the base rate, see r 36.21.

Defendants may also make a Part 36 offer or payment, though for any monetary claim, once proceedings have commenced, the defendant must make a Part 36 payment into court. As before, the claimant has 21 days in which to decide whether or not to accept the offer. If, however, he chooses not to accept the offer and he fails to better the Part 36 payment at trial, then, pursuant to r 36.20, the court will order the claimant to pay the defendant's costs for some or all of the period, starting with the latest date that the claimant could have accepted the offer or payment. This effectively means that, although the claimant will have been awarded some damages, a significant proportion of these will be used to pay the defendant's costs. If the claimant does better than the Part 36 payment at trial, then the usual order for costs will be made, ie costs follow the event.

Children and patients

It is appropriate to include a brief section on the additional procedures that need to be followed where children and patients are involved, given that a significant number of clinical negligence claims are brought on their behalf.

Part 21 of the CPR sets out the general principles to be followed when conducting a case on behalf of a 'child' or 'patient'.

(1) Under Part 21 a 'child' means a person under 18 and a 'patient' means a person who by reason of mental disorder within the meaning of the Mental Health Act 1983 is incapable of managing and administering his own affairs.

(2) Both a patient and a child must have a 'litigation friend' to conduct proceedings on their behalf. On occasions the court can make an order allowing a child to conduct proceedings without a litigation friend. This would depend upon the circumstances of the child and the nature of the claim. A person authorised under Part VII of the Mental Health Act 1983 to conduct legal proceedings on the patient's behalf can be the patient's litigation friend. A person can become a litigation friend without a court order if he:

(a) can fairly and competently conduct proceedings on behalf of the child or patient;

(b) has no interest adverse to that of the child or patient; and

(c) undertakes to pay the costs which the child or patient may be ordered to pay.

A person who wants to act as a litigation friend must file a certificate of suitability, unless they are authorised under the Mental Health Act 1983 in which case an official copy of document authorising him to act must be filed. Otherwise, the court can make an order appointing a litigation friend.

When a child reaches 18, the litigation friend's appointment ends. If a party ceases to be a patient the litigation friend's appointment will continue until a court order ends the appointment. Where a litigation friend's appointment ceases, notice must be served on the other parties within 28 days of the ending of the appointment, failing which the court can, if the opposing party makes an application, strike out the claim brought by the child or patient.

(3) No settlement, compromise, payment and no acceptance of money paid into court shall be valid, so far as it relates to a claim on behalf of a child or patient, without the court's approval (CPR r 21.10). Counsel's opinion or the solicitor's opinion on the merits of the settlement should be supplied to the court, together with further information the court will require concerning the claim (CPR PD 21, para 6.2). If an agreement is made to settle the claim

before proceedings have commenced the procedure set out in Part 8 of the CPR must be followed to obtain the court's approval of the settlement. The hearing of a decision to approve a settlement will usually take place in private. The decision to approve together with the basic reasons ought to be given in open court. Note: provisions dealing with the need for the court's approval of a structured settlement in respect of a child or patient are set out at p 288.

(4) If money is recovered on behalf of a child or patient that money will only be dealt with in accordance with the court's directions. The money can be paid into court and invested or otherwise dealt with. The Court of Protection is responsible for dealing with the property of a patient and is given extensive powers to administer the funds under the Mental Health Act 1983. The court can direct that certain sums should be paid direct to the child or patient, his litigation friend or legal representative for the immediate benefit of the child or patient or in respect of expenses incurred on his behalf. If the money is invested in court for a child, the money must be paid to the child when he reaches full age.

APPENDIX A

STATUTES

LAW REFORM (MISCELLANEOUS PROVISIONS) ACT 1934

1 Effect of death on certain causes of action

(1) Subject to the provisions of this section, on the death of any person after the commencement of this Act all causes of action subsisting against or vested in him shall survive against, or, as the case may be, for the benefit of his estate: Provided that this subsection shall not apply to causes of action for defamation.

(1A) The right of a person to claim under s 1A Fatal Accidents Act 1976 (bereavement) shall not survive for the benefit of his estate on his death.

(2) Where a cause of action survives as aforesaid for the benefit of the estate of a deceased person, the damages recoverable for the benefit of the estate of that person:

    (a) shall not include:

        (i) any exemplary damages;

        (ii) any damages for loss of income in respect of any period after that person's death;

    (b) [Repealed.]

    (c) where the death of that person has been caused by the act or omission which gives rise to the cause of action, shall be calculated without reference to any loss or gain to his estate consequent on his death, except that a sum in respect of funeral expenses may be included.

(3) [Repealed.]

(4) Where damage has been suffered by reasons of any act or omission in respect of which a cause of action would have subsisted against any person if that person had not died before or at the same time as the damage was suffered, there shall be deemed, for the purposes of this Act, to have been subsisting against him before his death such cause of action in respect of that act or omission as would have subsisted if he had died after the damage was suffered.

(5) The rights conferred by this Act for the benefit of the estates of deceased persons shall be in addition to and not in derogation of any rights conferred on the dependants of deceased persons by the Fatal Accidents Act 1846–1908 or the Carriage by Air Act 1932, and so much of this Act as relates to causes of action against the estate of deceased persons shall apply in relation to causes of action under the said Act as it applies in relation to other causes of action not expressly excepted from the operation of subsection (1) of this section.

(6) In the event of the insolvency of an estate against which proceedings are maintainable by virtue of this section, any liability in respect of the cause of action in respect of which the proceedings are maintainable shall be deemed to be a debt provable in the administration of the estate, notwithstanding that it is a demand in the nature of unliquidated damages arising otherwise than by a contract, promise or breach of trust.

FATAL ACCIDENTS ACT 1976

1 Right of action for wrongful act causing death

(1)   If death is caused by any wrongful act, neglect or default which is such as would (if death had not ensued) have entitled the person injured to maintain an action and recover damages in respect thereof, the person who would have been liable if death had not ensued shall be liable to an action for damages, notwithstanding the death of the person injured.

(2)   Subject to s 1A(2) below, every such action shall be for the benefit of the dependants of the person ('the deceased') whose death has been so caused.

(3)   In this Act 'dependant' means:

(a)   the wife or husband or former wife or husband of the deceased;

(b)   any person who:

(i)   was living with the deceased in the same household immediately before the date of the death; and

(ii)   had been living with the deceased in the same household for at least two years before that date; and

(iii)   was living during the whole of that period as the husband or wife of the deceased;

(c)   any parent or other ascendant of the deceased;

(d)   any person who was treated by the deceased as his parent;

(e)   any child or other descendant of the deceased;

(f)   any person (not being a child of the deceased) who, in the case of any marriage to which the deceased was at any time a party, was treated by the deceased as a child of the family in relation to that marriage;

(g)   any person who is, or is the issue of, a brother, sister, uncle or aunt of the deceased.

(4)   The reference to the former wife or husband of the deceased in subsection (3)(a) above includes a reference to a person whose marriage to the deceased has been annulled or declared void as well as a person whose marriage to the deceased has been dissolved.

(5)   In deducing any relationship for the purposes of subsection (3) above:

(a)   any relationship by affinity shall be treated as a relationship of consanguinity, any relationship of the half blood as a relationship of the whole blood, and the stepchild of any person as his child, and

(b)   an illegitimate person shall be treated as the legitimate child of his mother and reputed father.

(6)   Any reference in this Act to injury includes any disease and any impairment of a person's physical or mental condition.

1A Bereavement

(1)   An action under this Act may consist of or include a claim for damages for bereavement.

(2)   A claim for damages for bereavement shall only be for the benefit:

    (a) of the wife or husband of the deceased; and

    (b) where the deceased was a minor who was never married:

       (i) of his parents, if he was legitimate; and

       (ii) of his mother, if he was illegitimate.

(3)   Subject to subsection (5) below, the sum to be awarded as damages under this section shall be £7,500.

(4)   Where there is a claim for damages under this section for the benefit of both the parents of the deceased, the sum awarded shall be divided equally between them (subject to any deduction falling to be made in respect of costs not recovered from the defendant).

(5)   The Lord Chancellor may by order made by statutory instrument, subject to annulment in pursuance of a resolution of either House of Parliament, amend this section by varying the sum or the time being specified in subsection (3) above.

2 Persons entitled to bring the action

(1)   The action shall be brought by and in the name of the executor or administrator of the deceased.

(2)   If:

    (a) there is no executor or administrator of the deceased, or

    (b) no action is brought within six months after the death by and in the name of an executor or administrator of the deceased, the action may be brought by and in the name of all or any of the persons for whose benefit an executor or administrator could have brought it.

(3)   Not more that one action shall lie for and in respect of the same subject matter of complaint.

(4)   The plaintiff in the action shall be required to deliver to the defendant or his solicitor full particulars of the persons for whom and on whose behalf the action is brought and of the nature of the claim in respect of which damages are sought to be recovered.

3 Assessment of damages

(1)   In the action such damages, other than damages for bereavement, may be awarded as are proportioned to the injury resulting from the death to the dependants respectively.

(2)   After deducting the costs not recovered from the defendant any amount recovered otherwise than as damages for bereavement shall be divided among the dependants in such shares as may be directed.

(3)   In an action under this Act where there fall to be assessed damages payable to a widow in respect of the death of her husband there shall not be taken into account the re-marriage of the widow or her prospects of re-marriage.

(4)   In an action under this Act where there fall to be assessed damages payable to a person who is a dependant by virtue of section 1(3)(b) above in respect of the death of the person with whom the dependant was living as husband or wife there shall be taken into account (together with any other matter that appears to the court to

be relevant to the action) the fact that the dependant had no enforceable right to financial support by the deceased as a result of their living together.

(5) If the dependants have incurred funeral expenses in respect of the deceased, damages may be awarded in respect of those expenses.

(6) Money paid into court in satisfaction of a cause of action under this Act may be in one sum without specifying any person's share.

4 Assessment of damages: disregard of benefits

In assessing damages in respect of a person's death in an action under this Act, benefits which have accrued or will or may accrue to any person from his estate or otherwise as a result of his death shall be disregarded.

5 Contributory negligence

Where any person dies as the result partly of his own fault and partly of the fault of any other person or persons, and accordingly if an action were brought for the benefit of the estate under the Law Reform (Miscellaneous Provisions) Act 1934 the damages recoverable could be reduced under s 1(1) Law Reform (Contributory Negligence) Act 1945, any damages recoverable in an action under this Act shall be reduced to a proportionate extent.

CONGENITAL DISABILITIES (CIVIL LIABILITY) ACT 1976

1 Civil liability to child born disabled

(1) If a child is born disabled as a result of such an occurrence before its birth as is mentioned in subsection (2) below, and a person (other than the child's own mother) is under this section answerable to the child in respect of the occurrence, the child's disabilities are to be regarded as damage resulting from the wrongful act of that person and actionable accordingly at the suit of the child.

(2) An occurrence to which this section applies is one which:

(a) affected either parent of the child in his or her ability to have a normal healthy child; or

(b) affected the mother during pregnancy, or affected her or the child in the course of its birth, so that the child is born with disabilities which would not otherwise have been present.

(3) Subject to the following subsections, a person (here referred to as 'the defendant') is answerable to the child if he was liable in tort to the parent or would, if sued in due time, have been so; and it is no answer that there could not have been such liability because the parent suffered no actionable injury, if there was a breach of legal duty which, accompanied by injury, would have given rise to the liability.

(4) In the case of an occurrence preceding the time of conception, the defendant is not answerable to the child if at that time either or both of the parents knew the risk of their child being born disabled (that is to say, the particular risk created by the occurrence); but should it be the child's father who is the defendant, this subsection does not apply if he knew of the risk and the mother did not.

(5) The defendant is not answerable to the child, for anything he did or omitted to do when responsible in a professional capacity for treating or advising the parent, if he took reasonable care having due regard to then received professional opinion applicable to the particular class of case; but this does not mean that he is answerable only because he departed from received opinion.

(6) Liability to the child under this section may be treated as having been excluded or limited by contract made with the parent affected, to the same extent and subject to the same restrictions as liability in the parent's own case; and a contract term which could have been set up by the defendant in an action by the parent, so as to exclude or limit his liability to him or her, operates in the defendant's favour to the same, but no greater, extent in an action under this section by the child.

(7) If in the child's action under this section it is shown that the parent affected shared the responsibility for the child being born disabled, the damages are to be reduced to such extent as the court thinks just and equitable having regard to the extent of the parent's responsibility.

1A Extension of s 1 to cover infertility treatments

(1) In any case where:

(a) a child carried by a woman as the result of the placing in her of an embryo or of sperm and eggs or her artificial insemination is born disabled;

(b) the disability results from an act or omission in the course of the selection, or the keeping or use outside the body, of the embryo carried by her or of the gametes used to bring about the creation of the embryo; and

(c) a person is under this section answerable to the child in respect of the act or omission, the child's disabilities are to be regarded as damage resulting from the wrongful act of that person and actionable accordingly at the suit of the child.

(2) Subject to subsection (3) below and the applied provisions of section 1 of this Act, a person (here referred to as 'the defendant') is answerable to the child if he was liable in tort to one or both of the parents (here referred to as 'the parent or parents concerned') or would, if sued in due time, have been so; and it is no answer that there could not have been such liability because the parent or parents concerned suffered no actionable injury, if there was a breach of legal duty which, accompanied by injury, would have given rise to the liability.

(3) The defendant is not under this section answerable to the child if at the time the embryo, or the sperm and eggs, are placed in the woman or the time of her insemination (as the case may be) either or both of the parents knew the risk of their child being born disabled (that is to say, the particular risk created by the act or omission).

(4) Subsections (5)–(7) of s 1 of this Act apply for the purposes of this section as they apply for the purposes of that but as if references to the parent or the parents affected were references to the parent or parents concerned.

2 Liability of woman driving when pregnant

A woman driving a motor vehicle when she knows (or ought reasonably to know) herself to be pregnant is to be regarded as being under the same duty to take care for the safety of her unborn child as the law imposes on her with respect to the safety of other people; and if in consequence of her breach of that duty her child is born with disabilities which would not otherwise have been present, those disabilities are to be regarded as damage resulting from her wrongful act and actionable accordingly at the suit of the child.

3

(1) Section 1 of this Act does not affect the operation of the Nuclear Installations Act 1965 as to liability for, and compensation in respect of, injury or damage caused by occurrences involving nuclear matter or the emission of ionising radiations.

(2) For the avoidance of doubt anything which:

(a) affects a man in his ability to have a normal, healthy child; or

(b) affects a woman in that ability, or so affects her when she is pregnant that her child is born with disabilities which would not otherwise have been present, is an injury for the purposes of that Act.

(3) If a child is born disabled as the result of an injury to either of its parents caused in breach of a duty imposed by any of ss 7–11 of that Act (nuclear site licensees and others to secure that nuclear incidents do not cause injury to persons, etc) the child's disabilities are to be regarded under the subsequent provisions of that Act (compensation and other matters) as injuries caused in the same occasion, and by the same breach of duty, as was the injury to the parent.

(4) As respects compensation to the child, s 13(6) of that Act (contributory fault of person injured by radiation) is to be applied as if the reference there to fault were to the fault of the parent.

(5) Compensation is not payable in the child's case if the injury to the parent preceded the time of the child's conception and at that time either or both of the parents knew the risk of their child being born disabled (that is to say, the particular risk created by the injury).

4 Interpretation and other supplementary provisions

(1) References in this Act to a child being born disabled or with disabilities are to its being born with any deformity, disease or abnormality, including predisposition (whether or not susceptible of immediate prognosis) to physical or mental defect in the future.

(2) In this Act:

(a) 'born' means born alive (the moment of a child's birth being when it first has a life separate from its mother), and 'birth' has a corresponding meaning; and

(b) 'motor vehicle' means a mechanically propelled vehicle intended or adapted for use on roads; and references to embryos shall be construed in accordance with s 1 Human Fertilisation and Embryology Act 1990.

(3) Liability to a child under s 1, 1A or 2 of this Act is to be regarded:

(a) as respects all its incidents and any matters arising or to arise out of it; and

(b) subject to any contrary context or intention, for the purposes of construing references in enactments and documents to personal or bodily injuries and cognate matters, as liability for personal injuries sustained by the child immediately after its birth.

(4) No damages shall be recoverable under any of those section in respect of any loss of expectation of life, nor shall any such loss be taken into account in the compensation payable in respect of a child under the Nuclear Installations Act 1965 as extended by s 3, unless (in either case) the child lives for at least 48 hours.

(4A) In any case where a child carried by a woman as the result of the placing in her of an embryo or of sperm and eggs or her artificial insemination is born disabled, any references in s 1 of this Act to a parent includes a reference to a person who would be a parent but for ss 27–29 Human Fertilisation and Embryology Act 1990.

(5) This Act applies in respect of births after (but not before) its passing, and in respect of any such birth it replaces any law in force before its passing, whereby a person could be liable to a child in respect of disabilities with which it might be born; but in s 1(3) of this Act the expression 'liable in tort' does not include any reference to liability by virtue of this Act, or to liability by virtue of any such law.

(6) References to the Nuclear Installations Act 1965 are to that Act as amended; and for the purposes of s 28 of that Act (power by Order in Council to extend the Act to territories outside the United Kingdom) s 3 of this Act is to be treated as if it were a provision of that Act.

5 Crown application

This Act binds the Crown.

6 Citation and extent

(1)   This Act may be cited as the Congenital Disabilities (Civil Liability) Act 1976.

(2)   This Act extends to Northern Ireland but not to Scotland.

LIMITATION ACT 1980

PART I: ORDINARY TIME LIMITS FOR DIFFERENT CLASSES OF ACTION

1 Time limits under Part I subject to extension or exclusion under Part II

(1) This part of this Act gives the ordinary time limits for bringing actions of the various classes mentioned in the following provisions of this part.

(2) The ordinary time limits given in this part of this Act are subject to extension or exclusion in accordance with the provisions of Part II of this Act.

Actions founded on tort

2 Time limit for actions founded on tort

An action founded on tort shall not be brought after the expiration of six years from the date on which the cause of action accrued.

...

Actions founded on simple contract

5 Time limit for actions founded on simple contract

An action founded on simple contract shall not be brought after the expiration of six years from the date on which the cause of action accrued.

...

Actions in respect of wrongs causing personal injuries or death

11 Special time limit for actions in respect of personal injuries

(1) This section applies to any action for damages for negligence, nuisance or breach of duty (whether the duty exists by virtue of a contract or of provision made by or under a statute or independently of any contract or any such provision) where the damages claimed by the plaintiff for the negligence, nuisance or breach of duty consist of or include damages in respect of personal injuries to the plaintiff or any other person.

(2) None of the time limits given in the preceding provisions of this Act shall apply to an action to which this section applies.

(3) An action to which this section applies shall not be brought after the expiration of the period applicable in accordance with subsection (4) or (5) below.

(4) Except where subsection (5) below applies, the period applicable is three years from:

(a) the date on which the cause of action accrued; or

(b) the date of knowledge (if later) of the person injured.

(5) If the person injured dies before the expiration of the period mentioned in subsection (4) above, the period applicable as respects the cause of action surviving for the benefit of his estate by virtue of s 1 Law Reform (Miscellaneous Provisions) Act 1934 shall be three years from:

(a) the date of death; or

(b) the date of the personal representative's knowledge; whichever is the later.

(6) For the purposes of this section 'personal representative' includes any person who is or has been a personal representative of the deceased, including an executor who has not proved the will (whether or not he has renounced probate) but not anyone appointed only as a special personal representative in relation to settled land; and regard shall be had to any knowledge acquired by any such person while a personal representative or previously.

(7) If there is more than one personal representative, and their dates of knowledge are different, subsection (5)(b) above shall be read as referring to the earliest of those dates.

Actions in respect of defective products

11A

(1) This section shall apply to an action for damages by virtue of any provision of Part I of the Consumer Protection Act 1987.

(2) None of the time limits given in the preceding provisions of this Act shall apply to an action to which this section applies.

(3) An action to which this section applies shall not be brought after the expiration of the period of ten years from the relevant time, within the meaning of s 4 of the said Act of 1987; and this subsection shall operate to extinguish a right of action and shall do so whether or not that right of action had accrued, or time under the following provisions of this Act had begun to run, at the end of the said period of ten years.

(4) Subject to subsection (5) below, an action to which this section applies in which the damages claimed by the plaintiff consist of or include damages in respect of personal injuries to the plaintiff or any other person for loss of or damage to any property, shall not be brought after the expiration of the period of three years from whichever is the later of:

   (a) the date on which the cause of action accrued; and

   (b) the date of knowledge of the injured persons or, in the case of loss of or damage to property, the date of knowledge of the plaintiff or (if earlier) of any person in whom his cause of action was previously vested.

(5) If in a case where the damages claimed by the plaintiff consist of or include damages in respect of personal injuries to the plaintiff or any other person the injured person died before the expiration of the period mentioned in subsection (4) above, that subsection shall have effect as respects the cause of action surviving for the benefit of his estate by virtue of s 1 Law Reform (Miscellaneous Provisions) Act 1934 as if for the reference to that period there were substituted a reference to the period of three years from whichever is the later of:

   (a) the date of death; and

   (b) the date of the personal representative's knowledge.

(6) For the purposes of this section 'personal representative' includes any person who is or has been a personal representative of the deceased, including an executor who has not proved the will (whether or not he has renounced probate) but not anyone appointed only as a special personal representative in relation to settled land, and regard shall be had to any knowledge acquired by any such person while a personal representative or previously.

(7) If there is more than one personal representative and their dates of knowledge are different, subsection (5)(b) above shall be read as referring to the earliest of those dates.

(8) Expressions used in this section or s 14 of this Act and in Part I of the Consumer Protection Act 1987 have the same meanings in this section or that section as in that part; and s 1(1) of that Act (Part I to be construed as enacted for the purpose of complying with the product liability Directive) shall apply for the purpose of construing this section and the following provisions of this Act so far as they relate to any action by virtue of any provision of that part as it applies for the purpose of construing that part.

12 Special time limits for actions under Fatal Accidents legislation

(1) An action under the Fatal Accidents Act 1976 shall not be brought if the death occurred when the person injured could no longer maintain an action and recover damages in respect of the injury (whether because of a time limit in this Act or in any other Act, or for any other reason).

Where any such action by the injured person would have been barred by the time limit in s 11 or 11A of this Act, no account shall be taken of the possibility of that time limit being overridden under s 33 of this Act.

(2) None of the time limits given in the preceding provisions of this Act shall apply to an action under the Fatal Accidents Act 1976, but no such action shall be brought after the expiration of three years from:

(a) the date of death; or

(b) the date of knowledge of the person for whose benefit the action is brought; whichever is the later.

(3) An action under the Fatal Accidents Act 1976 shall be one to which ss 28, 33 and 35 of this Act apply, and the application to any such action of the time limit under subsection (2) above shall be subject to section 39; but otherwise Parts II and III of this Act shall not apply to any such action.

13 Operations of time limit under s 12 in relation to different dependants

(1) Where there is more than one person for whose benefit an action under the Fatal Accidents Act 1976 is brought, s 12(2)(b) of this Act shall be applied separately to each of them.

(2) Subject to subsection (3) below, if by virtue of subsection (1) above the action would be outside the time limit given by s 12(2) as regards one or more, but not all, of the persons for whose benefit it is brought, the court shall direct that any persons as regards whom the action would be outside that limit shall be excluded from those for whom the action is brought.

(3) The court shall not give such a direction if it is shown that if the action were brought exclusively for the benefit of the person in question it would not be defeated by a defence of limitation (whether in consequence of s 28 of this Act or an agreement between the parties not to raise the defence, or otherwise).

14 Definition of date of knowledge for purposes of ss 11 and 12

(1) Subject to subsection (1A) below in ss 11 and 12 of this Act references to a person's date of knowledge are references to the date on which he first had knowledge of the following facts:

(a) that the injury in question was significant; and

(b) that the injury was attributable in whole or in part to the act or omission which is alleged to constitute negligence, nuisance or breach of duty; and

(c) the identity of the defendant; and

(d) if it is alleged that the act or omission was that of a person other then the defendant, the identity of that person and the additional facts supporting the bringing of an action against the defendant; and knowledge that any acts or omissions did or did not, as a matter of law, involve negligence, nuisance or breach of duty is irrelevant.

(1A) In s 11A of this Act and in s 12 of this Act so far as that section applies to an action by virtue of s 6(1)(a) Consumer Protection Act 1987 (death caused by defective product) references to a person's date of knowledge are references to the date on which he first had knowledge of the following facts:

(a) such facts about the damage caused by the defect as would lead a reasonable person who had suffered such damage to consider it sufficiently serious to justify his instituting proceedings for damages against a defendant who did not dispute liability and was able to satisfy a judgment; and

(b) that the damage was wholly or partly attributable to the facts and circumstances alleged to constitute the defect; and

(c) the identify of the defendant; but, in determining the date on which a person first had such knowledge there shall be disregarded both the extent (if any) of that person's knowledge on any date of whether particular facts or circumstances would or would not, as a matter of law, constitute a defect and, in a case relating to loss of or damage to property, any knowledge which that person had on a date on which he had no right of action by virtue of Part I of that Act in respect of the loss or damage.

(2) For the purposes of this section a person's knowledge includes knowledge which he might reasonably have considered it sufficiently serious to justify his instituting proceedings for damages against a defendant who did not dispute liability and was able to satisfy a judgment.

(3) For the purposes of this section a person's knowledge includes knowledge which he might reasonably have been expected to acquire:

(a) from facts observable or ascertainable by him; or

(b) from facts ascertainable by him with the help of medical or other appropriate expert advice which it is reasonable for him to seek; but a person shall not be fixed under this subsection with knowledge of a fact ascertainable only with the help of expert advice so long as he has taken all reasonable steps to obtain (and, where appropriate, to act on) that advice.

14A Special time limit for negligence actions where facts relevant to cause of action are not known at date of accrual

(1) This section applies to any action for damages for negligence, other than one to which s 11 of this Act applies, where the starting date for reckoning the period of limitation under subsection (4)(b) below falls after the date on which the cause of action accrued.

(2) Section 2 of this Act shall not apply to an action to which this section applies.

(3) An action to which this section applies shall not be brought after the expiration of the period applicable in accordance with subsection (4) below.

(4) That period is either:

(a) six years from the date on which the cause of action accrued; or

(b) three years from the starting date as defined by subsection (5) below, if that period expires later than the period mentioned in paragraph (a) above.

(5) For the purposes of this section, the starting date for reckoning the period of limitation under subsection (4)(b) above is the earliest date on which the plaintiff or any person in whom the cause of action was vested before him first had both the knowledge required for bringing an action for damages in respect of the relevant damage and a right to bring such an action.

(6) In subsection (5) above 'the knowledge required for bringing an action for damages in respect of the relevant damage' means knowledge both:

(a) of the material facts about the damage in respect of which damages are claimed; and

(b) of the other facts relevant to the current action mentioned in subsection (8) below.

(7) For the purposes of subsection (6)(a) above, the material facts about the damage are such facts about the damage as would lead a reasonable person who had suffered such damage to consider it sufficiently serious to justify his instituting proceedings for damages against a defendant who did not dispute liability and was able to satisfy a judgment.

(8) The other facts referred to in subsection (6)(b) above are:

(a) that the damage was attributable in whole or in part to the act or omission which is alleged to constitute negligence; and

(b) the identity of the defendant; and

(c) if it is alleged that the act or omission was that of a person other than the defendant, the identity of that person and the additional facts supporting the bringing of an action against the defendant.

(9) Knowledge that any acts or omissions did or did not, as a matter of law, involve negligence is irrelevant for the purposes of subsection (5) above.

(10) For the purposes of this section a person's knowledge includes knowledge which he might reasonably have been expected to acquire:

(a) from facts observable or ascertainable by him; or

(b) from facts ascertainable by him with the help of appropriate expert advice which it is reasonable for him to seek;

(c) but a person shall not be taken by virtue of this subsection to have knowledge of a fact ascertainable only with the help of expert advice so long as he has taken all reasonable steps to obtain (and, where appropriate, to act on) that advice.

14B Overriding time limit for negligence actions not involving personal injuries

(1) An action for damages for negligence, other than one to which s 11 of this Act applies, shall not be brought after the expiration of 15 years from the date (or, if

more than one, from the last of the dates) on which there occurred any act or omission:

(a) which is alleged to constitute negligence; and

(b) to which the damage in respect of which damages are claimed is alleged to be attributable (in whole or in part).

(2) This section bars the right of action in a case to which subsection (1) above applies notwithstanding that:

(a) the cause of action has not yet accrued; or

(b) where s 14A of this Act applies to the action, the date which is for the purposes of that section the starting date for reckoning the period mentioned in subsection (4)(b) of that section has not yet occurred; before the end of the period of limitation prescribed by this section.

PART II: EXTENSION OR EXCLUSION OF ORDINARY TIME LIMITS

Disability

28 Extension of limitation period in case of disability

(1) Subject to the following provisions of this section, if on the date when any right of action accrued for which a period of limitation is prescribed by this Act, the person to whom it accrued was under a disability, the action may be brought at any time before the expiration of six years from the date when he ceased to be under a disability or died (whichever first occurred) notwithstanding that the period of limitation has expired.

(2) This section shall not affect any case where the right of action first accrued to some person (not under a disability) through whom the person under a disability claims.

(3) When a right of action which has accrued to a person under a disability accrues, on the death of that person while still under a disability, to another person under a disability, no further extension of time shall be allowed by reason of the disability of the second person.

(4A) If the action is one to which s 4A of this Act applies, subsection (1) above shall have effect as if for the words from 'at any time' to 'occurred') there were substituted the words 'by him at any time before the expiration of three years from the date when he ceased to be under a disability'.

...

(6) If the action is one to which ss 11 or 12(2) of this Act applies, subsection (1) above shall have effect as for the words 'six years' there were substituted the words 'three years'.

(7) If the action is one to which s 11A of this Act applies or one by virtue of s 6(1)(a) Consumer Protection Act 1987 (death caused by defective product), subsection (1) above:

(a) shall not apply to the time limit prescribed by subsection (3) of the said s 11A or to that time limit as applied by virtue of s 12(1) of this act; and

(b) in relation to any other time limit prescribed by this Act shall have effect as if for the words 'six years' there were substituted the words 'three years'.

28A Extension for cases where the limitation period is the period under s 14A(4)(b)

(1) Subject to subsection (2) below, if in the case of any action for which a period of limitation is prescribed by s 14A of this Act:

    (a) the period applicable in accordance with subsection (4) of that section is the period mentioned in paragraph (b) of that subsection;

    (b) on the date which is for the purposes of that section the starting date for reckoning that period the person by reference to whose knowledge that date fell to be determined under subsection (5) of that section was under a disability; and

    (c) section 28 of this Act does not apply to the action;

the action may be brought at any time before the expiration of three years from the date when he ceased to be under a disability or died (whichever first occurred) notwithstanding that the period mentioned above has expired.

(2) An action may not be brought by virtue of subsection (1) above after the end of the period of limitation prescribed by s 14B of this Act.

Postponement of limitation period in case of fraud, concealment or mistake

32

(1) Subject to subsections (3) and (4A) below, where in the case of any action for which a period of limitation is prescribed by this Act, either:

    (a) the action is based upon the fraud of the defendant; or

    (b) any fact relevant to the plaintiff's right of action has been deliberately concealed from him by the defendant; or

    (c) the action is for relief from the consequences of a mistake;

the period of limitation shall not begin to run until the plaintiff has discovered the fraud, concealment or mistake (as the case may be) or could with reasonable diligence have discovered it.

References in this subsection to the defendant include references to the defendant's agent and to any person through whom the defendant claims and his agent.

(2) For the purposes of subsection (1) above, deliberate commission of a breach of duty in circumstances in which it is unlikely to be discovered for some time amounts to deliberate concealment of the facts involved in that breach of duty.

(3) Nothing in this section shall enable any action:

    (a) to recover, or recover the value of, any property; or

    (b) to enforce any charge against, or set aside any transaction affecting any property;

to be brought against the purchaser of the property or any person claiming through him in any case where the property has been purchased for valuable consideration by an innocent third party since the fraud or concealment or (as the case may be) the transaction in which the mistake was made took place.

(4) purchaser is an innocent third party for the purposes of this section:

    (a) in the case of fraud or concealment or any fact relevant to the plaintiff's right of action, if he was not a party to the fraud or (as the case may be) to the concealment of that fact and did not at the time of the purchase know or have reason to believe that the fraud or concealment had taken place; and

(b) in the case of mistake, if he did not at the time of the purchase know or have reason to believe that the mistake had been made.

(4A) Subsection (1) above shall not apply in relation to the time limit prescribed by s 11A(3) of this Act or in relation to that time limit as applied by virtue of s 12(1) of this Act.

(5) Section 14A and 14B of this Act shall not apply to any action to which subsection (1)(b) above applies (and accordingly the period of limitation referred to in that subsection, in any case to which either of these sections would otherwise apply, is the period applicable under s 2 of this Act).

33 Discretionary exclusion of time limit for actions in respect of personal injuries or death

(1) If it appears to the court that it would be equitable to allow an action to proceed having regard to the degree to which:

(a) the provisions of ss 11 [or 11A] or 12 of this Act prejudice the plaintiff or any person whom he represents; and

(b) any decision of the court under this subsection would prejudice the defendant or any person whom he represents;

the court may direct that those provisions shall not apply to the action, or shall not apply to any specified cause of action to which the action relates.

(1A) The court shall not under this section disapply:

(a) subsection 3 of s 11A; or

(b) where the damages claimed by the plaintiff are confined to damages for loss of or damage to any property, any other provision in its application to an action by virtue of Part I Consumer Protection Act 1987.

(2) The court shall not under this section disapply s 12(1) except where the reason why the person injured could no longer maintain an action was because of the time limit in s 11 or subsection (4) of s 11A.

If, for example, the person injured could at his death no longer maintain an action under the Fatal Accidents Act 1976 because of the time limit in Article 29 in Schedule 1 to the Carriage by Air Act 1961, the court has no power to direct that s 12(1) shall not apply.

(3) In acting under this section the court shall have regard to all the circumstances of the case and in particular to:

(a) the length of, and the reasons for, the delay on the part of the plaintiff;

(b) the extent to which, having regard to the delay, the evidence adduced or likely to be adduced by the plaintiff or the defendant is or is likely to be less cogent than if the action had been brought within the time allowed by s 11, s 11A or (as the case may be) by s 12;

(c) the conduct of the defendant after the cause of action arose, including the extent (if any) to which he responded to requests reasonably made by the plaintiff for information or inspection for the purpose of ascertaining facts which were or might be relevant to the plaintiff's cause of action against the defendant;

(d) the duration of any disability of the plaintiff arising after the date of the accrual of the cause of action;

(e) the extent to which the plaintiff acted promptly and reasonably once he knew whether or not the act or omission of the defendant, to which the injury was attributable, might be capable at that time of giving rise to an action for damages;

(f) the steps, if any, taken by the plaintiff to obtain medical, legal or other expert advise and the nature of any such advice he may have received.

(4) In a case where the person injured died when, because of s 11 or subsection 4 of s 11A, he could no longer maintain an action and recover damages in respect of the injury, the court shall have regard in particular to the length of, and the reasons for, the delay on the part of the deceased.

(5) In a case under subsection (4) above, or any other case where the time limit, or one of the time limits, depends on the date of knowledge of a person other than the plaintiff, subsection (3) above shall have effect with appropriate modifications, and shall have effect in particular as if references to the plaintiff included references to any person whose date of knowledge is or was relevant in determining a time limit.

(6) A direction by the court disapplying the provisions of s 12(1) shall operate to disapply the provisions to the same effect in s 1(1) Fatal Accidents Act 1976.

(7) In this section, 'the court' means the court in which the action has been brought.

(8) References in this section to s 11 or 11A include references to that section as extended by any of the preceding provisions of this part of this Act or by any provision of Part III of this Act.

PART III: MISCELLANEOUS AND GENERAL

35 New claims in pending actions: rules of court

(1) For the purposes of this Act, any new claim made in the course of any action shall be deemed to be a separate action and to have been commenced:

(a) in the case of a new claim made in or by way of third part proceedings, on the date on which those proceedings were commenced; and

(b) in the case of any other new claim, on the same date as the original action.

(2) In this section, a 'new claim' means any claim by way of set-off or counterclaim and any claim involving either:

(a) the addition or substitution of a new cause of action; or

(b) the addition or substitution of a new party;

and 'third party proceedings' means any proceedings brought in the course of any action by any party to the action against a person not previously a party to the action, other than proceedings brought by joining any such person as defendant to any claim already made in the original action by the party bringing the proceedings.

(3) Except as provided by s 33 of this Act or by rules of court, neither the High Court nor any county court shall allow a new claim within subsection (1)(b) above, other than an original set-off or counterclaim, to be made in the course of any action after the expiry of any time limit under this Act which would affect a new action to enforce that claim.

For the purposes of this subsection, a claim is an original set-off or an original counterclaim if it is a claim made by way of set-off or (as the case may be) by way of counterclaim by a party who has not previously made any claim in the action.

(4)   Rules of court may provide for allowing a new claim to which subsection (3) above applies to be made as there mentioned, but only if the conditions specified in subsection (5) below are satisfied, and subject to any further restrictions the rules may impose.

(5)   The conditions referred to in subsection (4) above are the following:

(a) in the case of a claim involving a new cause of action, if the new cause of action arises out of the same facts or substantially the same facts as are already in issue on any claim previously made in the original action; and

(b) in the case of a claim involving a new party, if the addition or substitution of the new party is necessary for the determination of the original action.

(6)   The addition or substitution of a new party shall not be regarded for the purposes of subsection (5)(b) above as necessary for the determination of the original action unless either:

(a) the new party is substituted for a party whose name was given in any claim made in the original action in mistake for the new party's name; or

(b) any claim already made in the original action cannot be maintained by or against an existing party unless the new party is joined or substituted as plaintiff or defendant in that action.

(7)   Subject to subsection (4) above, rules of court may provide for allowing a party to any action to claim relief in a new capacity in respect of a new cause of action notwithstanding that he had no title to make that claim at the date of the commencement of the action.

This subsection shall not be taken as prejudicing the power of rules of court to provide for allowing a party to claim relief in a new capacity without adding or substituting a new cause of action.

(8)   Subsections (3)–(7) above shall apply in relation to a new claim made in the course of third party proceedings as if those proceedings were the original action, and subject to such other modification as may be prescribed by rules of court in any case or class of case.

(9)   [Repealed.]

38 Interpretation

(1)   In this Act, unless the context otherwise requires:

'action' includes any proceedings in a court of law, including an ecclesiastical court;

'land' includes corporeal hereditaments, tithes and rent-charges and any legal or equitable estate or interest therein, including an interest in the proceeds of the sale of land held upon trust for sale, but except as provided above in this definition does not include any incorporeal hereditament;

'personal estate' and 'personal property' do not include chattels real;

'personal injuries includes any disease and any impairment of a person's physical or mental condition, and 'injury' and cognate expression shall be construed accordingly;

'rent' includes a rentcharge and a rent service;

'rentcharge' means any annuity or periodical sum of money charged upon or payable out of land, except a rent service or interest on a mortgage on land;

'settled land', 'statutory owner' and 'tenant for life' have the same meanings respectively as in the Settled Land Act 1925;

'trust' and 'trustee' have the same meanings respectively as in the Trustee Act 1925; and

'trust for sale' has the same meaning as in the Law of Property Act 1925.

(2) For the purposes of this Act a person shall be treated as under a disability while he is an infant, or of unsound mind.

(3) For the purposes of subsection (2) above a person is of unsound mind if he is a person who, by reason of mental disorder within the meaning of the Mental Health Act 1983, is incapable of managing and administering his property and affairs.

(4) Without prejudice to the generality of subsection (3) above, a person shall be conclusively presumed for the purposes of subsection (2) above to be of unsound mind:

   (a) while he is liable to be detained or subject to guardianship under the Mental Health Act 1983 (otherwise than by virtue of ss 35 or 89); and

   (b) while he is receiving treatment as an in-patient in any hospital within the meaning of the Mental Health Act 1983 or mental nursing home within the meaning of the Nursing Homes Act 1975 without being liable to be detained under the said Act of 1983 (otherwise than by virtue of ss 35 or 89), being treatment which follows without any interval a period during which he was liable to be detained or subject to guardianship under the Mental Health Act 1959, or the said Act of 1983 (otherwise than by virtue of ss 35 or 89) or by virtue of any enactment repealed or excluded by the Mental Health Act 1959.

(5) Subject to subsection (6) below, a person shall be treated as claiming through another person if he became entitled by, through, under, or by the act of that other person to the right claimed, and any person whose estate or interest might have been barred by a person entitled to an entailed interest in possession shall be treated as claiming through the person so entitled.

(6) A person becoming entitled to any estate or interest by virtue of a special power of appointment shall not be treated as claiming through the appointor.

(7) References in this Act to a right of action to recover land shall include references to a right to enter into possession of the land or, in the case of rentcharges and tithes, to distrain for arrears of rent or tithe, and references to the bringing of such an action shall include references to the making of such an entry or distress.

(8) References in this Act to the possession of land shall, in the case of tithes and rentcharges, be construed as references to the receipt of the tithe or rent, and references to the date of dispossession or discontinuance of possession of land shall, in the case of rentcharges, be construed as references to the date of the last receipt of rent.

(9) References in Part II of this Act to a right of action shall include references to:

   (a) a cause of action;

   (b) a right to receive money secured by a mortgage or charge on any property;

(c) a right to recover proceeds of the sale of land; and

(d) a right to receive a share or interest in the personal estate of a deceased person.

(10) References in Part II to the date of the accrual or a right of action shall be construed:

    (a) in the case of an action upon a judgment, as references to the date on which the judgment became enforceable; and

    (b) in the case of an action to recover arrears of rent or interest, or damages in respect of arrears of rent or interest, as references to the date on which the rent or interest became due.

SUPREME COURT ACT 1981

32 Orders for interim payment

(1) As regards proceedings pending in the High Court, provision may be made by rules of court, in such circumstances as may be prescribed, to make an order requiring a party to the proceedings to make an interim payment of such amount as may be specified in the order, with provision for the payment to be made to such other party to the proceedings as may be so specified or, if the order so provides, by paying it into court.

(2) Any rules of court which make provision in accordance with subsection (1) may include provision for enabling a party to any proceedings who, in pursuance of such an order, has made an interim payment to recover the whole or part of the amount of the payment in such circumstances, and from such other party to the proceedings, as may be determined in accordance with the rules.

(3) Any rules made by virtue of this section may include such incidental, supplementary and consequential provisions as the rulemaking authority may consider necessary or expedient.

(4) Nothing in this section shall be construed as affecting the exercise of any power relating to costs, including any power to make rules of court relating to costs.

(5) In this section, 'interim payment', in relation to a party to any proceedings, means a payment on account of any damages, debt or other sum, (excluding any costs) which that party may be held liable to pay to or for the benefit of another party to the proceedings if a final judgment or order of the court in the proceedings is given or made in favour of that other party.

32A Orders for provisional damages for personal injuries

(1) This section applies to an action for damages for personal injuries in which there is proved or admitted to be a chance that at some definite or indefinite time in the future the injured person will, as a result of the act or omission which gave rise to the cause of action, develop some serious disease or suffer some serious deterioration in his physical or mental condition.

(2) Subject to subsection (4) below, as regards any action for damages to which this section applies in which a judgment is given in the High Court, provision may be made by rules of court for enabling the court, in such circumstances as may be prescribed, to award the injured person:

    (a) damages assessed on the assumption that the injured person will not develop the disease or suffers the deterioration in his condition; and

    (b) further damages at a future date if he develops the disease or suffers the deterioration.

(3) Any rules made by virtue of this section may include such incidental, supplementary and consequential provisions as the rulemaking authority may consider necessary or expedient.

(4) Nothing in this section shall be construed:

    (a) as affecting the exercise of any power relating to costs, including any power to make rules of court relating to costs; or

(b) as prejudicing any duty of the court under any enactment or rule of law to reduce or limit the total damages which would have been recoverable apart from any such duty.

...

35A Power of High Court to award interest in debts and damages

(1) Subject to rules of court, in proceedings (whenever instituted) before the High Court for the recovery of a debt or damages there may be included in any sum for which judgment is given simple interest, at such rate as the court thinks fit or as rules of court may provide, on all or any part of the debt or damages in respect of which judgment is given, or payment is made before judgment, for all or any part of the period between the date when the cause of action arose and:

(a) in the case of any sum paid before judgment, the date of the payment; and

(b) in the case of the sum for which judgment is given, the date of the judgment.

(2) In relation to a judgment given for damages for personal injuries or death which exceed £200 subsection (1) shall have effect:

(a) with the substitution of 'shall be included' for 'may be included'; and

(b) with the addition of 'unless the court is satisfied that there are special reasons to the contrary' after 'given,' where first occurring.

(3) Subject to rules of court, where:

(a) there are proceedings (whenever instituted) before the High Court for the recovery of a debt; and

(b) the defendant pays the whole debt to the plaintiff (otherwise than in pursuance of a judgment in the proceedings),

the defendant shall be liable to pay the plaintiff simple interest at such rate as the court thinks fit or as rules of court may provide on all or any part of the debt for all or any part of the period between the date when the cause of action arose and the date of the payment.

(4) Interest in respect of a debt shall not be awarded under this section for a period during which, for whatever reason, interest on the debt already runs.

(5) Without prejudice to the generality of s 84, rules of court may provide for a rate of interest by reference to the rate specified in s 17 Judgment Act 1838 as that section has effect from time to time or by reference to a rate for which any other enactment provides.

(6) Interest under this section may be calculated at different rates in respect of different periods.

(7) In this section, 'plaintiff' means the person seeking the debt or damages and 'defendant' means the person from whom the plaintiff seeks the debt or damages and 'personal injuries' includes any disease and any impairment of a person's physical or mental condition.

(8) Nothing in this section affects the damages recoverable for the dishonour of a bill of exchange.

COUNTY COURTS ACT 1984

50 Orders for interim payments

(1) Provision may be made by [rules of court] for enabling the court, in such circumstances as may be prescribed, to make an order requiring a party to the proceedings to make an interim payment of such amount as may be specified in the order, with provision for the payment to be made to such other party to the proceedings as may be so specified or, if the order so provides, by paying it into court.

(2) Any [rules of court] which make provision in accordance with subsection (1) may include provision for enabling a party to any proceedings who, in pursuance of such an order, has made an interim payment to recover the whole or part of the amount of the payment in such circumstances, and from such other party to the proceedings, as may be determined in accordance with the rules.

(3) Any rules made by virtue of this section may include such incidental, supplementary and consequential provisions as the [Civil Procedure Rule Committee] may consider necessary or expedient.

(4) Nothing in this section shall be construed as affecting the exercise of any power relating to costs, including any power to make [rules of court] relating to costs.

(5) In this section 'interim payment', in relation to a party to any proceedings, means a payment on account of any damages, debt or other sum (excluding any costs) which that party may be held liable to pay to or for the benefit of another party to the proceedings if a final judgment or order of the court in the proceedings is given or made in favour of that other party; and any reference to a party to any proceedings includes a reference to any person who for the purposes of the proceedings acts as next friend or guardian of a party to the proceedings.

51 Orders for provisional damages for personal injuries

(1) This section applies to an action for damages for personal injuries in which there is proved or admitted to a be a chance that at some definite or indefinite time in the future the injured person will, as a result of the act or omission which gave rise to the cause of action, develop some serious disease or suffer some serious deterioration in his physical or mental condition.

(2) Subject to subsection (4), as regards any action for damages to which this section applies in which a judgment is given in the county court, provision may be made by [rules of court] for enabling the court, in such circumstances as may be prescribed, to award the injured person –

(a) damages assessed on the assumption that the injured person will not develop the disease or suffer the deterioration in his condition; and

(b) further damages at a future date if he develops the disease or suffers the deterioration.

(3) Any rules made by virtue of this section may include such incidental, supplementary and consequential provisions as the [Civil Procedure Rule Committee] may consider necessary or expedient.

(4)   Nothing in this section shall be construed –

(a)   as affecting the exercise of any power relating to costs, including any power to make [rules of court] relating to costs; or

(b)   as prejudicing any duty of the court under any enactment or rule of law to reduce or limit the total damages which would have been recoverable apart from any such duty.

(5)   In this section 'personal injuries' includes any disease any impairment of a person's physical or mental condition.

...

69 Power to award interest on debts and damages

(1)   Subject to [rules of court], in proceedings (whenever instituted) before a county court for the recovery of a debt or damages there may be included in any sum for which judgment is given simple interest, at such rate as the court thinks fit or as may be prescribed, on all or any part of the debt or damages in respect of which judgment is given, or payment is made before judgment, for all or any part of the period between the date when the cause of action arose and –

(a)   in the case of any sum paid before judgment, the date of the payment; and

(b)   in the case of the sum for which judgment is given, the date of the judgment.

(2)   In relation to a judgment given for damages for personal injuries or death which exceed £200 subsection (1) shall have effect –

(a)   with the substitution of 'shall be included' for 'may be included'; and

(b)   with the addition of 'unless the court is satisfied that there are special reasons to the contrary' after 'given', where first occurring.

(3)   Subject to [rules of court], where –

(a)   there are proceedings (whenever instituted) before a county court for the recovery of a debt; and

(b)   the defendant pays the whole debt to the plaintiff (otherwise than in pursuance of a judgment in the proceedings).

the defendant shall be liable to pay the plaintiff simple interest, at such rate as the court thinks fit or as may be prescribed, on all or any part of the debt for all or any part of the period between the date when the cause of action arose and the date of payment.

(4)   Interest in respect of a debt shall not be awarded under this section for a period during which, for whatever reason, interest on the debt already runs.

(5)   Interest under this section may be calculated at different rates in respect of different periods.

(6)   In this section 'plaintiff' means the person seeking the debt or damages and 'defendant' means the person from whom the plaintiff seeks the debt or damages and 'personal injuries' includes any disease and any impairment of a person's physical or mental condition.

(7)   Nothing in this section affects the damages recoverable for the dishonour of a bill of exchange.

[(8) In determining whether the amount of any debt or damages exceeds that prescribed by or under any enactment, no account shall be taken of any interest payable by virtue of this section except where express provision to the contrary is made by or under that or any other enactment.]

ACCESS TO MEDICAL REPORTS ACT 1988

1 Right of access

It shall be the right of an individual to have access, in accordance with the provisions of this Act, to any medical report relating to the individual which is to be, or has been, supplied by a medical practitioner for employment purposes or insurance purposes.

2 Interpretation

(1) In this Act:

'the applicant' means the person referred to in s 3(1) below;

'care' includes examination, investigation or diagnosis for the purposes of, or in connection with, any form of medical treatment;

'employment purposes', in the case of any individual, means the purposes in relation to the individual of any person by whom he is or has been, or is seeking to be, employed (whether under a contract of service or otherwise);

'health professional' has the same meaning as in the Data Protection (Subject Access Modification) (Health) Order 1987;

'insurance purposes', in the case of any individual, means the purposes in relation to the individual of any person carrying on an insurance business with whom the individual has entered into, or is seeking to enter into, a contract of insurance, and 'insurance business' and 'contract of insurance' have the same meaning as in the Insurance Companies Act 1982;

'medical practitioner' means a person registered under the Medical Act 1983;

'medical report', in the case of an individual, means a report relating to the physical or mental health of the individual prepared by a medical practitioner who is or has been responsible for the clinical care of the individual.

(2) Any reference in this Act to the supply of a medical report for employment or insurance purposes shall be construed:

(a) as a reference to the supply of such a report for employment or insurance purposes which are purposes of the person who is seeking to be supplied with it; or

(b) (in the case of a report that has already been supplied) as a reference to the supply of such a report for employment or insurance purposes which, at the time of its being supplied, were purposes of the person to whom it was supplied.

3 Consent to applications for medical reports for employment or insurance purposes

(1) A person shall not apply to a medical practitioner for a medical report relating to any individual to be supplied to him for employment or insurance purposes unless:

(a) that person ('the applicant') has notified the individual that he proposes to make the application; and

(b) the individual has notified the applicant that he consents to the making of the application.

(2) Any notification given under subsection (1)(a) above must inform the individual of his right to withhold his consent to the making of the application, and of the following rights under this Act, namely:

(a) the rights arising under ss 4(1)–(3) and 6(2) below with respect to access to the report before or after it is supplied,

(b) the right to withhold consent under subsection (1) of s 5 below, and

(c) the right to request the amendment of the report under subsection (2) of that section, as well as of the effect of s 7 below.

4 Access to reports before they are supplied

(1) An individual who gives his consent under s 3 above to the making of an application shall be entitled, when giving his consent, to state that he wishes to have access to the report to be supplied in response to the application before it is so supplied; and, if he does so, the applicant shall:

(a) notify the medical practitioner of that fact at the time when the application is made, and

(b) at the same time notify the individual of the making of the application; and each such notification shall contain a statement of the effect of subsection (2) below.

(2) Where a medical practitioner is notified by the applicant under subsection (1) above that the individual in question wishes to have access to the report before it is supplied, the practitioner shall not supply the report unless:

(a) he has given the individual access to it and any requirements of s 5 below have been complied with, or

(b) the period of 21 days beginning with the date of the making of the application has elapsed without his having received any communication from the individual concerning arrangements for the individual to have access to it.

(3) Where a medical practitioner:

(a) receives an application for a medical report to be supplied for employment or insurance purposes without being notified by the applicant as mentioned in subsection (1) above, but

(b) before supplying the report receives a notification from the individual that he wishes to have access to the report before it is supplied, the practitioner shall not supply the report unless:

(i) he has given the individual access to it and any requirements of s 5 below have been complied with, or

(ii) the period of 21 days beginning with the date of that notification has elapsed without his having received (either with that notification or otherwise) any communication from the individual concerning arrangements for the individual to have access to it.

(4) References in this section and s 5 below to giving an individual access to a medical report are references to:

(a) making the report or a copy of it available for his inspection; or

(b) supplying him with a copy of it; and where a copy is supplied at the request, or otherwise with the consent, of the individual the practitioner may charge a reasonable fee to cover the costs of supplying it.

5 Consent to supplying of report and correction of errors

(1) Where an individual has been given access to a report under s 4 above the report shall not be supplied in response to the application in question unless the individual has notified the medical practitioner that he consents to its being so supplied.

(2) The individual shall be entitled, before giving his consent under subsection (1) above, to request the medical practitioner to amend any part of the report which the individual considers to be incorrect or misleading; and, if the individual does so, the practitioner:

   (a) if he is to any extent prepared to accede to the individual's request, shall amend the report accordingly;

   (b) if he is to any extent not prepared to accede to it but the individual requests him to attach to the report a statement of the individual's views in respect of any part of the report which he is declining to amend, shall attach such a statement to the report.

(3) Any request made by an individual under subsection (2) above shall be made in writing.

6 Retention of reports

(1) A copy of any medical report which a medical practitioner has supplied for employment or insurance purposes shall be retained by him for at least six months from the data on which it was supplied.

(2) A medical practitioner shall, if so requested by an individual, give the individual access to any medical report relating to him which the practitioner has supplied for employment or insurance purposes in the previous six months.

(3) The reference in subsection (2) above to giving an individual access to a medical report is a reference to:

   (a) making a copy of the report available for his inspection; or

   (b) supplying him with a copy of it; and where a copy is supplied at the request, or otherwise with the consent, of the individual the practitioner may charge a reasonable fee to cover the costs of supplying it.

7 Exemptions

(1) A medical practitioner shall not be obliged to give an individual access, in accordance with the provisions of ss 4(4) or 6(3) above, to any part of a medical report whose disclosure would in the opinion of the practitioner be likely to cause serious harm to the physical or mental health of the individual or others or would indicate the intentions of the practitioner in respect of the individual.

(2) A medical practitioner shall not be obliged to give an individual access, in accordance with those provisions, to any part of a medical report whose disclosure would be likely to reveal information about another person, or to reveal the identity of another person who has supplied information to the practitioner about the individual, unless:

   (a) that person has consented; or

   (b) that person is a health professional who has been involved in the care of the individual and the information relates to or has been provided by the professional in that capacity.

(3) Where it appears to a medical practitioner that subsection (1) or (2) above is applicable to any part (but not the whole) of a medical report:

(a) he shall notify the individual of that fact; and

(b) references in the preceding sections of this Act to the individual being given access to the report shall be construed as references to his being given access to the remainder of it; and other references to the report in ss 4(4), 5(2) and 6(3) above shall similarly be construed as references to the remainder of the report.

(4) Where it appears to a medical practitioner that subsection (1) or (2) above is applicable to the whole of a medical report:

(a) he shall notify the individual of that fact; but

(b) he shall not supply the report unless he is notified by the individual that the individual consents to its being supplied; and accordingly, if he is so notified by the individual, the restrictions imposed by ss 4(2) and (3) above on the supply of the report shall not have effect in relation to it.

8 Application to the court

(1) If a court is satisfied on the application of an individual that any person, in connection with a medical report relating to that individual, has failed or is likely to fail to comply with any requirement of this Act, the court may order that person to comply with that requirement.

(2) The jurisdiction conferred by this section shall be exercisable by a county court or, in Scotland, by the sheriff.

9 Notifications under this Act

Any notification required or authorised to be given under this Act:

(a) shall be given in writing; and

(b) may be given by post.

10 Short title, commencement and extent

(1) This Act may be cited as the Access to Medical Reports Act 1988.

(2) This Act shall come into force on 1st January 1989.

(3) Nothing in this Act applies to a medical report prepared before the coming into force of this Act.

(4) This Act does not extend to Northern Ireland.

MEDICAL (PROFESSIONAL PERFORMANCE) ACT 1995

1 Professional performance

After s 36 Medical Act 1983 (professional misconduct and criminal offences), there shall be inserted:

36A(1)   Where the standard of professional performance of a fully registered person is found by the Committee on Professional Performance to have been seriously deficient, the Committee shall direct:

(a) that his registration in the register shall be suspended (that is to say, shall not have effect) during such period not exceeding 12 months as may be specified in the direction; or

(b) that his registration shall be conditional on his compliance, during such period not exceeding three years as may be specified in the direction, with the requirements so specified.

SOCIAL SECURITY (RECOVERY OF BENEFITS) ACT 1997

INTRODUCTORY

1 Cases in which this Act applies

(1) This Act applies in cases where –

   (a) a person makes a payment (whether on his own behalf or not) to or in respect of any other person in consequence of any accident, injury or disease suffered by the other, and

   (b) any listed benefits have been, or are likely to be, paid to or for the other during the relevant period in respect of the accident, injury or disease.

(2) The reference above to a payment in consequence of any accident, injury or disease is to a payment made –

   (a) by or on behalf of a person who is, or is alleged to be, liable to any extent in respect of the accident, injury or disease, or

   (b) in pursuance of a compensation scheme for motor accidents;

   but does not include a payment mentioned in Part I of Schedule 1.

(3) Subsection (1)(a) applies to a payment made –

   (a) voluntarily, or in pursuance of a court order or an agreement, or otherwise, and

   (b) in the United Kingdom or elsewhere.

(4) In a case where this Act applies –

   (a) the 'injured person' is the person who suffered the accident, injury or disease,

   (b) the 'compensation payment' is the payment within subsection (1)(a), and

   (c) 'recoverable benefit' is any listed benefit which has been or is likely to be paid as mentioned in subsection (1)(b).

2 Compensation payments to which this Act applies

This Act applies in relation to compensation payments made on or after the day on which this section comes into force, unless they are made in pursuance of a court order or agreement made before that day.

3 'The relevant period'

(1) In relation to a person ('the claimant') who has suffered any accident, injury or disease, 'the relevant period' has the meaning given by the following subsections.

(2) Subject to subsection (4), if it is a case of accident or injury, the relevant period is the period of five years immediately following the day on which the accident or injury in question occurred.

(3) Subject to subsection (4), if it is a case of disease, the relevant period is the period of five years beginning with the date on which the claimant first claims a listed benefit in consequence of the disease.

(4)   If at any time before the end of the period referred to in subsection (2) or (3) –

(a) a person makes a compensation payment in final discharge of any claim made by or in respect of the claimant and arising out of the accident, injury or disease, or

(b) an agreement is made under which an earlier compensation payment is treated as having been made in final discharge of any such claim,

the relevant period ends at that time.

CERTIFICATES OF RECOVERABLE BENEFITS

4 Applications for certificates of recoverable benefits

(1)   Before a person ('the compensator') makes a compensation payment he must apply to the Secretary of State for a certificate of recoverable benefits.

(2)   Where the compensator applies for a certificate of recoverable benefits, the Secretary of State must –

(a) send to him a written acknowledgement of receipt of his application, and

(b) subject to subsection (7), issue the certificate before the end of the following period.

(3)   The period is –

(a) the prescribed period, or

(b) if there is no prescribed period, the period of four weeks,

which begins with the day following the day on which the application is received.

(4)   The certificate is to remain in force until the date specified in it for that purpose.

(5)   The compensator may apply for fresh certificates from time to time.

(6)   Where a certificate of recoverable benefits ceases to be in force, the Secretary of State may issue a fresh certificate without an application for one being made.

(7)   Where the compensator applies for a fresh certificate while a certificate ('the existing certificate') remains in force, the Secretary of State must issue the fresh certificate before the end of the following period.

(8)   The period is –

(a) the prescribed period, or

(b) if there is no prescribed period, the period of four weeks,

which begins with the day following the day on which the existing certificate ceases to be in force.

(9) For the purposes of this Act, regulations may provide for the day on which an application for a certificate of recoverable benefits is to be treated as received.

5 Information contained in certificates

(1)   A certificate of recoverable benefits must specify, for each recoverable benefit –

(a) the amount which has been or is likely to have been paid on or before a specified date, and

(b) if the benefit is paid or likely to be paid after the specified date, the rate and period for which, and the intervals at which, it is or is likely to be so paid.

(2) In a case where the relevant period has ended before the day on which the Secretary of State receives the application for the certificate, the date specified in the certificate for the purposes of subsection (1) must be the day on which the relevant period ended.

(3) In any other case, the date specified for those purposes must not be earlier than the day on which the Secretary of State received the application.

(4) The Secretary of State may estimate, in such manner as he thinks fit, any of the amounts, rates or periods specified in the certificate.

(5) Where the Secretary of State issues a certificate of recoverable benefits, he must provide the information contained in the certificate to –

(a) the person who appears to him to be the injured person, or

(b) any person who he thinks will receive a compensation payment in respect of the injured person.

(6) A person to whom a certificate of recoverable benefits is issued or who is provided with information under subsection (5) is entitled to particulars of the manner in which any amount, rate or period specified in the certificate has been determined, if he applies to the Secretary of State for those particulars.

LIABILITY OF PERSON PAYING COMPENSATION

6 Liability to pay Secretary of State amount of benefits

(1) A person who makes a compensation payment in any case is liable to pay to the Secretary of State an amount equal to the total amount of the recoverable benefits.

(2) The liability referred to in subsection (1) arises immediately before the compensation payment or, if there is more than one, the first of them is made.

(3) No amount becomes payable under this section before the end of the period of 14 days following the day on which the liability arises.

(4) Subject to subsection (3), an amount becomes payable under this section at the end of the period of 14 days beginning with the day on which a certificate of recoverable benefits is first issued showing that the amount of recoverable benefit to which it relates has been or is likely to have been paid before a specified date.

7 Recovery of payments due under section 6

(1) This section applies where a person has made a compensation payment but-

(a) has not applied for a certificate of recoverable benefits, or

(b) has not made a payment to the Secretary of State under section 6 before the end of the period allowed under that section.

(2) The Secretary of State may –

(a) issue the person who made the compensation payment with a certificate of recoverable benefits, if none has been issued, or

(b) issue him with a copy of the certificate of recoverable benefits or (if more than one has been issued) the most recent one,

and (in either case) issue him with a demand that payment of any amount due under section 6 be made immediately.

(3) The Secretary of State may, in accordance with subsections (4) and (5), recover the amount for which a demand for payment is made under subsection (2) from the person who made the compensation payment.

(4) If the person who made the compensation payment resides or carries on business in England and Wales and a county court so orders, any amount recoverable under subsection (3) is recoverable by execution issued from the county court or otherwise as if it were payable under an order of that court.

(5) If the person who made the payment resides or carries on business in Scotland, any amount recoverable under subsection (3) may be enforced in like manner as an extract registered decree arbitral bearing a warrant for execution issued by the sheriff court of any sheriffdom in Scotland.

(6) A document bearing a certificate which –

(a) is signed by a person authorised to do so by the Secretary of State, and

(b) states that the document, apart from the certificate, is a record of the amount recoverable under subsection (3),

is conclusive evidence that that amount is so recoverable.

(7) A certificate under subsection (6) purporting to be signed by a person authorised to do so by the Secretary of State is to be treated as so signed unless the contrary is proved.

8 Reduction of compensation payment

(1) This section applies in a case where, in relation to any head of compensation listed in column 1 of Schedule 2 –

(a) any of the compensation payment is attributable to that head, and

(b) any recoverable benefit is shown against that head in column 2 of the Schedule.

(2) In such a case, any claim of a person to receive the compensation payment is to be treated for all purposes as discharged if –

(a) he is paid the amount (if any) of the compensation payment calculated in accordance with this section, and

(b) if the amount of the compensation payment so calculated is nil, he is given a statement saying so by the person who (apart from this section) would have paid the gross amount of the compensation payment.

(3) For each head of compensation listed in column 1 of the Schedule for which paragraphs (a) and (b) of subsection (1) are met, so much of the gross amount of the compensation payment as is attributable to that head is to be reduced (to nil, if necessary) by deducting the amount of the recoverable benefit or, as the case may be, the aggregate amount of the recoverable benefits shown against it.

(4) Subsection (3) is to have effect as if a requirement to reduce a payment by deducting an amount which exceeds that payment were a requirement to reduce that payment to nil.

(5) The amount of the compensation payment calculated in accordance with this section is –

(a) the gross amount of the compensation payment,

less

(b) the sum of the reductions made under subsection (3),

(and, accordingly, the amount may be nil).

9 Section 8: supplementary

(1)   A person who makes a compensation payment calculated in accordance with section 8 must inform the person to whom the payment is made –

(a) that the payment has been so calculated, and

(b) of the date for payment by reference to which the calculation has been made.

(2)   If the amount of a compensation payment calculated in accordance with section 8 is nil, a person giving a statement saying so is to be treated for the purposes of this Act as making a payment within section 1(1)(a) on the day on which he gives the statement.

(3)   Where a person –

(a) makes a compensation payment calculated in accordance with section 8, and

(b) if the amount of the compensation payment so calculated is nil, gives a statement saying so,

he is to be treated, for the purpose of determining any rights and liabilities in respect of contribution or indemnity, as having paid the gross amount of the compensation payment.

(4)   For the purposes of this Act –

(a) the gross amount of the compensation payment is the amount of the compensation payment apart from section 8, and

(b) the amount of any recoverable benefit is the amount determined in accordance with the certificate of recoverable benefits.

REVIEWS AND APPEALS

10 Review of certificates of recoverable benefits

[(1)   Any certificate of recoverable benefits may be reviewed by the Secretary of State –

(a) either within the prescribed period or in prescribed cases or circumstances, or

(b) either on the application made for the purpose or on his own initiative.]

(2)   On a review under this section the Secretary of State may either –

(a) confirm the certificate, or

(b) (subject to subsection (3)) issue a fresh certificate containing such variations as he considers appropriate.

(3)   The Secretary of State may not vary the certificate so as to increase the total amount of the recoverable benefits unless it appears to him that the variation is required as a result of the person who applied for the certificate supplying him with incorrect or insufficient information.

11 Appeals against certificates of recoverable benefits

(1)   An appeal against a certificate of recoverable benefits may be made on the ground –

(a) that any amount, rate or period specified in the certificate is incorrect, or

(b) that listed benefits which have been, or are likely to be, paid otherwise than in respect of the accident, injury or disease in question have been brought into account.

(2) An appeal under this section may be made by –

  (a) the person who applied for the certificate of recoverable benefits, or

  (b) (in a case where the amount of the compensation payment has been calculated under section 8) the injured person or other person to whom the payment is made.

(3) No appeal may be made under this section until –

  (a) the claim giving rise to the compensation payment has been finally disposed of, and

  (b) the liability under section 6 has been discharged.

(4) For the purposes of subsection (3)(a), if an award of damages in respect of a claim has been made under or by virtue of –

  (a) section 32A(2)(a) of the Supreme Court Act 1981,

  (b) section 12(2)(a) of the Administration of Justice Act 1982, or

  (c) section 51(2)(a) of the County Courts Act 1984,

(orders for provisional damages in personal injury cases), the claim is to be treated as having been finally disposed of.

(5) Regulations may make provision –

  (a) as to the manner in which, and the time within which, appeals under this section may be made,

  (b) as to the procedure to be followed where such an appeal is made, and

  (c) for the purpose of enabling any such appeal to be treated as an application for review under section 10.

12 Reference of questions to medical appeal tribunal

[(1) The Secretary of State must refer an appeal under section 11 to an appeal tribunal.]

...

(3) In determining [any appeal under section 11], the tribunal must take into account any decision of a court relating to the same, or any similar, issue arising in connection with the accident, injury or disease in question.

(4) On [an appeal under section 11 an appeal tribunal] may either –

  (a) confirm the amounts, rates and periods specified in the certificate of recoverable benefits, or

  (b) specify any variations which are to be made on the issue of a fresh certificate under subsection (5).

(5) When the Secretary of State has received [the decision of the tribunal on the appeal under section 11, he must in accordance with that decision] either –

  (a) confirm the certificate against which the appeal was brought, or

  (b) issue a fresh certificate.

...

(7) Regulations may (among other things) provide for the non-disclosure of medical advice or medical evidence given or submitted following a reference under subsection (1).

13 Appeal to Social Security Commissioner

(1)   An appeal may be made to a Commissioner against any decision of [an appeal tribunal] under section 12 on the ground that the decision was erroneous in point of law.

(2)   An appeal under this section may be made by –

(a) the Secretary of State,

(b) the person who applied for the certificate of recoverable benefits, or

(c) (in a case where the amount of the compensation payment has been calculated in accordance with section 8) the injured person or other person to whom the payment is made.

(3)   [Subsections (7) to (10) of section 14 of the Social Security Act 1998] apply to appeals under this section as they apply to appeals under that section.

14 Reviews and appeals: supplementary

(1)   This section applies in cases where a fresh certificate of recoverable benefits is issued as a result of a review under section 10 or an appeal under section 11.

(2)   If –

(a) a person has made one or more payments to the Secretary of State under section 6, and

(b) in consequence of the review or appeal, it appears that the total amount paid is more than the amount that ought to have been paid,

regulations may provide for the Secretary of State to pay the difference to that person, or to the person to whom the compensation payment is made, or partly to one and partly to the other.

(3)   If –

(a) a person has made one or more payments to the Secretary of State under section 6, and

(b) in consequence of the review or appeal, it appears that the total amount paid is less than the amount that ought to have been paid,

regulations may provide for that person to pay the difference to the Secretary of State.

(4)   Regulations under this section may provide –

(a) for the re-calculation in accordance with section 8 of the amount of any compensation payment,

(b) for giving credit for amounts already paid, and

(c) for the payment by any person of any balance or the recovery from any person of any excess,

and may provide for any matter by modifying this Act.

COURTS

15 Court orders

(1)   This section applies where a court makes an order for a compensation payment to be made in any case, unless the order is made with the consent of the injured person and the person by whom the payment is to be made.

(2)   The court must, in the case of each head of compensation listed in column 1 of Schedule 2 to which any of the compensation payment is attributable, specify in the order the amount of the compensation payment which is attributable to that head.

16 Payments into court

(1)   Regulations may make provision (including provision modifying this Act) for any case in which a payment into court is made.

(2)   The regulations may (among other things) provide –

    (a) for the making of a payment into court to be treated in prescribed circumstances as the making of a compensation payment,

    (b) for application for, and issue of, certificates of recoverable benefits, and

    (c) for the relevant period to be treated as ending on a date determined in accordance with the regulations.

(3)   Rules of court may make provision governing practice and procedure in such cases.

(4)   This section does not extend to Scotland.

17 Benefits irrelevant to assessment of damages

In assessing damages in respect of any accident, injury or disease, the amount of any listed benefits paid or likely to be paid is to be disregarded.

REDUCTION OF COMPENSATION: COMPLEX CASES

18 Lump sum and periodical payments

(1)   Regulations may make provision (including provision modifying this Act) for any case in which two or more compensation payments in the form of lump sums are made by the same person to or in respect of the injured person in consequence of the same accident, injury or disease.

(2)   The regulations may (among other things) provide –

    (a) for the re-calculation in accordance with section 8 of the amount of any compensation payment,

    (b) for giving credit for amounts already paid, and

    (c) for the payment by any person of any balance or the recovery from any person of any excess.

(3)   For the purposes of subsection (2), the regulations may provide for the gross amounts of the compensation payments to be aggregated and for –

    (a) the aggregate amount to be taken to be the gross amount of the compensation payment for the purposes of section 8,

    (b) so much of the aggregate amount as is attributable to a head of compensation listed in column 1 of Schedule 2 to be taken to be the part of the gross amount which is attributable to that head;

and for the amount of any recoverable benefit shown against any head in column 2 of that Schedule to be taken to be the amount determined in accordance with the most recent certificate of recoverable benefits.

(4)   Regulations may make provision (including provision modifying this Act) for any case in which, in final settlement of the injured person's claim, an agreement is entered into for the making of –

(a) periodical compensation payments (whether of an income or capital nature), or

(b) periodical compensation payments and lump sum compensation payments.

(5) Regulations made by virtue of subsection (4) may (among other things) provide –

(a) for the relevant period to be treated as ending at a prescribed time,

(b) for the person who is to make the payments under the agreement to be treated for the purposes of this Act as if he had made a single compensation payment on a prescribed date.

(6) A periodical payment may be a compensation payment for the purposes of this section even though it is a small payment (as defined in Part II of Schedule 1).

19 Payments by more than one person

(1) Regulations may make provision (including provision modifying this Act) for any case in which two or more persons ('the compensators') make compensation payments to or in respect of the same injured person in consequence of the same accident, injury or disease.

(2) In such a case, the sum of the liabilities of the compensators under section 6 is not to exceed the total amount of the recoverable benefits, and the regulations may provide for determining the respective liabilities under that section of each of the compensators.

(3) The regulations may (among other things) provide in the case of each compensator –

(a) for determining or re-determining the part of the recoverable benefits which may be taken into account in his case,

(b) for calculating or re-calculating in accordance with section 8 the amount of any compensation payment,

(c) for giving credit for amounts already paid, and

(d) for the payment by any person of any balance or the recovery from any person of any excess.

MISCELLANEOUS

20 Amounts overpaid under section 6

(1) Regulations may make provision (including provision modifying this Act) for cases where a person has paid to the Secretary of State under section 6 any amount ('the amount of the overpayment') which he was not liable to pay.

(2) The regulations may provide –

(a) for the Secretary of State to pay the amount of the overpayment to that person, or to the person to whom the compensation payment is made, or partly to one and partly to the other, or

(b) for the receipt by the Secretary of State of the amount of the overpayment to be treated as the recovery of that amount.

(3) Regulations made by virtue of subsection (2)(b) are to have effect in spite of anything in section 71 of the Social Security Administration Act 1992 (overpayments- general).

(4) The regulations may also (among other things) provide –

(a) for the re-calculation in accordance with section 8 of the amount of any compensation payment,

(b) for giving credit for amounts already paid, and

(c) for the payment by any person of any balance or the recovery from any person of any excess.

(5) This section does not apply in a case where section 14 applies.

21 Compensation payments to be disregarded

(1) If, when a compensation payment is made, the first and second conditions are met, the payment is to be disregarded for the purposes of sections 6 and 8.

(2) The first condition is that the person making the payment –

(a) has made an application for a certificate of recoverable benefits which complies with subsection (3), and

(b) has in his possession a written acknowledgment of the receipt of his application.

(3) An application complies with this subsection if it –

(a) accurately states the prescribed particulars relating to the injured person and the accident, injury or disease in question, and

(b) specifies the name and address of the person to whom the certificate is to be sent.

(4) The second condition is that the Secretary of State has not sent the certificate to the person, at the address, specified in the application, before the end of the period allowed under section 4.

(5) In any case where –

(a) by virtue of subsection (1), a compensation payment is disregarded for the purposes of sections 6 and 8, but

(b) the person who made the compensation payment nevertheless makes a payment to the Secretary of State for which (but for subsection (1)) he would be liable under section 6,

subsection (1) is to cease to apply in relation to the compensation payment.

(6) If, in the opinion of the Secretary of State, circumstances have arisen which adversely affect normal methods of communication –

(a) he may by order provide that subsection (1) is not to apply during a specified period not exceeding three months, and

(b) he may continue any such order in force for further periods not exceeding three months at a time.

22 Liability of insurers

(1) If a compensation payment is made in a case where –

(a) a person is liable to any extent in respect of the accident, injury or disease, and

(b) the liability is covered to any extent by a policy of insurance,

the policy is also to be treated as covering any liability of that person under section 6.

(2) Liability imposed on the insurer by subsection (1) cannot be excluded or restricted.

(3) For that purpose excluding or restricting liability includes –

(a) making the liability or its enforcement subject to restrictive or onerous conditions,

(b) excluding or restricting any right or remedy in respect of the liability, or subjecting a person to any prejudice in consequence of his pursuing any such right or remedy, or

(c) excluding or restricting rules of evidence or procedure.

(4) Regulations may in prescribed cases limit the amount of the liability imposed on the insurer by subsection (1).

(5) This section applies to policies of insurance issued before (as well as those issued after) its coming into force.

(6) References in this section to policies of insurance and their issue include references to contracts of insurance and their making.

23 Provision of information

(1) Where compensation is sought in respect of any accident, injury or disease suffered by any person ('the injured person'), the following persons must give the Secretary of State the prescribed information about the injured person –

(a) anyone who is, or is alleged to be, liable in respect of the accident, injury or disease, and

(b) anyone acting on behalf of such a person.

(2) A person who receives or claims a listed benefit which is or is likely to be paid in respect of an accident, injury or disease suffered by him, must give the Secretary of State the prescribed information about the accident, injury or disease.

(3) Where a person who has received a listed benefit dies, the duty in subsection (2) is imposed on his personal representative.

(4) Any person who makes a payment (whether on his own behalf or not) –

(a) in consequence of, or

(b) which is referable to any costs (in Scotland, expenses) incurred by reason of,

any accident, injury or disease, or any damage to property, must, if the Secretary of State requests him in writing to do so, give the Secretary of State such particulars relating to the size and composition of the payment as are specified in the request.

(5) The employer of a person who suffers or has suffered an accident, injury or disease, and anyone who has been the employer of such a person at any time during the relevant period, must give the Secretary of State the prescribed information about the payment of statutory sick pay in respect of that person.

(6) In subsection (5) 'employer' has the same meaning as it has in Part XI of the Social Security Contributions and Benefits Act 1992.

(7) A person who is required to give information under this section must do so in the prescribed manner, at the prescribed place and within the prescribed time.

(8) Section 1 does not apply in relation to this section.

24 Power to amend Schedule 2.

(1) The Secretary of State may by regulations amend Schedule 2.

(2) A statutory instrument which contains such regulations shall not be made unless a draft of the instrument has been laid before and approved by resolution of each House of Parliament.

...

29 General interpretation

In this Act –

'benefit' means any benefit under the Social Security Contributions and Benefits Act 1992, a jobseeker's allowance or mobility allowance,

'compensation scheme for motor accidents' means any scheme or arrangement under which funds are available for the payment of compensation in respect of motor accidents caused, or alleged to have been caused, by uninsured or unidentified persons,

'listed benefit' means a benefit listed in column 2 of Schedule 2,

'payment' means payment in money or money's worth, and related expressions are to be interpreted accordingly,

'prescribed' means prescribed by regulations, and

'regulations' means regulations made by the Secretary of State.

SCHEDULE 1
COMPENSATION PAYMENTS

Part I
Exempted payments

1   Any small payment (defined in Part II of this Schedule).

2   Any payment made to or for the injured person under section 35 of the Powers of Criminal Courts Act 1973 or section 249 of the Criminal Procedure (Scotland) Act 1995 (compensation orders against convicted persons).

3   Any payment made in the exercise of a discretion out of property held subject to a trust in a case where no more than 50 per cent. by value of the capital contributed to the trust was directly or indirectly provided by persons who are, or are alleged to be, liable in respect of –

(a)   the accident, injury or disease suffered by the injured person, or

(b)   the same or any connected accident, injury or disease suffered by another.

4   Any payment made out of property held for the purposes of any prescribed trust (whether the payment also falls within paragraph 3 or not).

5   Any payment made to the injured person by an insurance company within the meaning of the Insurance Companies Act 1982 under the terms of any contract of insurance entered into between the injured person and the company before –

(a)   the date on which the injured person first claims a listed benefit in consequence of the disease in question, or

(b)   the occurrence of the accident or injury in question.

6   Any redundancy payment falling to be taken into account in the assessment of damages in respect of an accident, injury or disease.

7   So much of any payment as is referable to costs.

8   Any prescribed payment.

Part II
Power to disregard small payments

9(1) Regulations may make provision for compensation payments to be disregarded for the purposes of sections 6 and 8 in prescribed cases where the amount of the compensation payment, or the aggregate amount of two or more connected compensation payments, does not exceed the prescribed sum.

(2) A compensation payment disregarded by virtue of this paragraph is referred to in paragraph 1 as a 'small payment'.

(3) For the purposes of this paragraph –

(a) two or more compensation payments are 'connected' if each is made to or in respect of the same injured person and in respect of the same accident, injury or disease, and

(b) any reference to a compensation payment is a reference to a payment which would be such a payment apart from paragraph 1.

SCHEDULE 2
CALCULATION OF COMPENSATION PAYMENTS

(1) Head of compensation	(2) Benefit
1 Compensation for earnings lost during the relevant period	...
	Disablement pension payable under section 103 of the 1992 Act
	Incapacity benefit
	Income support
	Invalidity pension and allowance
	Jobseeker's allowance
	Reduced earnings allowance
	Severe disablement allowance
	Sickness benefit
	Statutory sick pay
	Unemployability supplement
	Unemployment benefit
2 Compensation for cost of care incurred during the relevant period	Attendance allowance
	Care component of disability living allowance
	Disablement pension increase payable under section 104 or 105 of the 1992 Act
3 Compensation for loss of mobility during the relevant period	Mobility allowance
	Mobility component of disability living allowance

Notes

1

(1) References to incapacity benefit, invalidity pension and allowance, severe disablement allowance, sickness benefit and unemployment benefit also include any income support paid with each of those benefits on the same instrument of payment or paid concurrently with each of those benefits by means of an instrument for benefit payment.

(2) For the purpose of this Note, income support includes personal expenses addition, special transitional additions and transitional addition as defined in the Income Support (Transitional) Regulations 1987.

2

Any reference to statutory sick pay –

(a) includes only 80 per cent of payments made between 6th April 1991 and 5th April 1994, and

(b) does not include payments made on or after 6th April 1994.

3

In this Schedule 'the 1992 Act' means the Social Security Contributions and Benefits Act 1992.

DATA PROTECTION ACT 1998

An Act to make new provision for the regulation of the processing of information relating to individuals, including the obtaining, holding, use or disclosure of such information.

[16th July 1998]

BE IT ENACTED by the Queen's most Excellent Majesty, by and with the advice and consent of the Lords Spiritual and Temporal, and Commons, in this present Parliament assembled, and by the authority of the same, as follows: –

Part I

Preliminary

1 Basic interpretative provisions

(1) In this Act, unless the context otherwise requires –

'data' means information which –

(a) is being processed by means of equipment operating automatically in response to instructions given for that purpose,

(b) is recorded with the intention that it should be processed by means of such equipment,

(c) is recorded as part of a relevant filing system or with the intention that it should form part of a relevant filing system, or

(d) does not fall within paragraph (a), (b) or (c) but forms part of an accessible record as defined by section 68;

'data controller' means, subject to subsection (4), a person who (either alone or jointly or in common with other persons) determines the purposes for which and the manner in which any personal data are, or are to be, processed;

'data processor', in relation to personal data, means any person (other than an employee of the data controller) who processes the data on behalf of the data controller;

'data subject' means an individual who is the subject of personal data;

'personal data' means data which relate to a living individual who can be identified –

(a) from those data, or

(b) from those data and other information which is in the possession of, or is likely to come into the possession of, the data controller,

and includes any expression of opinion about the individual and any indication of the intentions of the data controller or any other person in respect of the individual;

'processing', in relation to information or data, means obtaining, recording or holding the information or data or carrying out any operation or set of operations on the information or data, including –

(a) organisation, adaptation or alteration of the information or data,

(b) retrieval, consultation or use of the information or data,

(c) disclosure of the information or data by transmission, dissemination or otherwise making available, or

(d) alignment, combination, blocking, erasure or destruction of the information or data;

'relevant filing system' means any set of information relating to individuals to the extent that, although the information is not processed by means of equipment operating automatically in response to instructions given for that purpose, the set is structured, either by reference to individuals or by reference to criteria relating to individuals, in such a way that specific information relating to a particular individual is readily accessible.

(2)   In this Act, unless the context otherwise requires –

(a) 'obtaining' or 'recording', in relation to personal data, includes obtaining or recording the information to be contained in the data, and

(b) 'using' or 'disclosing', in relation to personal data, includes using or disclosing the information contained in the data.

(3) In determining for the purposes of this Act whether any information is recorded with the intention –

(a) that it should be processed by means of equipment operating automatically in response to instructions given for that purpose, or

(b) that it should form part of a relevant filing system,

it is immaterial that it is intended to be so processed or to form part of such a system only after being transferred to a country or territory outside the European Economic Area.

(4)   Where personal data are processed only for purposes for which they are required by or under any enactment to be processed, the person on whom the obligation to process the data is imposed by or under that enactment is for the purposes of this Act the data controller.

2 Sensitive personal data

In this Act 'sensitive personal data' means personal data consisting of information as to –

(a) the racial or ethnic origin of the data subject,

(b) his political opinions,

(c) his religious beliefs or other beliefs of a similar nature,

(d) whether he is a member of a trade union (within the meaning of the Trade Union and Labour Relations (Consolidation) Act 1992),

(e) his physical or mental health or condition,

(f) his sexual life,

(g) the commission or alleged commission by him of any offence, or

(h) any proceedings for any offence committed or alleged to have been committed by him, the disposal of such proceedings or the sentence of any court in such proceedings.

3 The special purposes

In this Act 'the special purposes' means any one or more of the following –

(a) the purposes of journalism,

(b) artistic purposes, and

(c) literary purposes.

4 The data protection principles

(1) References in this Act to the data protection principles are to the principles set out in Part I of Schedule 1.

(2) Those principles are to be interpreted in accordance with Part II of Schedule 1.

(3) Schedule 2 (which applies to all personal data) and Schedule 3 (which applies only to sensitive personal data) set out conditions applying for the purposes of the first principle; and Schedule 4 sets out cases in which the eighth principle does not apply.

(4) Subject to section 27(1), it shall be the duty of a data controller to comply with the data protection principles in relation to all personal data with respect to which he is the data controller.

5 Application of Act

(1) Except as otherwise provided by or under section 54, this Act applies to a data controller in respect of any data only if –

(a) the data controller is established in the United Kingdom and the data are processed in the context of that establishment, or

(b) the data controller is established neither in the United Kingdom nor in any other EEA State but uses equipment in the United Kingdom for processing the data otherwise than for the purposes of transit through the United Kingdom.

(2) A data controller falling within subsection (1)(b) must nominate for the purposes of this Act a representative established in the United Kingdom.

(3) For the purposes of subsections (1) and (2), each of the following is to be treated as established in the United Kingdom –

(a) an individual who is ordinarily resident in the United Kingdom,

(b) a body incorporated under the law of, or of any part of, the United Kingdom,

(c) a partnership or other unincorporated association formed under the law of any part of the United Kingdom, and

(d) any person who does not fall within paragraph (a), (b) or (c) but maintains in the United Kingdom-

(i) an office, branch or agency through which he carries on any activity, or

(ii) a regular practice;

and the reference to establishment in any other EEA State has a corresponding meaning.

6 The Commissioner and the Tribunal

(1) The office originally established by section 3(1)(a) of the Data Protection Act 1984 as the office of Data Protection Registrar shall continue to exist for the purposes of this Act but shall be known as the office of Data Protection Commissioner; and in this Act the Data Protection Commissioner is referred to as 'the Commissioner'.

(2) The Commissioner shall be appointed by Her Majesty by Letters Patent.

(3) For the purposes of this Act there shall continue to be a Data Protection Tribunal (in this Act referred to as 'the Tribunal').

(4)   The Tribunal shall consist of –

(a)   a chairman appointed by the Lord Chancellor after consultation with the Lord Advocate,

(b)   such number of deputy chairmen so appointed as the Lord Chancellor may determine, and

(c)   such number of other members appointed by the Secretary of State as he may determine.

(5)   The members of the Tribunal appointed under subsection (4)(a) and (b) shall be –

(a)   persons who have a 7 year general qualification, within the meaning of section 71 of the Courts and Legal Services Act 1990,

(b)   advocates or solicitors in Scotland of at least 7 years' standing, or

(c)   members of the bar of Northern Ireland or solicitors of the Supreme Court of Northern Ireland of at least 7 years' standing.

(6)   The members of the Tribunal appointed under subsection (4)(c) shall be –

(a)   persons to represent the interests of data subjects, and

(b)   persons to represent the interests of data controllers.

(7)   Schedule 5 has effect in relation to the Commissioner and the Tribunal.

Part II

Rights of data subjects and others

7 Right of access to personal data

(1)   Subject to the following provisions of this section and to sections 8 and 9, an individual is entitled –

(a)   to be informed by any data controller whether personal data of which that individual is the data subject are being processed by or on behalf of that data controller,

(b)   if that is the case, to be given by the data controller a description of –

(i) the personal data of which that individual is the data subject,

(ii) the purposes for which they are being or are to be processed, and

(iii) the recipients or classes of recipients to whom they are or may be disclosed,

(c)   to have communicated to him in an intelligible form-

(i)   the information constituting any personal data of which that individual is the data subject, and

(ii)   any information available to the data controller as to the source of those data, and

(d)   where the processing by automatic means of personal data of which that individual is the data subject for the purpose of evaluating matters relating to him such as, for example, his performance at work, his creditworthiness, his reliability or his conduct, has constituted or is likely to constitute the sole basis for any decision significantly affecting him, to be informed by the data controller of the logic involved in that decision-taking.

(2) A data controller is not obliged to supply any information under subsection (1) unless he has received –

   (a) a request in writing, and

   (b) except in prescribed cases, such fee (not exceeding the prescribed maximum) as he may require.

(3) A data controller is not obliged to comply with a request under this section unless he is supplied with such information as he may reasonably require in order to satisfy himself as to the identity of the person making the request and to locate the information which that person seeks.

(4) Where a data controller cannot comply with the request without disclosing information relating to another individual who can be identified from that information, he is not obliged to comply with the request unless –

   (a) the other individual has consented to the disclosure of the information to the person making the request, or

   (b) it is reasonable in all the circumstances to comply with the request without the consent of the other individual.

(5) In subsection (4) the reference to information relating to another individual includes a reference to information identifying that individual as the source of the information sought by the request; and that subsection is not to be construed as excusing a data controller from communicating so much of the information sought by the request as can be communicated without disclosing the identity of the other individual concerned, whether by the omission of names or other identifying particulars or otherwise.

(6) In determining for the purposes of subsection (4)(b) whether it is reasonable in all the circumstances to comply with the request without the consent of the other individual concerned, regard shall be had, in particular, to –

   (a) any duty of confidentiality owed to the other individual,

   (b) any steps taken by the data controller with a view to seeking the consent of the other individual,

   (c) whether the other individual is capable of giving consent, and

   (d) any express refusal of consent by the other individual.

(7) An individual making a request under this section may, in such cases as may be prescribed, specify that his request is limited to personal data of any prescribed description.

(8) Subject to subsection (4), a data controller shall comply with a request under this section promptly and in any event before the end of the prescribed period beginning with the relevant day.

(9) If a court is satisfied on the application of any person who has made a request under the foregoing provisions of this section that the data controller in question has failed to comply with the request in contravention of those provisions, the court may order him to comply with the request.

(10) In this section –

   'prescribed' means prescribed by the Secretary of State by regulations;

   'the prescribed maximum' means such amount as may be prescribed;

'the prescribed period' means forty days or such other period as may be prescribed;

'the relevant day', in relation to a request under this section, means the day on which the data controller receives the request or, if later, the first day on which the data controller has both the required fee and the information referred to in subsection (3).

(11) Different amounts or periods may be prescribed under this section in relation to different cases.

8 Provisions supplementary to section 7

(1) The Secretary of State may by regulations provide that, in such cases as may be prescribed, a request for information under any provision of subsection (1) of section 7 is to be treated as extending also to information under other provisions of that subsection.

(2) The obligation imposed by section 7(1)(c)(i) must be complied with by supplying the data subject with a copy of the information in permanent form unless –

(a) the supply of such a copy is not possible or would involve disproportionate effort, or

(b) the data subject agrees otherwise;

and where any of the information referred to in section 7(1)(c)(i) is expressed in terms which are not intelligible without explanation the copy must be accompanied by an explanation of those terms.

(3) Where a data controller has previously complied with a request made under section 7 by an individual, the data controller is not obliged to comply with a subsequent identical or similar request under that section by that individual unless a reasonable interval has elapsed between compliance with the previous request and the making of the current request.

(4) In determining for the purposes of subsection (3) whether requests under section 7 are made at reasonable intervals, regard shall be had to the nature of the data, the purpose for which the data are processed and the frequency with which the data are altered.

(5) Section 7(1)(d) is not to be regarded as requiring the provision of information as to the logic involved in any decision-taking if, and to the extent that, the information constitutes a trade secret.

(6) The information to be supplied pursuant to a request under section 7 must be supplied by reference to the data in question at the time when the request is received, except that it may take account of any amendment or deletion made between that time and the time when the information is supplied, being an amendment or deletion that would have been made regardless of the receipt of the request.

(7) For the purposes of section 7(4) and (5) another individual can be identified from the information being disclosed if he can be identified from that information, or from that and any other information which, in the reasonable belief of the data controller, is likely to be in, or to come into, the possession of the data subject making the request.

9 Application of section 7 where data controller is credit reference agency

(1) Where the data controller is a credit reference agency, section 7 has effect subject to the provisions of this section.

(2) An individual making a request under section 7 may limit his request to personal data relevant to his financial standing, and shall be taken to have so limited his request unless the request shows a contrary intention.

(3) Where the data controller receives a request under section 7 in a case where personal data of which the individual making the request is the data subject are being processed by or on behalf of the data controller, the obligation to supply information under that section includes an obligation to give the individual making the request a statement, in such form as may be prescribed by the Secretary of State by regulations, of the individual's rights –

(a) under section 159 of the Consumer Credit Act 1974 , and

(b) to the extent required by the prescribed form, under this Act.

10 Right to prevent processing likely to cause damage or distress

(1) Subject to subsection (2), an individual is entitled at any time by notice in writing to a data controller to require the data controller at the end of such period as is reasonable in the circumstances to cease, or not to begin, processing, or processing for a specified purpose or in a specified manner, any personal data in respect of which he is the data subject, on the ground that, for specified reasons –

(a) the processing of those data or their processing for that purpose or in that manner is causing or is likely to cause substantial damage or substantial distress to him or to another, and

(b) that damage or distress is or would be unwarranted.

(2) Subsection (1) does not apply –

(a) in a case where any of the conditions in paragraphs 1 to 4 of Schedule 2 is met, or

(b) in such other cases as may be prescribed by the Secretary of State by order.

(3) The data controller must within twenty-one days of receiving a notice under subsection (1) ('the data subject notice') give the individual who gave it a written notice –

(a) stating that he has complied or intends to comply with the data subject notice, or

(b) stating his reasons for regarding the data subject notice as to any extent unjustified and the extent (if any) to which he has complied or intends to comply with it.

(4) If a court is satisfied, on the application of any person who has given a notice under subsection (1) which appears to the court to be justified (or to be justified to any extent), that the data controller in question has failed to comply with the notice, the court may order him to take such steps for complying with the notice (or for complying with it to that extent) as the court thinks fit.

(5) The failure by a data subject to exercise the right conferred by subsection (1) or section 11(1) does not affect any other right conferred on him by this Part.

11 Right to prevent processing for purposes of direct marketing

(1) An individual is entitled at any time by notice in writing to a data controller to require the data controller at the end of such period as is reasonable in the circumstances to cease, or not to begin, processing for the purposes of direct marketing personal data in respect of which he is the data subject.

(2) If the court is satisfied, on the application of any person who has given a notice under subsection (1), that the data controller has failed to comply with the notice, the court may order him to take such steps for complying with the notice as the court thinks fit.

(3) In this section 'direct marketing' means the communication (by whatever means) of any advertising or marketing material which is directed to particular individuals.

12 Rights in relation to automated decision-taking

(1) An individual is entitled at any time, by notice in writing to any data controller, to require the data controller to ensure that no decision taken by or on behalf of the data controller which significantly affects that individual is based solely on the processing by automatic means of personal data in respect of which that individual is the data subject for the purpose of evaluating matters relating to him such as, for example, his performance at work, his creditworthiness, his reliability or his conduct.

(2) Where, in a case where no notice under subsection (1) has effect, a decision which significantly affects an individual is based solely on such processing as is mentioned in subsection (1) –

(a) the data controller must as soon as reasonably practicable notify the individual that the decision was taken on that basis, and

(b) the individual is entitled, within twenty-one days of receiving that notification from the data controller, by notice in writing to require the data controller to reconsider the decision or to take a new decision otherwise than on that basis.

(3) The data controller must, within twenty-one days of receiving a notice under subsection (2)(b) ('the data subject notice') give the individual a written notice specifying the steps that he intends to take to comply with the data subject notice.

(4) A notice under subsection (1) does not have effect in relation to an exempt decision; and nothing in subsection (2) applies to an exempt decision.

(5) In subsection (4) 'exempt decision' means any decision –

(a) in respect of which the condition in subsection (6) and the condition in subsection (7) are met, or

(b) which is made in such other circumstances as may be prescribed by the Secretary of State by order.

(6) The condition in this subsection is that the decision –

(a) is taken in the course of steps taken-

(i) for the purpose of considering whether to enter into a contract with the data subject,

(ii) with a view to entering into such a contract, or

(iii) in the course of performing such a contract, or

(b) is authorised or required by or under any enactment.

(7)   The condition in this subsection is that either –

   (a) the effect of the decision is to grant a request of the data subject, or

   (b) steps have been taken to safeguard the legitimate interests of the data subject (for example, by allowing him to make representations).

(8)   If a court is satisfied on the application of a data subject that a person taking a decision in respect of him ('the responsible person') has failed to comply with subsection (1) or (2)(b), the court may order the responsible person to reconsider the decision, or to take a new decision which is not based solely on such processing as is mentioned in subsection (1).

(9)   An order under subsection (8) shall not affect the rights of any person other than the data subject and the responsible person.

13 Compensation for failure to comply with certain requirements

(1)   An individual who suffers damage by reason of any contravention by a data controller of any of the requirements of this Act is entitled to compensation from the data controller for that damage.

(2)   An individual who suffers distress by reason of any contravention by a data controller of any of the requirements of this Act is entitled to compensation from the data controller for that distress if –

   (a) the individual also suffers damage by reason of the contravention, or

   (b) the contravention relates to the processing of personal data for the special purposes.

(3)   In proceedings brought against a person by virtue of this section it is a defence to prove that he had taken such care as in all the circumstances was reasonably required to comply with the requirement concerned.

14 Rectification, blocking, erasure and destruction

(1)   If a court is satisfied on the application of a data subject that personal data of which the applicant is the subject are inaccurate, the court may order the data controller to rectify, block, erase or destroy those data and any other personal data in respect of which he is the data controller and which contain an expression of opinion which appears to the court to be based on the inaccurate data.

(2)   Subsection (1) applies whether or not the data accurately record information received or obtained by the data controller from the data subject or a third party but where the data accurately record such information, then –

   (a) if the requirements mentioned in paragraph 7 of Part II of Schedule 1 have been complied with, the court may, instead of making an order under subsection (1), make an order requiring the data to be supplemented by such statement of the true facts relating to the matters dealt with by the data as the court may approve, and

   (b) if all or any of those requirements have not been complied with, the court may, instead of making an order under that subsection, make such order as it thinks fit for securing compliance with those requirements with or without a further order requiring the data to be supplemented by such a statement as is mentioned in paragraph (a).

(3)   Where the court –

   (a) makes an order under subsection (1), or

   (b) is satisfied on the application of a data subject that personal data of which he was the data subject and which have been rectified, blocked, erased or destroyed were inaccurate,

   it may, where it considers it reasonably practicable, order the data controller to notify third parties to whom the data have been disclosed of the rectification, blocking, erasure or destruction.

(4)   If a court is satisfied on the application of a data subject –

   (a) that he has suffered damage by reason of any contravention by a data controller of any of the requirements of this Act in respect of any personal data, in circumstances entitling him to compensation under section 13, and

   (b) that there is a substantial risk of further contravention in respect of those data in such circumstances,

   the court may order the rectification, blocking, erasure or destruction of any of those data.

(5)   Where the court makes an order under subsection (4) it may, where it considers it reasonably practicable, order the data controller to notify third parties to whom the data have been disclosed of the rectification, blocking, erasure or destruction.

(6)   In determining whether it is reasonably practicable to require such notification as is mentioned in subsection (3) or (5) the court shall have regard, in particular, to the number of persons who would have to be notified.

15 Jurisdiction and procedure

(1)   The jurisdiction conferred by sections 7 to 14 is exercisable by the High Court or a county court or, in Scotland, by the Court of Session or the sheriff.

(2)   For the purpose of determining any question whether an applicant under subsection (9) of section 7 is entitled to the information which he seeks (including any question whether any relevant data are exempt from that section by virtue of Part IV) a court may require the information constituting any data processed by or on behalf of the data controller and any information as to the logic involved in any decision-taking as mentioned in section 7(1)(d) to be made available for its own inspection but shall not, pending the determination of that question in the applicant's favour, require the information sought by the applicant to be disclosed to him or his representatives whether by discovery (or, in Scotland, recovery) or otherwise.

Part III
Notification by data controllers

16 Preliminary

(1)   In this Part 'the registrable particulars', in relation to a data controller, means –

   (a) his name and address,

   (b) if he has nominated a representative for the purposes of this Act, the name and address of the representative,

   (c) a description of the personal data being or to be processed by or on behalf of the data controller and of the category or categories of data subject to which they relate,

(d) a description of the purpose or purposes for which the data are being or are to be processed,

(e) a description of any recipient or recipients to whom the data controller intends or may wish to disclose the data,

(f) the names, or a description of, any countries or territories outside the European Economic Area to which the data controller directly or indirectly transfers, or intends or may wish directly or indirectly to transfer, the data, and

(g) in any case where-

  (i) personal data are being, or are intended to be, processed in circumstances in which the prohibition in subsection (1) of section 17 is excluded by subsection (2) or (3) of that section, and

  (ii) the notification does not extend to those data,

a statement of that fact.

(2) In this Part –

'fees regulations' means regulations made by the Secretary of State under section 18(5) or 19(4) or (7);

'notification regulations' means regulations made by the Secretary of State under the other provisions of this Part;

'prescribed', except where used in relation to fees regulations, means prescribed by notification regulations.

(3) For the purposes of this Part, so far as it relates to the addresses of data controllers –

(a) the address of a registered company is that of its registered office, and

(b) the address of a person (other than a registered company) carrying on a business is that of his principal place of business in the United Kingdom.

17 Prohibition on processing without registration

(1) Subject to the following provisions of this section, personal data must not be processed unless an entry in respect of the data controller is included in the register maintained by the Commissioner under section 19 (or is treated by notification regulations made by virtue of section 19(3) as being so included).

(2) Except where the processing is assessable processing for the purposes of section 22, subsection (1) does not apply in relation to personal data consisting of information which falls neither within paragraph (a) of the definition of 'data' in section 1(1) nor within paragraph (b) of that definition.

(3) If it appears to the Secretary of State that processing of a particular description is unlikely to prejudice the rights and freedoms of data subjects, notification regulations may provide that, in such cases as may be prescribed, subsection (1) is not to apply in relation to processing of that description.

(4) Subsection (1) does not apply in relation to any processing whose sole purpose is the maintenance of a public register.

18 Notification by data controllers

(1) Any data controller who wishes to be included in the register maintained under section 19 shall give a notification to the Commissioner under this section.

(2)   A notification under this section must specify in accordance with notification regulations –

(a) the registrable particulars, and

(b) a general description of measures to be taken for the purpose of complying with the seventh data protection principle.

(3)   Notification regulations made by virtue of subsection (2) may provide for the determination by the Commissioner, in accordance with any requirements of the regulations, of the form in which the registrable particulars and the description mentioned in subsection (2)(b) are to be specified, including in particular the detail required for the purposes of section 16(1)(c), (d), (e) and (f) and subsection (2)(b).

(4)   Notification regulations may make provision as to the giving of notification –

(a) by partnerships, or

(b) in other cases where two or more persons are the data controllers in respect of any personal data.

(5)   The notification must be accompanied by such fee as may be prescribed by fees regulations.

(6)   Notification regulations may provide for any fee paid under subsection (5) or section 19(4) to be refunded in prescribed circumstances.

19 Register of notifications

(1)   The Commissioner shall –

(a) maintain a register of persons who have given notification under section 18, and

(b) make an entry in the register in pursuance of each notification received by him under that section from a person in respect of whom no entry as data controller was for the time being included in the register.

(2)   Each entry in the register shall consist of –

(a) the registrable particulars notified under section 18 or, as the case requires, those particulars as amended in pursuance of section 20(4), and

(b) such other information as the Commissioner may be authorised or required by notification regulations to include in the register.

(3)   Notification regulations may make provision as to the time as from which any entry in respect of a data controller is to be treated for the purposes of section 17 as having been made in the register.

(4)   No entry shall be retained in the register for more than the relevant time except on payment of such fee as may be prescribed by fees regulations.

(5)   In subsection (4) 'the relevant time' means twelve months or such other period as may be prescribed by notification regulations; and different periods may be prescribed in relation to different cases.

(6)   The Commissioner –

(a) shall provide facilities for making the information contained in the entries in the register available for inspection (in visible and legible form) by members of the public at all reasonable hours and free of charge, and

(b) may provide such other facilities for making the information contained in those entries available to the public free of charge as he considers appropriate.

(7) The Commissioner shall, on payment of such fee, if any, as may be prescribed by fees regulations, supply any member of the public with a duly certified copy in writing of the particulars contained in any entry made in the register.

20 Duty to notify changes

(1) For the purpose specified in subsection (2), notification regulations shall include provision imposing on every person in respect of whom an entry as a data controller is for the time being included in the register maintained under section 19 a duty to notify to the Commissioner, in such circumstances and at such time or times and in such form as may be prescribed, such matters relating to the registrable particulars and measures taken as mentioned in section 18(2)(b) as may be prescribed.

(2) The purpose referred to in subsection (1) is that of ensuring, so far as practicable, that at any time –

(a) the entries in the register maintained under section 19 contain current names and addresses and describe the current practice or intentions of the data controller with respect to the processing of personal data, and

(b) the Commissioner is provided with a general description of measures currently being taken as mentioned in section 18(2)(b).

(3) Subsection (3) of section 18 has effect in relation to notification regulations made by virtue of subsection (1) as it has effect in relation to notification regulations made by virtue of subsection (2) of that section.

(4) On receiving any notification under notification regulations made by virtue of subsection (1), the Commissioner shall make such amendments of the relevant entry in the register maintained under section 19 as are necessary to take account of the notification.

21 Offences

(1) If section 17(1) is contravened, the data controller is guilty of an offence.

(2) Any person who fails to comply with the duty imposed by notification regulations made by virtue of section 20(1) is guilty of an offence.

(3) It shall be a defence for a person charged with an offence under subsection (2) to show that he exercised all due diligence to comply with the duty.

22 Preliminary assessment by Commissioner

(1) In this section 'assessable processing' means processing which is of a description specified in an order made by the Secretary of State as appearing to him to be particularly likely –

(a) to cause substantial damage or substantial distress to data subjects, or

(b) otherwise significantly to prejudice the rights and freedoms of data subjects.

(2) On receiving notification from any data controller under section 18 or under notification regulations made by virtue of section 20 the Commissioner shall consider –

(a) whether any of the processing to which the notification relates is assessable processing, and

(b) if so, whether the assessable processing is likely to comply with the provisions of this Act.

(3) Subject to subsection (4), the Commissioner shall, within the period of twenty-eight days beginning with the day on which he receives a notification which relates to assessable processing, give a notice to the data controller stating the extent to which the Commissioner is of the opinion that the processing is likely or unlikely to comply with the provisions of this Act.

(4) Before the end of the period referred to in subsection (3) the Commissioner may, by reason of special circumstances, extend that period on one occasion only by notice to the data controller by such further period not exceeding fourteen days as the Commissioner may specify in the notice.

(5) No assessable processing in respect of which a notification has been given to the Commissioner as mentioned in subsection (2) shall be carried on unless either –

   (a) the period of twenty-eight days beginning with the day on which the notification is received by the Commissioner (or, in a case falling within subsection (4), that period as extended under that subsection) has elapsed, or

   (b) before the end of that period (or that period as so extended) the data controller has received a notice from the Commissioner under subsection (3) in respect of the processing.

(6) Where subsection (5) is contravened, the data controller is guilty of an offence.

(7) The Secretary of State may by order amend subsections (3), (4) and (5) by substituting for the number of days for the time being specified there a different number specified in the order.

23 Power to make provision for appointment of data protection supervisors

(1) The Secretary of State may by order –

   (a) make provision under which a data controller may appoint a person to act as a data protection supervisor responsible in particular for monitoring in an independent manner the data controller's compliance with the provisions of this Act, and

   (b) provide that, in relation to any data controller who has appointed a data protection supervisor in accordance with the provisions of the order and who complies with such conditions as may be specified in the order, the provisions of this Part are to have effect subject to such exemptions or other modifications as may be specified in the order.

(2) An order under this section may –

   (a) impose duties on data protection supervisors in relation to the Commissioner, and

   (b) confer functions on the Commissioner in relation to data protection supervisors.

24 Duty of certain data controllers to make certain information available

(1) Subject to subsection (3), where personal data are processed in a case where –

   (a) by virtue of subsection (2) or (3) of section 17, subsection (1) of that section does not apply to the processing, and

   (b) the data controller has not notified the relevant particulars in respect of that processing under section 18, the data controller must, within twenty-one days of receiving a written request from any person, make the relevant particulars available to that person in writing free of charge.

(2) In this section 'the relevant particulars' means the particulars referred to in paragraphs (a) to (f) of section 16(1).

(3) This section has effect subject to any exemption conferred for the purposes of this section by notification regulations.

(4) Any data controller who fails to comply with the duty imposed by subsection (1) is guilty of an offence.

(5) It shall be a defence for a person charged with an offence under subsection (4) to show that he exercised all due diligence to comply with the duty.

25 Functions of Commissioner in relation to making of notification regulations

(1) As soon as practicable after the passing of this Act, the Commissioner shall submit to the Secretary of State proposals as to the provisions to be included in the first notification regulations.

(2) The Commissioner shall keep under review the working of notification regulations and may from time to time submit to the Secretary of State proposals as to amendments to be made to the regulations.

(3) The Secretary of State may from time to time require the Commissioner to consider any matter relating to notification regulations and to submit to him proposals as to amendments to be made to the regulations in connection with that matter.

(4) Before making any notification regulations, the Secretary of State shall –

   (a) consider any proposals made to him by the Commissioner under subsection (1), (2) or (3), and

   (b) consult the Commissioner.

26 Fees regulations

(1) Fees regulations prescribing fees for the purposes of any provision of this Part may provide for different fees to be payable in different cases.

(2) In making any fees regulations, the Secretary of State shall have regard to the desirability of securing that the fees payable to the Commissioner are sufficient to offset –

   (a) the expenses incurred by the Commissioner and the Tribunal in discharging their functions and any expenses of the Secretary of State in respect of the Commissioner or the Tribunal, and

   (b) to the extent that the Secretary of State considers appropriate-

      (i) any deficit previously incurred (whether before or after the passing of this Act) in respect of the expenses mentioned in paragraph (a), and

      (ii) expenses incurred or to be incurred by the Secretary of State in respect of the inclusion of any officers or staff of the Commissioner in any scheme under section 1 of the Superannuation Act 1972.

Part IV
Exemptions

27 Preliminary

(1) References in any of the data protection principles or any provision of Parts II and III to personal data or to the processing of personal data do not include references to data or processing which by virtue of this Part are exempt from that principle or other provision.

(2) In this Part 'the subject information provisions' means –

(a) the first data protection principle to the extent to which it requires compliance with paragraph 2 of Part II of Schedule 1, and

(b) section 7.

(3) In this Part 'the non-disclosure provisions' means the provisions specified in subsection (4) to the extent to which they are inconsistent with the disclosure in question.

(4) The provisions referred to in subsection (3) are –

(a) the first data protection principle, except to the extent to which it requires compliance with the conditions in Schedules 2 and 3,

(b) the second, third, fourth and fifth data protection principles, and

(c) sections 10 and 14(1) to (3).

(5) Except as provided by this Part, the subject information provisions shall have effect notwithstanding any enactment or rule of law prohibiting or restricting the disclosure, or authorising the withholding, of information.

28 National security

(1) Personal data are exempt from any of the provisions of –

(a) the data protection principles,

(b) Parts II, III and V, and

(c) section 55,

if the exemption from that provision is required for the purpose of safeguarding national security.

(2) Subject to subsection (4), a certificate signed by a Minister of the Crown certifying that exemption from all or any of the provisions mentioned in subsection (1) is or at any time was required for the purpose there mentioned in respect of any personal data shall be conclusive evidence of that fact.

(3) A certificate under subsection (2) may identify the personal data to which it applies by means of a general description and may be expressed to have prospective effect.

(4) Any person directly affected by the issuing of a certificate under subsection (2) may appeal to the Tribunal against the certificate.

(5) If on an appeal under subsection (4), the Tribunal finds that, applying the principles applied by the court on an application for judicial review, the Minister did not have reasonable grounds for issuing the certificate, the Tribunal may allow the appeal and quash the certificate.

(6) Where in any proceedings under or by virtue of this Act it is claimed by a data controller that a certificate under subsection (2) which identifies the personal data

to which it applies by means of a general description applies to any personal data, any other party to the proceedings may appeal to the Tribunal on the ground that the certificate does not apply to the personal data in question and, subject to any determination under subsection (7), the certificate shall be conclusively presumed so to apply.

(7)   On any appeal under subsection (6), the Tribunal may determine that the certificate does not so apply.

(8)   A document purporting to be a certificate under subsection (2) shall be received in evidence and deemed to be such a certificate unless the contrary is proved.

(9)   A document which purports to be certified by or on behalf of a Minister of the Crown as a true copy of a certificate issued by that Minister under subsection (2) shall in any legal proceedings be evidence (or, in Scotland, sufficient evidence) of that certificate.

(10) The power conferred by subsection (2) on a Minister of the Crown shall not be exercisable except by a Minister who is a member of the Cabinet or by the Attorney General or the Lord Advocate.

(11) No power conferred by any provision of Part V may be exercised in relation to personal data which by virtue of this section are exempt from that provision.

(12) Schedule 6 shall have effect in relation to appeals under subsection (4) or (6) and the proceedings of the Tribunal in respect of any such appeal.

29 Crime and taxation

(1)   Personal data processed for any of the following purposes –

   (a) the prevention or detection of crime,

   (b) the apprehension or prosecution of offenders, or

   (c) the assessment or collection of any tax or duty or of any imposition of a similar nature,

are exempt from the first data protection principle (except to the extent to which it requires compliance with the conditions in Schedules 2 and 3) and section 7 in any case to the extent to which the application of those provisions to the data would be likely to prejudice any of the matters mentioned in this subsection.

(2)   Personal data which –

   (a) are processed for the purpose of discharging statutory functions, and

   (b) consist of information obtained for such a purpose from a person who had it in his possession for any of the purposes mentioned in subsection (1),

are exempt from the subject information provisions to the same extent as personal data processed for any of the purposes mentioned in that subsection.

(3)   Personal data are exempt from the non-disclosure provisions in any case in which –

   (a) the disclosure is for any of the purposes mentioned in subsection (1), and

   (b) the application of those provisions in relation to the disclosure would be likely to prejudice any of the matters mentioned in that subsection.

(4)   Personal data in respect of which the data controller is a relevant authority and which –

(a) consist of a classification applied to the data subject as part of a system of risk assessment which is operated by that authority for either of the following purposes –

    (i) the assessment or collection of any tax or duty or any imposition of a similar nature, or

    (ii) the prevention or detection of crime, or apprehension or prosecution of offenders, where the offence concerned involves any unlawful claim for any payment out of, or any unlawful application of, public funds, and

(b) are processed for either of those purposes,

are exempt from section 7 to the extent to which the exemption is required in the interests of the operation of the system.

(5) In subsection (4) –

'public funds' includes funds provided by any Community institution;

'relevant authority' means –

(a) a government department,

(b) a local authority, or

(c) any other authority administering housing benefit or council tax benefit.

30 Health, education and social work

(1) The Secretary of State may by order exempt from the subject information provisions, or modify those provisions in relation to, personal data consisting of information as to the physical or mental health or condition of the data subject.

(2) The Secretary of State may by order exempt from the subject information provisions, or modify those provisions in relation to –

(a) personal data in respect of which the data controller is the proprietor of, or a teacher at, a school, and which consist of information relating to persons who are or have been pupils at the school, or

(b) personal data in respect of which the data controller is an education authority in Scotland, and which consist of information relating to persons who are receiving, or have received, further education provided by the authority.

(3) The Secretary of State may by order exempt from the subject information provisions, or modify those provisions in relation to, personal data of such other descriptions as may be specified in the order, being information –

(a) processed by government departments or local authorities or by voluntary organisations or other bodies designated by or under the order, and

(b) appearing to him to be processed in the course of, or for the purposes of, carrying out social work in relation to the data subject or other individuals;

but the Secretary of State shall not under this subsection confer any exemption or make any modification except so far as he considers that the application to the data of those provisions (or of those provisions without modification) would be likely to prejudice the carrying out of social work.

(4) An order under this section may make different provision in relation to data consisting of information of different descriptions.

(5) In this section –

'education authority' and 'further education' have the same meaning as in the Education (Scotland) Act 1980 ('the 1980 Act'), and

'proprietor'

(a) in relation to a school in England or Wales, has the same meaning as in the Education Act 1996,

(b) in relation to a school in Scotland, means-

(i) in the case of a self-governing school, the board of management within the meaning of the Self-Governing Schools etc. (Scotland) Act 1989,

(ii) in the case of an independent school, the proprietor within the meaning of the 1980 Act,

(iii) in the case of a grant-aided school, the managers within the meaning of the 1980 Act, and

(iv) in the case of a public school, the education authority within the meaning of the 1980 Act, and

(c) in relation to a school in Northern Ireland, has the same meaning as in the Education and Libraries (Northern Ireland) Order 1986 and includes, in the case of a controlled school, the Board of Governors of the school.

31 Regulatory activity

(1) Personal data processed for the purposes of discharging functions to which this subsection applies are exempt from the subject information provisions in any case to the extent to which the application of those provisions to the data would be likely to prejudice the proper discharge of those functions.

(2) Subsection (1) applies to any relevant function which is designed –

(a) for protecting members of the public against-

(i) financial loss due to dishonesty, malpractice or other seriously improper conduct by, or the unfitness or incompetence of, persons concerned in the provision of banking, insurance, investment or other financial services or in the management of bodies corporate,

(ii) financial loss due to the conduct of discharged or undischarged bankrupts, or

(iii) dishonesty, malpractice or other seriously improper conduct by, or the unfitness or incompetence of, persons authorised to carry on any profession or other activity,

(b) for protecting charities against misconduct or mismanagement (whether by trustees or other persons) in their administration,

(c) for protecting the property of charities from loss or misapplication,

(d) for the recovery of the property of charities,

(e) for securing the health, safety and welfare of persons at work, or

(f) for protecting persons other than persons at work against risk to health or safety arising out of or in connection with the actions of persons at work.

(3) In subsection (2) 'relevant function' means –

(a) any function conferred on any person by or under any enactment,

(b) any function of the Crown, a Minister of the Crown or a government department, or

(c) any other function which is of a public nature and is exercised in the public interest.

(4) Personal data processed for the purpose of discharging any function which –

(a) is conferred by or under any enactment on –

(i) the Parliamentary Commissioner for Administration,

(ii) the Commission for Local Administration in England, the Commission for Local Administration in Wales or the Commissioner for Local Administration in Scotland,

(iii) the Health Service Commissioner for England, the Health Service Commissioner for Wales or the Health Service Commissioner for Scotland,

(iv) the Welsh Administration Ombudsman,

(v) the Assembly Ombudsman for Northern Ireland, or

(vi) the Northern Ireland Commissioner for Complaints, and

(b) is designed for protecting members of the public against –

(i) maladministration by public bodies,

(ii) failures in services provided by public bodies, or

(iii) a failure of a public body to provide a service which it was a function of the body to provide,

are exempt from the subject information provisions in any case to the extent to which the application of those provisions to the data would be likely to prejudice the proper discharge of that function.

(5) Personal data processed for the purpose of discharging any function which –

(a) is conferred by or under any enactment on the Director General of Fair Trading, and

(b) is designed –

(i) for protecting members of the public against conduct which may adversely affect their interests by persons carrying on a business,

(ii) for regulating agreements or conduct which have as their object or effect the prevention, restriction or distortion of competition in connection with any commercial activity, or

(iii) for regulating conduct on the part of one or more undertakings which amounts to the abuse of a dominant position in a market,

are exempt from the subject information provisions in any case to the extent to which the application of those provisions to the data would be likely to prejudice the proper discharge of that function.

32 Journalism, literature and art

(1) Personal data which are processed only for the special purposes are exempt from any provision to which this subsection relates if –

(a) the processing is undertaken with a view to the publication by any person of any journalistic, literary or artistic material,

(b) the data controller reasonably believes that, having regard in particular to the special importance of the public interest in freedom of expression, publication would be in the public interest, and

(c) the data controller reasonably believes that, in all the circumstances, compliance with that provision is incompatible with the special purposes.

(2) Subsection (1) relates to the provisions of –

(a) the data protection principles except the seventh data protection principle,

(b) section 7,

(c) section 10,

(d) section 12, and

(e) section 14(1) to (3).

(3) In considering for the purposes of subsection (1)(b) whether the belief of a data controller that publication would be in the public interest was or is a reasonable one, regard may be had to his compliance with any code of practice which –

(a) is relevant to the publication in question, and

(b) is designated by the Secretary of State by order for the purposes of this subsection.

(4) Where at any time ('the relevant time') in any proceedings against a data controller under section 7(9), 10(4), 12(8) or 14 or by virtue of section 13 the data controller claims, or it appears to the court, that any personal data to which the proceedings relate are being processed –

(a) only for the special purposes, and

(b) with a view to the publication by any person of any journalistic, literary or artistic material which, at the time twenty-four hours immediately before the relevant time, had not previously been published by the data controller,

the court shall stay the proceedings until either of the conditions in subsection (5) is met.

(5) Those conditions are –

(a) that a determination of the Commissioner under section 45 with respect to the data in question takes effect, or

(b) in a case where the proceedings were stayed on the making of a claim, that the claim is withdrawn.

(6) For the purposes of this Act 'publish', in relation to journalistic, literary or artistic material, means make available to the public or any section of the public.

33 Research, history and statistics

(1) In this section –

'research purposes' includes statistical or historical purposes;

'the relevant conditions', in relation to any processing of personal data, means the conditions –

(a) that the data are not processed to support measures or decisions with respect to particular individuals, and

(b) that the data are not processed in such a way that substantial damage or substantial distress is, or is likely to be, caused to any data subject.

(2) For the purposes of the second data protection principle, the further processing of personal data only for research purposes in compliance with the relevant conditions is not to be regarded as incompatible with the purposes for which they were obtained.

(3) Personal data which are processed only for research purposes in compliance with the relevant conditions may, notwithstanding the fifth data protection principle, be kept indefinitely.

(4) Personal data which are processed only for research purposes are exempt from section 7 if –

(a) they are processed in compliance with the relevant conditions, and

(b) the results of the research or any resulting statistics are not made available in a form which identifies data subjects or any of them.

(5) For the purposes of subsections (2) to (4) personal data are not to be treated as processed otherwise than for research purposes merely because the data are disclosed –

(a) to any person, for research purposes only,

(b) to the data subject or a person acting on his behalf,

(c) at the request, or with the consent, of the data subject or a person acting on his behalf, or

(d) in circumstances in which the person making the disclosure has reasonable grounds for believing that the disclosure falls within paragraph (a), (b) or (c).

34 Information available to the public by or under enactment

Personal data are exempt from –

(a) the subject information provisions,

(b) the fourth data protection principle and section 14(1) to (3), and

(c) the non-disclosure provisions,

if the data consist of information which the data controller is obliged by or under any enactment to make available to the public, whether by publishing it, by making it available for inspection, or otherwise and whether gratuitously or on payment of a fee.

35 Disclosures required by law or made in connection with legal proceedings etc

(1) Personal data are exempt from the non-disclosure provisions where the disclosure is required by or under any enactment, by any rule of law or by the order of a court.

(2) Personal data are exempt from the non-disclosure provisions where the disclosure is necessary –

(a) for the purpose of, or in connection with, any legal proceedings (including prospective legal proceedings), or

(b) for the purpose of obtaining legal advice,

or is otherwise necessary for the purposes of establishing, exercising or defending legal rights.

...

39 Transitional relief

Schedule 8 (which confers transitional exemptions) has effect.

Part V
Enforcement

40 Enforcement notices

(1)   If the Commissioner is satisfied that a data controller has contravened or is contravening any of the data protection principles, the Commissioner may serve him with a notice (in this Act referred to as 'an enforcement notice') requiring him, for complying with the principle or principles in question, to do either or both of the following –

(a)   to take within such time as may be specified in the notice, or to refrain from taking after such time as may be so specified, such steps as are so specified, or

(b)   to refrain from processing any personal data, or any personal data of a description specified in the notice, or to refrain from processing them for a purpose so specified or in a manner so specified, after such time as may be so specified.

(2)   In deciding whether to serve an enforcement notice, the Commissioner shall consider whether the contravention has caused or is likely to cause any person damage or distress.

(3)   An enforcement notice in respect of a contravention of the fourth data protection principle which requires the data controller to rectify, block, erase or destroy any inaccurate data may also require the data controller to rectify, block, erase or destroy any other data held by him and containing an expression of opinion which appears to the Commissioner to be based on the inaccurate data.

(4)   An enforcement notice in respect of a contravention of the fourth data protection principle, in the case of data which accurately record information received or obtained by the data controller from the data subject or a third party, may require the data controller either –

(a)   to rectify, block, erase or destroy any inaccurate data and any other data held by him and containing an expression of opinion as mentioned in subsection (3), or

(b)   to take such steps as are specified in the notice for securing compliance with the requirements specified in paragraph 7 of Part II of Schedule 1 and, if the Commissioner thinks fit, for supplementing the data with such statement of the true facts relating to the matters dealt with by the data as the Commissioner may approve.

(5)   Where –

(a)   an enforcement notice requires the data controller to rectify, block, erase or destroy any personal data, or

(b)   the Commissioner is satisfied that personal data which have been rectified, blocked, erased or destroyed had been processed in contravention of any of the data protection principles,

an enforcement notice may, if reasonably practicable, require the data controller to notify third parties to whom the data have been disclosed of the rectification, blocking, erasure or destruction; and in determining whether it is reasonably practicable to require such notification regard shall be had, in particular, to the number of persons who would have to be notified.

(6) An enforcement notice must contain –

   (a) a statement of the data protection principle or principles which the Commissioner is satisfied have been or are being contravened and his reasons for reaching that conclusion, and

   (b) particulars of the rights of appeal conferred by section 48.

(7) Subject to subsection (8), an enforcement notice must not require any of the provisions of the notice to be complied with before the end of the period within which an appeal can be brought against the notice and, if such an appeal is brought, the notice need not be complied with pending the determination or withdrawal of the appeal.

(8) If by reason of special circumstances the Commissioner considers that an enforcement notice should be complied with as a matter of urgency he may include in the notice a statement to that effect and a statement of his reasons for reaching that conclusion; and in that event subsection (7) shall not apply but the notice must not require the provisions of the notice to be complied with before the end of the period of seven days beginning with the day on which the notice is served.

(9) Notification regulations (as defined by section 16(2)) may make provision as to the effect of the service of an enforcement notice on any entry in the register maintained under section 19 which relates to the person on whom the notice is served.

(10) This section has effect subject to section 46(1).

41 Cancellation of enforcement notice

(1) If the Commissioner considers that all or any of the provisions of an enforcement notice need not be complied with in order to ensure compliance with the data protection principle or principles to which it relates, he may cancel or vary the notice by written notice to the person on whom it was served.

(2) A person on whom an enforcement notice has been served may, at any time after the expiry of the period during which an appeal can be brought against that notice, apply in writing to the Commissioner for the cancellation or variation of that notice on the ground that, by reason of a change of circumstances, all or any of the provisions of that notice need not be complied with in order to ensure compliance with the data protection principle or principles to which that notice relates.

42 Request for assessment

(1) A request may be made to the Commissioner by or on behalf of any person who is, or believes himself to be, directly affected by any processing of personal data for an assessment as to whether it is likely or unlikely that the processing has been or is being carried out in compliance with the provisions of this Act.

(2) On receiving a request under this section, the Commissioner shall make an assessment in such manner as appears to him to be appropriate, unless he has not been supplied with such information as he may reasonably require in order to –

   (a) satisfy himself as to the identity of the person making the request, and

   (b) enable him to identify the processing in question.

(3)   The matters to which the Commissioner may have regard in determining in what manner it is appropriate to make an assessment include –

    (a) the extent to which the request appears to him to raise a matter of substance,

    (b) any undue delay in making the request, and

    (c) whether or not the person making the request is entitled to make an application under section 7 in respect of the personal data in question.

(4)   Where the Commissioner has received a request under this section he shall notify the person who made the request –

    (a) whether he has made an assessment as a result of the request, and

    (b) to the extent that he considers appropriate, having regard in particular to any exemption from section 7 applying in relation to the personal data concerned, of any view formed or action taken as a result of the request.

43 Information notices

(1)   If the Commissioner –

    (a) has received a request under section 42 in respect of any processing of personal data, or

    (b) reasonably requires any information for the purpose of determining whether the data controller has complied or is complying with the data protection principles,

he may serve the data controller with a notice (in this Act referred to as 'an information notice') requiring the data controller, within such time as is specified in the notice, to furnish the Commissioner, in such form as may be so specified, with such information relating to the request or to compliance with the principles as is so specified.

(2)   An information notice must contain –

    (a) in a case falling within subsection (1)(a), a statement that the Commissioner has received a request under section 42 in relation to the specified processing, or

    (b) in a case falling within subsection (1)(b), a statement that the Commissioner regards the specified information as relevant for the purpose of determining whether the data controller has complied, or is complying, with the data protection principles and his reasons for regarding it as relevant for that purpose.

(3)   An information notice must also contain particulars of the rights of appeal conferred by section 48.

(4)   Subject to subsection (5), the time specified in an information notice shall not expire before the end of the period within which an appeal can be brought against the notice and, if such an appeal is brought, the information need not be furnished pending the determination or withdrawal of the appeal.

(5)   If by reason of special circumstances the Commissioner considers that the information is required as a matter of urgency, he may include in the notice a statement to that effect and a statement of his reasons for reaching that conclusion; and in that event subsection (4) shall not apply, but the notice shall not require the information to be furnished before the end of the period of seven days beginning with the day on which the notice is served.

(6)   A person shall not be required by virtue of this section to furnish the Commissioner with any information in respect of –

(a)   any communication between a professional legal adviser and his client in connection with the giving of legal advice to the client with respect to his obligations, liabilities or rights under this Act, or

(b)   any communication between a professional legal adviser and his client, or between such an adviser or his client and any other person, made in connection with or in contemplation of proceedings under or arising out of this Act (including proceedings before the Tribunal) and for the purposes of such proceedings.

(7)   In subsection (6) references to the client of a professional legal adviser include references to any person representing such a client.

(8)   A person shall not be required by virtue of this section to furnish the Commissioner with any information if the furnishing of that information would, by revealing evidence of the commission of any offence other than an offence under this Act, expose him to proceedings for that offence.

(9)   The Commissioner may cancel an information notice by written notice to the person on whom it was served.

(10)   This section has effect subject to section 46(3).

44 Special information notices

(1)   If the Commissioner –

(a)   has received a request under section 42 in respect of any processing of personal data, or

(b)   has reasonable grounds for suspecting that, in a case in which proceedings have been stayed under section 32, the personal data to which the proceedings relate –

(i)   are not being processed only for the special purposes, or

(ii)   are not being processed with a view to the publication by any person of any journalistic, literary or artistic material which has not previously been published by the data controller,

he may serve the data controller with a notice (in this Act referred to as a 'special information notice') requiring the data controller, within such time as is specified in the notice, to furnish the Commissioner, in such form as may be so specified, with such information as is so specified for the purpose specified in subsection (2).

(2)   That purpose is the purpose of ascertaining –

(a)   whether the personal data are being processed only for the special purposes, or

(b)   whether they are being processed with a view to the publication by any person of any journalistic, literary or artistic material which has not previously been published by the data controller.

(3)   A special information notice must contain –

(a)   in a case falling within paragraph (a) of subsection (1), a statement that the Commissioner has received a request under section 42 in relation to the specified processing, or

(b) in a case falling within paragraph (b) of that subsection, a statement of the Commissioner's grounds for suspecting that the personal data are not being processed as mentioned in that paragraph.

(4) A special information notice must also contain particulars of the rights of appeal conferred by section 48.

(5) Subject to subsection (6), the time specified in a special information notice shall not expire before the end of the period within which an appeal can be brought against the notice and, if such an appeal is brought, the information need not be furnished pending the determination or withdrawal of the appeal.

(6) If by reason of special circumstances the Commissioner considers that the information is required as a matter of urgency, he may include in the notice a statement to that effect and a statement of his reasons for reaching that conclusion; and in that event subsection (5) shall not apply, but the notice shall not require the information to be furnished before the end of the period of seven days beginning with the day on which the notice is served.

(7) A person shall not be required by virtue of this section to furnish the Commissioner with any information in respect of –

(a) any communication between a professional legal adviser and his client in connection with the giving of legal advice to the client with respect to his obligations, liabilities or rights under this Act, or

(b) any communication between a professional legal adviser and his client, or between such an adviser or his client and any other person, made in connection with or in contemplation of proceedings under or arising out of this Act (including proceedings before the Tribunal) and for the purposes of such proceedings.

(8) In subsection (7) references to the client of a professional legal adviser include references to any person representing such a client.

(9) A person shall not be required by virtue of this section to furnish the Commissioner with any information if the furnishing of that information would, by revealing evidence of the commission of any offence other than an offence under this Act, expose him to proceedings for that offence.

(10) The Commissioner may cancel a special information notice by written notice to the person on whom it was served.

45 Determination by Commissioner as to the special purposes

(1) Where at any time it appears to the Commissioner (whether as a result of the service of a special information notice or otherwise) that any personal data –

(a) are not being processed only for the special purposes, or

(b) are not being processed with a view to the publication by any person of any journalistic, literary or artistic material which has not previously been published by the data controller,

he may make a determination in writing to that effect.

(2) Notice of the determination shall be given to the data controller; and the notice must contain particulars of the right of appeal conferred by section 48.

(3) A determination under subsection (1) shall not take effect until the end of the period within which an appeal can be brought and, where an appeal is brought, shall not take effect pending the determination or withdrawal of the appeal.

46 Restriction on enforcement in case of processing for the special purposes

(1) The Commissioner may not at any time serve an enforcement notice on a data controller with respect to the processing of personal data for the special purposes unless –

(a) a determination under section 45(1) with respect to those data has taken effect, and

(b) the court has granted leave for the notice to be served.

(2) The court shall not grant leave for the purposes of subsection (1)(b) unless it is satisfied –

(a) that the Commissioner has reason to suspect a contravention of the data protection principles which is of substantial public importance, and

(b) except where the case is one of urgency, that the data controller has been given notice, in accordance with rules of court, of the application for leave.

(3) The Commissioner may not serve an information notice on a data controller with respect to the processing of personal data for the special purposes unless a determination under section 45(1) with respect to those data has taken effect.

47 Failure to comply with notice

(1) A person who fails to comply with an enforcement notice, an information notice or a special information notice is guilty of an offence.

(2) A person who, in purported compliance with an information notice or a special information notice –

(a) makes a statement which he knows to be false in a material respect, or

(b) recklessly makes a statement which is false in a material respect,

is guilty of an offence.

(3) It is a defence for a person charged with an offence under subsection (1) to prove that he exercised all due diligence to comply with the notice in question.

48 Rights of appeal

(1) A person on whom an enforcement notice, an information notice or a special information notice has been served may appeal to the Tribunal against the notice.

(2) A person on whom an enforcement notice has been served may appeal to the Tribunal against the refusal of an application under section 41(2) for cancellation or variation of the notice.

(3) Where an enforcement notice, an information notice or a special information notice contains a statement by the Commissioner in accordance with section 40(8), 43(5) or 44(6) then, whether or not the person appeals against the notice, he may appeal against –

(a) the Commissioner's decision to include the statement in the notice, or

(b) the effect of the inclusion of the statement as respects any part of the notice.

(4) A data controller in respect of whom a determination has been made under section 45 may appeal to the Tribunal against the determination.

(5)   Schedule 6 has effect in relation to appeals under this section and the proceedings of the Tribunal in respect of any such appeal.

49 Determination of appeals

(1)   If on an appeal under section 48(1) the Tribunal considers –

  (a) that the notice against which the appeal is brought is not in accordance with the law, or

  (b) to the extent that the notice involved an exercise of discretion by the Commissioner, that he ought to have exercised his discretion differently,

  the Tribunal shall allow the appeal or substitute such other notice or decision as could have been served or made by the Commissioner; and in any other case the Tribunal shall dismiss the appeal.

(2)   On such an appeal, the Tribunal may review any determination of fact on which the notice in question was based.

(3)   If on an appeal under section 48(2) the Tribunal considers that the enforcement notice ought to be cancelled or varied by reason of a change in circumstances, the Tribunal shall cancel or vary the notice.

(4)   On an appeal under subsection (3) of section 48 the Tribunal may direct –

  (a) that the notice in question shall have effect as if it did not contain any such statement as is mentioned in that subsection, or

  (b) that the inclusion of the statement shall not have effect in relation to any part of the notice,

  and may make such modifications in the notice as may be required for giving effect to the direction.

(5)   On an appeal under section 48(4), the Tribunal may cancel the determination of the Commissioner.

(6)   Any party to an appeal to the Tribunal under section 48 may appeal from the decision of the Tribunal on a point of law to the appropriate court; and that court shall be –

  (a) the High Court of Justice in England if the address of the person who was the appellant before the Tribunal is in England or Wales,

  (b) the Court of Session if that address is in Scotland, and

  (c) the High Court of Justice in Northern Ireland if that address is in Northern Ireland.

(7)   For the purposes of subsection (6) –

  (a) the address of a registered company is that of its registered office, and

  (b) the address of a person (other than a registered company) carrying on a business is that of his principal place of business in the United Kingdom.

...

57 Avoidance of certain contractual terms relating to health records

(1)   Any term or condition of a contract is void in so far as it purports to require an individual –

  (a) to supply any other person with a record to which this section applies, or with a copy of such a record or a part of such a record, or

(b) to produce to any other person such a record, copy or part.

(2) This section applies to any record which –

(a) has been or is to be obtained by a data subject in the exercise of the right conferred by section 7, and

(b) consists of the information contained in any health record as defined by section 68(2).

INFORMATION PROVIDED TO COMMISSIONER OR TRIBUNAL

58 Disclosure of information

No enactment or rule of law prohibiting or restricting the disclosure of information shall preclude a person from furnishing the Commissioner or the Tribunal with any information necessary for the discharge of their functions under this Act.

59 Confidentiality of information

(1) No person who is or has been the Commissioner, a member of the Commissioner's staff or an agent of the Commissioner shall disclose any information which –

(a) has been obtained by, or furnished to, the Commissioner under or for the purposes of this Act,

(b) relates to an identified or identifiable individual or business, and

(c) is not at the time of the disclosure, and has not previously been, available to the public from other sources,

unless the disclosure is made with lawful authority.

(2) For the purposes of subsection (1) a disclosure of information is made with lawful authority only if, and to the extent that –

(a) the disclosure is made with the consent of the individual or of the person for the time being carrying on the business,

(b) the information was provided for the purpose of its being made available to the public (in whatever manner) under any provision of this Act,

(c) the disclosure is made for the purposes of, and is necessary for, the discharge of-

(i) any functions under this Act, or

(ii) any Community obligation,

(d) the disclosure is made for the purposes of any proceedings, whether criminal or civil and whether arising under, or by virtue of, this Act or otherwise, or

(e) having regard to the rights and freedoms or legitimate interests of any person, the disclosure is necessary in the public interest.

(3) Any person who knowingly or recklessly discloses information in contravention of subsection (1) is guilty of an offence.

GENERAL PROVISIONS RELATING TO OFFENCES

60 Prosecutions and penalties

(1) No proceedings for an offence under this Act shall be instituted –

(a) in England or Wales, except by the Commissioner or by or with the consent of the Director of Public Prosecutions;

(b) in Northern Ireland, except by the Commissioner or by or with the consent of the Director of Public Prosecutions for Northern Ireland.

(2) A person guilty of an offence under any provision of this Act other than paragraph 12 of Schedule 9 is liable –

    (a) on summary conviction, to a fine not exceeding the statutory maximum, or

    (b) on conviction on indictment, to a fine.

(3) A person guilty of an offence under paragraph 12 of Schedule 9 is liable on summary conviction to a fine not exceeding level 5 on the standard scale.

(4) Subject to subsection (5), the court by or before which a person is convicted of –

    (a) an offence under section 21(1), 22(6), 55 or 56,

    (b) an offence under section 21(2) relating to processing which is assessable processing for the purposes of section 22, or

    (c) an offence under section 47(1) relating to an enforcement notice,

may order any document or other material used in connection with the processing of personal data and appearing to the court to be connected with the commission of the offence to be forfeited, destroyed or erased.

(5) The court shall not make an order under subsection (4) in relation to any material where a person (other than the offender) claiming to be the owner of or otherwise interested in the material applies to be heard by the court, unless an opportunity is given to him to show cause why the order should not be made.

...

68 Meaning of 'accessible record'

(1) In this Act 'accessible record' means-

    (a) a health record as defined by subsection (2),

    (b) an educational record as defined by Schedule 11, or

    (c) an accessible public record as defined by Schedule 12.

(2) In subsection (1)(a) 'health record' means any record which –

    (a) consists of information relating to the physical or mental health or condition of an individual, and

    (b) has been made by or on behalf of a health professional in connection with the care of that individual.

69 Meaning of 'health professional'

(1) In this Act 'health professional' means any of the following –

    (a) a registered medical practitioner,

    (b) a registered dentist as defined by section 53(1) of the Dentists Act 1984,

    (c) a registered optician as defined by section 36(1) of the Opticians Act 1989,

    (d) a registered pharmaceutical chemist as defined by section 24(1) of the Pharmacy Act 1954 or a registered person as defined by Article 2(2) of the Pharmacy (Northern Ireland) Order 1976,

    (e) a registered nurse, midwife or health visitor,

    (f) a registered osteopath as defined by section 41 of the Osteopaths Act 1993,

(g) a registered chiropractor as defined by section 43 of the Chiropractors Act 1994,

(h) any person who is registered as a member of a profession to which the Professions Supplementary to Medicine Act 1960 for the time being extends,

(i) a clinical psychologist, child psychotherapist or speech therapist,

(j) a music therapist employed by a health service body, and

(k) a scientist employed by such a body as head of a department.

(2) In subsection (1)(a) 'registered medical practitioner' includes any person who is provisionally registered under section 15 or 21 of the Medical Act 1983 and is engaged in such employment as is mentioned in subsection (3) of that section.

(3) In subsection (1) 'health service body' means –

(a) a Health Authority established under section 8 of the National Health Service Act 1977,

(b) a Special Health Authority established under section 11 of that Act,

(c) a Health Board within the meaning of the National Health Service (Scotland) Act 1978,

(d) a Special Health Board within the meaning of that Act,

(e) the managers of a State Hospital provided under section 102 of that Act,

(f) a National Health Service trust first established under section 5 of the National Health Service and Community Care Act 1990 or section 12A of the National Health Service (Scotland) Act 1978,

(g) a Health and Social Services Board established under Article 16 of the Health and Personal Social Services (Northern Ireland) Order 1972,

(h) a special health and social services agency established under the Health and Personal Social Services (Special Agencies) (Northern Ireland) Order 1990, or

(i) a Health and Social Services trust established under Article 10 of the Health and Personal Social Services (Northern Ireland) Order 1991.

...

73 Transitional provisions and savings

Schedule 14 (which contains transitional provisions and savings) has effect.

SCHEDULE 1
THE DATA PROTECTION PRINCIPLES

Part I
The principles

1 Personal data shall be processed fairly and lawfully and, in particular, shall not be processed unless –

(a) at least one of the conditions in Schedule 2 is met, and

(b) in the case of sensitive personal data, at least one of the conditions in Schedule 3 is also met.

2 Personal data shall be obtained only for one or more specified and lawful purposes, and shall not be further processed in any manner incompatible with that purpose or those purposes.

3   Personal data shall be adequate, relevant and not excessive in relation to the purpose or purposes for which they are processed.

4   Personal data shall be accurate and, where necessary, kept up to date.

5   Personal data processed for any purpose or purposes shall not be kept for longer than is necessary for that purpose or those purposes.

6   Personal data shall be processed in accordance with the rights of data subjects under this Act.

7   Appropriate technical and organisational measures shall be taken against unauthorised or unlawful processing of personal data and against accidental loss or destruction of, or damage to, personal data.

8   Personal data shall not be transferred to a country or territory outside the European Economic Area unless that country or territory ensures an adequate level of protection for the rights and freedoms of data subjects in relation to the processing of personal data.

Part II
Interpretation of the principles in Part I

1 The first principle

(1)   In determining for the purposes of the first principle whether personal data are processed fairly, regard is to be had to the method by which they are obtained, including in particular whether any person from whom they are obtained is deceived or misled as to the purpose or purposes for which they are to be processed.

(2)   Subject to paragraph 2, for the purposes of the first principle data are to be treated as obtained fairly if they consist of information obtained from a person who –

   (a) is authorised by or under any enactment to supply it, or

   (b) is required to supply it by or under any enactment or by any convention or other instrument imposing an international obligation on the United Kingdom.

2

(1)   Subject to paragraph 3, for the purposes of the first principle personal data are not to be treated as processed fairly unless –

   (a) in the case of data obtained from the data subject, the data controller ensures so far as practicable that the data subject has, is provided with, or has made readily available to him, the information specified in sub-paragraph (3), and

   (b) in any other case, the data controller ensures so far as practicable that, before the relevant time or as soon as practicable after that time, the data subject has, is provided with, or has made readily available to him, the information specified in sub-paragraph (3).

(2)   In sub-paragraph (1)(b) 'the relevant time' means –

   (a) the time when the data controller first processes the data, or

   (b) in a case where at that time disclosure to a third party within a reasonable period is envisaged

      (i) if the data are in fact disclosed to such a person within that period, the time when the data are first disclosed,

     (ii) if within that period the data controller becomes, or ought to become, aware that the data are unlikely to be disclosed to such a person within that period, the time when the data controller does become, or ought to become, so aware, or

     (iii) in any other case, the end of that period.

(3)   The information referred to in sub-paragraph (1) is as follows, namely –

    (a) the identity of the data controller,

    (b) if he has nominated a representative for the purposes of this Act, the identity of that representative,

    (c) the purpose or purposes for which the data are intended to be processed, and

    (d) any further information which is necessary, having regard to the specific circumstances in which the data are or are to be processed, to enable processing in respect of the data subject to be fair.

3

(1)   Paragraph 2(1)(b) does not apply where either of the primary conditions in sub-paragraph (2), together with such further conditions as may be prescribed by the Secretary of State by order, are met.

(2)   The primary conditions referred to in sub-paragraph (1) are –

    (a) that the provision of that information would involve a disproportionate effort, or

    (b) that the recording of the information to be contained in the data by, or the disclosure of the data by, the data controller is necessary for compliance with any legal obligation to which the data controller is subject, other than an obligation imposed by contract.

4

(1)   Personal data which contain a general identifier falling within a description prescribed by the Secretary of State by order are not to be treated as processed fairly and lawfully unless they are processed in compliance with any conditions so prescribed in relation to general identifiers of that description.

(2)   In sub-paragraph (1) 'a general identifier' means any identifier (such as, for example, a number or code used for identification purposes) which –

(a)   relates to an individual, and

(b)   forms part of a set of similar identifiers which is of general application.

5 The second principle

The purpose or purposes for which personal data are obtained may in particular be specified –

    (a) in a notice given for the purposes of paragraph 2 by the data controller to the data subject, or

    (b) in a notification given to the Commissioner under Part III of this Act.

6

In determining whether any disclosure of personal data is compatible with the purpose or purposes for which the data were obtained, regard is to be had to the purpose or purposes for which the personal data are intended to be processed by any person to whom they are disclosed.

7 The fourth principle

The fourth principle is not to be regarded as being contravened by reason of any inaccuracy in personal data which accurately record information obtained by the data controller from the data subject or a third party in a case where –

    (a) having regard to the purpose or purposes for which the data were obtained and further processed, the data controller has taken reasonable steps to ensure the accuracy of the data, and

    (b) if the data subject has notified the data controller of the data subject's view that the data are inaccurate, the data indicate that fact.

8 The sixth principle

A person is to be regarded as contravening the sixth principle if, but only if –

    (a) he contravenes section 7 by failing to supply information in accordance with that section,

    (b) he contravenes section 10 by failing to comply with a notice given under subsection (1) of that section to the extent that the notice is justified or by failing to give a notice under subsection (3) of that section,

    (c) he contravenes section 11 by failing to comply with a notice given under subsection (1) of that section, or

    (d) he contravenes section 12 by failing to comply with a notice given under subsection (1) or (2)(b) of that section or by failing to give a notification under subsection (2)(a) of that section or a notice under subsection (3) of that section.

9 The seventh principle

Having regard to the state of technological development and the cost of implementing any measures, the measures must ensure a level of security appropriate to –

    (a) the harm that might result from such unauthorised or unlawful processing or accidental loss, destruction or damage as are mentioned in the seventh principle, and

    (b) the nature of the data to be protected.

10

The data controller must take reasonable steps to ensure the reliability of any employees of his who have access to the personal data.

11

Where processing of personal data is carried out by a data processor on behalf of a data controller, the data controller must in order to comply with the seventh principle –

    (a) choose a data processor providing sufficient guarantees in respect of the technical and organisational security measures governing the processing to be carried out, and

    (b) take reasonable steps to ensure compliance with those measures.

12

Where processing of personal data is carried out by a data processor on behalf of a data controller, the data controller is not to be regarded as complying with the seventh principle unless –

(a) the processing is carried out under a contract –

    (i) which is made or evidenced in writing, and

    (ii) under which the data processor is to act only on instructions from the data controller, and

(b) the contract requires the data processor to comply with obligations equivalent to those imposed on a data controller by the seventh principle.

13 The eighth principle

An adequate level of protection is one which is adequate in all the circumstances of the case, having regard in particular to –

(a) the nature of the personal data,

(b) the country or territory of origin of the information contained in the data,

(c) the country or territory of final destination of that information,

(d) the purposes for which and period during which the data are intended to be processed,

(e) the law in force in the country or territory in question,

(f) the international obligations of that country or territory,

(g) any relevant codes of conduct or other rules which are enforceable in that country or territory (whether generally or by arrangement in particular cases), and

(h) any security measures taken in respect of the data in that country or territory.

14

The eighth principle does not apply to a transfer falling within any paragraph of Schedule 4, except in such circumstances and to such extent as the Secretary of State may by order provide.

15

(1) Where –

(a) in any proceedings under this Act any question arises as to whether the requirement of the eighth principle as to an adequate level of protection is met in relation to the transfer of any personal data to a country or territory outside the European Economic Area, and

(b) a Community finding has been made in relation to transfers of the kind in question,

that question is to be determined in accordance with that finding.

(2) In sub-paragraph (1) 'Community finding' means a finding of the European Commission, under the procedure provided for in Article 31(2) of the Data Protection Directive, that a country or territory outside the European Economic Area does, or does not, ensure an adequate level of protection within the meaning of Article 25(2) of the Directive.

SCHEDULE 2
CONDITIONS RELEVANT FOR PURPOSES OF THE FIRST PRINCIPLE: PROCESSING OF ANY PERSONAL DATA

1   The data subject has given his consent to the processing.

2   The processing is necessary –

(a) for the performance of a contract to which the data subject is a party, or

(b) for the taking of steps at the request of the data subject with a view to entering into a contract.

3   The processing is necessary for compliance with any legal obligation to which the data controller is subject, other than an obligation imposed by contract.

4   The processing is necessary in order to protect the vital interests of the data subject.

5   The processing is necessary –

(a) for the administration of justice,

(b) for the exercise of any functions conferred on any person by or under any enactment,

(c) for the exercise of any functions of the Crown, a Minister of the Crown or a government department, or

(d) for the exercise of any other functions of a public nature exercised in the public interest by any person.

6   (1) The processing is necessary for the purposes of legitimate interests pursued by the data controller or by the third party or parties to whom the data are disclosed, except where the processing is unwarranted in any particular case by reason of prejudice to the rights and freedoms or legitimate interests of the data subject.

(2) The Secretary of State may by order specify particular circumstances in which this condition is, or is not, to be taken to be satisfied.

SCHEDULE 3
CONDITIONS RELEVANT FOR PURPOSES OF THE FIRST PRINCIPLE: PROCESSING OF SENSITIVE PERSONAL DATA

1   The data subject has given his explicit consent to the processing of the personal data.

2(1) The processing is necessary for the purposes of exercising or performing any right or obligation which is conferred or imposed by law on the data controller in connection with employment.

(2) The Secretary of State may by order –

    (a) exclude the application of sub-paragraph (1) in such cases as may be specified, or

    (b) provide that, in such cases as may be specified, the condition in sub-paragraph (1) is not to be regarded as satisfied unless such further conditions as may be specified in the order are also satisfied.

3   The processing is necessary –

    (a) in order to protect the vital interests of the data subject or another person, in a case where

       (i) consent cannot be given by or on behalf of the data subject, or

       (ii) the data controller cannot reasonably be expected to obtain the consent of the data subject, or

    (b) in order to protect the vital interests of another person, in a case where consent by or on behalf of the data subject has been unreasonably withheld.

4   The processing –

    (a) is carried out in the course of its legitimate activities by any body or association which-

       (i) is not established or conducted for profit, and

       (ii) exists for political, philosophical, religious or trade-union purposes,

    (b) is carried out with appropriate safeguards for the rights and freedoms of data subjects,

    (c) relates only to individuals who either are members of the body or association or have regular contact with it in connection with its purposes, and

    (d) does not involve disclosure of the personal data to a third party without the consent of the data subject.

5   The information contained in the personal data has been made public as a result of steps deliberately taken by the data subject.

6   The processing –

    (a) is necessary for the purpose of, or in connection with, any legal proceedings (including prospective legal proceedings),

    (b) is necessary for the purpose of obtaining legal advice, or

    (c) is otherwise necessary for the purposes of establishing, exercising or defending legal rights.

7

(1) The processing is necessary –

    (a) for the administration of justice,

    (b) for the exercise of any functions conferred on any person by or under an enactment, or

    (c) for the exercise of any functions of the Crown, a Minister of the Crown or a government department.

(2) The Secretary of State may by order –

    (a) exclude the application of sub-paragraph (1) in such cases as may be specified, or

    (b) provide that, in such cases as may be specified, the condition in sub-paragraph (1) is not to be regarded as satisfied unless such further conditions as may be specified in the order are also satisfied.

8(1) The processing is necessary for medical purposes and is undertaken by –

    (a) a health professional, or

    (b) a person who in the circumstances owes a duty of confidentiality which is equivalent to that which would arise if that person were a health professional.

(2) In this paragraph 'medical purposes' includes the purposes of preventative medicine, medical diagnosis, medical research, the provision of care and treatment and the management of healthcare services.

9(1) The processing –

    (a) is of sensitive personal data consisting of information as to racial or ethnic origin,

    (b) is necessary for the purpose of identifying or keeping under review the existence or absence of equality of opportunity or treatment between persons of different racial or ethnic origins, with a view to enabling such equality to be promoted or maintained, and

    (c) is carried out with appropriate safeguards for the rights and freedoms of data subjects.

(2) The Secretary of State may by order specify circumstances in which processing falling within sub-paragraph (1)(a) and (b) is, or is not, to be taken for the purposes of sub-paragraph (1)(c) to be carried out with appropriate safeguards for the rights and freedoms of data subjects.

10 The personal data are processed in circumstances specified in an order made by the Secretary of State for the purposes of this paragraph.

SCHEDULE 4
CASES WHERE THE EIGHTH PRINCIPLE DOES NOT APPLY

1   The data subject has given his consent to the transfer.

2   The transfer is necessary –

   (a) for the performance of a contract between the data subject and the data controller, or

   (b) for the taking of steps at the request of the data subject with a view to his entering into a contract with the data controller.

3   The transfer is necessary –

   (a) for the conclusion of a contract between the data controller and a person other than the data subject which-

      (i)   is entered into at the request of the data subject, or

      (ii) is in the interests of the data subject, or

   (b) for the performance of such a contract.

4(1) The transfer is necessary for reasons of substantial public interest.

(2)   The Secretary of State may by order specify –

   (a) circumstances in which a transfer is to be taken for the purposes of sub-paragraph (1) to be necessary for reasons of substantial public interest, and

   (b) circumstances in which a transfer which is not required by or under an enactment is not to be taken for the purpose of sub-paragraph (1) to be necessary for reasons of substantial public interest.

5   The transfer –

   (a) is necessary for the purpose of, or in connection with, any legal proceedings (including prospective legal proceedings),

   (b) is necessary for the purpose of obtaining legal advice, or

   (c) is otherwise necessary for the purposes of establishing, exercising or defending legal rights.

6   The transfer is necessary in order to protect the vital interests of the data subject.

7   The transfer is of part of the personal data on a public register and any conditions subject to which the register is open to inspection are complied with by any person to whom the data are or may be disclosed after the transfer.

8   The transfer is made on terms which are of a kind approved by the Commissioner as ensuring adequate safeguards for the rights and freedoms of data subjects.

9   The transfer has been authorised by the Commissioner as being made in such a manner as to ensure adequate safeguards for the rights and freedoms of data subjects.

....

SCHEDULE 8
TRANSITIONAL RELIEF

Part I
Interpretation of Schedule

1(1) For the purposes of this Schedule, personal data are 'eligible data' at any time if, and to the extent that, they are at that time subject to processing which was already under way immediately before 24th October 1998.

(2) In this Schedule –

'eligible automated data' means eligible data which fall within paragraph (a) or (b) of the definition of 'data' in section 1(1);

'eligible manual data' means eligible data which are not eligible automated data;

'the first transitional period' means the period beginning with the commencement of this Schedule and ending with 23rd October 2001;

'the second transitional period' means the period beginning with 24th October 2001 and ending with 23rd October 2007.

Part II
Exemptions available before 24th October 2001

Manual data

2(1) Eligible manual data, other than data forming part of an accessible record, are exempt from the data protection principles and Parts II and III of this Act during the first transitional period.

(2) This paragraph does not apply to eligible manual data to which paragraph 4 applies.

3(1) This paragraph applies to –

(a) eligible manual data forming part of an accessible record, and

(b) personal data which fall within paragraph (d) of the definition of 'data' in section 1(1) but which, because they are not subject to processing which was already under way immediately before 24th October 1998, are not eligible data for the purposes of this Schedule.

(2) During the first transitional period, data to which this paragraph applies are exempt from –

(a) the data protection principles, except the sixth principle so far as relating to sections 7 and 12A,

(b) Part II of this Act, except-

(i) section 7 (as it has effect subject to section 8) and section 12A, and

(ii) section 15 so far as relating to those sections, and

(c) Part III of this Act.

4(1) This paragraph applies to eligible manual data which consist of information relevant to the financial standing of the data subject and in respect of which the data controller is a credit reference agency.

(2) During the first transitional period, data to which this paragraph applies are exempt from –

   (a) the data protection principles, except the sixth principle so far as relating to sections 7 and 12A,

   (b) Part II of this Act, except-

      (i) section 7 (as it has effect subject to sections 8 and 9) and section 12A, and

      (ii) section 15 so far as relating to those sections, and

(c) Part III of this Act.

Processing otherwise than by reference to the data subject

5 During the first transitional period, for the purposes of this Act (apart from paragraph 1), eligible automated data are not to be regarded as being 'processed' unless the processing is by reference to the data subject.

Payrolls and accounts

6(1) Subject to sub-paragraph (2), eligible automated data processed by a data controller for one or more of the following purposes –

   (a) calculating amounts payable by way of remuneration or pensions in respect of service in any employment or office or making payments of, or of sums deducted from, such remuneration or pensions, or

   (b) keeping accounts relating to any business or other activity carried on by the data controller or keeping records of purchases, sales or other transactions for the purpose of ensuring that the requisite payments are made by or to him in respect of those transactions or for the purpose of making financial or management forecasts to assist him in the conduct of any such business or activity,

   are exempt from the data protection principles and Parts II and III of this Act during the first transitional period.

(2) It shall be a condition of the exemption of any eligible automated data under this paragraph that the data are not processed for any other purpose, but the exemption is not lost by any processing of the eligible data for any other purpose if the data controller shows that he had taken such care to prevent it as in all the circumstances was reasonably required.

(3) Data processed only for one or more of the purposes mentioned in sub-paragraph (1)(a) may be disclosed –

   (a) to any person, other than the data controller, by whom the remuneration or pensions in question are payable,

   (b) for the purpose of obtaining actuarial advice,

   (c) for the purpose of giving information as to the persons in any employment or office for use in medical research into the health of, or injuries suffered by, persons engaged in particular occupations or working in particular places or areas,

   (d) if the data subject (or a person acting on his behalf) has requested or consented to the disclosure of the data either generally or in the circumstances in which the disclosure in question is made, or

(e) if the person making the disclosure has reasonable grounds for believing that the disclosure falls within paragraph (d).

(4) Data processed for any of the purposes mentioned in sub-paragraph (1) may be disclosed –

   (a) for the purpose of audit or where the disclosure is for the purpose only of giving information about the data controller's financial affairs, or

   (b) in any case in which disclosure would be permitted by any other provision of this Part of this Act if sub-paragraph (2) were included among the non-disclosure provisions.

(5) In this paragraph 'remuneration' includes remuneration in kind and 'pensions' includes gratuities or similar benefits.

Unincorporated members' clubs and mailing lists

7   Eligible automated data processed by an unincorporated members' club and relating only to the members of the club are exempt from the data protection principles and Parts II and III of this Act during the first transitional period.

8   Eligible automated data processed by a data controller only for the purposes of distributing, or recording the distribution of, articles or information to the data subjects and consisting only of their names, addresses or other particulars necessary for effecting the distribution, are exempt from the data protection principles and Parts II and III of this Act during the first transitional period.

9   Neither paragraph 7 nor paragraph 8 applies to personal data relating to any data subject unless he has been asked by the club or data controller whether he objects to the data relating to him being processed as mentioned in that paragraph and has not objected.

10   It shall be a condition of the exemption of any data under paragraph 7 that the data are not disclosed except as permitted by paragraph 11 and of the exemption under paragraph 8 that the data are not processed for any purpose other than that mentioned in that paragraph or as permitted by paragraph 11, but –

   (a) the exemption under paragraph 7 shall not be lost by any disclosure in breach of that condition, and

   (b) the exemption under paragraph 8 shall not be lost by any processing in breach of that condition,

   if the data controller shows that he had taken such care to prevent it as in all the circumstances was reasonably required.

11   Data to which paragraph 10 applies may be disclosed –

   (a) if the data subject (or a person acting on his behalf) has requested or consented to the disclosure of the data either generally or in the circumstances in which the disclosure in question is made,

   (b) if the person making the disclosure has reasonable grounds for believing that the disclosure falls within paragraph (a), or

   (c) in any case in which disclosure would be permitted by any other provision of this Part of this Act if paragraph 8 were included among the non-disclosure provisions.

Back-up data

12   Eligible automated data which are processed only for the purpose of replacing other data in the event of the latter being lost, destroyed or impaired are exempt from section 7 during the first transitional period.

Exemption of all eligible automated data from certain requirements

13(1) During the first transitional period, eligible automated data are exempt from the following provisions –

    (a) the first data protection principle to the extent to which it requires compliance with –

        (i)   paragraph 2 of Part II of Schedule 1,

        (ii) the conditions in Schedule 2, and

        (iii) the conditions in Schedule 3,

    (b) the seventh data protection principle to the extent to which it requires compliance with paragraph 12 of Part II of Schedule 1;

    (c) the eighth data protection principle,

    (d) in section 7(1), paragraphs (b), (c)(ii) and (d),

    (e) sections 10 and 11,

    (f) section 12, and

    (g) section 13, except so far as relating to –

        (i)   any contravention of the fourth data protection principle,

        (ii) any disclosure without the consent of the data controller,

        (iii) loss or destruction of data without the consent of the data controller, or

        (iv) processing for the special purposes.

(2)   The specific exemptions conferred by sub-paragraph (1)(a), (c) and (e) do not limit the data controller's general duty under the first data protection principle to ensure that processing is fair.

Part III
Exemptions available after 23rd October 2001 but before 24th October 2007

14(1) This paragraph applies to –

    (a) eligible manual data which were held immediately before 24th October 1998, and

    (b) personal data which fall within paragraph (d) of the definition of 'data' in section 1(1) but do not fall within paragraph (a) of this sub-paragraph,

but does not apply to eligible manual data to which the exemption in paragraph 16 applies.

(2)   During the second transitional period, data to which this paragraph applies are exempt from the following provisions –

    (a) the first data protection principle except to the extent to which it requires compliance with paragraph 2 of Part II of Schedule 1,

(b) the second, third, fourth and fifth data protection principles, and

(c) section 14(1) to (3).

Part IV
Exemptions after 23rd October 2001 for historical research

15   In this Part of this Schedule 'the relevant conditions' has the same meaning as in section 33.

16(1) Eligible manual data which are processed only for the purpose of historical research in compliance with the relevant conditions are exempt from the provisions specified in sub-paragraph (2) after 23rd October 2001.

(2)   The provisions referred to in sub-paragraph (1) are –

(a) the first data protection principle except in so far as it requires compliance with paragraph 2 of Part II of Schedule 1,

(b) the second, third, fourth and fifth data protection principles, and

(c) section 14(1) to (3).

17(1) After 23rd October 2001 eligible automated data which are processed only for the purpose of historical research in compliance with the relevant conditions are exempt from the first data protection principle to the extent to which it requires compliance with the conditions in Schedules 2 and 3.

(2)   Eligible automated data which are processed –

(a) only for the purpose of historical research,

(b) in compliance with the relevant conditions, and

(c) otherwise than by reference to the data subject,

are also exempt from the provisions referred to in sub-paragraph (3) after 23rd October 2001.

(3)   The provisions referred to in sub-paragraph (2) are –

(a) the first data protection principle except in so far as it requires compliance with paragraph 2 of Part II of Schedule 1,

(b) the second, third, fourth and fifth data protection principles, and

(c) section 14(1) to (3).

18   For the purposes of this Part of this Schedule personal data are not to be treated as processed otherwise than for the purpose of historical research merely because the data are disclosed –

(a) to any person, for the purpose of historical research only,

(b) to the data subject or a person acting on his behalf,

(c) at the request, or with the consent, of the data subject or a person acting on his behalf, or

(d) in circumstances in which the person making the disclosure has reasonable grounds for believing that the disclosure falls within paragraph (a), (b) or (c).

Part V
Exemption from Section 22

19   Processing which was already under way immediately before 24th October 1998 is not assessable processing for the purposes of section 22.

HUMAN RIGHTS ACT 1998

An Act to give further effect to rights and freedoms guaranteed under the European Convention on Human Rights; to make provision with respect to holders of certain judicial offices who become judges of the European Court of Human Rights; and for connected purposes.

[9th November 1998]

BE IT ENACTED by the Queen's most Excellent Majesty, by and with the advice and consent of the Lords Spiritual and Temporal, and Commons, in this present Parliament assembled, and by the authority of the same, as follows: –

INTRODUCTION

The Convention rights

1(1) In this Act 'the Convention rights' means the rights and fundamental freedoms set out in –

(a) Articles 2 to 12 and 14 of the Convention,

(b) Articles 1 to 3 of the First Protocol, and

(c) Articles 1 and 2 of the Sixth Protocol,

as read with Articles 16 to 18 of the Convention.

(2) Those Articles are to have effect for the purposes of this Act subject to any designated derogation or reservation (as to which see sections 14 and 15).

(3) The Articles are set out in Schedule 1.

(4) The Secretary of State may by order make such amendments to this Act as he considers appropriate to reflect the effect, in relation to the United Kingdom, of a protocol.

(5) In subsection (4) 'protocol' means a protocol to the Convention –

(a) which the United Kingdom has ratified; or

(b) which the United Kingdom has signed with a view to ratification.

(6) No amendment may be made by an order under subsection (4) so as to come into force before the protocol concerned is in force in relation to the United Kingdom.

Interpretation of Convention rights.

2(1) A court or tribunal determining a question which has arisen in connection with a Convention right must take into account any –

(a) judgment, decision, declaration or advisory opinion of the European Court of Human Rights,

(b) opinion of the Commission given in a report adopted under Article 31 of the Convention,

(c) decision of the Commission in connection with Article 26 or 27(2) of the Convention, or

(d) decision of the Committee of Ministers taken under Article 46 of the Convention,

whenever made or given, so far as, in the opinion of the court or tribunal, it is relevant to the proceedings in which that question has arisen.

(2) Evidence of any judgment, decision, declaration or opinion of which account may have to be taken under this section is to be given in proceedings before any court or tribunal in such manner as may be provided by rules.

(3) In this section 'rules' means rules of court or, in the case of proceedings before a tribunal, rules made for the purposes of this section –

(a) by the Lord Chancellor or the Secretary of State, in relation to any proceedings outside Scotland;

(b) by the Secretary of State, in relation to proceedings in Scotland; or

(c) by a Northern Ireland department, in relation to proceedings before a tribunal in Northern Ireland-

(i) which deals with transferred matters; and

(ii) for which no rules made under paragraph (a) are in force.

LEGISLATION

Interpretation of legislation

3(1) So far as it is possible to do so, primary legislation and subordinate legislation must be read and given effect in a way which is compatible with the Convention rights.

(2) This section –

(a) applies to primary legislation and subordinate legislation whenever enacted;

(b) does not affect the validity, continuing operation or enforcement of any incompatible primary legislation; and

(c) does not affect the validity, continuing operation or enforcement of any incompatible subordinate legislation if (disregarding any possibility of revocation) primary legislation prevents removal of the incompatibility.

Declaration of incompatibility

4(1) Subsection (2) applies in any proceedings in which a court determines whether a provision of primary legislation is compatible with a Convention right.

(2) If the court is satisfied that the provision is incompatible with a Convention right, it may make a declaration of that incompatibility.

(3) Subsection (4) applies in any proceedings in which a court determines whether a provision of subordinate legislation, made in the exercise of a power conferred by primary legislation, is compatible with a Convention right.

(4) If the court is satisfied –

(a) that the provision is incompatible with a Convention right, and

(b) that (disregarding any possibility of revocation) the primary legislation concerned prevents removal of the incompatibility,

it may make a declaration of that incompatibility.

(5) In this section 'court' means –

(a) the House of Lords;

(b) the Judicial Committee of the Privy Council;

(c) the Courts-Martial Appeal Court;

      (d) in Scotland, the High Court of Justiciary sitting otherwise than as a trial court or the Court of Session;

      (e) in England and Wales or Northern Ireland, the High Court or the Court of Appeal.

(6) A declaration under this section ('a declaration of incompatibility') –

      (a) does not affect the validity, continuing operation or enforcement of the provision in respect of which it is given; and

      (b) is not binding on the parties to the proceedings in which it is made.

Right of Crown to intervene

5(1) Where a court is considering whether to make a declaration of incompatibility, the Crown is entitled to notice in accordance with rules of court.

(2) In any case to which subsection (1) applies –

      (a) a Minister of the Crown (or a person nominated by him),

      (b) a member of the Scottish Executive,

      (c) a Northern Ireland Minister,

      (d) a Northern Ireland department,

is entitled, on giving notice in accordance with rules of court, to be joined as a party to the proceedings.

(3) Notice under subsection (2) may be given at any time during the proceedings.

(4) A person who has been made a party to criminal proceedings (other than in Scotland) as the result of a notice under subsection (2) may, with leave, appeal to the House of Lords against any declaration of incompatibility made in the proceedings.

(5) In subsection (4) –

'criminal proceedings' includes all proceedings before the Courts-Martial Appeal Court; and

'leave' means leave granted by the court making the declaration of incompatibility or by the House of Lords.

PUBLIC AUTHORITIES

Acts of public authorities

6(1) It is unlawful for a public authority to act in a way which is incompatible with a Convention right.

(2) Subsection (1) does not apply to an act if –

      (a) as the result of one or more provisions of primary legislation, the authority could not have acted differently; or

      (b) in the case of one or more provisions of, or made under, primary legislation which cannot be read or given effect in a way which is compatible with the Convention rights, the authority was acting so as to give effect to or enforce those provisions.

(3) In this section 'public authority' includes –

      (a) a court or tribunal, and

      (b) any person certain of whose functions are functions of a public nature, but does not include either House of Parliament or a person exercising functions in connection with proceedings in Parliament.

(4) In subsection (3) 'Parliament' does not include the House of Lords in its judicial capacity.

(5) In relation to a particular act, a person is not a public authority by virtue only of subsection (3)(b) if the nature of the act is private.

(6) 'An act' includes a failure to act but does not include a failure to –

 (a) introduce in, or lay before, Parliament a proposal for legislation; or

 (b) make any primary legislation or remedial order.

Proceedings

7(1) A person who claims that a public authority has acted (or proposes to act) in a way which is made unlawful by section 6(1) may –

 (a) bring proceedings against the authority under this Act in the appropriate court or tribunal, or

 (b) rely on the Convention right or rights concerned in any legal proceedings,

 but only if he is (or would be) a victim of the unlawful act.

(2) In subsection (1)(a) 'appropriate court or tribunal' means such court or tribunal as may be determined in accordance with rules; and proceedings against an authority include a counterclaim or similar proceeding.

(3) If the proceedings are brought on an application for judicial review, the applicant is to be taken to have a sufficient interest in relation to the unlawful act only if he is, or would be, a victim of that act.

(4) If the proceedings are made by way of a petition for judicial review in Scotland, the applicant shall be taken to have title and interest to sue in relation to the unlawful act only if he is, or would be, a victim of that act.

(5) Proceedings under subsection (1)(a) must be brought before the end of –

 (a) the period of one year beginning with the date on which the act complained of took place; or

 (b) such longer period as the court or tribunal considers equitable having regard to all the circumstances,

 but that is subject to any rule imposing a stricter time limit in relation to the procedure in question.

(6) In subsection (1)(b) 'legal proceedings' includes –

 (a) proceedings brought by or at the instigation of a public authority; and

 (b) an appeal against the decision of a court or tribunal.

(7) For the purposes of this section, a person is a victim of an unlawful act only if he would be a victim for the purposes of Article 34 of the Convention if proceedings were brought in the European Court of Human Rights in respect of that act.

(8) Nothing in this Act creates a criminal offence.

(9) In this section 'rules' means –

 (a) in relation to proceedings before a court or tribunal outside Scotland, rules made by the Lord Chancellor or the Secretary of State for the purposes of this section or rules of court,

(b) in relation to proceedings before a court or tribunal in Scotland, rules made by the Secretary of State for those purposes,

(c) in relation to proceedings before a tribunal in Northern Ireland-

(i) which deals with transferred matters; and

(ii) for which no rules made under paragraph (a) are in force,

rules made by a Northern Ireland department for those purposes,

and includes provision made by order under section 1 of the Courts and Legal Services Act 1990.

(10) In making rules, regard must be had to section 9.

(11) The Minister who has power to make rules in relation to a particular tribunal may, to the extent he considers it necessary to ensure that the tribunal can provide an appropriate remedy in relation to an act (or proposed act) of a public authority which is (or would be) unlawful as a result of section 6(1), by order add to –

(a) the relief or remedies which the tribunal may grant; or

(b) the grounds on which it may grant any of them.

(12) An order made under subsection (11) may contain such incidental, supplemental, consequential or transitional provision as the Minister making it considers appropriate.

(13) 'The Minister' includes the Northern Ireland department concerned.

Judicial remedies

8(1) In relation to any act (or proposed act) of a public authority which the court finds is (or would be) unlawful, it may grant such relief or remedy, or make such order, within its powers as it considers just and appropriate.

(2) But damages may be awarded only by a court which has power to award damages, or to order the payment of compensation, in civil proceedings.

(3) No award of damages is to be made unless, taking account of all the circumstances of the case, including –

(a) any other relief or remedy granted, or order made, in relation to the act in question (by that or any other court), and

(b) the consequences of any decision (of that or any other court) in respect of that act,

the court is satisfied that the award is necessary to afford just satisfaction to the person in whose favour it is made.

(4) In determining –

(a) whether to award damages, or

(b) the amount of an award,

the court must take into account the principles applied by the European Court of Human Rights in relation to the award of compensation under Article 41 of the Convention.

(5) A public authority against which damages are awarded is to be treated –

(a) in Scotland, for the purposes of section 3 of the Law Reform (Miscellaneous Provisions) (Scotland) Act 1940 as if the award were made in an action of damages in which the authority has been found liable in respect of loss or damage to the person to whom the award is made;

(b) for the purposes of the Civil Liability (Contribution) Act 1978 as liable in respect of damage suffered by the person to whom the award is made.

(6) In this section –

'court' includes a tribunal;

'damages' means damages for an unlawful act of a public authority; and

'unlawful' means unlawful under section 6(1).

Judicial acts

9(1) Proceedings under section 7(1)(a) in respect of a judicial act may be brought only –

(a) by exercising a right of appeal;

(b) on an application (in Scotland a petition) for judicial review; or

(c) in such other forum as may be prescribed by rules.

(2) That does not affect any rule of law which prevents a court from being the subject of judicial review.

(3) In proceedings under this Act in respect of a judicial act done in good faith, damages may not be awarded otherwise than to compensate a person to the extent required by Article 5(5) of the Convention.

(4) An award of damages permitted by subsection (3) is to be made against the Crown; but no award may be made unless the appropriate person, if not a party to the proceedings, is joined.

(5) In this section –

'appropriate person' means the Minister responsible for the court concerned, or a person or government department nominated by him;

'court' includes a tribunal;

'judge' includes a member of a tribunal, a justice of the peace and a clerk or other officer entitled to exercise the jurisdiction of a court;

'judicial act' means a judicial act of a court and includes an act done on the instructions, or on behalf, of a judge; and

'rules' has the same meaning as in section 7(9).

REMEDIAL ACTION

Power to take remedial action

10(1) This section applies if –

(a) a provision of legislation has been declared under section 4 to be incompatible with a Convention right and, if an appeal lies –

(i) all persons who may appeal have stated in writing that they do not intend to do so;

(ii) the time for bringing an appeal has expired and no appeal has been brought within that time; or

(iii) an appeal brought within that time has been determined or abandoned; or

(b) it appears to a Minister of the Crown or Her Majesty in Council that, having regard to a finding of the European Court of Human Rights made after the coming into force of this section in proceedings against the United Kingdom, a provision of legislation is incompatible with an obligation of the United Kingdom arising from the Convention.

(2) If a Minister of the Crown considers that there are compelling reasons for proceeding under this section, he may by order make such amendments to the legislation as he considers necessary to remove the incompatibility.

(3) If, in the case of subordinate legislation, a Minister of the Crown considers –

(a) that it is necessary to amend the primary legislation under which the subordinate legislation in question was made, in order to enable the incompatibility to be removed, and

(b) that there are compelling reasons for proceeding under this section,

he may by order make such amendments to the primary legislation as he considers necessary.

(4) This section also applies where the provision in question is in subordinate legislation and has been quashed, or declared invalid, by reason of incompatibility with a Convention right and the Minister proposes to proceed under paragraph 2(b) of Schedule 2.

(5) If the legislation is an Order in Council, the power conferred by subsection (2) or (3) is exercisable by Her Majesty in Council.

(6) In this section 'legislation' does not include a Measure of the Church Assembly or of the General Synod of the Church of England.

(7) Schedule 2 makes further provision about remedial orders.

OTHER RIGHTS AND PROCEEDINGS

Safeguard for existing human rights

11 A person's reliance on a Convention right does not restrict –

(a) any other right or freedom conferred on him by or under any law having effect in any part of the United Kingdom; or

(b) his right to make any claim or bring any proceedings which he could make or bring apart from sections 7 to 9.

Freedom of expression

12(1) This section applies if a court is considering whether to grant any relief which, if granted, might affect the exercise of the Convention right to freedom of expression.

(2) If the person against whom the application for relief is made ('the respondent') is neither present nor represented, no such relief is to be granted unless the court is satisfied –

(a) that the applicant has taken all practicable steps to notify the respondent; or

(b) that there are compelling reasons why the respondent should not be notified.

(3) No such relief is to be granted so as to restrain publication before trial unless the court is satisfied that the applicant is likely to establish that publication should not be allowed.

(4) The court must have particular regard to the importance of the Convention right to freedom of expression and, where the proceedings relate to material which the respondent claims, or which appears to the court, to be journalistic, literary or artistic material (or to conduct connected with such material), to –

   (a) the extent to which-

      (i) the material has, or is about to, become available to the public; or

      (ii) it is, or would be, in the public interest for the material to be published;

   (b) any relevant privacy code.

(5) In this section –

   'court' includes a tribunal; and

   'relief' includes any remedy or order (other than in criminal proceedings).

Freedom of thought, conscience and religion

13(1) If a court's determination of any question arising under this Act might affect the exercise by a religious organisation (itself or its members collectively) of the Convention right to freedom of thought, conscience and religion, it must have particular regard to the importance of that right.

(2) In this section 'court' includes a tribunal.

DEROGATIONS AND RESERVATIONS

Derogations

14(1) In this Act 'designated derogation' means –

   (a) the United Kingdom's derogation from Article 5(3) of the Convention; and

   (b) any derogation by the United Kingdom from an Article of the Convention, or of any protocol to the Convention, which is designated for the purposes of this Act in an order made by the Secretary of State.

(2) The derogation referred to in subsection (1)(a) is set out in Part I of Schedule 3.

(3) If a designated derogation is amended or replaced it ceases to be a designated derogation.

(4) But subsection (3) does not prevent the Secretary of State from exercising his power under subsection (1)(b) to make a fresh designation order in respect of the Article concerned.

(5) The Secretary of State must by order make such amendments to Schedule 3 as he considers appropriate to reflect –

   (a) any designation order; or

   (b) the effect of subsection (3).

(6) A designation order may be made in anticipation of the making by the United Kingdom of a proposed derogation.

Reservations

15(1) In this Act 'designated reservation' means –

   (a) the United Kingdom's reservation to Article 2 of the First Protocol to the Convention; and

(b) any other reservation by the United Kingdom to an Article of the Convention, or of any protocol to the Convention, which is designated for the purposes of this Act in an order made by the Secretary of State.

(2) The text of the reservation referred to in subsection (1)(a) is set out in Part II of Schedule 3.

(3) If a designated reservation is withdrawn wholly or in part it ceases to be a designated reservation.

(4) But subsection (3) does not prevent the Secretary of State from exercising his power under subsection (1)(b) to make a fresh designation order in respect of the Article concerned.

(5) The Secretary of State must by order make such amendments to this Act as he considers appropriate to reflect –

(a) any designation order; or

(b) the effect of subsection (3).

Period for which designated derogations have effect

16(1) If it has not already been withdrawn by the United Kingdom, a designated derogation ceases to have effect for the purposes of this Act –

(a) in the case of the derogation referred to in section 14(1)(a), at the end of the period of five years beginning with the date on which section 1(2) came into force;

(b) in the case of any other derogation, at the end of the period of five years beginning with the date on which the order designating it was made.

(2) At any time before the period –

(a) fixed by subsection (1)(a) or (b), or

(b) extended by an order under this subsection,

comes to an end, the Secretary of State may by order extend it by a further period of five years.

(3) An order under section 14(1)(b) ceases to have effect at the end of the period for consideration, unless a resolution has been passed by each House approving the order.

(4) Subsection (3) does not affect –

(a) anything done in reliance on the order; or

(b) the power to make a fresh order under section 14(1)(b).

(5) In subsection (3) 'period for consideration' means the period of forty days beginning with the day on which the order was made.

(6) In calculating the period for consideration, no account is to be taken of any time during which

(a) Parliament is dissolved or prorogued; or

(b) both Houses are adjourned for more than four days.

(7) If a designated derogation is withdrawn by the United Kingdom, the Secretary of State must by order make such amendments to this Act as he considers are required to reflect that withdrawal.

Periodic review of designated reservations

17(1) The appropriate Minister must review the designated reservation referred to in section 15(1)(a) –

(a) before the end of the period of five years beginning with the date on which section 1(2) came into force; and

(b) if that designation is still in force, before the end of the period of five years beginning with the date on which the last report relating to it was laid under subsection (3).

(2) The appropriate Minister must review each of the other designated reservations (if any) –

(a) before the end of the period of five years beginning with the date on which the order designating the reservation first came into force; and

(b) if the designation is still in force, before the end of the period of five years beginning with the date on which the last report relating to it was laid under subsection (3).

(3) The Minister conducting a review under this section must prepare a report on the result of the review and lay a copy of it before each House of Parliament.

JUDGES OF THE EUROPEAN COURT OF HUMAN RIGHTS

Appointment to European Court of Human Rights

18(1) In this section 'judicial office' means the office of –

(a) Lord Justice of Appeal, Justice of the High Court or Circuit judge, in England and Wales;

(b) judge of the Court of Session or sheriff, in Scotland;

(c) Lord Justice of Appeal, judge of the High Court or county court judge, in Northern Ireland.

(2) The holder of a judicial office may become a judge of the European Court of Human Rights ('the Court') without being required to relinquish his office.

(3) But he is not required to perform the duties of his judicial office while he is a judge of the Court.

(4) In respect of any period during which he is a judge of the Court –

(a) a Lord Justice of Appeal or Justice of the High Court is not to count as a judge of the relevant court for the purposes of section 2(1) or 4(1) of the Supreme Court Act 1981 (maximum number of judges) nor as a judge of the Supreme Court for the purposes of section 12(1) to (6) of that Act (salaries etc);

(b) a judge of the Court of Session is not to count as a judge of that court for the purposes of section 1(1) of the Court of Session Act 1988 (maximum number of judges) or of section 9(1)(c) of the Administration of Justice Act 1973 ('the 1973 Act') (salaries etc);

(c) a Lord Justice of Appeal or judge of the High Court in Northern Ireland is not to count as a judge of the relevant court for the purposes of section 2(1) or 3(1) of the Judicature (Northern Ireland) Act 1978 (maximum number of judges) nor as a judge of the Supreme Court of Northern Ireland for the purposes of section 9(1)(d) of the 1973 Act (salaries etc);

(d) a Circuit judge is not to count as such for the purposes of section 18 of the Courts Act 1971 (salaries etc);

(e) a sheriff is not to count as such for the purposes of section 14 of the Sheriff Courts (Scotland) Act 1907 (salaries etc);

(f) a county court judge of Northern Ireland is not to count as such for the purposes of section 106 of the County Courts Act Northern Ireland) 1959 (salaries etc).

(5) If a sheriff principal is appointed a judge of the Court, section 11(1) of the Sheriff Courts (Scotland) Act 1971 (temporary appointment of sheriff principal) applies, while he holds that appointment, as if his office is vacant.

(6) Schedule 4 makes provision about judicial pensions in relation to the holder of a judicial office who serves as a judge of the Court.

(7) The Lord Chancellor or the Secretary of State may by order make such transitional provision (including, in particular, provision for a temporary increase in the maximum number of judges) as he considers appropriate in relation to any holder of a judicial office who has completed his service as a judge of the Court.

PARLIAMENTARY PROCEDURE

Statements of compatibility

19(1) A Minister of the Crown in charge of a Bill in either House of Parliament must, before Second Reading of the Bill –

(a) make a statement to the effect that in his view the provisions of the Bill are compatible with the Convention rights ('a statement of compatibility'); or

(b) make a statement to the effect that although he is unable to make a statement of compatibility the government nevertheless wishes the House to proceed with the Bill.

(2) The statement must be in writing and be published in such manner as the Minister making it considers appropriate.

SUPPLEMENTAL

Orders etc under this Act

20(1) Any power of a Minister of the Crown to make an order under this Act is exercisable by statutory instrument.

(2) The power of the Lord Chancellor or the Secretary of State to make rules (other than rules of court) under section 2(3) or 7(9) is exercisable by statutory instrument.

(3) Any statutory instrument made under section 14, 15 or 16(7) must be laid before Parliament.

(4) No order may be made by the Lord Chancellor or the Secretary of State under section 1(4), 7(11) or 16(2) unless a draft of the order has been laid before, and approved by, each House of Parliament.

(5) Any statutory instrument made under section 18(7) or Schedule 4, or to which subsection (2) applies, shall be subject to annulment in pursuance of a resolution of either House of Parliament.

(6) The power of a Northern Ireland department to make –

(a) rules under section 2(3)(c) or 7(9)(c), or

(b) an order under section 7(11),

is exercisable by statutory rule for the purposes of the Statutory Rules (Northern Ireland) Order 1979.

(7) Any rules made under section 2(3)(c) or 7(9)(c) shall be subject to negative resolution; and section 41(6) of the Interpretation Act Northern Ireland) 1954 (meaning of 'subject to negative resolution') shall apply as if the power to make the rules were conferred by an Act of the Northern Ireland Assembly.

(8) No order may be made by a Northern Ireland department under section 7(11) unless a draft of the order has been laid before, and approved by, the Northern Ireland Assembly.

Interpretation, etc

21(1) In this Act –

'amend' includes repeal and apply (with or without modifications);

'the appropriate Minister' means the Minister of the Crown having charge of the appropriate authorised government department (within the meaning of the Crown Proceedings Act 1947);

'the Commission' means the European Commission of Human Rights;

'the Convention' means the Convention for the Protection of Human Rights and Fundamental Freedoms, agreed by the Council of Europe at Rome on 4th November 1950 as it has effect for the time being in relation to the United Kingdom;

'declaration of incompatibility' means a declaration under section 4;

'Minister of the Crown' has the same meaning as in the Ministers of the Crown Act 1975;

'Northern Ireland Minister' includes the First Minister and the deputy First Minister in Northern Ireland;

'primary legislation' means any –

(a) public general Act;

(b) local and personal Act;

(c) private Act;

(d) Measure of the Church Assembly;

(e) Measure of the General Synod of the Church of England;

(f) Order in Council –

(i) made in exercise of Her Majesty's Royal Prerogative;

(ii) made under section 38(1)(a) of the Northern Ireland Constitution Act 1973 or the corresponding provision of the Northern Ireland Act 1998; or

(iii) amending an Act of a kind mentioned in paragraph (a), (b) or (c);

and includes an order or other instrument made under primary legislation (otherwise than by the National Assembly for Wales, a member of the Scottish Executive, a Northern Ireland Minister or a Northern Ireland department) to the extent to which it operates to bring one or more provisions of that legislation into force or amends any primary legislation;

'the First Protocol' means the protocol to the Convention agreed at Paris on 20th March 1952;

'the Sixth Protocol' means the protocol to the Convention agreed at Strasbourg on 28th April 1983;

'the Eleventh Protocol' means the protocol to the Convention (restructuring the control machinery established by the Convention) agreed at Strasbourg on 11th May 1994;

'remedial order' means an order under section 10;

'subordinate legislation' means any –

(a) Order in Council other than one –

    (i) made in exercise of Her Majesty's Royal Prerogative;

    (ii) made under section 38(1)(a) of the Northern Ireland Constitution Act 1973 or the corresponding provision of the Northern Ireland Act 1998; or

    (iii) amending an Act of a kind mentioned in the definition of primary legislation;

(b) Act of the Scottish Parliament;

(c) Act of the Parliament of Northern Ireland;

(d) Measure of the Assembly established under section 1 of the Northern Ireland Assembly Act 1973;

(e) Act of the Northern Ireland Assembly;

(f) order, rules, regulations, scheme, warrant, byelaw or other instrument made under primary legislation (except to the extent to which it operates to bring one or more provisions of that legislation into force or amends any primary legislation);

(g) order, rules, regulations, scheme, warrant, byelaw or other instrument made under legislation mentioned in paragraph (b), (c), (d) or (e) or made under an Order in Council applying only to Northern Ireland;

(h) order, rules, regulations, scheme, warrant, byelaw or other instrument made by a member of the Scottish Executive, a Northern Ireland Minister or a Northern Ireland department in exercise of prerogative or other executive functions of Her Majesty which are exercisable by such a person on behalf of Her Majesty;

'transferred matters' has the same meaning as in the Northern Ireland Act 1998; and

'tribunal' means any tribunal in which legal proceedings may be brought.

(2) The references in paragraphs (b) and (c) of section 2(1) to Articles are to Articles of the Convention as they had effect immediately before the coming into force of the Eleventh Protocol.

(3) The reference in paragraph (d) of section 2(1) to Article 46 includes a reference to Articles 32 and 54 of the Convention as they had effect immediately before the coming into force of the Eleventh Protocol.

(4) The references in section 2(1) to a report or decision of the Commission or a decision of the Committee of Ministers include references to a report or decision made as provided by paragraphs 3, 4 and 6 of Article 5 of the Eleventh Protocol (transitional provisions).

(5) Any liability under the Army Act 1955, the Air Force Act 1955 or the Naval Discipline Act 1957 to suffer death for an offence is replaced by a liability to imprisonment for life or any less punishment authorised by those Acts; and those Acts shall accordingly have effect with the necessary modifications.

Short title, commencement, application and extent

22(1) This Act may be cited as the Human Rights Act 1998.

(2) Sections 18, 20 and 21(5) and this section come into force on the passing of this Act.

(3) The other provisions of this Act come into force on such day as the Secretary of State may by order appoint; and different days may be appointed for different purposes.

(4) Paragraph (b) of subsection (1) of section 7 applies to proceedings brought by or at the instigation of a public authority whenever the act in question took place; but otherwise that subsection does not apply to an act taking place before the coming into force of that section.

(5) This Act binds the Crown.

(6) This Act extends to Northern Ireland.

(7) Section 21(5), so far as it relates to any provision contained in the Army Act 1955, the Air Force Act 1955 or the Naval Discipline Act 1957, extends to any place to which that provision extends.

SCHEDULE 1
THE ARTICLES

Part I
The Convention rights and freedoms

Article 2 Right to life

1   Everyone's right to life shall be protected by law. No one shall be deprived of his life intentionally save in the execution of a sentence of a court following his conviction of a crime for which this penalty is provided by law.

2   Deprivation of life shall not be regarded as inflicted in contravention of this Article when it results from the use of force which is no more than absolutely necessary:

(a) in defence of any person from unlawful violence;

(b) in order to effect a lawful arrest or to prevent the escape of a person lawfully detained;

(c) in action lawfully taken for the purpose of quelling a riot or insurrection.

Article 3 Prohibition of torture

No one shall be subjected to torture or to inhuman or degrading treatment or punishment.

Article 4 Prohibition of slavery and forced labour

1   No one shall be held in slavery or servitude.

2   No one shall be required to perform forced or compulsory labour.

3   For the purpose of this Article the term 'forced or compulsory labour' shall not include:

   (a) any work required to be done in the ordinary course of detention imposed according to the provisions of Article 5 of this Convention or during conditional release from such detention;

   (b) any service of a military character or, in case of conscientious objectors in countries where they are recognised, service exacted instead of compulsory military service;

   (c) any service exacted in case of an emergency or calamity threatening the life or well-being of the community;

   (d) any work or service which forms part of normal civic obligations.

Article 5 Right to liberty and security

1   Everyone has the right to liberty and security of person. No one shall be deprived of his liberty save in the following cases and in accordance with a procedure prescribed by law:

   (a) the lawful detention of a person after conviction by a competent court;

   (b) the lawful arrest or detention of a person for non-compliance with the lawful order of a court or in order to secure the fulfilment of any obligation prescribed by law;

   (c) the lawful arrest or detention of a person effected for the purpose of bringing him before the competent legal authority on reasonable suspicion of having committed an offence or when it is reasonably considered necessary to prevent his committing an offence or fleeing after having done so;

   (d) the detention of a minor by lawful order for the purpose of educational supervision or his lawful detention for the purpose of bringing him before the competent legal authority;

   (e) the lawful detention of persons for the prevention of the spreading of infectious diseases, of persons of unsound mind, alcoholics or drug addicts or vagrants;

   (f) the lawful arrest or detention of a person to prevent his effecting an unauthorised entry into the country or of a person against whom action is being taken with a view to deportation or extradition.

2   Everyone who is arrested shall be informed promptly, in a language which he understands, of the reasons for his arrest and of any charge against him.

3   Everyone arrested or detained in accordance with the provisions of paragraph 1(c) of this Article shall be brought promptly before a judge or other officer authorised by law to exercise judicial power and shall be entitled to trial within a reasonable time or to release pending trial. Release may be conditioned by guarantees to appear for trial.

4   Everyone who is deprived of his liberty by arrest or detention shall be entitled to take proceedings by which the lawfulness of his detention shall be decided speedily by a court and his release ordered if the detention is not lawful.

5   Everyone who has been the victim of arrest or detention in contravention of the provisions of this Article shall have an enforceable right to compensation.

Article 6 Right to a fair trial

1   In the determination of his civil rights and obligations or of any criminal charge against him, everyone is entitled to a fair and public hearing within a reasonable time by an independent and impartial tribunal established by law. Judgment shall be pronounced publicly but the press and public may be excluded from all or part of the trial in the interest of morals, public order or national security in a democratic society, where the interests of juveniles or the protection of the private life of the parties so require, or to the extent strictly necessary in the opinion of the court in special circumstances where publicity would prejudice the interests of justice.

2   Everyone charged with a criminal offence shall be presumed innocent until proved guilty according to law.

3   Everyone charged with a criminal offence has the following minimum rights:

   (a) to be informed promptly, in a language which he understands and in detail, of the nature and cause of the accusation against him;

   (b) to have adequate time and facilities for the preparation of his defence;

   (c) to defend himself in person or through legal assistance of his own choosing or, if he has not sufficient means to pay for legal assistance, to be given it free when the interests of justice so require;

   (d) to examine or have examined witnesses against him and to obtain the attendance and examination of witnesses on his behalf under the same conditions as witnesses against him;

   (e) to have the free assistance of an interpreter if he cannot understand or speak the language used in court.

Article 7 No punishment without law

1   No one shall be held guilty of any criminal offence on account of any act or omission which did not constitute a criminal offence under national or international law at the time when it was committed. Nor shall a heavier penalty be imposed than the one that was applicable at the time the criminal offence was committed.

2   This Article shall not prejudice the trial and punishment of any person for any act or omission which, at the time when it was committed, was criminal according to the general principles of law recognised by civilised nations.

Article 8 Right to respect for private and family life

1   Everyone has the right to respect for his private and family life, his home and his correspondence.

2 There shall be no interference by a public authority with the exercise of this right except such as is in accordance with the law and is necessary in a democratic society in the interests of national security, public safety or the economic well-being of the country, for the prevention of disorder or crime, for the protection of health or morals, or for the protection of the rights and freedoms of others.

Article 9 Freedom of thought, conscience and religion

1 Everyone has the right to freedom of thought, conscience and religion; this right includes freedom to change his religion or belief and freedom, either alone or in community with others and in public or private, to manifest his religion or belief, in worship, teaching, practice and observance.

2 Freedom to manifest one's religion or beliefs shall be subject only to such limitations as are prescribed by law and are necessary in a democratic society in the interests of public safety, for the protection of public order, health or morals, or for the protection of the rights and freedoms of others.

Article 10 Freedom of expression

1 Everyone has the right to freedom of expression. This right shall include freedom to hold opinions and to receive and impart information and ideas without interference by public authority and regardless of frontiers. This Article shall not prevent States from requiring the licensing of broadcasting, television or cinema enterprises.

2 The exercise of these freedoms, since it carries with it duties and responsibilities, may be subject to such formalities, conditions, restrictions or penalties as are prescribed by law and are necessary in a democratic society, in the interests of national security, territorial integrity or public safety, for the prevention of disorder or crime, for the protection of health or morals, for the protection of the reputation or rights of others, for preventing the disclosure of information received in confidence, or for maintaining the authority and impartiality of the judiciary.

Article 11 Freedom of assembly and association

1 Everyone has the right to freedom of peaceful assembly and to freedom of association with others, including the right to form and to join trade unions for the protection of his interests.

2 No restrictions shall be placed on the exercise of these rights other than such as are prescribed by law and are necessary in a democratic society in the interests of national security or public safety, for the prevention of disorder or crime, for the protection of health or morals or for the protection of the rights and freedoms of others. This Article shall not prevent the imposition of lawful restrictions on the exercise of these rights by members of the armed forces, of the police or of the administration of the State.

Article 12 Right to marry

Men and women of marriageable age have the right to marry and to found a family, according to the national laws governing the exercise of this right.

Article 14 Prohibition of discrimination

The enjoyment of the rights and freedoms set forth in this Convention shall be secured without discrimination on any ground such as sex, race, colour, language, religion, political or other opinion, national or social origin, association with a national minority, property, birth or other status.

Article 16 Restrictions on political activity of aliens

Nothing in Articles 10, 11 and 14 shall be regarded as preventing the High Contracting Parties from imposing restrictions on the political activity of aliens.

Article 17 Prohibition of abuse of rights

Nothing in this Convention may be interpreted as implying for any State, group or person any right to engage in any activity or perform any act aimed at the destruction of any of the rights and freedoms set forth herein or at their limitation to a greater extent than is provided for in the Convention.

Article 18 Limitation on use of restrictions of rights

The restrictions permitted under this Convention to the said rights and freedoms shall not be applied for any purpose other than those for which they have been prescribed.

Part II
The First Protocol

Article 1 Protection of Property

Every natural or legal person is entitled to the peaceful enjoyment of his possessions. No one shall be deprived of his possessions except in the public interest and subject to the conditions provided for by law and by the general principles of international law.

The preceding provisions shall not, however, in any way impair the right of a State to enforce such laws as it deems necessary to control the use of property in accordance with the general interest or to secure the payment of taxes or other contributions or penalties.

Article 2 Right to education

No person shall be denied the right to education. In the exercise of any functions which it assumes in relation to education and to teaching, the State shall respect the right of parents to ensure such education and teaching in conformity with their own religious and philosophical convictions.

Article 3 Right to free elections

The High Contracting Parties undertake to hold free elections at reasonable intervals by secret ballot, under conditions which will ensure the free expression of the opinion of the people in the choice of the legislature.

Part III
The Sixth Protocol

Article 1 Abolition of the death penalty

The death penalty shall be abolished. No one shall be condemned to such penalty or executed.

Article 2 Death penalty in time of war

A State may make provision in its law for the death penalty in respect of acts committed in time of war or of imminent threat of war; such penalty shall be applied only in the instances laid down in the law and in accordance with its provisions. The State shall communicate to the Secretary General of the Council of Europe the relevant provisions of that law.

SCHEDULE 2
REMEDIAL ORDERS

Orders

1(1) A remedial order may –

    (a) contain such incidental, supplemental, consequential or transitional provision as the person making it considers appropriate;

    (b) be made so as to have effect from a date earlier than that on which it is made;

    (c) make provision for the delegation of specific functions;

    (d) make different provision for different cases.

(2) The power conferred by sub-paragraph (1)(a) includes –

    (a) power to amend primary legislation (including primary legislation other than that which contains the incompatible provision); and

    (b) power to amend or revoke subordinate legislation (including subordinate legislation other than that which contains the incompatible provision).

(3) A remedial order may be made so as to have the same extent as the legislation which it affects.

(4) No person is to be guilty of an offence solely as a result of the retrospective effect of a remedial order.

Procedure

2 No remedial order may be made unless –

    (a) a draft of the order has been approved by a resolution of each House of Parliament made after the end of the period of 60 days beginning with the day on which the draft was laid; or

    (b) it is declared in the order that it appears to the person making it that, because of the urgency of the matter, it is necessary to make the order without a draft being so approved.

Orders laid in draft

3(1) No draft may be laid under paragraph 2(a) unless –

    (a) the person proposing to make the order has laid before Parliament a document which contains a draft of the proposed order and the required information; and

(b) the period of 60 days, beginning with the day on which the document required by this sub-paragraph was laid has ended.

(2) If representations have been made during that period, the draft laid under paragraph 2(a) must be accompanied by a statement containing –

(a) a summary of the representations; and

(b) if, as a result of the representations, the proposed order has been changed, details of the changes.

Urgent cases

4(1) If a remedial order ('the original order') is made without being approved in draft, the person making it must lay it before Parliament, accompanied by the required information, after it is made.

(2) If representations have been made during the period of 60 days beginning with the day on which the original order was made, the person making it must (after the end of that period) lay before Parliament a statement containing –

(a) a summary of the representations; and

(b) if, as a result of the representations, he considers it appropriate to make changes to the original order, details of the changes.

(3) If sub-paragraph (2)(b) applies, the person making the statement must –

(a) make a further remedial order replacing the original order; and

(b) lay the replacement order before Parliament.

(4) If, at the end of the period of 120 days beginning with the day on which the original order was made, a resolution has not been passed by each House approving the original or replacement order, the order ceases to have effect (but without that affecting anything previously done under either order or the power to make a fresh remedial order).

Definitions

5 In this Schedule –

'representations' means representations about a remedial order (or proposed remedial order) made to the person making (or proposing to make) it and includes any relevant Parliamentary report or resolution; and

'required information' means –

(a) an explanation of the incompatibility which the order (or proposed order) seeks to remove, including particulars of the relevant declaration, finding or order; and

(b) a statement of the reasons for proceeding under section 10 and for making an order in those terms.

Calculating period

6 In calculating any period for the purposes of this Schedule, no account is to be taken of any time during which –

(a) Parliament is dissolved or prorogued; or

(b) both Houses are adjourned for more than four days.

ACCESS TO JUSTICE ACT 1999

27 Conditional fee agreements

(1) For section 58 of the Courts and Legal Services Act 1990 substitute –

'Conditional fee agreements.

58(1) A conditional fee agreement which satisfies all of the conditions applicable to it by virtue of this section shall not be unenforceable by reason only of its being a conditional fee agreement; but (subject to subsection (5)) any other conditional fee agreement shall be unenforceable.

(2) For the purposes of this section and section 58A –

(a) a conditional fee agreement is an agreement with a person providing advocacy or litigation services which provides for his fees and expenses, or any part of them, to be payable only in specified circumstances; and

(b) a conditional fee agreement provides for a success fee if it provides for the amount of any fees to which it applies to be increased, in specified circumstances, above the amount which would be payable if it were not payable only in specified circumstances.

(3) The following conditions are applicable to every conditional fee agreement –

(a) it must be in writing;

(b) it must not relate to proceedings which cannot be the subject of an enforceable conditional fee agreement; and

(c) it must comply with such requirements (if any) as may be prescribed by the Lord Chancellor.

(4) The following further conditions are applicable to a conditional fee agreement which provides for a success fee –

(a) it must relate to proceedings of a description specified by order made by the Lord Chancellor;

(b) it must state the percentage by which the amount of the fees which would be payable if it were not a conditional fee agreement is to be increased; and

(c) that percentage must not exceed the percentage specified in relation to the description of proceedings to which the agreement relates by order made by the Lord Chancellor.

(5) If a conditional fee agreement is an agreement to which section 57 of the Solicitors Act 1974 (non-contentious business agreements between solicitor and client) applies, subsection (1) shall not make it unenforceable.

28 Litigation funding agreements

In the Courts and Legal Services Act 1990, after section 58A (inserted by section 27 above) insert –

'Litigation funding agreements

58B-(1) A litigation funding agreement which satisfies all of the conditions applicable to it by virtue of this section shall not be unenforceable by reason only of its being a litigation funding agreement.

(2) For the purposes of this section a litigation funding agreement is an agreement under which –

    (a) a person ('the funder') agrees to fund (in whole or in part) the provision of advocacy or litigation services (by someone other than the funder) to another person ('the litigant'); and

    (b) the litigant agrees to pay a sum to the funder in specified circumstances.

(3) The following conditions are applicable to a litigation funding agreement –

    (a) the funder must be a person, or person of a description, prescribed by the Lord Chancellor;

    (b) the agreement must be in writing;

    (c) the agreement must not relate to proceedings which by virtue of section 58A(1) and (2) cannot be the subject of an enforceable conditional fee agreement or to proceedings of any such description as may be prescribed by the Lord Chancellor;

    (d) the agreement must comply with such requirements (if any) as may be so prescribed;

    (e) the sum to be paid by the litigant must consist of any costs payable to him in respect of the proceedings to which the agreement relates together with an amount calculated by reference to the funder's anticipated expenditure in funding the provision of the services; and

    (f) that amount must not exceed such percentage of that anticipated expenditure as may be prescribed by the Lord Chancellor in relation to proceedings of the description to which the agreement relates.

(4) Regulations under subsection (3)(a) may require a person to be approved by the Lord Chancellor or by a prescribed person.

(5) The requirements which the Lord Chancellor may prescribe under subsection (3)(d) –

    (a) include requirements for the funder to have provided prescribed information to the litigant before the agreement is made; and

    (b) may be different for different descriptions of litigation funding agreements.

(6) In this section (and in the definitions of 'advocacy services' and 'litigation services' as they apply for its purposes) 'proceedings' includes any sort of proceedings for resolving disputes (and not just proceedings in a court), whether commenced or contemplated.

(7) Before making regulations under this section, the Lord Chancellor shall consult –

    (a) the designated judges;

    (b) the General Council of the Bar;

    (c) the Law Society; and

    (d) such other bodies as he considers appropriate.

(8) A costs order made in any proceedings may, subject in the case of court proceedings to rules of court, include provision requiring the payment of any amount payable under a litigation funding agreement.

(9) Rules of court may make provision with respect to the assessment of any costs which include fees payable under a litigation funding agreement.'

29 Recovery of insurance premiums by way of costs.

Where in any proceedings a costs order is made in favour of any party who has taken out an insurance policy against the risk of incurring a liability in those proceedings, the costs payable to him may, subject in the case of court proceedings to rules of court, include costs in respect of the premium of the policy.

APPENDIX B

STATUTORY INSTRUMENTS

NATIONAL HEALTH SERVICE (GENERAL MEDICAL SERVICES) REGULATIONS 1992 (SI 1992/635)

SCHEDULE 2: TERMS OF SERVICE FOR DOCTORS (REGULATION 3(2))

General

3 Where a decision whether any, and if so what, action is to be taken under these terms of service requires the exercise of professional judgment, a doctor shall not, in reaching that decision, be expected to exercise a higher degree of skill, knowledge and care than:

(a) in the case of a doctor providing child health surveillance services under regulation 28, maternity medical services under regulation 31 or minor surgery services under regulation 33, that which any general practitioner included in the child health surveillance list, the obstetric list or, as the case may be, the minor surgery list may reasonably be expected to exercise; and

(b) in any other case, that which general practitioners as a class may reasonably be expected to exercise.

A doctor's patients

4 (1) Subject to sub-paragraph (2) and to paragraphs 9, 10 and 11, a doctor's patients are:

(a) persons who are recorded by the FHSA as being on his list;

(b) persons whom he has accepted or agreed to accept on his list, whether or not notification of that acceptance has been received by the FHSA, and who have not been notified to him by the FHSA as having ceased to be on his list;

(c) for the limited period specified in sub-paragraph (4), persons whom he has refused to accept;

(d) persons who have been assigned to him under regulation 21;

(e) for the limited period specified in sub-paragraph (5), persons in respect of whom he has been notified that an application has been made for assignment to him in a case to which regulation 21(3)(b) applies;

(f) persons whom he has accepted as temporary residents;

(g) in respect of services under paragraph 8, persons to whom he has agreed to provide those services;

(h) persons to whom he may be requested to give treatment which is immediately required owing to an accident or other emergency at any place in his practice are, provided that:

(i) he is not, at the time of the request, relieved of liability to give treatment under paragraph 5; and

(ii) he is not, at the time of the request, relieved, under paragraph 19(2), of his obligation to give treatment personally; and

(iii) he is available to provide such treatment;

(iv) and any persons by whom he is requested, and agrees, to give treatment which is immediately required owing to an accident or other emergency at any place in the locality of any FHSA in whose medical list he is included, provided there is no doctor who, at the time of the request, is under an obligation otherwise than under this head to give treatment to that person, or there is such a doctor but, after being requested to attend, he is unable to attend and give treatment immediately required;

(i) persons in relation to whom he is acting as deputy for another doctor under these terms of service;

(j) during the period of an appointment under regulation 25, persons whom he has been appointed to treat temporarily;

(k) in respect of child health surveillance services, contraceptive services, maternity medical services, or minor surgery services persons for whom he has undertaken to provide such services; and

(l) during the hours arranged with the FHSA, any person whose own doctor has been relieved of responsibility during those hours under paragraph 19 and for whom he has accepted responsibility under that paragraph.

(2) Except in a case to which head (h), (i) or (j) of sub-paragraph (l) applies, no person shall be a patient for the purposes of that sub-paragraph if the doctor has been notified by the FHSA that he is no longer responsible for the treatment of that person.

(3) Where a person applies to a doctor for treatment and claims to be on that doctor's list, but fails to produce his medical card on request and the doctor has reasonable doubts about that person's claim, the doctor shall give any necessary treatment and shall be entitled to demand and accept a fee accordingly under paragraph 38(f), subject to the provision for repayment contained in paragraph 39.

(4) Where a doctor refuses to accept for inclusion on his list a person who lives in his practice area and who is not on the list of another doctor practising in that area, or refuses to accept as a temporary resident a person to whom regulation 26 applies, he shall on request give that person any immediately necessary treatment for one period not exceeding 14 days from the date when that person was refused acceptance or until that person has been accepted by or assigned to another doctor, whichever period is the shorter.

(5) Where the FHSA has notified a doctor that it is applying for the Secretary of State's consent under regulation 21(3)(b), the doctor shall give the person proposed for assignment any immediately necessary treatment until the FHSA has notified him that:

(a) the Secretary of State has determined whether or not the person is to be assigned to that doctor; and

(b) either the person has been accepted by, or assigned to, another doctor or another doctor has been notified that an application has been made, in a case to which regulation 21(3)(b) applies, to assign that person to him.

5 A doctor who is elderly or infirm or who has been exempted by the FHSA under regulation 21(11) from the liability to have persons assigned to him, may be relieved by the FHSA of any liability to give treatment which is immediately required owing to an accident or other emergency between 7 pm on weekdays and 8 am on the following

morning and between 1 pm on Saturday and 8 am on the following Monday to persons who are neither:

(a) on his list; nor

(b) temporary residents for whom he is responsible; nor

(c) accepted by him for the provision of maternity medical services.

Acceptance of patients

6 (1) Subject to sub-paragraph (2), a doctor may agree to accept a person on his list if the person is eligible to be accepted by him.

(2) Where a doctor is responsible for treating the patients of another doctor whose name has been removed from the medical list, he may not consent to the transfer of any of those patients under regulation 22 to his own list or to that of his partner.

(3) Where a doctor has agreed to accept a person on his list, he shall, within 14 days of receiving this person's medical card or form of application, or as soon after the expiry of that period as it practicable:

(a) sign the medical card or, as the case may be, the form of application; and

(b) send it to the FHSA.

(4) Where, for the purposes of sub-paragraph (3), any person signs a medical card or a form of application on behalf of a doctor he shall, in addition to his own signature, specify the name of the doctor on whose behalf he is signing.

7 A doctor may:

(a) undertake to provide contraceptive services to a women who has applied to him in accordance with regulation 29;

(b) accept as a temporary resident a person who has applied to him in accordance with regulation 26(1);

(c) undertake to provide maternity medical services to a woman who has made an arrangement with him in accordance with regulation 31(2).

8 Notwithstanding that the person concerned is not on his list, a doctor may:

(a) take a cervical smear from a woman who would be eligible for acceptance by him as a temporary resident or for whom he has undertaken to provide maternity medical services or contraceptive services; and

(b) vaccinate or immunise a person who would be eligible for acceptance by him as a temporary resident.

Termination of responsibility for patients

9 (1) A doctor may have any person removed from his list and shall notify the FHSA in writing that he wishes to have a person removed from his list and, subject to sub-paragraph (2), the removal shall take effect:

(a) on the date on which the person is accepted by or assigned to another doctor; or

(b) on the eighth day after the FHSA receives the notice,

whichever is the sooner.

(2) Where, at the date when the removal would take effect under sub-paragraph (1), the doctor is treating the person at intervals of less than seven days, the doctor shall inform the FHSA in writing of the fact and the removal shall take effect:

(a) on the eighth day after the FHSA receives notification from the doctor that the person no longer needs such treatment; or

(b) on the date on which the person is accepted by or assigned to another doctor,

whichever is the sooner.

10   Where a doctor informs the FHSA in writing that he wishes to terminate his responsibility for a temporary resident, his responsibility for that person shall crease in accordance with paragraph 9, as if the temporary resident were a person on his list.

11 (1) A doctor with whom an arrangement has been made for the provision of any or all of the maternity medical services mentioned in regulation 31(1)(a) may agree with the woman concerned to terminate the arrangement, and in default of agreement the doctor may apply to the FHSA for permission to terminate the arrangement.

(2) On an application under paragraph (1), the FHSA, after considering any representations made by either party and after consulting the Local Medical Committee, may terminate the arrangement.

(3) Where a doctor ceases to provide any or all of the maternity medical services mentioned in regulation 31(1)(a), he shall inform any woman for whom he has arranged to provide such services that he is ceasing to provide them and that she may make a fresh arrangement to receive those services from another doctor.

Services to patients

12 (1) Subject to paragraphs 3, 13, and 44, a doctor shall render to his patients all necessary and appropriate personal medical services of the type usually provided by general medical practitioners.

(2) The services which a doctor is required by sub-paragraph (1) to render shall include the following:

(a) giving advice, where appropriate, to a patient in connection with the patient's general health, and in particular about the significance of diet, exercise, the use of tobacco, the consumption of alcohol and the misuse of drugs or solvents;

(b) offering to patients consultations and, where appropriate, physical examinations for the purpose of identifying, or reducing the risk of, disease or injury;

(c) offering to patients, where appropriate, vaccination or immunisation against measles, mumps, rubella, pertussis, poliomyelitis, diphtheria and tetanus;

(d) arranging for the referral of patients, as appropriate, for the provision of any other services under the Act; and

(e) giving advice, as appropriate, to enable patients to avail themselves of services provided by a local social services authority.

(3) A doctor is not required by sub-paragraph (1) or (2):

(a) to provide to any person child health surveillance services, contraceptive services, minor surgery services nor, except in an emergency, maternity medical services, unless he has previously undertaken to the FHSA to provide such services to that person; or

(b) where he is a restricted services principal, to provide any category of general medical services which he has not undertaken to provide.

Provision of services to patients.

13 ...

Newly registered patients

14 ...

Patients not seen within three years

15 (1) Subject to sub-paragraph (2), a doctor shall, in addition to and without prejudice to any other obligation under these terms of service, invite each patient on his list who appears to him:

(a) to have attained the age of 16 years but who has not attained the age of 75 years; and

(b) to have neither:

(i) within the preceding three years attended either a consultation with, or a clinic provided by, any doctor in the course of his provision of general medical services; nor

(ii) within the preceding 12 months been offered a consultation pursuant to this sub-paragraph by any doctor,

to participate in a consultation at his practice premises for the purpose of assessing whether he needs to render personal medical service to that patient.

(2) Sub-paragraph (1) shall not apply in the case of a doctor who is a restricted services principal.

(3) When inviting a patient to participate in a consultation pursuant to subparagraph (1) a doctor shall comply with the requirements of paragraph 14(3).

(4) Where a patient agrees to participate in a consultation mentioned in sub-paragraph (1), the doctor shall, in the course of that consultation:

(a) where appropriate, seek details from the patient as to his medical history and, so far as may be relevant to the patient's medical history, as to that of his consanguineous family, in respect of:

(i) illnesses, immunisations, allergies, hereditary disease, medication and tests carried out for breast or cervical cancer;

(ii) social factors (including employment, housing and family circumstances) which may affect his health;

(iii) factors of his lifestyle (including diet, exercise, use of tobacco, consumption of alcohol, and misuse of drugs or solvents) which may affect his health; and

(iv) the current state of his health;

(b) offer to undertake a physical examination of the patient, comprising:

(i) the measurement of his blood pressure; and

(ii) the taking of a urine sample and its analysis to identify the presence of albumen and glucose; and

     (iii) the measurement necessary to detect any changes in his body mass;

  (c) record, in the patient's medical records, his findings arising out of the details supplied by, and any examination of, the patient under this sub-paragraph;

  (d) assess whether and, if so, in what manner and to what extent he should render personal medical services to the patient; and

  (e) in so far as it would not, in the opinion of the doctor, be likely to cause serious damage to the physical or mental health of the patient to do so, offer to discuss with the patient the conclusions the doctor has drawn as a result of the consultation as to the state of the patient's health.

  (5) In this paragraph, 'body mass' means the figure produced by dividing the number of kilograms in the patient's weight by the square of the number of metres in his height.

Patients aged 75 years and over

16 ...

17 ...

Absences, deputies, assistants and partners

18 (1) Subject to sub-paragraph (2), a doctor is responsible for ensuring the provision for his patients of the services referred to in paragraph 12 throughout each day during which his name is included in the FHSA's medical list.

  (2) A doctor who was, prior to 1 April 1990, relieved by the FHSA of such responsibility in respect of his patients during times approved by the FHSA may continue to enjoy such relief for so long as his name is included in the medical list.

19 (1) Subject to the following provisions of this paragraph, a doctor shall give treatment personally.

  (2) Subject to sub-paragraphs (3), (5), and (6), a doctor (in this sub-paragraph referred to as 'the patient's doctor') shall be under no obligation to give treatment personally to a patient provided that reasonable steps are taken to ensure the continuity of the patient's treatment, and in those circumstances treatment may be given:

  (a) by another doctor acting as a deputy, whether or not he is a partner or assistant of the patient's doctor; or

  (b) in the case of treatment which it is clinically reasonable in the circumstances to delegate to someone other than a doctor, by a person whom the doctor has authorised and who he is satisfied is competent to carry out such treatment.

  (3) Subject to sub-paragraph (4), in the case of maternity medical services a doctor on the obstetric list shall not arrange for the provision of such services by another doctor unless that doctor is a doctor on the obstetric list or satisfies one or more of the criteria set out in Part 1 of Schedule 5.

  (4) Sub-paragraph (3) shall not apply where there has been a summons to an obstetric emergency.

  (5) In the case of child health surveillance services, a doctor who has, pursuant to regulation 28, undertaken to provide such services shall not arrange for the provision of such services by:

(a) another doctor unless that doctor is included in a child health surveillance list; or

(b) any other person without the consent of the FHSA.

(6) In the case of minor surgery services, a doctor who has, pursuant to regulation 33, undertaken to provide such services shall not arrange for the provision of such services by:

(a) another doctor unless that doctor is included in a minor surgery list; or

(b) any other person.

(7) In this paragraph, 'a summons to an obstetric emergency' means a summons to the doctor by a midwife or on behalf of the patient to attend when medical attention is required urgently by a woman or her baby during pregnancy, labour or the post-natal period, as defined in regulation 31(7).

20 (1) In relation to his obligations under these terms of service, a doctor is responsible for all acts and omissions of:

(a) any doctor acting as his deputy;

(b) any deputising service while acting on his behalf; and

(c) any person employed by, or acting on behalf, of him or such a deputy or deputising service expect where the act or omission is one for which a deputy is responsible under sub-paragraph (2).

(2) Where a doctor whose name is included in the medical list is acting as deputy to anther doctor whose name is also included in the list, the deputy is responsible for:

(a) his own acts and omissions in relation to the obligations under these terms of service of the doctor for whom he acts as deputy; and

(b) the acts and omissions of any person employed by him or acting on his behalf.

21 (1) A doctor shall inform the FHSA of any arrangements for the engagement of a deputy on a regular basis unless the deputy:

(a) is an assistant of the doctor, or is a doctor included in the medical list of an FHSA; and

(b) is to carry out the arrangements at the doctor's practice premises.

(2) Where a doctor proposes to be absent form his practice for more that a week, he shall inform the FHSA of the name of any doctor responsible for his practice during his absence.

22 (1) Before entering into arrangements with a deputising service for the provision of any deputy, a doctor shall obtain the consent of the FHSA.

(2) In giving its consent, the FHSA may impose such conditions as it considers necessary or expedient to ensure the adequacy of such arrangements.

(3) Before refusing its consent or imposing any such conditions, the FHSA shall consult the Local Medical Committee.

(4) The FHSA may at any time, and shall periodically, review in consultation with the Local Medical Committee any such consent given or conditions imposed in relation to any doctor under this paragraph, and may withdraw such consent or vary such conditions.

(5)A doctor may appeal to the Secretary of State against refusal of consent or the imposition of a condition under this paragraph or against withdrawal of consent or variation of conditions under this paragraph.

(6)An appeal under sub-paragraph (5) shall be made in writing within 30 days of the decision of the FHSA and shall set out the grounds of appeal.

(7)In determining an appeal under sub-paragraph (5) the Secretary of State may substitute for the FHSA's decision such decision and conditions as he thinks fit.

23 A doctor shall take reasonable steps to satisfy himself that a doctor whom he proposes to employ as a deputy or assistant is not disqualified under s 46 of the Act from inclusion in the medical list of the FHSA and he shall not knowingly employ a doctor who is so disqualified.

24 (1)A doctor shall inform the FHSA of the name of any assistant he employs and of the termination of such employment, and shall not employ any one or more assistants for a total period of more than three months in any period of 12 months without the consent of the FHSA.

(2)The FHSA shall periodically review and may withdraw any consent given but, before refusing or withdrawing consent, the FHSA shall consult the Local Medical Committee.

(3)The doctor may appeal to the Medical Practices Committee against any refusal or withdrawal of consent.

(4)Any withdrawal of consent under this paragraph shall not have effect until the expiration of period of one month after the date of notification of the withdrawal, but if the doctor appeals to the Medical Practices Committee against the withdrawal and the Medical Practices Committee dismisses the appeal, the withdrawal shall not take effect until after such date as the Committee determines being a date falling not less than one month after the date of such dismissal.

25 A doctor acting as a deputy for another doctor may treat patients at places and at times other than those approved pursuant to paragraph 29 in relation to the doctor for whom he is acting, but when determining the places and times at which he is to provide such treatment, the deputy shall have regard to the convenience of the patients.

26 When issuing any document under these terms of service a deputy or assistant (other than a partner or assistant whose name is included in the medical list) shall, as well as signing the document himself, enter on it the name of the doctor for whom he is acting, if it does not already appear.

Arrangements at practice premises

27 A doctor shall:

(a)provide proper and sufficient accommodation at his practice premises, having regard to the circumstances of his practice; and

(b)on receipt of a written request from the FHSA, allow inspection of those premises at a reasonable time by a member or officer of the FHSA or Local Medical Committee or both, authorised by the FHSA for the purpose.

Employees

28 (1) A doctor shall, before employing any person to assist him in the provision of general medical services, take reasonable care to satisfy himself that the person in question is both suitably qualified and competent to discharge the duties for which he is to be employed.

(2) When considering the competence and suitability of any person for the purpose of sub-paragraph (1), a doctor shall have regard, in particular, to:

(a) that person's academic and vocational qualifications;

(b) that person's training and his experience in employment; and

(c) any guidance issued by the FHSA pursuant to regulation 39.

(3) A doctor shall afford to each employee reasonable opportunities to undertake appropriate training wit a view to maintaining that employee's competence.

Doctors' availability to patients

29 ...

Doctors' available for only four days a week

30 ...

Practice area

34 ...

Notification of change of place of residence

35 ...

Records

36 ...

Certification

37 ...

Fees

38 ...

Prescribing

43 ...

Practice leaflet

47 ...

Reports to medical officers, etc

48 ...

Inquiries about prescriptions and referrals

49 ...

Annual reports

50 ...

Incorporation of provisions of regulations, etc

51 ...

CONDITIONAL FEE AGREEMENT REGULATIONS 2000 (SI 2000/692)

1 Citation, commencement and interpretation

(1) These Regulations may be cited as the Conditional Fee Agreements Regulations 2000.

(2) These Regulations come into force on 1st April 2000.

(3) In these Regulations –

'client' includes, except where the context otherwise requires, a person who –

(a) has instructed the legal representative to provide the advocacy or litigation services to which the conditional fee agreement relates, or

(b) is liable to pay the legal representative's fees in respect of those services; and

'legal representative' means the person providing the advocacy or litigation services to which the conditional fee agreement relates.

2 Requirements for contents of conditional fee agreements: general

(1) A conditional fee agreement must specify –

(a) the particular proceedings or parts of them to which it relates (including whether it relates to any appeal, counterclaim or proceedings to enforce a judgement or order),

(b) the circumstances in which the legal representative's fees and expenses, or part of them, are payable,

(c) what payment, if any, is due –

(i) if those circumstances only partly occur,

(ii) irrespective of whether those circumstances occur, and

(iii) on the termination of the agreement for any reason, and

(d) the amounts which are payable in all the circumstances and cases specified or the method to be used to calculate them and, in particular, whether the amounts are limited by reference to the damages which may be recovered on behalf of the client.

(2) A conditional fee agreement to which regulation 4 applies must contain a statement that the requirements of that regulation which apply in the case of that agreement have been complied with.

3 Requirements for contents of conditional fee agreements providing for success fees

(1) A conditional fee agreement which provides for a success fee –

(a) must briefly specify the reasons for setting the percentage increase at the level stated in the agreement, and

(b) must specify how much of the percentage increase, if any, relates to the cost to the legal representative of the postponement of the payment of his fees and expenses.

(2) If the agreement relates to court proceedings, it must provide that where the percentage increase becomes payable as a result of those proceedings, then –

    (a) if –

        (i) any fees subject to the increase are assessed, and

        (ii) the legal representative or the client is required by the court to disclose to the court or any other person the reasons for setting the percentage increase at the level stated in the agreement,

he may do so,

    (b) if –

        (i) any such fees are assessed, and

        (ii) any amount in respect of the percentage increase is disallowed on the assessment on the ground that the level at which the increase was set was unreasonable in view of facts which were or should have been known to the legal representative at the time it was set,

that amount ceases to be payable under the agreement, unless the court is satisfied that it should continue to be so payable, and

    (c) if –

        (i) sub-paragraph (b) does not apply, and

        (ii) the legal representative agrees with any person liable as a result of the proceedings to pay fees subject to the percentage increase that a lower amount than the amount payable in accordance with the conditional fee agreement is to be paid instead,

the amount payable under the conditional fee agreement in respect of those fees shall be reduced accordingly, unless the court is satisfied that the full amount should continue to be payable under it.

(3) In this regulation 'percentage increase' means the percentage by which the amount of the fees which would be payable if the agreement were not a conditional fee agreement is to be increased under the agreement.

4 Information to be given before conditional fee agreements made

(1) Before a conditional fee agreement is made the legal representative must –

    (a) inform the client about the following matters, and

    (b) if the client requires any further explanation, advice or other information about any of those matters, provide such further explanation, advice or other information about them as the client may reasonably require.

(2) Those matters are –

    (a) the circumstances in which the client may be liable to pay the costs of the legal representative in accordance with the agreement,

    (b) the circumstances in which the client may seek assessment of the fees and expenses of the legal representative and the procedure for doing so,

    (c) whether the legal representative considers that the client's risk of incurring liability for costs in respect of the proceedings to which agreement relates is insured against under an existing contract of insurance,

    (d) whether other methods of financing those costs are available, and, if so, how they apply to the client and the proceedings in question,

    (e) whether the legal representative considers that any particular method or methods of financing any or all of those costs is appropriate and, if he considers that a contract of insurance is appropriate or recommends a particular such contract –

       (i) his reasons for doing so, and

       (ii) whether he has an interest in doing so.

(3) Before a conditional fee agreement is made the legal representative must explain its effect to the client.

(4) In the case of an agreement where –

    (a) the legal representative is a body to which section 30 of the Access to Justice Act 1999[2] (recovery where body undertakes to meet costs liabilities) applies, and

    (b) there are no circumstances in which the client may be liable to pay any costs in respect of the proceedings,

    paragraph (1) does not apply.

(5) Information required to be given under paragraph (1) about the matters in paragraph (2)(a) to (d) must be given orally (whether or not it is also given in writing), but information required to be so given about the matters in paragraph (2)(e) and the explanation required by paragraph (3) must be given both orally and in writing.

(6) This regulation does not apply in the case of an agreement between a legal representative and an additional legal representative.

5 Form of agreement

(1) A conditional fee agreement must be signed by the client and the legal representative.

(2) This regulation does not apply in the case of an agreement between a legal representative and an additional legal representative.

6 Amendment of agreement

Where an agreement is amended to cover further proceedings or parts of them –

    (a) regulations 2, 3 and 5 apply to the amended agreement as if it were a fresh agreement made at the time of the amendment, and

    (b) the obligations under regulation 4 apply in relation to the amendments in so far as they affect the matters mentioned in that regulation.

7 Revocation of 1995 Regulations

The Conditional Fee Agreements Regulations 1995[3] are revoked.

APPENDIX C

CIVIL PROCEDURE RULES 1998

PART 1
OVERRIDING OBJECTIVE

1.1 The overriding objective

(1)   These Rules are a new procedural code with the overriding objective of enabling the court to deal with cases justly.

(2)   Dealing with a case justly includes, so far as is practicable –

    (a) ensuring that the parties are on an equal footing;

    (b) saving expense;

    (c) dealing with the case in ways which are proportionate –

        (i)   to the amount of money involved;

        (ii) to the importance of the case;

        (iii) to the complexity of the issues; and

        (iv) to the financial position of each party;

    (d) ensuring that it is dealt with expeditiously and fairly; and

    (e) allotting to it an appropriate share of the court's resources, while taking into account the need to allot resources to other cases.

1.2 Application by the court of the overriding objective

The court must seek to give effect to the overriding objective when it –

(a)   exercises any power given to it by the Rules; or

(b)   interprets any rule.

1.3 Duty of the parties

The parties are required to help the court to further the overriding objective.

1.4 Court's duty to manage cases

(1)   The court must further the overriding objective by actively managing cases.

(2)   Active case management includes –

    (a) encouraging the parties to co-operate with each other in the conduct of the proceedings;

    (b) identifying the issues at an early stage;

    (c) deciding promptly which issues need full investigation and trial and accordingly disposing summarily of the others;

    (d) deciding the order in which issues are to be resolved;

    (e) encouraging the parties to use an alternative dispute resolution[(GL)] procedure if the court considers that appropriate and facilitating the use of such procedure;

    (f) helping the parties to settle the whole or part of the case;

    (g) fixing timetables or otherwise controlling the progress of the case;

(h) considering whether the likely benefits of taking a particular step justify the cost of taking it;

(i) dealing with as many aspects of the case as it can on the same occasion;

(j) dealing with the case without the parties needing to attend at court;

(k) making use of technology; and

(l) giving directions to ensure that the trial of a case proceeds quickly and efficiently.

PART 25
INTERIM REMEDIES

25.6 Interim payments – general procedure

(1) The claimant may not apply for an order for an interim payment before the end of the period for filing an acknowledgement of service applicable to the defendant against whom the application is made.

(Rule 10.3 sets out the period for filing an acknowledgement of service)

(Rule 25.1(1)(k) defines an interim payment)

(2) The claimant may make more than one application for an order for an interim payment.

(3) A copy of an application notice for an order for an interim payment must –

(a) be served at least 14 days before the hearing of the application; and

(b) be supported by evidence.

(4) If the respondent to an application for an order for an interim payment wishes to rely on written evidence at the hearing, he must –

(a) file the written evidence; and

(b) serve copies on every other party to the application,

at least 7 days before the hearing of the application.

(5) If the applicant wishes to rely on written evidence in reply, he must –

(a) file the written evidence; and

(b) serve a copy on the respondent,

at least 3 days before the hearing of the application.

(6) This rule does not require written evidence –

(a) to be filed if it has already been filed; or

(b) to be served on a party on whom it has already been served.

(7) The court may order an interim payment in one sum or in instalments.

(Part 23 contains general rules about applications)

25.7 Interim payments – conditions to be satisfied and matters to be taken into account

(1) The court may make an order for an interim payment only if –

(a) the defendant against whom the order is sought has admitted liability to pay damages or some other sum of money to the claimant;

(b) the claimant has obtained judgment against that defendant for damages to be assessed or for a sum of money (other than costs) to be assessed;

(c) except where paragraph (3) applies, it is satisfied that, if the claim went to trial, the claimant would obtain judgment for a substantial amount of money (other than costs) against the defendant from whom he is seeking an order for an interim payment; or

(d) the following conditions are satisfied –

  (i) the claimant is seeking an order for possession of land (whether or not any other order is also sought); and

  (ii) the court is satisfied that, if the case went to trial, the defendant would be held liable (even if the claim for possession fails) to pay the claimant a sum of money for the defendant's occupation and use of the land while the claim for possession was pending.

(2) In addition, in a claim for personal injuries the court may make an order for an interim payment of damages only if –

  (a) the defendant is insured in respect of the claim;

  (b) the defendant's liability will be met by –

    (i) an insurer under section 151 of the Road Traffic Act 1988; or

    (ii) an insurer acting under the Motor Insurers Bureau Agreement, or the Motor Insurers Bureau where it is acting itself; or

  (c) the defendant is a public body.

(3) In a claim for personal injuries where there are two or more defendants, the court may make an order for the interim payment of damages against any defendant if –

  (a) it is satisfied that, if the claim went to trial, the claimant would obtain judgment for substantial damages against at least one of the defendants (even if the court has not yet determined which of them is liable); and

  (b) paragraph (2) is satisfied in relation to each of the defendants.

(4) The court must not order an interim payment of more than a reasonable proportion of the likely amount of the final judgment.

(5) The court must take into account –

  (a) contributory negligence; and

  (b) any relevant set-off or counterclaim.

25.8 Powers of court where it has made an order for interim payment

(1) Where a defendant has been ordered to make an interim payment, or has in fact made an interim payment (whether voluntarily or under an order), the court may make an order to adjust the interim payment.

(2) The court may in particular –

  (a) order all or part of the interim payment to be repaid;

  (b) vary or discharge the order for the interim payment;

  (c) order a defendant to reimburse, either wholly or partly, another defendant who has made an interim payment.

(3) The court may make an order under paragraph (2)(c) only if –

  (a) the defendant to be reimbursed made the interim payment in relation to a claim in respect of which he has made a claim against the other defendant for a contribution[(GL)], indemnity[(GL)] or other remedy; and

(b) where the claim or part to which the interim payment relates has not been discontinued or disposed of, the circumstances are such that the court could make an order for interim payment under rule 25.7.

(4) The court may make an order under this rule without an application by any party if it makes the order when it disposes of the claim or any part of it.

(5) Where –

(a) a defendant has made an interim payment; and

(b) the amount of the payment is more than his total liability under the final judgment or order,

the court may award him interest on the overpaid amount from the date when he made the interim payment.

25.9 Restriction on disclosure of an interim payment

The fact that a defendant has made an interim payment, whether voluntarily or by court order, shall not be disclosed to the trial judge until all questions of liability and the amount of money to be awarded have been decided unless the defendant agrees.

PRACTICE DIRECTION – INTERIM PAYMENTS

This Practice Direction Supplements CPR Part 25

General

1.1 Rule 25.7 sets out the conditions to be satisfied and matters to be taken into account before the court will make an order for an interim payment.

1.2 The permission of the court must be obtained before making a voluntary interim payment in respect of a claim by a child or patient.

Evidence

2.1 An application for an interim payment of damages must be supported by evidence dealing with the following:

(1) the sum of money sought by way of an interim payment,

(2) the items or matters in respect of which the interim payment is sought,

(3) the sum of money for which final judgment is likely to be given,

(4) the reasons for believing that the conditions set out in rule 25.7 are satisfied,

(5) any other relevant matters,

(6) in claims for personal injuries, details of special damages and past and future loss, and

(7) in a claim under the Fatal Accidents Act 1976, details of the person(s) on whose behalf the claim is made and the nature of the claim.

2.2 Any documents in support of the application should be exhibited, including, in personal injuries claims, the medical report(s).

2.3 If a respondent to an application for an interim payment wishes to rely on written evidence at the hearing he must comply with the provisions of rule 25.6(4).

2.4 If the applicant wishes to rely on written evidence in reply he must comply with the provisions of rule 25.6(5).

Interim payment where account to be taken

2A.1 This section of this practice direction applies if a party seeks an interim payment under rule 25.7(b) where the court has ordered an account to be taken.

2A.2 If the evidence on the application for interim payment shows that the account is bound to result in a payment to the applicant the court will, before making an order for interim payment, order that the liable party pay to the applicant 'the amount shown by the account to be due'.

Instalments

3 Where an interim payment is to be paid in instalments the order should set out:

(1) the total amount of the payment,

(2) the amount of each instalment,

(3) the number of instalments and the date on which each is to be paid, and

(4) to whom the payment should be made.

Compensation recovery payment

4.1 Where in a claim for personal injuries there is an application for an interim payment of damages:

(1) which is other than by consent,

(2) which falls under the heads of damage set out in column 1 of Schedule 2 of the Social Security (Recovery of Benefits) Act 1997 in respect of recoverable benefits received by the claimant set out in column 2 of that Schedule, and

(3) where the defendant is liable to pay recoverable benefits to the Secretary of State, the defendant should obtain from the Secretary of State a certificate of recoverable benefits.

4.2 A copy of the certificate should be filed at the hearing of the application for an interim payment.

4.3 The order will set out the amount by which the payment to be made to the claimant has been reduced according to the Act and the Social Security (Recovery of Benefits) Regulations 1997.

4.4 The payment made to the claimant will be the net amount but the interim payment for the purposes of paragraph 5 below will be the gross amount.

Adjustment of final judgment figure

5.1 In this paragraph 'judgment' means:

(1) any order to pay a sum of money,

(2) a final award of damages,

(3) an assessment of damages.

5.2 In a final judgment where an interim payment has previously been made which is less than the total amount awarded by the judge, the order should set out in a preamble:

(1) the total amount awarded by the judge, and

(2) the amounts and dates of the interim payment(s).

5.3 The total amount awarded by the judge should then be reduced by the total amount of any interim payments, and an order made for entry of judgment and payment of the balance.

5.4 In a final judgment where an interim payment has previously been made which is more than the total amount awarded by the judge, the order should set out in a preamble:

(1) the total amount awarded by the judge, and

(2) the amounts and dates of the interim payment(s).

5.5 An order should then be made for repayment, reimbursement, variation or discharge under rule 25.8(2) and for interest on an overpayment under rule 25.8(5).

5.6 A practice direction supplementing Part 40 provides further information concerning adjustment of the final judgment sum.

PART 35
EXPERTS AND ASSESSORS

35.1 Duty to restrict expert evidence

Expert evidence shall be restricted to that which is reasonably required to resolve the proceedings.

35.2 Interpretation

A reference to an 'expert' in this Part is a reference to an expert who has been instructed to give or prepare evidence for the purpose of court proceedings.

35.3 Experts – overriding duty to the court

(1) It is the duty of an expert to help the court on the matters within his expertise.

(2) This duty overrides any obligation to the person from whom he has received instructions or by whom he is paid.

35.4 Court's power to restrict expert evidence

(1) No party may call an expert or put in evidence an expert's report without the court's permission.

(2) When a party applies for permission under this rule he must identify –

(a) the field in which he wishes to rely on expert evidence; and

(b) where practicable the expert in that field on whose evidence he wishes to rely.

(3) If permission is granted under this rule it shall be in relation only to the expert named or the field identified under paragraph (2).

(4) The court may limit the amount of the expert's fees and expenses that the party who wishes to rely on the expert may recover from any other party.

35.5 General requirement for expert evidence to be given in a written report

(1) Expert evidence is to be given in a written report unless the court directs otherwise.

(2) If a claim is on the fast track, the court will not direct an expert to attend a hearing unless it is necessary to do so in the interests of justice.

35.6 Written questions to experts

(1)   A party may put to –

    (a) an expert instructed by another party; or

    (b) a single joint expert appointed under rule 35.7,

    written questions about his report.

(2)   Written questions under paragraph (1) –

    (a) may be put once only;

    (b) must be put within 28 days of service of the expert's report; and

    (c) must be for the purpose only of clarification of the report,

    unless in any case,

        (i)   the court gives permission; or

        (ii) the other party agrees.

(3)   An expert's answers to questions put in accordance with paragraph (1) shall be treated as part of the expert's report.

(4)   Where –

    (a) a party has put a written question to an expert instructed by another party in accordance with this rule; and

    (b) the expert does not answer that question,

    the court may make one or both of the following orders in relation to the party who instructed the expert –

        (i)   that the party may not rely on the evidence of that expert; or

        (ii) that the party may not recover the fees and expenses of that expert from any other party.

35.7 Court's power to direct that evidence is to be given by a single joint expert

(1)   Where two or more parties wish to submit expert evidence on a particular issue, the court may direct that the evidence on that issue is to given by one expert only.

(2)   The parties wishing to submit the expert evidence are called 'the instructing parties'.

(3)   Where the instructing parties cannot agree who should be the expert, the court may –

    (a) select the expert from a list prepared or identified by the instructing parties; or

    (b) direct that the expert be selected in such other manner as the court may direct.

35.8 Instructions to a single joint expert

(1)   Where the court gives a direction under rule 35.7 for a single joint expert to be used, each instructing party may give instructions to the expert.

(2)   When an instructing party gives instructions to the expert he must, at the same time, send a copy of the instructions to the other instructing parties.

(3)   The court may give directions about –

    (a) the payment of the expert's fees and expenses; and

    (b) any inspection, examination or experiments which the expert wishes to carry out.

(4) The court may, before an expert is instructed –

    (a) limit the amount that can be paid by way of fees and expenses to the expert; and

    (b) direct that the instructing parties pay that amount into court.

(5) Unless the court otherwise directs, the instructing parties are jointly and severally liable(GL) for the payment of the expert's fees and expenses.

35.9 Power of court to direct a party to provide information

Where a party has access to information which is not reasonably available to the other party, the court may direct the party who has access to the information to –

    (a) prepare and file a document recording the information; and

    (b) serve a copy of that document on the other party.

35.10 Contents of report

(1) An expert's report must comply with the requirements set out in the relevant practice direction.

(2) At the end of an expert's report there must be a statement that –

    (a) the expert understands his duty to the court; and

    (b) he has complied with that duty.

(3) The expert's report must state the substance of all material instructions, whether written or oral, on the basis of which the report was written.

(4) The instructions referred to in paragraph (3) shall not be privileged(GL) against disclosure but the court will not, in relation to those instructions –

    (a) order disclosure of any specific document; or

    (b) permit any questioning in court, other than by the party who instructed the expert,

unless it is satisfied that there are reasonable grounds to consider the statement of instructions given under paragraph (3) to be inaccurate or incomplete.

35.11 Use by one party of expert's report disclosed by another

Where a party has disclosed an expert's report, any party may use that expert's report as evidence at the trial.

35.12 Discussions between experts

(1) The court may, at any stage, direct a discussion between experts for the purpose of requiring the experts to –

    (a) identify the issues in the proceedings; and

    (b) where possible, reach agreement on an issue.

(2) The court may specify the issues which the experts must discuss.

(3) The court may direct that following a discussion between the experts they must prepare a statement for the court showing –

    (a) those issues on which they agree; and

    (b) those issues on which they disagree and a summary of their reasons for disagreeing.

(4)   The content of the discussion between the experts shall not be referred to at the trial unless the parties agree.

(5)   Where experts reach agreement on an issue during their discussions, the agreement shall not bind the parties unless the parties expressly agree to be bound by the agreement.

35.13 Consequence of failure to disclose expert's report

A party who fails to disclose an expert's report may not use the report at the trial or call the expert to give evidence orally unless the court gives permission.

35.14 Expert's right to ask court for directions

(1)   An expert may file a written request for directions to assist him in carrying out his function as an expert.

(2)   An expert may request directions under paragraph (1) without giving notice to any party.

(3)   The court, when it gives directions, may also direct that a party be served with –

   (a)   a copy of the directions; and

   (b)   a copy of the request for directions.

35.15 Assessors

(1)   This rule applies where the court appoints one or more persons (an 'assessor') under section 70 of the Supreme Court Act 1981 or section 63 of the County Courts Act 1984.

(2)   The assessor shall assist the court in dealing with a matter in which the assessor has skill and experience.

(3)   An assessor shall take such part in the proceedings as the court may direct and in particular the court may –

   (a)   direct the assessor to prepare a report for the court on any matter at issue in the proceedings; and

   (b)   direct the assessor to attend the whole or any part of the trial to advise the court on any such matter.

(4)   If the assessor prepares a report for the court before the trial has begun –

   (a)   the court will send a copy to each of the parties; and

   (b)   the parties may use it at trial.

(5)   The remuneration to be paid to the assessor for his services shall be determined by the court and shall form part of the costs of the proceedings.

(6)   The court may order any party to deposit in the court office a specified sum in respect of the assessor's fees and, where it does so, the assessor will not be asked to act until the sum has been deposited.

(7)   Paragraphs (5) and (6) do not apply where the remuneration of the assessor is to be paid out of money provided by Parliament.

PRACTICE DIRECTION – EXPERTS AND ASSESSORS

This Practice Direction supplements CPR Part 35

Part 35 is intended to limit the use of oral expert evidence to that which is reasonably required. In addition, where possible, matters requiring expert evidence should be dealt with by a single expert. Permission of the court is always required either to call an expert or to put an expert's report in evidence.

Form and content of expert's reports

1.1   An expert's report should be addressed to the court and not to the party from whom the expert has received his instructions.

1.2   An expert's report must:

(1) give details of the expert's qualifications,

(2)   give details of any literature or other material which the expert has relied on in making the report,

(3) say who carried out any test or experiment which the expert has used for the report and whether or not the test or experiment has been carried out under the expert's supervision,

(4) give the qualifications of the person who carried out any such test

or experiment, and

(5) where there is a range of opinion on the matters dealt with in the report –

(i)   summarise the range of opinion, and

(ii) give reasons for his own opinion,

(6) contain a summary of the conclusions reached,

(7) contain a statement that the expert understands his duty to the court and has complied with that duty (rule 35.10(2)), and

(8) contain a statement setting out the substance of all material instructions (whether written or oral). The statement should summarise the facts and instructions given to the expert which are material to the opinions expressed in the report or upon which those opinions are based (rule 35.10(3)).

1.3   An expert's report must be verified by a statement of truth as well as containing the statements required in paragraph 1.2 (7) and (8) above.

1.4   The form of the statement of truth is as follows:

` I believe that the facts I have stated in this report are true and that the opinions I have expressed are correct.'

1.5   Attention is drawn to rule 32.14 which sets out the consequences of verifying a document containing a false statement without an honest belief in its truth.

(For information about statements of truth see Part 22 and the practice direction which supplements it.)

1.6   In addition, an expert's report should comply with the requirements of any approved expert's protocol.

Information

2   Under rule 35.9 the court may direct a party with access to information which is not reasonably available to another party to serve on that other party a document

which records the information. The document served must include sufficient details of all the facts, tests, experiments and assumptions which underlie any part of the information to enable the party on whom it is served to make, or to obtain, a proper interpretation of the information and an assessment of its significance.

Instructions

3   The instructions referred to in paragraph 1.2(8) will not be protected by privilege (see rule 35.10(4)). But cross-examination of the expert on the contents of his instructions will not be allowed unless the court permits it (or unless the party who gave the instructions consents to it). Before it gives permission the court must be satisfied that there are reasonable grounds to consider that the statement in the report of the substance of the instructions is inaccurate or incomplete. If the court is so satisfied, it will allow the cross-examination where it appears to be in the interests of justice to do so.

Questions to experts

4.1   Questions asked for the purpose of clarifying the expert's report (see rule 35.6) should be put, in writing, to the expert not later than 28 days after receipt of the expert's report (see paragraphs 1.2 to 1.5 above as to verification).

4.2   Where a party sends a written question or questions direct to an expert, a copy of the questions should, at the same time, be sent to the other party or parties.

4.3   The party or parties instructing the expert must pay any fees charged by that expert for answering questions put under rule 35.6. This does not affect any decision of the court as to the party who is ultimately to bear the expert's costs.

Single expert

5   Where the court has directed that the evidence on a particular issue is to be given by one expert only (rule 35.7) but there are a number of disciplines relevant to that issue, a leading expert in the dominant discipline should be identified as the single expert. He should prepare the general part of the report and be responsible for annexing or incorporating the contents of any reports from experts in other disciplines.

Assessors

6.1   An assessor may be appointed to assist the court under rule 35.15. Not less than 21 days before making any such appointment, the court will notify each party in writing of the name of the proposed assessor, of the matter in respect of which the assistance of the assessor will be sought and of the qualifications of the assessor to give that assistance.

6.2   Where any person has been proposed for appointment as an assessor, objection to him, either personally or in respect of his qualification, may be taken by any party.

6.3   Any such objection must be made in writing and filed with the court within 7 days of receipt of the notification referred to in paragraph 6.1 and will be taken into account by the court in deciding whether or not to make the appointment (section 63(5) of the County Courts Act 1984).

6.4   Copies of any report prepared by the assessor will be sent to each of the parties but the assessor will not give oral evidence or be open to cross-examination or questioning.

PART 36
OFFERS TO SETTLE AND PAYMENTS INTO COURT

36.7 Offer to settle a claim for provisional damages

(1) A defendant may make a Part 36 payment in respect of a claim which includes a claim for provisional damages.

(2) Where he does so, the Part 36 payment notice must specify whether or not the defendant is offering to agree to the making of an award of provisional damages.

(3) Where the defendant is offering to agree to the making of an award of provisional damages the payment notice must also state –

   (a) that the sum paid into court is in satisfaction of the claim for damages on the assumption that the injured person will not develop the disease or suffer the type of deterioration specified in the notice;

   (b) that the offer is subject to the condition that the claimant must make any claim for further damages within a limited period; and

   (c) what that period is.

(4) Where a Part 36 payment is –

   (a) made in accordance with paragraph (3); and

   (b) accepted within the relevant period in rule 36.11,

   the Part 36 payment will have the consequences set out in rule 36.13, unless the court orders otherwise.

(5) If the claimant accepts the Part 36 payment he must, within 7 days of doing so, apply to the court for an order for an award of provisional damages under rule 41.2.

   (Rule 41.2 provides for an order for an award of provisional damages.)

(6) The money in court may not be paid out until the court has disposed of the application made in accordance with paragraph (5).

PRACTICE DIRECTION-STRUCTURED SETTLEMENTS

This Practice Direction supplements CPR Part 40

1.1 A structured settlement is a means of paying a sum awarded to or accepted by a claimant by way of instalments for the remainder of the claimant's life. The payments are either funded by an annuity from an insurance company or, where the party paying is a government body, by payments direct from that body.

1.2 The agreed sum which purchases the annuity or provides for payments (including any sum to be retained as capital for contingencies) is based on the sum offered or awarded on a conventional basis, less an amount representing the tax benefits obtained by the structure.

1.3 This type of order may be used both on settlement of a claim and after trial where the judge has found in favour of the claimant. In the latter case the claimant or his legal representative should ask the judge:

(1) not to provide for entry of judgment,

(2) to state the total amount to which the judge has found the claimant to be entitled, and

(3) for an adjournment to enable advice to be sought as to the formulation of a structured settlement based on that amount.

1.4 Where a claim settles before trial, an application should be made in accordance with CPR Part 23 for the consent order embodying the structured settlement to be made, and for the approval of the structured settlement where the claimant is a child or patient.

1.5 If the claimant is not a child or patient, the consent order may be made without a hearing.

1.6 Where a hearing is required and as the annuity rate applicable to the structure may only remain available for a short time, the claimant's legal representative on issue of his application notice, should immediately seek an early date for the hearing.

1.7 At such a hearing the court will require the following documents and evidence to be filed not later than midday on the day before the hearing is to take place:

(1) Counsel's or the legal representative's opinion of the value of the claim on the basis of a conventional award (unless approval on that basis has already been given or the judge has stated the amount as in paragraph 1.3(2) above),

(2) a report of forensic accountants setting out the effect of a structured settlement bearing in mind the claimant's life expectancy and the anticipated cost of future care,

(3) a draft of the proposed structure agreement,

(4) sufficient information to satisfy the court that -

(a) enough of the agreed sum is retained as a contingency fund for anticipated future needs, and

(b) the structured settlement is secure and the annuities are payable by established insurers,

(5) details of any assets available to the claimant other than the agreed sum which is the subject of the application, and

(6) where the claimant is a patient, the approval or consent of the Court of Protection.

1.8 To obtain the approval of the Court of Protection the claimant's legal representative should lodge the documents and information set out in paragraph 1.7(1) to (5) above together with a copy of the claim form and any statements of case filed in the proceedings in the Enquiries and Acceptances Branch of the Public Trust Office, Stewart House, 24 Kingsway, London WC2B 6JH by midday on the fourth day before the hearing.

1.9 If an application for the appointment of a receiver by the Court of Protection has not already been made:

(1) two copies of the application seeking his appointment (form CP1),

(2) a certificate of family and property (form CP5), and

(3) a medical certificate (form CP3) should be lodged at the same time as the documents and information mentioned in paragraph 1.8 above. Forms CP1, 3 and 5 may be obtained from the address set out in paragraph 1.8.

1.10 Wherever possible a draft order should also be filed at the same time as the documents in paragraph 1.7 above.

1.11 Examples of structured settlement orders are set out in an Annex to this practice direction which may be adapted for use after trial or as the individual circumstances require. It should be noted that the reference in the second paragraph of the Part 2 – structured settlement order to the 'defendant's insurers' means the Life Insurer providing the annuity on behalf of the defendant.

1.12 Where it is necessary to obtain immediate payment out of money in court upon the order being made, the claimant's legal representatives should:

(1) contact the officer in charge of funds in court at the Court Funds Office at least 2 days before the hearing, and arrange for a cheque for the appropriate sum made payable to the insurers or government body to be ready for collection,

(2) notify the court office the day before the hearing so that the court is aware of the urgency, and

(3) bring to the hearing a completed Court Funds Office form 200 for authentication by the court upon the order being made.

Annex

Part 1 – Structured Settlement Order

(Order to settle for conventional sum and for an adjournment to seek advice on the formulation of a structured settlement)

Title of Claim

UPON HEARING (Counsel/solicitor) for the claimant and (Counsel/solicitor) for the defendant

AND UPON the defendant by (Counsel/solicitor) having undertaken to keep open an offer of £............... in full and final settlement of the claim and the claimant having undertaken to limit the claim to £....................

AND UPON the claimant's solicitors undertaking to instruct appropriate advisers to advise upon a structured settlement and to use their best endeavours promptly to make proposals to the defendant's solicitors as to the most equitable formulation of a structured settlement and after to seek further directions/approval) from the court if necessary

IT IS ORDERED that this claim is adjourned with permission to both parties to apply in respect of the further hearing relating to further directions providing for a structured settlement as undertaken by the claimant's solicitors and that these proceedings be reserved to the (trial judge) unless otherwise ordered

AND IT IS ORDERED that the costs of these proceedings together with the costs relating to any proposal for a structured settlement be (as ordered).

Part 2 – Structured Settlement Order

(Order giving effect to and approval of a structured settlement)

Title of Claim

> UPON HEARING (Counsel/solicitor) for the claimant and (Counsel/solicitor) for the defendant
>
> AND the claimant and defendant having agreed to the terms set forth in the Schedule to this order in which the claimant accepts the sum of £............. (overall sum) in satisfaction of the claim of which the sum of £............... is to be used by the [defendant's insurers for the purchase of an annuity][defendant for the provision of the appropriate payments]
>
> AND UPON the Judge having approved the terms of the draft minute of order, the agreement and the schedule to this order
>
> AND UPON the claimant and the insurer (name) undertaking to execute the agreement this day
>
> BY CONSENT
>
> IT IS ORDERED
>
> (1) that of the sum of £............... (total sum in court) now in court standing to the credit of this claim the sum of £............... be paid out to (insurers/payee) on behalf of the defendant for the purchase of an annuity as specified in the payment schedule to this order
>
> (2) (other relevant orders)
>
> ( ) that all further proceedings in this claim be stayed except for the purpose of carrying the terms into effect
>
> ( ) that the parties have permission to apply to carry the terms into effect

Schedule

(Attach draft agreement and set out any other terms of the settlement)

PART 41
PROVISIONAL DAMAGES

41.1 Application and definitions

(1)   This Part applies to proceedings to which SCA s.32A or CCA s 51 applies.

(2)   In this Part –

(a)   'SCA s.32A' means section 32A of the Supreme Court Act 1981;

(b)   'CCA s.51' means section 51 of the County Courts Act 1984; and

(c)   'award of provisional damages' means an award of damages for personal injuries under which –

(i)   damages are assessed on the assumption referred to in SCA s.32A or CCA s 51 that the injured person will not develop the disease or suffer the deterioration; and

(ii)   the injured person is entitled to apply for further damages at a future date if he develops the disease or suffers the deterioration.

41.2 Order for an award of provisional damages

(1)   The court may make an order for an award of provisional damages if –

   (a) the particulars of claim include a claim for provisional damages; and

   (b) the court is satisfied that SCA s 32A or CCA s 51 applies.

(Rule 16.4(1)(d) sets out what must be included in the particulars of claim where the claimant is claiming provisional damages)

(2)   An order for an award of provisional damages –

   (a) must specify the disease or type of deterioration in respect of which an application may be made at a future date;

   (b) must specify the period within which such an application may be made; and

   (c) may be made in respect of more than one disease or type of deterioration and may, in respect of each disease or type of deterioration, specify a different period within which a subsequent application may be made.

(3)   The claimant may make more than one application to extend the period specified under paragraph (2)(b) or (2)(c).

41.3 Application for further damages

(1)   The claimant may not make an application for further damages after the end of the period specified under rule 41.2(2), or such period as extended by the court.

(2)   Only one application for further damages may be made in respect of each disease or type of deterioration specified in the award of provisional damages.

(3)   The claimant must give at least 28 days written notice to the defendant of his intention to apply for further damages.

(4)   If the claimant knows –

   (a) that the defendant is insured in respect of the claim; and

   (b) the identity of the defendant's insurers,

   he must also give at least 28 days written notice to the insurers.

(5)   Within 21 days after the end of the 28 day notice period referred to in paragraphs (3) and (4), the claimant must apply for directions.

(6)   The rules in Part 25 about the making of an interim payment apply where an application is made under this rule.

PRACTICE DIRECTION – PROVISIONAL DAMAGES

This Practice Direction supplements CPR Part 41

Claims for provisional damages

1.1   CPR Part 16 and the practice direction which supplements it set out information which must be included in the particulars of claim if a claim for provisional damages is made.

Judgment for an award of provisional damages

2.1   When giving judgment at trial the judge will:

   (1) specify the disease or type of deterioration, or diseases or types of deterioration, which

(a) for the purpose of the award of immediate damages it has been assumed will not occur, and

(b) will entitle the claimant to further damages if it or they do occur at a future date,

(2) give an award of immediate damages,

(3) specify the period or periods within which an application for further damages may be made in respect of each disease or type of deterioration, and

(4) direct what documents are to be filed and preserved as the case file in support of any application for further damages.

2.2   The claimant may make an application or applications to extend the periods referred to in paragraph 2.1(3) above.

2.3   A period specified under paragraph 2.1(3) may be expressed as being for the duration of the life of the claimant.

2.4   The documents to be preserved as the case file ('the case file documents') referred to in paragraph 2.1(4) will be set out in a schedule to the judgment as entered.

2.5   Causation of any further damages within the scope of the order shall be determined when any application for further damages is made.

2.6   A form for a provisional damages judgment is set out in the Annex to this practice direction.

The case file

3.1   The case file documents must be preserved until the expiry of the period or periods specified or of any extension of them.

3.2   The case file documents will normally include:

(1) the judgment as entered,

(2) the statements of case,

(3) a transcript of the judge's oral judgment,

(4) all medical reports relied on, and

(5) a transcript of any parts of the claimant's own evidence which the judge considers necessary.

3.3   The associate/court clerk will:

(1) ensure that the case file documents are provided by the parties where necessary and filed on the court file,

(2) endorse the court file

(a) to the effect that it contains the case file documents, and

(b) with the period during which the case file documents must be preserved, and

(3) preserve the case file documents in the court office where the proceedings took place.

3.4   Any subsequent order:

(1) extending the period within which an application for further damages may be made, or

(2) of the Court of Appeal discharging or varying the provisions of the original judgment or of any subsequent order under sub-paragraph (1) above, will become one of the case file documents and must be preserved accordingly and any variation of the period within which an application for further damages may be made should be endorsed on the court file containing the case file documents.

3.5 On an application to extend the periods referred to in paragraph 2.1(3) above a current medical report should be filed.

3.6 Legal representatives are reminded that it is their duty to preserve their own case file.

Consent Orders

4.1 An application to give effect to a consent order for provisional damages should be made in accordance with CPR Part 23. If the claimant is a child or patient the approval of the court must also be sought and the application for approval will normally be dealt with at a hearing.

4.2 The order should be in the form of a consent judgment and should contain:

(1) the matters set out in paragraph 2.1(1) to (3) above, and

(2) a direction as to the documents to be preserved as the case file documents, which will normally be

(a) the consent judgment,

(b) any statements of case,

(c) an agreed statement of facts, and

(d) any agreed medical report(s).

4.3 The claimant or his legal representative must lodge the case file documents in the court office where the proceedings are taking place for inclusion in the court file. The court file should be endorsed as in paragraph 3.3(2) above, and the case file documents preserved as in paragraph 3.3(3) above.

Default judgment

5.1 Where a defendant:

(1) fails to file an acknowledgment of service in accordance with CPR Part 10, and

(2) fails to file a defence in accordance with CPR Part 15, within the time specified for doing so, the claimant may not, unless he abandons his claim for provisional damages, enter judgment in default but should make an application in accordance with CPR Part 23 for directions.

5.2 The Master or district judge will normally direct the following issues to be decided:

(1) whether the claim is an appropriate one for an award of provisional damages and if so, on what terms, and

(2) the amount of immediate damages.

5.3 If the judge makes an award of provisional damages, the provisions of paragraph 3 above apply.

Annex

(Example of an award of provisional damages after trial)

(Title of proceedings)

THIS CLAIM having been tried before [title and name of judge] without a jury at [the Royal Courts of Justice or as may be] and [title and name of judge] having ordered that judgment as set out below be entered for the claimant

IT IS ORDERED

(1) that the defendant pay the claimant by way of immediate damages the sum of £............... (being (i) £.............. for special damages and £............. [agreed interest][interest at the rate of ...... from...........to............] (ii) £.............. for general damages and £.............. [agreed interest][interest at the rate of 2% from......... to...........] and (iii) £............... for loss of future earnings and/or earning capacity) on the assumption that the claimant would not at a future date as a result of the act or omission giving rise to the claim develop the following disease/type of deterioration namely [set out disease or type of deterioration]

(2) that if the claimant at a further date does develop that [disease][type of deterioration] he should be entitled to apply for further damages provided that the application is made on or before [set out period]

(3) that the documents set out in the schedule to this order be filed on the court file and preserved as the case file until the expiry of the period set out in paragraph (2) above or of any extension of that period which has been ordered

(4) (costs)

Schedule

(list documents referred to in paragraph (3))

PRE-ACTION PROTOCOL FOR THE RESOLUTION OF CLINICAL DISPUTES

1 WHY THIS PROTOCOL?

MISTRUST IN HEALTHCARE DISPUTES

1.1　The number of complaints and claims against hospitals, GPs, dentists and private healthcare providers is growing as patients become more prepared to question the treatment they are given, to seek explanations of what happened, and to seek appropriate redress. Patients may require further treatment, an apology, assurances about future action, or compensation. These trends are unlikely to change. The Patients' Charter encourages patients to have high expectations, and a revised NHS Complaints Procedure was implemented in 1996. The civil justice reforms and new Rules of Court should make litigation quicker, more user friendly and less expensive.

1.2　It is clearly in the interests of patients, healthcare professionals and providers that patients' concerns, complaints and claims arising from their treatment are resolved as quickly, efficiently and professionally as possible. A climate of mistrust and lack of openness can seriously damage the patient/clinician relationship, unnecessarily prolong disputes (especially litigation), and reduce the resources available for treating patients. It may also cause additional work for, and lower the morale of, healthcare professionals.

1.3　At present there is often mistrust by both sides. This can mean that patients fail to raise their concerns with the healthcare provider as early as possible. Sometimes patients may pursue a complaint or claim which has little merit, due to a lack of sufficient information and understanding. It can also mean that patients become reluctant, once advice has been taken on a potential claim, to disclose sufficient information to enable the provider to investigate that claim efficiently and, where appropriate, resolve it.

1.4　On the side of the healthcare provider this mistrust can be shown in a reluctance to be honest with patients, a failure to provide prompt clear explanations, especially of adverse outcomes (whether or not there may have been negligence) and a tendency to 'close ranks' once a claim is made.

WHAT NEEDS TO CHANGE

1.5　If that mistrust is to be removed, and a more co-operative culture is to develop –

- healthcare professionals and providers need to adopt a constructive approach to complaints and claims. They should accept that concerned patients are entitled to an explanation and an apology, if warranted, and to appropriate redress in the event of negligence. An overly defensive approach is not in the long-term interest of their main goal: patient care;

- patients should recognise that unintended and/or unfortunate consequences of medical treatment can only be rectified if they are brought to the attention of the healthcare provider as soon as possible.

1.6   A protocol which sets out 'ground rules' for the handling of disputes at their early stages should, if it is to be subscribed to, and followed –

- encourage greater openness between the parties;
- encourage parties to find the most appropriate way of resolving the particular dispute;
- reduce delay and costs;
- reduce the need for litigation.

WHY THIS PROTOCOL NOW?

1.7   Lord Woolf in his *Access to Justice Report* in July 1996, concluded that major causes of costs and delay in medical negligence litigation occur at the pre-action stage. He recommended that patients and their advisers, and healthcare providers, should work more closely together to try to resolve disputes co-operatively, rather than proceed to litigation. He specifically recommended a pre-action protocol for medical negligence cases.

1.8   A fuller summary of Lord Woolf's recommendations is at Annex D.

WHERE THE PROTOCOL FITS IN

1.9   Protocols serve the needs of litigation and pre-litigation practice, especially –

- predictability in the time needed for steps pre-proceedings;
- standardisation of relevant information, including records and documents to be disclosed.

1.10 Building upon Lord Woolf's recommendations, the Lord Chancellor's Department is now promoting the adoption of protocols in specific areas, including medical negligence.

1.11 It is recognised that contexts differ significantly. For example: patients tend to have an ongoing relationship with a GP, more so than with a hospital; clinical staff in the National Health Service are often employees, while those in the private sector may be contractors; providing records quickly may be relatively easy for GPs and dentists, but can be a complicated procedure in a large multi-department hospital. The protocol which follows is intended to be sufficiently broadly based, and flexible, to apply to all aspects of the health service: primary and secondary; public and private sectors.

ENFORCEMENT OF THE PROTOCOL AND SANCTIONS

1.12 The civil justice reforms will be implemented in April 1999. One new set of Court Rules and procedures is replacing the existing rules for both the High Court and county courts. This and the personal injury protocol are being published with the Rules, practice directions and key court forms. The courts will be able to treat the standards set in protocols as the normal reasonable approach to pre-action conduct.

1.13 If proceedings are issued it will be for the court to decide whether non-compliance with a protocol should merit sanctions. Guidance on the court's likely approach will be given from time to time in practice directions.

1.14 If the court has to consider the question of compliance after proceedings have begun it will not be concerned with minor infringements, eg failure by a short period to provide relevant information. One minor breach will not entitle the 'innocent' party to abandon following the protocol. The court will look at the effect of non-compliance on the other party when deciding whether to impose sanctions.

2 THE AIMS OF THE PROTOCOL

2.1   The *general* aims of the protocol are –
- to maintain/restore the patient/healthcare provider relationship;
- to resolve as many disputes as possible without litigation.

2.2   The *specific* objectives are –

Openness

- to encourage early communication of the perceived problem between patients and healthcare providers;
- to encourage patients to voice any concerns or dissatisfaction with their treatment as soon as practicable;
- to encourage healthcare providers to develop systems of early reporting and investigation for serious adverse treatment outcomes and to provide full and prompt explanations to dissatisfied patients;
- to ensure that sufficient information is disclosed by both parties to enable each to understand the other's perspective and case, and to encourage early resolution;

Timeliness

- to provide an early opportunity for healthcare providers to identify cases where an investigation is required and to carry out that investigation promptly;
- to encourage primary and private healthcare providers to involve their defence organisations or insurers at an early stage;
- to ensure that all relevant medical records are provided to patients or their appointed representatives on request, to a realistic timetable by any healthcare provider;
- to ensure that relevant records which are not in healthcare providers' possession are made available to them by patients and their advisers at an appropriate stage;
- where a resolution is not achievable to lay the ground to enable litigation to proceed on a reasonable timetable, at a reasonable and proportionate cost and to limit the matters in contention;
- to discourage the prolonged pursuit of unmeritorious claims and the prolonged defence of meritorious claims.

Awareness of options

- to ensure that patients and healthcare providers are made aware of the available options to pursue and resolve disputes and what each might involve.

2.3   This protocol does not attempt to be prescriptive about a number of related clinical governance issues which will have a bearing on healthcare providers' ability to meet the standards within the protocol. Good clinical governance requires the following to be considered –

(a) **Clinical risk management:** the protocol does not provide any detailed guidance to healthcare providers on clinical risk management or the adoption of risk management systems and procedures. This must be a matter for the NHS Executive, the National Health Service Litigation Authority, individual trusts and providers, including GPs, dentists and the private sector. However, effective co-ordinated, focused clinical risk management strategies and procedures can help in managing risk and in the early identification and investigation of adverse outcomes.

(b) **Adverse outcome reporting:** the protocol does not provide any detailed guidance on which adverse outcomes should trigger an investigation. However, healthcare providers should have in place procedures for such investigations, including recording of statements of key witnesses. These procedures should also cover when and how to inform patients that an adverse outcome has occurred.

(c) **The professional's duty to report:** the protocol does not recommend changes to the codes of conduct of professionals in healthcare, or attempt to impose a specific duty on those professionals to report known adverse outcomes or untoward incidents. Lord Woolf in his final report suggested that the professional bodies might consider this. The General Medical Council is preparing guidance to doctors about their duty to report adverse incidents and to co-operate with inquiries.

3 THE PROTOCOL

3.1   This protocol is not a comprehensive code governing all the steps in clinical disputes. Rather it attempts to set out **a code of good practice** which parties should follow when litigation might be a possibility.

3.2   The **commitments** section of the protocol summarises the guiding principles which healthcare providers and patients and their advisers are invited to endorse when dealing with patient dissatisfaction with treatment and its outcome, and with potential complaints and claims.

3.3   The **steps** section sets out in a more prescriptive form, a recommended sequence of actions to be followed if litigation is a prospect.

GOOD PRACTICE COMMITMENTS

3.4   **Healthcare providers** should –

(i) ensure that **key staff**, including claims and litigation managers, are appropriately trained and have some knowledge of healthcare law, and of complaints procedures and civil litigation practice and procedure;

(ii) develop an approach to **clinical governance** that ensures that clinical practice is delivered to commonly accepted standards and that this is routinely monitored through a system of clinical audit and clinical risk management (particularly adverse outcome investigation);

(iii) set up **adverse outcome reporting systems** in all specialties to record and investigate unexpected serious adverse outcomes as soon as possible. Such systems can enable evidence to be gathered quickly, which makes it easier to provide an accurate explanation of what happened and to defend or settle any subsequent claims;

(iv) use the results of **adverse incidents and complaints positively** as a guide to how to improve services to patients in the future;

(v) ensure **that patients receive clear and comprehensible information** in an accessible form about how to raise their concerns or complaints;

(vi) establish **efficient and effective systems of recording and storing patient records**, notes, diagnostic reports and X-rays, and to retain these in accordance with Department of Health guidance (currently for a minimum of eight years in the case of adults, and all obstetric and paediatric notes for children until they reach the age of 25);

(vii) **advise patients** of a serious adverse outcome and provide on request to the patient or the patient's representative an oral or written explanation of what happened, information on further steps open to the patient, including where appropriate an offer of future treatment to rectify the problem, an apology, changes in procedure which will benefit patients and/or compensation.

3.5   **Patients and their advisers** should –

(i) **report any concerns and dissatisfaction** to the healthcare provider as soon as is reasonable to enable that provider to offer clinical advice where possible, to advise the patient if anything has gone wrong and take appropriate action;

(ii) consider the **full range of options** available following an adverse outcome with which a patient is dissatisfied, including a request for an explanation, a meeting, a complaint, and other appropriate dispute resolution methods (including mediation) and negotiation, not only litigation;

(iii) **inform the healthcare provider when the patient is satisfied** that the matter has been concluded: legal advisers should notify the provider when they are no longer acting for the patient, particularly if proceedings have not started.

PROTOCOL STEPS

3.6 The steps of this protocol which follow have been kept deliberately simple. An illustration of the likely sequence of events in a number of healthcare situations is at Annex A.

OBTAINING THE HEALTH RECORDS

3.7 Any request for records by the **patient** or their adviser should –

- **provide sufficient information** to alert the healthcare provider where an adverse outcome has been serious or had serious consequences;
- be as **specific as possible** about the records which are required.

3.8 Requests for copies of the patient's clinical records should be made using the Law Society and Department of Health approved **standard forms** (enclosed at Annex B), adapted as necessary.

3.9 The copy records should be provided **within 40 days** of the request and for a cost not exceeding the charges permissible under the Access to Health Records Act 1990 (currently a maximum of £10 plus photocopying and postage).

3.10 In the rare circumstances that the healthcare provider is in difficulty in complying with the request within 40 days, the **problem should be explained** quickly and details given of what is being done to resolve it.

3.11 It will not be practicable for healthcare providers to investigate in detail each case when records are requested. But healthcare providers should **adopt a policy on which cases will be investigated** (see paragraph 3.5 on clinical governance and adverse outcome reporting).

3.12 If the healthcare provider fails to provide the health records within 40 days, the patient or their adviser can then apply to the court for an **order for pre-action disclosure**. The new Civil Procedure Rules should make pre-action applications to the court easier. The court will also have the power to impose costs sanctions for unreasonable delay in providing records.

3.13 If either the patient or the healthcare provider considers **additional health records are required from a third party**, in the first instance these should be requested by or through the patient. Third party healthcare providers are expected to co-operate. The Civil Procedure Rules will enable patients and healthcare providers to apply to the court for pre-action disclosure by third parties.

LETTER OF CLAIM

3.14 Annex C1 to this protocol provides **a template for the recommended contents of a letter of claim**: the level of detail will need to be varied to suit the particular circumstances.

3.15 If, following the receipt and analysis of the records, and the receipt of any further advice (including from experts if necessary – see Section 4), the patient/adviser decides that there are grounds for a claim, they should then send, as soon as practicable, to the healthcare provider/potential defendant, a **letter of claim.**

3.16 This letter should contain a **clear summary of the facts** on which the claim is based, including the alleged adverse outcome, and the **main allegations of negligence**. It should also describe the **patient's injuries**, and present condition and prognosis. The **financial loss** incurred by the plaintiff should be outlined with an indication of the heads of damage to be claimed and the scale of the loss, unless this is impracticable.

3.17 In more complex cases a **chronology** of the relevant events should be provided, particularly if the patient has been treated by a number of different healthcare providers.

3.18 The letter of claim **should refer to any relevant documents**, including health records, and if possible enclose copies of any of those which will not already be in the potential defendant's possession, eg any relevant general practitioner records if the plaintiff's claim is against a hospital.

3.19 **Sufficient information** must be given to enable the healthcare provider defendant to **commence investigations** and to put an initial valuation on the claim.

3.20 Letters of claim are **not** intended to have the same formal status as a **pleading**, nor should any sanctions necessarily apply if the letter of claim and any subsequent statement of claim in the proceedings differ.

3.21 **Proceedings should not be issued until after three months from the letter of claim**, unless there is a limitation problem and/or the patient's position needs to be protected by early issue.

3.22 The patient or their adviser may want to make an **offer to settle** the claim at this early stage by putting forward an amount of compensation which would be satisfactory (possibly including any costs incurred to date). If an offer to settle is made, generally this should be supported by a medical report which deals with the injuries, condition and prognosis, and by a schedule of loss and supporting documentation. The level of detail necessary will depend on the value of the claim. Medical reports may not be necessary where there is no significant continuing injury, and a detailed schedule may not be necessary in a low value case. The Civil Procedure Rules are expected to set out the legal and procedural requirements for making offers to settle.

THE RESPONSE

3.23 Attached at Annex C2 is a template for the suggested contents of the **letter of response**.

3.24 The healthcare provider should **acknowledge** the letter of claim **within 14 days of receipt** and should identify who will be dealing with the matter.

3.25 The healthcare provider should, **within three months** of the letter of claim, provide a **reasoned answer** –

- if the **claim is admitted** the healthcare provider should say so in clear terms;
- if only **part of the claim is admitted** the healthcare provider should make clear which issues of breach of duty and/or causation are admitted and which are denied and why;
- if it is intended that any **admissions will be binding;**
- if the claim is denied, this should include specific comments on the allegations of negligence, and if a synopsis or chronology of relevant events has been provided and is disputed, the healthcare provider's version of those events;
- where additional documents are relied upon, eg an internal protocol, copies should be provided.

3.26 If the patient has made an offer to settle, the healthcare provider should **respond to that offer** in the response letter, preferably with reasons. The provider may make its own offer to settle at this stage, either as a counter-offer to the patient's, or of its own accord, but should accompany any offer by any supporting medical evidence, and/or by any other evidence in relation to the value of the claim which is in the healthcare provider's possession.

3.27 If the parties reach agreement on liability, but time is needed to resolve the value of the claim, they should aim to agree a reasonable period.

4 EXPERTS

4.1   In clinical negligence disputes expert opinions may be needed –

- on breach of duty and causation;
- on the patient's condition and prognosis;
- to assist in valuing aspects of the claim.

4.2   The civil justice reforms and the new Civil Procedure Rules will encourage economy in the use of experts and a less adversarial expert culture. It is recognised that in clinical negligence disputes, the parties and their advisers will require flexibility in their approach to expert evidence. Decisions on whether experts might be instructed jointly, and on whether reports might be disclosed sequentially or by exchange, should rest with the parties and their advisers. Sharing expert evidence may be appropriate on issues relating to the value of the claim. However, this protocol does not attempt to be prescriptive on issues in relation to expert evidence.

4.3   Obtaining expert evidence will often be an expensive step and may take time, especially in specialised areas of medicine where there are limited numbers of suitable experts. Patients and healthcare providers, and their advisers, will therefore need to consider carefully how best to obtain any necessary expert help quickly and cost-effectively. Assistance with locating a suitable expert is available from a number of sources.

5 ALTERNATIVE APPROACHES TO SETTLING DISPUTES

5.1 It would not be practicable for this protocol to address in any detail how a patient or their adviser, or healthcare provider, might decide which method to adopt to resolve the particular problem. But, the courts increasingly expect parties to try to settle their differences by agreement before issuing proceedings.

5.2 Most disputes are resolved by discussion and negotiation. Parties should bear in mind that carefully planned face-to-face meetings may be particularly helpful in exploring further treatment for the patient, in reaching understandings about what happened, and on both parties' positions, in narrowing the issues in dispute and, if the timing is right, in helping to settle the whole matter.

5.3 Summarised below are some other alternatives for resolving disputes –

- The revised NHS Complaints Procedure, which was implemented in April 1996, is designed to provide patients with an explanation of what happened and an apology if appropriate. It is not designed to provide compensation for cases of negligence. However, patients might choose to use the procedure if their only, or main, goal is to obtain an explanation, or to obtain more information to help them decide what other action might be appropriate.

- Mediation may be appropriate in some cases: this is a form of facilitated negotiation assisted by an independent neutral party. It is expected that the new Civil Procedure Rules will give the court the power to stay proceedings for one month for settlement discussions or mediation.

- Other methods of resolving disputes include arbitration, determination by an expert, and early neutral evaluation by a medical or legal expert. The Lord Chancellor's Department has produced a booklet on 'Resolving Disputes Without Going to Court', LCD 1995, which lists a number of organisations that provide alternative dispute resolution services.

ANNEX A ILLUSTRATIVE FLOWCHART

Patient (P)   *Healthcare Provider* (HCP)

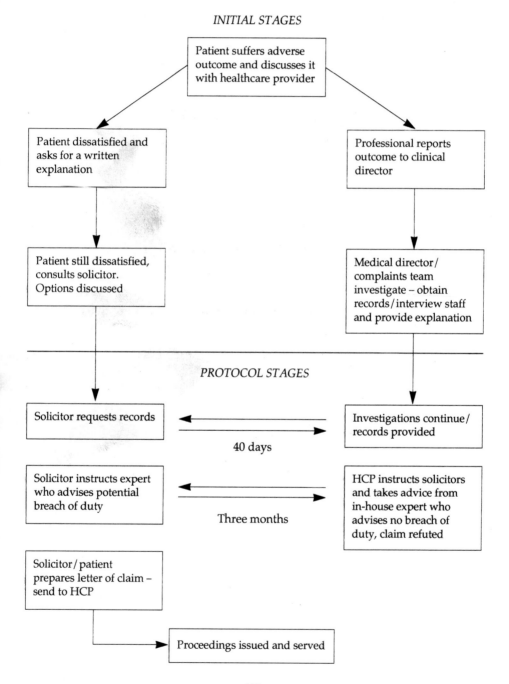

INITIAL STAGES

Patient suffers adverse outcome and discusses it with healthcare provider

Patient dissatisfied and asks for a written explanation

Professional reports outcome to clinical director

Patient still dissatisfied, consults solicitor. Options discussed

Medical director/ complaints team investigate – obtain records/interview staff and provide explanation

PROTOCOL STAGES

Solicitor requests records

Investigations continue/ records provided

40 days

Solicitor instructs expert who advises potential breach of duty

HCP instructs solicitors and takes advice from in-house expert who advises no breach of duty, claim refuted

Three months

Solicitor/patient prepares letter of claim – send to HCP

Proceedings issued and served

ANNEX B MEDICAL NEGLIGENCE AND PERSONAL INJURY CLAIMS

A PROTOCOL FOR OBTAINING

HOSPITAL MEDICAL RECORDS

CIVIL LITIGATION COMMITTEE

REVISED EDITION

JUNE 1998

THE LAW SOCIETY

APPLICATION ON BEHALF OF A PATIENT FOR HOSPITAL MEDICAL RECORDS FOR USE WHEN COURT PROCEEDINGS ARE CONTEMPLATED

PURPOSE OF THE FORMS

This application form and response forms have been prepared by a working party of the Law Society's Civil Litigation Committee and approved by the Department of Health for use in NHS and Trust hospitals.

The purpose of the forms is to standardise and streamline the disclosure of medical records to a patient's solicitors, who are investigating pursuing a personal injury claim against a third party, or a medical negligence claim against the hospital to which the application is addressed and/or other hospitals or general practitioners.

USE OF THE FORMS

Use of the forms is entirely voluntary and does not prejudice any party's right under the Access to Health Records Act 1990, the Data Protection Act 1984, or ss 33 and 34 of the Supreme Court Act 1981. However, it is Department of Health policy that patients be permitted to see what has been written about them, and that healthcare providers should make arrangements to allow patients to see all their records, not only those covered by the Access to Health Records Act 1990. The aim of the forms is to save time and costs for all concerned for the benefit of the patient and the hospital and in the interests of justice. Use of the forms should make it unnecessary in most cases for there to be exchanges of letters or other enquiries. If there is any unusual matter not covered by the form, the patient's solicitor may write a separate letter at the outset.

CHARGES FOR RECORDS

The Access to Health Records Act 1990 prescribes a maximum fee of £10. Photocopying and postage costs can be charged in addition. No other charges may be made.

The NHS Executive guidance makes it clear to healthcare providers that 'it is a perfectly proper use' of the 1990 Act to request records in that framework for the purpose of potential or actual litigation, whether against a third party or against the hospital or trust.

The 1990 Act does not permit differential rates of charges to be levied if the application is made by the patient, or by a solicitor on his or her behalf, or whether the response to the application is made by the healthcare provider directly (the medical records manager or a claims manager) or by a solicitor.

The NHS Executive guidance recommends that the same practice should be followed with regard to charges when the records are provided under a voluntary agreement as under the 1990 Act, except that in those circumstances the £10 access fee will not be appropriate.

The NHS Executive also advises –

- that the cost of photocopying may include 'the cost of staff time in making copies' and the costs of running the copier (but not costs of locating and sifting records);

- that the common practice of setting a standard rate for an application or charging an administration fee is not acceptable because there will be cases when this fails to comply with the 1990 Act.

RECORDS: WHAT MIGHT BE INCLUDED

X-rays and test results form part of the patient's records. Additional charges for copying X-rays are permissible. If there are large numbers of X-rays, the records officer should check with the patient/solicitor before arranging copying.

Reports on an 'adverse incident' and reports on the patient made for risk management and audit purposes may form part of the records and be disclosable: the exception will be any specific record or report made solely or mainly in connection with an actual or potential claim.

RECORDS: QUALITY STANDARDS

When copying records healthcare providers should ensure –

1   All documents are legible, and complete, if necessary by photocopying at less than 100% size.

2   Documents larger than A4 in the original, eg ITU charts, should be reproduced in A3, or reduced to A4 where this retains readability.

3   Documents are only copied on one side of paper, unless the original is two sided.

4   Documents should not be unnecessarily shuffled or bound and holes should not be made in the copied papers.

ENQUIRIES/FURTHER INFORMATION

Any enquiries about the forms should be made initially to the solicitors making the request. Comments on the use and content of the forms should be made to the Secretary, Civil Litigation Committee, The Law Society, 113 Chancery Lane, London WC2A 1PL, telephone 0171 320 5739, or to the NHS Management Executive, Quarry House, Quarry Hill, Leeds LS2 7UE.

The Law Society
May 1998

APPLICATION ON BEHALF OF A PATIENT FOR HOSPITAL MEDICAL RECORDS FOR USE WHEN COURT PROCEEDINGS ARE CONTEMPLATED

This should be completed as fully as possible

Insert
Hospital
Name
and
Address

TO: Medical Records Officer

Hospital

1 (a)	Full name of patient (including previous surnames)	
(b)	Address now	
(c)	Address at start of treatment	
(d)	Date of birth (and death, if applicable)	
(e)	Hospital ref no if available	
(f)	NI number, if available	
2	This application is made because the patient is considering	
(a)	a claim against your hospital as detailed in para 7 overleaf	YES/NO
(b)	pursuing an action against someone else	YES/NO
3	Department(s) where treatment was received	
4	Name(s) of consultant(s) at your hospital in charge of the treatment	
5	Whether treatment at your hospital was private or NHS, wholly or in part	
6	A description of the treatment received, with approximate dates	

7	If the answer to Q2(a) is 'Yes' details of	
	(a) the likely nature of the claim	
	(b) grounds for the claim	
	(c) approximate dates of the events involved	
8	If the answer to Q2(b) is 'Yes' insert	
	(a) the names of the proposed defendants	
	(b) whether legal proceedings yet begun	YES/NO
	(c) if appropriate, details of the claim and action number	
9	We confirm we will pay reasonable copying charges	
10	We request prior details of	
	(a) photocopying and administration charges for medical records	YES/NO
	(b) number of and cost of copying x-ray and scan films	YES/NO
11	Any other relevant information, particular requirements, or any particular documents not required (eg copies of computerised records)	
	Signature of Solicitor	
	Name	
	Address	
	Ref	
	Telephone Number	
	Fax number	

Please print name beneath each signature.
Signature by child over 12 but under
18 years also requires signature by parent

Signature of patient

Signature of parent or next friend if appropriate

Signature of personal representative where patient has died

FIRST RESPONSE TO APPLICATION FOR HOSPITAL RECORDS

NAME OF PATIENT Our ref Your ref		
1	Date of receipt of patient's application	
2	We intend that copy medical records will be dispatched within 6 weeks of that date	YES/NO
3	We require pre-payment of photocopying charges	YES/NO
4	If estimate of photocopying charges requested or pre-payment required the amount will be	£ /notified to you
5	The cost of x-ray and scan films will be	£ /notified to you
6	If there is any problem, we shall write to you within those 6 weeks	YES/NO
7	Any other information	
	Please address further correspondence to	
	Signed	
	Direct telephone number	
	Direct fax number	
	Dated	

SECOND RESPONSE ENCLOSING PATIENT'S
HOSPITAL MEDICAL RECORDS

Address

Our ref

Your ref

	NAME OF PATIENT:	
1	We confirm that the enclosed copy medical records are all those within the control of the hospital, relevant to the application which you have made to the best of our knowledge and belief, subject to paras 2–5 below	YES/NO
2	Details of any other documents which have not yet been located	
3	Date by when it is expected that these will be supplied	
4	Details of any records which we are not producing	
5	The reasons for not doing so	
6	An invoice for copying and administration charges is attached	YES/NO
	Signed	
	Date	

ANNEX C TEMPLATES FOR LETTERS OF CLAIM AND RESPONSE

C1 LETTER OF CLAIM

Essential contents

1   Client's name, address, date of birth, etc.

2   Dates of allegedly negligent treatment

3   Events giving rise to the claim:
- an outline of what happened, including details of other relevant treatments to the client by other healthcare providers.

4   Allegation of negligence and causal link with injuries:
- an outline of the allegations or a more detailed list in a complex case;
- an outline of the causal link between allegations and the injuries complained of.

5   The Client's injuries, condition and future prognosis

6   Request for clinical records (if not previously provided)
- use the Law Society form if appropriate or adapt;
- specify the records require;
- if other records are held by other providers, and may be relevant, say so;
- state what investigations have been carried out to date, e.g. information from client and witnesses, any complaint and the outcome, if any clinical records have been seen or experts advice obtained.

7   The likely value of the claim
- an outline of the main heads of damage, or, in straightforward cases, the details of loss.

Optional information

What investigations have been carried out:

    An offer to settle without supporting evidence

    Suggestions for obtaining expert evidence

    Suggestions for meetings, negotiations, discussion or mediation

Possible enclosures

    Chronology

    Clinical records request form and client's authorisation

    Expert report(s)

    Schedules of loss and supporting evidence

C2 LETTER OF RESPONSE

Essential contents

1   Provide **requested records** and invoice for copying:
   - explain if records are incomplete or extensive records are held and ask for further instructions;
   - request additional records from third parties.

2   **Comments on events and/or chronology:**
   - if events are disputed or the healthcare provider has further information or documents on which they wish to rely, these should be provided, eg internal protocol;
   - details of any further information needed from the patient or a third party should be provided.

3   **If breach of duty and causation are accepted:**
   - suggestions might be made for resolving the claim and/or requests for further information;
   - a response should be made to any offer to settle.

4   **If breach of duty and/or causation are denied:**
   - a bare denial will not be sufficient. If the healthcare provider has other explanations for what happened, these should be given at least in outline;
   - suggestions might be made for the next steps, eg further investigations, obtaining expert evidence, meetings/ negotiations or mediation, or an invitation to issue proceedings.

Optional matters

An offer to settle if the patient has not made one, or a counter offer to the patient's with supporting evidence

Possible enclosures:

Clinical records

Annotated chronology

Expert reports

ANNEX D LORD WOOLF'S RECOMMENDATIONS

1   Lord Woolf in his *Access to Justice Report* in July 1996, following a detailed review of the problems of medical negligence claims, identified that one of the major sources of **costs and delay** is **at the pre-litigation stage** because –

(a) Inadequate incident reporting and record keeping in hospitals, and mobility of staff, make it difficult to establish facts, often several years after the event.

(b) Claimants must incur the cost of an expert in order to establish whether they have a viable claim.

(c) There is often a long delay before a claim is made.

(d) Defendants do not have sufficient resources to carry out a full investigation of every incident, and do not consider it worthwhile to start an investigation as soon as they receive a request for records, because many cases do not proceed beyond that stage.

(e) Patients often give the defendant little or no notice of a firm intention to pursue a claim. Consequently, many incidents are not investigated by the defendants until after proceedings have started.

(f) Doctors and other clinical staff are traditionally reluctant to admit negligence or apologise to, or negotiate with, claimants for fear of damage to their professional reputations or career prospects.

2   Lord Woolf acknowledged that under the present arrangements **healthcare providers**, faced with possible medical negligence claims, have a number of **practical problems** to contend with –

(a) Difficulties of finding patients' records and tracing former staff, which can be exacerbated by late notification and by the health care provider's own failure to identify adverse incidents.

(b) The healthcare provider may have only treated the patient for a limited time or for a specific complaint: the patient's previous history may be relevant but the records may be in the possession of one of several other healthcare providers.

(c) The large number of potential claims which do not proceed beyond the stage of a request for medical records, or an explanation; and that it is difficult for healthcare providers to investigate fully every case whenever a patient asks to see the records.

ANNEX E HOW TO CONTACT THE FORUM

The Clinical Disputes Forum

Chairman

>   Dr Alastair Scotland
>   Medical Director and Chief Officer
>   National Clinical Assessment Authority
>   9th Floor, Market Towers
>   London
>   SW8 5NQ

>>>>>>   Telephone: 020 7273 0850

Secretary

>   Sarah Leigh
>   c/o Margaret Dangoor
>   3 Clydesdale Gardens
>   Richmond
>   Surrey
>   TW10 5EG

>>>>>>   Telephone: 020 8408 1012

APPENDIX E

ETHICAL GUIDELINES

HIPPOCRATIC OATH

I will look upon him who shall have taught me this Art even as one of my parents. I will share my substance with him, and I will supply his necessities, if he be in need. I will regard his offspring even as my own brethren, and I will teach them this Art, if they would learn it, without fee or covenant. I will impart this Art by precept, by lecture and by every mode of teaching, not only to my own sons, but to the sons of him who taught me, and to disciples bound by covenant and oath, according to the Law of Medicine.

The regimen I adopt shall be for the benefit of my patients according to my ability and judgment, and not for their hurt or for any wrong. I will give no deadly drug to any, though it be asked of me, nor will I counsel such, and especially I will not aid a woman to procure abortion. Whatsoever house I enter, there will I go for the benefit of the sick, refraining from all wrongdoing or corruption, and especially from any act of seduction of male or female, of bond or free. Whatsoever things I see or hear concerning the life of men, in my attendance on the sick, or even apart therefrom, which ought not to be noised abroad, I will keep silence thereon, counting such things to be as sacred secrets.

DUTIES OF A DOCTOR – GUIDANCE FROM THE GENERAL MEDICAL COUNCIL'S *GOOD MEDICAL PRACTICE* (MAY 2001)

Patients must be able to trust doctors with their lives and well-being. To justify that trust, we as a profession have a duty to maintain a good standard of practice and care and to show respect for human life. In particular, as a doctor you must:

- make the care of your patient your first concern;
- treat every patient politely and considerately;
- respect patients' dignity and privacy;
- listen to patients and respect their views;
- give patients information in a way they can understand;
- respect the rights of patients to be fully involved in decisions about their care;
- keep your professional knowledge and skills up-to-date;
- recognise the limits of your professional competence;
- be honest and trustworthy;
- respect and protect confidential information;
- make sure that your personal beliefs do not prejudice your patients' care;
- act quickly to protect patients from risk if you have good reason to believe that you or a colleague may not be fit to practice;
- avoid abusing your position as a doctor;

- work with colleagues in the way that best serve patients' interests.

In all these matters you must never discriminate unfairly against your patients or colleagues. And you must always be prepared to justify your actions to them.

CONFIDENTIALITY – GUIDANCE FROM THE GENERAL MEDICAL COUNCIL'S *CONFIDENTIALITY* BOOKLET (SEPTEMBER 2000)

SECTION 1 – PATIENTS' RIGHT TO CONFIDENTIALITY

1. Patients have a right to expect that information about them will be held in confidence by their doctors. Confidentiality is central to trust between doctors and patients. Without assurances about confidentiality, patients may be reluctant to give doctors the information they need in order to provide good care. If you are asked to provide information about patients you should:

    a. Seek patients' consent to disclosure of information wherever possible, whether or not you judge that patients can be identified from the disclosure.

    b. Anonymise data where unidentifiable data will serve the purpose.

    c. Keep disclosures to the minimum necessary.

    You must always be prepared to justify your decisions in accordance with this guidance.

Protecting information

2. When you are responsible for personal information about patients you must make sure that it is effectively protected against improper disclosure at all times.

3. Many improper disclosures are unintentional. You should not discuss patients where you can be overheard or leave patients' records, either on paper or on screen, where they can be seen by other patients, unauthorised health care staff or the public. Whenever possible you should take steps to ensure that your consultations with patients are private.

SECTION 2 – SHARING INFORMATION WITH PATIENTS

4. Patients have a right to information about the health care services available to them, presented in a way that is easy to follow and use.

5. Patients also have a right to information about any condition or disease from which they are suffering. This should be presented in a manner easy to follow and use, and include information about diagnosis, prognosis, treatment options, outcomes of treatment, common and/or serious side-effects of treatment, likely time-scale of treatments and costs where relevant. You should always give patients basic information about treatment you propose to provide, but you should respect the wishes of any patient who asks you not to give them detailed information. This places a considerable onus upon health professionals. Yet, without such information, patients cannot make proper choices, as partners in the health care process. Our booklet *Seeking Patients' Consent: The Ethical Considerations* gives further advice on providing information to patients.

6. It is good practice to give patients information about how anonymised information about them may be used to protect public health, to undertake research and audit, to teach or train medical staff and students and to plan and organise health care services.

SECTION 3 – DISCLOSURE OF INFORMATION

Sharing information with others providing care

7. Where patients have consented to treatment, express consent is not usually needed before relevant personal information is shared to enable the treatment to be provided. For example, express consent would not be needed before general practitioners disclose relevant personal information so that a medical secretary can type a referral letter. Similarly, where a patient has agreed to be referred for an X-ray physicians may make relevant information available to radiologists when requesting an X-ray. Doctors cannot treat patients safely, nor provide the continuity of care, without having relevant information about the patient's condition and medical history.

8. You should make sure that patients are aware that personal information about them will be shared within the health care team, unless they object, and of the reasons for this. It is particularly important to check that patients understand what will be disclosed if it is necessary to share personal information with anyone employed by another organisation or agency providing health or social care. You must respect the wishes of any patient who objects to particular information being shared with others providing care, except where this would put others at risk of death or serious harm.

9. You must make sure that anyone to whom you disclose personal information understands that it is given to them in confidence, which they must respect. Anyone receiving personal information in order to provide care is bound by a legal duty of confidence, whether or not that they have contractual or professional obligations to protect confidentiality.

10. Circumstances may arise where a patient cannot be informed about the sharing of information, for example because of a medical emergency. In these cases you should pass relevant information promptly to those providing the patients' care.

SECTION 4 – DISCLOSURE OF INFORMATION OTHER THAN FOR TREATMENT OF THE INDIVIDUAL PATIENT

Principles

11. Information about patients is requested for a wide variety of purposes including education, research, monitoring and epidemiology, public health surveillance, clinical audit, administration and planning. You have a duty to protect patients' privacy and respect their autonomy. When asked to provide information you should follow the guidance in paragraph 1, that is:

   a. Seek patients' consent to disclosure of any information wherever possible, whether or not you judge that patients can be identified from the disclosure.

   b. Anonymise data where unidentifiable data will serve the purpose.

   c. Keep disclosures to the minimum necessary.

12. The paragraphs which follow deal with obtaining consent, and what to do where consent is unobtainable, or it is impracticable to seek consent.

OBTAINING CONSENT

13. Seeking patients' consent to disclosure is part of good communication between doctors and patients, and is an essential part of respect for patients' autonomy and privacy.

Consent where disclosures will have personal consequences for patients

14. You must obtain express consent where patients may be personally affected by the disclosure, for example when disclosing personal information to a patient's employer. When seeking express consent you must make sure that patients are given enough information on which to base their decision, the reasons for the disclosure and the likely consequences of the disclosure. You should also explain how much information will be disclosed and to whom it will be given. If the patient withholds consent, or consent cannot be obtained, disclosures may be made only where they can be justified in the public interest, usually where disclosure is essential to protect the patient, or someone else, from risk of death or serious harm.

Consent where the disclosure is unlikely to have personal consequences for patients

15. Disclosure of information about patients for purposes such as epidemiology, public health safety, or the administration of health services, or for use in education or training, clinical or medical audit, or research is unlikely to have personal consequences for the patient. In these circumstances you should still obtain patients' express consent to the use of identifiable data or arrange for members of the health care team to anonymise records (see also paragraphs 16 and 18).

16. However, where information is needed for the purposes of the kind set out in paragraph 15, and you are satisfied that it is not practicable either to obtain express consent to disclosure, nor for a member of the health care team to anonymise records, data may be disclosed without express consent. Usually such disclosures will be made to allow a person outside the health care team to anonymise the records. Only where it is essential for the purpose may identifiable records be disclosed. Such disclosures must be kept to the minimum necessary for the purpose. In all such cases you must be satisfied that patients have been told, or have had access to written material informing them:

   a. That their records may be disclosed to persons outside the team which provided their care.

   b. Of the purpose and extent of the disclosure, for example, to produce anonymised data for use in education, administration, research or audit.

   c. That the person given access to records will be subject to a duty of confidentiality.

   d. That they have a right to object to such a process, and that their objection will be respected, except where the disclosure is essential to protect the patient, or someone else, from risk of death or serious harm.

17. Where you have control of personal information about patients, you must not allow anyone access to them for the purposes of the kind set out in paragraph 15, unless the person has been properly trained and authorised by the health authority, NHS trust or comparable body and is subject to a duty of confidentiality in their employment or because of their registration with a statutory regulatory body.

Disclosures in the public interest

18. In cases where you have considered all the available means of obtaining consent, but you are satisfied that it is not practicable to do so, or that patients are not competent to give consent, or exceptionally, in cases where patients withhold consent, personal information may be disclosed in the public interest where the benefits to an individual or to society of the disclosure outweigh the public and the patient's interest in keeping the information confidential.

19. In all such cases you must weigh the possible harm (both to the patient, and the overall trust between doctors and patients) against the benefits which are likely to arise from the release of information.

20. Ultimately, the 'public interest' can be determined only by the courts; but the GMC may also require you to justify your actions if we receive a complaint about the disclosure of personal information without a patient's consent.

SECTION 5 – PUTTING THE PRINCIPLES INTO PRACTICE

21. The remainder of this booklet deals with circumstances in which doctors are most frequently asked to disclose information, and provides advice on how the principles in paragraphs 14–20 should be applied.

Disclosures which benefit patients indirectly

Monitoring public health and the safety of medicines and devices including disclosures to cancer and other registries

22. Professional organisations and government regulatory bodies which monitor the public health or the safety of medicines or devices, as well as cancer and other registries, rely on information from patients' records for their effectiveness in safeguarding the public health. For example, the effectiveness of the yellow card scheme run by the Committee on Safety of Medicines depends on information provided by clinicians. You must co-operate by providing relevant information wherever possible. The notification of some communicable diseases is required by law (see also paragraph 43), and in other cases you should provide information in anonymised form, wherever that would be sufficient.

23. Where personal information is needed, you should seek express consent before disclosing information, whenever that is practicable. For example, where patients are receiving treatment there will usually be an opportunity for a health care professional to discuss disclosure of information with them.

24. Personal information may sometimes be sought about patients with whom health care professionals are not in regular contact. Doctors should therefore make sure that patients are given information about the possible value of their data in protecting the public health in the longer-term, at the initial consultation or at another suitable occasion when they attend a surgery or clinic. Patients should be given the information set out in paragraph 16: it should be clear that they may object to disclosures at any point. You must record any objections so that patients' wishes can be respected. In such cases, you may pass on anonymised information if asked to do so.

25. Where patients have not expressed an objection, you should assess the likely benefit of the disclosure to the public and commitment to confidentiality of the organisation requesting the information. If there is little or no evident public

benefit, you should not disclose information without the express consent of the patient.

26. Where it is not practicable to seek patients' consent for disclosure of personal information for these purposes, or where patients are not competent to give consent, you must consider whether disclosures would be justified in the public interest, by weighing the benefits to the public health of the disclosure against the possible detriment to the patient.

27. The automatic transfer of personal information to a registry, whether by electronic or other means, before informing the patient that information will be passed on, is unacceptable save in the most exceptional circumstances. These would be where a court has already decided that there is such an overwhelming public interest in the disclosure of information to a registry that patients' rights to confidentiality are overridden; or where you are willing and able to justify the disclosure, potentially before a court or to the GMC, on the same grounds.

Clinical audit and education

28. Anonymised data will usually be sufficient for clinical audit and for education. When anonymising records you should follow the guidance on obtaining consent in paragraphs 15–17 above. You should not disclose non-anonymised data for clinical audit or education without the patient's consent.

Administration and financial audit

29. You should record financial or other administrative data separately from clinical information, and provide it in anonymised form, wherever that is possible.

30. Decisions about the disclosure of clinical records for administrative or financial audit purposes, for example where health authority staff seek access to patients' records as part of the arrangements for verifying NHS payments, are unlikely to bring your registration into question, provided that, before allowing access to patients' records, you follow the guidance in paragraphs 15–17. Only the relevant part of the record should be made available for scrutiny.

Medical research

31. Where research projects depend on using identifiable information or samples, and it is not practicable to contact patients to seek their consent, this fact should be drawn to the attention of a research ethics committee so that it can consider whether the likely benefits of the research outweigh the loss of confidentiality. Disclosures may otherwise be improper, even if the recipients of the information are registered medical practitioners. The decision of a research ethics committee would be taken into account by a court if a claim for breach of confidentiality were made, but the court's judgement would be based on its own assessment of whether the public interest was served. More detailed guidance is issued by the medical royal colleges and other bodies.

Publication of case-histories and photographs

32. You must obtain express consent from patients before publishing personal information about them as individuals in media to which the public has access, for

example in journals or text books, whether or not you believe the patient can be identified. Express consent must therefore be sought to the publication of, for example, case-histories about, or photographs of, patients. Where you wish to publish information about a patient who has died, you should take into account the guidance in paragraphs 40–41 before deciding whether or not to do so.

Disclosures where doctors have dual responsibilities

33. Situations arise where doctors have contractual obligations to third parties, such as companies or organisations, as well as obligations to patients. Such situations occur, for example, when doctors:

   a. Provide occupational health services or medical care for employees of a company or organisation.

   b. Are employed by an organisation such as an insurance company.

   c. Work for an agency assessing claims for benefits.

   d. Provide medical care for patients and are subsequently asked to provide medical reports or information for third parties about them.

   e. Work as police surgeons.

   f. Work in the armed forces.

   g. Work in the prison service.

34. If you are asked to write a report about and/or examine a patient, or to disclose information from existing records for a third party to whom you have contractual obligations, you must:

   a. Be satisfied that the patient has been told at the earliest opportunity about for the purpose of the examination and/or disclosure, the extent of the information to be disclosed and the fact that relevant information cannot be concealed or withheld. You might wish to show the form to the patient before you complete it to ensure the patient understands the scope of the information requested.

   b. Obtain, or have seen, written consent to the disclosure from the patient or a person properly authorised to act on the patient's behalf. You may, however, accept written assurances from an officer of a government department that the patient's written consent has been given.

   c. Disclose only information relevant to the request for disclosure: accordingly, you should not usually disclose the whole record. The full record may be relevant to some benefits paid by government departments.

   d. Include only factual information you can substantiate, presented in an unbiased manner.

   e. The Access to Medical Reports Act 1988 entitles patients to see reports written about them before they are disclosed, in some circumstances. In all circumstances you should check whether patients wish to see their report, unless patients have clearly and specifically stated that they do not wish to do so.

35. Disclosures without consent to employers, insurance companies, or any other third party, can be justified only in exceptional circumstances, for example, when they are necessary to protect others from risk of death or serious harm.

Disclosures to protect the patient or others

36. Disclosure of personal information without consent may be justified where failure to do so may expose the patient or others to risk or death or serious harm. Where third parties are exposed to a risk so serious that it outweighs the patient's privacy interest, you should seek consent to disclosure where practicable. If it is not practicable, you should disclose information promptly to an appropriate person or authority. You should generally inform the patient before disclosing the information.

37. Such circumstances may arise, for example:

   a. Where a colleague, who is also a patient, is placing patients at risk as a result of illness or other medical condition. If you are in doubt about whether disclosure is justified you should consult an experienced colleague, or seek advice from a professional organisation. The safety of patients must come first at all times. (Our booklet *Serious Communicable Diseases* gives further guidance on this issue.)

   b. Where a patient continues to drive, against medical advice, when unfit to do so. In such circumstances you should disclose relevant information to the medical adviser of the Driver and Vehicle Licensing Agency without delay. Fuller guidance is given in Appendix 2.

   c. Where a disclosure may assist in the prevention or detection of a serious crime. Serious crimes, in this context, will put someone at risk of death or serious harm, and will usually be crimes against the person, such as abuse of children.

Children and other patients who may lack competence to give consent

38. Problems may arise if you consider that a patient is incapable of giving consent to treatment or disclosure because of immaturity, illness or mental incapacity. If such patients ask you not to disclose information to a third party, you should try to persuade them to allow an appropriate person to be involved in the consultation. If they refuse and you are convinced that it is essential, in their medical interests, you may disclose relevant information to an appropriate person or authority. In such cases you must tell the patient before disclosing any information, and, where appropriate, seek and carefully consider the views of an advocate or carer. You should document in the patient's record the steps you have taken to obtain consent and the reasons for deciding to disclose information.

39. If you believe a patient to be a victim of neglect or physical, sexual or emotional abuse and that the patient cannot give or withhold consent to disclosure, you should give information promptly to an appropriate responsible person or statutory agency, where you believe that the disclosure is in the patient's best interests. You should usually inform the patient that you intend to disclose the information before doing so. Such circumstances may arise in relation to children, where concerns about possible abuse need to be shared with other agencies such as social services. Where appropriate you should inform those with parental responsibility about the disclosure. If, for any reason, you believe that disclosure of information is not in the best interests of an abused or neglected patient, you must still be prepared to justify your decision.

Disclosure after a patient's death

40. You still have an obligation to keep personal information confidential after a patient dies. The extent to which confidential information may be disclosed after a patient's death will depend on the circumstances. These include the nature of the information, whether that information is already public knowledge or can be anonymised, and the intended use to which the information will be put. You should also consider whether the disclosure of information may cause distress to, or be of benefit to, the patient's partner or family.

41. There are a number of circumstances in which you may be asked to disclose, or wish to use, information about patients who have died. For example:

    a. To assist a Coroner, Procurator Fiscal or other similar officer in connection with an inquest or fatal accident inquiry. In these circumstances you should provide relevant information (see also paragraph 19 of Good Medical Practice).

    b. As part of National Confidential Enquiries or other clinical audit or for education or research. The publication of properly anonymised case studies would be unlikely to be improper in these contexts.

    c. On death certificates. The law requires you to complete death certificates honestly and fully.

    d. To obtain information relating to public health surveillance. Anonymised information should be used unless identifiable data is essential to the study.

42. Particular difficulties may arise when there is a conflict of interest between parties affected by the patient's death. For example, if an insurance company seeks information in order to decide whether to make a payment under a life assurance policy, you should release information in accordance with the requirements of the Access to Health Records Act 1990 or with the authorisation of those lawfully entitled to deal with the person's estate who have been fully informed of the consequences of disclosure. It may also be appropriate to inform those close to the patient.

SECTION 6 – DISCLOSURE IN CONNECTION WITH JUDICIAL OR OTHER STATUTORY PROCEEDINGS

43. You must disclose information to satisfy a specific statutory requirement, such as notification of a known or suspected communicable disease.

44. You must also disclose information if ordered to do so by a judge or presiding officer of a court. You should object to the judge or the presiding officer if attempts are made to compel you to disclose what appear to you to be irrelevant matters, for example matters relating to relatives or partners of the patient, who are not parties to the proceedings.

45. You should not disclose personal information to a third party such as a solicitor, police officer or officer of a court without the patient's express consent, except in the circumstances described at paragraphs 36–37, 39 and 41.

46. You may disclose personal information in response to an official request from a statutory regulatory body for any of the health care professions, where that body determines that this is necessary in the interests of justice and for the safety of other patients. Wherever practicable you should discuss this with the patient. There may be exceptional cases where, even though the patient objects, disclosure is justified.

If you decide to disclose confidential information you must be prepared to explain and justify your decision.

APPENDIX 1
ELECTRONIC PROCESSING

1. You must be satisfied that there are appropriate arrangements for the security of personal information when it is stored, sent or received by fax, computer, e-mail or other electronic means.

2. If necessary, you should take appropriate authoritative professional advice on how to keep information secure before connecting to a network. You should record the fact that you have taken such advice.

3. You must make sure your own fax machine and computer terminals are in secure areas. If you send data by fax you should satisfy yourself, as far as is practicable, that the data cannot be intercepted or seen by anyone other than the intended recipient.

4. When deciding whether, and in what form to transmit personal information, you should note that information sent by e-mail through the internet may be intercepted.

APPENDIX 2
DISCLOSURE OF INFORMATION ABOUT PATIENTS TO THE DRIVER AND VEHICLE LICENSING AGENCY (DVLA)

1. The DVLA is legally responsible for deciding if a person is medically unfit to drive. The Agency needs to know when driving licence holders have a condition which may now, or in the future, affect their safety as a driver.

2. Therefore, where patients have such conditions you should:

    a. Make sure that patients understand that the condition may impair their ability to drive. If a patient is incapable of understanding this advice, for example because of dementia, you should inform the DVLA immediately.

    b. Explain to patients that they have a legal duty to inform the DVLA about the condition.

3. If patients refuse to accept the diagnosis or the effect of the condition on their ability to drive, you can suggest that the patients seek a second opinion, and make appropriate arrangements for the patients to do so. You should advise patients not to drive until the second opinion has been obtained.

4. If patients continue to drive when they are not fit to do so, you should make every reasonable effort to persuade them to stop. This may include telling their next of kin.

5. If you do not manage to persuade patients to stop driving, or you are given or find evidence that a patient is continuing to drive contrary to advice, you should disclose relevant medical information immediately, in confidence, to the medical adviser at the DVLA.

6. Before giving information to the DVLA you should try to inform the patient of your decision to do so. Once the DVLA has been informed, you should also write to the patient, to confirm that a disclosure has been made.

SERIOUS COMMUNICABLE DISEASES – GUIDANCE FROM THE GENERAL MEDICAL COUNCIL'S BOOKLET (OCTOBER 1997)

Use of term 'serious communicable disease'

In this guidance the term serious communicable disease applies to any disease which may be transmitted from human to human and which may result in death or serious illness. It particularly concerns, but is not limited to, infections such as human immunodeficiency virus (HIV), tuberculosis and hepatitis B and C.

Providing a good standard of practice and care

1. All patients are entitled to good standards of practice and care from their doctors, regardless of the nature of their disease or condition.

2. You must not deny or delay investigation or treatment because you believe that the patient's actions or lifestyle may have contributed to their condition. Where patients pose a serious risk to your health or safety you may take reasonable, personal measures to protect yourself before investigating a patient's condition or providing treatment. In the context of serious communicable diseases these will usually be infection control measures. You must follow the guidance in paragraph 4 on consent to testing.

3. You must keep yourself informed about serious communicable diseases, and particularly their means of transmission and control. You should always take appropriate measures to protect yourself and others from infection. You must make sure that any staff for whom you are responsible are also appropriately informed and co-operate with measures designed to prevent transmission of infection to other patients.

Consent to testing for a serious communicable disease

4. You must obtain consent from patients before testing for a serious communicable disease, except in the rare circumstances described in paragraphs 6, 7, 9, 11 and 17 below. The information you provide when seeking consent should be appropriate to the circumstances and to the nature of the condition or conditions being tested for. Some conditions, such as HIV, have serious social and financial, as well as medical, implications. In such cases you must make sure that the patient is given appropriate information about the implications of the test, and appropriate time to consider and discuss them.

Children

5. When testing patients under 16 for a serious communicable disease, you must follow the guidance in paragraph 4 if you judge that they have sufficient maturity to understand the implications of testing.

6. Where a child cannot give or withhold consent, you should seek consent from a person with parental responsibility for the child. If you believe that that person's

judgement is distorted, for example, because he or she may be the cause of the child's infection, you must decide whether the medical interests of the child override the wishes of those with parental responsibility. Whenever possible you should discuss the issues with an experienced colleague before making a decision. If you test a child without obtaining consent, you must be prepared to justify that decision.

Unconscious patients

7. You may test unconscious patients for serious communicable diseases, without their prior consent, where testing would be in their immediate clinical interests – for example, to help in making a diagnosis. You should not test unconscious patients for other purposes.

Injuries to health care workers

8. If you or another health care worker has suffered a needlestick injury or other occupational exposure to blood or body fluids and you consider it necessary to test the patient for a serious communicable disease, the patient's consent should be obtained before the test is undertaken. If the patient is unconscious when the injury occurs consent should be sought once the patient has regained full consciousness. If appropriate, the injured person can take prophylactic treatment until consent has been obtained and the test result is known.

9. If the patient refuses testing, is unable to give or withhold consent because of mental illness or disability, or does not regain full consciousness within 48 hours, you should reconsider the severity of risk to yourself, or another injured health care worker, or to others. You should not arrange testing against the patient's wishes or without consent other than in exceptional circumstances, for example where you have good reason to think that the patient may have a condition such as HIV for which prophylactic treatment is available. In such cases you may test an existing blood sample, taken for other purposes, but you should consult an experienced colleague first. It is possible that a decision to test an existing blood without consent could be challenged in the courts, or be the subject of a complaint to your employer or the GMC. You must therefore be prepared to justify your decision.

10. If you decide to test without consent, you must inform the patient of your decision at the earliest opportunity. In such cases confidentiality is paramount: only the patient and those who have been exposed to infection may be told about the test and its result. In these exceptional circumstances neither the fact that test has been undertaken, nor its result, should be entered in the patient's personal medical record without the patient's consent.

11. If the patient dies you may test for a serious communicable disease if you have good reason to think that the patient may have been infected, and a health care worker has been exposed to the patient's blood or other body fluid. You should usually seek the agreement of a relative before testing. If the test shows the patient was a carrier of the virus, you should follow the guidance in paragraphs 21–23 of this booklet on giving information to patients' close contacts.

Testing in laboratories

12. It is the responsibility of the doctor treating the patient to obtain consent to testing for diagnostic purposes. If you work in a laboratory you may test blood or other specimens for serious communicable diseases only for the purposes for which the samples have been obtained, or for closely related purposes which are in the direct interests of the patient. See paragraph 14 for guidance on testing undertaken for research purposes.

Unlinked anonymised screening

13. In unlinked anonymised surveillance programmes for serious communicable diseases, you should make sure that patients are provided with information which covers:

    • Their right to refuse inclusion of the sample in the programme.

    • The fact that their blood sample cannot be identified and there is no way of tracing it back to them.

    • The benefits of seeking a test if they think they have been exposed to infection.

Research

14. You may undertake research only where the protocol has been approved by the appropriate, properly constituted research ethics committee. It remains your responsibility to ensure that research does not infringe patients' rights.

Deceased patients

15. When a patient who is brain stem dead is being considered as an organ donor, you should explain to relatives that assessing the suitability of organs for transplantation will involve testing for certain infections, including HIV.

Post-mortem testing

16. Where a post-mortem has been authorised or ordered you may test the deceased patient for communicable diseases where relevant to the investigation into the causes of death.

17. You should not routinely test for serious communicable diseases before performing post-mortems; but you should take precautions to protect yourself and other health care workers. If you have reason to believe the deceased person had a serious communicable disease, you should assume the body to be infectious.

Confidentiality

Informing other health care professionals

18. If you diagnose a patient as having a serious communicable disease, you should explain to the patient:

    a. The nature of the disease and its medical, social and occupational implications, as appropriate.

    b.   Ways of protecting others from infection.

    c.   The importance to effective care of giving the professionals who will be providing care information which they need to know about the patient's disease or condition. In particular you must make sure that patient understands that general practitioners cannot provide adequate clinical management and care without knowledge of their patients' conditions.

19.   If patients still refuse to allow other health care workers to be informed, you must respect the patients' wishes except where you judge that failure to disclose the information would put a health care worker or other patient at serious risk of death or serious harm. Such situations may arise, for example, when dealing with violent patients with severe mentally illness or disability. If you are in doubt about whether disclosure is appropriate, you should seek advice from an experienced colleague. You should inform patients before disclosing information. Such occasions are likely to arise rarely and you must be prepared to justify a decision to disclose information against a patient's wishes.

Disclosures to others

20.   You must disclose information about serious communicable diseases in accordance with the law. For example, the appropriate authority must be informed where a notifiable disease is diagnosed. Where a communicable disease contributed to the cause of death, this must be recorded on the death certificate. You should also pass information about serious communicable diseases to the relevant authorities for the purpose of communicable disease control and surveillance.

21.   As the GMC booklet *Confidentiality* makes clear, a patient's death does not of itself release a doctor from the obligation to maintain confidentiality. But in some circumstances disclosures can be justified because they protect other people from serious harm or because they are required by law.

Giving information to close contacts

22.   You may disclose information about a patient, whether living or dead, in order to protect a person from risk of death or serious harm. For example, you may disclose information to a known sexual contact of a patient with HIV where you have reason to think that the patient has not informed that person, and cannot be persuaded to do so. In such circumstances you should tell the patient before you make the disclosure, and you must be prepared to justify a decision to disclose information.

23.   You must not disclose information to others, for example relatives, who have not been, and are not, at risk of infection.

Doctors' responsibilities to protect patients from infection

24.   You must protect patients from unnecessary exposure to infection by following safe working practices and implementing appropriate infection control measures. This includes following the Control of Substances Hazardous to Health Regulations 1994 and other health and safety at work legislation. These regulations

may require you to inform your employer, or the person responsible for health and safety in your organisation, if there are any deficiencies in protection measures in your work place. Failure to do so may amount to a criminal offence.

25. You must follow the UK Health Departments' advice on immunisation against hepatitis B. If you are in direct contact with patients you should protect yourself and your patients by being immunised against other common serious communicable diseases, where vaccines are available.

26. You must always take action to protect patients when you have good reason to suspect that your own health, or that of a colleague, is a risk to them.

27. You must consider how any infection you have may put patients at risk. You must take particular care if you work with patients for whom exposure to infection may be serious, for example pregnant women or immuno-suppressed patients.

28. You must comply promptly with appropriate requests to be tested for serious communicable diseases when there is an investigation into an outbreak of disease amongst patients.

Responsibilities of doctors who have been exposed to a serious communicable disease

29. If you have any reason to believe that you have been exposed to a serious communicable disease you must seek and follow professional advice without delay on whether you should undergo testing and, if so, which tests are appropriate. Further guidance on your responsibilities if your health may put patients at risk is included in our booklet *Good Medical Practice*.

30. If you acquire a serious communicable disease you must promptly seek and follow advice from a suitably qualified colleague – such as a consultant in occupational health, infectious diseases or public health on:

   • Whether, and in what ways, you should modify your professional practice.

   • Whether you should inform your current employer, your previous employers or any prospective employer, about your condition.

31. You must not rely on your own assessment of the risks you pose to patients.

32. If you have a serious communicable disease and continue in professional practice you must have appropriate medical supervision.

33. If you apply for a new post, you must complete health questionnaires honestly and fully.

Treating colleagues with serious communicable diseases

34. If you are treating a doctor or other health care worker with a serious communicable disease you must provide the confidentiality and support to which every patient is entitled.

35. If you know, or have good reason to believe, that a medical colleague or health care worker who has or may have a serious communicable disease, is practising, or has practised, in a way which places patients at risk, you must inform an appropriate person in the health care worker's employing authority, for example an

occupational health physician, or where appropriate, the relevant regulatory body. Such cases are likely to arise very rarely. Wherever possible you should inform the health care worker concerned before passing information to an employer or regulatory body.

The authors extend their grateful thanks to the General Medical Council for permission to reproduce the above material.

BMA PRACTICAL GUIDE TO GAINING PATIENT CONSENT

MARCH 2001

The British Medical Association has published a brief working guide to gaining patient consent, designed to help doctors work through the practical problems, ethical dilemmas and legal pitfalls.

About this toolkit

This Tool Kit has been produced by a Working Party established by representatives at the BMA's Annual Meeting. A consultation exercise undertaken by the Working Party confirmed that there is already a significant amount of guidance on the relevant legal and ethical principles relating to consent, but that such guidance is not always adhered to. This Tool Kit is just one method by which, it is hoped, the practice of obtaining valid consent can be improved.

The purpose of this Tool Kit is to act as a prompt to doctors when they are seeking consent by providing answers to common questions raised by this process. The Tool Kit consists of a series of cards relating to specific areas of consent such as providing treatment to children; consent and research; and obtaining consent for teaching purposes. Separate cards have been produced identifying factors to be considered when assessing competence and determining 'best interests'. Each card is intended to stand alone, although there are some areas of overlap. Cards 1, 2 and 3 will be relevant to all doctors.

The Tool Kit is not intended to provide definitive guidance on all issues surrounding consent. Indeed, all cards refer to useful guidance, from bodies such as the GMC, BMA and the medical defence bodies, that should be used in conjunction with the cards. In addition, many of the Royal Colleges produce specific advice for their members: Card 13 lists contact details for organisations from whom further advice can be obtained. The Tool Kit is designed to raise doctors' awareness about the ethical and legal principles that apply, to dispel some common misconceptions surrounding consent and to help doctors to obtain valid consent from their patients.

CARD 2
GENERAL INFORMATION

1. When is it necessary to seek patient consent?

Patient consent is required on every occasion the doctor wishes to initiate an examination or treatment or any other intervention, except in emergencies or where the law prescribes otherwise (such as where compulsory treatment is authorised by mental health legislation). Consent can be verbal, written or implied by acquiescence by a person who understands what will be undertaken. Acquiescence when a patient does not know what the intervention entails, or is unaware that he or she can refuse, is not 'consent'. Consent should be considered as a process, not an event, and it is important that there is continuing discussion to reflect the evolving nature of treatment.

2. Who should seek consent from a patient prior to an examination or treatment?

The BMA considers that the doctor who recommends that the patient should undergo the intervention should have responsibility for providing an explanation to the patient and obtaining his or her consent. In a hospital setting this will normally be the senior clinician. In exceptional circumstances the task of reaffirming consent (see question 4) can be delegated to a doctor who is suitably trained and qualified, is sufficiently familiar with the procedure and possesses the appropriate communication skills.

The GMC makes it clear that the doctor who is providing the treatment or undertaking the investigation will be responsible for ensuring, before starting any treatment or intervention, that the patient has given valid consent. (See also Card 1 list: 'Consent.')

3. Do certain examinations or procedures require written consent?

Generally there is no legal requirement to obtain **written** consent. The consent form simply documents that some discussion about the procedure or investigation has taken place. The quality and clarity of the information given is the paramount consideration. Consent forms are evidence of a process, not the process itself. Any discussion, however, should be recorded in the patient's medical notes. (See also Card 1 list: 'Consent', 'DoH', 'MET', 'MDU', 'MPS.')

Some bodies, including the Royal Colleges and the GMC, recommend that written consent is obtained for certain types of procedure. Doctors should familiarise themselves with guidance relevant to their area of practice.

4. For how long is consent valid?

Consent should be perceived as a continuing process rather than a one-off decision. Where there has been a significant interval between the patient agreeing to a treatment option and its start, consent should be reaffirmed. In the intervening period, the patient may have changed his or her mind or there may have been clinical developments. It is therefore important that the patient is given continuing opportunities to ask further questions and to review the decision. (See also Card 1 list: 'Consent', 'MET', 'MDU', 'MPS', 'DoH.')

5. Can patients withdraw consent during a procedure?

Patients can change their minds about a decision at any time, as long as they have the capacity to do so.

6. Can a competent patient refuse treatment?

Competent adult patients are entitled to refuse consent to treatment even when doing so may result in permanent physical injury or death. Therefore, for example, a Jehovah's Witness can refuse a blood transfusion even where this is essential for survival. Where the consequences of refusal are grave, it is important that patients understand this, and also that, for clinical reasons, refusal may limit future treatment options (see also Card 1 list: 'Consent', 'DoH', 'MET', 'MDU', 'MPS'). Doctors must respect a refusal of treatment if the patient is an adult who is competent, properly informed and is not being coerced.

7. Are doctors obliged to follow an advance statement?

See Card 9 on Advance Statements.

CARD 3
INFORMATION PROVISION

1. How much information should patients be given in order for the consent to be valid?

The amount of information doctors provide to each patient will vary according to factors such as the nature of the condition, the complexity of the treatment, the risks associated with the treatment or procedure and the patient's own wishes. The GMC counsels doctors to take appropriate steps to find out what patients want to know and ought to know about their condition and its treatment. A careful balance needs to be struck between listening to what the patient wants and providing enough information in order that the patient's decisions are informed (see also question 2).

The GMC provides helpful guidance on the type of information doctors should provide, such as:

- the purpose of the investigation or treatment;
- details and uncertainties of the diagnosis;
- options for treatment including the option not to treat;
- explanation of the likely benefits and probabilities of success for each option;
- known possible side effects;
- the name of the doctor who will have overall responsibility; and
- a reminder that the patient can change his or her mind at any time.

The GMC also reminds doctors:

- to try to ascertain the patient's individual needs and wishes;
- not to exceed the scope of the authority given by the patient (except in an emergency where the patient's views are not known);
- to raise with patients the possibility of additional problems coming to light during the procedure and discuss possible action in this event.

Doctors should respond honestly to direct questions from patients and, as far as possible, answer as fully as the patients wish (see also Card 1 list: 'Consent'). Failure to provide sufficient relevant information could be challenged in law, including under the Human Rights Act (see also Card 1 list: 'HRA').

2. What should be done when a patient asks the doctor to make the decision on his or her behalf?

Doctors should explain to patients the importance of knowing the options open to them and what the treatment will involve. If patients still insist they do not want to know in detail about their condition and its treatment, the doctor must still provide basic information about the treatment before proceeding. (See also Card 1 list: 'Consent.')

3. What should be done where a patient's relative asks the doctor to withhold information from the patient?

In all cases, doctors should take the lead from the patient. The GMC counsels doctors to seek the views of the patient in such cases. It also reminds doctors that they should not withhold relevant information unless they consider that disclosure of this information would cause the patient serious harm. Although distress could constitute 'harm' to the patient in some circumstances, this is not generally accepted as sufficient reason to withhold relevant information. (See also Card 1 list: 'Consent.')

4. If a patient gives consent for blood to be taken during an examination, is it necessary to specify what tests are to be performed?

Patients should be informed about the purpose of the tests and doctors should be prepared to respond to patients' questions. If doctors need to take blood to test for evidence of a serious communicable disease, patients should be properly informed of the nature and implications of being tested, including the relative advantages and disadvantages, and their specific consent should be obtained. (See also Card 12 on HIV/AIDS, and Card 1 list: 'Communicable diseases', 'HIV.')

CARD 4
EMERGENCY TREATMENT

1. Can treatment be provided in an emergency situation where the patient is unable to give consent?

In an emergency, where consent cannot be obtained, doctors may provide medical treatment that is immediately necessary to save life or avoid significant deterioration in the patient's health. If, however, the patient is an adult and there is clear evidence of a valid advance refusal of a particular treatment (such as a refusal of blood by a Jehovah's Witness) that treatment should not be given. (See also Card 9 on Advance Statements and Card 1 list: 'Advance statements', 'Consent', 'DoH', 'MET', 'MDU', 'MPS.')

2. Can treatment be provided to a child in an emergency situation where there is nobody available to give consent?

Where the patient is under 18 years old and is unable to consent, either because of lack of capacity or because of illness, anyone with parental responsibility can provide consent (see Card 7 on Children and Young People and Card 1 list: 'Children'). If, however, treatment is required urgently and nobody with parental responsibility is available, doctors can proceed with treatment that is in the young person's best interests (see also Card 8 on Determining 'Best Interests' and Card 1 list: 'Children').

3. What action can be taken where a patient is unconscious and an unexpected finding is made during the course of a procedure that requires urgent attention?

When obtaining consent for any procedure, doctors should advise the patient of any foreseeable problems that could come to light while the patient is unconscious. This enables the doctor to obtain the patient's consent in advance for necessary treatment should the situation arise. The GMC warns doctors that where they treat outside patient consent their actions may be challenged. Where treatment which has not been discussed with the patient is required as a matter of urgency and it is not possible to wait until the patient has regained consciousness, the guidance contained in question 1 will apply. (See also Card 1 list: 'Consent.')

CARD 5
ASSESSMENT OF COMPETENCE

1. Are adults presumed to be competent The terms competence and capacity are used interchangeably **to give consent?**

Yes. All people aged 16 and over are presumed, in law, to have the capacity to consent to treatment unless there is evidence to the contrary. A patient who is suffering from a mental disorder or impairment does not, necessarily, lack the competence to consent to treatment. Equally, patients who would otherwise be competent may be temporarily incapable of giving valid consent due to factors such as fatigue, drunkenness, shock, fear, severe pain or sedation. The fact that an individual has made a decision that appears to others to be irrational or unjustified should not be taken as evidence that the individual lacks the mental capacity to make that decision. If, however, the decision is clearly contrary to previously expressed wishes, or is based on a misperception of reality, this may be indicative of a lack of capacity and further investigation will be required. (See also Card 1 list: 'Consent', 'Capacity', 'MET', 'MDU', 'MPS', 'DoH'.)

2. Are children and young people presumed to be competent to give consent?

No. There is no presumption of competence for people under 16 and those under this age must demonstrate their competence by meeting certain standards set by the Courts. In England, Wales and Northern Ireland, the central test is whether the young person has sufficient understanding and intelligence to understand fully what is proposed. In Scotland, a young person is considered competent to make treatment decisions if he or she is capable of understanding the nature and possible consequences of the procedure or treatment. (See also Card 7 on Children and Young People and Card 1 list: 'Children'.)

3. What factors should be taken into account when assessing competence to consent to treatment?

The assessment of a patient's capacity to make a decision about medical treatment is a matter for clinical judgement guided by professional practice and subject to legal requirements. To demonstrate capacity individuals should be able to:

- understand in simple language what the medical treatment is, its purpose and nature and why it is being proposed;
- understand its principal benefits, risks and alternatives;
- understand in broad terms what will be the consequences of not receiving the proposed treatment;
- retain the information for long enough to make an effective decision; and
- make a free choice (ie free from pressure).

(For other aspects of competence and for practical guidance, see Card 1 list: 'Children', 'Capacity'.)

CARD 6
ADULTS WHO LACK CAPACITY

1. Where a patient lacks capacity to consent to treatment, can consent be sought from the relatives?

Legally, in England, Wales and Northern Ireland, no person can give consent to medical treatment on behalf of another adult (although there are proposals for this to change in England and Wales). As the law currently stands, doctors may treat a patient who lacks capacity, without consent, providing the treatment is necessary and in the patient's best interests (see Card 8 on Determining 'Best Interests'). Even where the views of people who are close to the patient have no legal status in terms of actual decision making, it is good practice for the health care team to consult with them in assessing the patient's best interests. This may also be a requirement of the Human Rights Act. Any such enquiries should, however, be mindful of the duty of confidentiality owed to the patient (see also Card 1 list: 'HRA').

In Scotland, the Adults with Incapacity (Scotland) Act allows people over 16 to appoint a proxy decision maker who has the power to give consent to medical treatment when the patient loses capacity. Unless to do so is unreasonable or impracticable, the proxy must be consulted about treatment decisions. Proxy decision makers cannot demand treatment which is judged to be against the patient's interests. The Act also requires doctors to take account, so far as is reasonable and practicable, of the views of the patient's nearest relative and his or her primary carer.

For information about assessing competence see Card 5.

2. If a relative has an Enduring Power of Attorney can he or she consent to treatment on behalf of the patient?

No. Currently, an Enduring Power of Attorney empowers an individual to oversee the patient's property and affairs, but does not give him or her the right to consent to treatment. In Scotland, an appointed proxy decision maker may consent to medical treatment (see question 1).

3. Can treatment be provided to a patient without seeking consent if he or she is detained under mental health legislation?

Mental health legislation permits doctors to treat a patient compulsorily for a mental disorder, although it is still good practice to explain the treatment to be provided and, wherever possible, to seek the patient's agreement. The legislation does not provide the doctor with authority to proceed where the treatment is for a condition unrelated to the mental disorder. In those circumstances, the patient's competence should be assessed and, if he or she is deemed to lack decision-making capacity, the doctor should act in the patient's best interests. (See also Card 8 on Determining 'Best Interests', Card 5 on Assessment of Competence and Card 1 list: 'Capacity', 'Consent', 'MDU', 'MPS', 'DoH'.)

4. Can a patient who lacks capacity be sterilised if the health care team and relatives agree it is necessary?

The sterilisation of a minor or a mentally incompetent adult will, in virtually all cases, require the prior approval of a Court. Unless sterilisation is a necessary consequence of a procedure carried out for therapeutic purposes, such as treatment for cancer, doctors are advised to seek legal advice. (See also Card 5 on Assessment of Competence and Card 1 list: 'Capacity', 'Children.')

CARD 7
CHILDREN AND YOUNG PEOPLE

1. Who can consent to treatment where the patient is under 18?

A young person of any age can give a valid consent to treatment or examination provided he or she is considered to be competent to make the decision. At the age of 16 there is a presumption that the patient is competent to give a valid consent. Up to the age of 18, where the person lacks capacity, a person or local authority with parental responsibility can give consent on behalf of the patient. In some circumstances, the Courts will give consent to treatment and/or examination. (See also Card 5 on Assessment of Competence and Card 1 list: 'Children,' 'Consent', 'MET', 'MDU', 'MPS', 'DoH.')

2. Who has parental responsibility?

Not all parents have parental responsibility. Legally both parents will have parental responsibility if they were married at the time of the child's conception, or birth, or at some time after the child's birth. Neither parent loses parental responsibility on divorce. If the parents have never been married, only the mother automatically has parental responsibility, but the father may acquire that status by order or agreement. (There are proposals to change the law in this area.) Parents who do not have parental responsibility nonetheless play an essential role in determining best interests and may have a right, under the Human Rights Act to participate in the decision-making process (see Card 1 list: 'HRA', 'Children'). In some circumstances people other than parents may acquire parental responsibility, for example by the appointment of a guardian or on the order of a Court. If there is any doubt about whether the person giving consent is legally entitled to do so, legal advice should be sought.

3. When is a minor competent to give valid consent?

There is no presumption of competence for those under the age of 16 and those under this age must demonstrate their competence. A young person under 16 can consent to treatment provided he or she is competent to understand the nature, purpose and possible consequences of the treatment proposed (see also Card 5 on Assessment of Competence and Card 1 list: 'Children', 'Consent', 'DoH', 'MET', 'MDU', 'MPS'). Parental involvement should be encouraged, particularly for important or life-changing decisions, but a competent young person's request for confidentiality should be respected.

4. Can a competent minor refuse life-prolonging treatment?

In England, Wales and Northern Ireland, refusal of treatment by competent young people under the age of 18 is not necessarily binding upon doctors since the Courts have ruled that consent from people with parental responsibility, or a Court, still allows doctors to provide treatment. It is possible, however, that these cases may be approached differently since the implementation of the Human Rights Act (see also Card 1 list: 'HRA'). Where a competent young person refuses treatment, the harm caused by violating a young person's choice must be balanced against the harm caused by failing to treat. In Scotland, it is likely that neither parents nor the Courts are entitled to override a competent young patient's decision, although this matter cannot be considered settled. If a competent young person refuses life-prolonging treatment, it would be advisable to seek legal advice and it may be necessary to take the matter to Court. (See also Card 1 list: 'Children', 'Consent', 'DoH', 'MET', 'MDU', 'MPS.')

5. Where a minor lacks capacity is it necessary to obtain the consent of both parents?

Anyone with parental responsibility can consent to treatment on behalf of a minor who lacks capacity. Where the proposed intervention is controversial, agreement between parents is desirable. If this cannot be achieved, ethical and legal advice should be sought.

CARD 8
DETERMINING 'BEST INTERESTS'

1. What factors should be taken into account when considering what is in a patient's best interests?

A number of factors should be addressed including:

- the patient's own wishes and values (where these can be ascertained), including any advance statement;

- clinical judgement about the effectiveness of the proposed treatment, particularly in relation to other options;

- where there is more than one option, which option is least restrictive of the patient's future choices;

- the likelihood and extent of any degree of improvement in the patient's condition if treatment is provided;

- the views of the parents, if the patient is a child;

- the views of people close to the patient, especially close relatives, partners, carers or proxy decision makers about what the patient is likely to see as beneficial; and

- any knowledge of the patient's religious, cultural and other non-medical views that might have an impact on the patient's wishes.

(See also Card 1 list: 'Consent', 'DoH', 'Children', 'Capacity', 'MET', 'MDU', 'MPS'.)

CARD 9
ADVANCE STATEMENTS

1. What is an advance statement?

People who understand the implications of their choices can state in advance how they wish to be treated if they suffer loss of capacity. An advance statement (sometimes known as a living will) can be of various types:

- a requesting statement reflecting an individual's aspirations;
- a statement of general beliefs and aspects of life which an individual values;
- a statement that names another person who should be consulted at the time a decision has to be made;
- a clear instruction refusing some or all medical procedures (advance directive);
- a statement which, rather than refusing any particular treatment, specifies a degree of irreversible deterioration after which no life sustaining treatment should be given; or
- a combination of the above, including requests, refusals and the nomination of a representative.

2. What form should an advance statement take?

An advance statement can be a written document, a witnessed oral statement, a signed printed card, a smart card or a note of a particular discussion recorded in the patient's file.

3. Who can make an advance statement?

Any person can make an advance statement including an individual under the age of 18, although advance statements will only be legally binding in certain circumstances (see below).

4. Are advance statements legally binding?

A clear refusal of treatment by a competent adult, acting free from pressure, has potential legal force. General statements of preferences should be respected, if appropriate, but are not legally binding. Any advance statement is superseded by a clear and competent contemporaneous decision by the individual concerned. In the case of young people under the age of 18, advance statements should be taken into account and accommodated, if possible, but do not necessarily have the same status as those of adults. (See also Card 7 on Children and Young People and Card 1 list: 'Advance Statements', 'Children.')

5. Are all advance refusals of treatment legally binding?

An advance refusal is legally binding providing that the patient is an adult, the patient was competent and properly informed when reaching the decision, the statement is clearly applicable to the present circumstances and there is no reason to believe that the patient has changed his or her mind. If doubt exists about what the individual intended, the law supports a presumption in favour of providing clinically appropriate treatment, but where the situation that has arisen is clearly that which was envisaged by the patient, treatment should not be provided contrary to a valid advance refusal. (See Card 1 list: 'Advance statements.')

CARD 10
RESEARCH

1. Is separate consent required for research procedures?

Yes. Doctors must take care to ensure that any patient who is asked to consider taking part in research is given the fullest possible information presented in terms and a form that they can understand. Patients must be aware that they are being asked to participate in a research project and that the results are not predictable. Adequate time must be given for reflection prior to the patient giving consent. Where patients do not wish to receive full information about the research, this may affect the doctor's decision to involve them. (See also Card 1 list: 'Consent', 'DoH', MET', 'MDU', 'MPS', 'GCP.') Retention of human tissue for research or teaching requires consent from the donor, or the next of kin of deceased patients or those who cannot speak for themselves (see also card 1 list: 'MRC').

2. What information should be provided?

Information should preferably be provided in writing and should include: the purpose of the research; the probability of random allocation to treatment; information about trial-related procedures, particularly invasive procedures; arrangements for covering expenses of patients and compensation in the event of trial-related injury. Information should also be provided about confidentiality and the possibility of access to confidential notes by third parties such as regulatory authorities, auditors or ethics committees. Patients must also be aware that they can withdraw at any time without penalty. All written information should be approved in advance by a local research ethics committee (LREC) or multi-centre research ethics committee (MREC). (See also Card 1 list: 'GCP.')

3. Is there a relevant distinction between 'therapeutic' and 'non-therapeutic' research?

Research is often divided into two categories of 'therapeutic' and 'non-therapeutic' although this distinction is increasingly challenged. All research that involves particularly vulnerable people (such as children or incompetent adults) must have special safeguards. Whether or not the participant is likely to benefit personally (so-called 'therapeutic research') is one of a number of relevant factors for research ethics committees to consider.

4. Can patients who lack capacity participate in 'therapeutic' research?

It is the generally accepted view that it is lawful for a doctor to involve adults who lacks capacity in research provided the research is 'therapeutic' in nature (in terms of potentially benefiting the individual patient). Views should, however, be sought from the appropriate ethics committee. (See also Card 1 list: 'Capacity.')

5. Can adults who lack capacity participate in 'non-therapeutic' research?

The involvement of persons lacking capacity in some types of 'non-therapeutic' research is increasingly regarded as ethical provided certain strict safeguards are applied but, in England, Wales and Northern Ireland, it is doubtful that such research is lawful. In Scotland, a nominated proxy may give consent for this type of research in some circumstances. Observational research which is not contrary to the individual's interests may be approved by LRECs/MRECs. (See also Card 1 list: 'Capacity.')

6. Can a competent minor give consent to participate in 'therapeutic' research?

Current guidance emphasises that, even where the minor is competent to make this decision for him or herself, it would be inadvisable to proceed without the approval of someone with parental responsibility. Researchers should seek the views of the appropriate LREC/MREC. (See also Card 1 list: 'Children', 'Capacity.') 7. Can children who lack capacity to consent participate in 'non-therapeutic' research? There is general agreement that participation by immature minors in 'non-therapeutic' research is not necessarily unethical provided that: the research carries no more than minimal risk; it does not entail any suffering for the child; parental and LREC agreement is obtained; and the child does not appear to object. Nonetheless, researchers should be aware that the law is unclear and therefore legal advice should be sought. (See also Card 1 list: 'Children', 'Capacity.')

CARD 11
TEACHING

1. Is it necessary to seek the patient's consent for students to be present at a consultation?

Yes. The doctor carrying out the consultation should explain to the patient that an observer would like to sit in on the consultation, who that person is and why he or she wishes to observe. Patients should feel able to refuse consent to the presence of medical, or work observation, students during their consultation and/or examination. They should be reassured that their decision will, in no way, affect their treatment. Wherever possible, patients should be given the option of considering this request prior to the arrival of the students.

2. Is it necessary to seek consent prior to a patient being questioned and examined by medical students for teaching purposes?

Teaching hospitals should draw up detailed protocols about the extent to which medical students and other doctors in training will be present during, and involved with, treatment. Patients should be made aware of this in advance and, where those in training will be directly involved with providing treatment, specific consent should be sought.

3. Is specific consent required to teach additional practical procedures on a patient who has been anaesthetised?

Yes. A patient who is anaesthetised has the same right to give and withhold consent as any other patient. Before any anaesthetic is given, the specific consent of the patient should be obtained to additional practical procedures being carried out solely for teaching purposes.

4. Is it necessary to seek consent from patients for the use of video and audio recordings of procedures made for teaching purposes?

Yes. It is necessary to seek the consent of the patient prior to a recording being made and for its subsequent use for teaching purposes. If the recording is of a child unable to give consent him or herself, consent should be sought from someone with parental responsibility and consent to its continued use should be sought from the child him or herself when he or she is sufficiently mature to make a decision. Patients may vary or withdraw their consent to the use of video and audio recordings in teaching at any time. If consent is withdrawn, the recording should be erased. (See also Card 1 list: 'Recordings', 'Children.')

CARD 12
HIV / AIDS

1. Is patient consent required prior to testing for HIV/AIDS in all cases?

Doctors must obtain consent from patients before testing for HIV / AIDS except in the rare circumstances addressed in the questions below.

2. What information should be provided to the patient?

Doctors must make sure that the patient is given appropriate information about the implications of the test, including the advantages and disadvantages, and wherever possible allow the patient appropriate time to consider and discuss them. (See also Card 1 list: 'Communicable diseases', 'HIV.')

3. Where a child cannot give or withhold consent, can consent be sought from a person with parental responsibility?

Yes, if testing is in the child's best interests. If a parent refuses consent to testing, and the doctor believes that person's judgement to be distorted, for example because he or she may be the cause of the child's infection, the doctor must decide whether the medical interests of the child override the wishes of those with parental responsibility. Legal advice should be sought if testing is medically necessary, but parental consent is refused. The GMC also advises doctors to consult with an experienced colleague. (See also Card 1 list: 'Communicable diseases', 'Children.')

4. Can a patient be tested for HIV/AIDS where a health care worker has suffered a needlestick injury or other occupational exposure to blood or body fluids?

Yes, provided that the patient gives consent. Where the patient is unable to consent or refuses to do so, the doctor should proceed with testing only in exceptional circumstances. Further advice should be sought initially from the Trust's Occupational Health Department. (See also Card 1 list: 'Communicable diseases.')

5. Are there any circumstances when an unconscious patient can be tested for HIV/AIDS?

The GMC indicates that doctors may test unconscious patients for HIV / AIDS without their prior consent, where testing would be in their immediate clinical interests, for example to help in making a diagnosis. Where a health care worker has suffered a needlestick injury or other exposure to blood or body fluids, consent for the test should be sought once the patient has regained full consciousness. If the patient has not regained consciousness within 48 hours, the severity of risk should be carefully assessed and further advice sought, initially from the Trust's Occupational Health Department. In exceptional cases, testing without consent may be justified. (See also Card 1 list: 'Communicable diseases.')

6. Can a deceased patient be tested for HIV/AIDS where a health care worker has suffered a needle stick injury or other occupational exposure to blood or body fluids?

Doctors may test a deceased patient for HIV / AIDS if they have good reason to think that the patient may have been infected, and a health care worker has been exposed to the patient's blood or other body fluid. Doctors should usually seek the agreement of a relative before testing. Further advice should be sought, initially from the Trust's Occupational Health Department. (See also Card 1 list: 'Communicable diseases.')

APPENDIX F

GLOSSARY OF SOME COMMON ABBREVIATIONS AND HIEROGLYPHS

Common abbreviations

aa	of each (Greek)
AAL	Anterior Auxiliary Line
ac	before meals
ACTH	Adrenocorticotrophic Hormone
ad	up to
add	adduction
ADH	Antidiuretic Hormone
ADL	Activities of Daily Living
ad lib	to the desired amount
ADP	Adenosine Diphosphate
AE	Air Entry
AFB	Acid Fast Bacillus (TB)
AFP	Alphafetoprotein maternal serum and occasionally amniotic fluid levels tested in pregnancy to screen for neural tube defect in foetus
AID	Artificial Insemination–Donor
AIDS	Acquired Immune Deficiency Syndrome
AIH	Artificial Insemination–Husband
AJ	Ankle Jerk (reflex: see also BJ,KJ,SJ,TJ)
alt dieb	every other day
Al S	Alimentary System
anti-D	this gamma globulin must be given by injection to rhesus negative mother who delivers/aborts rhesus positive child/foetus, to prevent mother developing antibodies which would damage a subsequent rhesus positive baby
Apgar	Apgar score: means of recording baby's condition at birth by observing and 'scoring' (0, 1 or 2) five parameters
applic	applications
aq	water
aq dest/ster	distilled water/sterilised
aq dest	distilled water
AR	Analytical standard of Reagent purity
ARC	Aids Related Complex (less damage can result in full blown AIDS)
ARDS	Adult Respiratory Distress Syndrome
ARM	Artificial Rupture of Membranes

ASD		Atrial Septal Defect
AST		Aspartate Aminotransferase
ATP		Adenosine Triphosphate
aurist		ear drops
A/V		Anteverted
bd		both
b.d.		twice a day
BJ		Biceps Jerk (reflex: see AJ)
B.S.		British Standard
blood sugar		normal 2.5–5.5 mmol/1
blood urea		normal 2.5–6.6 mmol/1
BMR		Basal Metabolism Rate
BNF (plus date)		British National Formulary (prescriber's bible supplied free to all NHS doctors).
BO		Bowels Open
BP (plus date)		British Pharmacopoeia
BP		Blood Pressure
BS	(i)	Breath Sounds
	(ii)	Bowel Sounds
	(iii)	Blood Sugar
	(iv)	British Standard
c		with (Latin: cum)
C2H5OH		alcohol
Ca	(i)	Carcinoma/cancer
	(ii)	Calcium
Caps		Capsules
CAT scan		Computed Axial Tomograph
cp		compare
CIN		Cervical Intraepithelial Neoplasia (cervical cancer)
CMV		Cytomegalovirus
CNS		Central Nervous System
CO		Complaining Of
CO_2		carbon dioxide
COETT		Cuffed Oral Endotracheal Tube (see COT and ETT)
comp		compounded of
COT		Cuffed Oral Tube (endotracheal tube used for ventilating a patient who cannot breathe unaided)

CPD	Cephalo-pelvic Disproportion (baby too big to fit through pelvis)
crem	a cream
CSF	Cerebro-spinal Fluid
CTG	Cardiotocograph Trace (during labour – of baby's heart and mother's contractions)
CVA	Cardiovascular Accident (stroke)
CVS	Cardiovascular System
Cx	Cervix
CXR	Chest X-ray
D	Diagnosis (GOK–God Only Knows)
DES	Diethylstilbestrol
DIC	Disseminated Intravascular Coagulation (a serious complication of many conditions – relates to widespread thrombosis)
dil	dilute
DNA (i)	Did Not Attend
(ii)	Deoxyribonucleic Acid
D & V	Diarrhoea and Vomiting
DOA	Dead On Arrival
DOPA	Dopamine
DVT	Deep Vein Thrombosis
D/W	Discussed With
Dx	Diagnosis
ECG	Electrocardiography
ECT	Electroconvulsive Therapy
EDD	Expected Date of Delivery
emf	electromotive force
EM	Electron Micrography
EMG	Electromyo/gram/graph
emp	emplastrum (a plaster)
enem	enemata (enemas)
EOG	Electro-oculogram
ER	External Rotation
ERCP	Endoscopic Retrograde Cholangio-pancreatography/scope
ERPC	Evacuation of Retained Products of Conception
ERG	Electroretinogram
ESR	Erythrocyte Sedimentation Rate
Ex	Extension

FB	Finger's Breadth
FBC	Full Blood Count
FBS	Foetal Blood Sampling (ob)
FH	Family History
FHH	Foetal Heart Heard
FHHR	Foetal Heart Heard Regular
FHR	Foetal Heart Rate
Flex	Flexion
FLK	Funny Looking Kid
FMF	Foetal Movements Felt
FSE	Foetal Scalp Electrode
FSH	Family Social History or Follicle-stimulating Hormone
GA	General Anaesthetic
garg	gargles
glc	Gas Liquid Chromatography
GTT	Glucose Tolerance Test
GFR	Glomerular Filtration Rate
GIT	Gastrointestinal Tract
GM	Geiger Muller
GUT	Genitourinary Tract
Hb	Haemoglobin
HCG	Human Chorionic Gonadotrophin
HCO	History of Present Complaint (or HPC)
hn	hac nocte (Latin: tonight)
ha	hora somni (Latin: at bed time)
HS	Heart Sounds
HSA	Human Serum Albumin
HVS	High Vaginal Swab
Hx	History
ICF	Intracellular Fluid
ICS	Intercostal Space
IgA, IgB, IgG, IgM	Immunoglobins
IJV	Internal Jugular Vein
IM	Intramuscular
implant	implantation
in aq	in water

inj	injections
IP	Intraperitoneal
IR	Internal Rotation
irrig	irrigations
IVI	Intravenous Infusion
IVP	Intravenous Pyelogram
K	potassium
KJ	Knee Jerk
KPa	Kiloplascal, approx 7.5 mm Hg
L	Litre
LA	Local Anaesthetic
LATS	Long Acting Thyroid Stimulator
LFT	Liver Function Tests
LH	Lutenizing Hormone
LIH	Left Inguinal Hernia
linc	linctus
lin	liniments
liq	solutions
LMP	Last Menstrual Period
LN	Lymph Node
LOA	Left Occiput Anterior
LOC	Loss Of Consciousness
LOL	Left Occiput Lateral
LOP	Left Occiput Posterior
LSCS	Lower Segment Caesarean Section
LSK	Liver, Spleen, Kidneys
m	mix
mane	in the morning (Latin)
mcg	microgram
MCL	Mid Clavicular Line
ME	Myalgic Encephalomyelitis (chronic fatigue syndrome or post viral fatigue syndrome)
mg	milligram
mmttg	mm of mercury (unit of pressure)
ml	millilitres
MP	Melting Point

MS	Multiple Sclerosis
MSH	Melanophore Stimulating Hormone
MSU	Midstream Specimen of Urine
N & V	Nausea and Vomiting
NAD	Nothing Abnormal Detected
NBM	Nil By Mouth
Neb	a spray
ng	nanogram
NG	Neoplastic Growth
Ng	Nasogastric
NGT	Nasogastric Tube
NHL	non-Hodgkins Lymphoma
NMCS	No Malignant Cells Seen
NOF	Neck of Femur
N/S	Normal Size
O$_2$	oxygen
occulent	eye ointment
OA	Occupito-anterior
od	daily
OD	Outside Diameter
OE	On Examination
om	every morning
oe	every evening
OP	Occupito-posterior
PR	Pulse Rate
Pa	Pascal
PAS	Periodic Acid–Schiff reaction
pc	after meals
PCG	Phonocardiogram
PCV	Packed Cell Volume
PERLA	Pupils are Equal and React to Light and Accommodation
PE	Pulmonary Embolism
pes	pessaries
PET	Pre-eclampsia Toxaemia
ph	acidity/alkalinity scale
PH	Past History

PID	Pelvic Inflammatory Disease or
	Prolapsed Intravertebral Disc
PMH	Past Medical History
PN(R)	Percussion Note (Resonant)
PNS	Peripheral Nervous System
PPI	paternal preconception irradiation
PO	Per–or by–mouth
PR	Per Rectum
PV	Per Vagina
PVS	Persistent Vegetative State
prn	as required / as occasion arises
RBC	Red Blood Cells
Rh	Rhesus
RH	Relative Humidity
RIA	Relative Immune Assay
RIH	Right Inguinal Hernia
ROA	Right Occupit Anterior
ROL	Right Occupit Lateral
ROM	Range of Movement
RPF	Renal Plasma Flow
RQ	Respiratory Quotient
RS	Respiratory System
RT	Reaction Time
RTI	Respiratory Tract Infection
S/B	Seen By
S/D	Systolic/Diastolic
SEM	Scanning Electron Microscope
SH	Social History
SJ	Jerk
SOA	Swelling Of Ankles
SOB	Shortness Of Breath
SOS	Si Opus Sit (if necessary) or See Other Sheet
SROM	Spontaneous Rupture of Membranes
SVC	Superior Vena Cava
SVD	Spontaneous Vaginal Delivery

TCI 3/52	To Come In three weeks time
TGH	To Go Home
THR	Total Hip Replacement
TID	Three Times a Day
TJ	Triceps Jerk
TFTS	Thyroid Function Tests
TSH	Thyroid Stimulating Hormone
U & E	Urea and Electrolytes
ung	ointments
UG	Urogenital System
URTI	Upper Respiratory Tract Infection
VE	Vaginal Examination
VF	Ventrical Fibrillation
VT	Ventrical Tachycardia
V/V	Vulva and Vagina
WBC	White Blood Count/Corpuscle

Common hieroglyphs

#	fracture
D	diagnosis
R_x	treatment
o	nil/nothing
≠	up
Ø	down
1/7	one day
2/52	two days
3/12	three months

The authors extend their grateful thanks to AVMA for permission to reproduce this list of common abbreviations and hieroglyphs.

APPENDIX G

MISCELLANEOUS

INJURY	EXPERT
Brain damage/head injury	Neurologist/neurosurgeon preferably at a hospital with brain scan equipment.
Mother and baby	Obstetrician and gynaecologist, paediatrician.
Wrong drug treatment	Pharmacologist (and toxicologist if necessary) and appropriate expert.
Negligent surgery	A general surgeon expert in the field.
Chest complaints	Chest physician – most teaching hospitals have large chest clinics with modern equipment and post graduate expertise.
Ear, nose and throat	Otolaryngologist.
Eyes	Ophthalmologist.
Personality disorders	Psychiatrist/clinical psychologist.
Waterworks and related piping	Urologist.
Bones	Orthopaedic consultant expert in knees, hips, etc.
Children	Paediatrician, eg specialist in neurology, urology and note educational psychologist.
'Wrongful birth cases'	May involve haematologist, geneticist.
In anaesthetic cases	Anaesthetist as well as the speciality within which the anaesthetic problem arose.
In nursing cases	A senior nursing officer.
In GP cases	An experienced GP and/or university teachers of general practice.

ADVANCE DIRECTIVE

TO MY FAMILY AND MY PHYSICIAN

This Declaration is made by me (full name and address) at a time when I am of sound mind and after careful consideration.

If I am unable to take part in decisions about my medical care owing to my physical or mental incapacity and if I develop one or more of the medical conditions listed in Item 3 below and two independent physicians conclude that there is no prospect of my recovery, I declare that my wishes are as follows:

1. I request that my life shall not be sustained by artificial means such as life support systems, intravenous fluids or drugs, or by tube feeding.

2. I request that distressing symptoms caused by illness or by lack of food or fluid should be controlled by appropriate sedative treatment though such treatment may shorten my life.

*3. The said medical conditions are:
   (1) Severe and lasting brain damage sustained as a result of injury, including stroke, or disease.

   (2) Advanced disseminated malignant disease.

   (3) Advanced degenerative disease or of the nervous and/or muscular systems with severe limitations of independent mobility, and no satisfactory response to treatment.

   (4) Senile or pre-senile dementia, eg Alzheimer or multi-infarct type.

   (5) Other condition of comparable gravity.

* Cross out and initial any condition you do not wish to include.

I further declare that I hereby absolve my medical attendants from any civil liability arising from action taken in response to and in terms of this Declaration.

I reserve the right to revoke this Declaration at any time.

Signature:......................

Date:............................

Witnessed by:

Signature:........................... Signature:...........................

Name:......................... Name:.........................
(please print) (please print)

Address:......................... Address:.........................

....

....

The authors extend their appreciation to the Voluntary Euthanasia Society for giving their permission to reproduce their sample advance directive.

CONSENT FORM

Health Authority ....   **Patient's Surname**...........................

Hospital ....   **Other Names**...................................

Unit Number....................................   **Date of Birth**....................................

Sex: *(please tick)* **Male**   **Female**

DOCTORS OR DENTISTS *(This part to be completed by doctor or dentist. See notes on the reverse)*

TYPE OF OPERATION INVESTIGATION OR TREATMENT

I confirm that I have explained the operation investigation or treatment, and such appropriate options as are available and the type of anaesthetic, If any (general/regional/sedation) proposed, to the patient in terms which in my judgement are suited to the understanding of the patient and/or to one of the parents or guardians of the patient.

Signature.....................................   Date .../.../...

Name of doctor or dentist ....

PATIENT/PARENT/GUARDIAN

1. Please read this form and the notes overleaf very carefully.

2. If there is anything that you don't understand about the explanation, or if you want more information, you should ask the doctor or dentist.

3. Please check that all the information on the form is correct. If it is, and you understand the explanation, then sign the form.

I am the patient/parent/guardian *(delete as necessary)*.

I agree	to what is proposed which has been explained to me by the doctor/dentist named on this form.
	to the use of the type of anaesthetic that I have been told about.
I understand	that the procedure may not be done by the doctor/dentist who has been treating me so far.
	that any procedure in addition to the investigation or treatment described on this form will only be carried out if it is necessary and in my best interests and can be justified for medical reasons.
I have told	the doctor or dentist about any additional procedures I would not wish to be carried out straight way without my having the opportunity to consider them first.

Signature ....

Name...

Address ....

(if not the patient) ....

....

Crown Copyright is reproduced with the permission of the Controller of Her Majesty's Stationary Office.

INDEX

A

Abortion
    failed .... .243, 272
    regulations .... .31
    rights .... .46
    wrongful life .... .257, 260–61, 273

Acceptable medical
    practice 165–70,
                      171–74, 233

Accidents
    See Injury, Fatal accidents

Accommodation expenses ..... .252, 302

Adenocarcinoma .... .175

Aggravated damages 291–92

AIDS .... .12, 15, 27–29,
                     82, 168, 169

Alcohol intoxication .... .181

Allocation of track .... .304

Amenity loss .... .301

Amniocentesis
    See Prenatal diagnosis

Amoxil prescription .... .189

Amputation of limb .... .124, 183, 204

Anaesthesia
    complications .... .121, 163, 168
    dose error .... .192
    failure .... .269
    halothane .... .228
    inadequate .... .192, 228, 269
    muscle relaxants .... .155
    nupercaine .... .87
    spinal .... .168, 229

Angiography, complication .... .216

Anorexia nervosa .... .48

Application notice for
    court order 38–39

Arsenic poisoning .... .204

Artificial insemination .... .169

Asbestosis 207–09, 212

B

Australian case law
    causation .... .215, 225, 240
    confidentiality 6, 31
    damages .... .277
    duty of care 76–77, 87–88,
                  91–92, 104
    standard of care .... .163, 169,
                176–77, 183, 189

Avascular necrosis .... .217

Back injury .... .152, 168, 268

Behcet disease .... .189

Benefits for claimants 280–83

Benevolence benefit .... .283

Birth, wrongful 257–63, 301

Blindness .... .215

Blood disease 151–52, 183, 223

Blood transfusion
    infections .... .169, 180
    refusal 41–42, 47,
                 53, 67, 239
    screening 168–69

BMA
    See British Medical Association

Bolam test
    Bolitho defence .... .235
    duty of care .... .75, 194–95
    standard of care ...... .155, 165–67, 178

Bolitho defence 235–39

Brachial plexus injury .... .229

Brain damage
    complication 138–38, 269
    drug side effect .... .189
    late referral .... .182
    misdiagnosis .... .124

Breach of confidence
    application notice 38–39
    checklist for claim 34–35
    court orders 30–31
    defence 26–29, 40